# TEXT-BOOK

OF THE

# HISTORY OF DOCTRINES

BY

REINHOLD SEEBERG

TRANSLATED BY

CHARLES E. HAY

*COMPLETE IN TWO VOLUMES*

## VOL. I
HISTORY OF DOCTRINES IN THE ANCIENT CHURCH

BAKER BOOK HOUSE

Grand Rapids, Michigan

1961

Library of Congress Catalog Card Number: 56-7584

*First Printing, November 1952*
*Second Printing, August 1954*
*Third Printing, August 1956*
*Fourth Printing, August 1958*
*Fifth Printing, April 1961*

PHOTOLITHOPRINTED BY CUSHING - MALLOY, INC.
ANN ARBOR, MICHIGAN, UNITED STATES OF AMERICA
1961

# TRANSLATOR'S PREFACE.

THE appearance of the present work is in response to the expressed desire of the teachers of Dogmatic Theology in a number of institutions in various portions of the Church.

In a department which at so many points vitally affects the conceptions of fundamental truth, and which has to do with the entire historical development lying back of the Protestant Reformation, as well as with the formulations of doctrine then made, which have proved regulative in the sphere of dogmatics to the present day, it is imperative that our students of theology should enjoy the benefit of the very best modern scholarship, and that they should be led through the maze of conflicting views under the guidance of one who, while impartial as a historian, yet recognizes the validity of our ecclesiastical inheritance as embodying and expressing the essential results of both ancient and modern religious thought.

The "Lehrbuch" of Dr. Seeberg has since its appearance been constantly used as a book of reference in our theological seminaries. The unchallenged pre-eminence of the author in this his chosen field, the conservatism of his views, so well reflecting the spirit of our churches in America, and the condensation and lucidity of his style combine to commend his work as the most suitable for the purpose above indicated.

It is confidently expected that the Text-book will find a circulation far beyond the limits of the class-room. To the busy, working pastor it will prove a welcome companion as with ripened powers he reviews from time to time the field of his early studies, enabling also the intelligent layman to scan the field of ancient religious thought through the field-glass of a living historian of his own church.

The unusually full treatment of the doctrinal history of the Reformation will be found peculiarly helpful, displaying the lines of continuity connecting the theology of the Reformers with the central truths of the original Christian revelation, and indicating, at the same time, the sufficiency of the principles then enunciated to direct the religious activities of the present age.

It has been thought best, in order to facilitate the use of the work in wider circles, to translate the large number of citations

(iii)

from the Greek and Latin, but the pivotal words are in such cases also presented in the original form. The translation of citations has been made as literal as possible, sacrificing elegance of English idiom to exactness in reproducing the originals.

I desire gratefully to acknowledge the courtesy of the distinguished author in so cheerfully furnishing the large amount of valuable new material for this edition, thus anticipating future editions of the original.

CHARLES E. HAY.

# AUTHOR'S PREFACE TO ENGLISH EDITION.

THE extracts from the prefaces to the German edition, appearing upon the succeeding pages, give a sufficient indication of the character of the present work. I have not endeavored to present to the reader historical constructions of doctrine, but I have sought to display the actual course of doctrinal development as objectively as possible and in strict harmony with the sources. The prevalent and controlling view-points have, however, in each case been kept steadily in mind and prominently indicated.

I have carefully revised the present English edition, amending and enlarging it at many points. This is true especially of the first volume, which has in various parts been very largely re-written. I felt it to be particularly fitting to introduce a brief historical sketch of the development of the New Testament doctrine.

May the work in this English edition, by the blessing of God, prove a service to the church and to ecclesiastical science among my brethren in the faith in the distant West.

R. SEEBERG.

# FROM AUTHOR'S PREFACES TO GERMAN EDITION.

PREFACE VOL. I., 1895, PP. 5, 6.

THE work whose first volume is herewith presented to the theological public claims to be but a text-book, and I have been at special pains to adapt it in all parts to the requirements of academic study. I have endeavored to condense the material as far as possible without allowing it to become obscure or unintelligible. I have, therefore, commonly contented myself with literal quotation of the original sources, and it is my hope that the most important passages from them will be found here collected. Historic and dogmatic criticisms are merely suggested. In my lectures upon the History of Doctrines I am accustomed to lay stress upon the ecclesiastico-historical setting of doctrinal development and to accompany its presentation with the appropriate biblico-dogmatic criticism. But in this work, with the exception of a few brief hints, I have refrained from such attempts. Many comments of this kind which I had at first included were stricken out in the last revision of the manuscript, in order that the work, which has nevertheless, despite the compact printing, somewhat exceeded the dimensions originally contemplated, might not become too large for its designed use. Such discussions, moreover, are not, strictly speaking, in place in a work of the present character. Perhaps an opportunity may be elsewhere found to offer some "Comments upon the History of Doctrines." That I do not entirely agree with Baur and Harnack, nor with Kliefoth-Thomasius, will be evident from occasional hints in the following pages. As the work owes its existence to my desire to secure relief from the burdensome task of dictation in the delivery of my lectures, it takes for granted that students, at least, will in the use of it have the assistance of academic lectures. But it is my further hope that, even for advanced theologians, the earnest study of the material here furnished may bring vividly before the mind the wealth of questions and problems embraced within the range of the formula, "Faith and Doctrine." It cannot be sufficiently emphasized in our day that a real answering of these questions and an inward emancipation from these problems can never be attained without thorough-going studies in dogmatic history.    The revelations and " evidences " of that theological Dilettanteism, which selects the sphere of dogmatics as the field for its antics, must come to naught despite the favor or disfavor of parties.    The History of Doctrines demands a hearing and requires an intelligent understanding.

The general plan and arrangement of the present work have been fixed in my mind since the preparation of my lectures upon the History of Doctrines in the year 1885-1886.    That it is based upon a study of the original sources will be sufficiently evident to the reader.    I would not fail to acknowledge with gratitude the frequent suggestions and enlarged fund of information which I have derived from the newer works upon the History of Doctrines, especially from Baur, Thomasius and Harnack, as also from the many faithfully executed Patristic monographs of the last decennia.

### PREFACE VOL. II., 1898, PP. 3, 4.

It is manifest that the acquaintance of any single individual with the immense historical material embraced within the scope of the present volume must be far from exhaustive, especially since there is a great lack of preparatory monographs, such as exist in abundance for the earlier periods in the History of Doctrines.    It may be readily understood also that the historian, in seeking to delineate the course of development, should endeavor, so far as his time and strength may permit, to fill up the existing gaps by original research.    The delay in the appearance of the present volume is to be thus accounted for, as painstaking investigations were necessary in various fields, the results of which may, I trust, be recognized as constituting an enrichment of our Science.    I mention, for example, the full presentation of the Scholastic theology, particularly that of the later Scholasticism, and the attempt to give to the teaching of Luther and the other Reformers its rightful place in the History of Doctrines.    No one familiar with the subject can deny that it is amazing to find in the existing Histories of Doctrines very much about Anselm and Thomas, and but little, and that too often untrustworthy, about Duns Scotus and his followers—as though it were possible without a knowledge of this later development to understand the doctrinal construction in the Evangelical and Roman Catholic churches, either in its positive or in its negative aspects !    It is just as clearly out of keeping with the fitness of things that we may in many Histories of Doctrines read much of Origen and the Damascene, and even of Osiander and Chemnitz, but only passing sketches of the four

great Reformers, and these marred by strong dogmatic preju-
dices. I have here attempted to remedy this defect, although
the section upon Luther has thus grown almost to the dimensions of a small monograph, yet without exceeding the proper
limits of a History of Doctrines.

The reader will observe that the later portions of the work are
somewhat less condensed than the earlier sections. I have thus
sought to meet the wants of the general reader as well as of the
technical student, without sacrificing the clearness and exactness
necessary in a text-book. I have allowed myself also, as the
work advanced, somewhat more liberty in the critical estimate
of the positions reviewed. I have not concealed my own doctrinal views, but have nowhere given prominence to them,
seeking only to make proper comment upon the actual historical
phenomena. If the hand of the dogmatic theologian is more
evident in this than in the former volume, it is to be attributed
in part to the nature of the material under review.

R. SEEBERG.

# CONTENTS.

# BOOK I.

## DEVELOPMENT OF DOCTRINE IN THE ANCIENT CHURCH.

## PART I.

### CONCEPTION OF CHRISTIANITY IN THE POST-APOSTOLIC AND PRIMITIVE CATHOLIC AGES.

### CHAPTER I.

#### THE CONCEPTION OF CHRISTIANITY IN THE POST-APOSTOLIC AGE.

(ix)

## CHAPTER II.

### PERVERSIONS OF THE GOSPEL AND REFORMATORY MOVEMENTS DIRECTED AGAINST CATHOLIC CHRISTIANITY.

## CHAPTER III.

### BEGINNINGS OF THE CHURCH'S THEOLOGY.

## CHAPTER IV.

### SEPARATE DOCTRINES AND GENERAL CONCEPTION OF CHRISTIANITY IN THE THIRD CENTURY.

# PART II.

## DOCTRINAL CONSTRUCTION IN THE ANCIENT CHURCH.

### CHAPTER I.

#### THE DOCTRINE OF THE TRINITY.

## CHAPTER II.

### DOCTRINE OF ONE PERSON AND TWO NATURES IN CHRIST.

## CHAPTER III.

### GENERAL CONCEPTION OF CHRISTIANITY. COMPLETION OF DOCTRINAL CONSTRUCTION ON GREEK TERRITORY.

## CHAPTER IV.

FOUNDATION OF ANTHROPOLOGICAL DOGMA (SIN AND GRACE) AND DEVEL-
OPMENT OF THE CONCEPTION OF THE CHURCH IN THE WEST. DOC-
TRINE OF AUGUSTINE.

CONTENTS.

## CHAPTER V.

AUGUSTINIANISM AS THE DOCTRINE OF THE CHURCH. COMPLETION OF
DOCTRINAL DEVELOPMENT IN THE ANCIENT CHURCH OF THE WEST.

# GENERAL INTRODUCTION.

## DEFINITION, OFFICE, AND METHODS OF THE HISTORY OF DOCTRINES.

### § 1. *Definition and Office of the History of Doctrines.*

KLIEFOTH, Eine Einleitung in die Dogmengeschichte, 1839. R. SEE-BERG, Ein Gang durch die Dogmengeschichte, Neue kirchl. Zeitschr., 1890, 761 ff. G. KRÜGER, Was heisst u. zu welchem Ende studirt man Dogmengeschichte? 1895. STANGE, Das Dogma u. seine Beurteilung, 1898.

1. The theological term, Dogma,[1] designates either an ecclesiastical doctrine, or the entire structure of such doctrines, *i. e.*, the doctrinal system of the church. As Dogma is the formal expression of the truth held by the church at large, or by a particular church, the church expects the acknowledgment of it by her members, and, as legally organized, demands this of her recognized teachers. We apply the term, Dogma, not to every kind of theological propositions or formulas in which the general consciousness of the church may find utterance, but only to such propositions as have attained an ecclesiastical character, *i. e.*, such as have by a public declaration of the church at large, or some particular branch of it, been acknowledged as expressing Christian truth. Although the form of Dogma is the work of theology, its content is derived from the common faith of the Christian church.

2. Dogma is an exceedingly complicated historical structure. It has in its various constituent parts, constructed as they have been in the face of multifarious forms of opposition, and under the inspiration of many practical (ethical and devotional) impulses and external (political and canonical) occasions, received the impress of different theological tendencies. Thus dogmas have been "deepened," or "disintegrated" and super-

---

[1] Δόγμα is in ordinary Greek "commandment, precept" (Lk. 2. 1. Acts 17. 7; 16. 4. Eph. 2. 15. Col. 2. 14. Didache, ii. 3). The word is employed both in a political and in a philosophical sense. The theological conception accords most fully with the philosophical use of the term, as equivalent to "proposition, principle," *e. g.*, Cicero, Quaest. acad., iv. 9. Marc. Aurel., ii. 3. Ep. Barn., 1. 6; x. 9. Ignat. ad Magnes, 13. 1. See fuller discussion in Münscher, DG., p. 1, and Hagenbach, DG., p 1 f.

ficialized—logically developed, or, under the influence of advancing views, transformed, restored, and again newly interpreted. To delineate these historical processes is the office of the History of Doctrines—to show how the Dogma as a whole and the separate dogmas have arisen and through what course of development they have been brought to the form and interpretation prevailing in the churches of any given period.

3. It is a historical fact, that the church gives her faith a fixed form in Dogma. The continuity of her development and the necessity of unity and purity in the proclamation of her message, as well as in her decisions upon questions of morality, afford a sufficient explanation of this fact. But, theologically considered, the fallibility of Dogma must, at least upon Protestant territory, be acknowledged as an axiom. The Scriptures and the religious faith of the church are the criteria by which Dogma must submit to be judged. But to prove the harmony or disharmony of Dogma with these courts of appeal is not the office of the History of Doctrines, but rather that of Dogmatics and Practical Theology.[1] The History of Doctrines can only be required to present the arguments which have been adduced by the original advocates of any given dogma. History is not historical criticism.

The necessity for a strict observance of the historical character of our Science excludes, first of all, the Roman Catholic view, that the Dogma of the church is as such infallible—a view which is proven to be without historical foundation by the mere fact of the conflicting dogmas of the various particular churches. There is no divine Dogma, just as there is no divine church discipline nor divine liturgy. And just as little can the History of Doctrines be influenced by a desire to establish the Dogma of the Confession to which the historian himself adheres. This might practically be a very desirable achievement, but theoretically it is an invasion of the proper sphere of dogmatic theology.[2] But it is, on the other hand, just as serious an offense against the strictly historical character of the History of Doctrines to represent the Dogma of the church as necessarily tinctured with error, either because it originated in ancient, unilluminated periods (Rationalism), or because it marks only a stage of transition to the spirit of modern times (Baur), or because it presents Christianity as apprehended by antiquity, *i. e.*, a

---

[1] This question has a place in the discussions of Homiletics, Catechetics, and Liturgics, as well as in (practical) Apologetics.

[2] *E. g.*, KLIEFOTH. Compare Thomasius, DG. Wolff, Die Entwicklung der christlichen Kirche durch Athanasius, Augustine, Luther, 1889. (See Theol. Litt.-bl., 1890, col. 156 ff.)

secularized or Hellenistic form of Christianity (Harnack). It is, of course, to be freely acknowledged, that the dogmas of the church have attained their present form through the use of the intellectual apparatus of the times in which they originated.[1] This circumstance suggests the possibility of perversion or adulteration of the content by means of the scientific form. The statement of the principles of the religious life of Christianity in the form of dogmas is accompanied also by the danger that the religious formula may assume the place of religion itself, or that faith may cease to be understood as obedience to God and trust (*fiducia*) in him, and become instead the mere acknowledgment of a doctrine concerning God (*assensus*). It cannot be denied that the History of Doctrines furnishes an abundance of examples of both these forms of error. But this acknowledgment does not by any means condemn the Dogma of the church as unchristian. It merely warns us to discriminate clearly between the substance of doctrine and its form—between that which the framers of the Dogma have sought to express and the form adopted for the expression of their thought. Upon this principle, it may be possible for one to recognize the Christian and Biblical character of the ideas maintained by the Councils of Nice and Chalcedon (and these form the chief subjects of dispute), while unable to approve all the terminology employed by them. At the same time, it must be constantly kept in mind, that the sense and content of a dogma are to be historically understood in the first instance as in contrast with some particular doctrinal view. Agreement with a dogma does not by any means indicate the acknowledgment of the technical and theoretical method of its presentation, but extends only to a similar rejection of the opposite position excluded by the dogma and to a sharing of the religious tendency which demands such exclusion.[2]

Nor is it to be forgotten, finally, that Dogma is perpetually subject to ecclesiastical and theological interpretation, which prepares the forms suitable to each age, which can and does express the ancient content in these new forms, and which furthermore seizes upon and preserves the religious experiences peculiar to its own age in the harmony of the ancient faith.[3]

[1] There is yet much to be done in the investigation of this terminology (a field upon which the general History of Doctrines cannot enter). Efforts in this direction have not seldom been marred by a too pronounced dogmatic bias.

[2] See fuller discussion of this principle in SEEBERG, Die Grundwahrheiten der christl. Religion, ed. 3, 1903, p. 60 ff.

[3] This is in some sense true of the valuable thoughts of nearly all the leading theologians of the last century, *e. g.*, Schleiermacher, Ritschl, Hofmann, Frank.

The History of Doctrines is therefore a department of Historical Theology, and its office is the historical presentation of the origin and development of the dogmas which have been formulated up to the present time, and of the ecclesiastical Dogma in its relation to the various doctrinal systems.

## § 2. *Method and Divisions of the History of Doctrines.*

1. The History of Doctrines, being a historical science, must employ the strictly historical method.[1] What really occurred, and how it came to pass, must be impartially related upon the basis of original sources critically examined.[2] This requirement is not met by the simple arraying of facts side by side—which is not history at all—but by tracing the effective forces in their origin and influence, as well as the interpenetration and co-operation of the various forces. Only thus is it possible to set forth truthfully *how it really was.* In doing this, we must presume upon a general knowledge of the history of religion, of the church, and of philosophy, as well as some practice and facility in the sphere of historical criticism and objectivity. Every age, furthermore, will preserve its own version of the History of Doctrines, since our conception of the past is always conditioned by the views, problems, and questions of the present age.

2. We thus at once exclude the formerly accepted division of the science into the General and Special History of Doctrines, as well as the subdivision of the latter (as in Baur and Hagenbach) according to the arrangement of topics in the systematic theology of the day; for it is evident that this method of treating the subject is not historical. Believers have not in the various periods of history revised in turn all the separate topics of theology, but they have in each case fixed their attention upon some special vitalizing, fundamental thought, or some peculiar point of view, and in this one great principle, or revolv-

---

[1] Warning cannot be too earnestly sounded in the interest of historical truth, which must ever be one with Christian truth, against polemic, ecclesiastico-political and dogmatic Dilettanteism in the History of Doctrines.

[2] The original sources of the History of Doctrines are, besides the respective resolutions, decrees, bulls, and confessions, the records of the transactions of the bodies by which these were promulgated ; also the writings of the theologians who participated positively or negatively, directly or indirectly, in the origination of the respective doctrinal systems. Documents attesting the faith of the church, such as sermons, hymns, and liturgies, and the literature of church discipline must also be studied. The relation of the History of Doctrines to the history of theology will always be a shifting one. The History of Doctrines may be described as a branch of the history of theology, but must nevertheless, on account of its great importance, be treated independently and more exhaustively ; and it *can* be thus treated because its special material is subdivided and held in cohesion by an organizing principle peculiar to itself.

ing around it as a centre, they have seen the whole sum and substance of Christianity, thus attaining new conceptions of the truth and deepening or transforming earlier conceptions. The historical presentation of the results must adapt itself to the course of this development. Along with the "central dogma" of every age there comes to view, not indeed a peripheral system of doctrine (Thomasius), but a general conception of Christianity dependent upon and involved in the central, dominating thought.

3. It would seem proper to begin the History of Doctrines with the adoption of the first Dogma, in the strict sense of the term, *i. e.*, that of the Council of Nice. Since, however, the Nicene, as well as the later formulation of doctrinal statements, rests upon the ideas and views of the Primitive Catholic age, the History of Doctrines must begin with the Post-Apostolic period. It closes with the last Dogmas which the churches have produced, *i. e.*, with the Second Council of Nice (787), the Vatican Council (1870), the Formula of Concord (1580), and the Synod of Dort (1619).[1] That these formal statements all have the character of Dogmas, or complete doctrinal systems, cannot be denied. It follows that, while it is not justifiable, with Thomasius, to make the Lutheran confession the goal, it must be a thorough perversion of historic verity to represent the History of Doctrines as closed before the Reformation, referring the later material to the sphere of Symbolics, or to close it with a portrayal of Romanism, Socinianism, and a general characterization of the Christianity of Luther—the last method being based upon the ground "that the entirely conservative attitude of the Reformation toward the ancient Dogma belongs not to the Foundation but to History!" (HARNACK, DG., iii. 584). But we cannot recognize this fine distinction as valid,[2] in view of the clear facts in the case. Socinianism does not belong to the History of Doctrines at all, but to the history of theology (as the product of Nominalism). The view above taken of the limits of the period properly included within the range of the History of Doctrines may therefore be regarded as final. It is self-evident that it cannot be made to cover all

---

[1] So Hauck (Schmid, DG., ed. 4); Seeberg (Thomas. ii., ed. 2); Loofs.
[2] Ib. p. 585. "To present in detail a narration of historical events until the time of the Formula of Concord and the Decrees of Dort and then suddenly to drop the subject, I consider a serious error, inasmuch as countenance is thereby given to the prejudiced opinion that the dogmatic structures framed by the churches of the Reformation in the sixteenth century constituted the classical completion of the movement, whereas they can only be regarded as points of transition." Such an argument in a historical work must fill the unprejudiced reader with amazement.

the ecclesiastical and theological developments up to the present time (*e. g.*, Baur, Hagenbach), since these movements have not yet produced any dogmas, or authorized doctrinal statements. On the contrary, it has recently been demanded (see esp. G. KRÜGER, in loco) that the distinction between the History of Doctrines and the history of theology be entirely abandoned, since it is based upon the Catholic estimate of the dogmas of the church, with which Harnack and myself are supposed to treacherously sympathize. But, apart from purely practical considerations based upon convenience in the study of the subject, it must be acknowledged that the products in the history of theology have not to the same extent attained practical ecclesiastical significance. If Dogma is a tangible historical reality, it may very appropriately be also historically depicted. Catholic claims of infallibility have nothing to do with the matter.

We note Three Chief Periods in the History of Doctrines parallel with those of Church History :

1. *The Construction of Doctrine in the Ancient Church.*

In the study of this period we shall need to (*a*) Lay a secure foundation by tracing the theological and ecclesiastical development of doctrine in the Post-Apostolic and Primitive Catholic age. (*b*) Describe the origination of the separate dogmas upon the territory of Greek Christianity (Trinity, Christ, Images), in connection with the prevalent type of piety, incidentally noting the parallel lines of doctrinal opinion developing in the Eastern Church. (*c*) Depict the formulation of the doctrinal system upon the territory of the Western Church (Augustine : Sin, Grace, the Church).

2. *The Preservation, Transformation, and Development of Doctrine in the Church of the Middle Ages.*

(*a*) Beginning with the emasculated Augustinianism of Gregory the Great, we shall have occasion to describe the external conservation of Dogma until the eleventh century (with the conquest of various concurrent misunderstandings), and then (*b*) the abnormal refinement of Dogma by Scholasticism, together with the genuine developments (Theology, the Atonement, the Sacraments, the Church) and the perversions (the dissolution of Augustinianism, Hierarchism) of the doctrinal system which fall within this period.

3. *The Development of the Doctrinal System through the Reformation, and the Opposing Crystallization of Doctrine by Roman Catholicism.*

We shall here have to treat of (*a*) The reformatory ideas of Luther and Zwingle and the fixation of the same in symbolical form. (*b*) The development of these reformatory ideas, together with the doctrinal controversies, etc., up to the Formula of Concord and the Synod of Dort. (*c*) The conservation of the Doctrine of the Middle Ages by the Romish church (Trent, Jansenistic controversies, etc., Curialism, Episcopalism, the Vatican).

### § 3. *Literature of the History of Doctrines.*

S. BAUR, Lehrb. der DG., ed. 2, p. 19 ff., and Epochen der Kirchl. Geschichtsschreibung. HARNACK, DG., i. 23 ff. HAGENBACH, DG., p. 20 ff.

Neither the polemical works of the ancient church (Irenæus, Tertullian, Epiphanius, Philaster, Theodoret, etc.), nor Abelards' Sic et Non, Chemnitz' Examen Conc. Trid., nor Joh. Gerhard's Confessio Catholica (comp. Luther's Von den Concilien und Kirchen—a repetition of proofs drawn from the History of Doctrines [Weim. ed., vol. ii.], Melanchthon's tract, De eccl. et de autoritate verbi divini, C. R. xxiii.; also, the discourse upon bulls and the periods of church history, C. R. xi. 786), can be regarded as works upon the History of Doctrines. The first genuine attempt in this direction was made by the Jesuit, DIONYSIUS PETAVIUS : " De theologicis dogmatibus," 4 vols., Paris, 1644 ff. Before him may be mentioned CANUS, De locis theologicis, ll. 12. Salamanca, 1563. Beginnings were further made from different points of view by GOTTFRIED ARNOLD, Unparteiische Kirchen- u. Ketzer-historie ; J. W. ZIEROLD, Einleiting zur gründlichen Kirchenhistoria, Leipzig u. Stargardt, 1700, and Gründliche Kirchenhistoria von der wahren und falschen Theologie, Frankf. a. M., 1703 ; LAURENZ V. MOSHEIM (Dissert. ad hist. eccl. pertinent., 2 vols., 1731 ff.; De rebus christ. ante Const., 1753) ; CHARLES W. F. WALCH (Hist. der Ketzereien, etc., 11 vols., 1762 ff.; Gedanken von der Geschichte der Glaubenslehre, 1756), as also SEMLER (Einleitung zu Baumgartens Glaubenslehre und zu desselben Unters. theol. Streitigkeiten, 1762 ff.); comp. also PLANCK, Gesch. des prot. Lehrbegriffes, 6 parts, 1787 ff. All these attempts served to improve the traditional idea of doctrinal history, but in all of them there was lacking a generalized historical conception, and they did not get beyond monographical sketches and the gathering of materials. According to Semler, the causes for the constant modification of opinions are " of a purely subjective and accidental character, because one chooses to think this way, another that ; because the relations of things are now thus, now otherwise." It was from this point of view that the first delineations in the sphere of our Science were undertaken. It was then already quite generally recognized that the Christianity of the church was permeated with Platonic ideas (Logos, Trinity, etc.). To this result contributed in no small degree the book of SOUVERAIN, Le platonisme devoilé (1700, translated by Löffler, 1782). Historians as well as dogmaticians were influenced by this thought (cf. the 17th book of HERDER, Ideen zu einer Geschichte der Menschheit). We cite the separate works upon the History of Doctrines. LANGE, Ausführliche Gesch. d. Dogmen, 1796. MÜNSCHER, Handb. d. christl. DG., 4 vols., 1797 ff. (the first 6 Jahrbb.), and Lehrbuch d. DG., ed. 1, 1811; ed. 3, 1832 ff. (excellent quotations from the sources). Comp. also AUGUSTI (1805), BERTHOLDT (1822 f.), BAUMGARTEN-CRUSIUS (1832), F. K. MEIER (1840; ed. 2, 1854), C. H. LENTZ (i. 1834), J. G. V. ENGELHARDT (1839), et al.

The suggestive works of A. NEANDER and F. CHR. BAUR marked an epoch in our Science. Both have incorporated in their treatment the results of the great intellectual activity since the end of the eighteenth century. The one possessed the marks of personality ; the other applied Hegel's conception of development. The former's History of Doctrines was edited by Jacobi (1857). Similar is Hagenbach, DG. (1850, ed. 6, revised by BEURATH). Hegel's suggestions were soon followed by MARHEINEKE (DG., edited by Matthies and Vatke, 1849), then by BAUR, who handled the appalling mass of material in a thorough and independent fashion, and presented it in the form of a development (modified, however, by speculative considerations. See Lehrb. d. DG., 1847, ed. 3, 1867, and especially Vorlesungen über. d. chr. DG., ed. F. Baur, 3 parts, 1895 ff. Also the large monographs : Lehre von d. Versöhnung, 1838, and Lehre von d. Dreieinigk. u. Menschwerdung, 3 parts, 1841 ff.). The labors of Baur were both positively and negatively of the greatest importance in the development of the History of Doctrines. TH. KLIEFOTH wrote his Einleitung in d. DG. (1839) from the standpoint of revived Lutheranism, and G. THOMASIUS furnished a careful presentation of the subject, prepared with methodical skill and a fine perception of religious problems: Die chr. DG., als Entwicklungsgesch. d. kirchl. Lehrbegriffs, 2 vols., 1874, 1876 (Plitt edited vol. ii.) ; vol. i., ed. 2, published by BONWETSCH with many additions, 1886 ; vol. ii. revised by Seeberg, materially enlarged and extended in scope by including the Reformed and Roman Catholic DG., 1889. Compare with these, SCHMID, Lehrb. d. DG., 1860 ; ed. 4, revised by HAUCK (an excellent collection of quotations from the sources); also KAHNIS, Die luth. Dogmatik. (vol. ii., Der Kirchenglaube, 1864). F. NITZSCH has in his Grundriss der chr. DG., vol. i., 1870, given us a comprehensive and careful exhibition of the material, attempting also a new arrangement of it. Finally, we mention A. HARNACK, Lehrb. d. DG., 3 vols., 1886 ff., ed. 3, 1894, with which compare his Grundriss der DG., ed. 2, 1893, and LOOFS, Leitfaden z. Studium d. DG., 1889, ed. 3, 1894. In his great work distinguished by richness of material (especially in vols. i. and ii.), wide variety in the points of view, and vivacity in narration, Harnack attempts to present the History of Doctrines in the light of the theory, that the process of their development consisted in a Hellenizing of the Gospel, following the impulses of RITSCHL'S work against Baur: Entstehung d. altkath. Kirche, ed. 2, 1857, and of M. v. ENGELHARDT, in his Christentum Justins des Märtyrers, 1878. With this the History of Doctrines turned back to an idea of the era of Illumination. The criterion appeared to have been at the same time discovered for the criticism of dogma—again in the line of the Illumination theology. A Hellenizing influence upon dogma *was* a historical necessity, but it furnishes at the same time the ground upon which the church of the present is compelled to surrender the ancient Dogma.

Finally, we have a long list of such monographs, undertaking to follow particular conceptions through the whole course of history, but throwing light upon the ideas of entire periods. In addition to the writings of BAUR already referred to, we mention especially : F. A. DORNER, Entwicklungsgesch. d. Lehre v. d. Person Christi, 3 parts, ed. 2, 1851 ff. A. RITSCHL, Die Lehre v. d. Rechtfertig. und Versöhnung, vol. i., ed. 2, 1882. H. REUTER, Augustin. Studien, 1887 ; Gesch. d. Aufklärung im MA., 2 vols., 1875 ff. R. SEEBERG, Die Theologie des Duns Scotus. KÖSTLIN, Luther's Theol., 2 vols., ed. 2, 1901. TH. HARNACK, Luth. Theol., 2 vols., 1862, 1866. G. PLITT, Einleitung in die Augustana, 2 vols., 1867 f. F. FRANK, Die Theol. der Conc. Form, 4 parts, 1858 ff. A. SCHWEIZER, Centraldogmen, 2 parts, 1854, 1856. Excellent material is also furnished in many articles in the PRE (Herzog's Real-Encyklopädie für protest. Theologie und Kirche) and in the Dictionary of Christian Biography, 4 vols., 1877 ff.

From Roman Catholic sources we mention : KLEE, Lehrb. d. DG., 2 vols., 1837 f. SCHWANE, DG., 3 vols., 1862 ff. BACH, Die DG. des Kath. MA. v. christolog. Standp., 2 vols., 1873 ff. Also, the monographs of K. WERNER, Thomas v. Aq., 3 vols., 1859, and Die Scholastik des späteren MA., 4 vols., 1881 ff.

## HISTORICAL INTRODUCTION.

§ 4.  *Greek-Roman Heathenism in Its Relation to Christianity.*

Cf. CHANTEPIE DE LA SAUSSAYE, Lehrbuch der Religionsgesch., ii., ed. 2,
421 ff. CUMONT, Die Mysterien des Mithras (in German), 1903.  A. DIE-
TERICH, Eine Mithrasliturgie, 1903.  FRIEDLÄNDER, Darstellungen aus der
Sittengesch. Roms iii., ed. 6, 509 ff.  BOUSSIER, La religion romaine d'Auguste
aux Antonins, 2 vols., 1874.  RÉVILLE, La religion à Rome sous les Sevères,
1886.  ZELLER, Die Philos. der Griechen, 3 parts, ed. 3, 1869 ff.  LUT-
HARDT, Die antike Ethik, 1887.  BONHÖFER, Die Ethik Epiktets, 1894.
MOMMSEN, Röm. Gesch., vol. v.  HATCH, Griechentum u. Christentum,
translated by Preuschen, 1892.

But when the fullness of the time came, God sent forth his
Son, born of a woman, born under the law (Gal. 4. 4 f.).  To
make this declaration intelligible, and thus to secure a foundation
for the History of Doctrines, is the purpose of the following
paragraphs, which will present but a very rapid sketch, presum-
ing upon the possession of the requisite biblical and historical
knowledge upon the part of the reader.

We must first of all take a view of Greek-Roman Heathenism.
The religion of the period is exceedingly varied (see *e. g.*,
Lucian, Deorum concil.), and it is from the time of Augustus an
age of religious restoration.  Cosmopolitanism opens the door
to strange gods, and these are in wonderful speculations amalga-
mated with indigenous ideas and forms.  Strange rites of
worship, with their "wonderful tales and legends" (Strabo.;
cf. Acts 14. 11 ff.), flourish.  The divinities of the Orient
(Osiris, Isis, Mithras), with their strange, mysterious worship,
find devotees; the mysteries of old are revived as means of salvation (σωτηρία).  Above all, it was the worship of Mithras
which now became rapidly diffused, so that from the end of the
second century onward it met the wants of large sections and
enlisted in serious conflict with Christianity.  Regeneration
to a new life, or the counsel to live in heaven, became for
multitudes a real religion imparted to them in many symbols and
acts.  From the Orient was derived the worship of the Emperors as gods, which Augustus had already desired.  But the most
ancient forms of worship are also again practiced (*"antiquity
should be revered,"* Macrob. Saturn., iii. 4).  Interest in the
highest problems of existence sustained the popular philosophy
of Stoicism with its religious-ethical tendency among the great
mass of the educated (see especially Seneca and Epictetus).
God is the Spirit (πνεῦμα) which pervades the universe, the
νοῦς, λόγος, or world-sustaining Force (πρόνοια)—hence the Stoic
Determinism.  This Divinity, who was commonly conceived

with Plato as Being without attributes, but also as " Father," is after all nothing more than Natural Law. It is the office of the knowledge of the truth to make men good. He who desires to become good must first learn to know that he is bad. This comes to pass through reflection, or reason, by the help of God (to live agreeably to nature—ὁμολογουμένως τῇ φύσει ζῆν). Man must withdraw himself upon his inward life and die to the world, to the state, to sense (καθῆκον and κατόρθωμα). The world is our state ; we are "brothers to nature." The proper attitude is expressed in the familiar Ἀνέχου καὶ ἀπέχου, bear and forbear (Gellius, Noctes att., xvii. 19. 5, and ff., following chiefly Epictetus). Even the slave is free in soul. All men are members of the Greater Republic of this world. Man is a sacred object to man. All have God in themselves: "The sacred spirit has its seat within us." " What else is nature but God and divine reason implanted in the whole world and its parts." With this combine : "A happy life consists in this one thing, that reason be perfect in us." But between the reason (logos), or God within us, and the flesh (caro) there is a conflict : " None of us is without fault (culpa). But let man do what is good." Seneca's idea was : " Trust thyself and make thyself happy." To become free from the flesh is the highest goal of man : the way of escape stands open, and beyond it—great and eternal peace (Seneca).

In these conceptions of the philosophers, as in the great religious longings of the age, are embedded elements which prepared the way for Christianity (the unity of God, the Logos of God effectually working in the world, the emphasis upon the inner man, the great longing to become God's by becoming free from self and the world, the shattering of the ancient notions of state and rank in the interest of a spiritual fellowship of all men). But, freely as these conceptions were employed by the early Christians, the difference between them and the sphere of ancient Christian thought is no less clear (absence of the divine Person and of personal intercourse with him, and the consequent lack of the idea of moral guilt, resulting in the physical and moralistic conception of morality). The yearning after another world is the great feature of the " fullness of time," but the means by which this yearning might be made permanent and effectually satisfied—this the world did not produce from within itself. The moral life of even the better element seldom corresponded to the lauded ideals, as history testifies. It is, therefore, not difficult to understand the methods employed in the apologetic writings of the ancient church (harsh combating of idolatry, accommodation to the philosophical formulas, yet the constant affirmation that Christians are " a new generation ").

## § 5. *Judaism.*

Comp. SCHÜRER, Gesch. des jüd. Volkes, 2 vols., 1890, 1886. WELL-
HAUSEN, Israelit. u. jüd. Gesch., 1894. WEBER, System der altsynagogalen
paläst. Theol., 1880. HILGENFELD, Die jüd. Apokalyptik, 1857. SACK,
Die altjüd. Rel. im Uebergang v. Bibeltum z. Talmudism, 1889. STAPFER,
Les idées religieuses en Palestine à l'époque de Jés. Christ, 1878. SIEGFRIED,
Philo, 1875. ZELLER, Philos. d. Griech., iii. 2. BOUSSET, Die Religion
des Judentums in neutest. Zeitalter, 1903.

1. It is only the ideas of the later Judaism which are here of
interest to us. The relation between God and man is a legal
relation. God commands, and man obeys in order thereby to
merit the reward : לְפוּם עַצְרָא אַגְרָא (Pirqe aboth 5. 23) and
הֶשְׁבִּין וְדַע שֶׁהַכֹּל לְפִי (ib. 4. 22; cf. Tobit 4. 6; 2. 14; 12. 9;
14. 9; 13. 2). This connection of ideas explains the efficacy
attributed to the ordinances (הֲלָכָה tradition of the elders, Mk.
7. 3), deduced by exegesis from (מִדְרָשׁ) the text of the Thorah and
constantly multiplied without restraint. There are so many commandments, in order that there may be great reward (Makkoth
3. 16). For this we wait in perpetual humility (עוֹלָם חַבָּא)
Hence the scrupulous observance of the specific laws (δικαιοσύνη
προσταγμάτων, Ps. Sol., 14. 1) and the insistence upon the
value of good works (fasting, prayers, alms. Tobit 2. 18 f.; cf.
Matt. 6. 16; 6. 2, 1 ; 5. 20. Sir., 3. 28. Ps. Sol., 3. 9. 4.
Esra 7. 7: thesaurus operum repositus apud altissimum ; cf.
8. 36, and Tobit 4. 9; Weber, p. 273 ff.). This also in part
gave vitality to the Messianic hope of the nation, which looked
forward to the coming of Him who should deliver his people
from all the distress of the present time, bringing reward to the
pious and misery to the ungodly. This is the Christ of the
Lord (χριστὸς κυρίου, Ps. Sol., 18. 8, cf. 6 ; 17. 36), the Son of
David, the Son of Man (Par. of Enoch, *e. g.*, 46. 2 ; 63. 11 ;
69. 26 ; 62. 7, 14, cf. Son of a Woman, 62. 2, 3, 5 ; Son of a
Man, 71. 14 ; 65. 5 ; 69. 29), the Son of God (Enoch, 105. 2.
4. Esra 7. 28 f.; 13. 32 ; 37. 52 ; 14. 9). According to some,
the Messiah would come himself to bring the condition of
eternal blessedness (Sibyll., iii. 766. Ps. Sol., 17. 4. En., 62.
14 f. Jn. 12. 34). According to others, the Messiah but
prepares the way for the consummation. He was thought of as
a mighty king, who should rule Israel four hundred years and
then die (4. Esra, 7. 28, 29 ; cf. Apoc. Baruch, 39. 7 ; 40. 3);
only after this should follow the consummation of the world. He

is, therefore, a man of men (ἄνθρωπος ἐξ ἀνθρώπων—Trypho in Justin. Dial., 49).[1] The Messiah appears to have nothing in common with the spiritual beings who are the media of the divine presence in the world, with the angels who appear with increasing frequency, with the "great Scribe" of God, nor with the מיטטרון (probably μετάθρονος) and the מימרא (See Weber, p. 178.) But longing for the Messianic kingdom was awakened especially by the consciousness of sin, which oppresses the entire human race and from which man is absolutely unable to free himself. How can the law with its rewards bring help, if no man since Adam has fulfilled the law? Through the fall of Adam sin and guilt have come upon the human race (4. Esra; 3. 26; 4. 30; 7. 118 f.; 8. 35, 17. Apoc. Bar., 1703; 23. 4; 48. 42; 54. 15, 19. Cf. Weber, p. 216, 217).

We have nothing without the Almighty and his law (Apoc. Baruch, 85. 3). Thus there is a continual advance, as well in pessimistic estimate of self and the universe, as in the vividness of the hope centering in the kingdom of the royal Messiah. We may mention also the rich development attained by cosmology, by a peculiar metaphysics (everything earthly pre-exists in heaven), and in eschatological conceptions.

2. It is of the highest importance to observe the combination formed by Judaism with Greek philosophy, in which are foreshadowed many of the developments of the earlier Christian theology. Here the chief sources are the Wisdom of Solomon and Philo; cf. also 4 Macc., the Jewish Sibylline books, and the didactic poem of Phocylides: (a) God is conceived (Platonically) as abstract Being, without attributes. (b) There accordingly yawns a great gulf between God and the ὕλη (matter). (c) This is bridged by the intermediate existences, angels, demons, δυνάμεις (powers), λόγοι (words), comprehended in the ἰδέα ἰδεῶν (forms of forms) or the σοφία (wisdom) or the λόγος, ὁ λόγος πρωτόγονος, δεύτερος θεός (word, first-born word, other God), neither ungenerated as God nor generated as are we, the

---

[1] The representation of the birth of the Messiah from the virgin is also foreign to Judaism, vid. Seeberg, Glaube und Glaube, p. 28 f., note 2. The announcement of the pre-existence of the Messiah occasionally met with is to be understood in the light of Enoch, 46. 3 : "Before the sun and the constellations were created his Name was mentioned before the Lord of spirits." The later rabbinical literature similarly describes the Name of the Messiah as pre-existent (vid. Weber, l. c., pp. 333, 339 f.), as also the Thorah is declared, being involved in the divine wisdom, to be pre-existent and the "daughter of God." (See Weber, p. 14 ff.) This is all but a part of the later Jewish metaphysics, according to which everything Judaic has its origin in heaven.

high-priest mediating between the creature (dem Gewordenen) and him who has begotten it, and representing man as his advocate, the bread from Heaven, the source of the water of knowledge. He is the instrumentality (ὄργανον) through which the world was created. But the Logos is neither conceived as a person, nor as bearing any relation to the Messiah. (*d*) The dualism of this system is seen in its anthropology, in which the body of man is regarded as a prison and the cause of evil: "From the way in which it came to birth, sinning is natural (σομφυὲς) to it." Vit. Mos. iii., 157 Mangey. (*e*) Salvation is therefore deliverance from sensuality. This is experienced through the fulfillment of the law, whose external forms must maintain their validity (de migr. Abr., i. 450 Mangey), but ultimately through enthusiastic ecstasy. (*f*) All this is deduced by allegorical interpretation, after the manner of the Haggadah, from the Old Testament. Philo presents it as authorized in the strictest sense by inspiration: "For the prophets are the interpreters, God using their organs for the proclamation of whatever things he wished (de monarch., ii. 222, and, especially, Quis div. rer. her. i. 511 Mangey; cf. also Sanday, Inspiration (Bampton Lectures), ed. 2, 1894, p. 74 ff.[1] Nägelsbach, Nachhomer. Theol., p. 173 ff. Homer. Theol., ed. 2, p. 187 ff. Pauly Realencycl., ii. 1117).

Among the Essenes also similar Hellenistic conceptions exercised a formative influence.

### § 6. *The Primitive Christian Proclamation.*

Cf. B. WEISS, Bibl. Theol., ed. 2, 1901.  Die Religion des N. T., 1903. W. BEYSCHLAG, Neutest. Theologie, ed. 2, 1896.  H. J. HOLZMANN, Lehrbuch der neutest. Theologie, ed. 2, 1897.  HOFMANN, Bibl. Theol., ed. Volck, 1886.  A. RITSCHL, Rechtf. u. Vers. ii.  PFLEIDERER, Das Urchristentum, ed. 2, 1902.  WEIZSÄCKER, Das ap. Zeitalter, ed. 2, 1892. NÖSGEN, Gesch. d. neutest. Offenb., 1891-93.  P. WERNLE, Die Anfänge unserer Religion, 1901.  H. H. WENDT, Die Lehre Jesu, ed. 2, 1901. H. CREMER, Die paulinische Rechtfertigungslehre, 1898.  A. SCHLATTER, Der Glaube im N. T., ed. 2, 1895.  R. SCHMIDT, Die paulinische Christologie, 1870.  A. SEEBERG, Der Tod Christi in seiner Bedeutung für die Erlösung, 1895.

1. The prophecy of the Old Testament prophets culminates in the idea of the "new covenant" in Jeremiah (31. 31 ff.), and in the thought that God shall reign as king over his people and the whole world in righteousness and grace. Jesus Christ and his work constitute the realization of these ideas. He claimed for himself absolute authority. His words take a place of equal

---

1 This Platonic theory of inspiration, which influenced Christian theology in many ways, leads us back to the Platonic conception of the inspired seer. See Phaedrus, c. 22, p. 244 a.  Tim., c. 32, p. 71 e.

dignity by the side of the declarations of the law (Matt. 5. 7), and will outlast heaven and earth (Matt. 24. 25 f., 35). He announced himself as the promised Messiah. This is the meaning of the term which he applies to himself, the "Son of Man" (cf. Book of Enoch), and more than this is not in the first instance involved in his designation as the "Son of God." If the term "Son of man" describes the Messiah as of heavenly nature, origin, and goal (cf. Jn. 3. 12 f.), he is the "Son of God," as one who derives the content and motive of his inner life from God and therefore lives and works in the power of God (Matt. 11. 27; 3. 34 f.). Since now Christ as the Messiah lives, teaches, and works in God and by the power of God, he exercises divine dominion over men (Lk. 22. 29 f.; 17. 21, 23; 1. 33. Matt. 13; 12. 2, 8), and thereby establishes the blessed condition of men as a kingdom of God. Inasmuch as he exercises divine dominion, there belong to him the divine attributes of omnipotence and omniscience, the power to forgive sins—which did not according to Jewish teaching belong to the Messiah—absolute authority, power, over heaven and earth until the end of time. Although John often applies other terms, his ideas do not extend essentially beyond the synoptic representations. The conceptions of Christ as the light, the life, the truth and the way merely give fuller expression to the thought that he exercises the divine government of the world for the salvation of men.

2. Thus in Christ is the one expectation met. He rules with divine dominion for the salvation of men in the world, imparting to them life and righteousness, and gathering them into a kingdom of God. In this, one aspect of the new covenant is realized. But, according to Jeremiah, that covenant embraces a double purpose. The law is to be written by the power of the Spirit in the hearts of men, and their sins are to be forgiven. This second purpose was placed by Jesus in a peculiar relation to his death, the necessity for which he strongly emphasized (δεῖ). Jesus came into the world to minister. This ministry embraces the surrender of his soul to death as a λύτρον, so that many may be thereby delivered from death (Matt. 20. 28. Mk. 9. 35). Since now death may be regarded for us essentially as a penalty, Jesus has designated the giving of his life as a means of deliverance from the penalty of death, availing for many; or as a means of the forgiveness of sins (cf. Matt. 16. 26). The Gospel of John explains this by the illustration of a shepherd faithful unto death (Jn. 10. 11, 15, 17 f.; 12. 24 f.; 15. 13; 18. 11). His conception was, therefore, the same as that of Jesus himself, that the fidelity of Jesus even unto death and his obedi-

3

ence to the Father constitute the ground, or ransom, for the sake of which God forgives the sins of many ( Matt. 26. 28 ff.). The declaration in 1 Cor. 11. 25 expressly represents the new covenant established through the blood of Christ as embracing the forgiveness of sins ; but the shedding of the blood of Christ includes also the other aspect of the new covenant, *i. e.*, the awakening of new life and the implanting of the law within the heart. Each of these two cycles of thought—divine dominion and new covenant—thus of itself embraces the whole compass of the work of Christ. He is the King, who bestows a new life upon men ; and he does this by achieving for them, through his death, the forgiveness of sins.

An analysis of the manifold particulars in which Jesus has established the state of grace under his dominion, or in his kingdom, would carry us beyond our limits. The chief categories are as follows : (*a*) Repentance ($\mu\varepsilon\tau\dot{a}\nu\omega\iota a$), with faith, as the consciousness of the divine authority and power of Christ (Matt. 8. 11, 13 ; 9. 2, 22 ; 15. 28. Lk. 17. 19 ; 7. 48, 50)); as a receiving ($\lambda a\beta\varepsilon\dot{\iota}\nu$) in relation to Christ and his gifts (Jn. 1. 16 ; 13. 20 ; 17. 18). (*b*) The following of Christ, and that which it involves (Matt. 16. 16. Jn. 6. 68 f.; 8. 12). (*c*) The true fulfilling of the law, or true righteousness, love (Matt. 22. 23 f.; 23. 23). (*d*) A prayerful life. According to Matt. 16. 18 ; 13. 9 ff., Jesus anticipated a historical unfolding of the kingdom of God in the form of a congregation ($\dot{\varepsilon}x x\lambda\eta\sigma\dot{\iota}a$). In this congregation he will be present (Matt. 28. 20. 1 Cor. 11. 24 f.; 16. 22. Matt. 26. 26 ff.). He will also take part as her Lord in the last judgment. In the final days of his ministry he indicated the tokens which should herald the latter (Matt. 24. 6-31). In various parables he combined the general tenor of these prophecies. We should look for the return of him who will soon come and summon to account, in order that the eternal destiny of men may be determined (Matt. 24. 43 ff.; 25. 1 f., 14 ff., 31 ff.).

3. But, according to the Gospel narratives, the revelation of Christ was NOT completed in these declarations uttered before his death. And that which is said in the reports concerning the words of the RISEN CHRIST we find fully confirmed in the other New Testament writings. Everywhere we meet with the same ideas and assertions, which are simply inexplicable in this their absolute harmony if not derived from words of Christ himself ; for they cannot be accounted for by anything contained in the other sources accessible to the writers, *i. e.*, the Old Testament and Judaism. The risen Christ, first of all, convinced his disciples that he was really alive, and thus at the same time

awakened in them the conviction of his victory and his power over his enemies. He then instructed and exhorted them concerning his person and their mission. We unfortunately possess only very brief summarizing accounts of these instructions (Matt. 28. 18 ff. Lk. 24. 44 ff. Acts 1. 6 ff.). The task of their world-mission is revealed to the disciples. With it are combined preaching and baptism. At the same time there is imparted to them in the trinitarian formula a knowledge of the position of Christ and of the Spirit promised them in the life of the God-head. The term, "Son of God," received in consequence a new character. It no longer signifies merely, in the sense of the Old Testament usage, the man beloved and led by God, but the Son, who is in heaven with the Father, eternal and omnipresent as the Father. Thus the riddle of the person of Christ was solved for the disciples. His authority, claims, and promises during his earthly life now first attain for them their full significance and force. The Gospel of John in particular undertakes to present the human life of Christ in the light of the religious knowledge afterward attained. The last revelation of Christ serves to interpret his earlier revelations. This finds recognition when John discriminates between a state of divine glory (δόξα) belonging to the past, i. e., to the pre-existence of Christ, and his present existence (Jn. 12. 16, 23 ; 17. 5), but in such a way that this glory is manifested in Christ's earthly life (1. 14 ; 2. 11 ; 11. 4 ; 17. 10, 6-9), and especially in his sufferings as the consummation of his earthly life (13. 31 f.; 17. 1). The glory of Christ is the unlimited power of divine activity. To the pre-existent Son of God (8. 58 ; 10. 35 f.) belongs as his peculiar nature the divine glory. This was the knowledge of Christ which the disciples received through their communion with the risen Jesus, and by which they became fitted to interpret his earthly life and actions. The immense historical significance of the Gospel of John consists in the fact, that it makes it possible for us to understand how the disciples of Jesus were enabled and compelled to associate the historical events which they witnessed with the religious experience of the eternal, omnipotent Lord: "The Word became flesh."

The Spirit, hitherto regarded, in harmony with the Old Testament conception, as a revelation of the presence of the divine power (Matt. 1. 18. Lk. 1. 35), as a creative source of religious knowledge and power (Lk. 1. 15, 41, 67 ; 24. 49. Acts 1. 8. Matt. 10. 19 f.; 13. 11. Jn. 3. 6 ; 20. 22), or of miraculous works (Matt. 12. 28, 32), is by the last declarations of Christ described as likewise a personal principle, as the ἄλλος παράκλητος, who, coming from the Father (Jn. 15. 26), sent by

Christ (16. 7), makes the revelation of Christ effectual in the disciples, and thus becomes the medium of the coming of Christ to them (14. 18 f.; 16. 12 ff.).

These were the chief features of the revelation of Jesus Christ. He exercised divine dominion, or actualized the new covenant. He thus revealed his divine nature, and he expressly based this nature upon the conception of the unity of the Father with the Son and the Spirit. He opened up to the disciples a great task, while at the same time he held out the prospect of his presence and co-operation for its accomplishment through the coming of the Spirit.

4. In accordance with the prophecy of Christ, the Spirit produced a great awakening. Wonderful words and wonderful deeds were given to those who believed on Jesus. A sphere of the miraculous (see Acts) surrounds the church. But the Spirit did not exert his power as a revolutionary principle. On the contrary, he manifested himself as the Spirit of Christ, establishing the authority of Christ as Lord in the church. But in connection with this element of stimulation there were other and stable elements which preserved the work of the Spirit from subjective exaltation and onesidedness. These were the Old Testament; the authority of the words of Jesus and of the apostles as his historical witnesses (Acts 1. 22; 3. 15; 4. 33; 5. 32; 8. 12; cf. also Matt. 16. 19); the ordinances of baptism and the Lord's Supper, established by Jesus; and, finally, a complex of traditions (παραδόσεις), embracing the ordinances just named. These traditions included a formula of belief, of which 1 Cor. 15. 3 f. has preserved a fragment easily recognizable. This formula of belief stood in a peculiar relation to the administration of baptism. It had a confessional character. There was accordingly a formulated basis of instruction for those desiring to receive the sacrament of baptism, i. e., a baptismal confession (cf. Rom. 6. 3 f. Acts 19. 2. Heb. 10. 22, 23; cf. 4. 14. Eph. 4. 5 f. 1 Pet. 3. 21 f. 1 Tim. 6. 12. 1 Jn. 2. 20). 1 Cor. 15. 3 gives an indication as to the age of this formula. It was made known to Paul already at the time of his baptism. Since in the New Testament we meet very frequently with a triadic arrangement and formulation of ideas (1 Cor. 12. 4; 6. 11. 2 Cor. 13. 13. Rom. 15. 16, 30. Eph. 2. 19-22; 5. 19; 4. 4-6; 1. 3-14. 2 Thes. 2. 13-15. Jude 20 f. 1 Pet. 1. 2; .2. 5; 4. 13 f. Heb. 10. 29-31. Jn. 14. 15-17, 26; 15. 26; 16. 13-16. Rev. 1. 4 f. With the last passage compare 1 Cor. 14. 12, 32; 12. 10. Rev. 22. 6), and since the command to baptize as given by Matthew contains the trinitarian formula, it is in the highest degree probable that the

formula of belief was arranged in a triad, *i. e.*, that it formed the basis from which at a later day our Apostles' Creed was derived. In favor of the triadic formulation is to be reckoned, first of all, the later form of the confession, and also the facts, that this confession is a baptismal confession, and that Matthew expressly combines baptism and the Trinity, as is the case also in Didache 7. 1, 3; cf. 1 Cor. 6. 11. Further, Acts 19. 2 appears to be most easily understood upon the supposition of a triadically divided baptismal formula of instruction.[1]

To this formula was then added a "tradition" concerning the Lord's Supper (1 Cor. 11. 23), which stands in connection with the custom of admitting the baptized at once to the celebration of the latter. But, besides this doctrinal material, tradition has preserved a great deal of an ethical character in the form of the enumeration of vices and virtues. Outlines of this character run through the entire New Testament and lie at the foundation of the "Two Ways" of the Didache. Compare the paradoxes of 1 Cor. 11. 2. To these two great chief elements may have been

---

[1] ALFRED SEEBERG in his important work, Der Catechismus der Urchristenheit, 1903, disputed the triadic form of this confession, as also its derivation from the tradition attested in Matt. 28. His arguments are essentially as follows: That the New Testament speaks of a baptism into the name of Christ, but never into the name of the Father and of the Spirit, which would be utterly incomprehensible if the formulation of Matthew 28. 19 had been already known to the writers. Further, that since the reception of the Spirit occurred only after baptism at the laying on of hands, a confession of the Spirit before baptism would not have been possible (7. 235 ff.). In response to this it may be said, that Matt. 28. 19 is not at all supposed to be a "formula" in the strict sense of the word, but only a summary of the last teachings of Christ parallel with the other summary in Lk. 24. 46-49, except that Matthew, in distinction from Luke, has given this summary a definite reference to baptism, recognizing that baptism in fact transports man into the sphere of the personal influence of the Father, Son, and Spirit. The apostles were taught what was involved in their commission to the whole world and in the revelation of God which was at the same time made to them. In this connection there was given to them, according to Luke, the idea of the Trinity, which Matthew has placed in a special relation to baptism. The triadic formula is thus in any case traceable to the tradition attested by both Matthew and Luke; but the particular formulation of this tradition, as Matthew has it, can scarcely have been generally known in the time of Paul. Baptism was administered commonly only into the name of Christ. It must then have been only through Matthew that the triadic formula came into general use. This does not, however, by any means exclude the view that instruction and confession during this period recognized the Father, the Son, and the Spirit (let the tradition preserved by Luke be borne in mind). If the baptized person looked forward at once to the reception of the Spirit, then must the instruction which he received and the faith which he was to confess also have had reference to the Spirit. It is my conviction that the triadic formula has its roots in the words of Jesus of which Matthew and Luke, each in his own way, have formed an epitome, and that the original basis for baptismal instruction and confession was triadically arranged.

later added instructions concerning ordination and congregational offices, as is suggested by various turns of expression in the pastoral epistles (*e. g.*, Tit. 1. 7 f.; 2. 1 ff.   1 Tim. 3. 1, 8, 10, 13, 15, 16.   2 Tim. 2. 2).   Heb. 6. 1, 2 offers a summary of these fixed elements of the instruction given by the church, which are now regarded as a " foundation ; " and the Didache, in perfect harmony with the latter, presents us a revision of the material in a later form.[1]

Thus the Spirit of Christ and certain definite forms of proclamation, or of doctrinal and moral instruction, stood from the very beginning side by side in the Christian Church. They worked together, although there were not wanting at a quite early day collisions between the two principles. Whatever heresies or disorderly elements appeared in the congregations seem to have appealed to the " Spirit." Very early was heard the warning against " false prophets." In opposition to them, the body of common ideas and representations in the church became constantly more fixed. Even with such a genius as Paul, the elements of the common Christianity outweigh the original elements of his own conceptions of truth.

5. This brings us to the gospel of Paul, or to the elements of a Pauline theology. Natural endowments and talents, the culture which he had enjoyed, and the Christ whom he had been permitted to see, made this man the greatest of the apostles. The Pauline theology may be presented in the following categories : (1) Law and gospel, faith and works, atonement and justification. (2) Spirit and flesh, the new life. (3) The congregation of believers, or the church. These categories have for their common basis the apostle's ideas of God and Christ. The extraordinarily vivid conception of God which distinguished Paul is concentrated in the thought that God is the omnipotent, spiritual Will. To this Will are to be traced all events—whether it be the choice of the apostles and their mission, transformations in the religious and moral life, or the ordinary occurrences of daily life. It is God who works in us to will and to do (Phil. 2. 13). As everything comes to pass " according to the counsel of his will " (Eph. 1. 11), so revelation is a

---

[1] In a certain sense our Gospels might be also included in this category. If the Gospel of Mark, according to ancient tradition and reports, originated with Peter, and if Luke set himself the task of giving to Theophilus an orderly account of the things which he had been taught, the conclusion can scarcely be avoided that the synoptic Gospels have their common basis in collections of material which had been gradually formed in the missionary preaching of the apostles. The problem as to the Gospels is not indeed thereby solved, but the peculiar, and in principle similar, grouping of the material in the synoptic writers is thus placed in a new light.

"making known to us the mystery of his will" (Eph. 1. 9) and faith the "knowledge of his will" (Col. 1. 9), which however serves for the accomplishment of his "purpose according to election" (Rom. 9. 11 ; 8. 2, 8 ff.; 9. 23. Eph. 2. 9 ff.). This purpose includes an election made before all time (Eph. 1. 4. 2 Thes. 2. 13 f.), which, so far as individual men are concerned, is actualized in the calling, which latter is always conceived as being effectual (Rom. 8. 30 ; 9. 12, 23. 2 Thes. 2. 14). The absolute divine Will is therefore eternal and rational will. It is characterized further as loving-will (Rom. 5. 5, 8) or grace (Rom. 3. 24; 5. 15. 2 Cor. 1. 3 ; 6. 1. Col. 4. 18). At the same time God is represented as the Righteous One, in the double sense which this attribute bears in the Old Testament, *i. e.*, as he who, because he is always consistent with himself, is faithful toward the righteous but punishes the wicked (Rom. 3. 26 ; 2. 5. 2 Thes. 1. 5, 6).

To this spiritual almighty Will, which rules in the world in love and righteousness, all things which occur are therefore to be traced. This point of view is constantly recurring in the writings of Paul, and hence any presentation of his theology must most strongly emphasize it. To this the Pauline Christology also leads. Christ is the Lord, to whom belongs the fullness of the divine nature—the "Lord of Glory" (1 Cor. 2. 8 f. 2 Cor. 4. 4). In this designation of Christ as Lord the same idea finds expression which was presented in the words of Jesus when he spoke of the dominion (βασιλεία) which Christ exercises (cf. esp. Rom. 4. 9 ; 10. 12 ff. 2 Cor. 4. 5. 1 Cor. 15. 24. Heb. 2. 11). But Paul now thought of Christ as the ascended Lord, who from heaven, with divine omnipotence and omnipresence, permeates the world and rules in his church. Christ, "who is above all, God blessed forever" (Rom. 9. 5, cf. Tit. 1. 3 ; 2. 13 ; 3. 4), is in us (2 Cor. 13. 3, 5), as we on the other hand are in him (Rom. 8. 1. 1 Cor. 4. 16 ; 6. 17. Gal. 3. 27). He who fills all things, in whom all things exist, is the head of the church (Eph. 1. 22 ff.; 2. 14 ff. Col. 1. 9, 18 ; 3. 11). All of these variations of thought rest upon the conception, "the Lord is that Spirit" (2 Cor. 3. 17, cf. 1 Cor. 15. 45; 6. 17). The Christ of Paul is the spiritual Energy which forms the world and shapes history. He is related to the church as the governing head to the governed body. As all-penetrating power, he is in us, as we on the other hand are in him. In all these ideas we are to recognize, not highly wrought similes, but assertions in regard to realities to be understood in the most literal sense. But this Lord-Spirit is one with the Son of David, born of a woman (Gal. 4. 4), who came "in the likeness of the flesh'' (Rom. 1. 3 f.). Through the resurrection he has been transferred to the heavenly state of dominion (Eph. 1. 20 f.), which he at present exercises, and he will soon, at his Parousia, be manifest to all. This conception becomes comprehensible only when we remember that Paul speaks of a preexistence of Christ ''in the form of God'' (Phil. 2. 6 ff. 2 Cor. 8. 9), as the '' first-born of the whole creation,'' through whom all things were created (Col. 1. 15 ff.    1 Cor. 8. 6; 10. 4.   2 Cor. 4. 4). Christ, therefore, through the resurrection returned unto the state of the '' form of God,'' which originally belonged to him, after having in obedience to the Father borne for a time the '' form of a servant.'' Viewed theoretically, there yet remain here many questions unsolved. That the divinity of Christ, in the proper sense of the term, was firmly held by Paul is evident. The triadic formulas receive their interpretation from the principles above stated.    Prayer to Christ (Rom. 10. 12, 14. Phil. 2. 10.   1 Cor. 1. 2; 16. 22.    2 Cor. 12. 8) is the practical consequence. The History of Doctrines, if it is to understand the further development of Christology, must keep this constantly before it as the starting-point. It is one of the most certain fàcts of history, that the thought and feeling of the apostolic age was based, not upon the man Jesus, but upon the Lord in heaven, who pervades and governs the universe, omnipotent and omniscient. It is simply absurd to attempt to explain this in a psychological way from the immense impression made by the man Jesus; for no imagination could mistake the most powerful man for God. Just as little can the resurrection in and of itself suffice for explanation; for even a resurrected man remains a man. A historical explanation is conceivable only upon the supposition that the disciples received from the Risen One impressions and evidences of his power and presence which compelled them to believe : He in us and we in him—as Paul also realized in his experience. Only from this point of view does the faith of the apostolic age become comprehensible. Every other explanation fails to explain anything historically, and ignores the simple facts of the case in the sources of our knowledge, not only in Paul and John, but also in the closing chapters of Matthew and Luke. But, despite all this, the question, how divinity and humanity are related to one another in Christ, finds no solution. The ''fullness of the Godhead,'' the ''spirit of holiness'' (Heb. 2. 9.   Rom. 1. 4), which constitute his divine nature, are something different from the existence '' according to the flesh,'' but no definition is given of the relation of the one to the other.

Like the ascended Christ, the Spirit of Christ, or of God, is active, and that, too, in the hearts of believers, whether exciting within them the miraculous powers of the *charismata* (1 Cor. 12. 11; 14. 12. Col. 1. 29), or as the "demonstration and power of the Spirit" (1 Cor. 2. 4. 1 Thes. 1. 5 f.; 2. 13. Eph. 6. 17). And it was especially in the latter that Paul recognized the specific energy of the Spirit. Not outward miracles nor religious exaltation appeared to him as the peculiar domain of the Spirit; but the Word, which becomes effectual as a "power of God" (Rom. 1. 16). As Christ is for Paul divine energy, so too the Spirit. Thus Christ is the Spirit (2 Cor. 3. 17). The difference is, that Christ has the church at large as the object of his activity, whereas the Spirit is the divine energy, as apprehending and transforming individuals.

6. The first great group of ideas in the Pauline theology may be placed under the title: Spirit ($\pi\nu\varepsilon\tilde{\upsilon}\mu\alpha$) and Flesh ($\sigma\acute{\alpha}\rho\xi$). Man is flesh—in the first place, according to his natural, visible substance; but also because the latter by virtue of its lust ($\varepsilon\pi\iota\vartheta\upsilon\mu\acute{\iota}\alpha$) determines the character of man's spirit, and thus the flesh becomes the instrument of sin. To be "after the flesh" ($\kappa\alpha\tau\grave{\alpha}$ $\sigma\acute{\alpha}\rho\kappa\alpha$) denotes the immoral condition of the sinner; whereas to be "in the flesh" ($\varepsilon\nu$ $\sigma\alpha\rho\kappa\grave{\iota}$) belongs to human nature (2 Cor. 10. 3). Thus arises a "walking in the lusts of the flesh" (Eph. 2. 3), with a mind ($\varphi\rho\acute{\upsilon}\nu\eta\mu\alpha$) of the flesh (Rom. 8. 7) and a "minding earthly things" (Phil. 3. 19; 2. 4, 21), the "worldly lusts" (Tit. 3. 3; 2. 12), the "desires of the flesh" (Eph. 2. 3), and the "works of the flesh" (Gal. 5. 19 f.). It is not the idea of Paul, that the natural constitution of man produces sin in him; for sin came into the world by a particular act (Rom. 5. 12. 1 Cor. 15. 22). He means, on the contrary, that the historical power of sin ($\dot{\alpha}\mu\alpha\rho\tau\acute{\iota}\alpha$) gives a free rein to lust in man and thereby the flesh becomes the determining factor in his life. Sin, thus regarded, is for Paul a degradation of human nature, a perversity. From this condition, contrary to nature and unworthy of it, Christ as the Spirit sets free. His energy ($\varepsilon\nu\acute{\varepsilon}\rho\gamma\varepsilon\iota\alpha$) works with power ($\varepsilon\nu$ $\delta\upsilon\nu\acute{\alpha}\mu\varepsilon\iota$) within us (Col. 1. 29). We become in him a "new creature" (2 Cor. 5. 17. Gal. 6. 15). He lives in us (Phil. 1. 21. Rom. 8. 10. 2 Cor. 4. 10 f. Gal. 2. 20). Wisdom, righteousness, and sanctification proceed from him (1 Cor. 1. 30; 6. 11). He who puts on Christ ceases to obey the will ($\pi\rho\acute{\upsilon}\nu\upsilon\iota\alpha$) of the flesh. But as through Christ a new life is begun in us, so will he also make us alive through the resurrection. It is only when we have received eternal life that the redemption of Christ is completed (Rom. 13. 11; 8. 23 f.). We have merely more precise and concrete delineations of this thought,

when Paul describes in many aspects the creative activity of the divine Spirit in the soul of man (the Spirit reveals, teaches, witnesses, confirms, inspires, impels, vivifies, renews, strengthens, sanctifies, infuses love, fills us, sets us free, etc.). "As many as are led by the Spirit of God, these are sons of God" (Rom. 8. 14). Christians live and walk "in the Spirit" and "according to the Spirit." They serve God in him and they lead a new life through him (Gal. 5. 16, 22. Rom. 7. 6. Phil. 3. 3. Eph. 6. 18). They are spiritual (πνευματικοί), whereas other men are only natural (ψυχικοί) (Gal. 6. 1. 1 Cor. 2. 14, 18). They expect at the resurrection, instead of the merely natural body, a spiritual body σῶμα πνευματικόν (1 Cor. 15. 44).

But the organ for the reception of the spiritual influences of Christ, or of the Spirit, is faith (Eph. 3. 17 f.). Faith is also, according to Paul, a taking and receiving. It is further characterized as a purely spiritual activity ; as a knowledge of the will of God (Col. 1. 9, 6. Eph. 1. 17. Phil. 3. 8. 1 Tim. 2. 4. 2 Tim. 2. 25); as an obedience of faith, or to the faith (ὑπακοὴ πίστεως, Rom. 1. 5; 16. 26); as "the obedience (ὑπακοὴ) of your confession unto the Gospel of Christ" (2 Cor. 9. 13. Rom. 6. 17; 10. 3 f., 16 f. 2 Thes. 1. 8. 2 Cor. 10. 4 f.); as a personal conviction (Rom. 14. 23); as love for the truth (2 Thes. 2. 10); as also a full persuasion, boldness, confidence (πληροφορία, παρρησία, πεποίθησις) (Rom. 4. 20, 21. Eph. 3. 12). But as faith thus in manifold ways apprehends the spiritual gifts and influences of God, it is, since God is efficient Will, essentially to be defined as subjection to God in obedience, or trust. Even faith itself must according to Paul be received as an effect of the Spirit ; for it is a gift of God (Phil. 1. 29. 2 Cor. 4. 13) and comes from the Gospel (Rom. 10. 17. 1 Cor. 15. 14. Gal. 3. 2, 5), in which the effectual working of the Spirit is exercised.

Thus there is awakened in man by the Spirit through faith a new life : faith working by love (Gal. 5. 6). Inasmuch as the Spirit makes the will of God effectual in man, man becomes free from the authority of the law (2 Cor. 3. 17. Rom. 8. 2). Christian morality culminates in liberty (Gal. 5. 1-13). The letter kills, but the Spirit makes alive. Sin remains even in the believer. Hence sanctification still proceeds in his life (1 Thes. 4. 3. Rom. 6. 19, 22), as also conversion (μετάνοια—2 Cor. 7. 9 f.; 12. 21. 2 Tim. 2. 25); grace is increased (2 Cor. 9. 8. Eph. 3. 16), and the moral life is a constant striving (Phil. 3. 13 ff.). A process is begun in man through the Christ-Spirit, which finds its consummation in eternal glory (Rom. 8. 18, 30. 2 Cor. 3. 8).

7. We pass now to the second combination of ideas found in the writings of Paul. Sin (ἁμαρτία), as we have seen, manifests itself in man as a carnal being. But it displays itself also as disobedience (παρακοή), and hence, as incurring personal guilt. This guilt is incurred by both Jews and Gentiles (Rom. 1. 3). The law cannot free from guilt. It only awakens a sense of sin. It kills, as Paul knew by experience (1 Cor. 15. 56. Rom. 7. 7 f.; 3. 19; 2. 13, 25; 5. 13). Nevertheless it comes from God, but has been imposed upon men only for pedagogical reasons and for a definite time (Gal. 3. 19, 21, 24. Rom. 5. 20). For the present time the Gospel (εὐαγγέλιον) holds sway, it being identical with the ancient gospels (εὐαγγελία) which preceded the law (Gal. 3. 17 f. Rom. 1. 2. Eph. 3. 6. Acts 13. 22. Tit. 1. 2 f.).

But since the entire race rests under guilt, and hence under penalty of death, and the law can only serve to make us sensible of our guilt, we need the forgiveness of sins upon the part of God. But deliverance from the guilt of sin occurs through the forensic justifying act (δικαιοῦν; cf. λογίζεσθαι εἰς δικαιοσύνην) of God (Rom. 2. 13, 26; 3. 4; 4. 4 f. Gal. 3. 6). Judaism also possessed the forensic conception of righteousness (זְכוֹת and הַעֲלוֹת):

but whereas, according to Jewish ideas, the law is a living power and stimulates man to the good, which God then accepts as a basis for justification, according to Paul the law is incapable of making man good, and only faith justifies, and it does so simply because it accepts Christ. God pronounces righteous the ungodly man ἀσεβής (Rom. 4. 5), who has no righteousness of his own (Rom. 10. 3. Phil. 3. 9). The meaning of justification by faith and not by works is therefore, not that God recognizes faith as an ethical beginning, but that it is faith alone by virtue of which man apprehends the righteousness achieved by Christ (Gal. 2. 20; 3. 13. Rom. 5. 9; 4. 25; 3. 22 ff.). This is the sense in which we are to understand the "righteousness which is of God by (ἐπὶ) faith" (Phil. 3. 9). It is the righteousness of God, or his faithfulness (Rom. 1. 17; cf. 3. 3, 4, 26; 5. 21; 4. 16; 10. 3), which graciously accomplishes the non-attributing of guilt, or the pronouncing righteous (Rom. 4. 5 ff. 2 Cor. 5. 19. Col. 1. 14. Eph. 1. 7). The formula: Faith is accounted for righteousness (Rom. 4. 3 ff.; cf. Gen. 15. 6), in itself misleading—it is constructed in opposition to the Pharisaic idea: Works are accounted for righteousness—is therefore meant to indicate merely that the righteousness bestowed by God avails for man only upon condition of faith, because only faith can make it an inward possession of the man. "Of faith" (ἐκ πίστεως) is therefore (Rom. 4. 16) the same as "according to grace"

($\varkappa\alpha\tau\dot{\alpha}\ \chi\dot{\alpha}\rho\iota\nu$). Hence the thought of Paul is clear : The righteousness of God ($\vartheta\varepsilon\upsilon\tilde{\upsilon}$) bestows upon man the righteousness which is
of ($\dot{\varepsilon}\varkappa$) God ; but man possesses this as the righteousness of faith
($\dot{\varepsilon}\varkappa\ \pi\iota\sigma\tau\varepsilon\omega\varsigma$). But if faith itself is now a gift of God, there results a double connection with the line of thought developed
under item 6 : God works faith in us through the Spirit, and he
gives to faith righteousness as a conscious possession ; cf. also
Eph. 2. 8 ff. Tit. 3. 5-7. Phil. 3. 9 ff.

The justified man has peace with God (Rom. 5. 1 f.); sonship and right of inheritance (Rom. 8. 23, 15 f. Gal. 4. 5, 6 ;
3. 26 f., 29. Eph. 1. 5); freedom from the law (Gal. 2. 4 ; 4.
26 ff.; 5. 1), etc.

We are now, for Christ's sake, declared righteous. But is it
for the sake of his work of redemption ? On the one hand, Paul
defines the object of Christ, who, in obedience to God, gave himself to death on account of our sins, but was raised by God from
the dead, to have been deliverance from the world (Gal. 1. 4),
sanctification and purification (Eph. 5. 25. Tit. 2. 14), a life
dedicated to Christ (1 Thes. 5. 10); on the other hand, he
represents the death of Christ as the means through which we
receive forgiveness and are placed in a new relation to God.
The two conceptions stand side by side in 2 Cor. 5. 14 ff.: In
Christ we are a " new creature " and through him we have recon-
ciliation ($\varkappa\alpha\tau\alpha\lambda\lambda\alpha\gamma\dot{\eta}$), because God has dealt with Christ as per-
sonified sin. Thus in the one direction Christ's death and resur-
rection serve for the establishment of his redemptive dominion
(Rom. 14. 9) and for the awakening of zeal for good works (Tit.
2. 14), since the life of Christ in the flesh displays the divine condemnation of sin, and he, by his death, severed forever his relation to sin (Rom. 8. 3 ; 6. 10), and in death most fully attested
his obedience (Phil. 2. 8). Christ therefore died and rose again,
by his obedience condemning and abolishing sin. As he who has
done this, he acts in believers, enabling them to lead a new life
opposed to sin. Thus viewed, even Christ's sufferings serve for
the religious and moral regeneration of the race, of which we have
spoken under item 6.

This presupposes that Christ brings into a new relation with
God, or achieves for us the forgiveness of sins. But this has come
to pass, because God has made Christ in his blood a propitiator
($\iota\lambda\alpha\sigma\tau\dot{\eta}\rho\iota\sigma\varsigma$), in order that those who believe on him may be for
his sake declared righteous (Rom. 3. 24 f.). His death,
acknowledged by God through the resurrection, brings to us forgiveness and justification (Rom. 4. 25), and Christ continually
represents us as our advocate before the Father (Rom. 8. 26 f.,
34 f.). By virtue of the death of Christ we are thus translated

into the state of reconciliation ( 2 Cor. 5. 18 f. ), with the forgiveness of sins and justification.    We are thus again brought near to
God (Eph. 2. 13, 18 ; 3. 12).    But if this has occurred, then at
the same time we were made free from the law and its curse,
under which Christ fell, in accordance with the declaration in
Deut. 21. 23, since he bore the fate of the transgressor (Gal.
3. 13 f., 17 ; cf. also Col. 2. 14 f.).    What Paul thus means
to assert is this : Since Christ attested to the utmost his obedience in the condition which sin had brought about for the
race, he, in accordance with the appointment of God, covered
the sins of men from the sight of God, or atoned for them, so
that God now enters upon a new relation to the race, looking
upon them for Christ's sake as righteous, and no longer permits
the requirements of the law to determine his bearing toward mankind.    The one righteous man who preserved his righteousness
to the utmost is the basis upon which God, for his sake—for he
rules through his Spirit in the race—permits the race to enter
into a new relation to himself.    These conceptions are not constructed upon the line of the sacrificial idea, but in accordance
with the idea of the reconciling effect and the vicarious significance of the sufferings of the righteous one.

Even here Paul's teachings are not arranged as a "system."
They are controlled by concrete aims, and the History of Doctrines
proves how many interpretations may be placed upon them.
Nevertheless they do not appear to lack a certain unity.    Since
Christ as the Reconciler, by his obedience even unto death, appeared and continually appears for man as his advocate, he has
brought the race into the new relation to God.    The law is abrogated, sin is forgiven, man is pronounced righteous.    But since
this new relation has been established, the inner spiritual dominion of God in the race has also been made possible.    Thus the
two lines of thought which we have traced here unite.    But at
the same time it is clear that, for Paul also, the new covenant is
actualized through Christ.    The reconciliatior. ( *καταλλαγή* ) is the
new covenant.

8.  The idealism of Paul's faith beheld in the few Christian
congregations of his time the beginning of a new epoch of
history, and his practical sense saw in these congregations the
means for actualizing this epoch.    In this, Paul adopted the
conception of the church ( *ἐκκλησία* ) held by Christ.    This, as
viewed from the position of the History of Doctrines, is an idea
of immense significance.    Christianity, accordingly, does not
present the spectacle of a number of individuals accidentally
associated, but it is the Christ present in the world.    The ancient
idea of Menenius Agrippa, of a body of humanity organically

associated, was revived in many forms in that day. Paul gives
it a new aspect. Christ is the Head of this body, from whom
it derives its origin, its course, its life, its growth, and its goal
(Col. 1. 18 f., 24.   Eph. 2. 20 ff.; 5. 23 ff.; 1. 22 f.).   In this
community Christ works through the Spirit.  All the gifts of
the Spirit are present in it.   But, above all, is the power of the
Spirit actively exerted in the preaching of the Gospel.   Among
other functions of the church are to be mentioned baptism and
the Lord's Supper.   Paul in 2 Tim. 2. 20 testifies that there
are among the saints (ἅγιοι) in the church not only such as lead
a real Christian life, struggling and crucifying the flesh, but also
perverse members.

The Pauline eschatology cannot be here presented, further
than to note the suggestion in the sphere of the philosophy of
history, that the prophecies concerning Israel are yet to find
their fulfillment in the ingathering of the heathen into the church
in the present era and in the salvation of "all Israel" at the end
of the world (Rom. 11. 25, 26).

9. Having now noted the peculiar doctrinal points emphasized
by Paul, let us cast a brief glance upon the general views prevalent in the apostolic age.  These laid the foundations upon
which the post-apostolic age carried forward the work of construction.  The Old Testament, inspired by God (2 Tim. 3.
16.  2 Pet. 1. 20 f.), is the Holy Scripture of Christendom.  It
serves for edification (Rom. 15. 4.   2 Tim. 3.16).  From its
utterances doctrines are developed (see esp. Hebrews).  Its
prophecies serve as the source of apostolic evidences (see esp.
the Gospel of St. Matthew).  To the Old Testament are
added the historical sayings of Jesus (1 Thes. 4. 5.   1 Cor. 7.
12, 25; 9. 14.  Acts 20. 35), but also the Spirit (πνεῦμα) and
the spirits (πνεύματα).  But the spirits are to be tried (Matt. 7.
16 ff.  1 Thes. 5. 19-22.  1 Cor. 14. 34 f.  1 Jn. 4. 1).  The
historical apostolate and the traditions (παραδόσεις) set a limit
to the working of the spirits (see above).

The vivid conception of God which we have found in Paul
is manifest also in other literature of the period.  The loving-will
of God desires our salvation (2 Pet. 3. 9) and begets us into
a new life (Jas. 1. 18).  The all-working God is also holy and
just (Rev. 15. 3 f.; 16. 5, 7; 19. 1 f.  2 Pet. 1. 1, 3.  1 Pet.
2. 23).  Christ is the Lawgiver and Judge (Jas. 4. 12).
He is always thought of as now existing in the state
of exaltation.  Rev. 1. 12-17 (cf. 11. 15; 17. 14; 19. 16;
22. 1) presents the popular conception.  Having passed
through death, he has entered into glory (1 Pet. 1. 21).
He is the Lord of glory (Jas. 2. 1), our only Master and

Lord (δεσπότης και κύριος, Jude 4.), who is enthroned at the right hand of God (Heb. 8. 1; 10. 12; 12. 2), and to whom the angels are subject (2 Pet. 3. 18; 1. 14, 16). Interest centres, above all, in the power (δύναμις) and coming (παρουσία) of Christ (2 Pet. 1. 16). The latter is near at hand, but will occur unexpectedly (2 Pet. 3. 4, 10. Rev. 3. 11). Thus there will be a revelation (ἀποκάλυψις) of his glory (1 Pet. 4. 13; 1. 7). The present glory of Christ is in harmony with his pre-existent state (1 Pet. 1. 20, 11; 3. 19 f.).

That Christ died on account of our sin was the apostolic tradition (1 Cor. 15. 3) and the general belief (1 Pet. 3. 18). The death of Christ was universally regarded as the means by which we are transported into a new moral state of life, and this because Christ died the just for the unjust, in order that he, having died and risen again, might lead them to God and bring them into a new relation with God. The Epistle to the Hebrews follows a peculiar course. Its Christology recognizes Christ as pre-existent (Heb. 1. 2 f., 4 ff.) and locates his nature in the "power of an endless life" (7. 16, δύναμις ζωῆς ἀκαταλύτου), in his "eternal Spirit" (9. 14, πνεῦμα αἰώνιον). As such, he assumed flesh and blood (2. 14; 7. 14), in his earthly life experienced human emotions, and died in obedience (4. 15; 5. 7, 8). He is now at the right hand of God (1. 3; 8. 1; 10. 12; 12. 2). In the same way as in the writings of Paul, a discrimination is made also in this Christology between the human existence of Christ and a spiritual, eternal, divine element. The author has presented the exaltation of Christ in the light of his high-priesthood. The apologetic character of the work, which required this method of presentation, led him, first of all, to conceive of the death of Christ as a sacrifice. And this sacrifice is once for all and forever sufficient (5. 1 ff., 7 f.; 9. 12-14; 7. 27), as Christ also forever stands as our advocate before God (7. 25; 9. 24). The death of Christ, i. e., his blood, inaugurates the "new covenant" and purifies the heavenly sanctuary (9. 15 ff., 18 ff.). To this is added, as the object of his death, the purifying from sin (καθαρισμὸς ἁμαρτιῶν, 1. 3; 9. 14, 26), as also the expiatory covering over (ἱλάσκεσθαι) of sin and the despoiling of the power of the devil (2. 14 f.). If we leave out of account the emphasis laid upon the forms of the sacrificial ceremonies, the conceptions of the author do not carry us beyond the two-fold representation which we have already found in Paul, i. e., that God, by the death of Christ, establishes a new objective relation between himself and the human race, and that the death of Christ aids in establishing a subjectively new attitude of man toward God.

Christians are partakers (μέταχοι) of Christ and of the Holy
Spirit (Heb. 3. 14; 16.4). With this all the blessings of salvation are bestowed upon them, for God works in them what is
well-pleasing in his sight (Heb. 13. 21). The word is, however, the means through which the blessings of salvation are imparted to believers (Heb. 4. 2). It is a heavenly summons
(Heb. 3. 1. 1 Pet. 3. 21; 5. 10. 2 Pet. 1. 3) which penetrates to the ends of the earth (Heb. 4. 12), begetting a new
life (Jas. 1. 18. 1 Pet. 1. 3) and preserving us in it (1 Pet. 1.
23 ff.; 2. 2. Jas. 1. 21). This new life is to be conceived of,
first of all, as faith (Jas. 1. 3, 6, 8; 2. 1, 5. 1 Pet. 1. 7 f., 9,
21; 5. 9. Heb. 12. 7). This term is understood precisely as
by Jesus and Paul. Faith is called wisdom (σοφία, Jas. 3. 13;
cf. 2. 18); also knowledge (ἐπίγνωσις, 2 Pet. 1. 2, 3; 2. 20;
3. 18), and is exercised in "full assurance" (πληροφορία, Heb.
10. 22). But, above all, it possesses the trait of obedience (1
Pet. 1. 22. Heb. 11. 8; 5. 9). It is to be noted, however,
that faith constantly assumes more of the character of hope, and
directs its gaze upon the blessedness of the future (1 Pet. 1. 21.
Heb. 12. 1 f.; 10. 36; 6. 11, 12). Thus the spiritual attitude of
the Old Testament was revived. The well-known definition of
Heb. 11. 1 (cf. Rom. 8. 24) exhibits this tendency, and hence
does not express the New Testament conception with entire
fidelity. The modification which begins to appear at this point
appears contemporaneously with the constantly growing tendency to conceive of salvation (σωτηρία) as lying essentially in
the future. It is even designated "a salvation ready to be revealed in the last time" (1 Pet. 1. 4, 5; cf. Heb. 3. 1; 9. 15.
1 Pet. 5. 10; 1. 9, 13. 2 Pet. 1. 4).

The Pauline doctrine of justification is not found in any of
the other New Testament writers. Heb. 11. 7 furnishes a slight
reminder. The generally prevalent conception may be expressed
in the declaration of John: "He that doeth righteousness is
righteous" (1 Jn. 3. 7. Rev. 22. 11). God produces good
works in us (Heb. 13. 21). We are to become doers of the
word, or of the law (Jas. 1. 22; 4. 4). "A doer (ποιητής)
of the work, this man shall be blessed in his doing" (ποιήσει)
(Jas. 1. 25). Righteousness is the moral integrity which avails
before God, and which is recognized by him (Jas 1. 20. 1 Pet.
2. 24; 3. 14. 2 Pet. 3. 13). At the same time, the latter is
by no means to be accounted as constituting merit upon the part
of man. On the contrary, everything good is given by God, as
upon the other hand the law is meant only as a "law of liberty"
(νόμος ἐλευθερίας, Jas. 2. 12; cf. 1 Pet. 2. 16). From this
point of view, the theory of justification presented by James is by

no means to be considered particularly remarkable. James seeks to base the edict of justification, not exclusively upon faith, but upon the moral character which accompanies the latter. From Gen. 16. 5 it is directly inferred that "man is justified by works (ἐξ ἔργων) and not by faith alone" (ἐκ πίστεως μόνον) (Jas. 2. 17, 20 ff.). Distinctly as this view differs from the Pauline, we cannot see in it a falling back upon Judaism. But this must be the starting-point for anyone who desires to understand the history of the Pauline doctrine of justification in the following centuries.

The warnings to keep the life free from sin, to practice love, etc., are extraordinarily abundant, and attest the spiritual wealth of the period. The conception of the church as a "spiritual house" and a "chosen generation" (1 Pet. 2. 5, 9) embraces the assurance that it was in possession of all the gracious gifts of God, and was under obligation to discharge all the duties of love toward the members of the brotherhood. More and more the sanctified (ἡγούμενοι) take the place of the spiritual (πνευματικοί) as leaders of the church (Heb. 13. 7, 17, 24, 19). Officebearers begin to exercise the ministry of the word (1 Tim. 3. 1 ff.; 5. 17. 2 Tim. 2. 2. Tit. 1. 7, 5). But these features of the period do not indicate any increasing worldliness. Eschatology, on the contrary, is a powerful factor of the religious life. Two characteristics meet and combine in mutual support in the Christianity of the apostolic age : upon the one hand, the powerful impulse to establish the dominion of Christ by serving him and in his power pressing out to the ends of the earth ; and, upon the other hand, the conviction that only Christ himself can achieve this, and that he will soon do so. These two tendencies did not at first conflict, but aided one another. We may recall the vivid hope of Paul and his great labors in the service of this hope. In the Apocalypse is given in great pictures, with veiled imagery and many references to the great world-empires, a portrayal of the conflicts and the great victory of the last time, which was so varied in its forms that every period of history has been able to employ it as a mirror of its own age. The city of God, already prepared in heaven, will come down to the earth. It remains only for us to pray : "Come, Lord Jesus" (Rev. 22. 17, 20). Christ will soon be Lord alone (Rev. 11. 15, 17; 12. 9, 10; 14. 3 f.; 19. 2, 6, 16). This is the one controlling thought. But just because it is, the moral counsels and exhortations to conflict and devoted service gain the support of powerful motives. Of this, the letters to the churches, recorded in the Apocalypse, furnish an illustration.

10. At the end of the apostolic age we witness the active

4

ministry of John, which is of the greatest significance for the
History of Doctrines.   Standing between two eras, be impressed
the message of the days of revelation deeply upon his generation.   We may define his significance in three observations:
(1) The Christ, of whose historical revelation he has been a
witness, is the Lord of the world.   The apocalyptic hopes of his
youth, of which hitherto but few have been realized in their external form, yet remain.   He sees in great visions the final victory of Christ.   The apocalyptic traditions of his nation furnish
for him the forms of these visions.   (2) A separation begins to
appear between the historical Jesus and the heavenly Logos-
principle (Cerinthus).   In response to this, the Gospel proves
that the heavenly Lord was none other than the man Jesus.
John expresses this as paradoxically and bluntly as possible ·
"The Word became flesh."   From this resulted the peculiarity of his Gospel.   The religious knowledge which he had
gained in the course of a long life in communion with the exalted Christ enables him to interpret the life of Jesus, which he
depicts in a thoroughly human way, with many minute human
traits.   He carries backward the knowledge gained at a later
day.   He seeks out the words which establish it and apprehends the
words of Jesus in this higher sense.   Profound contemplation
characterizes this treatment of the life of Jesus.   It saved to
the church the history of Christ, since it made it possible to understand it religiously, as the Lord himself, when present, had
been known to his disciples.   (3) Vision and contemplation
were in this remarkable man united with a practical, simple temper, averse to all foolish vaporings and pretense.   To the watchwords of the age, such as "spirit" and "righteousness," he
opposed this simple knowledge of the truth.   Christianity is
summarized in the "old commandment" (1 Jn. 2. 7) or the
teaching (διδαχή) of Christ (2 Jn. 9 f.).   This is the primitive
Christian catechism, to which reference has been made above
(item 4).   Its contents are faith in God and love toward one
another (1 Jn. 3. 23; 4. 15).

John does not mean, however, that faith and love are only an
outward keeping of the commandments.   On the contrary, they
are given to man by the Spirit in the new birth, or regeneration.
The Spirit does not, as once thought, produce separate states of
excitement.   John goes even beyond Paul, for whom the
"power" of the word was, in the last analysis, the Spirit.
The Spirit effects in man a permanent condition of fellowship
(κοινωνία) with God (1 Thes. 4. 13).   This communion with
God is manifested in faith and love.   But he who believes, believes in harmony with the commandment (ἐντολή), and he who

loves, loves that which the commandment enjoins. Faith and
love are awakened in the heart of man by the Spirit, and not by
the commandment. But faith and love, if they be genuine and
right, can never contain anything else than the commandment
given by God. It is evident that John himself is far removed
from the ancient Catholic conception of Christianity as a "new
law," but that he yet helped to prepare the way for that conception.

But true faith is that which confesses that Jesus is really
Christ. The Logos, or God only-begotten (Jn. 1. 14), the
"true God and eternal life" (1 Jn. 5. 20), became the man
Jesus. Unless all indications are at fault, John borrowed his
conception of the Logos from Cerinthus, but he interpreted it in
his own sense. The Logos is the revealing God—God, because
he manifests himself not only in many words, uttered "in
divers portions and in divers manners," as those of the prophets,
but in an all-inclusive, complete revelation (cf. Rev. 19. 13 f.
Heb. 1. 2. Ignat ad Magnes, 8. 2; 9. 2; ad Rom. 8. 2).
This God became the man Jesus. He who denies this—*i. e.*,
two principles, the divine and human, separate from one another
(Cerinthus)—is the Antichrist (1 Jn. 2. 22; 4. 3, 15; 5. 1, 5.
2 Jn. 7; cf. Iren. i. 26. 1; iii. 11. 1).

And true love is the practical, active brotherly-love, which
walks according to the commandments of God (2 Jn. 6. 1 Thes.
2. 3 f.). He who doeth righteousness is righteous. From this
active righteousness may be known whether anyone has really
been born of God (1 Jn. 2. 29; 4. 7; 5. 1, 4). The regenerated, as such, does not sin (1 Jn. 3. 9, 6; 1. 6; 2. 6). Nevertheless, John assumes sin in his readers, as well as a regularly
observed confession of sin (1 Jn. 2. 1. f.; 1. 7 f.). This apparent contradiction may, if I am correct in my judgment, be
solved by discriminating between a "sin unto death" and a
"sin not unto death" (1 Jn. 5. 16, 17), *i. e.*, between the
sinful state of ungodliness which forever prevents communion
with God and the separate sinful acts which leave room for a
restoration through repentance (1 Jn. 5. 16; 1. 7 f.). This
conception also (cf. Heb. 6. 4, 8; 10. 26 f.; 12. 17) reminds
us of ideas in the primitive Catholic period.

11. John subjected the traditional Christian conceptions to a
noticeable redaction. In addition to him, only the Pauline type
can be presented in distinct outlines. Between the two lie the
conceptions of James, Peter, Jude, and Hebrews. These types
of doctrine differ from one another in many particulars, but the
elements common to all certainly outweigh the differences. And
it was not really the peculiar features (*e. g.*, Paul's doctrine of
justification, and the theories of the Epistle to the Hebrews),

but those which were common to all, which influenced the future. The Apostolic Fathers, *e. g.*, presuppose a general proclamation which embraced the common basis of the New Testament doctrine.

These common ideas may be summarized as follows: The acknowledgment of the Old Testament; the words of Christ, together with the apostolic tradition and teaching, as of binding authority; faith in the living God, who, in omnipotence and grace, directs the life of individuals as well as the course of history; faith in Christ as the celestial and omnipresent Lord, who became man, and, through the resurrection, entered again into glory; the conviction that God and Christ, through the Spirit, renew and quicken man religiously and morally, granting him also the *charismata*, which he needs for the upbuilding of the church. The work of Christ embraces the efficacious atonement for sin as well as the transformation of man through the power of the Spirit. Forgiveness and sonship with God, the filling with the Spirit, and eternal blessedness constitute the blessings of salvation, which are appropriated in faith and love. Love as an active disposition of soul finds exercise in the congregational life, in which Christ and the Spirit work through the word, baptism, and the Lord's Supper, and through the *charismata*, and the miracles wrought through the latter. The final goal of· the church is the glory of the divine kingdom, to be ushered in by the coming of Christ, which is near at hand.

If we compare this with the teaching of Christ himself, it is clear that it presupposes the resurrection of Christ and the manifestation of the risen Lord in his glory; and, further, that the revelation made by Christ during his earthly life gives shape to the whole structure. Christ exercises divine dominion, in that he brings to man the forgiveness of sins and a new life, and actualizes the new covenant wherever these blessings are received. Through the dominion of Christ, humanity is organized as the church, or kingdom of God, and thus conducted to its appropriate goal. He accomplishes the salvation of men, forgiving the evil and bestowing the good, and he brings the race to its divinely appointed goal. In faith man bows to this beatifying dominion and in love brings into active exercise his new attitude in the kingdom of God. These ideas embrace the whole revelation of the New Testament. The redemptive dominion of God and faith, the kingdom of God and love—this is the briefest possible expression of the Essence of Christianity in the sense of the New Testament.[1]

[1] Cf. Seeberg, Die **Grundwahrheiten der christl. Religion**, ed. 3, 1903; lectures iii.-vi.

# BOOK I.

DEVELOPMENT OF DOCTRINE IN THE ANCIENT
CHURCH.

# PART I.

## CONCEPTION OF CHRISTIANITY IN THE POST-APOSTOLIC AND ANCIENT CATHOLIC AGES.

### CHAPTER I.

#### THE CONCEPTION OF CHRISTIANITY IN THE POST-APOSTOLIC AGE.

##### § 7. *The Apostolic Fathers.*

SOURCES : 1. From Clemens Romanus we possess a manuscript of the Roman congregation, addressed to the church at Corinth. It was written probably early in A. D. 97. WREDE, Untersuchungen zum 1. Klemensbrief, 1891.

2. In Rome appeared also the Pastor of Hermas, a call to repentance divided into 5 visions, 12 mandates, and 10 similitudes. Its composition is, with great probability, located in A. D. 97-100, while others, upon the testimony of the so-called Canon of Muratori, place it so late as A. D. 140-145. Cf. ZAHN, Der Hirte des H., 1868. HÜCKSTÄDT, Der Lehrbegriff des Hirten, 1889.

3. The documents which follow carry us to Asia Minor. First, the 7 genuine Epistles of IGNATIUS OF ANTIOCH (to the Ephesians, Magnesians, Trallians, Romans, Philadelphians, Smyrnans, and Polycarp), written about A. D. 110. Cf. ZAHN, Ign. v. Ant., 1874; Von der GOLTZ, Ign. v. Ant. als Christ u. Theologe, in Texte u. Unters., xii. 3 (1894).

4. In the same time appeared the Epistle of POLYCARP OF SMYRNA.

5. PAPIAS, Bishop of Hierapolis, wrote, about A. D. 125, 5 books : λογίων κυριακῶν ἐξήγησις. Of these, unfortunately, only a few fragments have been preserved to us in Irenæus, Eusebius, etc. Vid. in the small Leipzig edition of the Apostolic Fathers, p. 69 ff. Cf. also C. de BOOR in Texte u. Unters., v. 2, p. 170, and also p. 176 ff.

6. An Epistle ascribed to BARNABAS carries us to Alexandria. Chap. 16. 1 gives no aid in fixing the date of its appearance. According to Chap. 4. 3 f., it may have been composed under Nerva (A. D. 96-98). It is commonly assigned to the time of Hadrian. The unity of the composition is to be maintained.

7. It was also probably in Alexandria that the little liturgical handbook, Διδαχὴ τῶν ιβ΄ ἀποστόλων, made its appearance. From a literary point of view, it is very closely related to the Epistle of Barnabas, as is especially manifest in the section upon " The Two Ways." It can be proved, however, that neither of the two made use of the other, but that an earlier document lay at the basis of both. The Didache most probably appeared in the first decennium of the second century. We refer to publications of it by HARNACK in Texten u. Unters., vol. ii., and FUNK, Patres apostolici, ii. ed. 2, 1901, and to the small edition : " Die Apostellehre u. die jüd. beiden Wege " (Leipzig, 1886), in which, p. 38 ff., is noted also the most important literature.

8. The so-called SECOND EPISTLE OF CLEMENT is in truth the most an-

cient church homily that has been preserved to us. It was probably delivered in Corinth (7. 1), hardly later than A. D. 140. Cf. ZAHN in Zeitschr. f. Prot. u. Kirche, 1876, no. 4. HARNACK, Zeitschr. f. Kirchengesch., 1877, p. 329 ff.

The best edition of the above-named documents, not including the Didache, is: Patrum apostolicorum opera rec. de GEBHARDT, HARNACK, ZAHN, 3 vols., Leipzig, 1876-1877; smaller edition, Leipzig, 1877; and FUNK, Patres Apostolici, 2 vols., ed. 2, Tübingen, 1901. LIGHTFOOT, The Apostolic Fathers (Clemens, 1890; Ignatius, 1885).

For estimates of their doctrinal contents, see RITSCHL, Die Entstehung der altkath. Kirche., 1857, p. 274 ff. LÜBKERT, Die Theol. d. ap. Väter, 1854. V. ENGELHARDT, Das Christenthum Justins, 1878, p. 375 ff. LECHLER, Das apostol. u. nachap. Zeitalter, ed. 3, 1885, p. 586 ff. PFLEIDERER, Das Urchristentum, 1887, p. 640 ff., 823 ff., 845 ff. HARNACK, DG., i. ed. 3, p. 140 ff. THOMASIUS, DG., i. ed. 2, p. 31 ff., with additions by Bonwetsch; cf. p. 141 ff. BEHM, Das christl. Gesetztum der ap. Vät. in Zeitschr. f. k. Wiss., 1886, p. 295 ff., 408 ff., 453 ff.

For the sake of clearness and in view of the importance of the matter, we deem it advisable to examine each of the above documents separately before attempting to present a summary account of their doctrinal contents.

### 1. CLEMENS ROMANUS.

(*a*) The leading thought is that of the One God, the Lord (δεσπότης; cf. 49. 6 and 47 fin. with 48 init.) of the world, the Creator, and, in this sense, the Father (*e. g.*, 35. 3; 19. 2). The conception of the latter term is different in 29. 1; 23. 1; 56. 16: the merciful and gracious Father by his holy discipline protects men and trains them for the reception of mercy. It is our duty to love him who elects us, and to draw near to him with a holy heart. God is θεὸς καὶ ὁ κύριος Ἰησοῦς Χριστὸς καὶ τὸ πνεῦμα τὸ ἅγιον (58. 2; 46. 6).

(*b*) Christ is sent from God to deliver us (42. 1; 59. 2). In that God elected Christ, he elected us through him as his own people (64; 59. 3). As to his nature, he is the Son of God, exalted above the angels (36, following Heb. 1. 3 ff.); the Lord Jesus Christ; the sceptre of the majesty of God: and yet he came as the Humble One into the world (16. 2). Already in the Old Testament he spoke through the Holy Ghost (22. 1). In harmony with this, his descent from Abraham is by the term τὸ κατὰ σάρκα discriminated from another descent (32.2). The sufferings of Christ are described as the sufferings of God (2. 1), unless in this passage we are to read παθήματα αὐτοῦ, instead of παθήματα θεοῦ (Funk).

(*c*) Christ is the only mediator of our salvation. Through him we have become God's possession (vid. *b*). He is to us a helper in weakness and a high-priest in the offering of gifts (prayers; cf. 61. 3). Through his mediation we are made capable of seeing God and tasting immortal knowledge ; through it, faith, (godly) fear, peace, patience, temperance, and wisdom (σωφροσύνη) become the portion of the Christian (64). Out of love Christ gave his blood for us—his flesh for our flesh, his soul for our souls (49. 6 ; 21. 6). "By the blood of the Lord there is redemption (λύτρωσις) to all that believe and hope in God" (12. 7). This blood, which was shed for the sake of our salvation, is so precious to the Father of Christ, that it has obtained the grace of repentance for the whole world. The humility and patience which Christ maintained in his life's work are an example for us, who have through him come "beneath the yoke of grace" (16. 17).

To summarize : In Christ we have become the possession of God. Through him the knowledge of God, faith, and all virtues have become ours. His blood has redeemed us, since it brought us the grace of repentance. His life is for us a pattern of humility. It may be said, indeed, that Clement has not grasped the saving efficacy of the death of Christ in its full biblical significance ; but it is going too far to maintain that he believed nothing more to be accomplished by it than blotting out of past sins (Behm, l.c., p. 304. Vid. 7. 4).

(d) As to the personal standing of the believer, Clement teaches: "They were all (Old Testament saints) therefore glorified and magnified not through themselves nor their works, nor the righteousness which they wrought, but through his will. And we therefore, being called through his will in Christ Jesus, are not justified through ourselves, neither through our wisdom nor knowledge nor piety nor works which we have done in the holiness of our hearts, but through the faith through which God Almighty has justified all men from the beginning" (32. 3, 4). Such are the paths of blessedness (31. 1); faith in Christ brings us everything good (22. 1). Clement writes thus with a full conception of the wide scope of his words, for he follows them immediately with the remark, that good works are not thereby excluded, but on the contrary zeal in such works is required (33. 1, 7, 8). This is as truly Pauline as the definition of faith as confidence (πεποίθησις, 35. 2 ; 26. 1; cf. 2. 3 ; 58. 1). The humble temper of mind (16-19) and believing trust in God, obedience to God, and unreserved self-surrender to him (10. 1 ; 11) obtain salvation. But this line of thought is limited by another : "Blessed are we, beloved, if we shall have fulfilled the commandments of God in the unity of love, that so through love our sins may be forgiven us" (50. 5). No great weight is to be laid upon the mention of "hospitality" along with faith in the cases of Abraham and Rahab (10. 7 ; 12. 1 ; cf. also 10. 1 ;

31. 2); more upon the strong emphasis laid upon the laws (νόμοι) and commandments (προστάγματα) of God and Christ (1. 3; 2. 8; 3, 4; 13. 3; 37. 1; 49. 1; 40. 1). When Clement is thinking of the origin and nature of human salvation, he is controlled by Pauline conceptions; in view of the realities of life and the judgment, he lays great weight upon the moral activity of man in harmony with the law of God (but cf. also 26. 1).

(e) The church is, in Clement, the people of God, which he has chosen for his own possession (e.g., 59. 4; 30. 1; 6. 1; 64); those called to be saints (inscription; 65. 2); the flock of Christ (16. 1). It is of importance to note the legal argument based upon the Old Testament by which Clement supports the authority of the elders. Their duty is (40) accordingly, the conduct of worship (λειτουργία) and sacrifice (θυσία). The fixed office and its authority here took the place of the free activity of the Spirit in the church. Problems were thus created which were destined to occupy the best energies of the church of the future (cf. also Did. 15. 1; 14. 1, 2). In this fellowship reign discipline and order (2. 6; 4-6; 47. 6; 21. 6; 40), subjection to leaders and to one another (1. 3; 21. 6; 38. 1), piety and practical hospitality (1. 2 ff.; 2), firm fellowship one with another (46. 4 ff.; 30. 3; 15. 1). For Clement's ideal of Christian character, vid. Chapters I. and II.

(f) It may be mentioned, finally, that the author distinctly and intelligently maintains the resurrection of the body (24 and 25).

This document makes it clear that the ideas embraced in the apostolic proclamation have been preserved in the church, but that there may be already traced a lack of independent scrutiny of these ideas and of deeper penetration into their significance. One does not receive the impression that the biblical conception of Christ's work and the significance of faith are really understood and inwardly appropriated. However, in passing this judgment, we should bear in mind the particular object of Clement in the preparation of the work.

### 2. HERMAS.

To understand the peculiarities of the "Shepherd," we must remember its character as an exhortation to repentance.

(a) Hermas associates salvation directly with the Person of Christ (Sim. 9. 12. 4-6). His views in regard to this, however, furnish nothing really new. It is a perversion to make him a representative of an adoptionistic Christology, as though teaching that Christ was a man chosen of God, in whom the Spirit of God dwelt, and who, after having proved himself worthy, was elevated to a position of lordship (Harnack, DG., ed. 3, p. 182 f.). Christ, the Son of God, is as well the ancient Rock, out of which the tower of the church is hewn, as the new Door through which we enter this tower. "The Son of God is, indeed, more ancient (προγενέστερος) than any creature; insomuch that he was in counsel with his Father at the creation of all things (Sim. 9. 12. 2, 3). He could very well have protected his people through an angel (Sim. 5. 6. 2; cf. 2. 2); but he did more, since he purified them by his own toil (Sim. 5. 6. 3). The angels are his to command (Sim. 5. 5. 13; cf. 2. 2), and he upholds the whole world (Sim. 9. 14. 5; cf. Heb. 1. 2). It cannot therefore be doubted that Christ is for Hermas a pre-existent Being, exalted above the angels.

It has been contended that, according to Hermas, Christ is not a separate divine person, but that the Holy Spirit dwelt in his flesh (BAUR, V. ENGELHARDT, p. 425 f. HARNACK, p. 185. HÜCKSTÄDT, p. 26 ff.). But Sim. 5 distinctly discriminates between the lord of the farm, i. e., the Father, the servant, i. e., the Son, and the son, i. e., the Holy Ghost. The lord commits to the servant the cultivation of the farm, and after this has been done, he rejoices over it with the son, i. e., the Holy Ghost (5. 2. 6; 5. 2). If it is said immediately after this (6. 5) that God caused the Holy Ghost to dwell in the flesh of Christ, and that the latter served the Spirit without defiling it, the meaning is not that the Holy Spirit constitutes the divine nature of Christ, but that the pre-existent Christ is holy spirit (τὸ πνεῦμα τὸ ἅγιον τὸ προόν, τὸ κτίσαν πᾶσαν τὴν κτίσιν), and that this flesh, since it did not defile the spirit, has been by God taken with the spirit to himself (6 ff.). The other passage adduced in support of the theory in question, Sim. 9. 1. 1: "For that spirit is the Son of God" means only to say that the holy spiritual being that spoke with Hermas was the Son of God. The pre-existent Christ was not "the Holy Spirit," but a pre-existent holy spiritual being. It was not uncommon to speak in this way in the second century. Christ is called Spirit of God (πνεῦμα θεοῦ) in 2 Clem. 9. 5. Iren. adv. haer., v. 1. 2; cf. Arist. Apol., 2. 6. Celsus in Orig. c. Cels., vi. 75. Theophil. ad Autol., ii. 10. Tertul. Apol., 21; adv. Prax. 8. 26; de orat. 1. See already 1 Cor. 3. 17. The view of Hermas is, therefore, not essentially different from that of the New Testament. It would have been incomprehensible that he should, in view of the baptismal formula, have fallen into such confusion. Vid. also Dorner, Christol., i., ed. 2, p. 200 ff., 194.

(*b*) Christ, the Son of God, placed men (evidently meaning believers of Old Testament times) under the protection of angels ; then himself became man in order to purify men : " And he himself labored very much and suffered much that he might blot out their offenses . . . wherefore having himself blotted out the sins of the people, he showed to them the paths of life, giving them the law which he had received from the Father " (Sim. 5. 6. 2, 3). Thus Christ brought forgiveness for the sins of the past, and for the future gave to men his commandments. Cf. Link, Christi Person u. Werk im Hirten des Hermas (Marburg, 1886).

(*c*) As to the personal state of the believer, we are taught : In the hearts of men, which are in themselves weak and full of sin (*e.g.*, Mand. 4. 3. 4.   Sim. 9. 23. 4), which turn away from God, do not know him, and will not obey him (Vis. 3. 7. 2. Sim. 4. 4. 4, etc.), God causes his Spirit to take up its abode, or the powers of the Son of God are imparted to them.   Only such as have obtained these are able to enter into the kingdom of God (Mand. 3. 1 ; 12. 4. 3 ; 6. 2, 1 ff.   Sim. 9. 32.4 ; 13. 2 ; cf. 25. 4).   But this good Spirit cannot live in man together with the evil spirits (Mand. 5. 1. 3 ; 2. 5 ff.   Sim. 10. 3. 2). Sim. 8 explains how this gift is imparted.   Branches from a willow-tree are given to believers.   Some bring them back fresh and blooming : others, withering and withered (both classes in various degrees).   The willow-tree is the law of God.   " But this law is the Son of God, preached throughout the whole earth " (3. 2).   It is therefore the preaching of Christ as a new code of moral life which accomplishes the above results in believers.   We are futher told that life is given us through the water of baptism, and this is so necessary that it must in some way be applied even to Old Testament believers (Vis. 3. 3. 5. Sim. 9. 16. 2, 3, 5).   Through baptism all the sins which a man has committed are forgiven (cf. below under *d*).

The fundamental subjective condition of the moral life in man is faith (Sim. 6. 12).   This comes from above, and equips man with power ; whereas its opposite, double-mindedness, is of the earth and has no power (Mand. 9. 11).   Since the latter, which leads to doubt, must be overcome, as well as care and trouble (λύπη), man turns in faith with his whole heart to God, praying and sure that his prayer is heard (Mand. 9. 1, 2, 5 ; cf. Vis. 4. 2. 4-6.   Mand. 10).   He who fears God becomes free from the fear of the devil (Mand. 7. 4).   Although faith may be apparently presented as one among the Christian virtues (Mand. 8. 9 ; 12. 3, 1.   Sim. 9. 15. 2), it is evident from the above that it is not so regarded.   The elect are saved through faith. The other virtues are daughters of faith (Vis. 3. 8. 3, 4 ; cf. Mand. 5. 2. 3).   The essential content of faith is presented in the passage quoted as Scripture by Irenæus, Origen and Athanasius, Mand. 1. 1 : " First of all, believe that there is one God, who created and framed all things, and made them from being nothing to be all things (cf. 2 Macc. 7. 28), and who comprehends all things, and who is alone incomprehensible (ἀχώρητος)." God created the world for the sake of men and the church (Mand. 12. 4. Vis. 2. 4. 2 ; 1. 4). That faith in Christ is not unknown to Hermas is of course to be taken for granted (vid. Sim. 8. 3. 2 extr.).

Faith is therefore not only a knowledge and acknowledgment of God as the Creator, but also an undivided turning of the heart to God, which makes man strong and is the root of all moral activity. It is " as truly fundamental duty as fundamental power" (ZAHN, p. 175. Cf. HÜCKSTÄDT, p. 59 f.).

But the relationship of faith and good works is not always observed by Hermas. " Take heed, therefore, ye that serve the Lord, and have him in your hearts : work the works of God, being mindful of his commandments and of the promises which he has given, and believe that he will perform these if his commandments are kept " (Sim. 1. 7). The moral activity commended is the fulfillment of the separate divine requirements. To such an observance of the commandments is attached the promise of life (Sim. 8. 11. 3 ; 6. 1. 1 ; 7. 6 ; 10. 1. 2 ; 2. 4 ; 4. 1. Mand. 4. 2. 4 ; 7. 5). Although this cannot be interpreted as equivalent to the later moralism, it yet distinctly prepares the way for it. Cf. also the designation of the preaching concerning Christ as law, νόμος (Sim. 8. 3. 2, 3).

The view of Hermas as to the possibility of fulfilling the divine commandments is not fairly represented in the assertion : " The power thereto is innate in man " (Schmid-Hauck, DG., p. 11). On the contrary, it is " the man having the Lord in his heart " (Mand. 12. 4. 3 ; cf. Sim. 10. 3. 1) who has this ability.

A certain narrowing of the moral horizon is manifest in Sim. 5. 3. 3 : " If thou shalt do some good thing not embraced in the commandment of God, thou shalt purchase to thyself the greater dignity, and thou shalt be more honored before God than thou shouldst otherwise have been " (cf. Mand. 4. 4. 2).

(d) Finally, for a proper understanding of the general view of Hermas, it is very important to note his conception of repentance, which is the dominating note in his discussions. His fundamental idea here is : " that there is no other repentance than this, that we go down into the water and receive the forgiveness of our past sins " (Mand. 4. 3. 1 ; cf. 4. 1. 8). It is a special favor of God, that now through the preaching of Hermas, in an exceptional way, a second repentance is granted the congrega-

tion of believers (Vis. 2. 2, 4, 5. Mand. 4. 4. 4. Sim. 8. 11.
1, etc.). He who from this time forward keeps the commandments shall find the forgiveness of his sins (Mand. 4. 4. 4) and
be saved. This idea of one repentance is based, indeed, upon
representations in the New Testament (1 Jn. 5. 16 ff. Heb.
6. 4. ff.). As Christianity was regarded as the consummation
upon which very shortly should follow the end of the world, there
seemed to be no further room for apostasy and repentance (cf.
Apoc. Baruch, 85. 12). Although Hermas in other connections
by no means regards sin as consisting merely in outward works, but
includes in it inward desire (ἐπιθυμία, Vis. 1. 1. 8; 3.
8. 4. Mand. 12. 1. 1 ; 2. 2; 4. 2. Sim. 5. 1. 5), yet of repentance he can say : " For he that hath sinned is conscious
that he hath done evil in the sight of the Lord, and his deed that
he has done comes into his heart, and he repents and no more
does evil, but does good most abundantly, and humbles his soul
and afflicts it, because he has sinned " (Mand. 4. 2. 2 ; cf. Sim.
7. 4). But it is not held that he whose sins have been forgiven
can thereafter live without sin. The " Shepherd " himself since
his conversion remains liable to many moral faults, and the
righteous as well as the wicked must, after every transgression,
take refuge to the Lord (Sim. 9. 31. 2 ; cf. Zahn, p. 355).
Hermas does not venture to condemn to death the man who, after
hearing the call to repentance, shall sin under pressure of temptation (ὑπο χεῖρα, Mand. 4. 3. 6). He has in mind such sins
as effect a surrender of the moral power of the Gospel, a complete corruption : he is thinking of apostasy, which is to be
followed by a new conversion (Sim. 9. 14. 1 ff.; cf. Mand. 4.
1. 8. Sim. 9. 26. 6). Accordingly, repentance is like conversion : " If ye turn to the Lord with your whole heart, and work
righteousness the remaining days of your life, and serve him
strictly according to his will, he will heal your former sins "
(Mand. 12. 6. 2 ; cf. Sim. 8. 11. 3). This is the starting-point
of the Catholic discrimination between venial and mortal sins.
The error lies not really in the general idea of repentance, but
in an underestimate of minor sins. But the chief defection
from the biblical standard lies in the failure to understand grace
as the forgiveness of sins extending continuously throughout the
whole life. Hence the moralism of Hermas.

(e) In connection with the preaching of repentance, Hermas
gives great prominence to the conception of the church. The
church rests upon Christ, the ancient rock with the new door
(Sim. 9. 2. 2 ; cf. 12. 2. 3), i. e., the pre-existent Son of
God, who became manifest only in the last time. It is built
upon the waters of baptism (Vis. 3. 3. 5. Sim. 9, 16. 2), and

is extended through the preaching of Christ (Sim. 8. 3. 2). The church is tne city of God with its own laws (Sim. 1. 1, 3, 9). But not all who receive branches from the great willow-tree, or the word concerning Christ (cf. above, under *c*), preserve them ; and not all who have been admitted to the tower of the church stand the test when tried by Christ (Sim. 9. 6). Thus the essence and the appearance of the church are often not in harmony. The task of the preaching of Hermas is the purification of the church (Sim. 9. 18. 3). There is a pause in the building of the church in order that sinners may be purified and again admitted to the structure of the church (*e. g.*, Sim. 9. 7. 2 ; 10. 4. 4). It is necessary to turn quickly to repentance, since the building of the church, and with it the time of the world, will soon be ended (*e. g.*, Vis. 3. 8. 9. Sim. 9. 9. 4 ; 26. 6 ; 10. 4. 4, etc.). Thus by repentance the contradiction between the essence and the appearance of the church may be overcome. In this way the ideal of the church would be attained : "After these (the wicked) are cast out, the church of God shall become one body, one understanding, one mind, one faith, one love : and then the Son of God shall exceedingly rejoice among them and receive his pure people " (Sim. 9. 18. 4). It is not hidden from Hermas, that this state shall never be attained on earth. As in winter dead and living trees look alike, so it is also in the church : " Neither the righteous nor the wicked are recognized in this world, but they are alike (Sim. 3. 2, 3). Only the future world will reveal the difference (Sim. 4. 2)."

We have thus attempted to translate the most important doctrinal views of Hermas from the prophetical form of speech into the language of precise thought. Whatever stress may be laid upon the prophetic-visionary elements which strike us so strangely, upon the moralistic and legalistic elements, and the fateful limitation of forgiveness—the fact remains, that genuine Christian ideas hold the central place in his faith and thought.

### 3. IGNATIUS.

The martyr bishop of Antioch furnishes in his seven genuine epistles a portrayal of Christianity delightful in its religious fervor and power. His general conception is closely related to the Johannine doctrinal type.

(*a*) Christ is God, "our God," and " my God " (Eph. inscr.; 18. 2. Rom. inscr.; 3. 3 ; 6. 3. Polycarp, 8. 3). He is God, ὁ θεός (Smyrn. 1. 1), θεός (Trall. 7. 1), the only Son of the Father, ὁ μόνος υἱὸς τοῦ πατρός, (Rom. inscr.), and the Lord, ὁ κύριος (Polyc. 1. 2). Ignatius uses the formula "in Son and Father and in Spirit" (Magn. 13. 1 ; in § 2 τὸ πνεῦμα is doubtful ; cf. Lightf.). He was with the Father before time began (Magn. 6. 1). At the end of the days he became man —and this as a revelation of the One God, the Father, "who has manifested himself through his Son Jesus Christ, who is his word, λόγος, proceeding from silence" (Magn. 8. 2 ; cf. 9. 2 : "our only teacher," and Rom. 8. 2 : "the genuine mouth in whom the Father truly spake").[1] Ignatius recognizes the reality of the earthly activity of Christ and confirms his presentation of its separate features by an emphatic "truly," ἀληθῶς (Smyrn. 1 and 2. Tral. 9. It is not allowable to say that he only seemed to suffer : Tral. 10. Smyrn. 2. Polyc. 3. 2 ; cf. Smyrn. 12. 2. Ephes. 7). But since Christ has completed his work on earth, he is now again with the Father (ἐν πατρὶ ὤν), but in consequence of this he may be but the better known (μᾶλλον φαίνεται, Rom. 3. 3) on earth. Even after his resurrection, which he himself effected (truly raised himself, ἀνέστησεν ἑαυτόν, Smyrn. 2, in contrast with which, however, vid. 8. 1 : "The Father raised ;" cf. Trall. 9. 2), although spiritually united (πνευματικῶς ἡνωμένος) with the Father, he is yet "in the flesh" (Smyrn. 3. 1, 3).

Ignatius was fond of combining these two classes of utterances. Christ is at once God and man : "The one Healer is both fleshly and spiritual, born and unborn. God became incarnate, true life in death, both from Mary and from God, first passible and then impassible, Jesus Christ our Lord" (Eph. 7. 2 ; cf. 18. 2. Smyrn. 1. 1). Upon the one hand he is, therefore, unborn, ἀγέννητος, but according to the flesh he is sprung from David's tribe, born of the Virgin according to the will of God (Eph. 19. 1), "conceived in the womb of Mary, according to the dispensation of God—on the one hand of the seed of David, on the other of the Holy Spirit" (Eph. 18. 2). He is, therefore, perfect (τέλειος) man (Smyrn. 4. 2) and just as truly God (cf. supra). It is impossible, in view of the above, to hold that Ignatius regarded Jesus as by nature a pre-existent spiritual being who, after completing his work on earth, returned again to heaven (the so-called "pneumatic" Christology, HARNACK i. 183 ff.). How could he describe such a being as his God and the God of Christendom? We should observe further that the title, Son of God, in Ignatius designates Christ, not only as begotten in eternity, but also as the One sprung, according to the

---

[1] Thus the Johannine term, Logos, was authentically interpreted. Christ is the Word, or the Mouth of God, i. e., the revelation of God. Remarkable, further, is the combination of faith and love with the triadic formula (e. g., Magn. 13. 1. Ep. 9. 1 ; cf. 1 Clem. 58. 2 ; 46. 6). Were both formulas —they possess something of the character of formulas already in the New Testament—handed down together in the instruction preceding baptism?

dispensation of God, at once "from Mary and God," "from David's tribe and the Holy Spirit," and entering upon a historical existence: "being truly of the tribe of David according to the flesh, the Son of God truly born of a virgin according to the will and power of God" (Smyrna 1. 1 ; cf. ZAHN, Ignat., p. 469 f.). By virtue of the double origin of his historical existence, he is "Son of man" and "Son of God." And, being this, he is "the new man" (ὁ καινὸς ἄνθρωπος, Eph. 20, a term further explained in 19. 3 : God appearing in the form of man unto newness, εἰς καινότητα, of eternal life).

(b) Christ became man in order that he might, as the Λόγος of God, reveal God to men (supra, and Eph. 3. 2 : the knowledge, γνώμη, of the Father; Eph. 17. 2 : the secret wisdom γνῶσις, of God ; Philad. 9. 1). His appearance itself is for us a revelation of God, inasmuch as he is God. This revelation is not nullified by the death of Christ, but is attested by it anew for the contemplation of faith (Magn. 9. 2). He who was himself impassible is for our sakes passible (Polyc. 3. 2). To the prince of this world, the virginity and motherhood of Mary and the death of Christ were alike incomprehensible (three mysteries). But faith knows that this all aims at the abolition of death (Eph. 19). Especially does our life now have its origin in the death of Christ (Magn. 9. 1); through this mystery we have obtained faith (ib. 2). Faith in his death enables us to escape death (Tral. 2. 1). Thus his suffering has in view and effects our salvation and peace (Smyrn. 2 ; 7. 1, cf. Tral. inscr. Philad. inscr. Smyrn. 6. 1).

Christ is our life, not only in that he will one day bestow immortality upon us, but in that he personally dwells in believers, working eternal life in them. This is the leading thought of Ignatius. Christ is our inseparable life (τὸ ἀδιάκριτον ἡμῶν ζῆν, Eph. 3. 2, cf. Magn. 15), our life forever (Magn. 1. 2), our true life (Smyrn. 4. 1. Eph. 11. 1, cf. Tral. 9. 2). Christ now dwells in the hearts of believers, as does also the Father (e. g., Eph. 15. 3. Magn. 8 ; 12 ; 14 : "ye are full of God," θεοῦ γέμετε. Rom. 6. 3). In harmony with this, Ignatius calls himself a God-bearer (θεοφόρος); and Christians are God-bearers, temple-bearers, Christ-bearers, bearers of the Holy One (ναοφόροι, χριστοφόροι, ἁγιοφόροι, Eph. 9. 2), the temple in which God and Christ dwell (Eph. 15. 3. Philad. 7. 2). The expressions: being in Christ, living and acting in him, constantly recur ; "without whom we have no true life" (τὸ ἀληθινὸν ζῆν οὐκ ἔχομεν, Tral. 9. 2, cf. Eph. 8. 2 ; 10. 3. Magn. 9. 2).

(c) The Gospel has in it something peculiarly excellent, the appearing of the Saviour, our Lord Jesus Christ, his suffering

5

and his resurrection.   For the beloved prophets prophesied of him, but the gospel is the perfection of incorruption.   For all these things are together good, if ye believe with love ($\dot{\epsilon}\nu$ $\dot{a}\gamma\dot{a}\pi\eta$, Philad. 9. 2).   Man is, therefore, to apprehend the gospel in faith.   He takes his refuge to the gospel as to the flesh of Jesus (Philad. 5. 1.   Cf. also 8. 2), or the presentation of his sufferings and his resurrection (Smyrn. 7. 2), and in faith in the death of Jesus he escapes death (Tral. 2. 1.   Cf. Smyrn. 5. 3). Faith leads to love :   " Faith is the beginning, love the end. And these two in union are divine.   But all other things relating to a holy life are consequences of these " (Eph. 14. 1). Faith and love are the entire sum ($\tau\dot{o}$ $\gamma\dot{a}\rho$ $\ddot{o}\lambda o\nu$) of Christian life (Smyrn. 6. 1).   The aim is the glory of God: " Let all things be done to the glory of God " (Pol. 5. 2).   It is thus the theory of Ignatius that the new life, which has become man's through the indwelling of God, consists in faith in the gospel message and in love, and that this life is an eternal one, continuing after death.   We may quote as summarizing his general view the passage, Eph. 9. 1 : " As being stones of the temple of the Father, prepared for a building of God the Father, drawn up on high by the engine of Jesus Christ, which is the cross, using for a rope the Holy Spirit.   But your faith is the line and love the way drawing up to God."

When being led out to execution, Ignatius is filled with holy longing through death to reach God.   He has only one passion, the Crucified (Rom. 7. 2 : my love, $\dot{o}$ $\dot{\epsilon}\mu\dot{o}\varsigma$ $\ddot{\epsilon}\rho\omega\varsigma$, was crucified), and desires to be united to him.   " Let me go," he begs the Romans, " to find pure light.   Arriving there, I shall be a man " (Rom. 6. 2 ; 5. 3 ; 2. 2).

(*d*) If the indwelling of God and Christ in us is for Ignatius the one focal point in Christianity, the other is his conception of church order.   He is the first, so far as is known to us, to employ the term "catholic church" ($\kappa a\vartheta o\lambda\iota\kappa\dot{\eta}$ $\dot{\epsilon}\kappa\lambda\eta\sigma\dot{\iota}a$): " Wherever the bishop appears, there let the people be ; " just as wherever Christ is, there is the catholic church (Symrn. 8. 2.   Cf. Martyr. Polyc. 8. 1).   It is certain that this does not at all involve the idea of the "binding of believers into an external unity " (ROTHE, D. Anfänge d. chr. Kirche u. ihrer Verfassung, 1837, i. 472 ff. Cf. RITSCHL, Entstehung d. altkath. Kirche, p. 459 f.). The $\dot{\epsilon}\kappa\kappa\lambda\eta\sigma\dot{\iota}a$ $\kappa a\vartheta o\lambda\iota\kappa\dot{\eta}$ is here the church universal in contrast with the single congregation.[1]   This church universal has Christ

---

[1] For other applications of the term "catholic," vid. Justin. Dial. 81 : $\kappa a\delta o\lambda\iota\kappa\dot{\eta}$ $\dot{a}\nu\dot{a}\sigma\tau a\sigma\iota\varsigma$; 102 : $\kappa a\vartheta o\lambda\iota\kappa a\dot{\iota}$ $\kappa a\iota$ $\mu\epsilon\rho\iota\kappa a\dot{\iota}$ $\kappa\rho\dot{\iota}\sigma\epsilon\iota\varsigma$. Cf. the Exposition of Cyril of Jerus.: "It is called catholic on account of being through the whole world from one end to the other "(Cat. 18. 23).   Similarly Martyr. Polyc. 8. 1,

as its centre and the apostles as its presbytery (Philad. 5. 1). But the episcopacy bears no relation to it. The idea of Ignatius is, on the contrary, that as the universal church has its centre in Christ, so the separate congregation should find its centre in its bishop. What the apostles are to the church at large, that is the presbytery to the individual congregation. Accordingly, the bishop is a type of God or of Christ, the presbyters types of the apostles (Tral. 2. 1 ; 3. 1. Magn. 2 ; 6. 1. Smyrn. 8. 1. Eph. 6). Christ, the unseen Bishop, is contrasted with the bishop who is seen (Magn. 3. 2, cf. Rom. 9. 1. Pol. inscr.). The individual congregation subject to the bishop and presbytery is a copy of the church universal, which is led by Christ and the preaching of the apostles. Christ and the preaching of the apostles, therefore, not the episcopacy, condition the unity of the church universal.

Ignatius, it is true, attaches great importance to the episcopate, but in doing so he has in mind only the relation of the individual bishop to his congregation. He has, evidently, two motives for thus emphasizing the authority of the bishops. First, he wished to maintain the moral principle of authority and subjection in human society (he demands the same subjection and reverence for the presbyters and deacons). Referring to the three offices, he says : "Without these it is not called a church " (Tral. 3. 1, cf. Eph. 2. 2 ; 20. 2. Polyc. 6. 1. Philad. inscr. 4. 7. Tral. 2. 2 ; 13. 2. Magn. 13. 1 and 2 : "Be subject to the bishop and to one another ''). Secondly, there was a special reason for supporting the bishops at that time, as they presented a fixed authority in opposition to the gnostic tendencies then spreading in Asia Minor (Tral. 7. Philad. 2. 3. 4. Smyrn. 9. 1). The unity and harmony of the members of a congregation in prayer and in temper, in love and faith, in subjection to one leader, the bishop, constitutes for him the ideal of congregational life (e. g., Philad. 7. 2 ; 8. 1. Polyc. 1. 2. Magn. 1. 2 ; 3. 2 ; 6. 2 ; 7. Eph. 4. 13). It is to be attained by attachment to the bishop and obedience to him. Cf. SEEBERG, Der Begriff d. Kirche, i., 1885, p. 11 ff.[1]

The principle applies not only in matters of doctrine and life,

where the "catholic church" is the churches throughout the world (κατὰ τὴν οἰκουμένην ἐκκλησίαι); but ibid. 16. 2 speaks of "the catholic church in Smyrna." Cf. 19. 2.

[1] It is historically incorrect to find here—the case is somewhat different with Clement—the beginning of the Catholic hierarchy or "divine church law," as does SOHM (Kirchenrecht i., 1893), a position to which he is led by his erroneous principle, that every form of ecclesiastical law is in conflict with the essential nature of the church and a source of all manner of evil. Cf. my critique of the work of Sohm in Theol. Lit. bl., 1893, Nos. 25-27.

but particularly in baptism and the celebration of the eucharist, in the Agapæ and in the celebration of marriage : " It is not allowed without the bishop to baptize or hold the Agape, but whatsoever he shall approve, that is also well-pleasing to God, in order that whatsoever is done may be safe and secure " (Smyrn. 8. 2. Cf. Pol. 5. 2). Referring to baptism, Ignatius says that Christ in his own baptism designed to purify the water by his passion (Eph. 18. 2), and that baptism is for those who receive it, like faith, love, and patience, a part of the Christian panoply (Pol. 6. 2). It belongs to the defensive armor ($\ddot{o}\pi\lambda a$) of the Christian life, and has, therefore, a practical daily significance. Of the Lord's Supper it is said : " The eucharist is the flesh of our Saviour, Jesus Christ, which suffered for our sins, which the Father in his goodness raised from the dead." Of those who deny this, it is said : " It were profitable for them to commune ($\dot{a}\gamma a\pi\tilde{a}\nu=\dot{a}\gamma\acute{a}\pi\eta\nu\ \pi o\iota\tilde{\epsilon}\iota\nu$, Smyrn. 8. 2. Apparently in the same sense we find $\dot{a}\gamma\acute{a}\pi\eta\ \ddot{a}\varphi\vartheta a\rho\tau o\varsigma$, Rom. 3, cf. ZAHN. p. 348 f. ), in order that they might rise again" (Smyrn. 7. 1. Cf. also Rom. 7. 3.). The effect of participating is thus described : " Breaking the one bread, which is the medicine of immortality, an antidote that we might not die, but live in Jesus Christ forever" (Eph. 20. 2). This view is based upon Jn. 6. 54-58. Considered in its connection, this asserts nothing especially new. It is the meaning of the author that the Lord's Supper is on earth already a means whereby we are made partakers of eternal life.

(e) Christianity is sharply opposed to Judaism as well as to heathenism. This also is a view closely related to the Johannine. " To live according to the law of Judaism " is to have not received grace (Magn. 8. 1). On the contrary, we must put away the old Jewish leaven in order that we may be salted in Christ ($\dot{a}\lambda\iota\sigma\vartheta\eta\tau\epsilon\ \dot{\epsilon}\nu$ $\dot{a}\upsilon\tau\tilde{\omega}$, Magn. 10, 2). " It is absurd to name Jesus Christ and to Judaize ; for Christianity did not confess ($\dot{\epsilon}\pi\iota\sigma\tau\epsilon\upsilon\sigma\epsilon\nu\ \epsilon\iota\varsigma$) Judaism, but Judaism Christianity, and every tongue confessing Christianity will be gathered together unto God" (ib. § 3, cf. Philad. 6. 1, 2). Judaism is thus only a positive, but now antiquated, stage of preparation for Christianity. Believers, whether Jews or heathen, belong to the one body of the church (Smyrn. 1. 2, cf. Paulus Eph. 2. 16). How impressive is this historic self-consciousness of Christianity, that Judaism is for Christianity simply a vanquished position.

Summarizing, we find that Ignatius in Christ worships God in person, who became man to reveal God to man, and through his passion and death to redeem men and make them partakers of eternal salvation. In the hearts of those who in faith receive the gospel message Christ henceforth dwells. The believer leads an eternal life, whose content is faith and love. Christ is his life, and death his gain ; and he who believes on Christ shall live though he die. The congregational life develops harmoniously, since believers are taught to be in subjection in life and doctrine to their bishops. Finally, we note a consciousness of living in the last times (ἔσχατοι καιροί, Eph. 11. 1. Cf. Magn. 6. 1).

### 4. POLYCARP.

(a) The epistle of Polycarp to the Philippians assumes that those to whom it is addressed acknowledge the divinity of Christ, the fulfillment of his mission on earth, and his subsequent glorification and exaltation above heaven and earth (1. 2 ; 2. 1 ; 9. 2). It is just as firmly held that Christ suffered on account of our sins for our redemption (1. 2 ; 8. 1). He knows also that we are saved by grace, not by our own works, through Jesus Christ (1. 3 extr.); and, further, that only upon the assumption that we now have faith can we attain the glory which should crown our earthly life ("if we walk worthily of him, we shall also reign with him, if we believe," 5. 2. Cf. 2. 1 ; 8. 2). Faith, love, and hope are the content of the Christian life (3. 3).

(b) But the practical force of his exhortations is laid upon the requirement that we walk in the commandment (ἐντολή) of the Lord (4. 1 ; 5. 1 ; 2. 2). Only he who possesses faith, love toward God and his neighbor, and hope fulfills the " commandment of righteousness." He who has love is far from all sin (3. 3). The righteousness (δικαιοσύνη) of the Christian consists in his moral activity, but the pledge (ἀρραβών) of our righteousness is Christ, who lifted up our sins in his body on the tree (8. 1. Cf. 1 Pet. 2. 24). Christians should follow Christ and suffer with him (8. 2 ; 9. 2, cf. 2. 2).

(c) These exhortations reach their culmination in the thought that God will raise from the dead all those who, following Christ, keep his commandments, and will permit them to share in the dominion of Christ. He that raised him up from the dead will raise us up also, if we do his will and walk in his commandments, and love what he loved, abstaining from all iniquity (2. 2, cf. 5. 1, 2).

The leading thoughts of Polycarp are thus seen to be thoroughly evangelical : The Christian, who has apprehended Christ in faith, will in love fulfill the law of Christ, following him with patience, in hope of being, like Christ, raised up by God to everlasting life and of enjoying eternal fellowship with Christ. The influence of Johannine ideas (especially from the Epistles) is in this disciple of St. John just as apparent as is the different spirit which animates him.

### 5. PAPIAS.

Among the fragments of Papias, only that preserved by Irenæus (v. 33. 3 sq.) is of special importance in the History of Doctrines. It paints in glowing colors the wonderful fertility of the earth during the millennial reign : " The kingdom of Christ being established bodily upon this very earth " (Euseb. h. e. iii. 39. 12). The description is drawn from the Jewish apocalyptic books (Enoch 10. 19. Apoc. Bar. 29), which accounts for the vivid eschatological expectations and the conformity to Jewish theology (Cf. Just. Dial. 80).

### 6. BARNABAS.

Despite the repulsive extravagances of Alexandrian exegesis found in this author, he preserves the fundamental ideas of the apostolic period in a relatively pure form.

(a) The pre-existence of Christ is affirmed, and with it his divine creative activity (5. 5, 6). He will one day return again as Judge in divine omnipotence (15. 5). He is not Son of man, but Son of God (12. 10; 7. 9). He appeared in the flesh, since men cannot look even upon the created and perishable sun (5. 10, 11).

(b) The Son of God, who thus assumed human flesh, suffered also upon the cross, according to the will of God. His sufferings are understood also as a sacrifice (5. 1 ; 7. 3 : and since he would make the tabernacle of his Spirit [i. e., his body] a sacrifice for our sins, § 5 ; c. 8). The object and result of the bodily sufferings are, first, the abolition of death and the demonstration of this in the resurrection (5. 6); but chiefly the forgiveness of sins and sanctifying of the heart, since we are thus made new creatures (5. 1 : " For to this end the Lord endured, that he might give his flesh to death, in order that we might be sanctified by the remission of sins, that is, by his blood of sprinkling ;" 6. 11 : " Since, therefore, he has renewed us by the remission of sins, he gave us another character, so that we might have the spirit of children, as he had moulded us anew "). Accordingly, the heralds of the gospel proclaim " the remission of sins and the sanctification of the heart ". (8. 3). Through his suffering for us Christ has bestowed upon us the covenant which Israel (see below) forfeited, and has made us heirs of the inheritance (14. 4). Although Barnabas has not made clear the necessity, nature, and object of Christ's sacrifice, there is no ground for attributing to him the idea that the Saviour's death has relation

only to sins of the past (BEHM, Ztschr. f. k. Wiss., 1886, p.
299 f.). His sufferings are represented as making death powerless and establishing in us the principle of a permanent renewal.
Barnabas, it is true, has, like the other Church Fathers, failed
to realize and teach distinctly that the forgiveness of sins remains
a vital element of the Christian's entire life.

(*c*) The believer enters upon the possession of the blessings
of redemption through baptism : "This he says in order that
we may go down into the water bewailing our sins and unclean-
ness, and come up from it having fruit in our hearts, having
reverence and hope in Jesus in our spirits" (11. 1, cf. § 8).
Through baptism, therefore, we become free from sin. Our
heart is thenceforth a dwelling of God (8. 15). As to the nature of this new state and the means (preaching) by which it is
produced, we are taught in 16. 7-9 : " Before we believed in
God, the abode of our hearts was perishable and weak . . . so
that it was full of idolatry and the home of devils because we
did the things which were against God. But it is to be builded
up in the name of the Lord. . . How ? Learn : Receiving the
remission of sins and hoping in his name, we are become new
creatures, created again from the beginning. Wherefore God
truly dwells within us in the abode of our hearts. How ? His
word of faith, his proclamation of the Gospel, the wisdom of (his)
pardons, the commandments of (his) doctrine, he himself speaking in us and dwelling in us, slaves to death as we are, opening to
us the gate of the temple, which is his mouth [for the proclamation of the word], giving to us repentance, leads us into the
imperishable temple." It will be observed that here also faith is
presented as a fundamental act in the reception of grace (Cf. 2.
2 ; 4. 8 ; 6. 17 ; 9. 4 ; 11. 11). But faith is in Barnabas most
intimately associated with hope. Faith and hope are but different
aspects of the same inner possession (1. 4, 6 ; 4. 8 : " In the
hope of his faith ;" 6. 3 ; 11. 11, *i. e.*, of baptism : " having in
our spirits reverence and hope in Christ ;" 8. 5 ; 11. 8 ; 12. 2,
3, 7; 16. 8 ; 19. 7. Cf. Heb. 11. 1). The expectation that
Barnabas will place a corresponding valuation upon justification
($\delta \iota \varkappa \alpha \iota o \sigma \acute{\nu} \nu \eta$ and $\delta \iota \varkappa \alpha \iota o \tilde{\nu} \nu$) is not gratified. With the above
presentation of faith he combines a portrayal of moral integrity
(1. 4 ; 4. 12 ; 5. 4 ; 20. 2 ; 4. 10 ; 15. 7. The passage 13. 7
is not decisive, nor is 1. 6, where the text is also fragmentary).

(*d*) He who has thus received with faith in Christ through
baptism the forgiveness of his sins and the renewing indwelling
of God will also seek to fulfill the " new law of our Lord Jesus
Christ " (2. 6). Barnabas describes such an one as " being without the yoke of necessity " (ib., cf. Jas. 1. 5. Gal. 5. 1). This

assertion must not be overlooked amid the very strong emphasizing of the divine commandments (2. 1 ; 4. 11. Cf. 21. 1, 5, 8). But that Barnabas was not free from moralistic overvaluation of good works in the Christian life is clearly evident from the language (not, indeed, original with him, but adopted with approval) of 19. 10 : "Or work with thy hands for the ransom (εἰς λύτρον) of thy sins." Christians should not bring outward but inward sacrifices (2. 9, 10); the insight which they have gained restrains them, as strangers, from observing the Jewish law (3. 6, cf. 4. 6).

We note, finally, as bearing upon the development of the moral life, the admonition : " Do not take it upon yourselves to live alone, as already justified ; but, assembling in one place, strive together for the common good " (4. 10, cf. 2).

(e) In one point Barnabas fails entirely to understand the connections of the traditional faith. He sees in Christianity the people of God, but does not recognize the historical relation of Israel in the development of the plan of salvation. According to his view, the covenant with Israel was never really concluded, since the tables of the law were broken by Moses (4. 8 ; 14). Likewise, the assertion that the elder shall serve the younger (Gen. 25. 21 ff.; 48. 14 ff.) shows that the covenant was turned over to us (c. 13). Circumcision is accordingly without divine sanction (9. 6), and the entire conception of the law among the Jews, based upon a literal interpretation of it, is a colossal misconception (e. g., 10. 9). They rested in the allegorical exterior without penetrating to the real meaning. Γνῶσις furnishes Barnabas the proper and profound understanding of the law. As Philo interprets it in the interest of philosophy, so Barnabas in the interest of Christianity. For example, the prohibition of the eating of swine's flesh really forbids the association with men who are like swine. The prohibition of hyæna flesh warns us not to become seducers or adulterers, since that animal changes its sex every year (10. 3, 7). The 318 servants whom Abraham circumcised are thus interpreted : Learn that he first says the 18, and, after leaving a space, the 300. The 18 : I is ten, H is eight. There thou hast Jesus ('Ι Ησοῦς). But because the cross in the T would indicate grace, he says, "·and 300." Thus he sets forth Jesus in the two letters and the cross in the third (9. 8), etc. This exegetical method, which soon became the prevalent one, prevented for 1500 years a historical interpretation of the Old Testament ; but it also forbade the acceptance of anything found in the Old Testament which was not thought to be in consonance with New Testament teaching.

( f ) Barnabas, too, looks forward to the end of the world as

near at hand (4. 9; 21. 3). The last "offense" (σκάνδαλον
τέλειον) of which Enoch speaks (4. 3—not found in our Book of
Enoch) is near. He calls attention to the signs of the end, as
given in Daniel 7. 24, 7 f. Cf. Barn. 4. 4 and § 9. The ten
kingdoms are the Roman emperors from Augustus to Domitian.
The "little king" is Nerva, as the eleventh emperor. The hu-
miliating of the three kings together ( ὑφ'ἕν ) is fulfilled in the three
Flavians, Vespasian, Titus, and Domitian, who are humbled together since their dynasty loses the throne. There is need of
watchfulness, lest the devil (ὁ μέλας, ὁ πονηρὸς ἄρχων) force his
way and gain power (4. 9, 13). To avoid this, Christians must
keep the commandments and cling to (προσέχειν) the fellowship
of the church (2. 1; 4. 10, 11; 21. 8). Barnabas undertakes
also to map out the future. As there were six days of creation,
so will God in six thousand years bring the present dispensation
of the world to an end, since one day is with him as a thousand
years. Then follows a seventh millennium, corresponding to the
Sabbath of creation, in which Christ renews the world and the
righteous (δικαιωθέντες καὶ ἀπολαβόντες τὴν ἐπαγγελίαν, ἁγιασθέντες)
hallow this last day of the world's week. Then dawns the eighth
day, the beginning of the other world (ἄλλου κόσμου ἀρχή). The
type of this is seen in the joyous celebration of Sunday, upon
which day also Christ arose from the dead and ascended (!) to
heaven (15. 5-9).

To summarize : Through his passion and death Christ brought
us forgiveness of sins and deliverance from death. Through
baptism the forgiveness of sins is imparted to us, God dwells in
us, and a new life begins. In this new life we—with free will—
fulfill the commandments of Christ. The author is writing for
those who are in danger of accepting the Jewish ordinances
(3. 6; 4. 6. Cf. his own description of the contents of his
epistle, 17. 1), but he is free from any subjection to the Old
Testament law. The nearness of the end of all things and
the severity of the account to be rendered should impel us to
zeal.

## 7. THE DIDACHE.

This document can be employed in tracing the History of
Doctrines only with the most extreme caution, since we know
that it was not designed to present a statement of Christian teaching—not even of any particular doctrines.

(a) The designations of Christ as the Son of God (16. 4), as
the God (or is υἱός the proper reading?) of David (10. 6), and as
the Servant of God (9. 3 ; 10. 2, 3) are to be interpreted in the
same sense as in the documents already examined. We have also

already met the representation of God as Father, Son, and Holy Ghost (7. 1, 3), preserved in the baptismal formula.

(*b*) Of the blessings of salvation bestowed upon us by God through Christ are here mentioned life, the deeper knowledge ($\gamma\nu\tilde{\omega}\sigma\iota\varsigma$), faith, and immortality (10. 2 ; 9. 3, cf. 16. 1 ; 4. 8), and also the indwelling of the name of God in our hearts (10. 2). Christians are those who hope in God ($\dot{\epsilon}\pi\dot{\iota}\,\tau\dot{o}\nu\,\theta\epsilon\dot{o}\nu$, cf. Barnabas). The Spirit of God prepares us for our Christian calling (4. 10).

(*c*) As means by which salvation is applied to the individual may be mentioned baptism (7); the eucharist (9. 10), which is spiritual food and drink (10. 3 : "upon us he has graciously bestowed spiritual food and drink and eternal life through his Son") and is received with consciousness of the personal presence of the Lord (10. 6. Whether we read מרנא תא as in Rev. xxii. 10, "Come, Lord Jesus," or מרן אתא, "The Lord is here," does not affect the question before us), through which presence there are given to men the blessings which we have above (*b*) enumerated. (It is, therefore, the Johannine conception of the Lord's Supper which is presented here as well as in Ignatius); the proclamation of salvation ("for the imparting of righteousness and knowledge " (11. 2) by traveling apostles (11. 1, 2), by prophets (speaking in the Spirit. Cf. the description of prophets in Hermas, Mand. 11, and the labors of Hermas himself. Also Ignat. Eph. 20. 1. Rom. 7. 2. Philad. 7. Vid. BONWETSCH, Die Prophetie im apostol. u. nachap. Zeitalter in Ztschr. f. k. Wiss., 1884, p. 460 ff.), by special teachers inspired by the Spirit (13.2), but also by bishops and deacons ("for these also minister ($\lambda\epsilon\iota\tau\sigma\upsilon\rho\gamma\sigma\tilde{\upsilon}\sigma\iota$) for you the ministry of the prophets and teachers," 15. 1), and, as well, by brotherly admonition (4. 2).

(*d*) In this free exercise of spiritual functions there can be no thought of hierarchical tendencies. Official positions stand upon the same footing as the free agencies of the Spirit, and it is especially noted that the latter may fittingly render such service, and are, therefore, to be accorded like honor (15). The church (or the saints, 4. 2) is the body of believers scattered throughout the world, who are to be gathered into the (eschatological) kingdom of God (9. 4, cf. 10. 5). This eschatological conception of the kingdom of God is a peculiarity of the apostolic fathers (the view of Barnabas is different, 8. 6). Here, too, we find a vivid expectation of the approaching end of the world. Cf. in the communion-prayer : " Let grace come and this world pass away" (11. 6).[1] The last chapter of the Didache treats of the

---

[1] It is possible, indeed, that these words have reference to the blessings bestowed in the Eucharist, in which case the petitioner expresses his desire that

Christian duty of watchfulness, of false prophets which shall come, of Antichrist (then shall appear the κοσμοπλάνος as the Son of God), of the final testing of the church, of the signs in heaven, the sound of the trumpets, the resurrection, and the coming of the Lord upon the clouds of heaven.

(*e*) In the introductory counsel to candidates for baptism ("The Two Ways," c. 1-6, cf. Barnab. 18-20) the Didache presents a formula which was frequently used, in which the chief features of the moral life of the believer are stated in a condensed form : (1) Love to God and one's neighbor, (2) avoiding gross sins, (3) opposing sins of physical and spiritual lust, (4) proper conduct toward teachers, the church, the needy, children and servants. The exhortation to the confession of sins in the congregation before prayer, and also before receiving the eucharist (4. 14 ; 14. 1, cf. 10. 6), indicates a vivid sense of sin. The Didache also quotes with approval the counsel which we have found adopted by Barnabas : "If thou hast by (the work of) thy hands, thou shalt give a ransom for thy sins" (4. 6). The moralism of the document is sufficiently indicated in the above.

God has through Christ bestowed upon Christians an immortal life, which is displayed in faith, hope, and knowledge. This is produced and preserved in man through baptism and the Lord's Supper, and through teaching and instruction given in many ways. He maintains this life in earnest moral striving and in perpetual penitence, and is thus prepared for the approaching judgment and its terrors.

## 8. THE HOMILY OF CLEMENT.

(*a*) The sermon opens with the demand : "It is necessary for us to think of Jesus Christ as of God, as of the Lord of the living and the dead" (1. 1). In proportion as we underestimate him will we also underestimate the salvation to come (1. 2). Of his person, it is said : "Christ the Lord who saves us, being first spirit, became flesh and thus called us" (9. 5). That is, he who was at first a spiritual being became flesh. But the author appears to regard this spiritual being, and likewise the Holy Ghost, as a creature of the Father. "Male" and "female" (Gen. 1. 27) are applied respectively to Christ and to the church as a spiritual entity (14. 2).

(*b*) God sent Christ to us as Saviour and author of immortality (ἀρχηγὸς τῆς ἀφθαρσίας) and through him reveals to us "the truth and the heavenly life" (20. 5). It is said, indeed, that

the world may fade from his view and the gifts of grace (χάρις used, as often for χάρισμα) come to him.

Christ suffered for our sakes (1. 2), and that he had compassion
upon the lost (2. 7). But these ideas are, for the author, mere
formulas. The work of redemption means for him that Christ has
abolished the darkness of foolish creature-worship (1. 6, 7) and
brought us instead the knowledge of the Father of Truth (3. 1 ;
17. 1) and imparted to us his laws (3. 4). The promise of immortality is added as a reward for the keeping of his commandments (11. 1).

(c) The conception of the Christian life corresponds with the
above. The controlling thought is : " that we give to him some
recompense (ἀντιμισθίαν), or some fruit worthy of what he has
given to us " (1. 3 ; 9. 7, cf. 15. 2). This consists herein :
that we, in view of the magnitude of the work of Christ, confess him as the Saviour (3. 3), and that we thus confess him " by
doing what he says and not disregarding his commandments "
(3. 4), or " we confess him by our works " (ἐν τοῖς ἔργοις, 4. 3).
Doing thus, we may live without fear of death (5. 1). The
Christian should preserve his baptism without stain. It has
publicly cleansed him from his sins (6. 9 ; 8. 6, here called a
" seal "). He who in this way serves God is righteous
(11. 1, 7 ; 12. 1), and he who does righteousness shall be saved
(19. 3). But he who transgresses Christ's commandments in-
curs eternal punishment (6. 7). No person nor thing can then
save him : " nor anyone be our comforter, if we shall not be
found having holy and righteous works " (6, 9 and 7). For
doing such works men must, it is true, have faith as a prerequi-
site ; but faith is nothing more (in contrast with doubt.
διψυχία) than a believing of the divine promise of reward (11. 1,
5. 6).

But now, since men are sinful and full of evil lust (13. 1 ;
19. 2), this demand takes the form of a call to repentance. To
this the preacher summons (8. 1 f.; 9. 8 ; 13. 1 ; 16. 1 ; 17. 1 ;
19. 1). This embraces, first, the forsaking of the former sins
(13. 1), and then at once the fulfilling of the Lord's commandments (8. 3, 4). Repentance is for the author not a change of
mind, but a change of habits by good works. This repentance
(μετάνοια) is the " recompense " which we owe to God and
Christ (9. 8).

The externalizing of the moral life is further manifest in the
fact that the orator (on the basis of Tobit 12. 8, 9) recommends
certain particular works as peculiarly suited to repentance for
sins : " Almsgiving is, therefore, excellent as a repentance for
sins ; fasting is better than prayer ; but almsgiving better than
either . . . for almsgiving becomes a lightening of the burden
(κούφισμα) of sin " (16. 4).

If man has thus fulfilled the will of God, or Christ, striven against his evil passions, and done good, he receives from God eternal life in the kingdom of God (eschatologically conceived) as the reward for his works (8. 4 and 11. 7 ; 12. 1 ; 6. 7 ; 9. 6 ; 10. 4). The day of judgment is already approaching (16. 3). But the Christian receives his reward in the body in which he was called. The resurrection of the body dare not be called in question (9. 1-5, cf. also 9. 4). The kingdom of God will begin at the second coming of Jesus. Terrible tortures are impending over those who deny Jesus and do not keep his commandments (17. 4. 7).[1]

This last and latest book of the so-called " Apostolic Fathers " is beyond question the furthest removed from the Christianity of the apostolic age. What we have been able to detect in incipient form in the other " Fathers " here meets us in clear and undisguised form. Christ is essentially the Teacher of the knowledge of God and the new Lawgiver. Christianity is the reception of this teaching and this law into the heart and life. The motives prompting to the keeping of the law thus given are the consideration of the magnitude of the gift of God and faith in the promise of reward.

### 9. General Estimate.

It has been necessary to examine the Apostolic Fathers at such length, both on account of the nature of the documents and because the material thus secured forms the starting-point for any proper presentation of the History of Doctrines. It places us in position to picture vividly to ourselves the faith of the Christian church at the close of the first and the beginning of the second century. The picture thus constructed can lay claim to fidelity, since its features have been drawn from the most diverse sections of the church and from writings of most various character— congregational epistles and hand-books, martyrs, teachers wandering widely in their conceptions of Christian truth, prophets, and preachers.

The common features thus elicited are :

(1) Faith in the One God, the Creator of the world,[2] the

---

[1] Incidentally we refer to the abstruse discussion of the church in c. 14. "The first spiritual church" is a creature of God, created like Christ before the creation of the world. It is the Holy Ghost. The rest of the text (especially § 4) is probably interpolated. The passage as it stands appears to identify Christ with the Holy Ghost (§ 4), but § 2 requires the recognition of a difference.

[2] Compare also the *Prædicatio Petri*, which probably dates from about the same time (in Clem. Al. Strom. vi. 5): " Know therefore that there is one God, who made the beginning of all things and who has the power of the

Father, the Governor of the earth and the church, who has chosen Christians as his people, who takes up his abode in their hearts and guides their lives. (2) Faith in Jesus Christ the Son of God, who was already actively engaged at the creation and under the old covenant ; who is God, and appeared in the flesh at the end of the days. We find, however, nothing doctrinally definite in regard to his pre-existence (according to 2 Clem., he is a creature), his relation to the Father, the method of the incarnation, or the relationship of the divine and the human in his person. The New Testament proclamation of salvation is reproduced, but no doctrinal conclusions are drawn from it. (3) The designation of God as Father, Son, and Holy Ghost is preserved in connection with the baptismal formula, and is occasionally employed, but not made (especially as to the Holy Ghost) a subject of particular study. (4) There is a general agreement also as to the sinfulness and misery (especially death) of the human race, which is, through its disobedience, lost to God and given over to the folly of idolatry, the power of devils, and eternal perdition. (5) Jesus Christ is the Redeemer. He revealed the Father and taught the new moral law ; but, above all, he by his passion and death freed mankind from sin and death. He brought to men a new life, forgiveness of sins, knowledge of God and confidence in him : he gave the impulse to true morality, the hope of immortality. Although this is made dependent upon his sufferings and death, we fail to find any distinctive conception, or original religious apprehension, of the latter. The death of Christ arouses and moves religious feeling, but it is not understood nor pursued to its consequences. Our authors miss entirely that interpretation of the Old Testament premises which is so prominent in the canonical Scriptures. (6) The salvation which Christ has obtained and brought to men is quite differently described : (a) Forgiveness of sins through baptism, new creation. In Hermas and 2 Clement, only the sins of the past are included. There is a great lack of clearness in conception ; it is particularly noticeable that the significance of the forgiveness of sins for the whole subsequent Christian life is greatly obscured. "Righteousness" is always merely an active, actual righteousness. Paul is not understood, but even the influence of his specific doctrinal ideas falls noticeably into the background. The type of doctrine which is followed corresponds generally— though in a cruder form—with that of the catholic epistles of

end ; the Unseen, who beholdeth all things ; the Unmoved, who moveth all things ; needing nothing, whom all things need and for whom they exist ; intangible, eternal, incorruptible, uncreated, who made all things by the word of his power."

the New Testament. (*b*) Communion with God, the indwelling of the Father, or Christ, or the Spirit in the heart (Ignatius, Hermas). (*c*) Knowledge of God as the One God, the Creator, Lord, Father, etc. (*d*) The new law. (*e*) Eternal life as the reward of moral living.

(7) The means by which these blessings of salvation are appropriated by the church, as the people of God, are particularly : (*a*) Baptism, for the begetting of a new life and for the forgiveness of sins. (*b*) The Word of God, as a message of salvation and as doctrine (Old Testment proverbs ; the works, cross, and commandments of Christ ; promises of life and threatenings of judgment), presented in many ways, as sermon or fraternal admonition, by teachers, apostles, prophets, ecclesiastical officials, etc. No theory is offered, however, as to the connection of the divine energy with this proclamation of the Word. But, since it is chiefly through these means that salvation is imparted to men, we must, of course, understand the divine working upon man as essentially an actual religious influence corresponding to man's moral nature. (*c*) The Lord's Supper, as a means to immortality. This is not connected by these authors with the forgiveness of sins, just as the proclamation of the Word is not clearly made subordinate to that end. (*d*) We may mention further the influence of good angels (Hermas), the providential dealings of God, the moral efforts of man himself, etc.

(8) The individual Christian apprehends God in faith, which is a knowledge of God, self-committal to him and confidence in him, *i. e.*, in his grace, nearness, readiness to help, and the sincerity of his promises and threatenings. These conceptions are also traceable to the New Testament, but, as the Pauline idea of justification was lost sight of, a moralistic element readily became interwoven with them. This faith is the first step. Upon it depends the moral development of the individual. But the knowledge of God is obscured. Sin, whose forgiveness has been effected in baptism, remains in man as a power, a difference being traceable between willful and accidental sins (Hermas). This sin man must conquer and overcome ; but he accomplishes this not through faith in the continuous forgiveness of sins, but through the sense of the nearness of God, through confidence in his help, and, above all, through love as the obedient fulfillment of the divine commandments. The connection with faith is by no means lost sight of, but it is not clearly apprehended, nor preserved in purity. After the forgiveness of sins has once been granted to man, he thereafter merits it by his good works. The latter take their place as a second and independent principle by the side of faith, since the fixed relation of faith to the for-

giveness of sins vanishes. Thus we note the second great defect in the doctrinal conceptions of the period. As the work of Christ is not understood as having directly in view the forgiveness of sins, so there is naturally a failure to retain this forgiveness as an essential object of faith. Good works are considered necessary in order to become sure of the forgiveness of sins. It is perfectly proper to speak of the "moralism" of such views. Faith is more and more robbed of its significance. Love assumes the leading place in the soul, but, having by the depreciation of faith lost the inner impulsive power, it turns to the fulfillment of the commandments and the performing of good works. Thus was lost, however, the attitude of soul which distinguished primitive Christianity, the sense of receiving everything from God and by his gift. Instead of this, man's own works now occupy the foreground. This moralistic modification of the primitive Christian position was, indeed, brought about by means of the popular Greek-Roman ideal of human freedom. It Hellenized, but at the same time it proved a doorway through which Judaic legalism forced its way into the church.

(9) The Christian lives in connection with a congregation, or church. (*a*) In this reign harmony of spirit (especially in the celebration of the eucharist), brotherly love, readiness to teach and admonish, to help the poor, etc. (*b*) It presents a sharp contrast to the heathen world, which is to be converted by the efforts of Christian love. (*c*) It affords just as sharp a contrast to Judaism, which represents an antiquated stage of development, led by national pride to imagine itself still in possession of its ancient prerogatives.[1] (*d*) The unity of the church at large is based upon Christ and the preaching of the apostles, to which is to be added the influence of a common history and a common destiny. The inner unity finds expression in letters and pilgrimages, admonitions and mutual intercessory prayers. The church polity, especially the episcopate, has only a local significance for each particular congregation. Whilst the clerical office is highly esteemed, there is the fullest recognition also of the free activity of all believers in spiritual things (Did., Herm.). But we may already observe the beginning of the conflict between tradition (παράδοσις) and succession (διαδοχή) on the one hand, and the Spirit and *charismata* upon the other (1 Clem., Did.).

(10) There is a vivid sense of the vanity and the perishable nature of this world, and of the glory of the eternal world, as

---

[1] Cf. the portraiture of Jewish piety in the *Prædicatio Petri* (in Clem. Al. Strom. 6. 5): "Do not worship after the manner of the Jews, for they, thinking to know God, do not really know him, worshiping angels and archangels, the moon, Selene, etc."

well as the terrible character of the torments of hell (see especially Apocal. Petri.). The end of all things is thought to be
very near. Eschatology is moulded by the figures of Old Testament prophecy and the declarations of Christ. The kingdom
of God, or the supreme good, is, in accord with the whole tendency of the prevailing religious conceptions, regarded as a purely
future entity. The more ancient the document examined, the
more fervent is the expression of longing for this kingdom.
Before the end lies the millennial kingdom (Barnabas, Papias),
which is, after the Jewish pattern, depicted in a fantastic way.
It is going too far, however, to find in this expectation one of
the leading impulses of the Christian propaganda of the first
century (Harnack, i. ed. 3, 158, note). It is, on the other
hand, perfectly proper to assert, with the same author (i. ed. 3,
165), that : " The chief thing remained the final judgment of the
world, and the certainty that the holy shall go to heaven to God,
and the unholy to hell." This was involved in the idea of reward
for earthly conduct.

Such are the leading thoughts of the age discovered by candid
dissection of the sources. The circuit of thought inherited from
the apostolic age is preserved in outward form and in general
content, but the connection of the component thoughts is destroyed ; and the apprehension of truth becomes at decisive
points uncertain, when it does not entirely vanish. Faith, grace,
and the forgiveness of sins fall into the background, and in their
stead the new law and good works come into prominence. The
thoughts which we have rapidly sketched are not always a real
possession, but in some cases merely titles of possession, not understood by those who hold them.

A lack of comprehensive understanding and profound apprehension of the gospel itself (as related to its Old Testament
antecedents) is here undeniable. And this defect certainly
reaches far back into the apostolic age. But, as the most reliable
result of the study of the period under review, it may be asserted that the variations of the range of Christian thought from
the views of the apostles are not to be ascribed directly to Judaistic tendencies. The conclusion thus directly drawn from the
general character of the prevalent conception is enforced by the
fact, that in not a single point can any specific influence of Jewish-Christian thought or of the ceremonial law be detected. The
legality which here appears is not of the Jewish sort, but it,
nevertheless, without awakening suspicion, prepared the way for
the intrusion of Judaic influences. The moralism is that of the
heathen world, particularly in that age, and it has its origin in
the state of the natural man as such. The misconceptions of the

6

gospel may be traced directly to the fact that the Gentile Christians did not understand the Old Testament ideas presupposed in the apostolic proclamation of the gospel. But moralism always serves the interests of legalism. Making much of man's own works, the age accepted (*e. g.*, from the Book of Tobit) the legalistic works of the later Jewish piety.

## § 8. *Rules of Faith.*

Already in the period of the Apostolic Fathers, the Holy Scriptures and the baptismal formula began to be regarded as presenting the norm of Christian faith.

We can here consider only the earliest traces of the recognition granted to these two sources of authority. The problems associated with them in the course of historical development will demand our attention at a later period.

(1) Jesus himself describes and employs the Old Testament as an infallible authority (*e. g.*, Matt. 5. 17. Lk. 24. 44), and the apostles also use it as such (*e. g.*, Rom. 1. 2. Gal. 3. 8, 22 ; 4. 30, etc.). But the Lord says of his own words also, that they shall outlast heaven and earth, and asserts the same of the principles to be proclaimed by his apostles (Matt. 10. 40 ; 16. 19). In harmony with this, the apostles appeal to Christ's words as of binding authority (1 Thes. 4. 15. Gal. 6. 2. 1 Cor. 7. 10 ; 9. 14. Acts 20. 35), but claim also like authority for their own utterances (*e. g.*, 2 Thes. 2. 15. 2 Cor. 2. 9 ; 7. 15). There is, indeed, a manifest desire to have authoritative words of Jesus himself (1 Cor. 7. 10, 12, 25). The epistles of Paul and the books of the Old Testament are λοιπαὶ γραφαί (2 Pet. 3. 15, 16).

The Apostolic Fathers still view the matter in the same light. With them, too, the Old Testament is regarded as primarily the absolute authority and norm of truth, however constantly it is interpreted in a New Testament sense. Quotations from it are introduced with the traditional formulas, "the Scripture" (ἡ γραφή) and "it is written" (γέγραπται). If this formula, which, in accordance with New Testament usage, was associated peculiarly with the Old Testament, was very seldom applied to the sayings of Christ (Barn. 4. 14. 2 Clem. 2. 4. Cf. Polyc. 12. 1), yet the authority of the latter is just as fully recognized. The words of Christ are appealed to in controversy as decisive. "Of some who say : Unless I find it in the originals (τοῖς ἀρχείοις) in the gospel, I do not believe, and when I said to them, 'It is written,' they answered me, 'That settles it'" (Ign. Philad. 8. 2. Cf. Smyrn. 7. 2). The same is true of the writings of the apostles, which are regarded as final au-

thorities for the church of all places and all ages (Ign. Tral. 2. 2 ;
3. 1, 3 ; 7. 1.   Magn. 6. 1.   Phil. 5. 1.   Smyrn. 8. 1. Rom.
4. 3.   The Didache announces itself as the " Teaching of the
Apostles ").   The gospel is the flesh of Christ ; the apostles
are the presbytery of the church (Ign. Philad. 5. 1).   That
such was the esteem in which the writings of the apostles were
held is confirmed by the facts, that the documents which we have
just examined abound throughout in references to nearly all of
the New Testament books, and that the latter as well as the Gospels themselves were read in the assemblies for worship (cf.
1 Thes. 5. 27.   Col. 4. 16.   Jas. 1. 1.   1 Pet. 1. 1.   Rev. 1.
3.   1 Clem. 47. 1.   Cf. 2 Clem. 19. 1.   Homily of Aristides,
vid. ed. Seeberg, 1894.   Just. Apol. i. 67.   Iren. adv. haer.
ii. 27. 2 ; iii. 21. 4.   Can. Mur. l. 77 f.).   The Antignostic
Fathers at the end of the second century regard this recognition
of the authority of the New Testament as having been always
prevalent in the church.   Cf. below : Marcion's Canon and
Montanism.

The canon of Scripture was in this period by no means a
clearly defined whole, nor even a distinct dogmatic postulate.
As, on the one hand, not all of the New Testament books were
everywhere in use ; so, on the other hand, various other writings
soon came to be regarded with equal veneration, *i. e.*, Hermas,
Barnabas, the Didache, 1 and 2 Clement, the Apocalypse of Peter,
the Prædicatio of Peter.   These were read in public as the other
books (*e. g.*, Herm. Vis. ii. 4. 3.   Dionys. of Cor. in Euseb.
h. e., iv. 23. 11.   Hegesip., ib. 22. 1).   This was carried so
far that a like authority was thought to attach to every prophetic
utterance under the impulse of the Spirit (Hermas, Did. 11. 7).
Ignatius, in Philad. 7. 1, cites such a sentence uttered by himself :
" Crying out in the midst of them, I said with a loud voice, the
voice of God : Give heed to the bishop, and to the presbytery,
and to the deacons."   (Cf. Eph. 20. 1.   Rom. 7. 2 (?) and the
Montanistic prophetism.)   Thus the author of the Epistle of
Barnabas regards himself as a pneumatic teacher (9. 9 ff.).
The conflict with Gnosticism, Marcion, and Montanism led to
the gradual development of the conception of the canon in the
dogmatic sense of the term.   That which had always been held
in the church was thus distinctly recognized and expressed with
fixed design (see Irenæus).

Cf. CREDNER, Gesch. d. n. tl. Kanons, 1860.   KIRCHHOFER, Quellen-
sammlung zur Gesch. d. n. tl. Kanons, 1844.   OVERBECK, Zur Gesch. des
Kanons, 1880.   WEISS, Einleitung in d. N. T., 1886, p. 21 ff.   ZAHN,
Gesch. d. n. tl. Kanons, vols. i. and ii., 1888 ff.   HARNACK, Das N. T.
um 200, 1889.

(2) The current text of the so-called Apostles' Creed may be traced in substantially the same form to the close of the fifth century.  Its origin is located with great probability in Southern Gaul.  But this form, as many others prevalent in the East, leads back to the old Roman symbol, from which it differs only in embracing a few additions.  The latter was the common form in Rome in the fourth and fifth centuries (see the creed of Marcellus in Epiph. haer. 52 al. 72); but it may be traced back with certainty to the middle of the third century (cf. Novatian de trinitate).  Since, moreover, the most ancient form is devoid of all theological, antignostic elements; since an Irenæus and a Tertullian declare that the rule of faith has been handed down from the time of the apostles; since not only the Western, but also very probably the various independently framed and theologically detailed rules of faith in the East, have all their prototype in a confession very similar to the ancient Roman one—it is to be concluded that this most ancient form still preserved and others similar to it were in common use at the beginning of the second and the end of the first century, and were then imported from the East, *i. e.*, Asia Minor, to Rome.  About the middle of the second century a fixed form was in use in Rome. This view is confirmed by the fact that Ignatius and Justin employ various formulas which remind us of the Symbol (Ign. Magn. 11.   Eph. 7.   Trall. 9.   Smyrn. 1.   Just. Apol. 1. 13, 31, 46.   Dial. 85).[1]  Finally, we must bear in mind the suggestions above made (§ 6. 4), indicating the existence of a baptismal confession in the early apostolic age.  In this we have, therefore, beyond doubt the basis of the so-called Apostles' Creed. But the form of this oldest confession can no more be reconstructed with certainty than can the actual wording be certainly established from the oldest patristic parallels.  For us, the oldest form which is positively attested is the ancient Roman.

Since Greek was the ecclesiastical language at Rome until toward the middle of the third century, the most ancient text of the Roman creed within our reach is that employed by Marcellus (A. D. 337 or 338).   We here reproduce this form, indicating emendations as seen in the traditional wording of the ancient Roman confession (the Psalterium of Rufinus):

Πιστεύω εἰς θεὸν [πατέρα] παντοκράτορα· καὶ εἰς Χριστὸν Ἰησοῦν τὸν υἱὸν αὐτοῦ τὸν μονογενῆ, τὸν κύριον ἡμῶν, τὸν γεννηθέντα ἐκ πνεύματος ἁγίου καὶ Μαρίας τῆς παρθένου, τὸν ἐπὶ Ποντίου Πιλάτου σταυρωθέντα καὶ ταφέντα, [καὶ] τῇ τρίτῃ ἡμέρᾳ ἀναστάντα ἐκ τῶν νεκρῶν, ἀναβάντα εἰς

---

[1] Fixed formulas appear to be found also in Aristides.   Vid. SEEBERG in ZAHN's Forsch., v. p. 270, note.

τοὺς ουρανούς, [καὶ] καθήμενον ἐν δεξιᾷ τοῦ πατρὸς ὅθεν ἔρχεται κρῖναι ζῶντας καὶ νεκρούς· καὶ εἰς τὸ ἅγιον πνεῦμα, ἁγίαν ἐκκλησίαν, ἄφεσιν ἁμαρτιῶν, σαρκὸς ἀνάστασιν, [ζωὴν αἰώνιον].

Such is the usual wording,[1] from which there are slight variations in the churches of various countries.[2] It was explained and expanded with perfect freedom in theological argument. That this "rule of truth" (κανών τῆς ἀληθείας) has been identical, and everywhere employed in the church, since the time of the apostles, is maintained by Irenæus and Tertullian (Iren. adv. haer. i. 10. 1, 2 ; iii. 4. 1, 2. Tertul. de praescr. haeret. 37, 44, 42, 14, 26, 36 ; de virg. vel. 1). But this creed is nothing more than a historical development of the current baptismal formula (Matt. 28. 19. Did. 7. 1. Just. Apol. 1. 61 ; hence Tertul. de praescr. 9, 13, 37, 44, credits it to Christ himself). The "rule of truth," as it was afterward called, is thus in content only the primitive baptismal confession, no doubt variously interpreted.[3] "And he who thus holds inflexibly for himself the canon of truth which he received by his baptism,"—here

---

[1] The received text differs in one modification and several additions : (1) creatorem coeli et terrae, (2) qui conceptus est de spiritu sancto, (3) passus, mortuus, (4) descendit ad inferna, (5) catholicam, (6) sanctorum communionem, (7) vitam eternam. ZAHN, on the ground of reproductions of the rule of faith in Iren. and Tertul., concludes that the first clause originally stood : εἰς ἕνα θεὸν παντοκράτορα ; vid. also Eus. h. e., v. 28, p. 23 ff. But cf. HARNACK, Zur Gesch. der Entstehung des ap. Symb., in Ztschr. f. Th. u. K., 1894, p. 130 ff. In various ancient citations the term, μονογενής, is wanting (ZAHN, p. 45, note), and it is doubtful whether it was in the original formula.

[2] The majority of theologians of the present day hold, indeed, a view of the origin of the Apostles' Creed which is at variance with the account here given. According to HARNACK : (1) About A. D. 150 a confessional formula appeared at Rome, and was from that point spread through the churches of the West. (2) Simular formulas were also used in the East, but there was in that section of the church no commonly accepted confession. Against this it is to be said : (1) That Irenæus and Tertullian regard the confession as thoroughly ecumenical. (2) That they locate its origin in the apostolic age. (3) That the New Testament, as we have seen, testifies to the existence of such a confession. (4) That Ignatius and Justin appear to presuppose a fixed formula of this kind. Upon my hypothesis all the traditional facts in the case may be most simply explained.

[3] KUNZE has denied this (Glaubensregel, heil. Schrift u. Taufbekenntniss, 1899), as he does not regard the "canon of the truth" as limited to the baptismal confession, but as also including the Holy Scriptures. An anti-heretical character is thus given to the baptismal confession. In this there is the element of truth, that the "canon of the truth" at least represents the ecclesiastically interpreted baptismal confession ; but the Scriptures were by no means formally embraced in the "canon," for (1) This is said to be "apostolic," whereas the "Scriptures" of that age notoriously included non-apostolic elements, as e. g., Hermas. (2) In the Ante-nicene period the term "canon" is but very seldom used to designate the Scriptures (see JAHN, Grundriss der Geschichte des n. t. Kanons, p. 4 f.).

follows a short summary of the creed, which must, accordingly, be the content of the baptismal confession. (Iren. i. 9. 4, cf. 10. 1. Tert. de spectac. 4 ; de coron. 3 ; de bapt. 11 ; praescr. 14. See also Justin Apol. i. 61 extr. Clem. Al. Strom. viii. 15, p. 887. Potter. vi. 18, p. 826. Paed. i. 6, p. 116. Cf. Caspari : Hat die Alex. Kirche zur Zeit des Clem. ein Taufbek. besessen oder nicht, in Ztschr. f. k. Wiss., 1886, p. 352 ff. Also esp. Cyprian Ep. 69. 7 ; 70. 2 ; 75. 10 fin.)

This briefest and unbiased summary of the great realities of the Christian faith, which Irenæus rightly calls " the brief embodiment (σωμάτιον) of truth " (i. 9. 4), at once interprets and is interpreted by the creed of the Apostolic Fathers. They received from the time of the apostles the unquestioning conviction of the historical events thus related, and this has by means of the symbol remained as a possession of the church in all ages. As to the dogmatic use of the symbol by Irenæus, etc., see below. But even at this point of our investigation, it must be borne in mind that the historic significance of this brief summary of saving truth was very great. It preserved intact the consciousness that salvation is dependent upon the deeds of Christ ; it taught the church to construct Christian doctrine as the doctrine of the deeds of God ; and, finally, taught men to view the deeds of God under the three-fold conception of Father, Son, and Holy Spirit. How different—may we imagine—would have been the form assumed by dogmatics in the church without the fixed background of this formula, which the very first dogmatician known to us, Origen (de principiis), placed at the centre of his doctrinal system !

Cf. CASPARI, Ungedruckte, unbeachtete, u. wenig beachtete Quellen z. Gesch. d. Taufsymbols, Christiania, 1866, 1869, 1875, and Alte u. Neue Quellen z. Gesch. d. Taufsymbols, ib. 1879. V. ZESCHWITZ, Katechetik ii. ed. 1, § 19 ff. HAHN, Bibl. der Symbole u. Glaubensregeln, ed. 2, 1877. Patr. ap. opp., ed. Lips. i. ed. 2, 115 ff. A. HARNACK PRE. ed. 3, i. 41 ff. ZAHN, Glaubensregel u. Taufbek. in d. alt. K., in Ztschr. f. k. Wiss., 1881, p. 302 ff. ZAHN, Das ap. Symb., 1892. KATTENBUSCH, Das ap. Symb. i., ii. ff., 1894. SWETE, the Apostles' Creed, 1894. KUNZE, Glaubensregel, heil. Schrift u. Taufbekenntniss. A. SEEBERG, Der Katechismus der Urchristenheit, 1903.

## CHAPTER II.

PERVERSIONS OF THE GOSPEL AND REFORMATORY MOVEMENTS
DIRECTED AGAINST CATHOLIC CHRISTIANITY.

### § 9. *Judaic Christianity.*

CHIEF SOURCES. Justin. Dialogus c. Tryphone, c. 47. Iren. adv.
haereses i. 26. 2. Origenes contra Celsum 2. 1, 3; v. 71. Hippolyt. Refut.
vii. 34. Epiphan. Panarion haer. 29, 30. Euseb. hist. eccl., iii. 27. Jerome,
esp. Ep. 112 (or 89) and occasionally. Upon the testimony of the Twelve
Patriarchs and the Clementines, see below. Cf. HILGENFELD, Ketzergesch.
d. Urhristent., 1884, p. 421 ff. Judent. u. Judenchristent., 1886. RITSCHL,
Altkath. Kirche, ed. 2, p. 152 ff. HARNACK, DG., i. ed. 3, 271 ff. ZAHN,
Gesch. d. n. tl. Kan. ii. 642 ff.

Inasmuch as Judaic Christianity, confined practically to the
territory east of the Jordan and to Syria, exerted no more important influence upon the development of doctrinal views or
tendencies in the church, it presents little material for the History of Doctrines, and a brief review must here suffice.[1]

The terms, " Ebionite " and "Nazarene," applied to different groups of Jewish Christians, cannot be sharply discriminated.
We may note three general groups, indications of which may be
traced as early as the apostolic period.

(*a*) Justin speaks of Jewish Christians who require of all believers a strict observance of the law, as well as of others who,
while observing it strictly themselves, do not demand this of all
Christians. He himself does not maintain that the latter class
are excluded from salvation, but he knows that some Christians
so believe (Dial. 47). Jerome still knows of these as a " heresy
widely spread throughout all the synagogues of the Jews in the
East, called Nazarenes, who believe Christ to be the Son of God,
born of the Virgin Mary, and say that it was he who suffered
under Pontius Pilate and arose from the dead, and in whom we
also believe." But his opinion of them is : "While they wish
to be both Jews and Christians, they are neither Jews nor Christians" (Ep. 112. 13 [or 89]. Cf. Epiph. h. 29. 7-9). It appears thus that for centuries a Jewish Christianity maintained
itself in the East, whose confessors agreed in faith with the

[1] We may properly take account of the influence of the " Jewish " element
upon the church, as is customary at the present day. But this influence is not
exerted directly through Jewish Christianity, and just as little by Judaism itself,
which has from the beginning, and especially since the Cochebean war, stood
in opposition to Christianity. Its influence has, on the contrary, been exerted
through the later Jewish literature, with its legalism and apocalypticism.

Catholic Church,[1] used only a Hebrew Gospel, acknowledged
Paul and his work, but in their practice remained faithful to
their national law, without demanding an observance of the latter by all Christians. They were really Jewish Christians, whereas
the two following groups were only Christian Jews.

(b) The second group is represented by the Jewish-Christian
opponents of St. Paul. They are Christian Pharisees. They
held to circumcision and the law, demanding the practice of
these by all Christians (Just. Dial. 47). They rejected Paul as
an apostate from the law (apostata legis) and used only a recension of Matthew's Gospel, the Ebionite Gospel of the Hebrews
(Iren. adv. haer. i. 26. 2. Cf. ZAHN, Gesch. d. Kanons, ii. 724 ff.).
Besides this, the divinity of Christ and his birth from the Virgin
were denied (Iren. iii. 21. 1; v. 3). This is not to be understood as indicating a conservative tendency, but as a concession
to Judaism. Origen classifies the "two kinds of Ebionites" according to their attitude toward the birth of Christ (c. Celsus,
v. 61). The son of Joseph and Mary was through his baptism
endued with the Spirit of God. He then assumed the prophetic
office, and through his piety became the Son of God (Epiph. h.
30. 14, 18. Hipp. Ref. vii. 34. p. 406, ed. Duncker-Schneidewin).[2]  In this path we should strive to follow after Christ,

---

[1] Eusebius (h. e. iii. 27. 3) says of these Christians, whom he discriminates
sharply from the "Ebionites," that they held indeed to the birth of Christ
from the Virgin, but did not acknowledge the pre-existence of the Logos:
"And these likewise do not acknowledge that he pre-existed, being God,
Logos, and Wisdom," etc. Cf. Orig. in Matth. tom. 16. 12 Delarue iii. 733.
This cannot offset the above testimony of Jerome. It may be based upon a
confusion with Ebionite views, or merely upon the lack of speculations in regard to the Logos, for which the Jewish Christians had little inclination.
Origen testifies that the Jews know nothing of the identification of the Logos
with the Son of God (Celsum ii. 31). Even the מֵימְרָא of Jewish theology
has no such reference (cf. Weber, System d. altsynag. paläst. Theolog.,
1880, pp. 178, 339).

[2] Traces of this position are to be found in the Testamenta duodecim patri-
archarum (ed. Sinker, also Migne gr. ii., 1037 ff.). I remark in passing that
this originally Jewish document, after having perhaps been revised by a Jew,
A. D. 70-130, was again interpolated by an Ebionite Jewish Christian in view
of the destruction of Jerusalem. Brief additions were again made to it about
the beginning of the third century by a patripassian Monarchist. The passage
of chief interest for us is as follows: Test. Jud. 24: "And there shall arise
a man of my seed (i. e., of a Jew) as the sun of righteousness, associating
(συμπορευόμενος) with the sons of men in meekness and righteousness, and no
sin shall be found in him. And the heavens shall be opened upon him, pouring out the Spirit, the blessing of the Holy Father (i. e., at his baptism. Cf.
Levi 18), and he shall pour out the spirit of grace upon you, and ye shall be
to him sons in the truth, and ye shall walk in his commandments first and last"
(cf. Zabul. 9. Naph. 3). This man "renewing (ἀνακαινοποιοῦντα) the law
with power from on high," the Jews (specifically the descendants of Levi)

"confessing that we are justified according to the law" (Hippol.). With this are combined the crass conceptions of the millennium, derived, it is claimed, from the prophets of the Old Testament (Iren. i. 26. 2. Jerome, on Isa. l. 18, chap. 66. 20).

(c) As it has not been found possible always to draw the line accurately between the first and second groups, a similar difficulty is met in contrasting the second and* third groups, the latter of which presents a type of Jewish Christianity marked by theosophic speculations and strict asceticism. The existence of this class is implied in the Epistle to the Collosians (cf. the Alexandrian Judaism and the Essenes). This tendency appears to have received a strong impulse during the reign of Trajan at the beginning of the second century through a man named Ἠλχασαί (according to Wellhausen, a man Alexius, Skizzen iii. p. 206, note, or הֵיל בְּסָי δύναμις κεκαλυμμένη, hidden power, Epiph. haer. 19.2. Hippol. Ref. ix. 16, p. 468. Epiph., h. 30. 17, applies the same name to the book itself). An angel of terrible dimensions (Christ), accompanied by a female angel (the Holy Ghost), is said to have handed to Elkesai, in the land of the Seri, a book with new revelations. In this was enjoined a second baptism in the name of the Most High God and his Son, the great king, for the forgiveness (καινὴ ἄφεσις ἁμαρτιῶν) of all sins, even the greatest (adultery), and for the healing of wounds from the bite of mad dogs, and of severe diseases (in their clothing into the water with appeal to the heavens, the water, holy spirits, the angels of prayer, the olive tree, the salt, and the earth, accompanied with the promise to forsake evil). The doctrine to be accepted, and which must be kept secret, related to the observance of the law and the reception of circumcision. Christ was not born of the Virgin, but as other men. He had often appeared (an angel) at earlier periods. Paul was rejected, as were bloody sacrifices. The eucharist was celebrated with water (cf. Epiph. h. 30. 16; 19. 3). To this were added various astrological superstitions. In general, we must conclude that this Jewish-Christian movement is an attempt to aid Jewish Christianity to attain the ascendency by adapting it to the syncretistic tendency of the age. The whole movement falls, then, into a close parallel to Gnosticism. It is Gnosticism in the sphere of Jewish Christianity. (See Hippol. Ref. ix. 13 ff. Orig. in Euseb. h. e., 6. 38. Epiph. h. 19, cf. 53. 1; 30. 17.)

---

persecute and slay as a vagabond, not dreaming of his majesty (Levi 16). Israel is, therefore, cast off and Jerusalem destroyed (Levi 10. 14), until in the last time God will have compassion upon her (Zabul. 9. Asser 7. Joseph 19). Then the kingdom of the enemy will be destroyed (Dan. 6).

Alcibiades, of Apamea in Syria, attempted about A. D. 220, by employing the manner of a public crier, to establish a propaganda for this theory at Rome. The effect was but transient. But greater success attended its promulgation in the territory in which Jewish Christianity prevailed. Epiphanius, for example, in the second half of the fourth century, applies the term "Ebionite" to a tendency which, in all respects, manifests the closest relation to the teaching of Elkesai. For particulars, see haer. 30. 2, 3, 14, 15, 16, 17, 18. Cf. h. 53. 1, where his judgment is : "being neither Christians nor Jews nor Greeks, but being simply midway, they are nothing."

Here belongs also the complex of compositions known under the name, "Clementines."[1] It consists of a didactic romance preserved in various recensions, whose hero is the Roman, Clement. (1) The so-called TWENTY HOMILIES, introduced by a letter of Peter to James, the so-called διαμαρτυρία, edited by DRESSEL, Gœttingen, 1853, and DE LAGARDE, Leipzig, 1865. (2) The same material is worked over in the RECOGNITIONES, in which i. 27-74 is wrought in with the 'Αναβαθμοὶ 'Ιακώβου. We possess only the Latin translation of Rufinus, ed. GERSDORF, Bibl. patr. i., Leipzig, 1838. (3) Extracts from the material in the Epitomæ, of which DRESSEL edited two forms. (4) A Syrian recension compiled from the Homilies and Recognitiones, ed. de LAGARDE, 1861. Cf. SCHLIEMANN, Die Clementinen, etc. HILGENFELD, Die clem. Homil. u. Recogn., 1848. UHLHORN, Die Hom. u. Recogn., 1854. LEHMANN, Die clem. Schriften, 1869. LANGEN, Die Clemensromane, 1890. BIGG, The Clem. homilies, in Studia bibl. et ecclesiast. ii. 157 ff.

In these documents we find Popular-Catholic elements commingling with ideas of a gnosticizing Judaism. The world has emanated from God, who is the All (τὸ πᾶν). It moves dually and antagonistically. The devil as well as Christ is sprung from a change (τροπή) in God (Hom. 2. 15 ff., 33 ; 17. 7, 8, 9 ; 20. 8). God possesses, as in the Stoic conception, a body (σῶμα) and an outward form (σχῆμα) (Hom. 17. 7). In accordance

---

[1] In regard to the almost hopelessly complicated questions of literary and historical character clustering around the Clementine literature, I present but a few points in a tentative way. (1) Both the Homilies and the Recognitiones are dependent upon a comprehensive Jewish-Christian document. (2) This latter had a pronounced gnosticizing and Ebionite character. It had absorbed certain Jewish-Christian writings, such as the Περίοδοι Πέτρου (Epiph. h. 30. 15, 16), the 'Αναβαθμοὶ 'Ιακώβου (preserved in Recog. I. 27-74), etc. It was composed for the purpose of establishing a propaganda in the East (the Roman Clement, the mask of an Antimarcionite tendency), and in the latter half of the second century. (3) The document was, in the latter half of the third century, revised by two Catholic Christians (the time being estimated from the circumstances attending its composition). The Homilies were written first. The author of the Recognitiones made use of the primary document and of the revised Homilies. If this view be correct, we are justified in using—with caution—the Jewish-Christian primary document, which has, as a whole, been better conserved than the Homilies at large, for determining the character of the Jewish Christianity of about A. D. 200.

with the law of antagonism, there is a double line of prophets, male and female. The latter have a representative in Eve, the former in Adam. From the feminine line comes heathendom, and also false Judaism. From this false line of prophecy originate war and bloody sacrifices (parallel with menstruation), as well as idolatry (Hom. 3. 20-27. Cf. the double line in Recogn. 8. 52 ; 3. 61 ; 5. 9). On the other hand, the true prophet (Adam or Christ), "continually changing ever since the beginning of the world both his name and his form, proceeds through the world, until he shall have reached the times appointed, and, anointed by the mercy of God for his toil, shall find rest forever " (Hom. 3. 20. Cf. Recogn. 2. 22). This true prophet has, especially in Adam, Moses, and, above all, in Christ, taught the truth, that there is One God, who created the world, and is our righteous Judge. The idea that Christ is God is thus excluded (ούτε έαυτόν θεόν είναι ανηγόρευσεν). Although he is son of God, he is not God ; since God is an unbegotten entity, he, a begotten (Hom. 16. 15, 16). Man has free will : "It has been enjoined what things it is proper to think and to do : choose therefore what lies in your power " (Hom. 11. 11 ; 10. 4 ff., cf. 2. 36 fin.; 3. 22, 23, cf. 8. 48). It is our duty now to fulfill the commandments of God. The Homilies do not mention circumcision (but see Diamart. Jak. 1); the Recognitiones (5. 34) distinctly discredit it. We have, however, frequent washings (Hom. 9. 23 ; 10. 26. Recog. 4. 3 ; 5. 36), vegetable diet (Hom. 12. 6 ; 15. 7 ; 8. 15 ; 14. 1), prohibition of marriage (Hom. 3. 68. Ep. ad. Jac. 7). A characteristic mode of dealing with the Old Testament led to the rejection of bloody sacrifices (Hom. 2. 52 f.; 3. 42).

The documents before us constitute a special foreshadowing of Elkesaism. Although their preparation appears to have been undertaken with a view of winning the West, and especially Rome, we have no evidence that such a result was in any measure attained. This form of Judaism exercised a historical influence only upon the genesis of Mohammedanism. (Cf. Wellhausen, Skizzen u. Vorarbeiten H. iii. 197 ff.) Out of the combination of the two great monotheistic religions of the Semitic race arose the third.

### § 10. Gentile-Christian Gnosis.

SOURCES. Of the abundant Gnostic literature there have been preserved for us in complete form only the Epistle of PTOLEMÄUS to Flora in Epiph. h. 33. 3 ff.—the PISTIS-SOPHIA (Copt.), ed. Schwartze-Petermann, 1853, from the latter half of the third century (cf. HARNACK, Texte u. Unters. 7. 2), and two other Gnostic works in the Coptic language, edited by Schmidt, Texte u. Unters. viii. 1. 2. Besides these we have only fragments. See the account

given by BONWETSCH in Thomasius DG. i. 153 f.; a comprehensive collection
in GRABE, Spicilegium ii.; HILGENFELD, Ketzergesch. des Urchristent., 1884.
Also, STIEREN, Irenæus i. 900 ff. (Ptol. Valent. Heracleon; fragments of
the last named were collected by BROOKE in Texts and Studies, I. 4. The
most ancient of the works directed against the heretics have been lost, *e. g.*,
AGRIPPA CASTOR (Eus. h. e. iv. 7. 5 ff.). JUSTIN'S Syntagma wider alle
Haeresien (cf. Apol. i. 26) and his writing against Marcion (Iren. adv. haer.
iv. 6. 2), etc. These have been preserved in Latin, and many Greek
fragments are found in Epiph., Eus., etc. In Irenæus we have Ἐλεγχος
καὶ ἀνατροπὴ τῆς ψευδωνύμου γνώσεως ll. 5 (edd. Massuet; Stieren; Harvey),
written about A. D. 180; in TERTULLIAN, de praescriptione haerticorum,
adv. Valentinianos, de carne Christi, de resurrectione carnis, de anima.
From HIPPOLYTUS we possess κατὰ πασῶν αἱρέσεων ἐλεγχος, ll. 10 ca. 230
(Refutatio oder Philosophumena, ed. Duncker-Schneidewin. Cf. STÄHELIN
in Texte u. Unters. vi. 3); his earlier Syntagma wider alle Häresien, Photius
Bibl. Cod. 121, written after A. D. 200 (to be reconstructed from Ps.-Tertul.
adv. omn. haeres., Philastrius and Epiphanius), has been lost. Further,
PHILASTRIUS, de haeresibus. ca. A. D. 380. EPIPH. Panarion, written A. D.
374-376 (both in Oehler, Corp. haeresiologie). ADAMANTIUS, de recta in deum
fide, Delarue Opp. Origen i. 803; Latin translation by Rufinus in CASPARI,
Kirchenhist. Anekdota, 1883. Cf. ZAHN, Ztschr. f. Kirch.-Gesch. ix. 193 ff.
ca. 310. Also the works of CLEMENS, ALEX., ORIGEN, EUSEBIUS, h. e.,
PLOTINUS, Ennead. ii. 9 (ed. Müller i. 133 ff.), Porphyr. Vita Plotin, 16.
    For Critical Estimates of the Sources, see VOLKMAR, Quellen d. Ketzer-
gesch., 1855. LIPSIUS, Zur Quellenkrit. d. Epiph., 1865. LIPSIUS, Die
Quellen der ältest. Ketzergesch., 1875. HARNACK, Zur Quellenkrit. der
Gesch. d. Gnostic., 1873; also in Ztschr. f. hist. Th., 1874, 143 ff. HILGEN-
FELD, Ketzergesch. des Urchristent., 1884. KUNZE, de historiæ gnosticismi
fontibus, 1894.
    Important works are : NEANDER, Entwickl. der vornehmst. gnost. Systeme,
1818. BAUR, die christl. Gnosis, 1835. LIPSIUS, Der Gnostic., sein Wesen,
Ursprung u. Entwicklungsgang, 1860. KOFFMANE, die Gnosis nach Ten-
denz u. Organis., 1881. HILGENFELD, loc. cit. THOMASIUS, DG., i. ed. 2,
62 ff. HARNACK, DG., i. ed. 3, 211 ff. RENAN, Origines du christianisme
vi. 140 ff.; vii. 112 ff. ANRICH., Das antike Mysterienwesen in s. Einfluss
auf. d. Christent., 1894, p. 74. ff. WOBBERMIN, Religionsgeschichtl. Studien,
1896. ANZ, Ursprung des Gnosticismus, Texte u. Unters. 15. 4. LICHTENHAN,
Die Offenbarung im Gnosticismus, 1901. KRUEGER, PRE. vi. ed. 3, 723.

    1. Already in the apostolic age there arose, particularly in
Asia Minor and Antioch, heretical teachers, who drew their immediate impulse from Judaism. They were characterized by
speculations in regard to the realm of angels and spirits, a dualistically ascetic, ethical tendency, or immoral libertinism, a spirit-
ualizing of the resurrection, and mockery of the church's hope
(Col. 2. 18 ff. 1 Tim. 1. 3-7; 4. 1-3; 6. 3 f. 2 Tim. 14-18.
Tit. 1. 10-16. 2 Pet. 2. 1-3, 4. Jud. 4-16. Rev. 2. 6, 15, 20 ff.
Cf. Acts 20. 29 f.). By the end of the apostolic period, about
the close of the first century, these views had taken a more fixed
form. This is the first type of Gnosticism : opposition to the
sensuous, freedom of the Spirit. John combats a theory which
discriminates between Christ and Jesus, denying that Jesus came
in the flesh as Christ (Ἰησοῦν Χριστὸν ἐν σαρκὶ ἐληλυθότα, 1 Jn. 4.

2 ; 2. 22 ; 4. 15 ; 5. 1, 5, 6. 2 Jn. 7. Jn. 1. 14). He refers
to the heresy of CERINTHUS (Iren. i. 26. 1 ; iii. 11. 1). This is
the second type : religious philosophical speculation. To the
apostolic period belongs also the Samaritan Pseudo-Messiah Simon
(Acts 8. 9 ff. Just. Ap. i. 26. 56. Iren. i. 23. Cf. perhaps
Joseph. Antiq. xviii. 4. 1), whose doctrine was transplanted to
Antioch by his disciple, MENANDER. He also practiced magic,
taught that the world was created by angels, which are sprung
from the divine intelligence (ἔννοια). He promised immortality
to those who should follow him (Just. Ap. i. 26. Iren. iii. 23, 5).
Similarly, SATORNIL, who, however, assigns a less important
position to the Jewish God (Iren. i. 24. 1 f.). This third type
bears the character of the magic of asceticism. The false
teachers cited by Ignatius do not deny their indebtedness to
Jewish ideas. As their chief error appears the theory that Christ
only seemed to suffer ( τὸ δοχεῖν πεπονθέναι, Smyrn. 2-4. Tral.
10. Phil. 6-9. Cf. Magn. 8-11. Phil. 6. 1). But they are
themselves only in seeming (τὸ δοχεῖν), i. e., ascetics.

2. From the early part of the second century these errors were
openly proclaimed and immediately secured an amazingly wide
circulation (Hegesip. in Eus. h. e. iv. 22. 4 ; iii. 27. 7 f.).
This rapid growth is probably to be ascribed to wandering teachers (cf. 1 Jn. 4. 1. 2 Jn. 10. 3 Jn. 5 f. 10. Did. 11, 12.
Ign. Sm. 4. 1. Eph. 9. 1 ; 7. 1. Pist.-Soph., pp. 253, 372).
The particulars of its development are shrouded in uncertainty.
Only this much is clear—that within a few decades this mode of
thought had become very widespread among Gentile Christians,
and was still further developed in a specifically Gentile-Christian
way. The most important Gnostic " systems" are those of
BASILIDES, VALENTINE and his disciples (HERACLEON, PTOLE-
MÆUS, and THEODOTUS as the chief representatives of the Italian
school ; AXIONICUS and BARDESANES of the Eastern school), the
OPHITES, KAINITES, PERATES, SETHIANS, the Gnostic JUSTIN,
the NAASSENES. To these are to be added the ultras, such as
MARCION, CARPOCRATES, etc. (See a comprehensive classification in Möllers KG. i. 136 ff.)

The title, γνωστικοί, was assumed by some of these schools
themselves (e. g., Iren. i. 25. 6. Hippol. Ref. v. 11 ; 23).
Irenæus rightly applied it to all these tendencies exalting knowledge above faith (cf. Hilgenfeld, p. 343 f.).

3. In order to understand Gnosticism, it is necessary above all
to bear in mind the syncretism of that period in the church.
The religious unrest of the age eagerly absorbed all possible religious ideas and sought to generalize and harmonize them.
Preference was given in this process especially to the oriental

wisdom. It was by no means the aim merely to satisfy the thirst for knowledge, but it was sought to realize the upper world in personal experience through religious revelation and through the formulas and forms of the mysteries, and at the same time to secure a sure path for the soul in its ascent to the upper world at death. As the Gnostic religion addressed itself to this undertaking, so Christianity seemed to be seeking—in parallel lines and success-fully—to accomplish the same task. And this tendency found support in the universality of Christianity, in the idea that the latter as the absolute religion was to be everything to all men and bring all religions to their consummation. This Gnosticism sought to achieve. It sought to elevate Christianity to the position of the universal religion, by combining in it all the tendencies and energies of the age, and thus adapting it to the comprehension of all and satisfying the needs of all. Thus revelation was to be combined with the wisdom of the world, and Christianity by this means become a modern religion. It was the first attempt in the history of the church to bring the world into subjection to the church by interpreting Christianity in harmony with the wisdom of the world. Under the conditions then existing, this attempt appeared to be assured of success, and it seemed to oppose to the gospel of the church a tremendous combination of forces.

*Gnosis* is characterized by the following features : (1) It does not profess to be properly speculation or religious philosophy, but it is divine revelation. The "Spirit" lives in it, and it brings revelations of the Spirit. (2) It seeks to be the world-religion, in that it combines in itself all truth and all the religious revelation of the race. (3) It seeks to save the soul by impart-ing the truth, but just as truly—this feature is universally promi-nent—to teach men the formulas of enchantment by means of which they may find entrance through the various gates of the upper world. (4) It presents the truth in the form of mysteries, and hence often combines its adherents in the form of mystery-unions.

The religious questions which the heathenism of the second century propounded, and whose solution it was very widely thought was to be found in the religions of the Orient, Gnosti-cism thus undertakes to answer by the aid of a proper valuation of Christian ideas. It addresses itself to problems, not of Christian, but of heathenish religious thought. "Whence evil, and in what does it consist ? Whence man and how, and what is the highest thing?" asks Valentine—"Whence God?" (Tertul. de praescr. 7). "Baptism is not only the setting free (pardon), but also the knowledge (γνῶσις) what we are and why we were created, where we are or whither we shall be cast, what we are to understand by creation and regeneration" (Clem. Excerpta ex. Theod. 78).

This leads to a discussion of the origin of this world, and particularly of the mysterious commingling of spirit and matter in man, and to a pointing out of the way to deliverance from this condition, or to the attainment of immortality. To this end a phantastic cosmogony is devised, colored by a leaning toward oriental speculation, and with this is combined a corresponding "gospel history." The doctrine thus evolved is the content of Christianity. Following the pattern of the mysteries, and impelled by the same spirit which called them into being, the effort was made, by introducing a variety of symbolical ceremonies, magical miracles, and magical formulas, supposed to have significance for this life and for that which is to come, to secure the personal acceptance of these views.[1] They were attested as Christian by allegorical exegesis of the Old and New Testaments, and by appeals to the writings and secret traditions of the new teachers themselves. It was not philosophical knowledge which was thus offered to the individual, but intuitive, experimental knowledge, and experience of the divine life, and with these the inclination to view all things in a religious light.[2] "An astonishing spectre, this Gnosticism, begotten by the rising sun of Christianity in the evening shadows of departing heathendom!" (Graul, D. chr. Kirche and Schwelle d. ir. Ztalters, p. 91).

Without entering into the details of the various systems, we must examine somewhat more closely their chief features.

4. (1) The world of spirit and that of matter stand dualistically opposed to each other, as above and below, as good and bad.

(2) From the spirit-world (profundity, βύθος, the self-father, αὐτοπάτωρ, pleroma, πλήρωμα), which is internally agitated by the aeons (αἰῶνες, sensations and emotions—movements of the primal spirit, or even personal entities, *substantiæ*, Tert. adv. Val. 4. Iren. ii. 13. 10; 28. 4), the present world appeared by emanation or evolution.

(3) The creator of this world was not the supreme God, but a subordinate being, the Demiurge, or God of the Jews (*e. g.*, Ep. Ptol. ad. Flor.: "And this Demiurge is hence also the creator of the whole world, being different from those other beings

---

[1] Cf. Hippol. Refut. i. proem : But the things esteemed by them had their origin in the σοφια of the Greeks, from their speculative teachings and attempted mysteries and warning astrologers.

[2] We may recall the opinion of Celsus : "Certain dancing syrens and sophistriennes, sealing up the ears (a Gnostic rite) and turning the heads of their victims, etc. Orig. contra Cels. v. 64.

[the supreme God and the devil], occupying properly a place between them''), or even an angel.

(4) In the world of matter there exists a remnant from the
spirit-world, and the deliverance of this remnant is the aim of
the soteriological process.  According to the proportion of spirit
in the matter in their composition, men are spiritual ($\pi\nu\varepsilon\upsilon\mu\alpha\tau\iota\varkappa o\iota$),
psychical ($\psi\upsilon\chi\iota\varkappa o\iota$), and carnal ($\sigma\omega\mu\alpha\tau\iota\varkappa o\iota$) (e. g., Iren. i. 7. 5.
Tert. adv. Val. 29). This classification may be used to character-
ize Christianity, Judaism, and Heathenism.

(5) Sensuousness constitutes (in true heathen fashion) the evil
in men.  The spirit is imprisoned in the body : " It explains the
conflict in the body, that its structure ($\pi\lambda\acute{\alpha}\sigma\mu\alpha$) is composed of
warring elements (Hippol. Ref. v. 8, p. 154. Cf. the hymn of
the Naasenes, ib. c. 10, p. 176 : " From thy breath it wanders
away—it seeks to flee from the black chaos—and does not know
how to pass through," etc. ).  Demons of many kinds have their
abode in the soul of man, and injure and defile it as travelers an
inn (Valent. in Clem. Al. Str. ii. 20. 114). From this results
the universality of sin, and the fact that it is so natural to man
(Basilid. in Clem. Al. Str. iv. 12. 83, in Hilgenfeld, p. 208.
Iren. iv. 27. 2).

(6) Redemption originates in the world of spirit.  The Redeemer is Jesus Christ.  There are many and greatly variant delineations of his person.  He is a celestial aeon, which inhabits
a body, practices self-restraint, and thus comes to be of the same
nature as the latter : " For we say of that which is seen, and of
that which is unseen, that they are one nature '' (Valent. in
Clem. Al. Str. iii. 7. 59, and in Photius Bibl. cod. 230.  Vid.
Hilgenf. 297, 302).  Or he is an aeon which assumed a body
formed of a psychic substance : being impassible, he did not
suffer, but only his psychic body,—thus the school of Valentine
(Iren. i. 6. 1 ; 7. 2. Otherwise, Tertul. adv. Val. 39. 1).  Or
the man Jesus, bearing the image of God, and by a special dispensation born through Mary, is chosen by God ; with him at
his baptism the aeon Christ, also called " Man '' or " Son of
man,'' unites himself,—thus Marcion in Iren. i. 15. 3. Cf. Cerinthus in Iren. i. 26. 1.  Carpocrates, Iren. i. 25. 1, 2.  Ps.-
Tert. adv. omn. h. 15.—Satornil (" He held that the unbegotten Saviour was both incorporeal and invisible, but he
thought that he appeared a man," Iren. i. 24. 2) and Basilides
(" That Christ came in phantasm, was without substance of flesh,
did not suffer at the hands of the Jews, but instead of him Simon
was crucified ; whence we are not to believe in him who was
crucified," Ps.-Tert. 4.  Cf. Iren. i. 24. 4.  Philaster 32, etc.)
agree in discriminating sharply between the historical Jesus and

the celestial Christ, either considering the celestial aeon as dwelling in an apparent body, or regarding the man Jesus as led and prompted by the aeon.

(7) In regard to the object of Christ's coming, it is to be said: "For the Father of all wished to dispel ignorance and destroy death. But the recognition of himself became the dispelling of ignorance" (Iren. i. 15. 2, Marcion). In the hymn of the Naasenes, Christ says to the Father: "Having the seals I shall affirm: I travel through all ages. I shall unfold all mysteries—I shall show the forms of the gods—the hidden things of the holy way—I shall summon wisdom ($\gamma\nu\tilde{\omega}\sigma\iota\varsigma$) and teach"[1] (Hipp. Ref. v. 10. Cf. also Pist.-Soph., p. 1 f. 182, 232: "Verily I say unto you, that ye shall know how the world, $\varkappa\acute{o}\sigma\mu\sigma\varsigma$, was formed," vid. the enumeration, p. 206 ff.). The gospel is the knowledge of supermundane things ($\dot{\eta}$ $\tau\tilde{\omega}\nu$ $\dot{\upsilon}\pi\varepsilon\rho\varkappa\sigma\sigma\mu\acute{\iota}\omega\nu$ $\gamma\nu\tilde{\omega}\sigma\iota\varsigma$, Hipp. Ref. vii. 27, p. 376). At the beginning of the Jeû-books, p. 142, it is said: "This is the book of the knowledges of the invisible God by means of the hidden mysteries which lead to the elect generation." "This is the doctrine in which the entire sum of knowledge dwells." Christ thus brings knowledge to the world, and thereby the spiritual elements are strengthened to release themselves from matter. The self-consciousness of the human spirit begins, and it now recognizes the means of grace and sacred formulas which aid it to rise from this world into that above.

(8) Redemption has to do chiefly with the pneumatic. "They teach that these are not only by practice, but by nature pneumatic, and will everywhere and absolutely be saved" (Iren. i. 6. 2. Cf. Cl. Al. Str. v. 1. 3). The "only good Father" himself looks upon the heart of man in Christ, and it is illuminated and blessed in the vision of God. The man now lives bound to the Saviour in mutual fellowship, and has become in himself immortal (Val. in Cl. Al. Str. ii. 20. 114; v. 6. 52; iv. 13. 91 in Hilgenfeld, pp. 296, 301, 298). The knowledge ($\varepsilon\pi\acute{\iota}\gamma\nu\omega\sigma\iota\varsigma$) of the great Unutterable is redemption, but it has to do only with the spirit, and not with the soul or body (Iren. i. 21. 4; 7. 5). Thus the spirit by knowledge becomes free from the oppression of the sensuous and mounts to God. The psychic, *i. e.*, ordi-

---

[1] This hymn pictures the distress and anxiety of a soul which has fallen under the "dense darkness," and seeks like a trembling hart to escape from it, and yet does not know how to go in or out. Then comes Christ, the Saviour. He brings knowledge and shows the way of escape, *i. e.*, the ascent of the soul to God through the realm of the planetary spirits—which are the gods. The hymn furnishes a fine example of the practical religious temper of the Gnostic circles.

7

nary Christians in the church, may be saved through faith and
works, but the hylic will all be lost (Iren. i. 6. 2). In practical
life the Gnostics regarded all their actual adherents as pneumatic
(cf. Iren. i. 6. 1 fin.; iii. 15. 2. Hipp. Ref. v. 9, p. 174).

(9) The moral philosophy accompanying these views of redemption was dominated by the false estimate of sensuousness,
and assumed a double form (Iren. iii. 15. 2), either a strict
ascetic abstinence (Iren. i. 24. 2. Hipp. Ref. v. 9, p. 170.
Pist.-Soph., pp. 250, 254 f.), or a lax carnality, confident that
nothing could harm these favored ones, with scornful criticism of
the strict morality of the church, as, for example, on the subject of martyrdom (Iren. i. 6. 2, 3; 25. 3; 28. 2; 31. 2. Cl.
Al. Str. iv. 9. 73. Agrippa Cast., in Eus. h. e. iv. 7. 7.
Isadore, in Cl. Al. Str. iii. 1. 1, assails the "theatric ascetics."
Cf. also Plot. ii. 9. 15).

(10) In keeping with the whole trend of the system of Gnosticism, there is found in it no recognition of the resurrection of
the dead, nor of the early Christian eschatology as a whole.[1]
The return of the spirit freed from matter to the pleroma marks
the end (cf. Iren. i. 7. 1, 5. Tert. c. Val. 32).

5. The attempt was made in various special associations to
popularize this general cosmical theory by symbolic rites, mystic
ceremonies, and the teaching of magic formularies, etc. Members
of the orthodox church were particularly cultivated (Iren. iii.
15. 2. Tert. praescr. 42). The Gnostics either formed congregations outside the church or secret organizations within her
pale (Iren. iii. 4. 3; 15. 2; i. 13. 7). At the reception of
persons into these associations, and in their worship, strange
forms and formulas played an important part. It was taught to
have been the design of Christ to grant to his followers such
"mysteries" as a means of protection and as powers to be
effectually employed against sin, death, and the cosmic forces
opposing in the state of death : "Jesus said . . . coming into
the world I have brought nothing but this fire and this water,
and this wine and this blood" (Pist.-Soph., pp. 372, 219. Cf.
Jeû i. pp. 142,198). We note the principal rites observed :—
(1) The redemption ($\dot{a}\pi o\lambda\acute{v}\tau\rho\omega\sigma\iota\varsigma$), or leading into a bridal
chamber, among the Marcosians (spiritual marriage) (Iren. i.
21. 2, 3). (2) Touching of the glove as a sign of recognition
(Epiph. h. 26. 4). (3) Branding of the right ear (Iren. i. 25.
6. Cl. Al. Excerpt. ex proph., § 25. Celsus in Orig. c. Cels.
v. 64). (4) Three-fold baptism with water, fire, and spirit
(e. g., Jeû, pp. 195, 198, 200 ff. Pist.-Soph., 375 ff.). (5)

---

[1] What a difference is thus revealed between this system and the church !

Anointing with oil (Iren. i. 21. 3. Hippol. v. 7. Orig. c. Cels. vi. 27. Acta Thom. ed. Bonnet, pp. 20, 68, 73, 82). (6) The "mystery of the forgiveness of sins" (*e. g.*, Jeû, p. 206 f.): "Therefore must every man who would believe on the Son of Light receive the mystery of the forgiveness of sins, in order that he may become entirely perfect and complete in all mysteries . . . therefore now I also declare that, if ye have received the mystery of the forgiveness of sins, all the sins which ye have consciously or unconsciously committed, which ye have committed from the time of your childhood until the present day, and until the severing of the bond of the flesh of fate, are altogether blotted out, because ye have received the mystery of the forgiveness of sins." (Vid. Pist.-Soph., pp. 300, 375 f.) (7) The obscene rite (menstrual blood and male semen, Pist.-Soph., p. 386. Epiph. h. 26. 4. 2 Book Jeû, p. 194. Vid. Cyril. Catech. 6. 33 ; also August. de haeres. 46, de morib. Manich. 18. 66.) (8) Pictures (Iren. i. 25. 6). (9) Magic charms and sentences (Plot. Ennead. ii. 9. 14. Orig. c. Celsus vi. 31, Cels. ib. 39, 40. Cf. the various formulas preserved in the Coptic Gnostic works). (10) Hymns (Acta Joh. ed. Zahn, p. 220 f. Acta Thom. vid. Lips. Apokr. Apostelgesch. i. 292 ff. Hippol. v. 6. 10; vi. 37. Tertul. de carn. Chr. 17, 20, cf. Can. Mur. i. 81 ff. Pist.-Soph. 33 ff., 53-180). (11) Magic (Iren. ii. 32. 3). (12) Prophecy (Iren. i. 13. 3. Eus. h. e. iv. 7. 7).[1] (13) Miracles, such as the changing of wine into blood (Iren. i. 13. 2. Hipp. vi. 39, p. 296. Clem. Exc. ex Theodot. 82. Cf. the changing of wine into water, 2 Bk. Jeû, p. 200). (14) Anointing of the dying with oil (Iren. i. 21. 5. Cf. Orig. c. Cels. vi. 27. Epiph. h. 36. 2). The practical importance attached to all this ceremonial is evident from the original Gnostic works preserved in the Coptic language. It rested above all upon the belief that this was a means of gaining security in the world to come. It is at the same time very plain that this entire foolish trifling with symbols and formulas has an exact parallel in the heathen mysteries of the age. It is, really, only in view of this fact that we can estimate the true essential character of Gnosticism. It is an attempt to transform the gospel into a religious philosophy and

---

[1] In the unarticulated and senseless formulas of prayer and magic which are often met in the Pist.-Soph. and the Jeû books, we may be tempted to see an echo, *i. e.*, an imitation, of the speaking with tongues among the primitive Christians (cf. Harnack, T. u. U. vii. 2. 86 ff.). We are not compelled to so regard them, however, since similar formulas are very frequently found in the magic sentences of Jews and heathen nations. See *e. g.*, Dieterich, Abraxas, 1891, pp. 138, 139, etc. Also the Mithrasliturgie published by Dieterich, 1903.

into mystic wisdom—to make heathenism the Christianity of the enlightened.

6. Yet Gnosticism claimed to be Christian in character. The only way to establish this claim was that prevalent in the church, *i. e.*, by proving that the views held were based upon the Scriptures and the traditions of primitive Christianity. Appeal was made for this purpose wherever possible to the words of Jesus (Ep. Ptol. ad. Flor. fin.: "worthy of the apostolic tradition, which we also have in turn adopted, together with the establishing of all our words by the teaching of the Saviour''). To this end they employed freely the method of allegorical exegesis, then equally prevalent among heathen and Christian writers (*e. g.*, loc. cit. and Iren. i. 3. 8. Cf. Tert. de praescr. 38. 17. resur. carn. 63). Appeal was taken also to the professed secret tradition handed down from apostolic times (Iren. iii. 2. 1 ; i. 25. 5. Cl. Al. Str. vii. 17. Hipp. Ref. 7. 20 ; v. 7. Tert. de praescr. 25 f. Cf. in Pist.-Soph. and Jeû books). Upon this basis then arose a literature of sacred books ( "an unutterable mass of apocryphal and spurious writings'' (Iren. 20. 1 ; 25. 5. Gospels, see Zahn, Gesch. d. n. tl. Kan. i. 770 ff., 744 ff. See also the Sources of Hipp. Ref. whatever may be the opinion in regard to them). By thus treating the accepted writings of the church, it was not difficult to impose upon many of her members (to the amazement of the unthinking and those who do not understand the Scriptures of truth, Iren. i. 20. 1), and represent the Gnostic teachings as genuine Christianity.

Gnosticism is a coarse, anti-judaistic (cf. the condemnation of the demiurge) development upon the territory of Gentile Christianity. It is not merely Gentile Christian in character, but essentially heathenish. The fundamental problem to which it addresses itself originates in the religious thought of the heathen world, as well as the peculiar means employed for the solution of this problem. Its character is not altered by the fact that it applies the instruments of Christian and Jewish tradition to the problem in hand. Its claim to recognition as Christian is supported primarily by the high estimate which it places upon the person of Christ. His person marks the decisive turning-point in human history, and his teaching is the absolute truth. We may compare the attitude of Philo toward Judaism (there Moses, and here Christ), and the peculiar zeal of the age for oriental religious forms. It is misleading to designate Gnosis as "the acute Hellenizing of Christianity" (Harnack), or, with the same author, to call its leaders "the first Christian theologians."

Gnosticism is Hellenizing in so far as the problems of Greek and Roman culture influence its course, but the means by which it seeks to solve these problems are of essentially oriental origin. There were, indeed, systems—such as that of Valentine—in which the Hellenistic philosophical tendency was the controlling element; but, judged as a historical phenomenon, Gnosticism was the attempt to establish the universal religion, in which the religious problems of the educated world in that age should be answered by means of the ancient oriental mythology and magic, with the addition of the gospel of the church. We may, accordingly, instead of a Hellenizing, speak rather of an *Ethnicizing* of Christianity.

The historical significance of Gnosticism is very great. Christianity is here first conceived as " doctrine " and as a " mystery." Thus the church was compelled to determine positively what is Christian doctrine. And since the Gnostics used for their own purposes the standards of the church, the Scriptures, and tradition (which they were by no means the first to use in this way), the necessity of a clearer definition of the latter was early recognized. On the other hand, the positive influence of the Gnostics must not be overestimated.[1]

It is customary to count MARCION of Sinope also among the Gnostics; but it is better to treat separately of him. There were two

---

[1] We might here enter into many details, *e. g.:* the universality of sin. Of the Father of All it is said among the later Valentinians : It pleased him at one time that the most beautiful and perfect thing which he had in him should be born and proceed from him ; for he was not a lover of solitude. For love, they say, was all; but love is not love unless there be something loved. Hence the begetting of the intelligence ($νοῦς$) and truth ($ἀλήθεια$) (Hipp. Ref. vi. 29, p. 272). Basilides used the formula : "That in consequence of the supermundane election, the cosmic faith of all nature has arisen (Cl. Al. Str. ii. 3, p. 434). But this election signifies only an advantage of nature " (ib. cf. Str. v. 1, p. 645). Cf. also the interesting formulas of Origen's Gnostic opponents : "To live virtuously is not our work, but entirely divine grace," or, " salvation ($τὸ σώζεσθαι$) is not from anything in us, but from the planning or choice of him who has mercy when he will." Cf. Rom. 9. 16 (Orig. de princ. iii. 1. 8 ff., 15, 18, ed. Redepenning, pp. 28, 33). But no one will think Augustine historically dependent upon these formulas, whose sense is so far different (cf. c. Cels. v. 61). Gnostic teachers were, perhaps, the first to use the term, $ὁμοούσιος$ (*e.g.*, Ep. Ptol. ad Flor. in Epiph. h. 33. 7. Iren. i. 5. 1, 5, 6 ; 11. 3. Hipp. Ref. vii. 22. Cf. Clem. Hom. 20. 7. Iren. ii. 17. 2 ="of the same substance " (*ejusdam substantiæ*). Thus also Augustine translates it in Joh. tr. 97. 4. Cf. "*consubstantialis*" in Tert. adv. Hermog. 44. The Gnostic doctrine of the "two natures" has nothing in common with the teaching of the church, but the Gnostics (as early as Cerinthus) were the first to recognize the problem which is presented to the mind by the presence of the divine and the human in Christ. The relationship between the later Catholic doctrine of the sacraments and the Gnostic mysteries cannot, however, be denied. Both were influenced by the same models and the same necessities.

attempts at reform about the middle of the second century, that of Marcion and that of MONTANISM. The former finds the justification of his undertaking in the writings of St. Paul ; the latter draws its inspiration from St. John. The former takes up arms against the increasing tendency to legality (cf. the Apostolic Fathers and the Apologists); the latter points out a certain spiritual torpidity in contrast with the spirituality of the primitive church and a decay of eschatological expectations. Such was the condition of things about A. D. 150 (cf. supra, under "Apologists").

## § 11. *Marcion's Attempt at Reform.*

. SOURCES. Iren. i. 27. 2-4 ; iii. 12. 12, fin. Celsus, in Orig. c. Cels. vi. 74. 53. Tert. adv. Marc. ll. 5. Ps.-Tert. 17. Philast. h. 44, 45. Epiph. h. 41, 42. Hippol. Ref. vii. 29-31. Adamantius, Dial. de orth. fid. i., ii. Esnik (Arm. bishop of fifth century). Against the Sects, transl. by Schmid, Vienna, 1900. Cf. also Rhodon, upon Marcion's disciple Apelles, in Eus. h. e. v. 13, and fragments of the latter in Texte u. Unters. vi. 3. 111 ff. Cf. HARNACK, De ap. gnosi monarch., 1874 ; DG., i. ed. 3. 254 ff. and Ztschr. f. wiss. Th., 1876, p. 80 ff. BONWETSCH in Thomas. DG. i. 81 ff. ZAHN, Gesch. des n. tl. Kan. i. 585 ff.; ii. 409 f. HILGENFELD, Ketzergesch., p. 316 ff. MEYBOOM, Marcion en de Marcionieten, 1888.

About A. D. 140, Marcion came to Rome, apparently driven from his home church in Sinope on account of adultery. He became a member of the Roman congregation (Tert. iv. 4). One question burns within him, *i. e.*, how can the new wine be poured into the old bottles ? or, to put it in another form, the conviction that no good tree can bring forth evil fruit, nor evil tree good fruit (Matt. 9. 16 f. ; 7. 18). The replies of the elders to his inquiries did not satisfy him. His eyes were opened as he read the Epistle to the Galatians (Tert. iv. 3 ; i. 20). He there finds Paul opposed by the Judaistic teachers, who corrupt the gospel through the law, among whom are to be numbered the other apostles. In this way is the preaching of the gospel corrupted, the latter being commingled with the law (Iren. iii. 2. 2). "The separation of the law and the gospel is the peculiar and principal work of Marcion" (Tert. i. 19 ; iv. 1, 6). The Old Testament and the New, the law and the gospel, he held, are absolutely distinct the one from the other. Perhaps he already felt the bold contrast between the natural life and the kingdom of grace. His doctrinal views assumed their final form when he learned of the Gnostic teachings from the Syrian Gnostic CERDO (Iren. iv. 27. 1, 2. Tert. i. 2 ; iv. 17). His theory of opposites could be best explained upon the supposition of a double God. The one God is imperfect, full of wrath, a wild and warlike sovereign, subject to error, mistakes, and regrets (Tert. i. 6 ; 2. 20-26. Adam. i. 11). This is the creator of the world. Of grace he knows nothing ; he rules with rigor and justice only. All the misery of human existence results from the character of this God (e. g., Tert. iii. 11, Cl. Al. Str. iv. 7, p. 584). The Old Testament comes from him : the Messiah whom it foretells has not yet come, since the prophecies do not agree with the record of Christ's life. (He was not called Immanuel, and did not rule in Samaria and Damascus, Tert. iii. 12-23), and since he speaks against the law of the God of the Jews, and died on the cross which the latter had cursed (Adamant. i. 10 ff.; ii. 10. 15 ff.). Over against this creator is the other God, who is good and merciful (Tert. i. 6. 26, etc.). He was "the unknown God" until the 15th year of Tiberius, when he revealed himself in Christ (Iren. i. 27. 2. Tert. iii. 3 ; iv. 6 ; i. 19).

Christ is frequently called the " Saving Spirit " (sp. salutaris, Tert. i. 19). He is the manifestation of God himself. As to his relation to God, there are no plain deliverances. He is commonly spoken of as the good God himself (Tert. i. 11. 14 ; ii. 27 ; iii. 9 ; iv. 7). He did not defile himself with the body of the demiurge, but—merely in order to make himself intelligible —assumed an apparent body (Tert. iii. 8. 11). Thus his work was a conflict with the ancient God. Because he revealed the good God, and abrogated the law and all the works of the demiurge (Iren. i. 27. 2. Tert. iv. 25-27 ; i. 8. 19. Epiph. h. 42. 4), the latter secured his execution on the cross. Christ thereupon went into the nether world and there liberated the Gentiles, even the Sodomites and Egyptians, but not the pious of the Old Testament (Iren. i. 27. 3). Paul has faithfully preserved the truth. It is to be received in faith (cf. Apelles in Eus. h. e. v. 13. 5, 7. Adam. ii. 6 : "he changed them through faith, that, believing in him, they might become good"). Thus one attains the forgiveness of sins and becomes a child of God (Adam. ii. 2. 19). An earnest spirit prevailed among the adherents of Marcion, and the strictest asceticism was advocated, particularly celibacy (Tert. i. 29. Cl. Al. Str. iii. 3, p. 515). But the majority of men will finally be lost (Tert. i. 24), i. e., they will be consigned to the fire of the demiurge (Tert. i. 28). The good God does not punish ; but he does not desire to have the wicked. This is his judgment (Tert. i. 27, cf. Adam. ii. 4 f.). The bodily resurrection is denied (Iren i. 27. 3. Tert. i. 29).

Such was the teaching of Marcion. The contrasts of law and gospel, Judaism and Christianity, nature and grace, the just and the good God, dominate all his utterances. He has presented this distinctly in his "Antithesen" (Tert. i. 19 ; iv. 6. 9). His understanding of the Epistle to the Galatians led him to the idea that the apostolic writings in use in the church were partly interpolated and partly spurious. Inasmuch as he held firmly to the literal interpretation of Scripture, the only remedy lay in criticism of the texts of the accepted books. This led to the publication of Marcion's New Testament, which, besides a revised Gospel of Luke, contained ten similarly emended Pauline Epistles (Iren. i. 27. 2. Tert. iv. 2, 3, 5 ; v.). This undertaking is an evidence of the high place which the New Testament writings held at that time in the regard of the church.

Marcion was a practical genius. After leaving the church, he began to work. He proposed to reform the church and restore the pure gospel. "For they say that Marcion did not so much change the rule [of faith] by the separation of the law and the gospel, as restore it again to an unadulterated form"(Tert. i. 20). He established congregations (Tert. iv. 5, etc.), and as early as A. D. 150 his doctrine was spread "through the whole race of men" (Just. Apol. i. 26). In the sixth century, Marcionite congregations still existed in the East, their doctrinal views having been modified by either Gnostic or Catholic influences (μία ἀρχή, Apelles in Rhodon, Eus. h. e. v. 13. Between ἀγαθόν and κακόν as τρίτη ἀρχή=δίκαιον, Prepon. Hipp. Ref. vii. 31. The sufferings of Christ redeem men from the power of the demiurge. The Hyle as third principle, Adam. i. 27. Esnik, cf. Adam. i. 3. Cl. Al. Str. iii. 3, p. 515). The Marcionite controversy led the church to the clearer apprehension of two thoughts : that the Creator and the Redeemer are the same God, and that in God justice and mercy are combined.

## § 12. *The Montanist Reformation.*

LITERATURE. The Montanistic oracles have been collected by BONWETSCH, Gesch. d. Montan., p. 197 ff. and HILGENFELD, Ketzergesch., p. 591 ff. As to other documents, see BONWETSCH, l. c. p. 16, note. TERTULLIAN, de corona, de fuga, de exhort. castitatis, de virg. veland., de monogamia, de jejunio adv. psych., de pudicitia. The 7 books, DE ECSTASI (cf. Jerome, de vir. ill. 24, 40, 53), are lost. The most ancient replies have also been lost, *e. g.*, those, APOLINARIUS, MELITO, APOLLONIUS, MILTIADES, an ANONYMOUS WRITER from whom Eusebius gives large excerpts, SERAPION (vid. Eus. h. e. v. 16-19 ; iv. 26. 2). IREN. adv. haer. iii. 11. 9. Hippol. Ref. viii. 6. 19 ; x. 25. Ps.-Tert. 21. Philast. h. 49. Epiphan. h. 48, 49 (from ancient sources, cf. Voigt, Eine verschollene Urkunde des antimont. Kampfes, 1891). ORIGEN. de princ. ii. 7. 3 f. DIDYMUS, De trinitate iii. 41 (Migne Gr. 39. 984 ff.). Jerome, p. 41. Theodoret haer. fab. iii. 2.

Cf. RITSCHL, Altkath. K. 402 ff. BONWETSCH, l. c. 1881. HILGENFELD, 560 ff. Belck, Gesch. d. M. 1883. HARNACK, DG., i. ed. 3. 389 ff.

For Chronology, see ZAHN, Forschungen, v. p. 1 ff.

In A. D. 156 (Epiph. h. 48. 1. According to Eus. Chron. ed. Schoene ii. 172 f., not until January, 172. Cf. h. e. iv. 27 with v. 5. 4) Montanus appeared in Phrygia, and there first found a following. Hence the designation of his teaching as the Phrygian (κατὰ Φρύγας) heresy. He and the women, Prisca and Maximilla, announced themselves as prophets. The style of this prophecy is indicated by the claim of Montanus: "Behold man is as a lyre, and I play upon him as a plectron. Man is asleep, and I arouse him. It is the Lord who changes the hearts of men and gives a heart to men" (In Epiph. h. 48. 4, cf. 11, 12, 13; 49. 1. Anon. in Eus. h. e. v. 16. 7, 9, 8). On the basis of the writings of John, it was held that the last and highest stage of revelation had been reached. The age of the Paraclete had come, and he spoke in Montanus. The descent of the heavenly Jerusalem was near at hand. It would be located at Pepuza and Tymios (Epiph. h. 49. 1. Cf. Apollon. in Eus. v. 18. 2). In view of this, Christians should dissolve the bonds of wedlock, fast strictly, and assemble in Pepuza to await the descent of the New Jerusalem. Money was gathered for the support of the preachers of the new doctrine.

Such was probably the original form of Montanism. It soon spread through Asia Minor, and extended into Thrace, Rome, and North Africa, where Tertullian accepted its teachings. The fate of Montanism was that of all eschatological movements. When the end, whose imminence it had declared, failed to appear, the certainty of its coming became a mere dogma. The expectation of the immediate coming of the end was supplanted by a complex of statutory moral precepts. And instead of the Spirit which was to be imparted to all, men were obliged to content themselves with the belief that it has been manifested in certain persons. Instead of the original enthusiasm, the movement gained greater fixity in form and a theoretical determination of its essential character and significance, which may be thus summarized:

1. The last period of revelation has opened. It is the day of spiritual gifts. The recognition (*agnitio*) of spiritual *charismata* is a distinguishing trait of Montanism (Tert. monog. 1. adv. Prax. 1. Passio Perpetuae 1). This involves primarily the acknowledgment of the Paraclete. Maximilla said: "After me there will be prophecy no longer, but fulfillment" (Epiph. h. 48. 2). But there were visionary prophecies also at a later day. Prisca had prophesied this (Tert. de exh. cast. 10), and accordingly such actually appeared (Tert. de anima 9. Pas. Perp. 1, 14, 21, 4, 7 f., 10, 11 f.). Thus the possession of the charisms is a badge of Montanism. "It is necessary, say they, that we

also receive the charisms" (Epiph. h. 48. 1). These ideas were propagated by collections of Montanistic writings (Hip. Ref. viii. 19 : βίβλοι ἄπειροι. Eus. h. e. v. 16. 17 ; 18. 5 [the Catholic Epistle of Themison]. Pas. Perp. 1).

2. The orthodoxy of the Montanists is acknowledged—their acceptance of the rule of faith (Tert., cf. Epiph. h. 48. 1. Philast. h. 49). The Monarchianism in utterances of Montanus (Did. de tr. iii. 41. 1. Epiph. h. 48. 11) is due to lack of theological culture (cf. Tert. adv. Prax. 3. Orig. c. Cels. viii. 14), but was here and there retained at a later day (Hip. viii. 19. Ps.-Tert. 21. Theodoret h. f. iii. 2. Did. de tr. iii. 41. 1. Jerome ep. 41. 3).

3. The nearness of the end of the world is strongly emphasized.

4. There are strict moral requirements. (a) Marriage to be but once. (b) Fasting to be strictly observed (Tert. de jej. 1). (c) Strict moral discipline. The Paraclete said : " The church is able to pardon an offense, but I cannot prevent the commission of other offenses " (Tert. de pud. 21). There is no pardon for gross sins (especially fornication) committed after baptism. Another regulation, however, covers the " faults that daily beset " (Tert. de pud. 6, 7, 19). In the West this conception led to a conflict, as it was maintained that only the " church of the Spirit through a spiritual man, and not the church as a number of bishops," can forgive sins ·(Tert. pud. 21). Only martyrdom can atone for mortal sins (ib. 9. 22). (d) Martyrdom is extraordinarily exalted (Anon. in Eus. v. 16. 20). Flight from persecution (Tert.) is forbidden. A prophetic warning urges: " Do not wish to die upon couches nor from mild ailments and fevers, but in martyrdoms, in order that he may be glorified who has suffered for you " (Tert. de fug. 9 ; de an. 55).

5. In the later period, the organization of separate congregations was effected. Pepuza was the central point, where assemblies were annually held (Jerom. ep. 41. 3. Epiph. h. 49. 2).

The church was placed in a very embarrassing position (cf. the attitude of the Roman bishop in Tert. adv. Prax. 1). The Montanists were orthodox and opponents of Gnosticism. In the days of Irenæus, the church still recognized special charisms (Justin Dial. 39, 82, 87, 88 ; Ap. ii. 6. Iren. adv. h. i. 13. 4 ; ii. 31. 2 ; 32. 4 ; v. 6. 1. Eus. h. e. v. 1. 49 ; 3. 2, 3, 4. Anon. in Eus. h. e. v. 17. 4). But such manifestations grew less and less frequent : " But signs of the Holy Spirit were shown at the beginning of the teaching of Jesus, more after his ascension, and afterward fewer : except that there are yet traces of this in a few whose souls have been purified by the word and by their lives in accordance with it " (Orig. c. Cels. vii. 8, cf. ii. 8 ; i. 46 ; cf. also Iren. adv. h. iii. 11. 9 : " They [the so-called 'Alogi'] at the same time reject both the gospel and the prophetic Spirit "). There was also a noticeable relaxation of moral earnestness and of expectation of an early end of all things (cf. Tert. Apol. 39 : " we pray . . . for a delay of the end." Hip. Com. on Dan. ed. Bratke, p. 18 : " Tell me if thou knowest the day of thy departure, that thou mayest be so much concerned for the consummation of the whole world." Just., Dial. 80, declares that even many orthodox Christians take no interest in the millennial kingdom). It is not difficult, therefore, to understand the favorable reception of the Montanistic prophecy. The Scriptures, they said, teach that the end is at hand. Charisms are necessary for the church. Her life on earth is but a pilgrimage, and she should hence keep her members free from contamination with the natural secular life of the world. It was thought to be in full accord with Scripture to hold that with the prophetism of Montanus the age of the promised Paraclete had come, and it was felt that through this form of Christianity the secularized church (adherents of the church were regarded as *psychic*, and the Montanists spiritual, Tert. monog. 1) was being reformed. While Marcion based his efforts at reform upon the teachings of the greatest apostle, Montanus made similar appeal to the authority of the last apostle. But this reformation was a revolution (cf. the Irvingites), as the church gradually came to understand very fully.

From the eighth decade of the second century raged the conflict by which Montanism was driven out of the church. The confessors of Lyons, A. D. 177, write in condemnation of it to the Roman bishop (Eus. h. e. v. 3. 4. Cf. Voigt, l. c., p. 71 ff.). The fanaticism involved in the new prophetism (νέα προφετεία), as it was called, is easily seen. An attempt was made to reclaim Maximilla by exorcism (Eus. v. 16. 16, 17, here a saying of Maximilla). Miltiades published a book : " That it is not necessary for a prophet to speak in ecstasy " (Eus. v. 17. 1). The prophets of the Old and New Testaments, it was said, as those of the later church, were not in such a state when uttering their prophecies. The new prophetism was pronounced a pseudo-prophetism, inspired by the devil (Anon. in. Eus. v. 16. 4, 7, 8 ; 17. 2 ff. Apollon., ib. 18. 1. Epiph. h. 48. 1-8. Cf. Orig. de princ. ii. 7. 3). It was also felt to be impossible that this enthusiastic prophetism should usher in a new era of the world (Eus. v. 16. 9. Epiph. h. 48. 8, 11, 12. Did. de tr. iii. 41. 2). It is quite easy to understand that this opposition should be carried too far, and that with the false prophetism the genuine gift of prophecy should be discredited (Iren. iii. 11. 9: "they are imprudent who deny that pseudo-prophetism is anything, but reject prophetic grace from the church").[1] The Muratori fragment says: "I consider the prophets a finished thing" (l. 79). And Tertullian writes: "And hence the offices have ceased, as also their benefits; therefore thou mayest deny that he has continued the endowments until the present age, because this *law and the prophets* were also until John. It remains that ye put away from you whatever in you is so profitless" (de jej. 11 fin.). The church sees herself compelled to surrender one element of her former experience, the *charismata*. She in principle abandons her claim to the Spirit. Tradition triumphs over the Spirit. It was charged upon the Montanists that their teachings were unknown to tradition (Eus. h. e. v. 16. 7, 9). The Spirit expressed in the word and historical tradition triumphs over the Spirit which had become fanaticism. Synods—the first known to us—were held in Asia Minor, and the adherents of the new prophetism excluded from the church (Anon. in Eus. v. 16. 10. Thus also later in Iconium, Cypr. ep. 75. 19). Thus was Montanism expelled from the church. After the fourth century it began to feel the pressure of the civil power. With the sixth century it disappeared (BONWETSCH, l. c., p. 171 ff.).

The church rejected Montanism because she recognized these reformatory efforts as out of harmony with the principles of the gospel, her judgment being here entirely correct. She freed herself from responsibility for the charisms still claimed by a few, asserted more clearly the authority of biblical revelation (cf. the peculiar remark of the anonymous writer in Eus. h. e. v. 16. 3), and prepared the way for the forms of a compact organization. The conflict had, therefore, a most important influence upon the development of the church.

---

[1] This is "the heresy which rejects the books of John" (Hippol., vid. Epiph. h. 51. 3), whose adherents Epiphanius called the "Alogi" (cf. Epiph. h. 51. Phil. h. 60. Iren. iii. 11. 9). About A. D. 170 in Asia Minor they rejected the Gospel of John and the Apocalypse as spurious, and as composed by Cerinthus. As to their critical arguments, vid. Epiph. h. 51. 2, 18 f., 21 f., 32. 34. They are Catholic Christians, who sought in this way to undermine the foundations of Montanism. Cf. ZAHN, Gesch. d. ntl. Kan. i. 237 ff.; ii. 967 ff. A similar attempt was made at Rome about A. D. 210 by Caius, who, however, rejected only the Apocalypse as Cerinthian. Of the writings of Hippolytus against him, Capitula adv. Caium, GWYNN has published five Syrian fragments, found in ZAHN, l. c. ii. 974 ff.

# CHAPTER III.

### BEGINNINGS OF THE CHURCH'S THEOLOGY.

§ 13. *Christianity as Portrayed by the Apologists of the Ancient Church.*

SOURCES. The Greek WW. in Corpus apologetarum, ed. Otto, 9 vols., 1842 ff. Vols. 1-6 in 3d ed., 1876 ff. Tatian, Athenagoras and Aristides also in Texte u. Unters. iv. Cf. HARNACK, Die Ueberlieferung der griech. Apol., in Texte u. Unters. i. SEPARATELY: QUADRATUS ca. A. D. 125, a sentence in Eus. h. e. iv. 3. 2; cf. ZAHN in Neue kirchl. Ztschr., 1891, 281 ff. MARCIANUS ARISTIDES, his Apol. syr., edited by HARRIS, in Texts and Studies, i. 1. A Greek revision in Vita Barlaami et Joasaph. 26 fin. 27 (Migne, Gr. 96. 1108 ff.). A large Armenian fragment in S. Aristides philos. Atheniens. sermon. duo, ed. Mechitaristae, Venet., 1878, of which a good German translation by HIMPEL is found in Th. Quartalschr., 1880, p. 110 ff.—most correctly preserved in the Syrian text, ca. A. D. 140-145; vid. SEEBERG, Die Apol. d. Arist. untersucht u. wiederhergestellt, in Zahn's Forschungen, v., pp. 159-414, and SEEBERG, der Apol. Arist., 1894, where also the homily of Arist. and a fragment. The apologies of MELITO of Sardes (Eus. h. e., iv. 26—the Syrian apology bearing his name which has been preserved is not genuine), of APOLINARIUS of Hieropolis (ib. iv. 26. 1; 27), of MILTIADES (ib. v. 17. 5, cf. SEEBERG, l. c. 238 ff.) have been lost. They were all addressed to Marcus Aurelius (A. D. 161-180). The most important apologetic writer of the period is JUSTIN MARTYR, born ca. A. D. 100. About A. D. 150 he wrote his two apologies; somewhat later, the Dialogus contra Tryphone. Of his book, περὶ ἀναστάσεως, two fragments appear in Otto, ii. 208 ff. His Σύνταγμα κατὰ πασῶν αἱρέσεων has been lost. Cf. ZAHN, Ztschr. f. KG., viii. 1 ff. VEIL, Just. Rechtfertigung des Christ., prefaced, translated into German and elucidated, 1894; vid. SEEBERG in Theol. Littbl. Febr., 1895. VON ENGELHARDT, D. Christent. Just. d. Märt., 1878. Also STÄHLIN, Just. d. Märt. u. s. neuester Beurtheiler, 1880. FLEMMING, Zur Beurtheilung d. Christent. Just., 1893. DUNCKER, Logoslehre Just., 1848. BOSSE, der präex. Christus d. Just., 1891. TATIAN, a pupil of Justin, wrote: λόγος πρὸς Ἕλληνας. Upon his "Diatessaron," vid. ZAHN, Forschungen, i. ATHENAGORAS, about A. D. 170, addressed to Marcus Aurelius his Πρεσβεία περὶ χριστιανῶν. He wrote also, περὶ ἀναστάσεως. THEOPHILUS of Antioch: ad Antolycum, ll. 3. Book iii. was not written until A. D. 181 (iii. 27). As to the commentary upon the gospels attributed to him, vid. ZAHN, Forsch. ii. HARNACK, Texte u. Unters., i. 4. HAUCK, Ztschr. f. k. Wiss., 1884, 561 ff. BORNEMANN, Ztschr. f. KG., 1889, p. 169 ff. The Epistle to Diognetus does not appear to belong to this period. We possess an apology of MINUCIUS FELIX, written in Latin and entitled, Octavius. It was written after A. D. 180; edited by Dombart, also by Halm in Corp. scr. eccl. lat., ii. Cf. KÜHN, Der Octav. d. Min. Fel., 1882. TERTULLIAN'S Apologeticum is dependent upon the latter (cf. EBERT, Gesch. d. chr. lat. Litt., i. 25 ff. SCHWENKE, in Jahrbb. f. prot. Th., 1883, 263 ff. RECK, in Th. Quartalschr., 1886, 64 ff. On the other hand, HARTEL, in Ztschr. f. österr. Gymn., 1869, 348 ff. WILHELM, De Minuc. Fel Octavii et Tert. apol., Breslau, 1887). Cf. also the apologetic material in the Martyrium of Apollonius in HARNACK in the reports of sessions of Berl. Acad., 1893, p. 721 ff., and SEEBERG, in the Neue kirchl. Ztschr., 1893, p. 836 ff. HILGENFELD, in his Ztschr., 1894, p. 58 ff.

1. We are now to note the beginnings of Christian theology. It was the pressure of practical necessity, no less than the force of inward development, which gave birth to theology. It was, on the one hand, necessary to assume a positive position against the assaults from without and the efforts of the age to produce a new Christianity. On the other hand, in proportion as Christianity became more widely diffused and permeated the thinking of the world, was it compelled to explain what it claimed to possess in its revelation. The Apologists undertook in their biblical writings to set forth Christianity in forms intelligible to the cultured classes of their age, while at the same time repelling all unjust accusations. The Antignostic Fathers displayed the unbiblical and unchristian character of Gnosticism, and in opposition to it gave form to an ecclesiastical and biblical Christianity. The Alexandrian theology first presented Christianity in the forms of science, and thus proved that the faith of the church is a Gnosis superior to the pretended Gnosis of their adversaries. We must first consider the Apologists.

2. To outline the Christianity of the early Apologists is a task to be undertaken with great caution. They defended Christianity after the traditional fashion against certain definite traditional charges.[1] In doing this, those features of Christianity which might most readily be comprehended and acknowledged by cultivated heathen (the unity of God, the Logos, virtue, immortality) were expounded. There was danger that in this process Christ might be almost entirely overlooked (Theoph. Minuc. Ath. 10. Cf. the apology, 11 init.). Christian doctrines were skillfully presented as similar to heathen teachings (Polytheism, Just. i. 6. Ath. 10 fin.; per contra, Ath. 24. The sons of Zeus, Just. i. 20 ff.; 24 init. Tert. 21 ; per contra, Just. i. 53 f. Lat. 21). A choice was made of doctrines suitable to the purpose in view, and the material was adapted to the conceptions of those for whom the documents were written. That the Christian beliefs of the writers were not exhaustively presented under such circumstances is evident, and finds confirmation from the comparison of the apologetic writings in question with other productions of the same authors (Just. Dial., Tert.

---

[1] ἀθεότης, ἀσέβεια, secret immorality, vid. ep. eccl. Lugd. in Eus. h. e. v. 1. 9 : "that there is no atheistic nor impious person among us." Tert. Ap. 10 : "We are assembled for the sake of sacrilege and sedition. This is the chief, yea, the whole charge." Athenag. 3 : "they prefer three charges against us : atheism, Thyestian feasts, and Oedipean intercourse" (cf. Plinii ep. 10. 79. Aristid. 17. Just. Ap. i. 6. 26 f.; ii. 12. Dial. 10. Theoph. iii. 4. 15. Eus. h. e. v. 1. 9, 14, 19, 26, 52. Minuc. 8 ff.; 28 ff. Tert. Apol. 27 f.; 7 ff., 39. Orig. c. Cels. vi. 27 ; viii. 39, 41, 65, 67, etc.

in other works, Aristid. Hom.). It may be said of the majority
of these writers that they had no clearer conceptions of the gospel than had the Apostolic Fathers; but at the same time it
must be conceded that their views were no more defective. The
study of their works is instructive, not as adding anything to the
general faith of the church, but as furnishing the earliest attempts
of ecclesiastical theology. They have in common with the
Gnostics the attempt to make Christianity comprehensible to the
heathen, but they differ from them in that they do not admit the
syncretism of the age into their conception of Christianity. In
their view, Christianity stands in bold contrast with the religions
of the heathen world. Only in the case of philosophy is any
parallel conceded. The most important of their doctrinal views
may be classified as follows :

3. Christianity, Heathenism, and Judaism. Of Christianity
Justin Martyr declares: "I found that this philosophy only
is safe and useful" (Dial. 8, cf. Tatian. 31. Melito in Eus.
v. 26. 7, cf. Miltiades, ib. v. 17. 5). The "words of the
Saviour" should be observed, for they are full of power and
spirit (Dial. 8, 9). The attitude toward heathenism is one of
repulsion. When the purpose is to show the necessity for Christianity, the religious life of heathenism is characterized as folly
and immorality, and its gods as demons (cf. Just. Ap. i. 12, 14,
21. Dial. 79 fin., 83. Ath. 25 ff. 23. Minuc. 21 ff. Tert. 23.
For Scriptural proof, Ps. 95. 5 is quoted: "The gods of the
heathen are demons" (δαιμόνια), in connection with which the
different meanings of the term δαιμόνιον in heathen and Christian
parlance must not be overlooked).[1] The philosophers and poets
are only promoters of idolatry (Arist. 13), inspired by demons
(Theoph. ii. 8); their productions are nothing but self-contradictory frivolity (Tat. passim, Theoph. ii. 8; iii. 2 f., 5 ff.
Min. Fel. 38. Tert. 46). Whatever is undeniably good in
them has been borrowed from the Jewish prophets, who far excel
them in antiquity (Just. Ap. i. 44, 54, 59 f. Tat. 31, 40 f.
Theoph. i. 14; iii. 23; ii. 30, 37 fin. Minuc. 34. Tert. 47).
But, on the other hand, the Trinity, angels, and the Son of God
are represented as paralleled in Polytheism and in the heathen conception of "Sons of God" (vid. supra). In the philosophers
of Gentile nations the same Logos was supposed to have dwelt that
afterward appeared in Christ. "Our [doctrines] appear more
splendid than all human teaching because the Christ revealed
through us was the whole Logos-nature (τὸ λογικὸν τὸ ὅλον), body,

---

[1] Cf. e. g., the word as used by Celsus and by Origen in Orig. c. Celsus v.
2; viii. 24, 28, 33, 45, 58, etc. On the other hand, v. 5; vii. 67, 68 f.;
viii. 13, 25, etc.

intellect, and soul. For whatever things the philosophers and
lawgivers excellently uttered or invented were wrought out by
them through the co-operation of the Logos in discovery or contemplation'' (Just. Ap. ii. 10). Only germs (σπέρματα) of the
Logos dwelt in the prophets, whereas he revealed himself completely in Christ. Hence much is found in heathen authors
that is erroneous. Plato's teachings are thus related to the doctrines of Christ : "not alien (ἀλλότρια) to Christ, but that they
are not everywhere the same " (Just. Ap. ii. 13). Again, it is
said, " Those living according to the Logos are Christians,''
such as Socrates, Heraclitus, Abraham, Elijah,'' etc. (Just. Ap. i.
46 ; cf. Minuc. 20 init.). The entire truth is contained in
the primitive writings of the Old Testament prophets, for they
were inspired ; the Logos himself spoke in them ; they correctly prophesied of future things (Just. Ap. i. 30 f., 36. Ath.
9 : " Who, in the ecstasy of the thoughts within them, the
divine Spirit moving them, gave utterance to the things they
were impelled to utter, the Spirit using them as a flute-player
plays his flute. Cf. Just. Dial. 115). Their utterances are,
therefore, to be acknowledged even by the heathen as absolute
proof of the truth. Christianity, is, therefore, not a new religion, as Celsus charged (cf. Just. i. 53. Ath. 7, 9. Theoph.
ii. 9, cf. 36, the Sybils. As to this evidence from prophecy,
cf. also Celsus in Orig. c. Cels. iii. 26 ; viii. 12 ; vi. 2). The
prophets taught One God, true morality, and future rewards and
punishments (Theoph. ii. 34 fin.; iii. 9). Their writings contain the Christian truth (Just. Dial. 29). With their real
spiritual contents, however, was combined, on account of the
hardness of heart of the Jewish people, the ceremonial law
(Just. Dial. 19-22, 42, 44, 46, 67), which contains also veiled
references to Christ (" I say that a certain law was ordained for
the cultivation of piety and right living, and a certain law and
ceremony was also announced as a mystery of Christ, or on account of the hardness of your hearts,'' Dial. 44). The Jews
have, by their doctrines (διδάγματα) supplanted those of God
(Just. Dial. 78). They are, consequently, no more the people of
God.[1] In accordance with the prophecies, Christians from the
heathen world are now the people of God and the true Israel
(Just. Dial. 25, 26, 123, 135 fin.).

What are then the true Christian " doctrines? "

4. There is One God, the Creator, Adorner, and Preserver of
the world (Just. i. 6. Ath. 8. Theop. iii. 9). The invisible
God is an unbegotten, nameless, eternal, incomprehensible, un-

---

[1] The judgment of Aristides is less severe. Cf. Seeberg, l. c. 1, page 295 f.

changeable Being, without any needs and free from all passions
(Arist. 1. Just. i. 10, 13, 25, 49, 53 ; ii. 6. Dial. 127. Tat.
4. Ath. 10, 13, 16, 44, 21. Theoph. i. 4. 3 ; ii. 10, 3, 22 ).
He made everything for man's sake, and is therefore to be loved
(Arist. 2. Just. i. 10; ii. 4. Tat. 4. Theoph. i. 4 fin.; ii.
16). He created the world out of nothingness and gave form to
matter (Theoph. ii. 4, 13, 10 : "That in some way matter was
begotten, created by God, from which God made and formed the
world"). Yet, with all this, the true nature of the living God does
not find expression. There is no advance beyond the mere abstract
conception that the Divine Being is absolute attributeless Existence.

In both operations, God employed the Son as mediator. This
is not to be understood in a mythological sense (Ath. 10). He
is the Logos of God. This was a favorite term of the cultured
classes. Whenever it was mentioned, the interest of all was at
once secured. But that precisely this term was chosen proves
how entirely the thoughts of the church were centered in the
exalted Christ. If they had thought chiefly of the man Jesus,
they might have easily characterized him as a second Socrates.
But they thought of him as God, in God, and with God, and
hence selected a term such as "Logos," in order to make the
matter plain to the heathen. Originally God was alone, but by
virtue of the reasoning faculty ($\lambda o\gamma\iota\varkappa\grave{\eta}\ \delta\acute{\nu}\nu\alpha\mu\iota\varsigma$) belonging to him
he had in himself the Logos. By a simple exercise of his will,
the Logos sprang forth ($\pi\rho o\pi\eta\delta\tilde{\alpha}$). He is the first-born work of
the Father (Tat. 5 ; cf. Just. Ap. ii. 6. Dial. 100. Ath. 10 :
"The first begotten thing . . . not as coming into being, for
from the beginning God, being eternal intelligence, $\nu o\tilde{\nu}\varsigma$, had
in himself the Logos, being eternally Logos-natured, $\lambda o\gamma\iota\varkappa\acute{o}\varsigma$).
Of the manner in which the Logos originated, it is said : " This
power was begotten from the power of the Father and his counsel ;
but not by a separation, as though the nature of the Father were
distributed," i. e., somewhat as a fire does not diminish another
by which it is enkindled, "and that which is taken away from
it appears to be also the same and does not diminish that from
which it was taken " (Just. Dial. 128, 61, 100. Tat. 5). He is
not an angel, but divine ; divine ($\vartheta\varepsilon\acute{o}\varsigma$), but not God himself
($\acute{o}\ \vartheta\varepsilon\acute{o}\varsigma$) (Dial. 60 ; vid. per contra, Ap. i. 6). In respect to
the Father, he is something else ($\check{\varepsilon}\tau\varepsilon\rho\acute{o}\nu\ \tau\iota$) and another ($\check{\alpha}\lambda\lambda o\varsigma$
$\tau\iota\varsigma$), and is such in number but not in mind, $\gamma\nu\acute{\omega}\mu\eta$ (Just. Dial.
56, 50, 55, 62, 128, 129 : "And that which is begotten is
other in number than that which begets, as everyone must confess "). Thus the Logos is God together with the Father, and
to him alone, as to the Father, is worship due ( Just. Dial. 68,
63 f. Ap. ii. 13).

8

Through the Logos, God has revealed himself. He it is who
in the Old Testament period appears to men (Just. Dial. 56 ff.,
60. Ap. i. 36). He is the messenger of God, "our teacher and
apostle," God revealed, γνωριζόμενος [1] (Just. Dial. 60, 127. Ap.
i. 12. Dial. 64 ; cf. Theoph. ii. 22). When God determined
to create the world, he begat the word which he had in himself
(λογός ἐνδιάθετος) as the word uttering itself in speech (λόγος
προφορικός). For the use of the terms by the Stoics and Philo,
cf. HEINZE, Die Lehre vom Logos, p. 140 ff., 231 f.; Orig. c.
Cels. vi. 65 : ". . . the Logos always existing resident in the
heart of God. For before anything was created, he had this
counselor, which was his own reason (νοῦς) and purpose
(φρόνησις). But when God determined to make whatever he desired, he begat this Logos as the word (προφορικός), the first-
born of the whole creation, he himself not being emptied of the
Logos, but begetting the Logos, and always remaining associated
with his Logos " (Theoph. ii. 22 ; cf. 10. Ath. 10. Tert. adv.
Prax. 5 : *sermonalis* and *rationalis*). Christ is, therefore, the
Reason imminent in God, to which God granted a separate existence. As the divine Reason, he was not only operative at the
creation and in the Old Testament prophets, but also in the
wise men of the heathen world. The philosophical conception
of the Logos (cf. HEINZE in loco) here determines Christian
thought, although the important difference must not be overlooked, that the Logos of the Christian writers is an independent
personality. The divine person of Christ is acknowledged without any limitations ; and when the Johannine conception of the
Logos is presented as parallel with that of the Stoic philosophy,
it must be understood merely as an outward clothing of the
thought (momentous indeed in its consequences) in such garb as
to commend it to the heathen world.

Along with the "Word" is mentioned also the Wisdom of
God, or the holy prophetic Spirit; but comparatively little
prominence is given to the latter (Just. Ap. i. 6. 60. Ath. 12.
24). But the Trinity is certainly an article of the common
faith. The term, Τριάς, occurs first in Theoph. ii. 15. Although
the Apologists find little occasion to speak of this mystery,
the apprehension of it constitutes for them the profoundest
problem and the supreme desire of their hearts : "carried away
with this desire only, to see God and the Logos with him.
What is the unity of the Son with the Father? what the fellowship of the Father with the Son? what the Spirit? what the

[1] We here note the influence of the Logos-conception in the sense of John
and Ignatius.

union and the difference of those who are thus united—the Spirit, the Son, and the Father?'' (Ath. 12).

5. The Work of Christ.  The Logos of God, who, before the incarnation, was only a holy spirit (πνεῦμα ἅγιον), became man, born of the Virgin Mary (Arist. 2. 6.   Just. Ap. i. 22, 31, 32 f. Dial. 43, 45, 48, 63, 66, 76, 78, 84 f., 100).   The full reality of his bodily human nature is firmly held (Just. Ap. i. 21; ii. 10.   Dial. 85, 99: "He became a man, truly subject to suffering, made incarnate," σεσωματοποιῆσθαι, Dial. 70),[1] yet he was not by any means on that account only a man in the ordinary sense (Just. Dial. 54), but God and man (ib. 59); his divinity was concealed in his flesh (τὴν αὐτοῦ κεκρυμμένην ἐν σαρκὶ θεότητα) and he attested both in his life and work.   "For, being alike both God and perfect man, he placed his two natures over us."   It is said of him: "God suffered" (Melito, Corp. apol. ix. 415 f.  Cf. Tat. 13 fin., ὁ πεπονθὼς θεός).  Accordingly, he is now not a man executed upon the cross, but the Son of God, whom Christians honor next to the Father (ἐν δευτέρᾳ χώρᾳ ἔχοντες), and together with the prophetic Spirit (Just. Ap. i. 13, 53).  This view is supported by quotations from the prophets (Just. Ap. i. 30 ff.).

In defining the work of Christ, it is first of all emphasized that he became the teacher of the race (καινὸς νομοθέτης, Just. Dial. 18), as he had already shown himself before his incarnation.   The content of his teaching is found in the ideas of the One God ; the new law, requiring a virtuous life ; and immortality (αφθαρσία), more strictly speaking, the resurrection, bringing with it rewards and punishments (e. g., Just. Ap. i. 13-19).   Aristides thus reports to the Emperor what is contained in the Christian Scriptures : "But you may learn from their writings, O King, to know their words and their commandments, and the glorious character of their service, and the expectation of compensating reward according to the deeds done by each of them, which they expect in the other world " (c. 16. 3.  Cf. Just. Apol. i. 65 init.).

Man has the ability to keep these commandments, since God created him free (Just. Dial. 88, 102, 141.  Apol. i. 28.  Tat. 7).   Although man, by disobeying the commandments of God, fell and became subject to death (Theoph. ii. 25.  Tat. fin.), he is, nevertheless, still free to decide for God through faith and repentance (Just. Ap. i. 28, 43, 61 ; ii. 14 ; Dial. 141.  Theoph. ii.

---

[1] Justin, according to a quotation attributed to Jeremiah, taught a preaching of Christ in the Lower World (cf. Marcion): "And he went to them to preach his salvation to them "(Dial. 72 fin.; also Iren. v. 31. 1.  Cf. iv. 27. 2, 21. 1 ; iii. 20. 4.  Cf. also Herm. Sim. ix. 16. 5.  Barn. 5. 7.  Ignat. Philad. ix. 1 ; Tral. ix. 1).

27): "For just as the man who refuses to hear brings death upon himself, so he who willingly submits to the will of God is able to secure for himself eternal life. For God has given us the law and the holy commandments, everyone who keeps which can be saved (δύναται σωθῆναι) and, experiencing the resurrection, inherit immortality." Freedom here appears, it will be observed, as an inamissible element of man's endowment. However deeply the fall and corruption of man is conceived, his freedom yet remains unquestioned. From this it may be understood also that Justin includes grace, in the sense of the effectual power of God, in his conception of Christian doctrine. Grace is no more than the revelation of doctrine and of the law.

Although it does not appear from such presentations of the subject why the sufferings and death of Christ were necessary (except as in fulfillment of Old Testament prophecy), yet the Apologists very positively testify that the belief in the significance of these experiences of the Lord formed an essential part of the common Christian faith. The sufferings of Christ deliver men because he thereby took upon himself the curse which rested upon them; they bring forgiveness of sins and set free from death and the devil (Just. Ap. i. 63, 50, 32; ii. 13. Dial. 40, 41, 45, 95, 54, 80, 88, 111, 134. Melito, Corp. ap. ix. 418). He who now believes in the Crucified is purified from his past sins, the Spirit of God stands by his side to help in all assaults of the devil, and Christ will deliver him from all trouble and receive him to his kingdom if he will but keep his commandments (Dial. 116). The wood of the cross, the water of baptism, faith, and repentance are the means by which to escape from condemnation on the day of judgment (Dial. 138).[1] There was no attempt to enlarge upon these ideas in the controversial writings of the period; but there can be no doubt that they held the same place in moulding the life of the church at large as in the post-apostolic age.

6. The Christian Church is the people of God, the true Israel, the high-priestly generation of God (Just. Dial. 116, 123, 135). The churches are islands of safety in the stormy sea of the world, where the truth is taught (there are, it is true, also desert islands inhabited by ravenous wild beasts, i. e., heresies, Theoph. ii. 14). In the Christian world prevail strict morality, holy love, and readiness to suffer with rejoicing. Its members belong to another world. They are a "new generation," "the generation of the pious," winged to fly like birds above the things of this

---

[1] It appears exceedingly doubtful to me whether Justin already employed the conception of the ἀνακεφαλαίωσις. The citation from him in Iren. adv. haer. iv. 6. 2 would prove more than is intended.

world; but it is for their sake that the world is preserved (cf. Arist. 15 ff. Theoph. ii. 17. Just. Ap. ii. 7. Melito in Eus. h. e. iv. 26. 5, etc.).

7. Esoteric elements, which the Apology mentions only for the sake of completeness in its survey (vid. Just. Ap. i. 61 init.), are the means employed in public worship by which one becomes and remains a Christian. They consist of the reading of the prophets and the gospels, preaching and exhortation, united prayers (ib. 67), baptism, and the Lord's Supper. The candidate for baptism is washed in the name of the triune God, after having prayed for the forgiveness of his sins. Baptism brings repentance and the pardon ($\check{a}\varphi\varepsilon\sigma\iota\varsigma$) of sins, it transplants into a new existence, and without it there is no salvation (Just. Ap. i. 61 : being made new, $\varkappa\alpha\iota\nu\sigma\pi\sigma\iota\eta\vartheta\acute{\varepsilon}\nu\tau\varepsilon\varsigma$; 66 : the washing for the pardon of sins and unto regeneration, $\tau\grave{\sigma}\ \acute{\upsilon}\pi\varepsilon\rho\ \acute{\alpha}\varphi\acute{\varepsilon}\sigma\varepsilon\omega\varsigma\ \acute{\alpha}\mu\alpha\rho\tau\iota\tilde{\omega}\nu\ \varkappa\alpha\grave{\iota}\ \varepsilon\acute{\iota}\varsigma\ \acute{\alpha}\nu\alpha\gamma\acute{\varepsilon}\nu\nu\eta\sigma\iota\nu\ \lambda\sigma\upsilon\tau\rho\acute{\sigma}\nu$ cf. Dial. 19, 29, 44. Theoph. ii. 16 ; 61 : enlightenment, $\varphi\omega\tau\iota\sigma\mu\acute{\sigma}\varsigma$; Dial. 8 : becoming perfect, $\tau\acute{\varepsilon}\lambda\varepsilon\iota\sigma\nu\ \gamma\acute{\iota}\nu\varepsilon\sigma\vartheta\alpha\iota$). Of the Eucharist, Justin (Ap. i. 66) says : " We have been taught that the food blessed by the word of prayer employed by him (Christ), from which our bodies and blood are by its transformation ($\varkappa\alpha\tau\grave{\alpha}\ \mu\varepsilon\tau\alpha\beta\sigma\lambda\acute{\eta}\nu$) nourished, is also the body and blood of the same Jesus who was made flesh."[1]

8. The last article of the common faith of the church is the doctrine of the resurrection. Only upon the supposition of such an experience does the nature ($\varphi\acute{\upsilon}\sigma\iota\varsigma$) of man remain true to its essential character. As body and soul have become believing and done good, so shall both become participants in immortality (Just. Frag. de resur. 9, 10. Athenag. de resur. 15, 25, 21, cf. Theoph. ii. 13 f. Tat. 13. Tert. Ap. 48). As Christ promises immortality also to the body, he excels the philosophical representations upon the subject of the future life (Just. ib. 10).[2] The prophets foretold a first and a second coming

---

[1] These words, of course, do not teach transubstantiation. The meaning is only that the very same food, which, by virtue of its transformation, nourishes our bodies, is for faith the body and blood of Christ (see also Dial. 41. 70). The opinion of HARNACK, that " bread and water are the eucharistic elements in Justin" (Texte u. Unters. vii. 2. 117 ff.—Just. Ap. 65 fin. mentions "bread, wine, and water," as also 67. On the contrary, in 65, " $\check{\alpha}\rho\tau\sigma\varsigma\ \varkappa\alpha\grave{\iota}\ \pi\sigma\tau\acute{\eta}\rho\iota\sigma\nu\ \acute{\upsilon}\delta\alpha\tau\sigma\varsigma\ \varkappa\alpha\grave{\iota}\ \varkappa\rho\acute{\alpha}\mu\alpha\tau\sigma\varsigma$"—the last two words being wanting in Cod. Ottob. Harnack declares that they, as well as the $\sigma\check{\iota}\nu\sigma\varsigma$, are later interpolations. Cf. especially Cypr. ep. 63), is refuted by critical textual examination, as well as by the unvarying historical tradition. Cf. ZAHN, in Neue Kirchl. Ztschr., 1892, 261 ff. JÜLICHER, in the Theol. Abhandlungen, dedicated to Weizsäcker, 1892, p. 215 ff.

[2] There was a wavering of opinion upon the question whether the soul is essentially immortal (Theoph. ii. 19 fin.). Justin (Dial. 6) and Tat. (13) deny

($\pi\alpha\rho o\upsilon\sigma\acute{\iota}\alpha$) of Christ (Just. Ap. i. 52. Dial. 40, 49, 110 f.). Christ will return again in glory and as judge; the world will perish in fire; and after the resurrection, both the righteous and the wicked shall receive their just reward (Just. Ap. i. 20, 52; ii. 7). For entire orthodoxy (and if any are in all respects right-thinking Christians) Justin thinks necessary also an acknowledgment of the millennial kingdom in the restored, adorned, and enlarged Jerusalem (Dial. 81 f.; also Ap. i. 11).

9. The Apologists are of importance to us from a double point of view. In the first place, they make it evident that the general conception of Christianity in their day labored under the same defects and limitations as in the generation immediately preceding them (the work of Christ; moralism). In the second place, we discover here the beginnings of theology in the church. In order to bring the Christian religion within the comprehension of the cultivated in heathen lands, it was forced into a foreign framework (the religion of reason) and remoulded after foreign patterns. The prominent ideas thus employed were the abstract (Platonic) conception of God, the attempt to make the divinity of Christ comprehensible by utilizing the (Stoic) conception of the Logos, and the theory that man's fallen state consisted essentially in his ignorance and subjection to death, and redemption in instruction and the granting of immortality ($\dot{\alpha}\varphi\vartheta\alpha\rho\sigma\acute{\iota}\alpha$). It is upon these attempts that the significance of the Apologists for the History of Doctrines rests. That back of their formulations lay a richer fund of religious belief, of which we find only hints in the formal theological statements, has been already emphasized.

## § 14.  *Theology of the Antignostic Fathers.*

SOURCES. IRENÆUS adv. haeres,, vid. supra, § 10. Cf. ZIEGLER, Iren. der Bisch. von Lyon, 1871. WERNER, der Paulinism. d. Ir., Texte u. Unters. vi. 2. ZAHN, PRE. vii. 129 ff. TERTULLIAN, born ca. A D. 160; 197 at the latest, a writer; 199 Montanist; died ca. 230. Cf. HAUCK, Tert. Leben u. Schriften, 1877. BONWETSCH, die Schriften Tert., 1878. NÖLDECHEN, Tert. 1890. Here esp., de praescriptione haereticorum; adv. Valentinianos; adv. Marcionem ll. 5; adv. Hermogenem; de carne Christi; de resurrectione; de anima, cf. adv. Praxeam, written 206-211. Opp. ed. Oehler, 3 vols., 1851 ff. HIPPOLYTUS, after ca. A. D. 190 active at Rome; 235, banished to Sardinia. Upon the Refutatio and the Syntagma, vid. § 10. Also parts of De Anti-christo; comm. upon Dan. l. iv., after Georgiades, in the Ἐκκλησιαστικὴ ἀλήθεια, 1885 f., reprinted by BRATKE, 1891 (cf. BARDENHEWER, des H. Comm. z. Dan., 1877); c. Noētum. Also perhaps the so-called "Small Labyrinth" in Eus. h. e. v. 28. 6 (cf. Refut. X proem.). His writings were edited by de LAGARDE, 1858, and recently by BONWETSCH and ACHELIS,

this, and Theoph. (ii. 24, 27) writes: "He made it, therefore, neither immortal nor mortal, but . . . capable of both."

1897. Cf. BUNSEN, H. u. seine. Zeit. DÖLLINGER, H. u. Kallist, 1853. VOLKMAR. H. u. die röm. Zeitgenossen, 1855. FICKER, Studien z. Hippolytfrage, 1893. Cf. esp., THOMASIUS DG., i. ed. 2, 88 ff. HARNACK DG., i. ed. 3, 507 ff.

For almost a century Gnosticism had extended its sway before the church met it with a harmonious formulation of her own doctrine.

From the writings of the Antignostic Fathers we are now made familiar with this formulation of the common faith of the church, and also the motives and means for the vanquishing of Gnosticism.[1] Here for the first time a churchly theology comes into conflict with a modern but unchurchly theology.

1. It was not deemed necessary to construct a new system in the church in imitation of the Gnostic method, but it was thought sufficient to establish more firmly the truth which the church had possessed from the beginning, and to gain a clearer understanding of it. The Christian is not to be forever searching. Seeking finds its end in faith. He seeks no more, who believes what he should believe (Tert. de praescr. 11, 10). The problems with which Gnosticism toils are of heathen origin (Ir. ii. 14. 1-6. Tert. praescr. 7). Christianity knows nothing of them : " What have Athens and Jerusalem in common, the Academy and the Church? What heretics and Christians? . . . They have produced a Stoic, and Platonic, and dialectic Christianity " (Tert. ib. 7; adv. Herm. 1. Cf. Plot. Ennead. ii. 9. 6, 17). Hence that which in their writings sounds like Christian truth has a different meaning (Ir. i. proem. 2 : " saying like things indeed, but thinking unlike things "). Over against this "gnosis falsely so called," the proper course is to believe what the church has always taught. Thus an ecclesiastical theology rises to confront the philosophical theology.

2. Doctrine of God (cf. KUNZE, die Gotteslehre d. Iren., 1891). The separation of God and the Creator appears as the fundamental error of the Gnostics. It was the guile of the devil which gave birth to the blasphemous conception of a Creator other than God himself (*blasphemia creatoris*, Iren. i. praef.; i. 22. 1; 31. 3; ii. 10. 2; iii. 24. 2; v. 26. 2; cf. already Just. Ap. i. 26, 58, 35. Dial. 80). The setting forth of the true faith must begin with the One God, the Creator (Ir. ii. 1. 1; cf. Hipp. Ref. x. 34).

(*a*) God is One, at once Creator, Preserver, and Redeemer. The supreme God is the Creator. This is testified by the crea-

[1] We must moreover bear in mind that the first Antignostic work was the Gospel of John.

tion itself, and even by the faith of the heathen (Ir. iii. 9-15; iv. 9. 3. Tert. de praescr. 13; adv. Jud. 2 init.). The definition of God demands his unity. "If God is not One, he does not exist" (Tert. adv. Marc. i. 3; cf. adv. Hermog. 17. 7). It is the same God who gave both the law and the gospel (Ir. iv. 9. 3; iii. 12. 11). (*b*) God is an intelligent spirit; νοῦς, *spiritus*, and ἔννοια are accordingly not separate beings, but different aspects of his being (Ir. ii. 13. 3-6, 8; i. 12. 2. Tert. adv. Val. 4). Referring to the Stoic maxim, that everything real is corporeal (Tert. de carne Chr. 11; cf. ZELLER, Philos. der Griechen iii. 1. ed. 3, 124), Tertullian queries: "For who denies that God is a body (*corpus*), although God is a Spirit?" (adv. Prax. 7; also de bapt. 4: "but God is not flesh," *caro*, adv. Prax. 27). (*c*) God is not known through speculation, but from revelation. Hence we should not concern ourselves with idle questions as to what God did before the creation, how the Son was begotten, etc. (Ir. ii. 28. 3, 6 f.; cf. 25. 4; 26. 1; 28. 1). "Without God, God is not known" (Ir. iv. 6. 4). In his greatness God remains incomprehensible; but in his love we learn to known him in Christ: "Who is unknown according to his greatness by all those who have been made by him . . . but according to his love he is always known through him through whom he formed all things. But this is his Word" (Ir. iv. 20. 4). "Just as those who look upon the light are within the light and partake of its brilliance, so those who look upon God are within God, partaking of his brilliance" (ib. § 5). We learn to know God by way of revelation and experience, not through speculation. (*d*) The justice and the goodness of God are not to be ascribed to two separate gods: "The Creator was from the beginning both good and just" (Tertul. adv. Marc. ii. 12). True goodness is controlled by justice. He who is good is an enemy of that which is evil: "Not otherwise is one fully good unless jealous of evil" (ib. i. 26. Cf. Ir. iii. 25. 1-3; ii. 30. 9; iv. 38. 3, adding wisdom). As against sin, justice becomes severity and wrath (Tert. adv. Marc. ii. 11; i. 26). Thus the moral character of the divine Person is preserved (Ir. iii. 25. 2). (*e*) The aim of the ways of God is the salvation of the human race: "Nothing is so worthy of God as the salvation of man" (Tert. adv. Marc. ii. 27; cf. de poenit. 2. Ir. iii. 20. 2). The world was created for man's sake (Ir. v. 29. 1; cf. supra, p. 113). The goodness, justice, and wisdom of God are all enlisted in the effort to make man capable of beholding God: "God determining all things in advance for the perfection of man and for the efficacy and manifestation of his own plans, so that his goodness might be displayed and his justice executed, and the church be assembled as a figure of the likeness of his Son, and that somehow at length man might become mature in such things, ripening to the capacity of seeing and apprehending God " ( Ir. iv. 37. 7). (ƒ) God is the Creator and the Framer of the world. He created it by his Word and his will (Ir. ii. 30. 9; 2. 4; 3. 2. Hipp. c. Noët. 10); out of nothing (Tert. c. Hermog. 8, 45). The creation is not bad; all the contradictions which appear in it harmonize like the different tones of the cithara (Ir. ii. 25. 2). The same God provides redemption (*e. g.*, Ir. iv. 7. 2). In contrast with Gnosticism, this conception of God displays again concrete, living features, particularly in Irenæus. He is the active God, who accomplishes creation and redemption. He is the living God, who is just and merciful (contrast to Marcion), and he is the God historically revealed in Christ.

(*g*) The consciousness that God is a living God was also preserved intact by means of the triadic conception, which always compels the recognition of a spiritual life in God. The one God is the triune God (τριάς, Hipp. c. Noët. 14; *trinitas*, Tert. adv. Prax. 2, 3, 11, 12, etc.). Thus the church teaches (Ir. i. 10. 1). It is presupposed in the baptismal ceremony (Tert. adv. Prax. 26 extr.). The believer finds it in the Scriptures (Ir. iv. 33. 15). God, that is to say, was never alone: "but he, being the Only One, was many. For he was not wordless, nor wisdomless, nor powerless, nor counsel-less" (Hipp. c. Noët. 10; cf. Tert. adv. Prax. 5). "For God was not without his *Horae* (the angels) for doing the things which he had by himself pre-determined should be done, as though he had not his own hands. For there are always present to him the Word and Wisdom, the Son and the Spirit, through whom and in whom he made all things freely and spontaneously " (Ir. iv. 20. 1, 3; cf. v. 6. 1). These three are one God, because there belongs to them one power (δύναμις, Hipp. c. Noët. 8, 11). Tertullian expressed the thought more precisely in asserting that two *personae* partake of the one divine *substantia* in the second and third places, viz., the Son and the Spirit (*consortes substantiae patris*, adv. Prax. 3). "Everywhere I hold one substance in three cohering " (ib. 12). Thus in the one substance dwell three persons. Ib. 2 : "Not as if the One were thus all things because all things are from the One, but through unity of substance ; and yet there is preserved the mystery of the economy (οἰκονομίας) which disposes the unity in a trinity, placing in order the Father, the Son, and the Holy Ghost— three, not in condition but in order (*gradu*), not in substance but in form (*forma*), not in power but in aspect (*specie*), but of one substance, and of one condition, and of one power, because one God, from whom are derived these orders and forms and aspects in the name of the Father, and the Son, and the Holy Ghost.'' By expressing the problem in these fixed and simple formulas, Tertullian first presented it clearly to the mind of the Western church; but, as always, so here the completed formula might serve to arrest the process of thought.

3. Doctrine of Man. (a) Good and evil in man are not to be accounted for by different natural endowments. If evil were in man's nature, it would be impossible to pass moral judgment upon him (Ir. iv. 37. 2). On the contrary, sin is a free act of man, who was endowed with independence (τὸ αὐτεξούσιον) and "made free in his will and having power of his own" (Ir. iv. 37. 1, 3; 4. 3). As to the original state, it is held that man, as created, was not in a condition to receive from God at the very beginning of his career perfection. This consists in immortality: "For things just begotten could not be unbegotten. But in so far as they are not unbegotten, in so far do they fall short of perfection" (Ir. iv. 38. 1). This is a Greek idea, not a Christian one. But here, too, we must yet note the resemblance to the Johannine conception of life. (b) Free but mortal man must be obedient to God in order to become immortal. Since he was free, he must learn to know evil. To be good, is to obey God; to be evil, is to be disobedient to him. Man could not become God (i. e., immortal) until he should first have become a proper man (Ir. iv. 39. 1, 2; 38. 4). Sin is disobedience. But disobedience brings death (Ir. v. 23. 1), whereas obedience is immortality (iv. 38. 3). Sins are carnal or spiritual (delicta voluntatis), but we dare not regard the latter as of small moment in comparison with the former (Tertul. de poenit. 3, 7). (c) In Adam the whole race was disobedient. In him it became subject to sin and death (Ir. iii. 23. 3; v. 12. 3. Tert. de anima 40; de carn. Chr. 16). As to the connection of our sin with that of Adam, Tertullian makes some significant suggestions. Evil became, as it were, a natural element in man. "Evil has, therefore, the start of the soul . . . naturally, as it were, from the blemish of origin; for, as we have said, the corruption of nature is a second nature." But to this it is added: "Yet so that good pertains to the soul as the chief, the divine, and the real thing, and in the proper sense natural; for that which is from God is not so much extinguished as obscured" (Tert. de an. 41, 16. Cf. also de test. an. 2; de bapt. 18). This condition passes over through generation upon the entire human race, "through whom (i. e., the devil) man, having been in the beginning enticed to transgress the commandment of God, and having been in con-

sequence given over to death, made the whole race from that
time onward, infected from his seed, the bearer also of his condemnation" (Tert. de test. an. 3). Tertullian speaks also of a
"birth-mark of sin" (de carn. Chr. 16). These occasional
hints are the incipient stages of the doctrine of original sin.
They did not, however, prevent Tertullian from emphasizing in
the strongest manner the freedom of man's will. "To us pertains a will and choice of selecting the opposite" (Sir. 15. 18)
. . . "to will is in us alone" (Exh. cast. 2). "Therefore
entire liberty of choosing either part has been granted to him"
(c. Marc. ii. 6).

4. History of Redemption. God from motive of grace expelled fallen man from paradise and suffers him to die in order
that the injury sustained may not remain forever (Ir. iii. 23. 6).
God has from the beginning been deeply concerned for the salvation of the race, increasing from time to time the blessings
bestowed upon it (Ir. iv. 9. 3). He has remained ever the
same. The race, with its necessities, was constantly changing
(Ir. iv. 16. 3; 38; 36. 2). God has by means of three
covenants (διαθῆκαι, foedera. Ir. iii. 11. 8 fin. names four,
corresponding to the four gospels) sought to win the race.

(a) The first covenant embraced the natural requirements of
the law (naturalia legis, Ir. iv. 13. 1; 15. 1). This is the inherited, rational, natural law, as understood by the philosophers and jurists of the age. Its content, not differing from the
Decalogue and the commandments of Christ, was love to God
and one's neighbor. The patriarchs, who carried this law in
their hearts, were through it righteous before God (Ir. iv. 16. 3,
cf. Tert. adv. Jud. 2; also adv. Prax. 31). (b) As this covenant faded from the hearts of men, God renewed it through the
Decalogue, or second covenant (1. c.). It was the covetous
disposition of the nation of Israel, manifested in their sin in
connection with the golden calf, and in their hankering after the
bondage of Egypt, which gave occasion for the establishment
of the ceremonial law : "They received another bondage suited
to their concupiscence, not indeed severing them from God, but
controlling them in his yoke of bondage" (Ir. iv. 15. 1). As
the law prepares for the following of Christ and friendship with
God (Ir. iv. 12. 5; 16. 3), so the prophets prophesy for the
same purpose—the Spirit of God works through them in order
to accustom men to bear the Spirit of God in their hearts (Ir.
iv. 14. 2; 20. 5, 11 f.). But the law was diluted by the Pharisees and robbed of its chief content, love (Ir. iv. 12. 1, 4).
(c) In the third covenant, Christ restored the original moral law
—the law of love (Ir. iv. 12. 2, 5; cf. Tert. adv. Jud. 6). This

third covenant is related to the second as freedom to bondage
(iv. 13. 2); as the requirement of action to mere speech ; as
right disposition to the outward act (iv. 28. 2 ; 13. 1, 3); as
fulfillment to prophecy, or harvest to seed-sowing (iv. 34. 1 ;
11. 3, 4 ; 25. 3). Accordingly, it is our duty to believe, not
only on the Father, but also on the Son, who has now appeared
(iv. 13. 1 ; 28. 2). As the old covenant had validity for one
nation, so is the new valid for the whole race (iv. 9. 2). Christians have inherited a stricter law than did the Jews, and have
more to believe than they (iv. 28. 2 ; cf. Tert. de orat. 22 :
" our law is amplified and supplemented "); but they have also
received a greater donation of grace (iv. 11. 3) through the ad-
vent of Christ, who has brought to them life and salvation (iv.
34. 1). To this, Tertullian, in his Montanistic age, adds the era
of the Paraclete. This line of thought is important, first of all
on account of the historical significance of the whole movement
which it represents, and also because the attempt is here again
made to establish a positive relation between the religion of the
Old Testament and Christianity.

5. Person of Christ. (*a*) The Christology of IRENÆUS (cf.
DUNCKER, die Christol. d. h. Ir. 1843. ZAHN, Marcell v.
Ancyra, 1867, p. 235 ff.) is, in a marked degree, superior to
that of Tertullian and Hippolytus, upon whom it exerted great
influence. He does not begin with speculation as to the
origination of the Logos and his relation to the Father. As to
this, we know nothing, or have only probable guesses (ii. 28.
6 ; 13. 8). The starting-point in his study is the historically
revealed Son of God, who was actually born, lived and suffered as a man, and died.

(*a*) Nothing can be said, therefore, as to the mode of generation of the Logos. It is sufficient for us to know that he has
been from eternity with the Father, " the Son always co-existing
with the Father" (ii. 30. 9 ; 25. 3 ; iii. 18. 1). It has been
his nature from eternity to reveal the Father—to the angels and
archangels, and then to men, and to the latter from the beginning of the race (ii. 30. 9 ; iv. 6. 5 ff.; 20. 7). He is the
"measure (*mensura*) of the Father " (iv. 4. 2). He alone
knows the Father and reveals him : God (hence also the Son)
can be known only through God. The Son is God the Revealer.
Thus he acts in accordance with the Father's will, as well as in
accordance with his own (iv. 6. 3-7). The Logos has, therefore, been from all eternity God, as has the Father, by whose
determination and his own self-determination he acts as the revelation of the Father. All further questions are excluded. It is
to be observed in passing that Irenæus constantly maintained for

the Spirit, as the Wisdom of God, a special personal position by
the side of the Son (iv. 20. 1, 3 ; 33. 1). (β) The eternal
Logos became through the incarnation the historical Jesus.
Jesus was Christ, a fact emphasized in opposition to the Gnostics
(iii. 16-22). The Son of God is the Son of man (iv. 33. 11).
Jesus Christ is *vere homo, vere deus* (iv. 6. 7 ; cf. : "the Word
united to the flesh, iv. 34. 4). He became a real man, assuming not only the body but the soul" (iii. 22. 1 ; v. 1. 1). This
is maintained, not only as expressing a traditional conception,
but from practical religious interest, since the reality of the work
of redemption depends upon the real humanity of Christ and his
personal experience (*e. g.*, v. 21 ; 16. 3 ; 31, cf. under 6) of
human life in its entirety (ii. 22. 3, 5). Especially with respect
to his sufferings and death, the passible Jesus dare not be separated in Gnostic fashion from the impassible Christ : "(The
gospel) recognizes not that the Christ departing from Jesus before
the passion, but that he who was born Jesus Christ is the Son of
God, and that the same who suffered arose from the dead" (iii.
16. 5 ; cf. 18. 5). This union of God with the human nature is,
for Irenæus, of the greatest religious significance. Thus God himself has entered the race and become an active force in it. Inasmuch as the Logos assumed flesh of our flesh, he united all
flesh to God. From this point of view we must interpret the life
of the Lord : "For in what way could we have been able to be
partakers of this adoption as sons, unless through the Son we
had received from him that communion which brings us to him
—unless his Word,. made flesh, had communicated it to us?
Wherefore he comes also to every age, restoring to all that communion which brings to God" (iii. 18. 7 ; 19. 1 ; v. 14. 2).

(*b*) TERTULLIAN starts with the Logos theory of the Apologists, but he develops it in a most remarkable and historically
significant way. (*a*) The Logos of Christians is, in distinction
from that of the philosophers, a real subsistence (*propria substantia*) to which belong word, reason, and power (*sermo, ratio,
virtus*, Ap. 21 ; cf. adv. Prax. 5, 6). He is an independent
person, who proceeded from God—was begotten by him. He had
a beginning : "There was a time when . . . the Son was not
. . . who made the Lord a Father" (adv. Hermog. 3, 18). In
his relation to the Father, emphasis is to be laid upon the unity
and identity of the divine existence and nature—the *substantia*
("other . . . in the designation of person, not of substance—
for distinction, not for division," adv. Prax. 12); but also upon
the separateness and difference of his peculiar existence and mode
of existence—the *persona* ("the *distinctio* of the two persons,"
adv. Prax. 21 ; "the *conjunctio* of the two persons," 24). Since

Father and Son are the same divine substance (*unitate substan-tiae*—Ap. 21 ; adv. Prax. 25, 26), they are to be discriminated not by *divisio* nor by *separatio*, but by *distinctio* and *dispositio* (οἰκονομία, adv. Prax. 8, 11, 12, 19 fin., 21, 22): "he proves two—as truly two as they are inseparate ; for a testimony of two individuals"). Hence : "'I and the Father are one'—as to *unity of substance*, not as to singularity of number" (adv. Prax. 25), and: "Father and Son are *two*, and this not from separation of substance, but from arrangement (*dispositio*), as we pronounce the Son an individual and separate from the Father ; other, not in condition (*statu*), but in order" (*gradu*) (ib. 19).

This relation is supposed to be made more plain by the idea that the Logos is only a part of the Father's substance ("For the Father is the whole substance, but the Son a derivation and portion of the whole," adv. Prax. 9, 26, adv. Marc. iii. 6), or by the illustrations of the sun and its rays, the root and the stalk, the fountain and the stream (Ap. 21. adv. Prax. 8 ; cf. Hipp. c. Noët. 11). If the Father is, so to speak, the God of the philosophers, the Son is the tangible revelation of the Father ; "the executive (*arbiter*) and minister of the Father" (c. Marc. ii. 27). Tertullian is a Subordinationist. (β) The pre-existent Logos became man when he was born of the Virgin Mary (de carn. Chr. 17, 18, 20 ff.). "How was 'the Word made flesh'— by transformation, so to speak, in the flesh, or by assuming flesh? Certainly by assuming." This reply is given in view of the immutability of the divine substance (adv. Prax. 27). Christ, in order that he might be able to die and to deliver man (de carn. Chr. 5, 6, 11, 14), assumed actual human flesh (ib. 6 ff.; 15, 18 f.), together with a human soul (ib. 12 f.; but cf. 18 fin.). He was, therefore, a real man. His flesh was sinless, since he made it his own (ib. 16). Its genuinely human character was concealed by his divinity (ib. 9). There are two substances, the divine and the human, the latter of which contains again two substances, the bodily and the spiritual, united in itself (ib. 13 extr.); but these two are combined in a unity in one person. "Thus a consideration of the two substances presents man and God—here born, there unborn ; here carnal, there spiritual ; here weak, there mighty ; here dying, there living" (ib. 5, 18). Now these two substances have not by a *mixtura* become a third, but "we behold a double condition (*status*), not confused, but combined *in one person*, Jesus, God and man" (adv. Prax. 27). Each nature here retains its peculiarity of substance (*proprietas substantiae*, ib.), and each acts for itself ("the two substances act separately, each in its own *status*," ib.). Accordingly, the sufferings and death pertain only to the human substance ("we say that he was mortal from the human substance," adv. Prax. 29); the divine is not capable of suffering (the Son is also impassible by virtue of that condition by which he is God," ib.). On the other hand, Tertullian can speak of the "sufferings of God," and declare that "God was truly crucified, truly dead" (de carn. Chr. 5). (γ) To the question as to the possibility of the humanity of Christ, Tertullian responded by referring to the inconceivableness, unsearchableness, and impossibility of the entire transaction: "The Son of God was crucified; he was not ashamed, because it was a thing to be ashamed of. And the Son of God died; it is credible, just because it is unfitting. And, having been buried, he rose again; it is certain, because it is impossible" (de carn. Chr. 5).

It cannot be said that Tertullian gave really greater depth to Christian thought upon these points, but he sketched a formula for it (see already Melito supra, p. 115), which was sufficiently capacious to receive the richer thought of a later age, i. e.: A divine substance, in which three persons subsist; and, again, the divine and human substances in Christ, which are combined in the unity of the person.[1] Tertullian established the Christology of the West.

(c) We notice briefly the Christology of HIPPOLYTUS. The Father begat the Logos out of his own substance, when he desired to create the world (c. Noët. 10. Refut. x. 33. De Chr. et Antichr. 26. Hom. in theoph. 2, 7). In distinction

---

[1] Harnack has endeavored to explain Tertullian's contrasting of *substantia* and *persona* by the latter's use of juristic language (DG., ii., ed. 3, 286 n.), *i. e.*, he supposes Tertullian to have used *substantia* in the sense of possession (*e. g.*, Cant. 8. 7), in which case he could, indeed, ascribe one possession to three persons, or also two possessions to one person. But this supposition cannot be established, as this sense cannot be proved in any passage that may be cited, while other passages make the meaning of Tertullian perfectly clear (adv. Hermog. 3: "God is the name of his [Christ's] *substantia, i. e.*, of his divinity." Apol. 21: "We have taught that he was produced from God and generated by production, and for that reason called the Son of God and God from the unity of substance;" adv. Marc. iii. 6, he calls Christ "the Son and the Spirit and the substance of the Creator;" de carn. Chr. 9: "the human substance of his body;" adv. Prax. 2: "but three, not in condition but in order; not in substance but in form; . . . but of one substance and of one condition, etc.;" de carn. Chr. 13 fin. : "If one flesh and one soul . . . the number of two substances is preserved." According to these citations, the meaning which Tertullian attaches to the term *substantia* is beyond question. To this we may add the usage of Melito: "his two natures;" see .the passage cited, supra, p. 115. Tertullian had in mind, therefore, the divinity and the humanity of Christ. If now it was necessary to maintain the unity of these substances in one nature (cf. Iren. iii. 16. 5: "They divide the Lord . . . saying that he is composed of one and another substance"), the origin of the formula in question is not hard to understand.

from all creatures, he shares the nature ($o\dot{v}\sigma la$) of God (Ref. x.
33. Hom. 7: "the only-begotten according to the divine
nature "). Here, too, the relation is conceived in the mode of
Subordinationism (*e. g.*, c. Noët. 14 : " For the Father is one,
but the persons two ; because there is also the Son and the third,
the Holy Spirit. Here the Father is the Godhead "). The unincarnate Logos became man, in that he assumed flesh and a
rational soul ($\psi v \chi \dot{\eta} \lambda o \gamma \iota x \dot{\eta}$, de Chr. et Antichr. 4. c. Noët. 4,
17, 12. 15 : " the Logos incarnated and made man, made flesh,
the incarnate Logos," $\sigma \varepsilon \sigma a \rho x \omega \mu \acute{\varepsilon} v o v$ $\tau o \tilde{v}$ $\lambda \acute{o} \gamma o v$ $x a \grave{\iota}$ $\grave{\varepsilon} v a v \vartheta \rho \omega \pi \acute{\eta} \sigma a v \tau o \varsigma$,
$\sigma a \rho x \omega \vartheta \varepsilon \acute{\iota} \varsigma$, $\lambda \acute{o} \gamma o \varsigma$ $\check{\varepsilon} v \sigma a \rho x o \varsigma$). He assumed the actual nature of
man. " God himself having for our sakes become man " (ib.
18), and : "And the impassible ($\grave{a} \pi a \vartheta \acute{\eta} \varsigma$) Logos of God went
under suffering" ($\pi \acute{a} \vartheta o \varsigma$, ib. 15). Having become man, he is the
perfect Son ; but his flesh is conditioned upon the Logos for its
continued existence (" for the Logos unincarnate and of itself was
not the perfect Son—although the Logos was perfect as the Only-
begotten—nor was the flesh able to continue without the Logos,
because it had its constitution in the Logos," ib. 15).

6. **Work of Redemption.** Irenæus described the work of
Christ under various aspects. The premise is always the reality
of the divinity and humanity of the Saviour. Only upon this
basis could he furnish certain deliverance and deliver the particular race of man (Ir. iii. 18. 7). The leading ideas are : (1)
That the Logos, entered into humanity, brought to the latter the
sure knowledge of God, and by this vanquished it. (2) That
he did and suffered for the whole race what it ought to do, and
what it should have had to suffer, and that he thus became the
source of a new estimate of man in the sight of God. (3)
That he became a leaven through which humanity was purified,
sanctified, and made immortal. The ideas which Irenæus here
presents are Pauline and Johannine (cf. Methodius and Athanasius).

(*a*) The Son reveals the Father in his love, and teaches men
to observe the primeval law of love (iv. 12. 5=of the *nova lex,*
*e. g.*, Tert. praescr. 13). He shows God to men, and presents
them before God (iv. 20. 7 ; v. 1. 1). United to God through
him, we attain to the faith of Abraham and learn to know and
properly honor God (iv. 7. 2 ; iii. 10. 2). But to this man
could not attain unless freed from the forces of evil under whose
dominion and bondage he had fallen. These are sin, alienation
from God, and the devil. (*b*) Christ, therefore, became man
in order to recapitulate (cf. Eph. 1. 10) the whole human race
in himself. He thereby becomes a source of a new relation between God and man and the leaven of a new life in the latter

(vid. supra, p. 125). He embraces in himself the entire human race and all human life: "When he became incarnate and was made man, he recapitulated in himself the long line of men, standing surety in compendium for our salvation, so that what we had lost in Adam, *i. e.*, our being in the image and likeness of God, this we might receive in Christ Jesus" (iii. 18. 1; cf. 21. 10; v. 23. 2). Jesus became nearly fifty years old, "sanctifying every age through that likeness which he bore to it" (ii. 22. 4; 3, 5 f.). As the human race was thus combined in him, he became a new progenitor like Adam (iii. 22. 4; 18. 1). He did what we and Adam should have done (v. 21. 1, 2). He, as the representative of the race, presented his obedience before God for our disobedience. By his blood Christ redeemed us from the unrighteous dominion of sin ("By his blood effectually redeeming us, he gave himself a ransom for those who have been led into captivity," v. 1. 1; 2. 1). Through this fellowship of Christ with the race, it becomes reconciled to God (v. 14. 3; 16. 3: "For in the first Adam we offended, not observing his commandment; in the second Adam we have been reconciled again, having become obedient unto death"). Through the fall, the race was brought under the dominion, though unlawful, of the devil. Christ has lawfully (*juste*) as a man, by the application and observance of the divine commandment (at his temptation), conquered the devil, and he has by his resurrection broken the power of death over the race (v. 21. 1-3; iii. 23. 1; 18. 7). Thus the race became free from the power of death and the devil and from condemnation (iii. 23. 1). In this way man became again the image of God (v. 16. 2) and the son of God (iii. 19. 1; 20. 1). And thus man became again precious in God's sight (v. 16. 2), and intercourse and fellowship between God and man was restored through the forgiveness of sins (*e.g.*, iv. 33. 2; v. 17. 1: "And having relieved (*consolatus*) our disobedience by his obedience, giving also to us that manner of life and subjection which is in accord with our Creator," v. 1. 1; iii. 18. 7; iv. 13. 1: "who leads man into the communion and unity of God;" iv. 14. 2: "communion with God;" iv. 20. 4: "through whom occurs a commingling and communion of God and man." (*c*) In Christ, who has become a member of our race, we are now united with God, and lead a new, eternal life: "For to this end the Logos became man . . . in order that man, having taken to himself the Logos and received sonship, might be the son of God." "For not otherwise could we have received incorruptibility and immortality, unless we had been united to incorruptibility and immortality" (iii. 19. 1). As fellowship with the first Adam brought death to us, so fellowship with the second

9

Adam brings life and perfection. "The Word, having been united to the substance of the ancient creation of Adam, made man alive and perfect, receiving the perfect God (v. 1. 1). In Christ we stand in fellowship with the God by whom we have been adopted as sons. We thus contend against our sins, and follow after Jesus in holy love" (iv. 12. 5; v. 1. 1; iv. 14. 1; 16. 5: "generously granting to men through adoption to know the Father, and to love him with the whole heart . . . But he also increased fear (*timorem*), for it becomes sons to fear more than servants, and to have greater love for their father"). This union of God and man has its more immediate basis in the activity of the Holy Spirit, whom Christ gives to the race as its guiding Head (v. 20. 2, vid. under e). (*d*) But in all this the emphasis falls, not upon the forgiveness of sins, but upon the fact that man has through fellowship with Christ become *immortal*. This, primarily, is the result of the fellowship thus established (iii. 24. 1), of this union with God (iii. 187), of the overcoming of the devil (iii. 23. 7) and of sin (v. 12. 6). This is the consummation toward which Irenæus directs every thought, the real object of the redeeming work of Christ (cf. iii. 19. 1; 23. 7: "for his (man's) salvation is the evacuation of death"). In that God became a member of our race, we have through fellowship with him become immortal (v. 1. 1 fin.). This is a perversion of the Johannine idea, that Christ is the life and gives life, resulting from the fact that the term life is understood by Irenæus in a one-sided way. But yet there is always thus preserved something of the important thought, that Christ gives us a new life and consummates our existence. Finally, as the curse of sin consisted in mortality, so salvation is immortality (iii. 20. 2). Thus men become gods ("first indeed men; then at length gods;" cf. Ps. 81. 6 f.), *i. e.*, like God the Creator (iii. 38. 4). (*e*) The union of man with God occurs through the Spirit of God, through whom God descends to us and we ascend to him. The Spirit has through Christ become the Head of the race (v. 1. 1: "pouring out the Spirit of the Father for the uniting and communion of God and man, bringing down God to man through the Spirit, and again lifting up man to God through his incarnation." v. 20. 2: "giving the Spirit to be the Head of man, for through him we have seen and heard and spoken."). The Spirit brings faith and produces fruits in man. He sanctifies a man's works and makes him a spiritual man (*homo spiritalis*). Only through the infusion (*infusio*) of the Spirit can we please God. But the Spirit in us is also a pledge cf immortality (v. 10. 1, 2).

Irenæus accordingly means that Christ has taught us to know

God, and that he, by entering the race and becoming a member
of the body of humanity, has, as the new Adam, made the latter
acceptable to God and freed it from the devil, death, and the
dominion of sin. Through fellowship with him the Spirit of
God is brought to us, who begins in us a new life in holy works.
But the aim in view is the immortality of man; and thus the
scope of apostolic teaching is, after the Greek fashion, contracted.
Yet, as means to this end, biblical ideas find recognition as of
fundamental importance.

TERTULLIAN does not give such a comprehensive and varied portraiture of the work of redemption (the death of Christ as the
ground of salvation, and as a sacrifice, *e. g.*, c. Marc. iii. 8. adv.
Jud. 13. scorp. 7. de bapt. 11; instruction and fellowship through
the incarnation of Christ, c. Marc. 11. 27. praescr. 13. de orat. 4;
the proposer of a new law and new sacrifices, adv. Jud. 6).
HIPPOLYTUS represents the bestowal of immortality (c. Noët. 17)
as the object of the incarnation. It is this which is effected by
the impartation of the Spirit in baptism (hom. in theoph. 8).
To this end Christ granted the gift of the Spirit in baptism, as
well as his holy ordinances requiring obedience. Whoever obeys
him will become a god, *i. e.*, immortal (Hipp. Ref. x. 34:
"deified, made immortal;" cf. hom. 8, 10).

7. State of Grace. Through the redeeming work of Christ
the believer is in baptism[1] endowed with the Holy Spirit and
with the expectancy of eternal life (Ir. iv. 36. 4; iii. 17. 2).
Sins are washed away and the man regenerated. He can now
live in accordance with the word of Christ. For the attainment
of this condition, faith in Christ is necessary (Ir. iv. 2. 7; cf.
Hipp. hom. in theoph. 10: "he confesses that Christ is God").
Faith is the acknowledgment of Christ and the Father, attachment to his person and doctrine (Ir. iv. 5. 4 f.; 7. 2; 13. 1).
This recognition and acknowledgment, which, however, carry
with them the observance of the primitive moral law, or the commandments of Christ (Ir. iv. 13. 1 : "because the Lord did not
abrogate, but extended and completed . . . the natural requirements of the law, through which man is justified, which even
before the giving of the law those who were justified by
faith and pleased God observed;" cf. 16. 3), are sufficient to
make man righteous before God. Abraham knew Christ and the
Father; he believed on the Logos, and this was accounted to
him for righteousness: "for faith, which reposes upon the Most
High God, justifies man" (iv. 5. 5, 3, 4; cf. 34. 2; also 16. 3).

[1] As to infant baptism, vid. Ir. ii. 22. 4; also Tert. bapt. 18. Orig. in
Lev. hom. 8. 3; in Rom. comm. 5. 9: "The church received from the
apostles the tradition to give baptism also to infants."

Faith itself falls under the category of the commandment (iv.
13. 1 ; cf. 16. 5), and justifying faith in Christ is defined as " to
believe him and do his will" (iv. 6. 5). It cannot, therefore,
be maintained that Irenæus understood the Pauline conception of
the righteousness of faith, as he held simply that God regards as
righteous everyone who acknowledges Christ and is ready to follow his teaching.

The Spirit of God fills the Christian with new life and elevates
him into the fellowship of God (v. 9. 1, 2). But yet the fundamental characteristic of this new life is that it brings the fruits
of righteousness in good works. " And thus men, if, indeed,
they have advanced to better things through faith, and have assumed the Spirit of God, and have allowed his fructifying power
to develop, will be spiritual" (v. 10. 1). " Man, implanted
by faith and assuming the Spirit of God, does not, indeed, lose
the substance of the flesh, but changes the quality of the fruits
of his works" (ib. 2). Irenæus compares true Christians to
clean beasts. They are beasts dividing the hoof, who with firm
step come to the Father and the Son in faith, and, like the animals that chew the cud, they meditate day and night upon God's
word in order to adorn themselves with good works (v. 8. 31).

The Soteriology of Tertullian is of special interest at this point,
since it became (through Cyprian) normative for the Western
church, and, like his doctrine of the Trinity and his Christology,
anticipates the later development in many particulars. He regards the relation of man to God from the legal point of view.
The gospel is the " law peculiarly ours" (monog. 7, 8. praes.
13); God is the Lawgiver and the Avenger of transgressions of
the law (exhort. cast. 2. c. Marc. i. 26). Hence the fundamental relation of man to God is that of fear : " but the fear of
man is the honor of God" (paenit. 7, 2, 4, 5, 6. ad ux. ii. 7).
But for the sinner remains, as a means of salvation, repentance, as a floating board for the shipwrecked (paen. 3). The
sinner by his repentance earns for himself salvation in baptism
(paen. 6 : " offers impunity to be purchased by this compensation
of repentance"). Hereby baptism gains a fixed position in the
order of salvation. The grace of God is necessarily connected with
this sacrament. By baptism, guilt and punishment are removed :
"death having been destroyed through the washing away of
sins, and guilt thus removed, punishment is also removed. Man
is restored to the likeness of God, as he receives again the breathing of the Spirit which was experienced in paradise, but since
lost " (bap. 5). We are born in the water, not otherwise than
we are saved by remaining in the water (ib. 1). Baptism brings
"remission of sins, abolition of death, regeneration of the man,

the obtaining of the Holy Spirit " (c. Marc. i. 28). Tertullian, in Stoic fashion, conceives of the Spirit as something material, which, on account of its tenuity, can enter the water and impart to it the power of sanctifying : " to penetrate and permeate easily on account of the subtility of its substance. Thus the nature of the waters, being sanctified by that which is holy, has itself received (power) to sanctify. The sanctified (waters) imbibe the power of sanctifying " (bapt. 4). The impartation of the Spirit can therefore scarcely be regarded otherwise than as the infusion of a spiritual substance, as, *e. g.*, in de pat. 1 : " for the apprehending and performing of these (*i. e.*, good) things, only the grace of the divine inspiration (*inspirationis*) is effectual " (cf. Loofs, DG., 104). We " remain " in baptismal grace if we do not sin, but fulfill the law of God (bapt. 15). If we, nevertheless, sin, we offend God (*deum offendere*, ad ux. ii. 7. exh. cast. v. dejejun. 3. c. Marc. i. 26 : "if he is offended, he ought to be angry "). Satisfaction must now be rendered in view of this wrath of God. This technical term also—derived from Roman law—was introduced into dogmatics by Tertullian. "Thou hast offended, but thou mayest yet be reconciled. Thou hast one to whom thou mayest render satisfaction, and he, too, is willing " (paen. 7 extr.). It is necessary " to satisfy the offended Lord " (ib. 10): " in order that I may reconcile to myself God, whom by sinning I have offended " (ib. 11). This is done by repentance : " by repentance God is appeased (*mitigatur*; ib. 9, 5 : " to satisfy the Lord through repentance of offenses "). But repentance consists of heartfelt sorrow (*paenitere ex animo*) and confession (*confessio*), which embraces a purpose of satisfaction (*satisfactionis*), ib. 9. The sinner humbles himself by the confession (*confessio*, ἐξομολόγησις); he sighs, weeps, fasts, and thus atones for his transgression. He makes satisfaction to God and earns for himself forgiveness (ib. 9 ; jejun. 3). He even brings a sin-offering to God (paen. 12. scorp. 7 ; resur. 8), and thus satisfaction is rendered to God. Since man thus punishes himself, he frees himself from eternal punishment. " By temporal affliction eternal punishments are —I will not say, frustrated—but expunged " (paen. 9).

The entire moral life is regarded from the same legal point of view. Man is to fulfill the law—not only its precepts (*praecepta*), but, if possible, also its counsels (*consilia*) (c. Marc. ii. 17. ad ux. ii. 1). Thus he becomes holy and righteous, and recompenses Christ for his redeeming work (resur. 8 ; patient. 16 fin.). " By continence thou shalt negotiate a great substance of sanctity ; by parsimony of the flesh thou shalt acquire the Spirit " (exh. cast. 10 in.). Let man acquire for himself *merits* before God.

"No one is advanced by practical indulgence, but by obeying his will ; the will of God is our sanctification " (ib. 1 ; cf. paen. 6. jej. 3 in.). This is to be done in view of the divine recompense, especially from fear of the judgment ; for the reward will always be according to the merits. "Good done has God as debtor, just as has evil also, because the Judge is a rewarder of every case " (paen. 2). Why many mansions with the Father, if not on account of the variety of merits ? (scorp. 6 ; vid. also orat. 2, 4 ; resur. 8. ad Scapul. 4 extr.). Such is the program of the practical Christianity of the West ! Christianity, according to Tertullian, is salvation ; and it is such by the giving of *sacraments* and *laws*. The sacraments (baptism and repentance) are the properly saving element. The law points out to those who have been reconciled the way to meritorious works and holy life. In the sacraments is concentrated the religious element in Christianity ; in the law and good works the moral element. Thus there is, to a certain extent, a balance established between religion and morality, between the grace of God and man's deed, although there is wanting an inner connection between the two elements. In all of this, Tertullian's view became normative. Compare HARNACK, DG., iii. 13 ff. WIRTH, Der Verdienstbegriff in d. chr. Kirche, i. (d. Verdienstbegr. in Tert), 1892.

8. Eschatology. The resurrection of the flesh is, in harmony with the rule of faith, championed against the Gnostics. Irenæus adduces in its support the resurrection of Christ (v. 31. 2), the indwelling of the Spirit in our body (v. 13. 4), and also the Lord's Supper, since the latter, after God has been invoked upon it, is the body and blood of Christ (cf. in explanation : "the eucharist, consisting of two things, the earthly and the heavenly," iv. 18. 5), and as such nourishes our flesh (v. 2. 3 ; iv. 18. 5).[1] The end will come when the devil shall have once more recapitulated the entire apostate throng in the Antichrist (v. 25. 1: "recapitulating in himself the diabolic apostasy . . . he will tyrannically attempt to prove himself God "). Then will Christ appear, and the six thousand years of the world will

---

[1] Irenæus, as is from the entire context of the passages cited beyond question, thinks of a real presence of the body of Christ in the eucharist. The case appears to be the same, though not so evidently, with Tertullian. De orat. 6: "Thereby by praying for daily bread (4th petition) we ask for perpetuity and personal life from his body ; " c. Marc. 1. 14: "bread, in which he presents (*repraesentat=praesentat*) his very body." Ib. iv. 40: "This is my body, *i. e.*, a figure of my body (*figura corporis mei*, vid. LEIMBACH, Beiträge zur Abendmahlslehre Tert. 1874. Baptism and the Lord's Supper are often combined in such connections, *e. g.*, Tert. c. Marc. iv. 34 ; resur. 8 ; de virg. oel. 9 ; de exhort. cast. 7 ; de praescr. 40 ; de corona 3.

be followed by the first resurrection and the rest of the seventh millennium (v. 28. 3 ; 33. 2). In Palestine believers will refresh themselves with the marvelously rich fruits of the land (following Papias, cf. Matt. 26. 29 ; v. 33. 3 f. 1). Then follows the end, the new heavens and the new earth (v. 36. 1). The blessed will live in graded order in the "many mansions" in the Father's house, ascending from the Spirit to the Son, and through the Son to the Father (as learned from pupils of the apostles, v. 36. 2). Then will occur what is described in 1 Cor. 15. 26 ff. (ib.). Thus upon this subject also the teaching of the church stands in sharp and conscious contrast with the general Gnostic view (v. 36. 3).

9. Methods of Proof (cf., in addition to Irenæus, especially Tert., de praescr. haeret.). (*a*) The church professes to teach the truth concerning God, Christ, and salvation. This is attested by the prophets, apostles, and all disciples of Christ (Ir. iii. 24. 1). Thus the decisive authority rests with the Scriptures of the Old and New Testaments.[1] The idea that Gnosticism and Montanism forced the church to fix the canon of the New Testament is erroneous. The limits of the New Testament were not more positively fixed at the end of the second century than at its beginning (Jas. and Heb., *e. g.*, were wanting in many national churches ; others used Hermas [Ir. iv. 20. 2. Tert. de or. 16 ; cf. de pud. 10. Can. Mur. l. 73 ff.], Barnabas [Cl. Strom. ii. 31, 35], and the Didache [Cl. ib. i. 100. Orig. de princ. iii. 2. 7 ; cf. Clem. in Ir. iii. 33]—as canonical (cf. ZAHN i. 326 ff.). Appeal might be made to an established custom in citing the authority of these writings as conclusive. But the peculiar nature of the opposition encountered in Gnosticism led to the attaching of a special importance to the source of these documents—and this, not so much as coming from the apostles, as because they dated from the primitive period of the church, and hence contained the real gospel (Ir. iii. 1. Serap. in Eus. h. e. vi. 12. 3). Hence it is that Irenæus lays such stress upon the utterances of the "elders" (*i. e.*, ad Florin. in Eus. h. e. v. 20. 4. adv. haer. iv. 27. 1 in.; 32. 1 ; v. 36. 2). It was but a natural consequence of this high estimation of the New Testament writings, when inspiration ("Spirit-bearers," πνευματοφόροι; "spoken by the Word of God and his Spirit ; " "the Spirit

---

[1] In addition to the authority of Scripture, Tertullian appealed also to the testimony of reason : "Reason is a thing of God . . . he has wished nothing to be considered or known without reason" (paen. 1). Words have character, not only by their sound, but by their sense, and they are heard not so much by the ear as by the mind. "He who knows nothing believes that God is cruel" (scorp. 7); vid. also corona 4 f. 10, and Cyprian, sub.

through the apostle,'' etc.; "God-inspired,'' θεόπνευστος) was expressly ascribed to them (Theophil. ad. Autol. ii. 22. 9; iii. 11, 12, 13, 14. Ir. 28. 2; iii. 16. 2, 9. Tert. de pat. 7; de orat. 20, 22; c. Marc. v. 7. Clem. Al. Protr. § 87). The conception of inspiration is found frequently in Judaism, as among the Greeks, but it received its specific meaning only when Christianity had adopted from Judaism the conception of the canon : *i. e.*, that certain books are holy and every word in them is authoritative.[1] To this was, however, now added the Christian principle, that this authority attaches only to the original Christian documents. That from this time there should be also a constant tendency to greater definiteness in marking the limits of the canon may be easily understood. What was relatively new was really only the recognition of the canon, consciously and upon principle, as the legacy of primitive Christianity— as the norm and basis of the church's teaching (cf.: "in harmony with the Scriptures,'' σύμφωνα ταῖς γραφαῖς, Ir. in Eus. h. e., v. 20. 6). But since the heretics, apparently, in this particular followed the praxis of the primitive church, but introduced garbled writings, or misinterpreted those which were genuine, or appealed to private traditions of the apostolic circle, the appeal to the New Testament did not prove sufficient in controversy : "Therefore appeal is not to be taken to the Scriptures, nor a controversy instituted in those things in which there is either no victory, or a victory uncertain, or as good as uncertain'' (Tert. de praescr. 19; cf. Ir. iii. 2. 2 fin.).

(*b*) A criterion must be found for the right understanding of the Scriptures, which will prove that the heretics have no right to them (Tert. de praescr. 15, 19, 37. Ir. i. 9. 5; 10. 1; iv. 20. 2). This criterion is the ancient baptismal confession, or the "canon of truth'' (Tert. de praescr. 13, 16). This was paraphrased and interpreted in the free way which had up to this time been customary. All the reproductions of this rule in Irenæus and Tertullian are free, expanded references. It is not this confession as such which is the criterion, but the confession as interpreted. But just on this account the church could not abide by the confession, but was driven to tradition and the episcopacy (see below under d). (*c*) In regard to this confession, it was held that it could be traced back through the medium of the apostles to Christ (Ir. iii. praef.; v. praef.; i. 10. 1. Tert. praescr. 20 f. 37). It is not the formula itself, but its content, which is had in mind. It was thought that a histori-

---

[1] This idea of the canon appears nowhere, as far as I have observed, in the whole history of religion except in Judaism and Christianity.

cal support for this opinion could be deduced from the unbroken succession of bishops in the "mother-churches" since the days of the apostles (Iren. iii. 3 ; 4. 1 ; v. 20. 1). Tertullian (praescr. 21. 36, 32) says : "Let them [the heretics] therefore produce the origins of their churches ; let them display the order of their bishops, running through succession from the beginning in such a way that the first bishop had as his teacher and predecessor some one of the apostles or of the apostolic men who were closely associated with the apostles !" This applies most especially—and the praxis harmonized—to the church of Rome : "For it is necessary that the whole church, *i. e.*, those from all places who are believers, should come, on account of its more potent headship, to that church in which has been preserved by believers from all places those things which are a tradition from the apostles" (Ir. iii. 3. 2).[1] The old doctrine is the true doctrine : "Wherefore it is to be henceforth equally urged in advance against all heresies, that whatever is the first is true, and whatever is later is adulterated" (Tert. adv. Prax. 2, 20). (*d*) If the bishops are the successors of the apostles, we must learn the apostolic truth at their hand, as they have received the apostolic doctrine, "the sure charisma of truth" through succession from the apostles. Their daily life, moreover, remains confessedly irreproachable (Ir. iv. 26. 2, 4, 5 ; 33. 8 ; 32. 1. Tert. 32. Hipp. Ref. prooem.). Where the gifts (*charismata*) of the Lord have been deposited, there we ought to learn the truth, among whom is that succession of the church which comes from the apostles, and among whom that is preserved which is wholesome and irreproachable in life and unadulterated and incorruptible in speech" (Ir. iv. 26. 5). In place of the ancient *charismata* comes the *charisma veritatis*, peculiar to the bishops. This consists in the possession of the traditional faith, and also in the ability to interpret it (iv. 26. 5). Thus not only the confession, but its interpretation also, became authoritative. It was a historically comprehensible and necessary, but an abnormal path into which these ideas conducted.

(*e*) But of this there was, as yet, no consciousness. Since the church is, as thus historically attested, the possessor of evangelical saving truth, it may be said : "For where the church is, there is the Spirit of God ; and where the Spirit of God is, there

---

[1] The meaning of this noted passage is evidently : Since two great apostles labored at Rome, there attaches to it a special pre-eminence. Accordingly, every church must be in harmony with Rome. In Rome, also, the apostolic tradition was known by people who had come from all parts of the world. The two apostles granted to Rome its primacy, and this is binding upon all, as people from all parts of the world have at Rome held fast the true tradition.

is the church and all grace.    But the Spirit is truth " (Ir. iii.
24. 1), and : "who are beyond the bounds of the truth, *i. e.*,
beyond the bounds of the church " (iv. 33. 7).    This conception of the church is, therefore, not as yet hierarchical, for the
episcopacy comes into consideration only as the bearer of the
historical truth.    The church is not " essentially the episcopacy "
(ROTHE, Anfänge der chr. K., 1837, p. 486.    RITSCHL,
Entstehung d. altkath. K. 442 ; per contra, SEEBERG, Begriff der
chr. K. i. 16 ff.), but the congregation of those who believe in
God and fear him, and who receive the Spirit of God (Ir. v. 32.
2 ; iv. 36. 2 ; iii. 3. 2).    They are all priests (Ir. v. 34. 3 ; iv.
8. 3 : " for all the righteous have sacerdotal rank."    Tert. de
orat. 28. exh. cast. 7 : " Are not we laymen also priests ? . . .
where there are three, though they be laymen, there is a church ").
But the Spirit and faith are imparted to man only through the
preaching of the church.    " For this gift of God has been en-
trusted to the church, just as that of breathing at the creation,
to the end that all the members receiving it should be vivified ;
and in it is included the communication of Christ, *i. e.*, the
Holy Spirit, the pledge of incorruptibility and confirmation of
our faith and the ladder of ascension to God " (Ir. iii. 24. 1.
Hipp., de Chr. et Antichr. 59, compares the church to a ship in
which Christ is the pilot ; the rudder, the two testaments ; the
cable, the love of Christ ; the accompanying boat, regeneration ;
the iron anchor, the commandments of Christ ; the ladder representing the sufferings of Christ and inviting us to ascend to heaven,
etc.    The church gives birth to the Logos, ib. 61 : " The church
does not cease from her heart to give birth to the Logos . . .
the Son of God . . . always bringing forth, the church teaches
all the nations ").    But the proclamation of this truth has been
committed to the successors of the apostles : it is found only where
their words are obeyed.

The unity of the church is not yet traced to the one episcopacy.    It is based upon the one Spirit, the one truth, the one confession.    " Our bodies have, through that washing, received that
union which makes for incorruption ; but our souls through the
Spirit " (Ir. iii. 17. 2).    Tertullian says : " Therefore such and
so many churches has become that one first from the apostles,
from which they all are derived.    Thus all are first, and all are
apostolic, since all are one.    The communication of peace and the
title of brotherhood, and the friendship of hospitality, which
laws no other rule controls than the one tradition of the same
sacrament, prove the unity " (praescr. 20 ; cf. de virg. vel. 2.
Apol. 39 init.—" sacrament " here refers to the rule of faith).

Let us now glance backward.    We have discovered the ele·

ments of the common faith of the church at the close of the second century. The church found herself in a position to establish a positive doctrine ("I believed what it was proper for me to believe") in opposition to Gnosticism. It traced the Gnostic view to heathen influences. The fundamental features of the church's doctrine were as follows: (1) One God, who is righteous and good, the Creator, Preserver, Ruler, and Saviour of the world. The one God is not a lonely God. In maintaining this, reference was had to the speculations of the Apologists concerning the Logos, but, independently of these, it was regarded as fixed that we are to acknowledge a three-fold Ego in God (Iren.). Tertullian endeavored to explain this relation by introducing the conceptions of substance and person. (2) The evil in man is not implied in the fact of his sensuous nature, but is an act of his free will. The connection with the sin of Adam is emphasized, but no way is found to consistently carry out the idea. Even fallen man is free to choose "either part." (3) The reality of the divinity and humanity of Christ is to be maintained unconditionally in the interest of redemption. His personal life is composed of two substances (Tert.). The salvation which he brought consists, first, in the law of love which he taught, and whose observance he made possible; then, in immortality. Upon the latter the emphasis is laid. Together with this, other scriptural ideas, especially of a Pauline and Johannine type, are still influential and of practical significance, *e. g.*: Christ, as the second Adam, the source for us and the leaven in us; the Spirit, as making the fulfillment of the law possible and bringing to us fellowship with God; sonship to God; the forgiveness of sins; the weakening of the devil; our reconciliation with God, etc. (4) The preaching of the gospel imparts salvation, and baptism applies it to the individual. It is apprehended in faith. It is, indeed, a portentous turn of thought, when faith is represented as the acceptance and acknowledgment of Christ, or as obedience, and its object as "doctrine;" but this position is, after all, practically neutralized in part by the assertion that faith cannot be awakened without the operation of the Spirit, and is inconceivable without a life in union with God and holy love. If it is said that faith justifies man, this is meant substantially in the sense of an inciting to the fulfillment of the divine commandments. Tertullian, by treating the relation of God and man in a legal scheme, prepared the way for the later development of doctrine in the Western church. (5) These ideas find their consummation in the resurrection of the flesh, which the teachers of the period seek not only to propagate as a doctrine, but to understand in its relation to the practical religious life of

believers.  (6) In all of this, these men were conscious that they
represented the original Christianity, and were able to attest their
views as primitively Christian by the customary criteria of Scripture and the baptismal confession.  These positions were, indeed, further developed in the acknowledgment of the episcopacy
as the bearer and guarantor of the truth thus held, and in the
admission of ecclesiastical tradition to a place by the side of
scriptural authority.  It is a result of the great conflict with
Gnosticism, that the church first attained her unity as a
teaching church—in her doctrine.  The unity of the church embraces the elements absolutely essential if the church and Christianity are to continue in existence.  That this unity consists in
the pure doctrine is, leaving separate considerations out of view,
a result of the conflict with Gnosticism.

The Antignostic Fathers were, broadly speaking, right in their
general conception, as against the position of their opponents.
They did not really present anything new, not even a distinctly
enlarged understanding of Christianity.  Their conception of
Christian truth and life is that which prevailed already at the
close of the first and the beginning of the second century.  The
only peculiarity is that the opposition encountered compelled
them to greater distinctness and lucidity, as well as to deliberate
utterances with respect to the canon and doctrinal tradition.
The essential content of Christianity is still held to be faith in
the Triune God and in Christ, the Son of God and man, observance of the new law, and the hope of immortality.  As formerly,
so now, religious life found nourishment in the reflections, that
Christ has delivered us and brought to us the forgiveness of sins ;
that grace saves us ; that the believer leads a life in Christ and
with Christ, etc.: but there was no certainty in the treatment of
these ideas.  In the last analysis, it is the chief thing that he who
observes the commandment of love becomes a child of God and
a partaker of immortality.  In reality, use was made for spiritual
edification of more material than was taken account of in the
books of the age—a fact which is of great importance in explain-
ing the vigorous opposition to Gnosticism.

## § 15.  *The Theology of the Alexandrine Fathers.*

LITERATURE :  CLEMENS ALEXANDRINUS († ca. A. D. 215).  Λόγος
προτρεπτικὸς πρὸς Ἕλληνας ; Παιδαγωγός, ll.  3 ; Στρωματεῖς, ll.  8 ; ἐκ τῶν
προφητικῶν ἐκλογαί ; ἐκ τῶν Θεοδότου καὶ τῆς ανατολικῆς καλουμένης διδασκαλιας
κατὰ τοὺς Οὐαλεντίνου χρόνους ἐπιτομαί.  Also the homily, Τίς ὁ σωζόμενος
πλούσιος.  Finally, a large fragment from the Ὑποτυπώσεις, preserved in Latin
(Adumbrationes); editions by Potter, 1715 (citations of chapter and page in
present work refer to this edition), and Dindorf, 1868, in Migne, t. 8, 9.  ORIGEN
(† A. D. 254).  We make use especially of his Περὶ ἀρχῶν, ll. 4, preserved

in the Latin translation of Rufinus, of which we have also large Greek fragments. Also κατὰ Κέλσον, ll. 8 ; editions by DE LA RUE, 1733, reprinted by LOMMATZSCH, 1831 ff., in Migne, t. 11-17. Compare GUÉRIKE, de schola quae Alex. floruit cat., 1824, 1825. BIGG, The christ. Platonists of Alex., 1886. LUTHARDT, Gesch. d. chr. Ethik, i. 113 ff. ZAHN, Forschungen iii. (Supplementum Clementinum), 1884. COGNAT, Clement d'Alexandrie, 1859. WINTER, Die Ethik d. Clem. v. Alex., 1882. MERK, Clem. Alex. in s. Abh. v. d. griech. Philos., Leipz. Diss., 1879. HUETIUS, Origeniana, 1668. THOMASIUS, Orig., 1837. REDEPENNING, Orig., 2 vols., 1841, 1846. H. SCHULTZ, Die Christol. d. Orig. in Zusammenh. s. Weltanschauung, in Jahrb. f. prot. Theol., 1875, 193 ff., 369 ff. DENIS, La philosophie d' Origène, 1884. Möller, PRE. xi. 92 ff. HOLL, Enthusiasmus u. Bussgewalt, p. 228 ff.

We have noted the league formed in Alexandria between the Jewish spirit and the Hellenic philosophy, which produced the type of thought represented by Philo. A similar compact appears in the same locality toward the end of the second century. Hellenistic learning and gospel truth are associated in the most astonishing way. The catechetical schools at Alexandria provided the basis for this movement, and it was promoted by Pantaenus, Clement, and Origen (cf., as to the pedagogical method of Origen, the Panegyricus of Greg. Thaum., c. 6-15). It was sought to secure what had been attained by the most profound researches of the Gnostics, in the belief that this could be done without surrendering the church's rule of faith. The Gnostics and Apologists were here excelled. Christianity became a science in literary forms which assumed a place of equal rank by the side of secular literature. This explains the unbounded veneration and admiration with which Origen was regarded. The movement was of inestimable significance in the history of Greek theology. It is associated distinctly with the name of Origen. The teachings of Clement claim our attention only as preparatory in their character.

The Greek spirit is in Clement combined with the faith of the church in a way characteristically fresh and unsophisticated. The difficulties encountered do not disturb him. He was a talented dilettante, with the virtues and the vices which belong to such a character. He held that there is but one truth, in which all lines eventually converge. God gave to the Jews the law, and to the Greeks philosophy. "For it (philosophy) led the Grecian world to Christ as did the law the Hebrews" (Str. i. 5. p. 331 ; vi. 17. 823 ; 5. 762). He spoke of the philosophers as borrowing material from the Old Testament (Str. v. 14. 699 ff. This was not the case, however, with their idolatry, Protr. 2). Philosophy he regarded as still possessing a pedagogical signifi‐ cance for every Christian who rises from bare faith (ψιλὴ πίστις) to *Gnosis*. But this occurs according to the canon of the

church (κατὰ κάνονα ἐκκλησιαστικόν, Str. vii. 7. 855 ; vi. 15. 803).
Following Philo, Clement effects a compromise with the letter
of the Old and New Testaments by allegorical interpretation
(cf. Str. vi. 15. 806 f.). Faith in revelation is necessary to
salvation. Such faith is sufficient, but points beyond itself to
*Gnosis* (Str. ii. 2. 432 ; v. 1. 643 ; vii. 10. 864 f.: "to believe
is the foundation of gnosis"). Hence, "to know is more than
to believe" (Str. vi. 14. 794). Faith is the outward acceptance of God and of the doctrine of Christ in the literal sense,
from fear and respect for authority (*e. g.*, Str. ii. 12 ; v. 1. 643 ;
vii. 12. 873 f.). The Gnostic, on the other hand, lives in
initiated vision (ἐποπτικὴ θεωρία), apprehending salvation
inwardly and comprehending it (Str. vi. 10 ; i. 2. 327). He
does not do that which is good for the sake of expected reward,
but for its own sake, in love to God (Str. iv. 18. 614 ; iv. 22.
625). He avoids not only actual sin, but also every motion of
sinful desire (Str. ii. 11. 455 ; vi. 12. 789 f.). He regards
himself, not as a servant, but as a child of God (Str. vii. 2. 831).
He prays always, for prayer is companionship with God (Str.
vii. 7. 851 ff., 854 ; vii. 12. 875). If he who simply believes
(ἁπλῶς πεπιστευκώς) requires the purifications (καθάρσια), or
minor mysteries (μικρὰ μυστήρια) of the church, the Gnostic
needs the great (μεγάλα) mysteries, the ἐποπτεία (Protr. § 1, p.
9 ; § 12. Str. v. 11. 689). This is the royal way. "By as
much as anyone loves God, by so much the more does he make
his way into God (Quis div. salv. 27 fin.). Thus there result
two forms of Christianity. In contrast with the barely believing, uncultivated beginner, inclined to externalities, stands the
Christian who beholds the mysteries of God, and who, with heart
and understanding, receives God to abiding fellowship. The Stoic
discrimination between the wise and the advancing (προκόπτοντες)
is here transferred to Christianity. There are now Christians of a
first and of a second class. Thus the evacuation of the conception
of faith by means of the bare orthodoxy which is satisfied with
outward belief (Str. i. 9. 342 f.) is noted, but also granted
honorable recognition, while at the same time a way of escape,
although a dangerous one, from that error is discovered. The
"Gnostic" of Clement really stands higher than his "believer."

The separate doctrines in Clement—as the objects of faith and
knowledge—may be readily passed in review. The One God,
who is Being beyond nature (ἐπέκεινα τῆς οὐσίας), and without
attributes (*e. g.*, Str. v. 12. 695 f.; v. 11. 689), is the Creator
of the world. The formula and the conception of the Trinity
constantly recur (Str. v. 14. 710 ; cf. Exc. ex Theod. 80. Protr.
12 init. Paed. i. 6. 123 ; also iii. 12. 311. Quis div. salv. 42

fin. Adumbr., p. 88, Zahn). Christ is the Logos of God (distinct from the paternal Logos, πατριχὸς λόγος, Hypot. in Photius Bibl. cod. 109). In him God is known. He has been from the beginning present and active in the world, giving it existence and offering the truth in prophets and philosophers. He has now become man. "Christ was, indeed, in ancient times this Logos and [the cause] of our being . . . and of our well-being; but now this same Logos has appeared to men, the only One both God and man, the cause of all things good to us, by whom, having been thoroughly instructed in right living, we are conducted to eternal life" (Protr. 1, p. 6). He was a man with a human body and soul (cf., "impassible as to his soul," Paed. 1. 2, p. 99). Clement seeks, although without success, to avoid Docetism : "But in the case of the Saviour [to suppose] that the body, as a body, demanded the aids necessary for duration would be ridiculous. For he ate, not for the sake of the body sustained by holy power, but in order that those with him might not be induced to think otherwise concerning him, just as, indeed, afterward some thought that he was manifested in seeming (δοχήσει). But he was entirely impassible, upon whom no emotional impulse, whether of joy or grief, could manage to exert its power" (Str. vi. 9. 775; cf. iii. 7. 538. Adumbr., p. 87, Zahn). Christ surrendered his life to death for us, became a ransom (λύτρον) for us, and overcame the devil (Quis div., p. 37. Paed. iii. 12, p. 310; i. 5. 111; i. 11 fin. Protr. 11 init.). Not much importance is, however, attached to the conception of Christ as the propitiation (ἱλασμός; vid. e. g., Paed. iii. 6, p. 310). He grows eloquent, on the other hand, in extolling the Logos as a teacher beyond compare, as leader and lawgiver, and as the way to immortality (Protr. 11, p. 86 : "For if the Teacher who has filled all things with his holy powers, creation, salvation, goodness, legislation, prophecy, instruction, now as Teacher instructs us in all things, Athens and Greece also already knew everything in the Logos," ib. p. 88 f., § 12, p. 91. Paed. i. 3, p. 102 f.; i. 6. 113. Protr. i. p. 8 : "The Logos . . . having become man, just in order that thou also mightest learn from a man how at any time a man might become divine ; " cf. Paed. i. 12. 156. Str. iv. 23. 632 ; vii. 10. 865). Christ, as God, forgives sins, and his humanity serves the purposes of moral instruction : "As God, forgiving sins ; but as man, leading to avoid continuance in sin" (Paed. i. 3 init.).

Man, upon his part, is to render obedience to the teaching of Christ, and, with a view to reward, exercise love toward others, in accordance with the commandments (Protr. 11, p. 89 f. Paed. i. 3. 102). Clement knows full well that man lies bound

in the fetters of sin (Protr. ii. init. Paed. iii. 12. 307 : "For
to sin continually is natural and common to all"), but this
does not prevent him from most strongly emphasizing his free-
will (αὐτεξούσιον) or the "in our power" (ἐφ' ἡμῖν, Str. vi.
12. 788). "But he desires that we may be saved from ourselves" (ib.). Thus man is free to do good and to exercise
faith (Str. iv. 24. 633; ii. 15. 462 ; iii. 9. 540). God offers
salvation, and man has power to grasp it: "Just as the physician furnishes health to those who labor with him for health, so
also does God furnish eternal salvation to those working with
him for knowledge and prosperity" (Str. vii. 7. 860). The
first right inclination (ἡ πρώτη πρὸς σωτηρίαν νεῦσις) is faith.
Then follow fear, hope, repentance (μετάνοια). The goal is
reached in love (ἀγάπη) and knowledge (γνῶσις) (Str. ii. 6. 445).
Faith is an "assent" (συγκατάθεσις) and a "perception of the
mind (πρόληψις διανοίας) concerning the things spoken" (Str. ii.
12. 458 ; 2. 437, 432). Inasmuch as faith is a necessary pre-
liminary to salvation, our salvation may be ascribed to it (Str. ii.
12. 457 f.: "Faith is strength for salvation and power for eternal life ;" Paed. i. 6. 116 : "The one universal salvation of
the human race is faith"). But this faith points beyond itself to
knowledge and love (vid. supra ; cf. Str. ii. 11. 454 : "reasonable," δοξαστικὴ, and "intelligent," ἐπιστημονική, faith). This
was a necessary inference when faith was regarded as merely an
assent, or a persuasion to comply with the commandments
(πείθεσθαι ταῖς ἐντολαῖς, ib.). With such an idea of faith, Paul's
doctrine of justification is untenable : "Righteousness is two-
fold : that produced by love and that produced by fear" (Str. vii.
12. 879). The "Gnostic" has complete righteousness. This is
illustrated in Abraham's faith and righteousness : "For example,
to Abraham, having become a believer, it was accounted for righteousness ; to him, having advanced to that which is greater and
more perfect than faith," etc. (Str. vi. 12. 791 ; cf. vii. 14. 885).
Thus, then, the believer of his free will decides for God and his
law, advancing from mere faith and the righteousness which
attaches to it to knowledge and love, to continual inward fellowship with God, to a life of faith and uninterrupted holy activity,
to genuine righteousness. Here the moral ideal is attained ; the
lust of the world has vanished : "He is not strenuous, but in a
state of calmness" (Str. iv. 22. 625). Yet, on the other hand,
it is maintained with all earnestness that "only the well-doing
which is for the sake of love, or for the sake of the beautiful
itself, is chosen by the Gnostic." He lives and labors in the
world without love for the world (e.g., Str. iii. 7. 537; vi.

12. 790; vii. 12. 874$^1$-878). He attains to right conduct ($\kappa\alpha\tau\delta\rho\vartheta\omega\mu\alpha$), whereas the simple believer ($\dot{\alpha}\pi\lambda\tilde{\omega}\varsigma$ $\pi\iota\sigma\tau\delta\varsigma$) reaches only median conduct ($\mu\dot{\epsilon}\sigma\eta$ $\pi\rho\tilde{\alpha}\xi\iota\varsigma$), according to the Stoic terminology (Str. vi. 14. 796).

The individual, however, secures his salvation only in connection with the church and its agency (Paed. iii. 12 fin.; i. 6. 123, 114: "His desire is the salvation of men; and this has been called the church"). Hierarchical aims are entirely foreign to Clement (cf. Str. vi. 13. 793). It is baptism which makes one a member of the church and a partaker of salvation. It brings the cleansing from sin, and thus the capability of apprehending the salvation which the teaching of the church offers. Thus one becomes through baptism a new man. Sonship, perfection, immortality have become his in faith (initially) through baptism (Paed. i. 6. 113: "Having been baptized, we are illuminated; having been illuminated, we are made sons; having been made sons, we are perfected; having been perfected, we are made superior to death." p. 114: "Thus nothing but believing and being born again is perfection in life." Ib.: "This doctrine, $\mu\dot{\alpha}\vartheta\eta\mu\alpha$, is the eternal salvation of the eternal Saviour. . . We, the baptized, having erased our beclouding sins, the condemnation of darkness, by the divine Spirit, have the free and unhindered and bright vision of the Spirit; by which alone we behold divine things, the Holy Spirit streaming in upon us from heaven." p. 116: "Therefore we have washed away all our sins, and are immediately no longer evil. This is the one grace of illumination, viz., to be no longer the same as before, or to have cleansed the way. But when knowledge, $\gamma\nu\tilde{\omega}\sigma\iota\varsigma$, appears, together with illumination . . . the unlearned are learned—whenever this learning may have been added; for thou hast not [power] to tell the time. For instruction indeed leads up to faith, but faith is taught together with baptism by the Holy

---

[1] A few sentences may be adduced in illustration: "Wherefore also he eats and drinks and marries, not from choice, but from necessity. As to marrying, if reason may speak, I say, also because it is proper. For he who has become perfect has the apostles as examples; and he does not really show himself a man who enters upon a single life, but he conquers men who, in marriage and the rearing of children and providing for his house, has exercised himself without pleasure and without pain in the care of the house, constant in his experience of the love of God, and escaping every temptation besetting him through children and wife, domestics, and property. 'But it falls to the lot of the houseless man to be in many things without experience. Hence, caring for himself alone, he is weakened for that which is still lacking with respect to his own salvation, and abounds in the management of affairs pertaining to [the present] life."

10

Spirit "). God cleanses sins committed after baptism by disci-plinary sufferings (Str. iv. 24. 634).

The Eucharist, according to Clement, bestows participation in immortality. The communicant enters into fellowship with Christ and the divine Spirit. "On the one hand, the mixed wine nourishes to faith; on the other hand, the Spirit leads to immor-tality. The commingling anew in both of the potion and the Word is called the eucharist, a blessed and beautiful [gift of] grace, of which those who partake in faith are sanctified in both body and soul" (Paed. ii. 2. 177 f.; cf. i. 6. 125). These are the Christian mysteries (vid. Protr. 12, p. 91 ff.). But this all points beyond itself to the unshrouded knowledge of the "great mysteries" (vid. supra, p. 142). This is the Christian life: "right living, together with due appropriation of knowledge— for the perception of the truth and the fulfillment of the com-mandments" (Str. i. 1. 318; cf. vi. 12. 788: "both in learn-ing and in exercise").

Clement taught the resurrection of the body. He appears to have accepted the possibility of a conversion after death (Str. vii. 2 fin.; 16. 895), without giving prominence to the idea.[1]

ORIGEN is more positive than Clement, but Clement is more Christian than Origen. It was the age when Neoplatonism was beginning to control thought. Starting with God as the abstract Existence ($\tau\grave{o}$ $\H{\epsilon}\nu$), advance was made through the divine Thought ($\nu o \tilde{\upsilon} \varsigma$), the conceived order of things ($\varkappa \acute{o} \sigma \mu o \varsigma$ $\nu o \eta \tau \acute{o} \varsigma$), the uni-versal soul ($\acute{\eta}$ $\tau o \tilde{\upsilon}$ $\H{o} \lambda o \upsilon$ $\psi \upsilon \chi \acute{\eta}$), to this world, in which the souls of men live imprisoned in matter ($\H{\upsilon} \lambda \eta$). The task before them is escape from the sensuous by asceticism and ecstasy, through the medium of mystical symbolic rites. "The only salvation is a turn-ing toward God" (Porphyr. ad Marcell, 24). In the great longing which broods over this conception lies its significance. There is a gradation of being, extending from God to the soul, which penetrates through all things and all religions with their forms. All things are but copies of the infinite. Again, the soul aspires to God through all possible suggestions, means, and symbols. All things draw it upward. A wonderful musical rhythm resounds through this structure of thought: from God to the soul, and from the soul to God.

1. This trend of thought was not unknown to Origen. His work, *De principiis*—the first attempt to construct a system of dogmatics—contains a philosophical system, although not con-sistently adhered to. But Origen is an orthodox Christian. The

---

[1] Clement expresses himself as against the theory of the pre-existence of souls (Eclog. 17). It is not taught in Str. v. 16. 808, nor in Quis div. salv. 33 fin.

Scriptures contain the truth ; and he sends forth in advance of his own doctrinal conclusions a completed rule of faith, the teaching of the church, *ecclesiastica praedicatio* (De princ. praef).[1] "It seems necessary before [treating of] these separate points to lay down a certain line and a plain rule." These "elements and fundaments" are to be brought together, with the application of the things which the Scripture teaches, or which result from the teaching as a necessary consequence (praef. 10).[2] But the Scriptures are to be interpreted "spiritually," or allegorically. Thus Origen was enabled to find his peculiar opinions in them. He developed the allegorical interpretation systematically (de princ. iv.). Passages which seem contradictory, or which have a crass external sense, conceal a "deeper thought." The Holy Spirit veiled the thought by means of a "cloak of spiritual things." Impossible things are asserted in order to call attention to the fact that the occurrences could not have taken place corporeally ($\sigma\omega\mu\alpha\tau\iota\varkappa\tilde{\omega}\varsigma$), as, *e. g.*, the visible paradise and the walking of God therein ; Lk. 10. 4 ; Matt. 5. 39, 29 f.; 1 Cor. 9. 9 ; many narrations of the Old Testament ; some features in the history of Jesus ; and in the Gospels other things which did not happen ($\mathring{\varepsilon}\tau\varepsilon\rho\alpha\ \mu\mathring{\eta}\ \sigma\upsilon\mu\beta\varepsilon\beta\eta\varkappa\acute{o}\tau\alpha$ ; cf. iv. § 9-18). Appealing to Prov. 22. 20 f., Origen teaches a three-fold sense of Scripture : the somatic, literal sense ; the psychical, moral sense ; and the pneumatic, speculative sense. Historical and doctrinal passages are alike subject to this rule. He finds his own doctrine everywhere. Christian language adorns ideas

[1] One God, the Creator, the God of the Old and New Testaments, who gave Christ ; Christ, born of the Father before all creatures, truly born a man, who suffered, died and rose again ; the Holy Spirit, partaking of equal honor, his nature not clearly defined in tradition. The human soul has substance and life of its own, but there is nothing taught concerning its origin. Man is rewarded according to his merit. He has free will. The existence of angels and devils, together with the frequent expression of the opinion that the devil was an angel. The world was created, but not what was before it, nor what shall be after it. Holy Scriptures, which have not only the sense which lies upon the surface (*qui in manifesto ist*). The whole law is spiritual. Whether God is corporeal, what is the nature of the soul, if the stars are living beings, is not decided (de princ. praef. 4. 9; cf. the summary in Joh. xxxii. 9). A wide scope is here left for scientific exposition. The first dogmatician of the church assumed in his labors a position of fundamental subordination to the Rule of Faith. This has remained the case with his successors. The Rule of Faith became normative in the arrangement of doctrinal systems, and is so to the present day. This is the significance which it secured in the history of the world through the Antignostic controversies.

[2] Origen treats in the 4 Books of his De principiis, (1) Of God, (2) Of the Word, (3) Of Free Will, (4) Of the Allegorical Interpretation of Scripture. The first three books present—when viewed in a certain light—almost the whole content of his teaching.

which are but slightly Christian.   On the other hand, this method
enables him to conceal the foolishness of the gospel and to glorify
it as wisdom (*e. g.*, c. Cels. vi. 7 ; v. 60 ; iii. 19 ; cf. the estimate of Porphyry in Eus. h. e. vi. 19. 4, 7 f., and Cels. iv. 38).
The simpler class and the multitude depend upon the *ipse dixit*
(αὐτὸς ἔφα) and cling to the literal sense with their "bare and
unreasoning faith" (c. Cels. iv. 9 ; i. 42. 13 ; iii. 53).   They
speak of God as the Creator, but think of him as a coarse and
unjust man (de pr. iv. 8).   They understand literally, and not
in the sense of purifying, what the Scriptures say of judgment
(c. Cels. vi. 26 ; v. 16), and it is nothing but the fear of the
judgment which makes them Christians.   This is a lower plane,
above which the cultured believer rises, searching the Scriptures
as Christ has commanded, and learning to understand their spiritual contents (c. Cels. ii. 5 f.; iii. 79; iv. 71 ; v. 31 f., 18).
Thus, when contemplating the death of Christ, he reflects that he
is crucified with Christ (c. Cels. ii. 69).   He understands why
Christ heals the sick upon the plain, but ascends the mountain
with the disciples (ib. iii. 21).   Christ is for him the teacher,
and no longer the physician (ib. iii. 62 : "Therefore the divine
Logos was sent to be a physician to sinners, but to be a teacher of
divine mysteries to those already pure and no longer sinning").
The Christian starts out with faith based upon authority (cf. c.
Cels. i. 11) and with cleansing from sin in the fear of punishment ; there follows the higher stage, of understanding and insight (cf. also de orat. 27).   Origen thinks of this higher stage
as essentially intellectual, taking thus a step backward toward
Clement.   He has, however, the acuteness to recognize it as a
special advantage possessed by Christianity, compared with philosophy, that it is able to offer piety and salvation even to the
mass of the common people (c. Cels. vii. 60 ; iii. 53 f.).

   2.  (*a*)  "God is a Spirit," "God is light"—thus does Origen introduce his discussion of the doctrine of God.   Yet he remains within the limitations of the Grecian idea.   "God is Being,
and beyond Being" (ἐπέκεινα οὐσίας ; cf. c. Cels. vi. 64 ; in
Joh. xix. 1 ad fin.: "in the Over-beyond of Being, in the power
and nature of God").   He is an "intellectual nature" (de pr.
i. 1. 1-6), free from everything material, not limited by space
and time.   Accordingly, he is "incomprehensible, inestimable,
impassible, beyond want of anything," etc. (de pr. i. 1. 5 ; ii.
4. 4 ; iii. 5. 2.  c. Cels. viii. 8, 21).   "He is in every part sol-
itary (μονάς) and, so to speak, a unit (ἑνάς), at once mind and
the source whence is derived the beginning of all intellectual
nature or mind" (de pr. i. 1. 6).   But this Source of the world
is, on the other hand, conceived of as a personality.   He is

the Creator, Preserver, and Governor of the world (δημιουργήσας, συνέχων, κυβερνῶν; c. Cels. iii. 40; cf. vi. 79). In this government he is just and good : "This one and the same [God] is just and good, the God of the law and of the gospels ; he does good with justice, and punishes with goodness " (de pr. ii. 5. 3). The spirit of man attains a relative knowledge of God, and this in proportion as he severs himself from matter (de pr. i. 1. 7).

(b) The One God is primarily God the Father. We recognize him in the Son, who is his image, his radiant crown, his wisdom (sapientia) and his Logos (de princ. i. 2. 8, 2 f.). The Son proceeds from the Father, not by any kind of division, but in a spiritual way, somewhat as his will (de pr. i. 2. 6). Since everything in God is eternal, the begetting of the Son is also an eternal act : "The Father did not beget the Son and set him free after he was begotten, but he is always begetting him" (in Hierem. hom. ix. 4; de pr. i. 2. 4 : eterna ac sempiterna generatio). Accordingly the Son has no temporal beginning. "There is not when he was not" (Orig. in Athanas. de decr. syn. Nic. 27; de pr. i. 2. 9. f.; iv. 28; in Rom. i. 5. Afterward, in Joh. i. 22 : κτίσας; c. Cels. v. 37, fin. : "the eldest of all created things "). Upon the basis of this, the relation to the Father is that of unity of substance : "a vapor of the power, virtus, of God, an emanation of his glory . . . they show most clearly that there is in the Son a communion of substance with the Father. For an emanation (aporrhoea) is seen to be homousian,[1] i. e., of one substance with the body of which it is an emanation, or vapor " (in Hebrew fragment, Lommatzsch, xxiv. 359). If the Son is thus one with the Father through possession of the same nature (οὐσία), he is yet, on the other hand, himself a being, a separate hypostasis, or complete in his own subsistence (in propria subsistentia effectus) (de pr. i. 2. 2, 9).[2]  There are two hypos-

---

[1] Upon the term, ὁμοούσιος, whose meaning is here rightly given, compare supra, p. 101, n., and especially ZAHN, Marcell v. Ancyra, p. 11 ff. HATCH, Griechentum u. Christentum, pp. 202, 204. The word stood also, perhaps, in the original text of Clem. Adumbr. (Zahn, Forsch. iii. 87): secundum aequalitatem substantiae unum cum patre consistit (cf., for its signification, Clement, Str. ii. 16, p. 467).

[2] The terms, οὐσία and ὑπόστασις, are, in themselves, identical, both signifying primarily "substance." The former is Platonic, the latter Stoic. But a discrimination begins to appear in Origen, according to which ὑπόστασις indicates the οὐσία ἰδία, or personal mode of existence (e. g., in Joh. ii. 6; x. 21, it is held that "the Son does not differ from the Father in number, but the two are one, not only in nature, οὐσία, but also in attributes ; that for certain purposes, κατά τινας ἐπινοίας, the Father and the Son are said to be different, not according to hypostasis, c. Cels. viii. 12. in cant., cant. iii.) and οὐσία the substance. Cf. BIGG, l. c., p. 163 f.; also HATCH, Griechentum u. Christentum, p. 203 ff., and the terms substantia and persona in Tertullian.

tases here, but One God (Origen cites Acts 4. 32). "Therefore we worship the Father of truth and the true Son, being two
things in hypostasis, but one in sameness of thought and in harmony, and in sameness of will" (c. Cels. viii. 12). The two
hypostases have the same will and the same activity (cf. de pr.
i. 2. 12; in Joh. xiii. 36: "to there being no longer two wills,
but one will").

The ὁμοούσιος appears to require the complete equality of the
divinity of the Son and the Father. None the less, we meet with
Subordinationistic features in Origen. The Son is the "second
God" (c. Cels. v. 39; cf. in Joh. vi. 23). He is God, but as
the image of the Father. He is not the absolutely Good and
True, but he is good and true as an emanation and image of the
Father (de pr. i. 2. 13, a Greek fragment; iv. 35; in Joh. xiii.
25; xxxii. 18; in Matt. xv. 10, etc. Compare, on the contrary, in Matt. xiv. 7 init.; c. Cels. iii. 41; vi. 47 fin.). The
same is true of their activity. Christ is the executive officer
(ὑπηρέτης) of the Father, carrying out his instructions, as, e. g.,
at the creation (c. Cels. vi. 60; ii. 9). This tendency in Origen appears also in his refusal to sanction unconditionally the
addressing of prayer to Jesus. Petition is to be addressed to the
Father, and is presented to him by Christ (de orat. 15, 16 fin.,
14 fin.; c. Cels. viii. 13). Yet in other passages he maintains
that we should pray only to the Father and to Christ, to the latter that he may bear it before the Father (c. Cels. v. 4, 11; 8,
26). The prayer to Christ which is widely prevalent in the
church (e. g., Celsus in Origen viii. 12: ὑπερθρησκεύουσι. Origen himself, ib. viii. 67. de orat. 16 init.) is not forbidden, but
Origen has dogmatic objections to it. Thus Origen's doctrine
of the Logos reflects the conception of his age. Christ is God
as is the Father, like him eternal; yet he is the "second God,"
and dependent upon the Father.

(c) Whilst some philosophers thus agree with Christian teaching in the doctrine concerning the Son, the doctrine concerning
the Holy Ghost must be derived solely from revelation (de pr. 1.
3. 1-4). He is active, not like the Logos in all intelligent beings,
but only in the souls of the saints. It is in harmony with this
limitation that he is represented as inferior to the Logos: "The
Son is less than the Father . . . for he is second to the Father;
yet the Holy Spirit is lower, extending to the saints alone" (de
pr. i. 3. 5, 8). But he, too, is uncreated (de pr. i. 3. 3). As
everything else, so he was brought into being through the Son:
"all things having come into existence through the Son, the
Holy Spirit is more honorable than all, and in the [front] rank
of all those things created by the Father through the Son" (in

Joh. ii. 6). The hypostasis, as well as the divinity, of the Holy Spirit, is firmly maintained. There is a lack, however, of clear definition. The Father bestows existence, the Logos rationality, the Holy Spirit holiness (de pr. i. 3. 5), and also the " substance of the charismata which come from God " (in Joh. ii. 6).

Origen is, of course, familiar with the term, Trinity (in Joh. v. 17 ; vi. 17 ; in Jes. hom. i. 4 ; iv. 1, etc.). In the Latin translation, and also in De principiis, the term is often of doubtful genuineness.

3. God loved Jacob and hated Esau, and we constantly observe the most glaring contrasts in the fortunes of men. This is to be explained, not by the arbitrary decree of God, but by the freedom of the creature (de pr. ii. 9. 2, 5). Since everything in God is eternal, his creative activity must be so (ib. i. 2. 10). The Son serves him here as Mediator. A definite number of incorporeal spiritual beings, originally all alike, was at first created (ib. ii. 9. 6). To these belonged, however, free-will ($a\dot{v}\tau\varepsilon\xi o\acute{v}\sigma\iota o\nu$), which is inseparable from their existence. But their moral decisions were different. Man, who was intellect ($vo\ddot{v}s$), by reason of his fall from God, cooled down into soul ($\psi v\chi\acute{\eta}$), since he lost his participation in the divine fire (de pr. ii. 8. 3; Origen derives $\psi v\chi\acute{\eta}$ from $\psi v\chi\rho\acute{o}s$). The condition of all creatures is regulated by their respective merits (meritum, ib. i. 8. 2 ; ii. 9. 7). God has bestowed upon all creatures a material corporeity. Their bodies were framed to correspond with their merit—those of divinities, thrones, and powers were light and ethereal ; those of the stars, which are also living beings (cf. Plato and Philo), brilliant ; those of Satan and the devils, as being the creatures who fell first and more deeply than others, coarse and dark. Between the two classes is the corporeal being of men, "who, on account of the very great deficiencies of their minds, needed bodies more crass and substantial " (de pr. iii. 5. 4 ; ii. 1. 1-4). This accounts for the origination of the world, which hence had a beginning in time (ib. iii. 5. 3). This world itself is a judgment before the final judgment ; thus in the most literal sense, " the history of the world is the judgment of the world." The place and country, circumstances of birth, etc., are appointed to everyone in accordance with his condition in the pre-existent state (ib. ii. 9. 8). This explains the infinite variety in the world, which is a result of the exercise of free-will. But God thus attests his righteousness as well as his goodness. To everyone was given that to which he was entitled ; but God brought the countless contradictions "into the harmony of one world " (ib. ii. 9. 6 f.). This world, accordingly, makes an impression of harmony, and God finds means to

make even the sins of the wicked—for which he is not responsible
—serviceable to the whole (c. Cels. iv. 54, 70 ; in Num. hom.
xiv. 2).

4. The Logos, from eternity active as the principle of reason
and as the demiurge (c. Cels. iv. 81 ; vi. 47, 60 ; vii. 70 :
" governing all things ; " cf. in Joh. vi. 23), became man for
our deliverance.   He took upon himself human nature (ἀνθρωπίνη
φύσις, c. Cels. iii. 28), and was God and man (c. Cels. vii. 17),
the God-man (θεάνθρωπος, de pr. ii. 6. 3).   The divinity remains unchanged, continuing upon the throne (c. Cels. iv. 5).
Thus also Christ is a real man, with body and soul (c. Cels. iii. 28,
41 ; ii. 31).   The soul of Jesus was, like all others, free in the
state of pre-existence.   It, from the beginning, surrendered itself to the Logos ("the entire receiving the entire").   Yea, it
grew into an indissoluble union with the Logos (following 1 Cor.
6. 17): "It was made essentially one spirit with it" (de pr. ii.
6. 3, 6.   c. Cels. iii. 41 ; v. 39 ; vi. 47 f.).   This soul constituted the connecting link between the Logos and the flesh (de
pr. i. 1).   The flesh of Christ was produced in an unusual way
(c. Cels. 1. 69 f.), but was capable of suffering like any human
body (c. Cels. ii. 23 ; iii. 25 fin.).   It is a mystery beyond all
mysteries how we are to believe that the word and wisdom of
God were "within the limitations (*intercircumscriptionem*)
of that man who appeared in Judea . . . If one thinks him
God, he sees him to be mortal ; if one thinks him human, he
views him, having conquered the kingdom of death, returning
with spoils from the dead . . . thus is demonstrated the reality
of both natures in one and the same [person]" (de pr. ii. 6. 2).
After the incarnation, Logos, soul, and body constitute one
unity : " For the soul and the body of Jesus became, especially
after the incarnation (οἰκονομία), one with the Logos of God "
(c. Cels. ii. 9).   There was one person, which united in itself
divinity and humanity : " The one being was more than one in
mind " (ἐπινοίᾳ, c. Cels. ii. 64 init.).   He was a composite
being : "We say that he became something composite"
(σύνθετον τι χρῆμα; c. Cels. i. 66 ; cf. ib.: " Concerning the
composition, τοῦ συνθέτου, and of what [entities] the incarnate
Jesus was composed ").   Origen earnestly strives to maintain
intact the unity of the person and the integrity of the union of
the two natures.   In this he does not, indeed, succeed.   God
dwells in a man (c. Cels. i. 66, 68 ; de pr. iv. 3 : substantially
filled, *substantialiter repletus*, with God).   Divinity and humanity are yet not made one ; the divinity suffers nothing (c. Cels. iv.
15 : "Learn that the Logos remaining Logos in nature, τῇ οὐσίᾳ,
does not suffer any of the things which the body or the soul

suffers . . . as though it had become flesh;" cf. viii. 42).
"For the dying Jesus is a man" (in Joh. xxviii. 14. c. Cels.
vii. 16). As a man, he really suffered and really died (c. Cels.
ii. 16). His soul then preached in Hades (ib. ii. 43; cf. 16).
He really rose from the dead, and his body existed in a state
between the material and the psychic modes of existence (c.
Cels. ii. 62; cf. 64-66). After the ascension the human was
entirely absorbed in the divine. "But the exaltation of the
Son of man . . . this was the being no longer other than the
Logos, but the same with it" (in Joh. xxxii. 17; in Hierem.
hom. xv. 6; in Luc. hom. 29). The Lord now dwells omnipresent in the supramundane world : "Yet he is everywhere and
pervades the universe, but we cannot know him anywhere beyond that circumscribed body which, when located in our body
upon the earth, he possessed among men" (de pr. ii. 11. 6).
Cf. H. Schultz, loc. cit., 225 ff., 369 ff.

5. If we inquire for the work of Christ, we find the dominant thought to be, that Christ was physician, teacher, lawgiver,
and example. As he in olden time revealed the truth in philosophers and prophets, so he now brought to the world a new law,
which is designed for all and which has found acceptance from
all (e. g., c. Cels. iv. 4, 22, 32). Inasmuch as he brought the
saving doctrines (σωτήρια δόγματα, de pr. iv. 2), the precepts of
the gospel (praecepta evangelii, ib. 24), he is the lawgiver of
Christians (c. Cels. iii. 7). He is to Christianity what
Moses was to Israel (c. Cels. ii. 52, 75; iv. 4; v. 51; vii. 26;
viii. 5, 53). This law was intelligible, since, as the necessities
of the case required, reward and punishment were attached to it
(c. Cels. iii. 79). He appeared as a physician for sinners, as a
teacher of those who had become pure (c. Cels. iii. 62). His
law is "the law of nature, i. e., of God," as contrasted with
"the law written upon tablets" (ib. v. 37). Its essential contents are : the knowledge and worship of the One God, the Creator; faith in Jesus; the fulfilling of his commandments in a
virtuous life; the promise of salvation and threatening of eternal ruin (c. Cels. v. 51, 53; vii. 17, 48 f.; viii. 57, 51 : "The
whole foundation of the faith is God, with the promises through
Christ concerning the righteous and the announcements of punishment concerning the wicked"). To this is added the life of
Christ as the "model of a virtuous life" (c. Cels. i. 68; viii.
17, 56; de pr. iii. 5. 6), particularly as a pattern in the endur-
ance of suffering (c. Cels. ii. 42). By this means we may become partakers, as far as possible, of the divine nature (de pr.
iv. 31). Origen gives expression already to the underlying
thought of the mysticism of the Middle Ages : "And, speaking

corporeally and as flesh delivering his message, he calls to himself those who are flesh, in order that he may first cause them to be transformed into the likeness of the Logos made flesh, and after this elevate them to the beholding of himself as he was before he became flesh " (c. Cels. vi. 68).

Prominent as these ideas are in the writings of Origen, he yet recognizes the fact that the salvation of the believer is dependent upon the sufferings and death of Christ (*e. g.*, c. Cels. i. 54 ; cf. 61 fin.; ii. 23, 44 ; vii. 57): " His death is not only presented as a model for [our] dying on account of piety, but also effects the beginning and progress of our deliverance from the evil one, the devil" (ib. vii. 17). The death of Christ is accordingly presented in the light of deliverance from the power of the devil and the demons ; sacrifice for sin offered to God ; the purification of man from sin ; and the advocacy of man's cause before the Father (cf. THOMASIUS, Orig., p. 221 ff.). (*a*) Through sin the souls of men have surrendered themselves to the devil. Jesus gave his soul (life) to death as an exchange (ἀντάλλαγμα), or ransom (λύτρον), to redeem them from the devil (in Ex. hom. vi. 9 ; cf. c. Cels. i. 31. ad mart. 12 fin. in Matt. xii. 28 ; xvi. 8. LOMMATZSCH iv. 27 f. in Rom. iii. 7 ; iv. 11). But the devil was not able to retain these souls (" For he controlled us until the ransom for us, the soul of Jesus, was given to him, deceived as being able to rule over it, and not observing that he does not possess the touchstone for maintaining possession of it," in Joh. xvi. 8). Thus the souls of men —even those in Hades—became free from the power of the devil and his demons (vid. c. Cels. ii. 47 ; viii. 54, 27, 64 ; cf. as to the exorcism of demons, ib. vii. 4, 69 ; viii. 58 ; i. 67, etc.). An idea is thus expressed which was destined to play an important rôle in the History of Doctrines. (*b*) Sin requires a *propitiatio* before God, and this is effected by the bringing of a sacrifice. Christ is the high-priest, who offered to God in our behalf his own blood as a spotless sacrifice, in order that God might become gracious to us and forgive our sins (in Rom. iii. 8 ; in Num. hom. xxiv. 1). He bore in our stead the penalty belonging to us (in Joh. xxviii. 14, p. 355 : " And he assumed our sins and was bruised for our iniquities, and the penalty which was our due in order to our discipline and the reception of peace came upon him "). Since Christ thus, as the Head of the church, intervenes for us, God is reconciled to us and we to God (in Rom. iv. 8). This work of reconciliation extends beyond the world of men to the realm of the angels (in Joh. i. 40 ; in Matt. xiii. 8 ; c. Cels. vii. 17). Origen even seems to hint at a continuation of the sufferings of Christ in heaven (de pr. iv. 25, a

Greek fragment in Jerome). Thus the sufferings of Christ constitute a sacrifice which is offered to God as an atonement for sin,
while at the same time his soul was delivered to Satan as a ransom. (*c*) Christ continues through all ages his redeeming work.
The purification of the church is always a matter of deepest concern to him as its Head (in Lev. hom. vii. 2), although he binds
it together in unity in himself ("in himself embracing all who
are subject to the Father . . . and he is himself the Head of
all," de pr. iii. 5. 6). He works from heaven to purify his followers by his divine power and by his law (c. Cels. viii. 43 ; vii.
17). Thus the divine nature begins to unite itself again with
the human race : "From that time, the divine and the human
nature began to be associated, in order that the human nature
might in fellowship with that which is divine become divine, not
in Jesus alone, but in all those receiving with their faith (μετὰ τοῦ
πιστεύειν) the course of life which Jesus taught, which leads
to God in love and in fellowship with him everyone who lives
according to the foundations of Jesus" (c. Cels. iii. 28). In
these ideas we find the germs of the later conception of redemption as a ransom (Athanasius). Christ in himself again unites
human nature with the divine (cf. Irenæus); but, concretely expressed, he does this by teaching men divine truth. He imprints
upon the hearts of men a copy of his wounds ("an imprint of
the wounds appearing in the soul by virtue of the Logos, this is
the Christ in him," c. Cels. vi. 9). Thus effecting in us that
which is divine, he is, on the other hand, the mediator (μεταξὺ ὤν)
and high-priest who presents our prayers before God and leads
us to him (c. Cels. iii. 34 ; v. 4 ; vii. 46 ; viii. 4, 26, 34, 36 f.).

We have here the conception of the work of Christ which was
characteristic of the second and third centuries. But we may
trace in it a commingling of the ancient and the modern. Christ
is, above all else, the teacher and lawgiver, the pattern, in whom
begins the deification of humanity. But he is this for us, after
all, only because he has snatched us from the power of the devil
and demoniac powers, has reconciled God to us and us to God,
and stands as mediator and high-priest between us and God.

6. (*a*) The Logos is actively engaged in imparting this salvation to men, as formerly through the moral law and the Mosaic
code, so now through the gospel (in Rom. iii. 7. 3 ; v. 1. c.
Cels. vi. 78 ; vii. 26). The latter, as has been shown, is conceived of as essentially a lawgiving and instruction. To the
doctrines are added, as further means of salvation, the mysteries.
He who has in faith accepted the teachings of Christianity is
baptized : "The washing by water, being a symbol of the
cleansing of a soul washed from every defilement (which comes)

from evil, is no less and precisely, to him who surrenders himself
to the power of the names of the adorable Trinity, the beginning and fountain of divine charismata" (in Joh. vi. 17).[1]
Baptism is not a "symbol" in the modern sense, but as Christ's
miracles of healing were symbols of the healing activity of the
Logos. Yet, as these miracles nevertheless brought real healing to
the individual in whose behalf they were performed, so baptism is
for the recipient nothing less than the beginning and fountain of
the divine blessings. It is a symbol of the purifying power of the
Logos, but for the individual it is actual purification. Through
its administration sins are forgiven and the Holy Spirit bestowed
(in Luc. hom. xxi.; in Matt. xv. 23 ; ad mart. 30 init.). It is
the "first remission of sins" (in Lev. ii. 4), which, in accordance with the custom (*observantiam*) of the church, is granted
also to children (in Lev. viii.). Above water-baptism stands
the fire-baptism of martyrdom. This washes away sins, and the
sacerdotal intercessions of the martyrs are heard by God (ad
mart. 30, 50, 34 ff.). But the mature Christian should partake
of the solid intellectual food ($\sigma\tau\epsilon\rho\epsilon\alpha\grave{\iota}\ \lambda o\gamma\iota\varkappa\alpha\grave{\iota}\ \tau\rho o\varphi\alpha\acute{\iota}$) of the eucharist (c. Cels. iii. 60). He here receives the Logos and his
words as the true food of the soul. "That bread which God
the Word declares to be his body is the nutritious word of souls,
the word proceeding from God the Word . . . And that drink
. . . is the word thirst-quenching and splendidly inebriating the
hearts of those who drink it . . . For not that visible bread
which he held in his hand, did God the Word call his body,
but the word in whose sacrament (*mysterium*) that bread was to
be broken. And not that visible drink did he call his blood, but
the word in whose sacrament that drink was to be poured out.
For the body or blood of God the Word, what else can it be
than the word which nourishes and the word which delights the
heart?" (in Matt. com. ser. 85). The word of Christ, of
which the elements are a symbol, is, therefore, the effectual
thing in the eucharist. Primarily Christ's own word, and consequently the words of the apostles and their successors, are the
body and blood of the Lord (in Lev. hom. vii. 5). According
to this, the elements possess merely a symbolical significance.
The word alone, which is spoken over them, brings benefit to
him who approaches the eucharist with a pure heart and conscience (in Matt. xi. 14).[2]

---

[1] The text of Lommatzsch is here amended to agree with the citation in
Basil. de spir. sanct. 29. 73.

[2] Origin himself occasionally employs another type of expression (*e. g.*,
c. Cels. viii. 33 : "We eat the bread which has, through the prayer, become
the body, a thing holy and hallowing those who receive it with a proper pur-

(*b*) The New Testament proffer of salvation through doctrine is accepted by man in faith. (*a*) He is able to do this by virtue of the freedom of will which is inseparable from human nature. It is true, the soul of man at the fall before the creation of the world became disobedient to God, and sin is hence universal (cf. under 3, p. 151). "We are born to sinning" (c. Cels. iii. 66, 62; cf. Clem., supra, p. 141). "No one is pure even immediately after birth, not even though his life should be but a single day," Job 14. 4 f. (in Matt. xv. 23). What need would there otherwise be for infant baptism? (in Lev. hom. viii. 3; in Rom. v. 9). To the sin of the pre-natal existence is now added the further defilement involved in the union of the soul with the body (in Luc. hom. xiv.; in Lev. viii. 3, 4; c. Cels. vii. 50). Account must be made, still further, of the dominion of the devil and demons over the human soul, and the entrenchment of sin in the soul through the power of evil passions and under the influence of evil example (de pr. iii. 2. 2; c. Cels. iii. 69). However positively the sinfulness of man is thus maintained, it does not exclude his free-will (αὐτεζούσιον), the continuous and inamissible capacity for freely deciding for the good or the evil; for the will has only the office, according to the Greek conception, of carrying out the decisions of the reason (de pr. iii. 1. 3). Only upon the recognition of human freedom can we understand the ethical exhortations of the Scriptures, and only thus is the moral character of man preserved (de pr. iii. 1. 20). There are, indeed, scriptural passages which appear to confirm the Gnostic doctrine of predestination (*e. g.*, Ex. 4. 21. Hos. 11. 19. Mk. 4. 12. Rom. 9. 16, 18 ff.), but these may be differently interpreted (de pr. iii. 1. 7 ff.). It remains, therefore, an indisputable fact, that free will is preserved in the salvation of man (ib. iii. 5. 8; 3. 4). Scripture varies in its representations of the subject: "It attributes everything to us," and "it seems to attribute everything to God" (de pr. iii. 1. 22). The truth is, that God endowed man, not with conquest (the *vincere*), but with the power of conquest (the *vincendi virtus;* ib. iii. 2. 3), *i. e.*, through the rational nature of man and the doctrine of Christ. As a teacher promises "to improve those who come to him, so the divine Logos promises to take away evil from those who come to him . . . not from those who are unwilling, but from those who, being sick, commit themselves to the physician " (de pr. iii. 1. 15). God offers salvation, but free man apprehends it, and is

pose;" cf. in Ex. hom. xiii. 3). He is also aware that the more simple have "a commoner interpretation" of the eucharist (in Joh. xxxii. 16).

always himself active in its appropriation (ib. iii. 1. 18). He
may, however, always rely upon the divine assistance (*adjutorium;*
ib. iii. 2. 5, 2). Cf. MEHLHORN, Die Lehre von d. menschl.
Freiheit, according to Origen's περὶ ἀρχῶν, Ztschr. f. KG., ii.
234 ff. (β) In this sense, faith itself is an act of the free-will
as well as an effect of divine grace (cf. c. Cels. viii. 43). The
object of faith is the doctrines (δόγματα) of the church (in Joh.
xxxii. 9; c. Cels. i. 13). This faith is confidence (συγκατάθεσις),
often dependent primarily upon outward motives, such as fear,
or the recognition of authority. It needs to be elevated to
knowledge and understanding. It is better to "assent to the
dogmas with the reason and wisdom" (μετὰ λόγου καί σοφίας)
than "with bare faith" (c. Cels. 1. 13; cf. also *supra*, under
1). Many gradations may be traced in this process (in Matt.
xii. 15). Knowledge is the goal. But the unfolding of faith
is inconceivable without a corresponding moral conduct upon
the part of the individual. The Logos acts not only as teacher,
but also as physician (cf. supra). Threats of punishment and
promise of reward are spurs to piety. Thus faith is also the
way to virtue (c. Cels. iii. 69). A faith without works is impossible (*e. g.*, in Joh. xix. 6). If with such a conception of
faith (lacking the decisive element of an inward, obedient, and
trustful acceptance), Paul's doctrine of justification does not
receive an unqualified acknowledgment, this must be regarded as
merely an evidence of religious tact and of real Christian temper. Origen, in his commentary upon Romans, reproduced the
Pauline doctrine of justification, but was not able to maintain
himself at the altitude of that conception. Faith is sufficient,
indeed, for righteousness, but it finds its consummation in works,
and suffices only because it has ever works in view. "Righteousness cannot be imputed to an unrighteous man. Christ
justifies only those who have received new life from the example
of his resurrection." Accordingly, the forgiveness of sins and
the salvation and eternal happiness of men depend, not only upon
faith, but more upon their repentance and good works (cf. *e. g.*,
in Lev. hom. xii. 3; ii. 4; c. Cels. iii. 71, 57; viii. 10). "The
salvation of believers is accomplished in two ways, through the
acknowledgment (*agnitionem*) of faith and through the perfection
of works" (in cant., p. 84; cf. *institutionibus ac disciplinis*, de
pr. i. 6. 3). Repentance consists primarily in the confession of
one's sins to God, since he is the true physician of souls (in Ps.
36; hom. 1. 5); but also to one's fellowmen (ib.). In the latter case it is necessary, however, to find a man, whether clerical
or lay, who has the Spirit, who is devoted to the service of God,
and who is like the merciful high-priest Christ, as were the

apostles (de or. 28. 8 ; in Ps. 37 ; hom. 6). Repentance has here, it will be observed, an inward character, not a legal, as in the West. Origen's moral ideal embraces, first of all, the Gnostic contemplation of God, and also a strongly ascetic element (emphasis upon virginity and a corresponding depreciation of marriage ; c. Cels. vii. 48 ; i. 26 fin.; viii. 55 ; commendation of those who, separate from the world, abstain from the cares of this life, in Lev. xi. 1 ; in different vein, Clem., supra, p. 145, n. ).

(c) The church is the congregation of believers, the assembly of the righteous, the "city of God " (c. Cels. iii. 30 ; cf. vii. 31). Outside the church there is no salvation (in Jos. hom. iii. 5). Individual Christians are, indeed, also priests (in Lev. hom. iv. 6 ; vi. 5 ; ix. 1, 8 ; xiii. 5); but to the priests in the special sense of the term belong special prerogatives. It is theirs to announce the forgiveness of sins ; but this may be done only by a pious priest (in Lev. hom. v. 3 ; cf. BIGG, p. 215 ff. ). Further, Origen discriminates between the empirical church and the church properly so called (κυρίως, e. g., de or. 20 ; in Num. hom. xxvi. 7 ; in Jos. hom. xxi. 1. Cf. SEEBERG, Begriff d. chr. Kirche, i. 27 ff. ).

7. The process of purification and instruction begun on earth is continued after death. The good, clothed in a refined spiritual body, enter "paradise," or "a certain place of education, an auditorium or school of souls." Now are solved for the spirit all the problems which have been presented here in nature, history, and faith (de pr. ii. 11. 4, 5). The wicked, on the other hand, experience the fire of judgment. This is a "flame of one's own fire " (proprii ignis), whose material is the individual's own sinfulness tortured by the conscience (de pr. ii. 10. 4). In this we are to see, not a permanent punishment, as imagined by the simple, but a process of purification : " The fire of God's vengeance avails for the purgation of souls " (ib. § 6). " It befits the good God to destroy wickedness by the fire of punishments " (c. Cels. vi. 72 ; cf. v. 15 ; vi. 26). It is a purifying fire (πῦρ καθάρσιον, c. Cels. v. 17).[1] While the wicked are thus purified, the good mount up from sphere to sphere to meet Christ (de pr. ii. 11. 5). But the former as well as the latter, although it be only after infinite ages, also attain the goal (de pr. iii. 6. 6). Then, with the day of the second coming of Christ, will come the end. Now occurs the resurrection of the

---

[1] This idea, which found recognition also in the West (Cypr. ep. 55. 20), reminds us of the ancient conception of the purifying power of the fire of Hades, e. g., Virgil Aen. vi. 742 : Wickedness unconsummated is purged or consumed by fire ; cf. Dieterich, Nekyia, 1893, p. 199 ff.; also, Rohde, Psyche, ii. ed. 2, 128 f.

bodies of men—glorified, pneumatic bodies (de pr. iii. 6. 4-9; but cf. ii. 3. 7 ; iii. 6. 1, in Jerome's translation in Redepenning's edition, p. 318 f., and also H. SCHULTZ, l. c., p. 220 f.). God is now all in all, and all created things live in full vision of the Godhead (iii. 6. 3). Here we shall understand the "everlasting gospel," which is related to the temporal gospel as is the latter to the law (ib. iii. 6. 8 ; iv. 25). But, since there is even yet the possibility of a change in the attitude of will of a free agent, it always remains possible that this consummation of earth's drama may prove to be but temporary, and that freedom of will may call other worlds into existence (cf. de pr. iii. 6. 3, in Jerome's translation ; also c. Cels. iv. 69 ; per contra, de pr. iii. 6. 6 : "in which state they always and immutably remain ").

8. Tested by the original teachings of Christianity, the Alexandrine theology, as compared with the doctrinal development of the second century, indicates in all points a progression, but in very few particulars an actual advance. The Alexandrine Fathers gave to Christian literature, in form as well as in scientific method, a position of equal rank with other literature of the age, and prescribed for the future the method of theological statement. They are the first dogmaticians. But they knew no other way of accomplishing their task than by recasting the permanent elements of the church's doctrine in harmony with a religious philosophy of Grecian character (cf. the judgment of Porphyry in Eus. h. e. vi. 19. 7 f.). What the Apologists were compelled to do, these men willingly sought to accomplish. In their philosophy the elements of the Christian tradition are commingled in an amazing way with ideas and problems of the heathen world. It is easy to show the wavering character of the movement and the illogical nature of the presentation. The traditional elements are retained *en masse* (by Origen in detail). But in regard to these, nothing more was required than a simple assent, which is the proper attitude toward *dogmas* and a *law*. Beyond this lay knowledge and understanding, *i. e.*, of the philosophically-framed doctrine. The curious fabric thus constructed was glorified as the wisdom of the wise ; not, indeed, without some perception of the real nature of Christianity, such as was in danger of vanishing from the consciousness of the unitiated (ἁπλούστεροι).

The significance of this theology for later times lay in the fact that it preserved the traditional doctrines of the church in a form which impressed its own generation (Trinity, divinity and humanity of Christ, soteriological formulas, baptism and its effect, elements in the appropriation of Christianity, resurrection). In Christology, inferences were drawn from the orthodox view which were genuine logical deductions (cf. Origen). On the other hand, no little foreign material was given currency as Christian, and the foreign elements of the preceding age were carried to the most extreme conclusions (definition of God, conception of faith, moralism and asceticism in Christian life, limitation of the work of redemption to doctrine and example, definitions of sin and free-will). But it was just in this way that this theology succeeded in delivering the death-blow to Gnosticism. Whatever was influential in the latter, it also possessed, and possessed in connection with the faith of the church.

A general view of the historical development thus far traced leads to the conviction that the Christianity of the Apostolic Fathers was that which had characterized the church of the second century. Everywhere we note a consciousness of the sinner's lost condition, and the conviction that he can be saved only through grace, through Christ, through the sacred ordinances of the church; but everywhere also the heathen moralism —everywhere the zealous effort to hold fast to the ideas of primitive Christianity and surrender to the enemy not an iota of the sacred tradition. The more objective an asserted fact, and the more distinctly it pointed upward, the greater was the certainty attaching to it; the profounder its appeal downward to the heart of the believer, the more waveringly was it received. The former became an object of contemplation; the latter was more and more misunderstood. To the former, assent was given only in connection with suspicious heterogeneous material, and with a portentous employment of heathen ideas (Logos, faith); but the truths of the "Rule of Faith," however perverted may have been the relation of the individual to them, were, at least in general outline, preserved intact against the assaults of heathenism and a heathenized Christianity. This, together with the initial attempts at a scholarly interpretation of these truths, constitutes the significance of the theology developing during the present period.[1]

[1] What has been said applies also, with some modifications, to the faith of the common people. Cf. the discussion of Celsus, written probably not long after the middle of the second century, and occasional remarks of Origen, *e. g.*, the sharp contrasting of the "Great Church" with the Gnostic parties (Cels. in Orig. c. Cels. v. 63); the faith in One God; the rude conception of his Person (de pr. iv. 8 fin.; Cels. c. Cels. iv. 71; vi. 61 ff.; the unique position assigned to the adorable Person of Christ ("your God," "they reverently worship," Cels. in Orig. c. Cels. viii. 41, 39, 12, 14; cf. iii. 41; vi. 10; vii. 36: Orig. de or. 16 init.); the hymns recognizing the divinity of Christ (Eus. h. e. v. 28. 5; vii. 30. 10; the hymn at the close of Clement's Paedag.; Tert. c. Jud. 7; Mart. Polyc. 17. 2; Lucian's de morte Peregrin. ii. 13; the Roman mock crucifix, etc.; the emphasis upon bare faith (Cels. l. c. i. 9, 12); the epitomizing of Christianity in the declaration, "the world is crucified to me,"

11

## CHAPTER IV.

### SEPARATE DOCTRINES AND GENERAL CONCEPTION OF CHRISTIANITY IN THE THIRD CENTURY.

The period under review had a decisive influence upon the construction of dogmatics. It was then that conditions and views asserted themselves in connection with the popular faith with which dogmatic theology was compelled to deal, which it could neither deny nor ignore. A method was inaugurated by which it was sought to harmonize these and explain their significance. There was now an ecclesiastical doctrine and a doctrinal church. Heresy had come to be definitely noted. Every new development of doctrine was so regarded. The great extension of the church produced new perils and new practical problems. A new outlook had been won, and new requirements must be met. The secularization of the church, which had been already deplored in the second century,[1] was greatly accelerated in the third, and with it there became manifest also a secularization of the religious sentiment. This explains both the general type of doctrine prevalent and the modifications in the views concerning repentance and the church, as also the strenuous opposition to all doctrinal differences, particularly to the attempts, reaching back into the second century, to reconcile the divinity of Christ with the principle of Monotheism. We begin with the latter.

### § 16. *Monarchianism.*

DYNAMISTIC Monarchians: Hippol. Refut. vii. 35. Ps.-Tert. adv. omn. haer. 23 (8). The small Labyrinth, Eus. h. e. v. 28. Epiph. h. 54.

PAUL OF SAMOSATA: Eus. h. e. vii. 27-30. Epiph. h. 65. Fragments in ROUTH, Reliq. sacr. iii. ed. 2, 300 ff. MAI, Vet. scr. nova coll. vii. 68 f.

PATRIPASSIANS: Tert. adv. Prax. Hippol. c. Noët. Refut. ix. 6 12. Epiph. h. 62. Eus. h. e. vi. 33. Compare HARNACK, PRE. x. 178 ff. HILGENFELD, Ketzergesch., p. 609 ff. THOMASIUS, DG. i. 168 ff.

The divinity of Christ is, in the second century, a recognized fact (cf. supra, pp. 63 f., 70, 75, 78, 113 f., 124 ff., 143, 149 f.,

etc. (Gal. 6. 4. Cels. l. c. v. 64); grace (Cels. l. c. iii. 71, 78); the vivid, sensuously-colored hopes of the future life (*e. g.*, Orig. de pr. ii. 11. 2; cf. in Method. de resur. 20. Cels. l. c., viii. 49; iv. 11; v. 14; vii. 28); the strong faith in the power of the devil and demons, who are to be overcome by Christian faith through the use of scriptural citations, etc. (Orig. c. Cels. i. 24, 25, 46, 67; ii. 8; iii. 24; v. 45; vii. 69; viii. 37, 58, 59, 61).

[1] Cf. the strictures of Irenæus upon those Christians who, for personal reasons and on account of false brethren, sever themselves from the church (iv. 33. 7; 30. 3; iii. 11. 9; iv. 26. 2; cf. Eus. h. e. v. 15, with 20. 1).

161, n.). The learned attempts to define the relation of Christ to the Father (Logos, second God) were, indeed, far from satisfactory. Christ was regarded as "a God," and his human nature was asserted. The Logos-christology was, in the main, framed in such a way as to guard the unity of God. But when the Logos, proceeding from the Father, assumes an independent existence, he is then regarded as "the second God," and thus Monotheism is endangered. Monarchianism made an effort to reconcile Monotheism, the most precious treasure of Christianity as contrasted with the heathen world, with the divinity of Christ without resort to the expedient of the "second God." In this consists its historical significance. It reminded the church that there is only One personal God. To this task it addressed itself, under the guidance of the two-fold principle: (1) making the man Jesus the bearer of the divine Spirit, (2) recognizing in Christ the person of the Father himself: "Since they reflected . . . that God is one, they thought it was not possible for them to maintain this opinion unless they should hold the belief, either that Christ was such a man, or that he was truly God the Father" (Novatian, de trin. 30; cf. Tert. adv. Prax. 3: "Therefore they charge that two or three Gods are preached by us, but imagine that they are worshipers of the one God . . . they say, ' We hold a monarchy.'" Hippol. Refut. ix. 11 : Ditheists, δίθεοι, Epiph. h. 62. 2 ; Hilar. de Trin. i. 16).

1. *Dynamistic Monarchianism.* The "Alogi" are generally treated under this heading, but improperly so. Epiphanius, indeed, was disposed thus to classify them (h. 54. 1), but, following the authority before him, recognizes their orthodoxy (h. 51. 4; cf. Iren. and supra, p. 108, n.).

(*a*) THEODOTUS, the Fuller, brought this doctrine to Rome about A. D. 190: "Maintaining in part the doctrines commonly held among those of the true church concerning the beginning of all things, confessing that all things were made by God, he yet holds . . . that Christ came into existence in some such way as this : that Jesus is, indeed, a man born of a virgin according to the counsel of the Father—living in common with all men, and most pious by birth ; and that afterward at his baptism in the Jordan, the Christ from above, having descended in the form of a dove, entered into him ; wherefore miraculous powers were not exerted by him before the Spirit, which he says is Christ, having descended, was manifested in him. Some think that he did not become God until the descent of the Spirit ; others, until after his resurrection from the dead " (Hipp. Ref. vii. 35 ; cf. Ps.-Tert. 8). Pope Victor excommunicated him (small Lab. in Eus. v. 28. 6). (*b*) In the time of Zephyrinus this view again

appeared under the leadership of Asclepiodotus and Theodotus,
the Money-changer (Eus. v. 28. 7 ; see also 17). Here again
it was held : "He asserts that this man Christ (springs) only
from the Holy Spirit and the Virgin Mary" (Ps.-Tert. 8). He
was inferior to Melchizedek (see Epiph. h. 55. 8). But this
"bare man" was at his baptism endowed with the Spirit of God
(Hipp. vii. 36). The attempt was made to prove this doctrine
exegetically, calling in the aid of textual criticism and subtle
logical distinctions (Eus. v. 28. 13-18 ; cf., for examples, Epiph.
h. 54). Nevertheless, these men claimed to teach the ancient
confessional doctrine. "For they say that all the former teachers, and the apostles themselves, both received and taught these
things which they now proclaim, and that the truth of the gospel
message was preserved until the times of Victor . . . but that
the truth was perverted by his successor, Zephyrinus" (small
Lab. in Eus. v. 28. 3 ; cf. the charge brought against them by
their orthodox opponent : "They have impiously slighted the
divine Scriptures and repudiated the canon of the ancient faith,
and have not known Christ," ib. § 13). It is beyond question
that the claim of conformity to the teachings of the church was,
speaking generally, without foundation. The Monarchian doctrine is not an attempt to reproduce the original Christian view,
as is evident from a comparison of its tenets with the apostolic
portrayal of Christ as the Lord of heaven and earth (per contra,
Harnack, DG.; ed. 3, 673 f.). The origin of this form of
Monarchianism may be very easily traced to the Logos-idea—the
Logos, or Spirit, being conceived not as a personal being, but as
a divine energy. The attempt to establish a congregation of adherents to this view, although made at personal sacrifice, was not
successful (small Lab. in Eus. v. 28. 8-12). (c) After the
middle of the third century we find this view still advocated by
Artemas (or Artemon) at Rome, and he appears to have gathered about him a congregation of his own (Eus. h. e. vii. 30. 17).

(d) But its most important representative is Paul of
Samosata. This imperious and worldly-minded Bishop of
Antioch (from about A. D. 260 ; cf. encycl. letter of Synod of
Antioch, in Eus. h. e. vii. 30. 7-15) taught "Jesus Christ from
below" (κάτωθεν, in contrast with ἀνωθεν, ib. vii. 30. 11). In
the man Jesus, born of the virgin, dwelt the divine Wisdom.
This is not a separate hypostasis, but exists in God as human
reason exists in man : "That in God is always his Logos and his
Spirit, as in the heart of man his own reason (logos); and that
the Son of God is not in a hypostasis, but is in God himself . . .
But that the Logos came and dwelt in Jesus, who was a man ; and
thus, they say, God is one . . . one God the Father, and his Son

in him, as the reason (*logos*) in a man " (Epiph. h. 65. 1). A parallel to this is seen in the indwelling of Wisdom in the prophets, except that this indwelling occurred in a unique way in Christ as the temple of God : " In order that neither might the anointed of David be a stranger to Wisdom, nor Wisdom dwell so largely in any other. For it was in the prophets, much more in Moses ; and in many leaders, but much more in Christ as in a temple." But also : "He who appeared was not Wisdom, for he was not susceptible of being found in an outward form . . . for he is greater than the things that are seen " (fragm. disput. c. Malchionem in Routh, Rel. sacr. iii. 301 ; in Leontius, ib. p. 311). As to the mode of this union, Paul teaches that the man Jesus was from his birth anointed with the Holy Ghost. Because he remained immovably steadfast in this relationship and kept himself pure, the power of working miracles became his, and, having been " born pure and righteous," he overcame the sin of Adam. It is a moral union (in the way of learning and fellowship, Routh iii. 312) in the will and in love, which here meets us, not a merely natural one : " Thou shculdst not wonder that the Saviour has one will with God. For just as nature shows us a substance becoming out of many one and the same, so the nature of love makes one and the same will out of many through one and the same manifested preference." (Also : " the things obtained by the natural reason have no praise, but the things obtained by the nature of love are exceedingly praiseworthy," frag. in Mai, Vet. scr. nov. coll. vii. 68 f.; cf. Athanas. c. Arian, or. iii. 10.) Thus Jesus in his moral development united himself intimately with God by the influence of the Spirit and unity of will, thus securing the power to perform miracles and fitness to become the Redeemer, and in addition attaining a permanent oneness with God. " The Saviour, born holy and righteous, having by his struggle and sufferings overcome the sin of our progenitor, succeeding in these things, was united in character ($\tau\tilde{\eta}$ $\dot{a}\rho\epsilon\tau\tilde{\eta}$) to God, having preserved one and the same aim and effort as he for the promotion of things that are good ; and he, having preserved this inviolate, his name is called that above every name, the prize of love having been freely bestowed upon him " (Mai, l. c.). Three synods were held at Antioch to consider the matter (264-269 ; Eus. h. e. vii. 30. 4, 5). Paul at first resorted to evasions and no conclusion was reached. Finally, the presbyter Malchion vanquished him at the third synod. " He did not formerly say this, that he would not grant that in the whole Saviour was existent the only-begotten Son, begotten before the foundation of the world " (frg. disp. adv. Paul. a Malch. hab. in Routh iii. 302 ; also Pitra, Analecta sacra iii. 600 f.; iv. 424. Eus.

h. e. vii. 28, 29). The decree of the synod proclaimed the heresy of Artemas and his exclusion from the fellowship of the church (Eus. h. e. vii. 30. 16, 17).[1] But Paul retained a following and his office until, in A. D. 272, the degree of Aurelian gave the church property to the control of the one who should be upon terms of epistolary correspondence with the bishops of Italy and Rome (Eus. vii. 30. 19). This was the first time that imperial politics carried into effect a condemnatory decree of the church.[2]

2. *Patripassian Monarchianism* is the more influential and more widely prevalent form of Monarchianism. It is this form chiefly which gives to the system the historical significance noted on p. 163. It is not accidental that Rome and Egypt were the breeding places of Sabellianism and the pillars of the *homousia*. The history of the separate representatives of this party is, to some extent, obscure, and it is, therefore, difficult to keep the peculiar tenets of each distinct in our minds. Here and there we may trace a connection with the primitive form of the doctrine. The prevalent term, "Patripassians," may be traced to Tertullian (adv. Prax.). Their fundamental idea is : "For thus it is proper to state Monarchianism, saying that he who is called Father and Son is one and the same, not one from the other, but he from himself, called by name Father and Son according to the figure of the times, but that this one appearing and born of a virgin remains one . . . confessing to those who behold him that he is a Son . . . and not concealing from those

---

[1] The synod rejected also the Origenistic term, ὁμοούσιος, according to the opinion of Athanasius, because Paul understood it as teaching an equality with the divine nature (οὐσία) and not with the Father, so that there would be three natures (οὐσίαι) to be acknowledged (de synodis 45 ff.), or because Paul himself expressed the relation of the impersonal Logos to the Father by this term (thus Hilar. de synod. 81, 86).

[2] In Pseudo-Cyprian, *De montibus Sina et Sion*, the fourth chapter (Opp. Cypr. ed. Hartel iii. 108) is by no means (as Harnack, DG., i. 676 holds) to be understood as presenting a Monarchian Christology. For when it is there said : "the Lord's flesh from God the Father is called Jesus ; the Holy Spirit who descended from heaven is called Christ," this is but phraseology such as we find, *e. g.*, in Hermas, Sim. ix. 1. 1 ; Arist. Apol. 2. 6 ; Cyprian, quod idola dii non sint 11 ("the Holy Spirit assumes flesh ; God is mingled with man"); Lactant. Instit. iv. 6. 1 ; 12. 1 ; Tertul. adv. Prax. 8, 26 ; Hippol. c. Noët. 4, 16 ; Celsus in Orig. c. Cels. vi. 69, 72, 73, 78, 79 ; Apollinar. in Greg. Nyss. Antirrh. 12. See my remarks upon Arist. 2. 6. The case is different with the Christology of the *Acta disputationis Archelai et Manetis* (ab. A. D. 300, in Routh, Reliq. sacr. v. ed. 2, 38-205). Here, c. 50, the Monarchian Christology really appears : "For he who was born the son of Mary, who resolved to undertake the whole conflict because it is great, is Jesus. This is the Christ of God who descended upon him who is sprung from Mary." But the author has at once brought this idea into connection with the teaching of the church : "For God alone is *his Father by nature*, who has deigned to manifest all things to us speedily by his *Word*" (c. 33).

who approach him that he is the Father" (Hipp. Ref. ix. 10).

(*a*) PRAXEAS, a martyr of Asia Minor, came with Victor to Rome, and gained an influence over this foe of Dynamistic Monarchianism by means of his Christology as well as by his anti-montanistic tendencies. His doctrine found acceptance also in Africa (Tert. c. Prax. 1). He taught: "After that time the Father was born and the Father suffered. Jesus Christ is proclaimed as the Father born, the Father suffering, God himself, the omnipotent Lord" (Tert. adv. Prax. 2 init.). Father and Son are therefore the same person(ib. 5 init.). In support of this the Scriptures were appealed to, particularly Isa. 45. 5; Jn. x. 30; xiv. 9, 10 (ib. 18, 20). It reveals a lean-ing toward the orthodox view, employing the term, Son of God, in the Biblical sense—but at the same time an inclination toward Dynamistic Monarchianism—when distinction is, after all, made between the Father and the Son: "And in like man-ner in the one person they distinguish the two, Father and Son, saying that the Son is the flesh, *i. e.*, the man ; *i. e.*, Jesus ; but that the Father is the Spirit, *i. e.*, God, *i. e.*, Christ" (ib. 27). In this way they avoided the assertion that the Father suffered ("Thus the Son indeed suffers (*patitur*), but the Father suffers with him" (*compatitur*); ib. 29 ; cf. Hipp. Ref. ix. 12).

(*b*) NOËTUS of Smyrna and the adherents of his theory, EPIGONUS and CLEOMENES, found again at Rome in the beginning of the third century an influential centre for the dissemination of their views (Hipp. Ref. i. 7), which were the same as those of Praxeas : "That when the Father had not yet been born, he was rightly called the Father ; but when it had pleased him to sub-mit to birth, having been born, he became the Son, he of him-self and not of another" (Hipp. Ref. ix. 10). "He said that Christ is himself the Father, and that the Father himself was born and suffered and died" (Hipp. c. Noët. 1). Thus the Father also called himself to life again (ib. 3). The Scriptures require us to believe this. Thus the Son is glorified (ib. 1) and thus salvation made possible : "For Christ was God and suffered for us, being the Father himself, in order that he might be able also to save us" (ib. 2). It was a religiously-inspired interest in the full divinity of Christ which led these men to insist upon their theory, and this accounts for their wide influence. They wished to maintain that Christ was God, and yet not waver in the asser-tion of the unity of God as confessed in the church's creed : "For some simple persons (not to say inconsiderate and ignor-ant, as is always the majority of believers) since the rule of faith itself leads us from the many gods of the world to the one and

true God (cf. p. 85, n.), not understanding that he is to be believed as being one but with his own economy (οἰκονομία), are
terrified at this economy.   They think that the number and order
of the Trinity implies a division of the unity" (Tert. adv.
Prax. 3 init.).

(c)  The final form of this doctrine appears in SABELLIUS of Pentapolis (?) at Rome (under Zephyrinus and Callistus).   Father,
Son, and Spirit are only different designations of the same person, corresponding to the degree and form of his revelation.
God is, in his nature, the Father of the Son (υἱοπάτωρ, Athan.
Expos. fid. 2): " He himself is the Father ; he himself is the
Son ; he himself is the Holy Spirit—as I say that there are
three names in one object (hypostasis), either as in man, body
and soul and spirit . . . or as, if it be in the sun, being in one
object (I say) that there are three, having the energies of light-
giving and heat and  the form of roundness " (Epiph. h. 62. 1 ;
also Athanas. Orig. c. Arian. iii. 36; iv. 2,  3, 9, 13, 25, 17).
Cf. ZAHN, Marcel. v. anc. 198-216.

(d)  The Patripassian Christology had its adherents in the
West as well as in the East.   In Rome, the bishops VICTOR
(Ps.-Tert. adv. omn. haer. 8 : " after all these a certain Praxeas
introduced a heresy, which Victorinus sought to corroborate "),
ZEPHYRINUS (Hipp. Ref. ix. 7, 11), and CALLISTUS (ib. ix. 11,
12) adopted it, with the assent of a large part of the local
church.   Hippolytus and his following, who opposed it, were
charged with Ditheism.   Callistus, indeed, as bishop, upon
grounds of ecclesiastical prudence, denied his agreement with
Sabellius ; but he felt himself compelled, for the sake of consistency, to advocate a somewhat modified Monarchianistic Christology.   Father, Son, and Spirit are, of course, "one and the
same," and the Spirit who became incarnate in the Virgin is
identical with the Father, but the flesh of Jesus is to be designated
as " the Son : " " For that which is seen, which is the man, this
is the Son ; but the Spirit dwelling in the Son, this is the Father."
Therefore we should not, indeed, speak of a suffering by the
Father, but " the Father suffered with (συρπεπονθέναι) the Son "
(Hipp. Ref. ix. 12, p. 458).   But this is simply the doctrine of
Praxeas (see p. 167) used by Callistus as a formula of compromise.[1]

---

[1] A representative of this Christology in the East may yet be mentioned,
BERYL OF BOSTRA.   As we have only one sentence of Eusebius setting
forth his view, it is difficult to form a clear idea of it.  " Beryl . . . attempted to introduce certain new articles of faith, daring to say that our Saviour
and Lord did not pre-exist according to his own form of being before his coming
among men, and that he did not possess a divinity of his own, but only that of

## § 17. *Ante-Nicene Christology.*

(*a*) But Monarchianism, even in the form last noted, failed in the East also to secure general acceptance. It meets us in the third century only in quite isolated cases (COMMODIAN, Carmen apol. 278 : "Neither was he called Father until he had become Son," 618, 94, 110 ff., 198, 358, 772, 257, 363 f., 634; but see also 340). CYPRIAN classed the Patripassians with the Valentinians and Marcionites, and designated them as "pests and swords, and poisons for the perverting of the truth " (Ep. 73. 4). That even in Rome the Tertullian view was triumphant as early as A. D. 250 is manifest from the tract of Novatian, *De trinitate:* Christ is the second person of the Trinity, the Son of God, preexistent and manifesting himself already under the old covenant, one with the Father by virtue of a communion of substance

the Father committed to him" (h. e. vi. 33. 1). Origen vanquished him at a synod at Bostra about A. D. 244. The synod took occasion, in refuting him, to lay emphasis upon the human soul of Jesus (Socrates h. e. iii. 7). According to this, Beryl (1) knew nothing of a personal divinity of his own inhering in Jesus; his divinity was that of the Father. (2) He taught that Christ became a separate personality only through his incarnation. (3) He does not appear to have been led to this conclusion by the study of the inner human life of Jesus during his incarnation (?). (4) He is not charged with teaching, as did the Dynamistic Monarchians, that Jesus was a "bare man." He, therefore, probably approximated the position of the Sabellians, that it was not until the incarnation that God assumed the special mode of existence as Son (cf. sub, Marcellus of Ancyra).

Of the Libyan Sabellians we shall have occasion to speak hereafter. It may be well at this point to call attention to the fact that the "Testaments of the Twelve Patriarchs" were, during this period, interpolated by a Patripassian writer. See Sim. 6. Levi 4 ($\pi\acute{a}\vartheta o\varsigma\ \tau o\tilde{v}\ \acute{v}\psi\acute{\iota}\sigma\tau o v$); Cf. Zabul 9. Aser. 7. Benj. 9. Napht. 8). It is with mingled feelings that we turn from the acute attempts of the Monarchian theologians. They do not satisfy us, but their statement of the problem attracts and holds us. They endeavored to understand the divine-human nature of Christ from the point of view of his historical appearance without regard to the prevalent formulas. They did not, indeed, attain their object, for their theory does not give due prominence to the scriptural idea of redemption, nor does it make it possible to understand the historical significance of the person and words of Jesus. But, on the other hand, we must give them credit for certain profound intuitions which their contemporaries did not understand, and, under the prevalent system of theology, could not comprehend. Of these the most important were : (1) The strong emphasis laid upon the personal unity of God and the attempt to reconcile it with the divinity of Christ. The Sabellian position may have been at this point not without significance for Athanasius. (2) The attempt to establish the divine-human nature of Christ, not from the point of view of the two natures, but from that of the personal life, and thus of the will (especially Paul of Samosata). At this point the Antiochians joined them, but in such a way that they, by the orthodox coloring of their teaching, only enforced the chief weakness of the Monarchians—the impossibility involved in their conception of the appearance of Jesus in the flesh.

(*communio substantiae*, c. 31). He received his human bodily substance from Mary. He is "joined together from both, woven and grown together from both" (*ex utroque connexus, ex utroque contextus atque concretus*, c. 24). Monarchianism is energetically rejected (c. 12, 26, 27, 28, 30). He lays great stress upon the fact that Christ is not the Father, nor yet a mere man (c. 30). He is the Son of God, who has united with himself the "substance of flesh" ("*as it were betrothed*, sponsus, *to the flesh*"). The bodily human nature constitutes his humanity (c. 21, 25). At this point he falls short of the positions of Irenæus and Tertullian (supra, pp. 124, 126).

The occasional references to the person and work of Christ in the other Latin writers previous to A. D. 325 reveal no dogmatic interest in the doctrine and do not in any way modify the statement of it. It is a settled matter that Christ is God (ARNOBIUS adv. nationes, i. 53, 39, 42; ii. 11, 60: "Christ, or, if you object, God—I say the God Christ—for this must be often said, in order that the ears of infidels may burst and be destroyed." Cyprian ep. 63. 14: "our Lord and God"), although this is taught in a way that savors strongly of Subordination, as, *e. g.*, when LACTANTIUS declares, that God begat his energy (*virtus*), reason (*ratio*), speech (*sermo*) (cf. Cypr. ep. 73. 18: "God, the Creator of Christ"), and through this created the world: "finally, of all the angels whom this God formed from his spirits, he alone has been admitted to a partnership in supreme power, he alone is called God" (Epit. 36 [42], 3. Instit. iv. 6. 2; 8. 7; 14 [20]: "On this account, because he was so faithful . . . that he fulfilled the commands of him who sent him . . . he also received the name of God;" cf. Cyprian, quod idola dii non sint 11). The incarnation is the assuming of human flesh. But this was necessary in order that he might be a mediator between God and man (Cypr. ib. 11), and in order that he might labor among men by word and example (Arnob. i. 62. Lactant. Epit. 38 [43], 8: "Therefore the supreme Father commanded him to descend to earth and assume a human body, in order that, being subject to the sufferings of the flesh, he might teach virtue and patience, not only by words but also by deeds." Just. iv. 12. 15). By virtue of his duplex origin—according to the Spirit from God, according to the flesh from the Virgin Mary—he is Son of God and of man (Lact. Epit. 38. 2. Instit. iv. 13. 6: "he was both God and man, compounded of both genera," *ex utroque genera permixtum*). Such are the essential ideas of this Christology. It is a reiteration of the faith professed in the baptismal confession, attempting, without great exertion, to in some measure justify the latter. But that the ideas of Tertullian were not without influence upon the Latin theologians is clearly seen in Novatian.

2. What Tertullian was for the Christology of the West, that was Origen for the East. His views upon the subject form the basis of the theories of the Greek theologians. Thus PIERIUS (Photius, Cod. 119), THEOGNOSTUS (Athanas. de decret. syn. Nic. 25, ad Serapion. ep. iv. 9, 11), GREGORY THAUMATUR-GUS : "One Lord, one of one, God of God, the impress and image of the Godhead, the effective Word . . . neither, there-fore, any created thing, nor a servant in the Trinity, nor brought in from without as though not having existed before but coming in afterward" (Conf. of faith in Caspari, Alte u. Neue Quellen, etc., p. 10). On the other hand, he also designates the Logos as created ($\varkappa\tau\iota\sigma\mu\alpha$) and formed ($\pi o\iota\eta\mu\alpha$) (Basil. ep. 210. 5). But his great earnestness in maintaining the divinity of Christ is attested by his discussions of "the susceptibility and unsuscepti-bility of God to suffering" (see RYSSEL, Greg. Thaum., p. 73 ff.), leading to the conclusion that the "divinity did, in-deed, suffer, but in an immortal and incapable-of-pain way, with-out experiencing pain" (c. 13 ff. 8 ff.).

Much light is thrown upon the views of the age by the mutual explanations of DIONYSIUS OF ALEXANDRIA and DIONYSIUS OF ROME (about A. D. 260).

Compare Athanasius, De sententia Dionysii and De decret. Syn. Nic. 25, 26; De Synodis 44 (fragments from Dionysius of Alex., Ep. ad Euphranorum et Ammonium, as also from the Elenchus et apol., in 4 books, and from the correspondence of Dionysius of Rome); see also DITTRICH, Dionys. d. Gr., 1867, p. 91 ff.

The doctrine of Sabellius had found very many adherents in the Libyan Pentapolis, even among the bishops (Ath. sent. Dion. 5). Dionysius felt himself, in consequence, impelled to make a literary demonstration against Sabellianism. He started with ideas of his master, Origen, and laid especial emphasis, in view of the nature of the doctrine which he was combating, upon the Subordinationist elements which he here found. He accordingly gave special prom-inence to the personal difference between the Father and the Son, and this seems to have been done also in the school of catechists at Alexandria (Athan. de decr. syn. Nic. 26). The Son is a creation of the Father, which has a different nature from the Father, somewhat as the vine differs from the husband-man, the ship from its builder, or children from their parents ("as a thing made was not existent before it was made," de sent. Dion. 4, 12, 13, 17, 18, 21). It was orthodox Alexan-drine Christians who regarded this teaching with suspicion and brought complaint against their bishop before DIONYSIUS OF

ROME (sent. Dion. 13). They accused the Alexandrine bishop of teaching that "he was not the Son before he was born, but there was a time when he was not, for he is not eternal" (sent. Dion. 14); and, further, that "when Dionysius says Father he does not name the Son ; and, again, when he says Son he does not name the Father, but discriminates and puts apart, and divides the Son from the Father" (ib. 16); and "as saying that the Son is one of those who are born (τῶν γενητῶν) and not of the same substance (ὁμοούσιος) with the Father" (ib. 18 ; de decret. syn. Nic. 25). These charges were, no doubt, well founded.[1] They prove beyond question that the eternal existence of the Son (the eternal generation), as well as the ὁμοούσιος, was already firmly established in the consciousness of intelligent Christians, since they followed in the footsteps of Origen.

It is interesting in this connection to observe the nature of the teaching of the Roman Dionysius. He rejects the view of certain Alexandrine teachers which destroys the monarchy (μοναρχία), and substitutes for it "three powers" (δυνάμεις), and in the last analysis "three gods" (as Marcion). He opposes the designation of the Son as a created being (ποίημα), as also the ascription to him of a temporal beginning. On the contrary, we must, according to the Scriptures, connect the Son and the Spirit very closely with the Father : "I say now that it is fully necessary that the divine Trinity be brought together and summed up in one, as in a sort of consummation, the one God, the almighty Ruler of all things." Therefore the divine Unit (μονάς) dare not be split up into three gods, but we must believe : "in God the Father Almighty, and in Christ Jesus his Son, and in the Holy Ghost ;" but the declaration must be unified (ἡνῶσθαι) in the God of all things. For thus the divine Trinity and the holy message of the Monarchy would be preserved (de decr. syn. Nic. 26). Regarded theologically, this discussion is non-committal (e. g., the ἡνῶσθαι); but it proves that the Roman bishop was in a position to approve and sanction the Origenistic formulas of the accusers of his Alexandrine colleague,[2] and that he was, on the other hand, accustomed to expound the baptismal formula in such a way as to give due prominence to the unity of God (cf. Tertullian, Novatian, and even Sabellius). The course of Dionysius is typical of the attitude of the Romish church in the Christological controver-

---

[1] That the Alexandrian bishop did not, as Athanasius suggests in his defense (e. g., de decr. syn. Nic. 25 ; sent. Dion. 21), think of the "economy (οἰκονομια) of the Saviour according to the flesh," is sufficiently evident from the situation. Cf. also Basil. ep. 9. 2.

[2] He appears (according to sent. Dion. 18, de decret. syn. Nic. 25) even to have laid emphasis upon the ὁμοούσιος.

sies : (1) The creed is regarded as a fixed quantity, and as expressing everything necessary upon all points, and hence upon the details of Christological statement. (2) Tertullian's apparatus of formulas is considered as helpful. (3) The subject itself is discussed as little as possible, as the final conclusion is supposed to have been reached.

It is particularly worthy of note how quickly Dionysius of Alexandria found his way back to the doctrine of Origen. The charges of his opponents appeared to him in reality as a monstrous misunderstanding. Influenced, indeed, by the opposition encountered, he had hitherto revealed only the half of his Origenistic soul. He does not deny that there was a certain onesidedness in his earlier expositions, and that his figures of speech were inappropriate. There are not wanting attempts to help himself by strained interpretations of his former statements. But, beyond this, he expresses entire accord with his opponents : " For there was no time when God was not the Father. Since Christ was the Logos and Wisdom and Power he always existed— being always the reflection of the eternal light, he himself also is eternal. The Son always being with the Father " (sent. Dion. 15). It is false that he denies the ὁμοούσιος, although, indeed, the expression is not biblical (ib. 18, 26). " For as I do not think that the Logos is a creation, I also do not say that God is his Creator, but his Father " (21). " We expand the Monity undivided into the Trinity, and again combine the Trinity undiminished into the Monity " (ib. 17).

Almost more instructive than the controversy itself is the readiness with which the opposing parties come to agreement. The Roman bishop agrees with the Alexandrine plaintiffs, and the bishop of Alexandria at once finds his way back to the standpoint of his opponents. A certain uniformity is beginning to appear in the views entertained of the person of Christ and its relation to the Father.

3. A glance must yet be given to the Christology of METHODIUS OF OLYMPUS († A. D. 311. Opp. ed. Jahn, 1865, in Migne Gr. 18 ; BONWETSCH, Meth. v. Ol. vol. i. Writings, 1891). Christ is the Son of God " through whom all things became " (urchin, 7. 3), since he is the executive hand of the Father (de creatis 9, in Bonw., p. 343 f.), who stands beside the Father and the Spirit (who embraces in himself the knowledge of the Father and the Son), and of whom believers lay hold (conv. dec. virg. viii. 11, 9, 10 ; v. 2 ; iii. 8 ; cf. de resur. iii. 23. 8, 12 ; leprosy, 11, 4 ; distinction of meats, etc., 12. 3 f.). He is the " pre-temporal Word " (leprosy, 11. 4 ; de resur. ii. 24. 5 ; cf. conv. vii. 4 ; viii. 9 ; pre-existing already before

the worlds), the first sprout (βλάστημα, conv. iii. 4), the "only-born Son " (de resur. iii. 23. 6), who is, however, " the beginning after his own unbegun beginning " (de creatis 11), the first of the archangels (the oldest of the aeons and the first of the archangels, conv. iii. 4 ; cf. urchin, 7. 3), the shepherd and leader of the angels (conv. iii. 6), who spoke to the prophets under the old covenant (ib. vii. 6), greater than all except the Father (conv. vii. 1). Prayers are addressed to him (de resur. iii. 23. 11 ; conv. 11. 2). According to the will of the Father he "truly" assumed the "unsuffering " yet "much suf-fering body " (cf. " he imitated the poor," vom Leben und vern. Handl. 6. 2), and truly died (de resur. ii. 18. 8 ; iii. 23. 4). " For this is Christ—a man filled with unadulterated and com-plete divinity, and God contained in man " (conv. iii. 4). But the Logos dwelt in Adam as well as in Jesus (ib.: but this same became Christ and this one [Adam]; cf. 8). The Lord had also the same "actual " body, consisting of the same substance, in his glorification (resur. iii. 7. 12 ; 12. 3 ff.). This Christology, imperfect as it is, represents the average faith of the age : the pre-temporal Son of God, conceived of in a Subordinationistic way, became a real man.

These are illy-defined ideas, falling considerably short of the position of Athanasius, and also of Origen. But it required only a concrete occasion—as shown by the controversy of the two Dionysius's—to produce a more definite and fixed formula-tion.[1]

## § 18. *Ordinance of Repentance and Advance in Conception of the Church.*

1. The church is the general body of men who believe the truth. The further development of the doctrine concerning the church by Irenæus and Tertullian started with this idea. The

[1] We may here notice briefly the Syrian, APHRAATES (A. D. 337-345), who was in time post-Nicene, but in principles ante-Nicene (WRIGHT, the homilies of Aphr., Lond., 1869, translated into German by BERT in Texte u. Unters. iii. 3, 4 ; we cite from the latter). Of Christ, it is said, "that he is Son of God, and that he is God, who came from God " (xvii. 2, p. 280), " and that through him we know his Father" (§ 6, p. 285). To the Jews it is pointed out that they have no occasion to regard this as anything " unusual " (§ 5), since the Old Testament also calls men gods and sons of God (§ 3). But the meaning here is not that Jesus was only a sort of prophet, etc. He " came from God," *i. e.*, the Father separated him from his own nature (ὀνσία) and sent him to men (xxiii. p. 402; also vi. 9, p. 102). It was a special act that he assumed a human body (ib. p. 378 f.), being born "of the Virgin Mary " and "of the Holy Spirit" (p. 388). Gabriel *took the Word from on high and came,* and *the Word became flesh* and *dwelt among us.* He is, there-fore, God by nature, "the first-born of all creatures " (xvii. 8 fin., p. 289),

bishops are the bearers of the truth. The Catholic church is the church of pure doctrines, guaranteed and represented by the bishops. But the church is also the holy people of God. The recognition of this truth led to consequences of historical importance. There were three possible interpretations of the holiness of the church, each of which found its advocates : (1) Every separate individual is holy (Novatian). (2) The bishops are holy (Cyprian). (3) The sacraments and ordinances of the church are holy (Rome).

2. Hermas had, in his day, in accordance with a special revelation (p. 61 f.), proclaimed the possibility of a " second repentance.'' The church did not lose sight of this idea, and it is almost certain that it was through the authority of this publication that the idea of the "second repentance'' secured such general acceptance (cf. Tertul. de pud. 10, 20). The resulting praxis was at about the close of the second century the following : A discrimination was made between " sins of daily occurrence '' (as anger, smiting, cursing, swearing, lies) and ''sins more serious and destructive,'' ''mortal'' (1 Jn. v. 16), ''capital'' and ''irremediable '' (homicide, idolatry, fraud, denial or false testimony, blasphemy, adultery, fornication, ''and if there be any other violation of the temple of God,'' Tert. de pud. 19 ; c. Marc. iv. 9). Sins of the first class might find at once forgiveness through the mediation of Christ, through prayer, good works and intercession, since the sinner by these means offered to the offended God sufficient satisfaction (see p. 133); but sins of the second group require an exclusion from the congregation of the ''saints '' (see Tert. de pud. 19). There was, however, a difference in the praxis of the church in regard to transgressors of the second class. To the greater number of these it granted the '' second repentance,'' but only (Tert de poenit. 7, 12) upon condition that they felt bitter regret, manifesting this by their outward deportment, requested intercession in their behalf, and made the required confession (*exomologesis*) in the presence of the assembled congregation. The church granted this privilege through her presbyters and confessors (Tert. de poenit. 9, 12, 22 ; Apol. 39). Thus is suitable satisfaction made to God ('' let him repent from the heart,'' *ex animo* . . . ''confession of sins,'' *confessio delictorum* . . . ''confession is the method of satisfaction,'' *satisfactionis consilium*, poen. 8 fin.). These are the elements of the Romish sacrament of penance. The worship of idols, murder, for-

---

''light of light'' (ib. 2, the only Nicene turn in Aphraates). Trinitarian formulas are found, *e. g.*, xxiii., pp. 411, 412 ; cf. i. 15. These are ideas that fit easily into the line of thought traced in the present section. For the somewhat earlier '' Acta Archelai,'' see p. 166.

nication, and adultery were absolutely excluded from this second repentance (Tert. pud. 5, 12, 22 ; cf. Orig. de orat. 28 fin.). Practically, the discussion centered about two offenses : in times of peace, especially fornication ; in times of persecution, denial of the faith and apostasy. The conflicts of the future naturally raged about these two centres. The opinions entertained concerning this "second repentance" were still for a time, indeed, quite fluctuating. Not to speak of the Montanists, Tertullian, even before joining their ranks, had only reluctantly accepted the theory ("I am afraid of the second, I should rather say, last hope," poen. 7). But others found fault with the strictness of the treatment (poen. 5, 10), and even thought that open sinners might be tolerated in the church, as the ark, which typifies the church, held unclean animals (Tert. de idololatr. 24 fin.; cf. remarks of Dionysius of Corinth in Eus. h. e. iv. 23. 6).

3. Such was about the situation when CALLISTUS of Rome (217-222), by the publication of a new penitential order, introduced a change of momentous import in the praxis of repentance, and thus also in the conception of the church.

LITERATURE. Hipp. Ref. ix. 12, p. 458 f. Tert. de pudic.; cf. HARNACK, Ztschr. f. Theol. u. K., 1891, p. 114 ff. PREUSCHEN, Tert. Schriften de paenit; et de pud. Giess. Diss. 1890. ROLFFS, Das Indulgenzedikt des röm. Bischof Callist, in Text. u. Unters. xi. 3.[1]

Callistus was the first to allow the second repentance in the case of fornication : "He first contrived to connive with men in matters pertaining to their lusts, saying that sins were forgiven to all men by him " (Hipp.), *i. e.*, he declared : "I remit by penitence to those who have committed them also sins of adultery and fornication " (Tert. 1). But this applied, as Tertullian's polemics prove, only to sins of. the flesh, and made provision for but *one* second repentance. In justification of this innovation, Callistus (or his adherents) presented a number of biblical arguments, *e. g.:* "God is merciful, and does not desire the death of the sinner," etc. (Ez. xxxiii. 11. Tert. ii. init.); it is not for us to judge our brethren (Rom. xiv. 4, ib.); the parables of the prodigal son and the lost sheep (7 f.); Christ's treatment of the woman taken in adultery (11); Paul's manner of dealing with such (2 Cor. ii. 5 ff. c. 13), etc. The aim of repentance is forgiveness (3); fellowship (*communicatio*) may be withdrawn

[1] The following analysis proceeds upon the supposition that the bishop whom Tertullian attacks in his *De pudicitia* was Callistus, and that we may, accordingly, from the work of Tertullian, fill out the portraiture given in Hippol. Ref. ix. 12. This was first done by ROSSI, Bulletino archeol. christ., 1866, p. 26. Extracts from the Edict of Callistus reveal the hand of Tertullian. ROLFFS attempted a reconstruction.

from the sinning, but only for the present (*ad presens*). If he repent, let it be granted him again according to the mercy of God (18). If the blood of Christ cleanses us from all sin (1 Jn. i. 7, c. 19), then it is also perfectly scriptural for Callistus to grant pardon to fornicators. The church has the authority to do this ("but the church has, I say, the power of pardoning sins," c. 21); particularly the bishops. "And, therefore, the church will indeed pardon sins, but the church as a spirit (*ecclesia spiritus*) through a spiritual man, not the church as a number of bishops" (c. 21). Callistus here appeals to Matt. xvi. 18 (ib.), and appears to have attributed to himself, as the successor of Peter, peculiar authority (cf. the form of address, *apostolice*, c. 21, and the titles, *pontifex maximus, episcopus episcoporum*, c. 1). A similar authority is also ascribed to the confessors (22).

The forgiveness of sins is thus practically given into the hand of the bishop, who exercises it as a divine right. His own moral character is not taken into consideration. He is not subject to removal : "If a bishop should commit some sin, even a mortal one, it is not permitted to remove him" (Hipp. ix. 12). If the bishop tolerates sinners in the church, no objection can be made. He must allow the tares to stand among the wheat, and the ark contained many kinds of animals (Hipp. ix. 12, p. 460 ; Tert. de idol. 24).

The innovation of Callistus was certainly in harmony with the spirit of the age. Many of his deliverances have an evangelical sound. But that such is not really their character is evident from subsequent developments—from the fact that he did not advance a single new idea looking to the awakening of penitence, but only changed the praxis in regard to fornication upon practical grounds, and, above all, from his conception of the church, which gave direction to all his thought. Callistus was evangelical— and even liberal—because he was the first conscious hierarch.[1] Henceforth the church is no longer the holy people of God, holding in common the faith of the apostles, *i. e.*, the faith of the bishops ; but it is an association of men, subject to the control of the bishop, whom he tolerates in the church, and this by virtue of the divine authority which has been given him to pardon or retain sins. He whom the bishop recognizes belongs to the church. The bishop is lord over the faith and life of the Christian world by virtue of an absolute supremacy divinely bestowed upon him.

---

[1] Hipp. ix. 12 fin.: "Callistus . . . whose school remains, guarding morals and the tradition." Perhaps these were watchwords among the Callistians. They sought to evangelize morals upon the basis of the misinterpreted tradition.

Callistus was the author of the Roman Catholic conception of
the church.

4. The penitential praxis introduced by Callistus had become
universal by about A. D. 250 (*e. g.*, Cypr. ep. 55. 20 ; 4. 4),
although there were still lingering recollections of opposition to
it (Cypr. ep. 55. 21). The circumstances of the congregations
during the Decian persecution produced a further and logically
consistent (cf. Tert. de pud. 22) step in advance. Even to such
as had denied the Christian faith must now be extended the opportunity of return to the church. It was chiefly CYPRIAN (†
A. D. 258) who justified this step, and, in doing so, developed
more fully the Catholic conception of the church.

Vid. collection of Cyprian's letters, his *De lapsis* and *De catholicae ecclesiae
unitate* (Cypr. Opp. omn. ed. Hartel, 1868), and the letter of Cornelius of
Rome to Fabius of Antioch, in Eus. h. e. vi. 43.   Dionysius of Alexandria to
Novatian, ib. vi. 45.   Ambrose, de poen. ll. 2.   Compare RETTBERG, Cypri-
anus, 1831.   PETERS, Der heil. Cypr. v. Karthago, 1877.   FECHTRUP, Der
heil. Cypr. vol. i., 1878.   O. RITSCHL, Cypr. v. K. u. die Verfassung der
Kirche, 1885.   GOETZ, Die Busslehre Cyprians, 1895.   K. MILLER, Ztschr. f.
KG., 1896, 1 ff., 187 ff.   HARNACK, PRE. viii. 417 ff.; x. 652 ff.

During the Decian persecution it became evident that it would
be impossible, in view of the number of backsliders (*lapsi*), to
maintain the ancient praxis, *i. e.*, to exclude all such from the
communion of the church (the eucharist, Cypr. ep. 57. 2), and
to refuse to allow them to receive the benediction (*pax*) with the
congregation.   Those who had fallen applied to their " confessors " for letters of recommendation (*libelli*), which were freely
granted (Cypr. ep. 20. 2 ; cf. 22. 2 ; 27. 1). Although these
were primarily intended only as letters of recommendation (ep.
15. 1 ; 16. 3 ; 18. 1 ; 19. 2 ; 22. 2 fin.; cf. 36. 2), this recommendation (cf. the more ancient praxis, Tert. de pud. 22, and
Dionys. of Alex. in Eus. h. e. vi. 42. 5 f.; ep. eccl. Lugd. in
Eus. h. e. v. 1. 45, 46 ; 2. 6, 7) soon came to have the force of
a command (see the letter of the confessor Lucian to Cyprian,
ep. 23 ; cf. 21. 3). Cyprian did not dispute the right of the
confessors, but he thought that an assembly of the bishops should
first consider the matter and lay down the principles to govern
such cases before any action was taken—particularly in the midst
of the distractions caused by the persecution (ep. 19. 2 ; 20. 3 ;
20, cf. 31. 6). This was also the position of the church at
Rome (ep. 30. 3, 5, 6 ; 21. 3 ; 36. 3). Meanwhile some presbyters at Carthage, during the absence of their bishop, Cyprian,
admitted certain of the lapsed to the communion upon the basis
of their *libelli*, without previous public confession (ep. 15. 1 ;
16. 2, 3 ; 17. 2 ; 20. 2), and in some cities the mass of the

people (*multitudo*), relying upon the testimonials of the martyrs and confessors, compelled the bishops to pronounce the benediction upon them (ep. 27. 3). In contrast with those who, with the testimonial of the confessors in their hands, believed themselves authorized to demand the benediction, stood others, who declared their purpose to repent and to await the bishop's declaration (ep. 33. 1, 2; 35, cf. 36. 1). Cyprian instructed that the presbyters who would not submit to the episcopal decision should be excluded from fellowship (*communicatio*, ep. 34. 3; cf. 42). Thus the episcopal authority on the one hand, and on the other the pastoral office of the presbyters and the prerogative of the confessors, stand arrayed in opposition (cf. 16. 1). It is not in reality a discord in the praxis of repentance which here comes to view, but a discord between the bishop and the presbyters. As a result, an opposition party was formed under the leadership of five presbyters and a certain FELICISSIMUS (ep. 41. 2).) If the latter was the "standard-bearer of sedition," the presbyter, NOVATUS, was the soul of the insurrection, "a torch and fire for kindling the flames of sedition" (52. 2). FORTUNATUS became the bishop of this party (59. 9). Their motto was, "to restore and recall the lapsed" (43. 5), and they were opposed to an episcopal decision in the matter and to a more prolonged probation for penitence (43. 2). In accordance with the ancient privilege of confessors, they admitted at once to fellowship those who were recommended by the latter.

About the same time a schism arose also in Rome, occasioned by an election for bishop (ep. 44. 1. Euseb. h. e. vi. 43), in which CORNELIUS and NOVATIAN (about A. D. 251) were the candidates. Novatian, otherwise an orthodox man, established a party in opposition to Cornelius by retaining the ancient praxis in relation to the lapsed. He sought to build up a congregation of the pure (καθαροί, Eus. h. e. vi. 43. 1), since the idolatrous worship of some contaminates the remaining members of the church: "They say that one is corrupted by the sin of another, and in their zeal contend that the idolatry of an offender passes over to the non-offending" (Cypr. ep. 55. 27). He proposes to have a congregation of actually holy men. Hence he has those who come to him from the church at large re-baptized (Cypr. ep. 73. 2; Dionys. of Alex. in Eus. h. e. vii. 8; Ambros. de poenit. i. 7. 30). His adherents were compelled at the reception of the Lord's Supper to bind themselves by oath to adhere to his church (Cornel. in Eus. h. e. vi. 43. 18). There should thus be established a congregation of saints, such as Montanism had endeavored to form. But to what an extent church politics and personal motives were involved on both sides

is manifest from the league formed by Novatian—after his "confessors" had forsaken him (Cornel. to Cypr. ep. 49. 1, 3 ; cf.
53, 54)—with Novatus (see ep. 47. 50).    Novatian appointed
opposition-bishops also in other places (ep. 55. 24 ; 68. 1), and
Novatianism ere long struck root also in the Orient (Eus. h. e.
vi. 46. 3 ; vii. 5).    A Novatian counter-church, which afterward extended its rigor toward the lapsed to all guilty of mortal
sins (see *e. g.*, Athanas. ad Serap. ep. iv. 13 ; Socrat. h. e. i. 10),
had soon spread, variously combined with Montanism, over the
whole church (see HARNACK PRE. x. p. 667 ff.).    But it never
gained a more than superficial influence.    It was an essentially
powerless reaction in the interest of an archaistic idea, which
never was nor could be applied with real seriousness in practical
life.

In Carthage, after Cyprian's return, the proposed assembly of
bishops was held (A. D. 252).    Its decrees present the actual
results of the agitation.    In expectation of a new persecution, it
is here held to be proper " that to those who have not departed
from the church of the Lord, and from the first day of their
lapse have not ceased to exercise repentance and lament and
pray to the Lord, the *pax* should be given."    Although this had
hitherto been granted only to those in immediate peril of death
(cf. Cypr. ep. 55. 13 ; 57. 1 ; de laps. 16), yet it is now, upon
the suggestion of the Holy Spirit and plain visions, extended to
all the lapsed (see Cypr. ep. 57 ; cf. 55. 6).    To this Rome
also agreed (ep. 55. 6).    This principle was not, indeed, at once
acted upon in all places (see ep. 55. 22 ; 59. 15), but as a principle it had carried the day.    It is not in this fact, however,
that the real significance of the decision lay.    In the question
concerning repentance, Cyprian accepted fully the position of
his opponents; but it was bishops who passed the final decree,
bishops were to decide in the case of individuals who had
lapsed; and from their authority the latter could not appeal.    In
these controversies, therefore, Cyprian's conception of the church
was perfected.    The whole heart of the great bishop was bound
up with this idea.    In it concentred all the elements of his religious thought and feeling.    He had the juristic, logical bent
of a Roman.    Tertullian was his instructor.    He had a warm
heart.    He was fanatically devoted to the hierarchy, and he
loved Christ.

5. Cyprian's conception of the church embraces the following :

(*a*) The successors of the apostles are the bishops, who, like the
former, are chosen by the Lord himself and inducted into their
office (Cypr. ep. 3. 3 ; cf. Firmil. 75. 16) as leaders (*prae-*

*positi*) or pastors (*pastores*) (ep. 8. 1 ; 19. 2 ; 20. 3 ; 27. 3 ; 33. 1 ; 13. 1 ; 59. 14). This is to be understood not merely in the sense of an "ordinance of succession," but every individual bishop is inducted into his office by a "divine decree, for his own sake" (59. 5). He is a bishop, however, and his sacrifices and prayers are effectual, only so long as he remains faithful and leads a holy life.[1] He who criticises the bishops presumes thereby to pass judgment upon the judgment of God and Christ: "This is not to believe in God ; this is to be a rebel against Christ and his gospel, as, when he says : ' Are not two sparrows,' etc. (Matt. 10. 29) . . . thou wouldst think that priests of God are ordained in the church without his knowledge . . . For to believe that those who are ordained are unworthy or corrupt, what else is this but to contend that his priests are not appointed in the church by God nor through him?" (66. 1).[2] In harmony with this, the bishops are said to be guided in their decisions by divine suggestions and visions (*e. g.*, ep. 11. 3, 4 ; 57. 5 ; 68. 5 ; 66. 10 ; 63. 1 ; 73. 26, cf. 40 ; 81 ; see also de aleat. 3. 2).[3] The bishop, according to Cyprian, is, upon the one hand, a successor of the historical apostolate and hence the legitimate teacher of the apostolical tradition. But he is also an inspired prophet, endowed with the *charismata*—a claim not found in the teachings of Irenæus. Thus the bishop discharges the office of the ancient Spirit-endowed men, for he receives revelations from the Spirit. The place of the former πνευματικόι is filled by the bishop, as afterward by the monastic system. But if the bishops have the

---

[1] Ep. 65. 4 : "to separate the brothers from the folly and remove them from the contagion of these, since neither can a sacrifice be consecrated where there is not a holy spirit, nor does the Lord favor anyone on account of the addresses and prayers of one who has himself offended the Lord." And in ep. 67. 3 (circular letter of 37 bishops) it is announced as a fundamental principle : "All are completely bound to sin who have been contaminated [according to Hos. 9. 4] by the sacrifice of a profane and wicked priest," and "a people obedient to the Lord's commands and fearing God ought to separate themselves from a sinful leader, *praepositus*, and not participate in the sacrifice of a sacrilegious priest" (Numb. xvi. 26). These are statements to which the Donatists could afterward appeal. Cf. REUTER, Augustin. Studien, p. 254 ff.

[2] The divine decision at elections does not exclude "the vote of the people, the consensus of associated bishops" (ep. 59. 5 ; 55. 8 ; 67. 4, 5 ; 49. 2). It is even said of the populace ( *plebs*): "Since it most fully possesses the power of electing worthy or rejecting unworthy priests " (ep. 67. 3).

[3] This is an archaistic feature. Visions are mentioned by Cyprian also in other connections (ep. 16. 4 ; 39. 1 ; de immortal. 19 ; ad Donat. 5 ; cf. Dionys. Alex. in Eus. h. e. vii. 7. 2, 3 ; Firmilian's letter, ep. 75. 10, and the criticism noted in ep. 66. 10 : "ridiculous dreams and absurd visions appear to some "). Cyprian has in mind, not a permanent official endowment, but illuminations granted from time to time. This patriarch was not far removed from superstitious fanaticism.

Spirit, it may be easily understood that all criticism must be forestalled by their deliverances, as formerly by those of the prophets (vid. Didache ; also supra, p. 181).

(*b*) According to Matt. xvi. 18 f., the church is founded upon the bishop and its direction devolves upon him :   " Hence through the changes of times and dynasties the ordination of bishops and the order of the church moves on, so that the church is constituted of bishops, and every act of the church is controlled by these leaders " (33. 1).   " One in the church is for the time priest and for the time judge, in the stead of Christ " (ep. 59. 5.).   How seriously these principles were accepted is evident from the controversy above noted.   The bishop decides who belongs to the church and who shall be restored to her fellowship (16. 1 ; 41. 2 ; de laps. 18, 22, 29).   He conducts the worship as the priest of God, who offers the sacrifice upon the altar (67. 1 ; Cyprian is the first to assert an actual priesthood of the clergy, based upon the sacrifice offered by them, vid. sub, p. 196), and cares for the poor.   He defends the pure tradition against errorists (ep. 63. 17, 19 ; 74. 10).   Cf. O. RITSCHL, l. c., 216 ff.   He is the leader (*praepositus*), whose office it is to rule the laity (*laici*, or *plebs*) by virtue of divine authority.

(*c*) The bishops constitute a college (*collegium*), the episcopate (*episcopatus*).   The councils developed this conception. In them the bishops practically represented the unity of the church, as Cyprian now theoretically formulated it.   Upon their unity rests the unity of the church.   " The episcopate is one, a part of which taken separately is regarded as the whole: the church is one, which is ever more widely extended into a multitude by the increase of reproductive energy " (de unit. eccl. 5).   " The church, which is one and catholic, is in a manner connected and joined together by the glue of the mutually cohering priests " (ep. 66. 8).   In this connection it is said : " These are the church united (*adunata*) to the priest and the flock adhering to the pastor.   Whence thou shouldst know that the bishop is in the church and the church in the bishop, and he who is not with the bishop is not in the church, and they flatter themselves in vain who, not having peace with the priests of God, deceive themselves and think that they may secretly hold fellowship with any persons whatsoever " (ib.).   This unity of the episcopate rests upon the divine election and endowment which the bishops have in common as successors of the apostles, and finds expression in the same sense (*e. g.*, 75. 3) in their united conferences and mutual recognition (cf. ep. 19. 2 ; 20. 3 ; 55. 1, 6, 7, 24, 30 ; cf. 75. 4, 45, etc.).   The unity is manifest in the fact that the Lord in

the first instance bestowed apostolic authority upon Peter :
"Here the other apostles were also, to a certain extent, what
Peter was, endowed with an equal share of both honor and
power ; but the beginning proceeds from unity, in order that the
church of Christ may be shown to be one" (de un. eccl. 4).
Accordingly, the Roman church is the "mother and root of the
catholic church" (ep. 48. 3; cf. 59. 14, etc.). The Roman bishop
made practical application of these ideas (ep. 67. 5 ; esp. 68. 1-
3; cf. also ep. 8; 71. 3; 75. 17; de aleatoribus 1, as well
as the ideas of Callistus, supra, p. 177). As understood by
Cyprian, no higher significance was attached to them than
by Irenæus (supra, p. 137). In reality all the bishops—regarded
dogmatically—stand upon the same level, and hence he maintained, in opposition to Stephanus of Rome, his right of independent opinion and action, and flatly repelled the latter's appeal to his primacy (ep. 71. 3 ; 74 ; cf. Firmilian's keen criticism, ep. 75. 2, 3, 17, 24 f.; see also 59. 2, 14 ; 67. 5).
The bond which holds the church to unity is thus the episcopate.

(a) Rebellion against the bishop is, therefore, rebellion against
God. The schismatic is also a heretic (59. 5 ; 66. 5 ; 52. 1 ;
69. 1; de unit. eccl. 10). He who does not submit to the rightful
bishop forfeits thereby his fellowship with the church and his
salvation. "Whosoever he is, and whatever his character, he is
not a Christian who is not in the church of Christ" (55. 24,
referring to Novatian ! cf. 43. 5 ; de unit. 17, 19). The
possession of the same faith, to which such persons are wont to
appeal, benefits them as little as it did the family of Korah (ep.
69. 8). It is always chaff which is blown from the threshing-
floor (de un. eccl. 9 ; ep. 66. 8), even though the individuals
concerned were martyrs for the faith (ep. 73. 21): "because
there is no salvation outside the church." The true members of
the church will, therefore, above all, recognize the bishop and
obey him. Thus they remain in the one church, outside of
which there is no salvation : "It is not possible that he should
have God for his father who has not the church for his mother"
(de un. 6). The members of the church are related to the
bishop as children to their father (ep. 41. 1); members of the
*fraternitas* to one another as brothers, in that they give full sway
to peace and love, and avoid all discord and divisions, praying
with one another in brotherly accord, and even sharing with one
another their earthly goods (de un. 8, 9, 12, 13, 15, 24 f.; de
orat. dom. 8, 30 ; de op. et eleem. 25 fin.; de pat. 15 ; de zel.
et liv. 6).

(e) A logical result of this conception of the church is seen in Cyprian's denial of the validity of *heretic baptism*. Tradition was here divided. The bishops, assembled three times (A. D. 255-256) at Carthage under Cyprian, supported their opposition by appeal to their predecessors (ep. 70. 1 ; 71. 4 ; 73. 3 ; cf. Tert. de bapt. 15), and, as Firmilian reports (ep. 75. 19), the synod at Iconium had taken the same view. The Roman usage was, however, different, and Stephanus followed it (" let there be no innovations, let nothing be done except what has been handed down," 74. 1; cf. Ps.-Cypr. de rebaptismate 1; also Alexandrines, Eus. vii. 7. 4), and appealed to the primacy of Peter (71. 3; cf. sent. episcoporum, proem.). When confronted by tradition,[1] Cyprian always appealed to the " decision (*consilium*) of a sane mind " (68. 2 and 71. 3 ; 73. 13 ; 74. 2, 3, 9 ; cf. 75. 19. Compare Tert., supra, 135, n.), *i. e.*, to the logical consequences of his conception of the church, according to which, it was evident, no one who was himself outside of the church could receive anyone into it. The baptism of heretics is a "sordid and profane bath " (*tinctio*, 70. 1 ; 72. 1 ; 73. 6, 21, etc.). On the other hand : " the water is purified and sanctified through the priest of Christ " (70. 1). Only the leaders, who receive the Spirit, have the power to impart the forgiveness of sins, and it is only in the church that the Spirit of God is received (73. 7 ; 74. 5 ; cf. 75. 9); therefore, in receiving those baptized by heretics, the term employed should be not re-baptism, but baptism (73. 1). Stephanus severed fellowship with the churches of Africa (75. 25 ; cf. FECHTRUP i., p. 236 ff.) and threatened to pursue the same course with the Orientals (Dionys. in Eus. h. e. vii. 5. 4). Thus Cyprian's conception of the church was used as a weapon against himself. Cyprian held in this controversy apparently the more logical position. But the instinct of Rome was keener. Individuals are changeable and open to assault. A principle is firmly established only when it has become rooted in institutions, and when these bring individuals into subjection. Accordingly, the seemingly more liberal praxis of Rome prevailed.

6. We have thus witnessed a momentous transformation in the general conception of the Church. By the term is no longer understood the holy people of God believing on Jesus Christ, but a group of men belonging to the episcopacy. They obey it, not because it advocates the truth proclaimed by the apostles, but because the bishops have been endowed and appointed by God to be the leaders of the congregations, ruling them in God's

---

[1] Hippolytus (Ref. ix. 12) says of Callistus : ἐπὶ τούτου πρώτως τετόλμηται δεύτερον αὐτοῖς βάπτισμα.

name and by virtue of divine authority.   This subjection under
the episcopacy is the essential feature in the church, for it constitutes her unity.   Only he who obeys the bishop belongs to the
church and has relationship with God and salvation.   The ideas
of Irenæus must now receive a new interpretation and be brought
into harmony with this new conception, and the holiness of the
church is more and more distinctly associated with her sacraments.   The evangelical definition of the church was superseded
by the catholic.   The church is no longer essentially the assembly of believers and saints, nor an object of faith, but a visible
body, controlled by divinely authorized " ecclesiastical law."
Much is yet in a crude state, but the foundation has been laid.

## § 19.   *General Conception of Christianity.*

1. If the definition of the church is the church's own description of herself, defects in the definition must all find their coun-
terpart in perverted views of Christian character, and the means
by which it may be secured and maintained.   We will find confirmation of this principle when we come to deal with the literature of the West, but we must first examine the writings of the
Eastern theologians.

2. Among these we mention : DIONYSIUS OF ALEXANDRIA († ca. A. D.
265.  Fragments in ROUTH, Reliq. sacr. iii., iv.   THEOGNOSTUS (ca. A. D.
280 ; cf. Phot. cod. 106).   PIERIUS (age of Diocletian, vid. Phot. Bibl. 118).
GREGORY THAUMATURGUS (vid. CASPARI, Quellen, etc., 1886, p. 1 ff.  Migne
gr. 10.  LAGARDE, Analecta syr., 1858.  RYSSEL, Greg. Thaum. Leben u.
Schriften.  PITRA, Analecta sacr. iii., iv.).  HIERACAS (Epiph. h. 67).  Above
all, METHODIUS of Olympus (Opp. edited by Bonwetsch, vid. supra, p. 173, and
cf. PANKAU, Meth. Bisch. v. Olymp.; in " Der Katholik," 1887, ii., p. 113 ff.,
225 ff.; BONWETSCH, Theologie des Meth., 1903.  With the latter, his contemporary, PETER († A. D. 311 ; fragments in ROUTH, Reliq. sacr. iv.  PITRA,
Analecta sacra, iv, 187 ff., 425 ff.  Cf. HARNACK, Gesch. d. altchr. Litt. i.,
p. 443 ff.).

The thought of Eastern theologians was largely moulded by
Origen, as may be clearly seen even in his most energetic opponents.   His dogmatic formulas and problems (creation, homousia
of the Son, spirit and body, freedom, resurrection, interpretation of Scripture, etc.) continue to exert a positive influence.
Compare, *e. g.*, the writings of DIONYSIUS OF ALEXANDRIA (his
Christology, supra, p. 130; his work, περὶ φύσεως, against the
atomic theory, frg. in Routh iv.; his exegetic method in
treatment of the Apocalypse, in Eus. h. e. vii. 25. 8, 21 ff.).
True, there was also energetic criticism (*e. g.*, NEPOS, who in his
work, ἔλεγχος ἀλληγοριστῶν, cf. Eus. h. vii. 24. 2, 5 ff., which
argues for a visible millennial kingdom and against the " lofty

and grand understanding '' of the parousia and the resurrection).
This opposition compelled orthodox theology to abandon the
'' Gnostic '' elements of Origen's teaching.    At first, indeed,
the Alexandrine theologians reproduced his ideas quite faithfully.
THEOGNOSTUS and PIERIUS, *e. g.*, are said to have held his theories
of Subordinationism and the pre-existence of souls (vid. Photius
cod. 105 ; cf. Athanas. ad Serap. ep. 4. 11 ; de decr. syn. Nic.
25 ; Phot. cod. 119 ; cf. Hieracas in Epiph. 67. 1, 3).[1]   But we
find PETER OF ALEXANDRIA already vigorously assailing the views
of Origen upon these topics (against the pre-existence of the
soul, see frg. from *de anima* in Routh iv. 49 f.; Pitra, anal.
sacr. iv. 193, 429.   Defending the resurrection of a body substantially identical with the present body, frg. from *de resur.* in
Pitra, anal. sacr. iv. 189 ff.; esp. 427 ff.).[2]   The wall of parti-
tion between the faith of the ignorant masses ($\dot{a}\pi\lambda o\acute{v}\sigma\tau\epsilon\rho o\iota$) and
that of the initiated ($\gamma\nu\omega\sigma\tau\iota\varkappa o\iota$) has been broken down.   Only
thus have the ideas of Origen become common property, and
that not without the repression of his protests against the popular Christianity.    This is, upon the one hand, a matter of inestimable significance ; but, on the other hand, it diminished the
influence of Origen's justifiable antagonism to the type of Christianity prevalent among the masses in his day.

A remarkable character now meets us.    In METHODIUS we find
a Greek theologian, under the general influence of Origen, yet
consciously in strong opposition to him, giving expression to
the Christian sentiment of the churches in Asia Minor.    In
his opposition to Origen, whom he calls a '' centaur '' (de
creat. 2, 6), he is at one with Peter of Alexandria.

---

[1] Theognostus published 7 books entitled $\dot{v}\pi o\tau\nu\pi\acute{\omega}\sigma\epsilon\iota\varsigma$, being the second to
attempt a scientific statement of the doctrines of Christianity.    According to
Photius he treated : (1) Of God the Father, the Creator, antagonizing
those who hold that the universe is co-eternal with him.    (2) Affirmed that it
was necessary for the Father to have a Son, describing the latter as created
($\varkappa\tau\acute{\iota}\sigma\mu a$), and as '' presiding alone over rational beings,'' according to
Origen's teaching.    (3) Of the Holy Ghost, endeavoring particularly to pre-
sent the proofs of his existence ; in other respects following Origen.    (4)
Also agreeing with Origen in his view of angels and demons, who have refined
($\lambda\epsilon\pi\tau\grave{a}$) bodies.    (5 and 6) Concerning the incarnation ($\epsilon\nu a\nu\vartheta\rho\omega\pi\acute{\eta}\sigma\iota\varsigma$) of
the Saviour, '' he undertakes, as is his custom, to show that the incarnation of
the Son was necessary,'' in this also following Origen.    (7) '' What he
writes about God, the Creator,'' made a more orthodox impression, especially
in the closing part referring to the Son.    The personal Christian life and the
order of salvation are not, therefore, regarded as subjects of Christian knowledge.    This is a characteristic omission.
[2] There are no doubts as to the genuineness of these fragments, but the
Armenian fragments (Pitra iv. 430) are exceedingly suspicious, *e. g.*, '' Both
the God and the body (of Christ) are one nature and one person, from whose
will and ordering the Spirit comes.''

He dislikes his method, and vigorously assails the allegorical exegesis (conv. iii. 2; resur. i. 39. 2; 54. 6; iii. 9. 4 ff.), but he himself employs the latter heroically when it suits his purpose (see his rules, resur. iii. 8. 3, 7; cf. leprosy, 4. 5). He proposes to advocate a "theology of facts" as against the "theology of rhetoric:" "For there is nothing sound, whole, nor solid in them, but only a specious display of words merely for the amazement of the hearers, and an ornamented Pitho" (res. 1. 27. 2). Of the pre-existence of souls, the pre-temporal fall, and the spiritual interpretation of the resurrection, which is for him a "destruction of the resurrection" (ib. i. 27. 1), he will therefore know nothing (e. g., res. i. 55. 4; iii. 1. 1; 2. 2 f.; 3. 3; 5; 7. 12; 12).

We present a brief outline of his views in general. (1) The almighty God, out of love, for man's sake, created this world out of nothing, as well the essences ($o\dot{v}\sigma iai$) as the properties ($\pi o\iota \acute{o}\tau \eta \tau \varepsilon \varsigma$) (de lib. arb. 7. 4-91; 22. 7, 8). The world is not eternal (de creat. 11. 2; de lib. arb. 22. 10, 11); but, as God was never inactive, the world existed in him potentially ($\delta v v \acute{a}\mu \varepsilon \iota$), from eternity (de lib. arb. 22. 9). He created it through the Logos. As to the Logos and the Holy Spirit, see supra, p. 173. (2) The essential marks of man as created by God in time are freedom and immortality: "For man being free ($a\dot{v}\tau \varepsilon \zeta o\dot{v}\sigma \iota o\varsigma$) and independent ($a\dot{v}\tau o\varkappa \rho \acute{a}\tau \omega \rho$), his will is both self-controlled ($a\dot{v}\tau o\delta \acute{\varepsilon}\sigma \pi o\tau o\varsigma$) and self-determining in regard to choice" (res. i. 38. 3). "Made free in regard to the choice of the good, etc., . . . for God created man for immortality, and made him the image of his own eternity" (res. i. 36. 2; 34. 3; 51. 5). In this consists his godlikeness ($\vartheta \varepsilon o\varepsilon \acute{\iota}\delta \varepsilon \varsigma$ and $\vartheta \varepsilon o\varepsilon \acute{\iota}\varkappa \varepsilon \lambda o\nu$, res. i. 35. 2). This freedom of choice has descended from the first man to his posterity. "From whom the subsequent members of the race also had allotted to them the like freedom" (lib. arb. 16. 2). This moral equipment of man involves that he was and is in position to fulfill the law of God: "For it belongs to him to be able to accept the commandment or not" (lib. arb. 16. 7). "For it lies with us to believe or not to believe . . . , with us to live aright or to sin, with us to do good or to do evil" (res. 57. 6; cf. conv. viii. 17). Since man was created for eternity, God sees to it that this becomes his portion (res. 1. 35. 2-4). This is the genuine Greek anthropology. (3) The devil's envy of man led to the fall (lib. arb. 17. 5; 18. 4 ff.), i. e., man employed his freedom in disobedience of God's command. "But wickedness is disobedience" (ib. 18. 8). The spirit of the world then gained control within him: "For thus first came about our condition; we were filled with strifes and vain reasoning ; on the one hand, emptied of the indwelling of God ; on the other, filled with worldly lust, which the plotting serpent infused into us" (res. ii. 6. 2). Thus man "chose evil from free choice" (res. i. 45. 2). Thus it is not the flesh, but the soul, that is responsible for sin (res. i. 29. 8 ; 59. 3), but "every sin and every way of life attains its end through the flesh" (res. ii. 4. 3). Henceforth evil lusts crowd in upon us, which we, indeed, ought to conquer : "For it does not lie wholly with us to desire or not to desire things improper, but to carry out or not carry out the desire" (res. ii. 3. 1). But in order that the evil in man might not become immortal, God graciously appointed death (res. i. 39. 5 ; 38. 1 ; 45. 5 ; ii. 6. 3), which is a penalty intended, as are all penalties, to lead to amendment (res. i. 31. 4). As an artist breaks to pieces a statue which has been maliciously defaced, in order to recast it, so God deals with man in appointing him to death (res. i. 43. 2 ff.). We may here again clearly trace the influence of Origen, despite all the polemical assaults upon him.

(4) Wherein now consists the salvation which Christ has brought to the race? The answer assumes many forms. The souls of men are cleansed by the blood of Christ. He is our "Helper" in the conflict (distinction of meats, 15 ; 11. 4 ; 2. 1). He is "helper, advocate, and physician," the "great Giver and great Helper" (res. iii. 23. 11). Christ announced through the prophets of the old covenant that he would bring forgiveness of sins and the resurrection of the flesh (conv. vii. 6). Thus the "Word" "directed us to the truth and brought us to immortality" (res. iii. 23. 4, 6). He brings to men the redemption of the body (res. ii. 18. 8 ; 24. 4). But the controlling idea of Methodius is different from these, i. e., Christ is born in those who are received by baptism into the church : "For since those illuminated (baptized) with the image of the Logos, impressed in figure upon them and begotten within them according to perfect knowledge and faith, receive also the marks and image and manhood of Christ, so, we may understand, is Christ born in everyone." Since they through the Holy Spirit enter into living fellowship with Christ, they themselves become, as it were, Christs : "As if having become Christs, being baptized according to their possession of the Spirit into Christ " (conv. viii. 8 ; cf. Ephes. 3. 14-17). "For to proclaim the incarnation of the Son of God by the holy virgin, but not at the same time to confess that he also comes into his church as into his flesh, is not perfect. For everyone of us must confess, not alone his parousia in that holy flesh which came from the pure virgin, but also a similar parousia in the spirit

of everyone of us" (urchin, 8. 2, 3). "Be moulded by
Christ, who is within you" (ib. 1. 6 ; cf. distinction of meats,
4. 1). Christ becomes known to us, because he dwells in us
(cf. conv. viii. 9). But this fellowship in the Holy Ghost
produces in us a new life and energy, which lead to immortality (urchin, 4. 4, 6 ; 8. 3-5. Conv. iii. 8 : "It is impossible for anyone to be a partaker of the Holy Spirit and be
accounted a member of Christ, unless the Logos, having first
come to him, has fallen asleep and risen, in order that, having
arisen from sleep with him who for his sake fell asleep, he also
having been formed anew may be enabled to share in the renewal and restoration of the Spirit." Conv. viii. 10 : "He
chooses the thought of the restored"). Thus Christ has come to
take up his abode in men. When this is done through the Holy
Spirit, men are renewed, incited to choose the good and thus to
attain immortality. As the Logos once dwelt in Adam (supra,
p. 174), so now he dwells again in believers. (5) Man is introduced into this new life through the church, which is primarily "the whole assembly (ἄθροισμα) and mass (στίφος) of
those who have believed" (conv. iii. 8 ; vii. 3); but the more
perfect and morally mature properly constitute the church of
Christ, which has the power to prosecute his work (ib.). Further, in this "robe of the Lord," the church, are discriminated
the spiritual and the laity : " He calls the more powerful rank
of the church, *i. e.*, the bishops and teachers, the warp ; but the
subjects and laity of the pasture, the woof" (leprosy, 15. 4).
This is not yet understood in a hierarchical sense (see complaint
against bishops, ib. 17. 2). The church in which Christ dwells
now bears children to him. This occurs through teaching
(διδασκαλία, conv. iii. 8) and through baptism (ib. viii. 6 ; cf.
dist. of meats, 11. 6 : "as the mysteries have been ordained for
the illuminating and vivifying of that which has been learned ").
Baptism introduces into the fellowship of the Spirit and bestows
immortality ("the illuminated [*i. e.*, baptized] have been duly
born again to immortality," conv. iii. 8). Thus the church increases and grows because it stands in living fellowship with the
Logos : "growing daily into loftiness and beauty and magnitude through the union and fellowship of the Logos" (ib.).
Thus she bears children to Christ—yea, even begets the Word
itself in the heart (ib. viii. 11 init.). (6) Evident as it is that man
has the ability to accept by the power of his will the salvation
proffered, it is just as certain that sin yet exerts its alluring and
stimulating power within him. " But now, even after believing
and going to the water of cleansing, we are often found yet in
sins." Faith only smothers sin, and does not root it out ; it cuts

off the suckers, but not the root itself (res. i. 41. 2-4). More than this man cannot accomplish (ib. i. 44. 4 ; only death can complete the work): but this much he must strive to do. He does so in the power of the Spirit working within him (*e. g.*, conv. viii. 10). Thus he represses the lusts that burn within him (res. ii. 3-5) and obeys not the world but God ("the law of God is self-control," res. i. 60. 3). In this conflict, Christ is helper and advocate (res. iii. 23. 11). God is called upon to grant "improvement of the heart," and "non-imputation and for-giveness of sins" (ib. iii. 23. 7-9). Thus, contending and re-penting (ib. iii. 21. 9), man struggles upward. Repentance has to do primarily with the lusts of the heart. These must be con-fessed to God. But if one is yet unable to overcome them, or if they issue in sinful acts, then one should entrust himself to the bishop and be by him subjected to the discipline of the church. This imposes upon the offender separation from church-fellowship and public confession. It is the duty of the bishop to note whether there be real penitence and a forsaking of sin, and, only in such case, to restore the offender to fellowship (leprosy, 5 ff.; cf. BONWETSCH, Theol. des Method., p. 103 ff.). It is important to observe how the point of view here as elsewhere differs from that of the West. The bishop is not a judge, and the aim in repentance is not to render satisfaction to God. The bishop is regarded as a spiritual adviser and official of the church, and the object of repentance is inward healing and amendment. The Christian's aim is : " that we may become strong and sound through faith to keep thy commandments " (ib. iii. 23. 11). All depends upon " the faith and the conduct," upon " orthodoxy,"[1] and " good works," and " an active and rational life " (leprosy, 15. 2 ; urchin, 8. 4 ; dist. of meats, 8. 2). At the same time there is running through the writings of Methodius a strong leaning toward asceticism and thoughts of the life to come. Suffering purifies (dist. of meats, 1-5). He esteems lightly "things present " (" a using, but no possession "), but he loves " things to come," which are eternal (life and rat. conduct, 5. 1 ; 6. 3). Of "lusts" the church will know nothing, for "they say that it is called ' church ' from having turned away from (ἐκκεκλικέναι) pleasures" (de creat. 8). But Methodius never tires of glorifying celibacy :[2] Virginity is nearness to God

---

[1] Cf. the value attached to orthodoxy, *e. g.*, res. i. 30. 2 : " For thou seest that the doctrines are not of small account to us, but in what way it is necessary to have believed ; for I think that nothing is so evil for a man as that of the nec-essary things he should believe anything false."

[2] The right to marry is not thereby curtailed, *e. g.*, conv. ii. 1. 2 ; iii. 11 ff.; lib. arb. 15. 1 f.

(παρθεία γὰρ ἡ παρθενία, conv. viii. 1).   Christ is the chief Virgin
(ib. 1. 5).   Virgins are the best portion of the church.   "For,
although many are evidently daughters of the church, there is one
rank alone chosen and most precious in her eyes above all others,
the rank of the virgins (conv. vii. 3).

(7) The goal of the Christian life is immortality attained
through the resurrection.   The latter term applies not to the
soul, but to the body, whose substance continues to exist, since
it was not the purpose of God to transform men into angels (res.
i. 50. 1 ; iii. 1 ff.).   Immortality is, therefore, to be attained after
the final conflagration, which will result in a reconstruction
(ἀναχτισθῆναι) of the original creation (χτίσις) (ib. i. 48. 3).   All
of this is in direct and designed opposition to Origen.

4.  Such are the principles which constituted the "Christianity" of a cultivated Greek of about A. D. 300.   It is a
unique mixture of ideas garnered from the popular philosophy of the Greeks, from the popular Christianity of the age,
from a glowing zeal for the ideals of asceticism, and from a
real interest in the problems which Origen had so forcibly stated.
Methodius has lost all conception of a righteousness to be attained
through faith.   Faith is the acceptance of that which is to be
believed, and is accompanied by the moral application to the life
by means of self-control (σωφροσύνη) and in obedience, through
good works and an ascetic life—with which is combined also the
hope of immortality.   But throughout all these assertions is felt
the force of a great primitive Christian experience, "the Christ
in us," who is our strength, who renews us in our hearts, and
draws our hearts upward from this earth toward himself.   "Up
to the heights of the regenerated who have been borne to the
throne of God . . . are lifted the hearts of the renewed, taught
there to see and be seen, in order that they may not be betrayed
into the depths of the mighty dragon" (conv. viii. 10).   But
this *Sursum Corda!* rests upon the thought that he is the Vine
and we the branches—he in us and we in him.   It is the legacy
of John and Ignatius which furnishes spiritual sustenance to this
theologian of Asia Minor.   It is, perhaps, erroneous to characterize his theology as "the theology of the future" (Harnack);
but it reveals to us one of the factors which explain the bitter
conflicts of the future as to the person of Christ.   We see here
the religious capital which was to bear the expenses of the long
campaign.

5.  The *Western Theologians* now claim our attention.

SOURCES.   The writings of Cyprian with the Pseudo-Cyprian works, De
montibus Sina et Sion, and the sermon, De aleatoribus (probably delivered at
Rome in the second half of the second century), ed. Hartel, vid. p. 178;

the best edition of De aleat. by Miodonski, 1889. Compare GÖTZ, Das Christentum Cyprians, 1896. COMMODIANUS, Instructionum ll. 2, and Carmen
apologeticum (ed. Dombart, 1887). ARNOBIUS, adv. nationes, ll. 7 (ed.
Reifferscheid, 1875). LACTANTIUS, divinarum institutionum, ll. 7. Epitome,
de ira dei (ed. Brandt and Laubmann, 1890).

" Christ . . . since he knew that the nature of mortals is
blind and not able to comprehend the reality of any things except
those placed before our eyes, . . . has commanded us to leave
and neglect all those things, and not to devote fruitless meditations to those things which are removed far from our knowledge,
but as far as possible to draw near with our whole mind and soul
to the Lord of all things . . . What is it to you, he says, to
investigate and search out who made man, what is the origin of
souls, who planned the schemes of the wicked, whether the sun
is larger than the earth . . . whether the moon shines with rays
from another luminary or with her own ?   Neither is it an advantage to know these things, nor any detriment to be ignorant
of them.   Commit these things to God, and allow him to know
what, why, and whence they are, whether they ought to be, or
ought not to be, whether anything is without origin, or has its
primordial beginnings . . . it is not permitted to your faculties to
implicate you in such things and to be uselessly concerned about
things so remote.   Your own interests are endangered, I say the
safety of your souls, and unless you apply yourselves to the
thought of the Lord God, evil death awaits you when freed from
the bonds of the flesh " (Arnobius, ii. 60, 61).

These remarkable words of a Western theologian direct the
interest of the Christian upon the salvation of souls, and deny
to him the consideration of physical and metaphysical problems.
There is here revealed a peculiar and growing tendency of Western Christianity, very clearly seen by a comparison of Tertullian
with Origen, or Cyprian with Methodius.   Even the theological
interest of Cyprian did not extend further than the salvation
of souls (*salus animarum*) and immortality (*perpetuitas*, Arnob.
ii. 65).   We note the same limitation in Commodian and Lactantius, in the naive heterodoxy of Arnobius and the correct
orthodoxy of Novatian.   The practical Christianity of these men
—notably that of Cyprian, who so largely moulded the thought
of the succeeding ages—moves within the lines marked out by
Tertullian[1] (supra, p. 132 f.).

(*a*) By the Western theologians as well as by the Orientals

---

[1] Even the emphasis laid upon the *salus animarum* as the content of Christianity is an echo of Tertullian : " Of these blessings there is one superscrip-
tion, the salvation of man " (paen. 2 ; cf., *e. g.*, ib. 10, 12 ; pud. 9 ; jej. 3 ;
bapt. 5 ; praescr. 14 ; c. Marc. ii. 27 ; res. 8, et supra).

the first and most important place is assigned to the doctrine of
the one almighty God, Creator of heaven and earth (*e. g.*, Commod. carm. ap. 90 ff.). Man is under obligation to obey him.
The relationship is viewed as a legal one (vid. sub: lex, satisfactio, meritum). (*b*) The sinner is one who has refused obedience. Sin and death passed from Adam upon his descendants
(Cypr. ep. 64. 5 ; Comm. carm. ap. 324 : " on account of whose
sin (*cujus de peccato*) we die." Cf. instr. i. 35. 3).[1] (*c*) God
now endeavors to deliver man from sin and death. This is first
attempted through the law, but finally through Christ, who as
teacher of the truth gives a " new law " and makes it impressive
by his example ; " by the grace of God we are incited to believe
the law " (Comm. carm. ap. 766 ; cf. instr. i. 35. 18 ; ii. 1. 6 ;
7. 5. Cypr. de op. et eleem. 1, 7, 23, 24 ; de laps. 21 ; unit.
eccl. 2, etc.). Lactantius scarcely gets beyond these ideas.
Both the incarnation and the death upon the cross find their purpose completely attained in instruction and example (vid. instr.
iv. 10. 1 ; 11. 14 : " When God had determined to send the
teacher of virtue to men, he then ordained that he should be re-
born in the flesh and become like to man himself, whose leader
and companion and teacher he was to be ; " iv. 13. 1 ; 14. 15 ;
16. 4; 26. 30 ; 24. 1, 5, 10, 7 : " God himself surely would
not be able to teach virtue, because outside of the body he cannot do the things which he shall teach, and on this account his
teaching will not be perfect ; " also epit. 38. 8 f.; 39. 7 ; 45 ;
46. 2 f.), if we except the peculiar power attributed to the cross
in the taking of an oath (epit. 46. 6-8. Inst. iv. 27 ; see also
iv. 20. 3). Cyprian and Commodian strike a deeper note.
Christ not only taught us the new law, but he suffered for our
sins (Cypr. laps. 17), and thereby made us children of God (ep.
58. 6). He has become our attorney and advocate, our mediator (ep. 11. 5 ; quod idola, 11), so that we find forgiveness of
our sins through him. His blood nullifies death (ep. 55. 22 ;
op. et al. 1). Thus Christ grants cleansing from sin (baptism),
forgiveness of sins (repentance), the new law and immortality.
He is the Saviour, because he establishes and imparts the grace
of the sacraments and of the church order.

(*d*) This salvation is imparted to man in baptism ; is preserved by faith, fear, and obedience ; and attested by repentance
and good works. Divine grace begins with baptism, " since thence

---

[1] " What he did of good or of evil, the leader of our nativity conferred upon
(*contulisset*) us ; we die likewise through him ; " cf. Instr. ii. 5. 8 : *genitalia*. Cypr. ad Donat. 3 : *genuinum*, op. et eleem. 1 : " He healed the
wounds which Adam had conveyed and cured the ancient poisons of the serpent," etc.

13

begins the whole origin (*origo*) of faith and the saving entrance
(*ingressio*) upon the hope of eternal life and the divine regard
(*dignatio*) for the purifying and vivifying of the servants of God "
(Cypr. ep. 73. 12).[1] In baptism man experiences the second birth
(*secunda nativitas*, Cypr. ad Donat. 4; orat. dom. 23). The
recipient receives the Holy Ghost (ep. 63. 8; 73. 9), becomes
free from the devil (ep. 69. 15), from death and hell (ep. 55.
22; op. et al. 2). The second birth secures for man health
(*sanitas*, Cypr. hab. virg. 2); inborn sins are forgiven (Comm.
instr. ii. 5. 8: "in baptism *genitalia* are forgiven thee." Cypr.
op. et al. 1); the subject really becomes another man (Cypr. ad
Don. 3. 4). The new law now applies to him, by obeying
which he is to preserve the purity attained: "he gives the law
of innocence after he has conferred health . . . that pardon
may no more be lacking after thou hast begun to know God "
(Cypr. hab. virg. 2; cf. Commod. instr. ii. 5. 11: "The conclusion for thee: Always avoid serious sins"). Christ, therefore,
imparts a two-fold blessing to man. By baptism he makes him
whole, and he grants to him as thus restored the law, by obeying which he may and should preserve himself in health. If he
fails to do this, repentance is offered to him as a means of salvation. It is now a question of forgiving grace and the preservation of the good will which desires amendment. Man fulfills his
duty toward God by faith and the fear of God: "the whole
basis of religion and faith begins in obedience and fear" (Cypr.
hab. virg. 2 init.; cf. op. et al. 8); by prayer (or. dom. 12);
and by the reception through faith of the gifts of grace now
richly granted (ad Don. 5: "it flows continually; it overflows
abundantly; it satisfies our utmost desire and yet flows on. As
much of receptive faith as we bring thither, so much of the over-
flowing grace do we imbibe"). Although these words of
Cyprian, which were written soon after his conversion, seem to
reveal a vivid sense of the supreme significance of faith, yet the
context leads us to a different conclusion. Faith is for him essentially the recognition of the divine law and belief in the veracity
of the promises (*e. g.*, de mortalit. 6. 22 fin., 24; ad Demetr.
20; de patient. 1; cf. Commod. carm. ap. 311 ff., 615; Lactant. epit. 61. 3 ff.; inst. vi. 17. 23 ff.; also epit. 61. 1: "faith

---

[1] As to the outward form of baptism, we note : It is administered in the
name of the triune God, not merely in the name of Christ (ep. 73. 18; cf.
69. 7); the baptismal confession (ep. 70. 2; 69. 7; cf. 75. 10 f.); sprinkling
or pouring, with the customary bath (*lavacrum*, ep. 69. 12); children to be
baptized, not on the eighth day, but as soon as possible (ep. 64. 2; cf. laps.
10); they also receive the Holy Ghost (ep. 64. 3); anointing with the consecrated oil (*chrisma*, ep. 70. 2); cf. const. ap. vii. 40 ff.

is, therefore, a great part of righteousness."(!) Hence we may thus summarize : Baptism brings forgiveness of sins and blots out sin in a man ; he is now equipped with the Spirit and fulfills the law of God, because he believes that God will reward this struggle to live virtuously and will bestow upon him eternal life. By good works man really wins for himself a merit (*meritum*) before God (op. et al. 26 : "to our merits and works contributing promised rewards "). He pays back what Christ has done for him (op. et al. 17. 23 ; cf. hab. virg. 2). He who performs the works of the law is righteous before God. It is the first concern of the Christian to be mindful of the law : " Nor let anything be considered in your hearts and minds except the divine precepts and the heavenly commandments " (ep. 6. 2).

(*e*) But the baptized also still commit sin. For this, too, grace offers a way of escape : " He has given to the restored one a law and commanded that he should now sin no more . . . we would have been constrained and brought into a strait by the law, nor could the infirmity and imbecility of our human frailty have accomplished anything, had not the divine goodness, again intervening, opened out a certain way of preserving salvation by performing works of righteousness and mercy, so that we may *by alms wash away* whatever stains we have afterward contracted " (Cypr. op. et al. 1). This is the idea entertained of repentance. True, sincere penitence (in case of the lapsed, see p. 180) and confession before the church are prescribed, but, at least in the case of trifling daily sins, good works, and particularly alms, remain the principal thing. By the giving of alms, the Christian repeats what was granted to him at his baptism : "just as in the bath of saving water the fire of hell is extinguished, so by alms and righteous works the flame of sin is quenched. And because in baptism the forgiveness of sins is once bestowed, diligent and continual working, imitating the pattern of baptism, bestows again the favor of God " (op. et al. 2 ; orat. dom. 32). By alms, the sinner renders to God suitable satisfaction (*satisfactio*, op. et al. 4, 5 ; cf. ep. 35 ; 43. 3 ; 55. 11 ; 59. 13 ; 64. 1 ; de laps. 17, 22, 34 ff.); reconciles God (*propitiando deo*) and merits (*mereri*) the mercy of God (op. et el. 5, cf. 13 fin.; 15, cf. Comm. instr. ii. 14. 14 ; de aleator. 11. 2).

If man thus by prayer and good works merits for himself the mercy of God in his battle with sin (*precibus et operibus suis satisfacere*, Cypr. 16.2), we find the Eucharist represented as a means of strengthening for the conflict. It is a safeguard (*tutela*) in the conflict (ep. 57. 2.) It elevates and inflames the spirit ("there is something lacking in the spirit which the recep-

tion of the eucharist does not uplift and inflame," ib. 4). It
unites the church with Christ, and the sorrowing heart is by it
filled with joy (ep. 63, 13, 11 : "Let there be a forgetting
of the former worldly life, and let the sad and sorrowful heart,
which was before oppressed by its increasing sins, be set free in
the joy of the divine forgiveness"). These are genuinely Christian sentiments, which we are not at liberty to discredit because
they give no direct answer to questions raised at a later period.
But the eucharist is also viewed in another light. It is the
"*sacrifice*" offered by the priest, and this can be done only in
the church. Fellowship (*communicatio*) with the church really
consists in the partaking of the eucharist. This sacrifice is
offered (*offerre*) also for penitent sinners, and in their name (*e.g.*,
ep. 16. 2 ; 17. 2). It is a repetition of the sacrifice of Christ :
"This priest acts in the stead of Christ, imitating that which
Christ did, and offering then a true and full sacrifice in the
church to God the Father" (ep. 63. 14). "For the passion of
the Lord is the sacrifice which we offer" (ib. 17). In earlier
times, the virtues and prayers of believers had been called gifts
(δῶρα, 1 Clem. 44. 4; 40. 2 ff.; 36. 1), particularly the eucharistic prayer (Did. 14. 1, 2 ; Just. Dial. 40, 70, 117). Thus also
the presentation of the elements of the Lord's Supper before
God (Iren. iv. 17. 5; 18. 1, 4), as well as the contributions
brought at such times as on the anniversaries of the death of rela-
tives, were looked upon as a sacrifice, and before long a peculiar
significance began to be attached to them as such (*e. g.*, Tert.
ad ux. ii. 8; de monog. 10 ; ex. cast. 11 ; de coron. 3 f.; de
orat. 28 ; cf. Cypr. 1. 2). The Lord's Supper was called
the "*sacrificium.*"[1] Cyprian—since the clergy were, in his
view, actual priests—adopted this idea with great earnestness.
Through the priest the sinner is received into the church, and
through the act of the priest the merit of Christ is applied to
him. In this, a distinctive idea of Catholicism again comes to
view. The history of the Lord's Supper is marked by two great
modifications. The first transformed the fraternal Agape into
the ecclesiastical sacrament ; the second designated as the chief
thing in the transaction the bringing of the sacrifice before God
as a repetition of the death of Christ, and not the gracious
presence of God in our behalf. The second was effected by

[1] Tert. de cultu fem. ii. 11 : "Either the sacrifice is offered, or the word of
God administered ; " cf. de orat. 19 ; ad uxor. 11. 8. See the association of
Word and Eucharist also in Ps.-Clem. de virg. ep. i. 5 ; cf. Abercius-title,
lines 6, 9, 12 ff. (word, baptism, eucharist), and Method., supra, p. 189. For
the sacrificial idea in ancient times, see Höfling, Die Lehre d. ältesten Kirche
von Opfer, Erl. 1851.

Origen, and in it we have another illustration of the complete externalizing of religion.   Instead of the act and agency of God appears the work of man, the ordinance of a holy legal system.   It was thus in the eucharist, and most distinctly thus in the doctrine and praxis of repentance.   The Romish sacrament of penance was constructed by Tertullian and Cyprian.   In the attempt to make repentance difficult, it is made easy.   For that which is the hardest thing in religion—repentance and faith—is substituted good works:  "the salutary guardian of our security —a thing placed within our power to do—a thing both grand and easy" (op. et al. 26).[1]

(f) The inevitable consequence of the conception of the Christian life as an obedience rendered to the "new law" is a double morality.   The highest self-surrender to God cannot be *demanded* of all, but only *advised*.   The first precept commands to increase and multiply, and the second counsels continence (hab. virg. 23).   Virginity is the blossom of the ecclesiastical seed (ib. 3).   However beautifully Cyprian may depict the ideal of the Christian life (see esp. orat. dom. 15 ; zel. et liv. 16 ; cf. Comm. instr. ii. 17. 17 ff.), yet the best Christians are those alone who have chosen the heavenly Bridegroom (hab. virg. 20. 22)—and the language here is not meant, as in Origen, to indicate a really higher plane of Christian character.

(g) But, while thus accommodating the Christian life to the world, the desire was strongly felt to escape from the world, and there was much thought of the approaching end (Cypr. un. eccl. 16 ; de mortal. 25 f.; ad Demetr. 3 f.).   The resurrection was the chief object of faith, for from it was expected the reward for good works (e. g., hab. virg. 21, also supra).   Great delight was found in drawing portraitures of the last times and the conflicts under the reign of the Antichrist (Nero), with the consolation of the millennial kingdom (see esp. Comm. carm. ap. 791 ff.; instr. ii. 2-4 ; 39 ; i. 27, 28, 41, etc.   Lactant. ep. 66, 67).   The gulf between the church, as it was then conceived, and the kingdom of God lying wholly in the future, became but the wider :  "He declares that they shall be permitted to see the kingdom who have performed works in his church" (op. et el. 9, cf. de zel. et liv. 18).

---

[1] Cyprian, like Origen, believed in a purifying fire after death : "It is one thing, tortured with prolonged misery for sins, to be cleansed and purged for a long time by fire, and another thing to have all sins purged in the passion" (*i. e.*, Lord's Supper).  Ep. 55. 20 ; cf. supra, p. 159, n.  Vid. also Tert. de monog., 10: "He prays for his (the deceased's) soul ; he implores for him meanwhile a cooling (in the flame)."  These are ideas borrowed from antiquity, *e. g.*, Plato, Phaed. 6, and the Orphic poems.

6. Such is Western Christianity in the third century. Cyprian's work, *De catholicae ecclesiae unitate*, and, in at least equal degree, his *De opere et eleemosyne*, may be designated landmarks of the course of development. But scarcely at a single point does he furnish more than a development of suggestions found in the father of Western Catholicism, Tertullian (cf. p. 132 f.). There exists a legal relationship between God and man. By baptism, God has in a magical way made man pure (the Stoic definition of spirit here influences the thought), and he is now under obligation to observe the new law of Christ. Since he does not do this, he must render satisfaction to God by good works, by which he merits mercy for himself and secures as his reward the resurrection. This is the chief content of the faith. But it is only in the church, *i. e.*, in obedience to the bishops, who have been ordained by God and by him endowed with peculiar powers and authority (priests and judges of God's grace), that a man can become and continue a Christian. This is the meaning of the "salvation of souls," which Christ has brought to man.

The Christianity of the West is thus marked by the following characteristics : (1) Sacramental grace. (2) The legal conception of the relationship between God and man. (3) The combination of the two ideas in the concentration of the whole energy of religion upon the salvation of souls (*salus animarum*). (4) The subjugation of the soul, for the attainment of its salvation, to the control of the hierarchical church with its sacramental ordinances. (5) But the sacraments in the hierarchy are held in balance by the merits (*merita*) of the individual. (6) The formulas of Tertullian and the authority of the Apostles' Creed. The theology of the East, on the contrary, is distinguished by : (1) The adoption of the theology of Origen. (2) The emphasis laid upon "orthodoxy" and delight in metaphysical problems. (3) The fixing of immortality as the practical goal. (4) The mystical conception of the work of Christ, as being born in us, dwelling in us, and permeating us with spiritual life.

The Christianity of the third century presents itself to us as a direct continuation of the doctrinal teaching of the second century. The roots of the ideas here developed may in almost every instance be traced back to the Apostolic Fathers. In fact, the departure of the teachers of this period from the views of the Apostolic Fathers was but small in comparison with that of the latter from the position of the Apostles. Yet the development during the third century progressed with. astonishing rapidity. The original Christian ideas of a life with God in Christ and of an intercourse of the heart with God through repenlance and faith, which in the second century still constantly assert themselves despite the general moralizing of the gospel, are now, particularly in the Western church, almost entirely forced into the background.   The practical aims in view have become different from those prescribed by the spirit of Christ and the teachings of Paul.   In the East, all stress is laid upon the acceptance of the pure doctrine, which is more and more reduced to abstract formulas and a life of celibacy—yet practical interest in the "Christ in us" does not altogether disappear. In the West, the controlling ideas are the preservation of a right relation to God and the Catholic church, the way in which man may come to God and remain in fellowship with him, and the ideal of celibacy—yet there persists a feeling that it is the highest duty of the church to care for the salvation of souls.   The perversion, although differing in character, is common to the two branches of the church.   The time will come when repentance will be held to consist only in good works, and yet, under the delusion of strange ideals, really good works will be neglected, and when an intellectual acceptance of doctrine shall take the place of faith.   Nevertheless, "orthodoxy" will pursue its course in the East and the "hierarchy" in the West, and both will bring unutterable sorrow to the hearts of true believers.   Yet it cannot be but that he who with a Christian's open heart seeks to realize and study the motives underlying the life of that age will stumble upon ideas and convictions which still attest the power of the ancient truth.   In the one case it will be the "Up to the heights!" (p. 191), and in the other the "Salvation of souls."   The Eastern church will endeavor to fathom the mysteries of the world above, and enjoy its raptures in mystic contemplation, while the salvation of the soul will remain the great problem in the West.

If we consider the course of development from the point of view of two prominent apostles, the East will be found following in the path marked out by John, while the West walks in the footsteps of Paul.   These points of view were often much obscured in the course of the development, but a keen interest in the Divine Logos, who imparts new life to us, remains the central feature among the Greeks, while in the West the central problem continues to be "How may the sinner become righteous before God?"   In the doctrines of the Trinity and in Christology the interest here centres in repentance and the church, and this continues to be the case in the last great religious agitation of the West, the Reformation of Luther (vid. vol. ii.).   So far-reaching is the outlook which we may gain from the study of the Christianity of the third century.

For the grace of God hath appeared, bringing salvation to all men, instructing us, to the intent that, denying ungodliness and worldly lusts, we should live soberly and righteously and godly in this present world; looking for the blessed hope and appearing of the glory of the great God and our Saviour Jesus Christ; who gave himself for us, that he might redeem us from all iniquity, and purify unto himself a people for his own possession, zealous of good works.—*Titus ii. 11-14.*

# PART II.

## DOCTRINAL CONSTRUCTION IN THE ANCIENT CHURCH.

### CHAPTER I.

#### THE DOCTRINE OF THE TRINITY.

§ 20. *Arianism and the Homousia of the Son (the First Council of Nice).*

1. We have had occasion to observe the diversity of views concerning the divinity of Christ which prevailed before the outbreak of the great controversy ; but we have also noted a certain unity of religious conviction at this point : " the church unanimously adoring the divinity of Christ." Although there was little attempt to fathom the procession of the Son from the Father, yet he, like the Father, was regarded as God, as the brightness of his glory and the image ($\chi\alpha\rho\alpha\varkappa\tau\acute{\eta}\rho$) of his person ($\acute{\upsilon}\pi\acute{o}\sigma\tau\alpha\sigma\iota\varsigma$) (Heb. i. 3). These were regarded as the " apostolic dogmas of the church " (vid. Alex. ep. ad Alex. in Theodoret. h. e. i. 3). Opposite conceptions must now inevitably lead to conflict, as had become evident in the Monarchian and Dionysian controversies. After the unity of the church had become a theory of practical importance, and the conception of " heresy " had, in consequence of the fixation of the church's doctrine, become more definite, the ancient indefinite formulas became unsatisfactory, especially as they left room for such interpretations as that of Arius. But we shall utterly fail to understand the conflicts of the period before us if we shall interpret them as merely a result of the metaphysical tendency of Grecian thought. On the contrary, beneath these controversies lay most thoroughly practical and religious motives. Christ was the centre of Greek piety ; the new immortal life, the periphery ; the idea of salvation, the radius. The centre must be so located that all the radii may actually meet in it. Christ must be conceived of as in nature and character capable of bestowing the new divine life upon men.

LUCIAN of Antioch was an adherent of Paul of Samosata, and hence out of harmony with the church (ib. in Theod. i. 3, p. 739).

ARIUS was his pupil, as was also EUSEBIUS OF NICOMEDIA (ep. Arii ad Eus. in Theod. h. e. i. 4 fin. and Alex. ib. 4). Traces of relationship with Paul may be found in Arius (see Athanas. c. Arian. or. iii. 10, 51); but the views of Paul were developed by him in harmony with the later age. The impersonal energy (δύναμις) in the Father has become a special personality, which, however, does not—to the gratification of heathen and Jews (ep. Alex. in Theod. h. e. i. 3)—call the unity of God in question, and yet, in keeping with the consciousness of the church and the prevalent theory of the Logos, preserves the independence of the second divine person. It is thus that the doctrine of Arius, which, in its main features, Lucian may have already taught, is to be understood. It is merely the Christology of the third century theoretically carried to its logical conclusion. But it was this very fact of the logical consistency of the theory which opened the eyes of the church. The same process has been repeated in the case of most heresies. The controversies to which they gave rise have led to the construction of dogmas.

1. The Doctrine of ARIUS.

LITERATURE. Of the writings of Arius himself we possess: a letter to Alexander, bishop of Alexandria, in Athanas. de synodis Arim. et Seleuc. 16 and Epiph. h. 69. 7, 8; a letter of Eusebius of Nicomedia in Theodoret. h. e. i. 4 (opp. ed. SCHULZE, iii. 2), and Epiph. h. 69. 6. Fragments from his θάλεια in Athanas. c. Arian. or. i.; de synod. Arim. et Seleuc. 15).[1] For statements of his teaching, vid. especially the writings of Athanasius and the letter from Alexander of Alexandria to Alexander of Byzantium, in Theodoret. h. e. i. 3, and the Ep. encyclica in Socrat. h. e. i. 6. Compare GWATKIN, Studies of Arianism, 1882. KÖLLING, Gesch. d. arian. Häresie, 2 vols., 1874, 1883. MÖLLER, PRE. i. 620 ff.

(a) The dominant idea in the views of Arius is the monotheistic principle of the Monarchians (cf. Athanas. c. Ar. or. iii. 7, 28; iv. 10).[2] There is One unbegotten God: "We know only one God, unbegotten." This axiom led to a keen criticism of the prevalent representations of the relation of Christ to the Father. The Son dare not be represented as an emanation (προβολή), nor a part of the Father having the same nature (μέρος ὁμοούσιον), nor as alike uncreated (συναγέννητος). For if the Father were compound, divided, or mutable (σύνθετος, διαίρετος, τρεπτός), we should have to think of him as corporeal, and be compelled to accept two uncreated beings (δύο ἀγέννητοι). The Son would then be a brother of the Father (ep. ad Al. and ep. ad Eus.; Athanas. c. Arian. or. 1. 14; iii. 2, 62, 67; de

---

[1] Also, ᾄσματά τε ναυτικὰ καὶ ἐπιμύλια καὶ ὁδοιπορικὰ γράψαι . . . εἰς μελῳδίας ἐκτεῖναι, Philostorgius h. e. ii. 2.

[2] Appeal was made, among others, to Hermas, Mand. i. (Athanas. in Theod. h. e. i. 7).

decr. syn. Nic. 10). (*b*) God alone is unoriginated, or unbegotten, without beginning. The Son had a beginning, and was from a non-existent state created by the Father before the beginning of the world : "The Son is not unbegotten, nor a part of the unbegotten One . . . nor from something previously existing, but he existed with will and design before times and ages, the complete, only-begotten, unchangeable God ; and before he began to be, or was either created or founded, he was not. The Son has a beginning, but God is without beginning . . . He is, out of things not being (ep. ad Eus.). God was not always Father, but there was [a time] when God was alone, and was not yet Father, and afterward he became Father. The Son was not always. For, all things coming into being from not being, and all things created and made having begun to be, this Logos of God also came into being from things not existing ; and there was [a time] when he was not, and he was not before he was begotten, but he also had a beginning of being created" (Thal. in Athan. or. 1. 5). (*c*) The Son is the Logos and the Wisdom of the Father, but he is to be distinguished from the Logos immanent in God. The latter is a divine energy (δύναμις), the Son a created divine being, having participation in the immanent Logos (cf. the Dynamistic Monarchianism). He says thus that there are two *sophias;* the one peculiar to God and co-eternal with him, and the Son was born in the *sophia,* and, sharing in it, he is called simply *sophia* and *Logos* . . . and he says thus also that there is another Logos besides the Son in God, and that the Son, sharing in this, is again by grace called Logos and the Son himself" (Athan. l. c. i. 5). (*d*) The Logos is, therefore, a creature of the Father, created by him as the medium in the creation of the world (ib. and ii. 24 ; ep. encycl. Alex. in Socr. h. e. i. 6). Accordingly, he is not God in the full sense of the word, but through his enjoyment of the divine favor he receives the names, God and Son of God, as do also others ("and although he is called God, he is yet not the true God, but by sharing in grace, just as all others also, he is called by name simply God," Thal. ib. 1. 6 ; cf. ep. Al. ad Al. in Theod. i. 3. p. 732). It is, therefore, clear that "the Logos is different from and unlike the substance (ὀυσία) and peculiar nature (ἰδιότητος) of the Father in all respects" (Thal. ib.). (*e*) In view of the significance of this unoriginated character (ἀγεννησία) for the divine nature of the Son, a further consequence is unavoidable. The Logos is by nature mutable. But since God foresaw that he would remain good, he bestowed upon him in advance the glory which he afterward as man merited by his virtue (Thal. in Ath. i. 5 ; cf. i. 35 init.; ep. Al. ad Al. in Theod. i. 3, p. 732 ; cf. ep. encycl. Alex. in Socr. i. 6 : mutable, $\tau\rho\varepsilon\pi\tau\acute{o}\varsigma$, and variable, $\dot{\alpha}\lambda\lambda o\acute{\iota}\omega\tau o\varsigma$, by nature).[1]   The Arians held, with Paul of Samosata, that Christ is through unity of will one with the Father (Athan. c. Arian. or. iii. 10).  (f) By the use of profane logic (Athan. c. Ar. or. ii. 68) and by the citation of passages of Scripture treating of the humility of Christ (Alex. in Theod. i. 3, p. 740), the Arians sought to establish their own view and disprove that which was becoming the accepted doctrine of the church.   It was the easier to carry out this purpose, since Arianism did not attribute a human soul to Christ (see Greg. Naz. ep. ad Cledon. i. 7.   Epiphan. ancor. 33).

If we contemplate this theory as a whole, we at once observe its relationship with Paul of Samosata and Dynamistic Monarchianism.   But the earlier views referred to, in the process of accommodation, became much worse.   What Paul taught concerning the man Jesus, Arius—and apparently Lucian before him— transferred to a median being, the Logos.   It is not the man Jesus who is endowed with divine energy ($\delta\acute{v}\nu\alpha\mu\iota\varsigma$) and preserves it in a moral life, but the Logos—the man Jesus does not even possess a human soul.  The Logos is, therefore, a "creature of God" and yet "complete God."  The unity of God is preserved, but only at the price of teaching "that there are three persons ($\acute{v}\pi o\sigma\tau\acute{\alpha}\sigma\varepsilon\iota\varsigma$), Father, Son, and Holy Ghost" (ep. ad Al. in Epiph. h. 69. 8).  Thus a mythological element is introduced into Christianity, and bare Monotheism is transformed into the Polytheism of heroes and demigods; cf. Athan. c. Ar. or. iii. 15, 16), or there is thought to be a necessity, with Philo, for a median being between the world and God (cf. ib. ii. 24). Arius reminds us at many points of the old Apologists (§ 13), but what was in their case apologetic art and necessity is here a deliberate theory, set up in opposition to other views.

There is also the further difference, that by the Apologists Christ, as the Divine Logos, is regarded as truly God ; whereas Arius makes him but a rational energy created by God.  If we look for the inspiring motive of this doctrine—which is the worst Christology imaginable—Athanasius is probably not wholly wrong in regarding it as Samosatianism modified by lack of courage (ib. iii. 51 ; i. 38).   Arius interpreted Paul of Samosata in the sense of the subordinationistic utterances of Origen and

---

[1] That this was the view of Arius is beyond question.   He veiled it in correspondence with Eusebius (see the $\dot{\alpha}\nu\alpha\lambda\lambda o\acute{\iota}\omega\tau o\varsigma$ above), just as the direct declaration of the temporality of the Son was avoided (see citations above, and cf. ep. ad Al. in Epiph. h. 69. 8 : being born achronously, and also Athan. c. Arian. or i. 13), or, despite the utterances above cited, Christ was described to Eusebius as "complete God."

pressed every point thus gained to its extreme logical conclusion.

With great activity, political sagacity, and tact, Arius made provision for the propagation of his theory. He not only gained a following in Egypt, among bishops and virgins (see ep. Al. ad Al. init.), but he succeeded in winning the schismatic Meletians (Alex. ep. encycl. Sozomen. h. e. i. 15), and also found comrades among the bishops in Palestine and Syria (Theod. h. e. i. 3; Sozomen. h. e. 1. 115. The mighty co-Lucianist, Eusebius of Nicomedia (see his letters to Paulinus of Tyre in Theod. i. 5), became the patron of this doctrine.

3. The first to oppose Arius was the Alexandrine bishop, ALEXANDER. He really understood the new doctrine (see his account of it in Theod. h. e. i. 3 and Socr. h. e. i. 6). He points out that the Word cannot itself have come into existence in time, since all things were made by it (Jn. i. 3). His person (ὑπόστασις) is beyond the comprehension of men (or angels, cf. Isa. liii. 8; xxiv. 16). If Christ is the effulgence of God (Heb. i. 3), then to deny his eternity is to deny the eternity of the Father's light. The sonship (υἱότης) is, therefore, different in kind from that of human beings. The theory of Arius is related to the heresies of Ebion, Paul, and Artemas. Against it, Alexander regards the claims of the "apostolic doctrines of the church," i. e., of the Apostles' Creed, as vindicated by his defense of the eternal divinity of the Son, together with that of the Holy Ghost (Theod. 1. 3, p. 745 f., 742). Less certain is his positive teaching. He appears himself to have at an earlier period recognized an existence of the Father before that of Christ ("and he exists therefore before Christ, as we taught in harmony with your preaching in the church," says Arius of him, Ar. ad Al. in Epiph. h. 69. 8). But he now taught concerning the Son : "Always God, always Son. . . . The Son exists unbegottenly (ἀγεννήτως) in God, always begotten (ἀειγεννής), unbegottenly begotten " (ἀγεννητογενής) (Ar. ep. ad Eus. in Epiph. 69. 3). He does not deny the birth of the Saviour ("that his unbegottenness is a property having relation to the Father alone ") ; but it is a birth "without beginning so far as the Father is concerned," an always being from the Father (τὸ ἀεὶ εἶναι ἐκ τοῦ πατρός). He is thus immutable and unvariable, and is rightly worshiped as is the Father. When John locates the Son in the bosom of the Father, he means to indicate "that the Father and the Son are two entities (πράγματα), inseparable from one another." There are in the person (ὑποστάσις) two natures (φύσεις). When the Lord declares himself one with the Father (Jn. x. 30), he wishes to make himself known as the

absolute image of the Father. The Son is therefore a nature (φύσις) separate from the Father; but, since he is untemporally begotten of the Father, he is God as is the Father. This view is not clear.

The whole controversy appears in the first instance as a repetition of the Dionysian dispute. Alexander attributed to Dionysius of Rome an emphasizing of the "apostolic doctrines," but we have no intimation that the opposition became more pronounced.

4. It seems proper at this point to present connectedly the teaching of ATHANASIUS [born before A. D. 300; died A. D. 373], which he maintained unswervingly and unyieldingly in a long life, subject to constant assault and persecution. Such a study will reveal to us the profoundest motives underlying the great controversy.

SOURCES. Apologia c. Arianos; expositio fidei; de decretis synodi Nicaenae; Ep. ad episc. Aeg. et Lib.; apol. ad Constant. imperat.; apol. de fuga sua; hist. Arianorum ad monach.; ep. ad Serapionem de morte Arii; ad Serapionem, ep. ii.; de synodis Arim. et Seleuc.; and especially his chief work, Orationes iv. c. Arianos. Opp. ed. Montfaucon, in Migne ser. gr. 25-28; the most important also in Thilo, Bibl. patr. graec. dogmat. i. Compare MÖHLER, Athanas., ed. 2, 1844. VOIGT, Die Lehre des Athanas., 1861. ATZBERGER, Die Logoslehre des Athanas., 1880. PELL, Die Lehre des Athanas. von der Sünde u. Erlösung, 1888. LOOFS, PRE. ii., ed. 3, 194 ff. HARNACK DG. ii., ed. 3, 155 ff., 202 ff. STÜLCKEN, Athanasiana, 1899. Hoss, Studien über das Christentum u. die Theologie des Athanasius.

The strength of Athanasius lay in the following particulars: (1) In the very great stability and genuineness of his character. In a long life, amid persecution and oppression, he remained immovable in his adherence to the truth which he had grasped, without resorting to political expedients and without any waverings. (2) He stood upon a secure foundation in his firm grasp upon the conception of the unity of God, and this preserved him from the subordinationism of the Logos-Christology. (3) He, with an unerring tact, taught men to recognize the nature of the person of Christ and its importance. He was able therefore to understand Christ as the Redeemer and to define his nature in accordance with the logical requirements of his redeeming work. Just here is located the peculiarity of his Christology, which assures it a permanent place in the teachings of the church. Since Christ effects in us the new supernatural life, therefore he must be God in the sense of the *homousia*. To understand the biblical character of Athanasius's statement of the problem, we need but recall the representations of John and the κύριος-πνεῦμα of Paul.

(*a*) We notice first the denunciation of Arianism. Athanasius

clearly recognized the unchristian and irreligious conclusions
to which this doctrine leads.   If Arius is right, then the
triune God is not eternal ; to the unity was added·in time the
Son and the Spirit.   The three-foldness has come into existence
from the non-existent.   Who can assure us that there may not
be a further increase?  (c. Ar. or. i. 17, 18).   According to
Arius, baptism would be administered in the name of a creature,
which can after all render us no aid (ib. ii. 41 ; iv. 25).   But
not only is the Trinity thus dissolved by the Arians ; even the
divinity of the Father is imperiled.   The Father has not always
been Father—some change has taken place in him in the course
of time, and he did not always have within him the Word,
Light, and Wisdom (ib. i. 20, 24, 25).   Further, Arianism
leads logically to the polytheism of the heathen world.   Only if
the Son partakes of the same nature and substance as the
Father, can we speak of One God.   The Arians, on the contrary, have two different Gods :  "It is necessary for them to
speak of two Gods, one the creator and the other the created,
and to worship two Lords," which leads to Greek polytheism
(ib. iii. 15, 16).[1]   This is illustrated particularly in the worship
rendered to Jesus in the church.   It is heathenish to worship the
creature instead of the Creator (ep. encycl. 4), and, according
to Rev. xxii. 9, worship is not to be rendered even to the angels
(c. Ar. or. ii. 23):  "Who said to them that, having abandoned
the worship of the created universe ($\dot{\eta}$ $\varkappa\tau\acute{\iota}\sigma\iota\varsigma$), they should proceed again to worship something created and made?" (ib. i.
8, 38, 42 ; de decr. 11 fin.).   But, above all, the Arian view destroys the certainty of salvation.   If the Logos is mutable, as the
Arians consistently maintain, how can he reveal to us the Father,
and how can we behold in him the Father?   "How can he who
beholds the mutable think that he is beholding the immutable?"
(ib. i. 35 ; cf. Jn. 14. 9).   In this way man can never reach the
assurance of salvation, of fellowship with God, the forgiveness
of his sins, and immortality :  "For if, being a creature, he became man, he as man remained none the less such as he was,
not partaking of God ; for how could a creature by a creature partake of God ?  .  .  And how, if the Logos was a
creature, would he be able to dissolve a decree of God and forgive sin?" (ii. 67 ; iv. 20).   "Again, the man partaking of
a creature would not be deified, unless the Son was truly God ;
and the man would not be equal with the Father, unless he who
assumed the body was by nature also the true Logos of the

---

[1] Cf. Basil. ep. 243. 4 : "Polytheism has conquered—with them [there is]
a great God and a small God."   Also Greg. Nyss., in his funeral oration for
Basil, Mi. 46. 796.   Aug. de symbol., 1. 2.

Father" (ii. 70). Finally, this median being (μεσίτης) between God and the world is an utterly useless and senseless invention. Neither is God too proud to come himself as Creator into direct touch with a creature, nor in that case would the matter be made any better by the supposed Logos, since at his creation also some median creature would have been necessary, and so on *ad infinitum* (ii. 25, 26; de decr. 8). Hence, if Christ is not the true God and one substance with the Father, then it is all over with the Trinity and the baptismal-symbol; then polytheism and the worship of creatures are again introduced into the church; then the salvation of Christian believers comes to naught; and yet, after all, no logically tenable position has been reached. Thus the theory of Arius is just as impious as it is unscientific.

(*b*) What then is the doctrine of Athanasius himself touching the divinity of the Son? (*a*) "And since Christ is God of God and the Logos, Wisdom, Son, and Power of God, therefore, One God is proclaimed in the Holy Scriptures. For the Logos, being the Son of the one God, is referred back to him from whom he is, so that Father and Son are two, yet the monad of divinity is unseparated (ἀδιαίρετος) and undivided (ἄσχιστος). Thus it might be said also that there is one original source of divinity and not two original sources, and hence, also correctly, that there is a monarchy . . . the nature (οὐσία) and the person (ὑπόστασις) are one" (c. Ar. or. iv. 1). These theses voice the conviction that the divinity of the Son must be understood with a distinct and conscious effort to guard the divine monad. No basis is left for the "second God." Athanasius was led to recognize the importance of this position by the conclusions which Arius had drawn from his "second God." He may, perhaps, have been influenced also by the significant part played by Sabellianism in Egypt (vid. supra, p. 168). In this case we have another illustration of the historical recognition of the element of truth lurking in a false theory. But the circumstance should not be overlooked that Athanasius labored in the West, where the consciousness of the unity of God was always more vivid than in the East, which was so unquestionably controlled by the formulas of the Logos idea. (*β*) But Athanasius will not recognize a Son-Father (υἱοπάτωρ) with the Sabellians, nor a sole-natured (μονοούσιος) God, for the existence of the Son would thus be excluded. On the contrary, the independent and eternally personal existence of the Son is a fixed premise, always bearing in mind that we are not to think of "three hypostases separated from one another," which would lead to Polytheism. The relationship between the Father and the Son is rather like that between a fountain and the stream that gushes from it: "Just as a river springing from a fountain is not separated from it, although there are two forms and two names, so neither is the Father the Son, nor the Son the Father " (expos. fid. 2 ; c. Ar. or. iii. 4). (γ) This distinction, as well as the unity, finds expression in the term " oneness of essence " (ἑνότης τῆς οὐσίας). The Logos is a production, or generation (γέννημα), from the nature (οὐσία) of the Father (de decr. 3, 22, 23 ; c. Ar. i. 29). As to his relation to created beings, it follows that "the Son is different in origin and different in nature from created beings, and, on the other hand, is the same and of the same nature (ὁμοφυὴς) as the nature of the Father " (ib. i. 58 ; de decr. 23, 12 ; de syn. 53). As he is thus other-natured (ἑτεροούσιος) than created beings, so he is same-natured (ὁμοούσιος)[1] with the Father, i. e., he shares with him the one divine substance (the Son is ὁμοούσιος and of the οὐσία of the Father, ad Serap. ep. ii. 5 ; de syn. 40). But if this is the case, then the Logos is immutable and eternal (de decr. 23. 12). (δ) The Son comes forth from the Father by a begetting, or birth. In view of the unique character of the divine nature, we cannot here think of any outflow from the Father, nor any dividing of his substance. " The begetting of men and that of the Son from the Father are different. For the things begotten of men are in some way parts of those who beget them . . . men in begetting pour forth from themselves. But God, being without parts, is without division and without passion the Father of the Son. For neither does there take place any outflowing of the incorporeal One, nor any inflowing upon him, as with men ; but, being simple in his nature, he is the Father of the one and only Son . . . This is the Logos of the Father, in whom it is possible to behold that which is of the Father without passion or division " (de decr. 11). Nor is it as though "the Son was begotten from the Father by purpose and will" (c. Ar. iii. 59), for thus the Son would be again degraded to the position of a creature created in time, one which the Father first determined to make and then made (iii. 60-63). All things were created by the will of God, but of the Son it is to be said : " He is outside of the things created by the purpose [of God], and, on the other hand, he is himself the living purpose of the Father, in which all these things come into being " (64). " But the Son of God is himself the Logos and wisdom, himself the counsel and the living purpose, and in him is the will of the Father ; he himself is the truth and the light and the power of the Father "

---

[1] Athanasius himself never attached a particular significance to this word (see, e. g., de syn. 41).

14

(65). As the very image (το ίδιον) of the Father's person
(ὑπυστάσις),[1] he did not originate in an arbitrary act of the
Father's will (ib.). But this does not imply that the Son was not
desired by the Father. "For it is one thing to say : he was begotten by desire (βουλήσει), and another thing to say that the
Father loves his Son, who is the same in nature as himself, and
desires him " (66). The Son is thus related to the Father as
radiance to the light : "the living Counsel and truly by nature
a production, as the radiance is a production of the light" (67).
Father and Son are, therefore, two persons (the Logos is not
impersonal, ἀνυπόστατος, as the word of man, de syn. 41 fin.),
the Begetting and the Begotten ; but they are again, by virtue of
this same relationship, one—a divine Being : "The Father is
Father and not himself Son, and the Son is Son and not himself
Father, but the nature (φύσις) is one. For that which is begotten is not unlike him who begets, for it is his likeness (εἰκών)
. . . therefore the Son is not another God. . . . For if, indeed,
the Son as a begotten being is another, yet as God he is the
same, and he and the Father are one in the peculiarity and
structure of their nature and in the identity of the one divinity "
(ib. iii. 4). But this relationship of the Begetting and the Begotten is an eternal one: "The Father was always by nature
generating" (γεννητικός) (iii. 66). "It is evident that the
Logos is both of himself and always existent with the Father "
(i. 27).

Athanasius starts with the conception of the One divine Being,
but this one God leads a double life (as to the triune feature, see
below, d). As Begotten and Begetting, Son and Father stand
opposed to one another as two persons, but not as two Gods.
They are one nature (μία ουσία), of the same nature (ὁμοούσιος).
In these declarations is really expressed all that the church had
believed and taught concerning Christ since the days of the
apostles : the one Godhead and the divine " I " of the Son.
The elements of truth in Monarchianism and in the popular
Christology, with their conceptions of the "second God," the
"divine part," and the Logos of the Father, are all here combined and the errors of thought and expression carefully avoided.
The ancient formulas can never recur in the church in the same
shape. Athanasius really furnished something new. He reduced
the manifold representations of Christ to a simple formula, and
he established the necessity of this formula firmly by displaying

---

[1] A discrimination between the terms, ὑπόστασις and ουσία, is yet unthought
of by Athanasius, as manifest from this passage and others already cited. Cf.
de decr. 27 ; de syn. 41 ; ad Afros 4. Cf. Harnack, DG., ii., p. 211. The
same remark applies to the Nicene Creed.

its relation to the doctrine of redemption. Imperfections, of course, still remain. The theologian of to-day will find fault, in addition to the defectiveness of the scriptural proof, chiefly with the indefiniteness of the term οὐσία; he will not fail to observe that the one personal God of Athanasius is, after all, to a certain degree, only the Father " ("and thus there will be proclaimed in the church one God, the Father of the Logos," ad Epict. 9 fin.; "the Father as the source" (ἀρχή) and fountain (πηγή), ad Serap. ep. i. 28); and he will demand a more distinct recognition of the divine personality, as well as a proper application of the principle of historical revelation in connection with the life of Christ. The problem which Athanasius endeavored to solve thus becomes more complicated. But it will not be denied that Athanasius made the best possible use of the materials then at hand. And we can in our day, with the New Testament in hand, scarcely do otherwise than acknowledge the problem of Athanasius as one well worthy of our study, and—perhaps from other points of view, in other terms, and with other methods of proof—hold fast to the ὁμοούσιος.

(*c*) It was not the demands of logical consistency, forced upon him alike by the assaults of his opponents and by the requirements of his own position, which inspired Athanasius. The arguments, both positive and negative, by which he justifies his discussions are primarily of a religious nature (see p. 207), and it is precisely this fact which constitutes the novelty and importance of his view. Only if Christ is God, in the full sense of the word and without qualification, has God entered humanity, and only then have fellowship with God, the forgiveness of sins, the truth of God, and immortality been certainly brought to men. (*a*) This will become clear, if we consider the soteriological ideas of Athanasius. The Logos assumed human flesh (σάρξ) and became man. He was true God and true man (ib. i. 70; iii. 32, 41, 30; iv. 35, 36). "He became man, and did not enter into man," as, for example, he visited the Old Testament believers (iii. 30; ad Epict. 11). "He who was God by nature was born a man, in order that both might be one" (c. Apollin. i. 7). But the union (ἕνωσις) between the flesh (σάρξ), *i. e.*, the entire human nature (ad Epict. 8; c. Ar. iii. 30) and the divinity (θεότης) exists "from the womb" (c. Apol. i. 4), and the union is indissoluble, but without leading to any mixture (c. Apol. 1. 6: "In order that the body might be according to its nature, and again, without division, might be according to the nature of the divinity of its Logos." He ascended in the body, c. Ar. i. 45; i. 10: "Shall it not suffice thee that the body in the undivided physical union with the Logos has been made his own?")

The Logos was not therefore in some way transformed into the flesh (ad Epict. 8), but he is so related to human nature as to use the latter as his instrument. Hence, the works of the divine nature are accomplished through the flesh. But, on the other hand, inasmuch as this impassible flesh belongs to the Logos, we may attribute to it that which, strictly speaking, applies only to the human nature, since the divine nature is not capable of suffering. " Being God, he had a body of his own, and, using this as an organ, he became man for our sakes ; and, therefore, the things properly spoken of [the body] are said of him, when he was in it, such as hunger, thirst, suffering, . . . of which things the flesh is susceptible ; but the works peculiar to the Logos himself, such as raising the dead and making the blind to see, . . . he did through his own body, and the Logos bore the infirmities of the flesh as though they were his own, for it was his flesh, and the flesh assisted in the works of the divine nature, because it was in the latter ; for it was the body of God " (c. Ar. or. iii. 31, 32, 35, 41 ; ad Epict. 5, 10, 11). We may therefore, in a certain sense, speak of the sufferings of the Logos. " For the things which the human body of the Logos suffered, the Logos, being one with it, transferred to himself, in order that we might be enabled to become partakers of the divine nature of the Logos. And it was a paradox, that he was a sufferer and not a sufferer—a sufferer, because his own body suffered and he was in it as it suffered ; and not a sufferer, because the Logos, being by nature God, cannot suffer " (ad Epict. 6 ; c. Ar. iii. 37, 35). Hence Athanasius designates even the human acts of Christ as good deeds (κατορθώματα) of God (c. Ar. or. iii. 41 ; cf. ad Serap. ep. iv. 14 : All things were connectedly, συνημμένως, done . . . for he spat like men, and his spittle was full of God), and he could speak of the " crucified God " (ad Epict. 10 ; cf. c. Ar. iii. 34), of worshiping the man Jesus (c. Apol. i. 6), and of Mary as the Mother of God (θεοτόκος).

(β) The object of this whole method of regarding the subject is to establish a firm foundation for the salvation (σωτηρία) of men. Inasmuch as Christ was really God, he could deify the flesh which he assumed ; and inasmuch as this was really human flesh (c. Epict. 7), human nature has thereby been deified. " Man could not have been deified, unless he who became flesh had been by nature of the Father and his true and peculiar Logos. Therefore such a conjunction was effected, in order that to that which was according to the nature of the divinity he might join that which was by nature man, and the salvation and deification of the latter might be secure " (c. Ar. ii. 70). " For as the Lord, having assumed the body, became man, so

we men are by the Logos deified, having been taken into partnership through his flesh, and, furthermore, we inherit eternal
life" (ib. iii. 34). Accordingly, since Christ assumed flesh, he
assumed human nature, and thereby deified and immortalized it :
"From the holy and God-bearing Virgin he raised up the new
form and creation of Adam, making it his own by union
(καθ' ἕνωσιν), and thus appeared the man Christ, God from
eternity, and we are members of Christ." 1 Cor. vi. 15 (c.
Apol. i. 13, cf. c. Ar. i. 43 ; ii. 61 ; iii. 33 ; iv. 36). He is
thus the second Adam (c. Ar. i. 44; ii. 65). The life of the
Lord is to be interpreted in the light of this purpose. He was,
according to the flesh, without knowledge, in order that to
his flesh, and thus to humanity, might be given power to know
the Father (c. Ar. or. iii. 38 ; ad Serap. ii. 9). He feared
death, in order that we might become free from the fear of
death and partakers of immortality (ib. iii. 54 ff.; cf. ii. 70).
He was baptized, anointed with the Spirit of God, received
grace, and ascended to heaven, in order that we through his
flesh might secure the Spirit, grace, and immortality (ib. i.
43-48). To all assertions of this kind must be added, to insure
a proper understanding, the words : "And all such things in the
flesh wholly for our sakes" (ib. iii. 34, 38 ff.; cf. iv. 6 : "for on
this account he became incarnate, that the things thus given to
him might pass over to us"). But this all happens to the flesh of
Christ, and thus to the human race, because that flesh is joined
with true divinity (ib. ii. 70, 67; iv. 36). Thus sin is destroyed (ἀνήλωται) and humanity becomes free from sin and immortal (ib. iii. 32 ; 2. 56).[1] Thus, too, we become a temple
and sons of God (i. 43 ; ii. 59), the Spirit of Christ dwells in
us and we are thereby made one with the Father (ii. 25). We
must in all these discussions avoid the erroneous idea that in this
deification of man Athanasius sees a magical process by which
the seeds of immortality are physically implanted in man. The
deification embraces, on the contrary, all the spiritual and mystical processes in which Christ operates by his word and his example upon the hearts of men (ib. iii. 19 ff.). What Athanasius
means to assert is that Christ dwells in us, and, by the power of
his Spirit, gives us a new, eternal life. But now, since God was
in Christ, and from him a divine life flowed out upon men, the
man Jesus has become in all things the representative of the

---

[1] To this end it was necessary that the Logos should himself dwell in the
race, for although "many were indeed holy and pure from all sin" (e. g.,
Jeremiah and John the Baptist), yet death reigned from Adam to Moses also
over those who had not sinned, after the similitude of Adam's transgression.
Similarly, c. Ar. iii. 33.

race, or the second Adam. His death is, therefore, the death of all, or he has given his body to death for all, and thereby fulfilled the divine sentence against sin (ii. 69). This guiltless self-surrender to death is designated as a "ransom of the sin of men and an abolition of death" (i. 45). He presented this ransom, or sacrifice, to God the Father, and by his blood cleansed us all from sin (ii. 7). Athanasius here adopts traditional ideas. His own thought remains clear. Since we have become one body with Christ, his death is our death, and his victory over death is ours: "All men being ruined in accordance with the transgression of Adam, the flesh of this one was first of all saved and set free, as being the body of the Logos itself, and thereupon we, as being of one body (σύσσωμοι) with him, are saved. . . . Having endured death for us and abolished it, he was the first man to arise, having raised up his own body for us. Furthermore, he having arisen, we also in our order arise from the dead on account of and through him" (ib. ii. 61). As in all these positions we can trace the influence of the general point of view above noted, so too in the passages in which Christ is represented as the only mediator of the knowledge of the Father (i. 12, 16; ii. 81), as the pattern of unvarying righteousness (i. 51), as the dispenser of the forgiveness of sins (ii. 67), and as the bestower of the Holy Spirit (iii. 23-25, 33; de decr. 14). But it still remains the matter of chief importance that, through the incarnation of the Logos, God himself has entered into the human race for abiding fellowship, and the latter have thereby secured grace and righteousness, the Holy Spirit, a new life, and with it immortality: "Therefore the perfect Logos of God assumes the immortal body . . . in order that, having paid the debt for us (ανθ' ημων την οφειλην αποδιδους), the things yet lacking to man might be perfected by him; but there was yet lacking immortality and the way to paradise" (ii. 66).

That these are really Christian ideas cannot be doubted. They follow the Johannine type of doctrine, and, at the same time, one of the lines of Pauline teaching (cf. Ignatius, Irenæus, Methodius). That the apostolic conception of the gospel is here reproduced, however, in a one-sided way, can as little be questioned. Yet it remains true, that it is a religious and Christian foundation from which the views of Athanasius are logically developed. Christ is God, or we cannot have God dwelling and operating in us and be sure of our salvation,[1] i. e., of the new eternal life and the forgiveness of our sins.

---

[1] Harnack's estimate is: "This absurdity (i. e., 'the Logos-ὁμοούσιος-formula') Athanasius endured; he thus unwittingly offered up to his faith a yet

(*d*) We mention here by anticipation that Athanasius at a later period employed the same means to prove the Homousia of the Holy Spirit (vid. ep. iv. ad Serap. and cf. tomi ad Antiochenos). As against the opinion that the Holy Spirit is a creature (*κτίσμα*) or an angelic being (ad Serap. i. 10. 12), it must be remembered that something of different nature (a *ἑτερούσιον*) would thus be introduced into the Trinity, and the latter thereby be destroyed, or transformed into a Diad (*δυάς*, i. 29). Whatever is true of the Son must therefore be true also of the Holy Spirit (i. 9, 20, 21). He is of like nature (*ὁμοούσιον*, i. 27), immutable (*ἄτρεπτον*, i. 26), and *ἀναλλοίωτον*, ib.). And, as in the case of the Son, this is manifest also from the nature of his work as attested by our experience. He sanctifies us, and enables us to participate in the divine nature (*θεία φύσις*, i. 23). " When now we are called partakers of Christ and partakers of God, the anointing within us bears witness and the seal, which is not of the nature of things made, but of the nature of the Son through the Spirit who in him unites us to the Father (cf. 1 Jn. 4. 13) . . . But if in the fellowship of the Spirit we become partakers of the divine nature, he would be mad who should say that the Spirit is of created nature and not of the nature of God. Therefore, indeed, they into whom he enters are deified ; and if he deifies, it is not doubtful that his nature is that of God " (i. 24).

Such is the doctrine of Athanasius. It, in his judgment, faithfully reproduces the teachings of the Scriptures, as well as of the Fathers (*e. g.*, Ignat. Ephes. 7, cited in de syn. 47), the " great councils," the baptismal command, and the baptismal confession (ad Serap. ep. i. 28, 30, 33 ; ii. 8 ; iii. 6 ; c. Apol. i. 2 ; ad Epict. i. 3). Its profound religious basis, as well as its simplicity and consistency, must be evident to all.

5. We turn back in our study to present the historical course of the controversy and the conclusions of the Council of Nice, A. D. 325.

SOURCES. The DECREES OF THE COUNCIL in Mansi, Acta concil. ii. 665 ff. Ep. CONSTANTINE ad Alex. et Ar. in Eus. Vita Const. ii. 64-72 and account there given (ib. iii. 6-22). EUSEBIUS ep. ad Caesareens. in Theodoret. h. e. i. 11. ATHANASIUS, de decretis syn. Nic. and epistle to Afros. EUSTHATHIUS, in Theod. h. e. i. 7. Further, the accounts of the later church historians : Socrat. h. e. i. 7-10. Sozomen. h. e. i. 16-25. Theodoret. h. e. i. 6-13. Philostorgius h. e. i. 7 ff.; ii. 15. Also Gelasius (ca. A. D. 476); Σύνταγμα τῶν κατὰ τὴν ἐν Νικαίᾳ ἁγίαν σύνοδον πραχθέντων, l. ii. (in Mansi, Acta concil. ii. 759 ff. Cf. the collection of decrees in Mansi, l. c. NEANDER,

greater sacrifice—the historical Christ " (DG. ii. 221). But the peculiarity of Athanasius which made his teaching normative for the future lay precisely in the fact that he strictly guarded the unity of God, and yet without wavering maintained the divinity of Christ—and of the historical Christ at that.

KG. ii. 790 ff.). Möller-Schubert, KG. i., ed. 2, 424 ff. HEFELE, Concilien-
gesch. i., ed. 2, 282 ff. BRAUN, de synode Nic. (Kirchengeschichtl. Studien
by Knöpfler, iv. 3). SEECK, in Ztschr. f. KG. xvii. 105 ff. 319 ff.

Already in A. D. 320 or 321, Alexander of Alexandria had
directed two ecclesiastical assemblies in Egypt against Arianism,
and it was condemned by them (Hefele, l. c. i. 268 ff.). Arius
was compelled to leave Alexandria. But the agitation was thus
only increased, as a synod in Bithynia enlisted in his cause (Soz.
i. 15). The Emperor Constantine now found occasion to take
part in the affair. He at first endeavored to treat it as an unimportant strife of words, and exhorted to mutual reconciliation,
as, in any event, no "one of the chief commandments of our
law" was in question (Eus. vit. Const. ii. 70). The emperor,
indeed, changed his opinion upon this point (ib. ii. 69, 71 and
iii. 12); but he remained faithful to the political interest in the
preservation of the unity of the church's faith, which had from
the first been his controlling motive (cf. vita Const. ii. 65 init.,
with iii. 17, 21). As the agitation continued to grow and
threatened to spread through the entire East (ib. ii. 73. Socr.
i. 8), he summoned a general council of the church to meet at
Nicaea. About 300 bishops (as to the number, see Hefele i. 291),
chiefly Orientals, but also Thracians, Macedonians, Achaeans, and
the Spaniard, Hosius of Cordova (Rome being represented by tw
presbyters) responded to the call (vit. Const. iii. 7). The order
of business and the course of the debate are alike obscure for us.
There were in the council many elements lacking in independence
(Socr. 1. 8). We can note with some measure of certainty three
groups. An Arian section led by Eusebius of Nicomedia (see
his view in Theod. h. e. i. 5), small in numbers (Theod. i. 6.
Soz. i. 20), first presented its confession of faith. This was rejected with indignation, and even the partisans of Arius, with
the exception of two, did not dare to adhere to it (Eustath. in
Theod. i. 7). A compromising party now entered the field.
Eusebius of Caesarea presented an indefinite Origenistic confession : "We believe . . . in one Lord Jesus Christ, the Logos
of God, *God of God, light of light, life of life, the only-begotten
Son, the first-born of all creation, begotten of the Father before all
the ages;* through whom also all things were made ; who for the
sake of our salvation was made flesh and dwelt among men, and
suffered and rose on the third day and returned to the Father,
and shall come again in glory to judge the quick and the dead,"
etc. (Eus. in Theod. i. 11). This confession, as the italicized
words indicate, has all the advantages and defects incident to a
compromise formula. The Homousians could find their views
expressed in it as well as the Arians (see Ath. ad Afros). Taken

as it stood, it undoubtedly presented the view of the majority.
The emperor approved it, but wished an acknowledgment of the
ὁμοούσιος (ib.). It is very probable that he was under the influence of Hosius (cf. Socr. iii. 7. Philostorg. i. 17), who, in turn,
was in sympathy with Alexander, and for whom, as a Western
man, the term presented no difficulty (vid. Tert., Novat., Dionys.
of Rome, supra, pp. 124 f., 169 f., 172). A basis was thus furnished and a program mapped out for the third group, that of
Alexander and Athanasius : "Under the pretext of the addition
of the ὁμοούσιον, they composed the writing," writes Eusebius,
(ib.). With the professed purpose of cutting away the foundation beneath the Arians, the confession of Eusebius was changed,
and finally read : "We believe in one God, the Father Almighty,
maker of all things visible and invisible. And in one Lord
Jesus Christ, the Son of God, *begotten of the Father, only begotten*, i. e., *of the nature of the Father.* God of God, Light of
Light, very God of very God, begotten, not made, of one
substance with the Father, by whom all things were made,
both things in heaven and things on earth ; who for us men and
for our salvation came down and was made flesh and assumed
man's nature, suffered and rose the third day, ascended to
heaven, [and] shall come again to judge the quick and the
dead. And in the Holy Ghost. *But the holy and apostolic
church anathematizes those who say that there was* [*a time*, ποτέ]
*when he was not, and that he was made from things not existing,
or from another person* (ὑποστάσεως) *or being* (οὐσίας), *saying
that the Son of God is mutable, or changeable*" (ib.). The
words which we have italicized indicate in what spirit this modification was undertaken. This formula was accepted, also for
the sake of peace, though not without some delay, by the median
party (Eus. l. c.). It became the confession of the council.
Besides Arius, only five persons refused to sign it (even Eusebius
of Nicomedia, who, however, was unwilling to approve the condemnatory portion). These were banished by the emperor.

Thus the Homousia of the Son became a dogma. When, indeed, we consider the immediate circumstances under which this
dogma was adopted, it was but natural that the real struggle
should only then begin. Nevertheless, the assembled representatives of the church had accepted the Homousia, and the emperor
deemed it his duty to give legal force to the decrees[1] of the coun-

---

[1] In addition to the decision as to the Houmosia, decrees were adopted upon
the question of the Passover (Eus. vit. Const. iii. 18-20), upon the Meletian
(Socr. h. e. i. 9 ; cf. Canon 6) and Novatian (Can. 8) schism and upon a
number of questions of church order and discipline (cf. Hefele, CG. i. p.
320-431).

cil, demanding obedience to them and punishing those who opposed them. The state church comes into power. The emperor summons the councils; the state guarantees traveling expenses and entertainment; the emperor, or an imperial commissioner, opens the councils and regulates the proceedings; and an imperial edict gives legal force to the decrees. It is for Church History to point out the significance of all this. A historical parallel to Constantine is seen in Augustus' work of restoration. Both served God and politics, and both crowned their work by the introduction of imperialism.

§ 21. *Further Development Until the Council of Constantinople,* A. D. 381.

1. The strife and contentions of this period belong in their details to the sphere of Church History and Patristics. We must, therefore, be content with a brief general view of them.

The Nicene Creed was really, after all, but the confession of a minority. The letter of Eusebius to his congregation at Caesarea (in Theod. h. e. i. 11) indicates what skill was required to make it appear acceptable. According to this explanation, the ὁμοούσιος means no more than that "the Son is of the Father," and that "the Son of God bears no likeness to begotten creatures, but is to be likened in every way alone to the Father who begat him, and that he is not from any other ὑπόστασις, or οὐσία, but from that of the Father." The rejection of the Arian formulas was interpreted to mean that "he was the Son of God also *before his birth according to the flesh,* . . . he was dynamically in the Father before he was actually born."

2. It may be easily understood from this why the adoption of the Nicene Creed did not bring peace, but became the signal for a violent renewal of the conflict. The inner dialectics of the conflicts of the ensuing years were as follows : (1) The decision of the matter lay in the hands of the Origenists, *i. e.*, of the larger middle party. (2) Upon these the Arians at first depended in their effort to secure the revocation of the Nicene Creed, and thus restore the *status quo ante.* To this end the Origenists cast their influence with the Arians. (3) When the Nicene Creed had been set aside, the Arians began to push their own positive dogmatic views to the front. (4) The Origenists now parted company with them, and the elements attached to the *homousios* were more strongly emphasized in their opposition to the Arians. (5) The middle party now joined Athanasius. It may be said that, in the development of the movement, the same inner legalism proved influential which had produced the

result attained at Nicaea itself. Since now, instead of the anticipated peace, the Nicene Creed but provoked further controversy, it is not to be wondered at that Constantine himself undertook to change the aspect of affairs. Eusebius of Nicomedia
was permitted to return ; Arius defended himself to the satisfaction of the emperor (Socr. i. 26); the leaders of the Nicene
party, Eustathius of Antioch and Athanasius (who had been
since A. D. 328 bishop of Alexandria) were removed from office
and banished upon the ground of slanderous treatment of their
opponents (the former A. D. 330 ; the latter by the Council of
Tyre, 335, being sent to Treves in 336). Constantine died A.
D. 337, shortly after the death of Arius had prevented the
solemn restoration of the latter to the fellowship of the church.

After the death of Constantine, Athanasius was permitted to
return ; but Constantius carried out in the East the ecclesiastical
policy of the last years of his father's life. Athanasius was
again, in A. D. 339, compelled to flee, and proceeded to Rome.
The Eusebians (Eus. of Nic. had meanwhile become bishop of
Constantinople) were now in control in the East. It was necessary to find a form of doctrinal statement which would at the
same time establish firmly their own view, and, out of regard for
the Western theologians, avoid extreme Arianism. This was
secured by the Council held at Antioch A. D. 341 in connection
with the dedication of the church, and that held in the same city
A. D. 344, at which the *formula macrostichos* was prepared.
The formulas of these two councils (see Athan. de syn. 22 ff.)
approach the Athanasian view as closely as possible ("complete
God of complete God, begotten of the Father before the
ages"), and reject the statement that the Son had a temporal
beginning, or is from any other hypostasis ; but the ὁμοούσιος is
avoided. Athanasius is not indeed directly assailed, but in the
person of the like-minded Marcellus of Ancyra (see the three
formulas of the former of these councils and the *formula macrostichos* of the latter).

3. In the West, on the contrary, the doctrine of Athanasius,
as also that of Marcellus, was unconditionally endorsed at the
councils at *Rome*, A. D. 341 (see the letter of Pope Julius in
Ath. Apol. c. Ar. 20-35), and *Sardica*, A. D. 343 (ib. 36-50).

This brings us to the peculiar teaching of one of the most
zealous of the Nicene party, MARCELLUS, bishop of Ancyra (s.
Eus. c. Marcel., from which are taken the fragments in RETT-
BERG, Marcelliana, 1794; cf. ZAHN, Marc. v. Anc., 1867).
This man is professedly a scriptural theologian. Not the
"dogmas" ("for the name, dogma, has something of human
counsel and knowledge," p. 21 A), nor the authority of the

Fathers (p. 21), but the Scriptures are decisive.  In the Arian
doctrine, like Athanasius, he sees disguised polytheism (p.
25 D; 26 A; 27 C, D; 28 A; 29 C).  From this it appears
that he is interested, no less than Athanasius, in preserving
the unity of God.  If we insist upon investigating the eternal
nature of Christ and his relation to the Father, we should take
for the basis of our study such terms as: Christ, Jesus, Life,
Way, Day (cf. Just. Dial. 150), Resurrection, Door, Bread—for
" this starts with that which is new in him and with his new relationship according to the flesh " (p. 92).  The same may be said
of the names " Son of God " (p. 54 B), " image of God " (p. 47
D).  His eternal nature finds expression only in the term Logos
(in John i. 1 ff.).  As the Word of God, he is eternal (p. 35 D).
This term expresses his entire pretemporal experience (p. 35 B;
40 C).  To speak of the " generation of the Logos " is not
scriptural (p. 37 B), but conception applies to him as incarnated.  John furnishes us three items of knowledge: "Where
he says, in the first place : ' In the beginning was the Word,'
he shows that the Word is *in power* ($\delta \upsilon \nu \acute{a} \mu \varepsilon \iota$) in the Father, for
in the beginning of all things created [is] God, of whom are all
things ; and in the second place : ' and the Word was with
God,' that the Word is *in energy* ($\grave{\varepsilon} \nu \varepsilon \rho \gamma \varepsilon \acute{\iota} q$) with God, for all
things were made by him . . . ; and, in the third place : ' the
Word is God,' he tells us *not to divide the divine Being,* since the
Word is in him and he in the Word ; for the Father, says he, is
in me and I in the Father " (p. 37 A.).  The terms $\delta \acute{\upsilon} \nu a \mu \iota \varsigma$ and
$\grave{\varepsilon} \nu \acute{\varepsilon} \rho \gamma \varepsilon \iota a$ are here used to designate the Logos as power reposing in
God and power in action, the $\grave{\varepsilon} \nu \acute{\varepsilon} \rho \gamma \varepsilon \iota a \delta \rho a \sigma \tau \iota \varkappa \acute{\eta}$ (p. 41 D.) (see
Zahn, p. 123 ff.).  The Logos is, therefore, on the one hand, a
personal power immanent in God, and, on the other hand, in
the interest of his historical work, he proceeds ($\grave{\varepsilon} \xi \varepsilon \lambda \vartheta \acute{\omega} \nu$,
$\grave{\varepsilon} \varkappa \pi o \rho \varepsilon \acute{\upsilon} \varepsilon \tau a \iota$, p. 167 f.) from the Father, but without thereby
changing in any way the first relationship.  We dare not start
with three hypostases and then combine them into a divine
unity : " For it is impossible that three, being hypostases, be
united in a monad, unless the triad has first originated from a
monad " (p. 167 D).  How is it to be accounted for, upon the
Arian theory of two separated persons ($\pi \rho \acute{o} \sigma \omega \pi a$), that the Holy
Spirit proceeds from the Father and yet is bestowed by the Son?
(ib.).  We have not to do with three different beings, but
the inexpressible relationship is to be regarded somewhat as an
extension of the one God : " Not distinctly and evidently then,
but in a mystic sense, the *monad* appears extended to a *triad*, but,
continuing to exist, is in no way divided " (ib. cf. Dionys. of
Rome in Ath. sent. Dion. 17 and Tert. Apol. 21).  These are

Nicene ideas : the one God leads a three-fold life ; only that
Marcellus, with greater exegetical prudence, refrains from applying directly to the prehistoric life of the divine nature the
knowledge of God which we have historically gained.    This is
evident also from the following statements : When God proposed
to establish the church and set apart the human race for sonship
(p. 12 D), the Logos proceeded from the Father as actively engaged in the creation, preservation, and redemption of the
world.    Less than 400 years ago he became the " Son of God,"
Christ and King (p. 50 D).    At the end of the days, since his
kingdom shall become the kingdom of God, he will return into
God (p. 41 C ; 42 A ; 52 C), ruling with the Father.    What
will then become of his body, Marcellus confesses that he does
not know (p. 53 A).

The significance of this theology lies in the fact that it gave
the Eusebians the opportunity of continually bringing the charge
of Sabellianism against their opponents ; but, on the other hand,
the fact that it was recognized by the Homousians as orthodox (in
Athan. Apol. 32, 47) indicates how sincere they were in their de-
votion to the strictly monotheistic conception of God, and that their
controlling interest centered in the three-fold historical self-revela-
tion of God. But this theory itself made no impression historically.
It was too original and archaistic to secure wide acceptance
(cf. Iren., p. 124 f.).    Athanasius (or. c. Ar. iv.) also attacked
the views of Marcellus without naming him, and, after review-
ing them, had only ridicule for the oddities of the "old man"
(Epiph. h. 72. 4).    It was further disastrous for them that they
were interpreted even by contemporaries in the sense of PHOTI-
NUS of Sirmium (Epiph. h. 71), according to whom Christ was
only a supernaturally (per contra, Marius Mercator, opp. ed.
Baluz., p. 164) begotten man, in whom the Logos dwelt.    This
was really the doctrine of Paul of Samosata.    The Eusebians as
well as the Nicene theologians rejected it.

4. PHOTINUS fell under condemnation (Council at Milan, A. D.
345 (?) and 347).    In other points the Western theologians, with
Athanasius, adhered to their views.    Constantius, held in check
by the Persians, was driven to the determination to recall
Athanasius (A. D. 346), and two prominent Eusebians, Ursacius
and Valens, deemed it prudent to make peace with Rome and
Athanasius (see Athan. Apol. 51-58).    On the other hand,
the (first) Sirmian Council in A. D. 347 (?) condemned Photinus,
indicating Marcellus as the source of his heresy (Hilar. frg. 2. 21-
23).    The death of Constans (A. D. 350), who had inclined to
the Nicene orthodoxy, changed the situation. Constantine at once
applied himself with energy to the suppression of the Nicene faith.

The Orientals had already, at the (second) Council at Sirmium (A. D. 351), again made themselves felt.   The Sirmian formula here adopted is in the positive portion identical with the Fourth Antiochian formula (p. 219), but a large number of Athanasianisms (see Ath. de syn. 27 ; Socr. h. e. ii. 30 ; Hilar. de syn. 38. ; cf. Hefele CG., i. 642 ff.) are appended.   The latter are in the line followed hitherto by the Eusebians.   The favorite phrases of the Arians were rejected (n. 1. 24), and also the views of Photinus and Marcellus.   Subordinationism appears in n. 18 : " For we do not co-ordinate the Son with the Father, but he is subordinate ($\dot{\upsilon}\pi o\tau\epsilon\tau\alpha\gamma\mu\epsilon\nu o\nu$) to the Father."   At Arles, A. D. 353, at Milan, 355 (at Biterrae, 356), the Western men were compelled to recognize the condemnation of the " sacrilegious Athanasius " (Mansi, iii. p. 236).   It was politically prudent to demand no more than this.   Those who resisted this (Eusebius of Vercelli, Dionysius of Milan, Lucifer of Calaris, the deacon Hilarius of Poitiers, Hosius of Cordova, Liberius of Rome) were banished.   Athanasius, deposed, fled into the wilderness, A. D. 356.   In response to protests, the emperor asserted : " But what I desire, that is canon " (Athan. hist. Arian. ad mon. 33 fin. ).   The orthodox now regarded him as the Antichrist and a monstrous wild beast (*e. g.*, Ath. l. c. 67, 64 ; Lucif. Bibl. max. iv. p. 247, 244, 246).

But victory is a most dangerous thing for a bad cause ; and this victory led to the downfall of Arianism.   Who then were these victors and what would they do ?   Now that their common opponent no longer compelled them to harmony of action, it at once became evident how uncertain and how various were their positive ideas.   One party spoke of the pretemporal and eternal birth of the Son, and asserted that he is like the Father in all things.   This was " the royal path " between Arius and Sabellius (thus Cyrill of Jer. Catech. iv. 7 ; xi. 4, 7, 10, 14, 17). They, therefore, strenuously advocated the Antioch formulas, except that they could not reconcile themselves to the $\dot{o}\mu oo\dot{\upsilon}\sigma\iota o\varsigma$. They thought to substitute for it $\dot{o}\mu o\iota o\dot{\upsilon}\sigma\iota o\varsigma$ (Sozom. h. e. iii. 18). In other words : they were willing to agree with Athanasius in the result attained by him, but they reached it by a different path.   Instead of starting as he did from the one divine nature, they, dreading Sabellianism,[1] followed Origen in beginning with two divine persons.   But the result itself might thus be brought into question, as these formulas could be approved also by elements more in sympathy with the left wing, *i. e.*, Origenistic and

---

[1] This is plainly seen in the question of the Anomæan in Apollinaris dial. de trin. (Draeseke, p. 264) : " What does $\dot{o}\mu oo\dot{\upsilon}\sigma\iota o\nu$ mean ?   I understand this to teach that the Son and Father are not the same."

Arianizing tendencies.    These formed the party of the Semi-arians or Homoiusians.    But the consistent Arians now came out in opposition to this party, as well as to the Homousians, under the leadership of AËTIUS of Antioch (vid. discussion by him, "concerning the unbegotten and the begotten God," in Epiph. h. 76. 11), and EUNOMIUS of Cyzicus (a confession of faith and an apologetic discourse in Fabricius, Bibl. graec. viii., and in Thilo, Bibl. patr. gr. ii. pp. 580-629 ; cf. Philostorg. h. e. iii. 15 ff.; iv. 12 ; v. 2 ; ix. 6; x. 6 ; v. 1, etc.).    Of Eunomius, Theodoret says : "He presented theology as tech-nology" (haer. fab. iv. 3); and this is a just comment.    Al-though it was, indeed, deemed proper to appeal to the authority of the Scriptures and the ancients (Eunom. Ap. 4, 12, 15 ; see the citations in Greg. Naz. or. 29, 18 and the discussion, or. 30), yet the thinking of these men was dominated by the profane logic which Athanasius had rebuked in Arius (cf. Greg. Naz. or. 27. 2).    God is the unbegotten ($\dot{a}\gamma\acute{\epsilon}\nu\nu\eta\tau\sigma\nu$).    If this is his nature, then the view that we may fully know God (Socr. h. e. iv. 7 ; Theod. haer. fab. iv. 3 ; Basil. ep. 235) is quite intelligible.    If now it be proper to designate the Son as begotten ($\gamma\epsilon\nu\nu\eta\tau\acute{o}\nu$, Eunom. Ap. 11, 12), then it necessarily follows that he is not God as is the Father, not derived from the substance of the Father, but as his creature, from his will (ib. 12, 15, 28).    But if the Son is the first creature of the Father, then it follows : "that he is neither $\dot{o}\mu oo\acute{v}\sigma\iota o\varsigma$ nor $\dot{o}\mu o\iota o\acute{v}\sigma\iota o\varsigma$, since the one indi-cates a beginning and a division of the nature, and the other an identity" (Eunom. l. c. 26 ; cf. Aët. l. c. 4).    Even a similarity ($\ddot{o}\mu o\iota o\nu$) is, in regard to the nature, impossible between the Begot-ten and the Unbegotten (Eunom. 11. 26), although we may speak of an imitative moral similarity (Eunom. ib. 24 and conf. fid. 3 : "This only one like, $\ddot{o}\mu o\iota o\nu$, to the Begetter . . . is not an unbegotten like to the Unbegotten, for the Creator of all things is alone unbegotten . . . but as Son to the Father, as the image and seal [*i. e.*, impression made by seal] of the whole energy and power of the Creator of all things, he is the seal of the Father's works and words and councils;" cf. Philostorg. vi. 1 and iv. 12).    This is all merely consistent Arianism, and when Euzoius of Antioch (A. D. 361) proposes the formula : "In all things the Son is unlike the Father," he is also but consistent (see similar utterances at the Council of Seleucia, in Hilar. c. Const. imp. 12).    Thus had Arius himself taught.

Yet the Nicene Creed still remained the doctrinal basis, and it was necessary to secure its abrogation.    This was accomplished by the Third Council of Sirmium, under Ursacius and Valens, who had long before again become Arians, in the Second Sirmian formula (A. D. 357): "But as to that which some or many thought concerning the substance, which is called *usia* in Greek, *i. e.*, that it be understood very expressly as *homousion*, or what is called *homoeusion*, it is proper that no mention at all be made and that no one teach it, for this reason . . . that it is not contained in the divine Scriptures, and that it is beyond the knowledge of man (Isa. 53. 8)". Furthermore, according to Jn. 14. 28, "There is no doubt that the Father is greater" (Hilar. de Syn. 11). Western men, among them Hosius, now almost a hundred years old, accepted this formula, and it was approved by a council at Antioch, A. D. 358 (Sozom. iv. 12). Thus the Nicene Creed, and the terms ὁμοούσιος and ὁμοιούσιος as well, appeared to be banished from the world.

5. But the development of ideas cannot be forced backward by decrees. At the council of Ancyra, under the leadership of Basil of Ancyra (A. D. 358, see the decree of the council in Epiph. h. 73. 2-11), it became evident that Arianism was not the faith of the Eastern church. As a son, the Son is not a creation of the Father (creator and creature are one thing, father and son another, c. 3). On the contrary, he is in his nature— in another way than other children of God—like the Father, in his ουσία and not only in his ἐνέργεια ("certainly, as Only-one from Only-one, like in nature, from the Father," c. 5; "of likeness to the Father according to nature," c. 8; "He had the attributes of divinity, being according to nature incorporeal (ἀσώματος), and like (ὅμοιος) to the Father according to the divinity and incorporeity and energy," c. 9. "And if anyone, professing to believe upon the Father and the Son, say that the Father is not his Father of like nature but of like energy . . . thus taking away his being truly a son, let him be anathema," c. 11. But also: "If anyone, saying that the Father is in authority and nature the Father of the Son, should say also that the Son is of like or of the same nature (ὁμοούσιον δὲ ἢ ταυτοούσιον) as the Father, let him be anathema," 11 fin.[1] These formulas won the ear of the emperor (Soz. iv. 13 f.). The fourth council of Sirmium now made an attempt, by means of the third Sirmian formula (A. D. 358), to establish peace by the revival of the fourth Antioch formula. It was hoped to confirm this peace at the double council at Ariminium and Seleucia (A. D. 359) by the presentation of a formula previously prepared at the Court at Sirmium (the fourth Sirmian), which was a compromise

---

[1] In the dual arrangement of these anathemas, placing the Arian extreme side by side with the Sabellian, there is very clearly revealed the basis of the mistrust of the term, ὁμοούσιος. They were afraid of being led into Sabellianism. Cf. Ath. de syn. 12; Socr. h. e. ii. 39.

between the second formula of Sirmium and that of Ancyra :
" The term, *οὐσία*, on account of its having been used only by
the Fathers, but being unknown among the common people, occasions scandal because the Scriptures do not contain it—request
that this be done away with . . . ; but we say that the Son is
like, *ὅμοιον*, the Father in all things, as the Holy Scriptures declare and teach " (Ath. de syn. 8.   Socr. ii. 37).   The Western
men were here aiming at the restoration of the Nicene Creed ;
the majority of the Eastern men were Homoiusians.   But the
emperor's will prevailed in the end.   The formula, conforming
thus to some extent to Nicene ideas, was finally adopted, but the
"in all things" was dropped [1] (Ath. de syn. 30).   Cf. HEFELE,
CG. i. 697-722.

The Arians under Acacius of Caesarea and Eudoxius of Antioch (later of Constantinople) now held sway at the court.
The council of Constantinople (A. D. 360) was under their
control.   The *ὅμοιος*, as well as the condemnation of the *οὐσία*,
was again proclaimed.   Aëtius was turned adrift (but Eunomius
honored with the bishopric of Cyzicus).   The leaders of the
Semi-arians were deposed (Socr. h. e. ii. 41, 42).

6. The Arians had carried the day and harmony was established, but it was only in appearance.   Over against the Arians
still stood the Homousians (council of Paris, A. D. 361; see
Hilar. frg. 11 and Mansi iii. 357-362), and also the old middle
party, or Homoiusians, who were constantly approaching the
right wing.   We may learn their position from a treatise of
Basil of Ancyra (in Epiph. h. 73. 12-22): "The Son is like
the Father in all things (*κατὰ πάντα*), *i. e.*, according to nature
(*κατ' οὐσίαν*) as being spirit (*πνεῦμα*), and not merely in will "
(*κατὰ βούλησιν*) (ib. 13, 17, 18, 22).   The term used by the
Orientals, *ὑπόστασις*, is only designed to indicate the separateness of Father, Son, and Spirit, but by no means to lead to the
introduction of three gods.   " And do not let the name subsistences, *ὑποστάσεις*, trouble any.   For the Orientals speak of
hypostases, in order to indicate the subsisting and existing attributes of the persons (*τὰς ἰδιότητας τῶν προσώπων ὑφεστώσας καὶ
ὑπαρχούσας*).   For if the Father is spirit and the Son is spirit
and the Holy Ghost is spirit, the Son is not thought to be the
Father ; there subsists also the Spirit, who is not thought to be,

---

[1] This brought the formula into entire harmony with the Arians, who could
now, as necessity might require, emphasize either the likeness or the un-
likeness, according as they referred to the nature or the attributes.   See supra,
p. 222, and especially Philostorg. h. e. iv. 12 ; cf. Basil of Anc. in Epiph. h.
73. 13, 15, 22.   The rejection of the *ἀνόμοιος* by Acacius at Seleucia was,
therefore, in reality only a pretense.   Cf. Hilar. c. Constant. 14.

15

and is not, the Son, etc., . . . not saying that the three hypostases are three sources or three gods . . . for they confess that there is one Godhead (*θεότητα*) . . . and one kingship and one source [of all things]. Likewise, they reverently indicate the persons by the attributes of the hypostases, regarding the Father as subsisting in the paternal dominion, and acknowledging the Son not as being a part of the Father, but as begotten and subsisting from the Father, perfect from perfect, and designating the Holy Spirit . . . as subsisting from the Father through the Son" (c. 16, cf. c. 12). The parallel with the incarnation, according to Phil. 2. 6 ; Rom. 8. 3, leads to the result, that Christ as Spirit is the same as the Father, and as flesh the same as human flesh ; but that, as an acting personality, he is like the Father and like the flesh : "According to the conception of spirit, the same . . . yet not the same, but like, because the Spirit which is the Son is not the Father" (18). Here the Homousia is really acknowledged, the *ὅμοιος* applying only to the different personages : "For whatever the Father does, that does also the Son, not in the same way as the Father does it, but in a like way" (*ὁμοίως*) (ib.).

Constantine died A. D. 361, and Julian the Apostate became his successor. The banished bishops, including Athanasius, were permitted to return. The latter at once arranged for a council at Alexandria (A. D. 362, see esp. Tomi ad Antiochenos, ep. ad Rufinianum ; also Socr. h. e. iii. 7. Rufin. h. e. x. 27-29). As early as A. D. 359 Athanasius had, in his report of the councils of Rimini and Seleucia, called the Homoiusians brethren (de syn. 41-43 ; cf. 12, 53). Inasmuch as they confess "that the Son is of the nature (*οὐσία*) of the Father and not of another hypostasis, that he is not a being created or made," he recognized that they have something to rely upon and are not far from the *homoousios* (41), although it is not distinct and clear to substitute *homoios* or *homoiousios* for *homoousios* ( "because that which is like (*homoios*) is said to be like not on account of the natures (*οὐσιῶν*) [of the objects], but on account of their forms and properties. Thus a man is said to be like a man, not according to nature, but according to form and character, for in nature he is same-natured," *ὁμοφυεῖς*, c. 53). The great bishop was concerned not for his formula, nor for any formula,[1] but for the real matter at issue. This was evident also at Alexandria. Here the justification of the "three hypostases" was approved, provided these be conceived, not as different in nature (*ἀλλοτριούσοι*) nor as separate natures (*διαφόροι οὐσίαι*) nor even as three sources and

---

[1] Cf. his ridicule of the making of formulas in these years—De syn. 32.

gods; but as of the same nature (ὁμοούσιοι) (tom. ad Ant. 5); but the "one hypostasis" ·was also justified, since many hold that "it is the same thing to say ὑπόστασις or οὐσία (6). The condemnation of Arius, Sabellius, Paul, Valentine, Basilides, and Manichaeus throws light upon the situation (ib.). The council taught also the *homousia* of the Spirit (3, 5) in opposition to MACEDONIUS of Constantinople, who had declared the Holy Ghost to be a servant and assistant, like the angels (Socr. ii. 45 ; Sozom. iv. 27) and the human soul of Christ (7). Leniency is urged toward those who have erred from the truth (3, 8, 9), the avoidance of strife about words, and contentment with the Nicene formulas (8).

Athanasius was finally banished again by Julian, but recalled by Jovian (A. D. 363). Immediately a council at Alexandria (A. D. 363) again endorsed the Nicene Creed (Ath. ep. ad Jovian), and also, although with some reserve (ὁμοούσιος═ὅμοιος κατ᾿ οὐσίαν), a council at Antioch (A. D. 363 : see Socr. h. e. iii. 25).

These transactions were of epochal significance for the History of Doctrines. (1) The combination of the middle party with the Homousians assures the defeat of the Arians. (2) The Nicene interpretation of the nature of the Holy Spirit assigns to the third person of the Trinity a fixed position in the theological system. (3) The incipient discrimination between *hypostasis* and *usia* will give rise to new problems. (4) The interpretation of the ὁμοούσιος in the sense of ὁμοιούσιος and of ὅμοιος κατ᾿ οὐσίαν will engender new ideas foreign to those of Athanasius and the Nicene Creed.

7. The *Three Cappadocians* wielded the controlling influence in the following period :

Zealous Christians, and equally zealous Hellenists,[1] these men

SOURCES. BASIL THE GREAT of Caesarea († A. D. 379 ; opp. ed. Garnier et Maran, 1721 ff., de Sinner 1839, 1840, Migne gr. 29-32). His brother, GREGORY OF NYSSA († after A. D. 394 ; opp. ed. Fronto Ducäus, 1615-1618, Migne gr. 44-46. Separate writings in Oehler, Greg. Nyss. opp. i., 1865, and Bibliothek d. Kirchenväter, i. 1858. Mai, Script. vet. nov. coll. viii. 2. 1 ff.). GREGORY OF NAZIANZEN († A. D. 389 or 390; opp. ed. Clemencet et Caillou, 1778, 1842, Migne gr. 35-38. See also the most important of the works of these Fathers in Thilo, Bibl. patr. gr. dogm. ii.). Here belongs also a part of the writings attributed by Draeseke, although upon insufficient grounds, to APOLLINARIS OF LAODICEA, especially the Antirrheticus c. Eunom. Dialogi de trinitate and De trinitate. On the other hand, κατὰ μέρος πίστις belongs beyond question, as Caspari has shown, to Apollinaris. Vid. these documents in Draeseke, Apollinaris v. Laod., in Texte u. Unters. vii. 3, 4. The citations below are from this edition.

[1] See, *e. g.*, the correspondence between Basil and Libanius (Basil ep. 335-359), the sermon 22 of Basil (de legendis libris gentilium) and the funeral sermon of Greg. Naz. upon Basil (or. 43, c. 17-22).

sympathized with the religious positions of Athanasius and had appreciation at the same time for the scientific dogmatics of Origen.[1] They understood and interpreted Athanasius in the sense of Origenistic theology.  In this consists their significance for us; for it was by this means and in this form that the positions of Athanasius were victorious in the Orient.  What Origen had sought to accomplish appears again in these men—Christianity and philosophy were to form a covenant with one another.  These men stood actually in a Christianized world, which, it would seem, should furnish the new and necessary modes and forms of thought for the combination of the truth of antiquity and the truth of the gospel.  With the gospel in hand, they thought themselves prepared to Christianize philosophy.  The dream thus cherished was, however, never realized.

(a) Athanasius starts with the one divine nature (οὐσία, or ὑπόστασις); the three-fold personal life within which, being a self-evident presupposition, he does not at all attempt to prove. The Cappadocians begin with the three divine hypostases (cf. Basil of Anc.) and attempt to bring these under the conception of the one divine usia.  The terms, hypostasis and usia are now carefully discriminated, the former being understood as indicating the individual separate existence, and the latter the substance common to all (e. g., Basil, ep. 38. 1-3; 9. 2; 125. 1; 236. 6.  Greg. Nyss. in Oehler. Bibl. ii. 218 f., 236, 234.  Cat. magn. 1 in.  Cf. Apollin. dialogi, p. 266 f., 271).

(b) There should be recognized three divine ὑποστάσεις, or πρόσωπα : Father, Son, and Holy Ghost.  The different names applied to them correspond to real differences : "According to which the hypostases are to be clearly and without commingling discriminated from one another " (Greg. Nyss. öhl. ii. 162). Each hypostasis has its peculiarity (ἴδιον, ἰδιάζον), or its property (ἰδιότης) or attribute (ἰδίωμα).  Thus, " the ἴδιον of the Father is unbegottenness ; that of the Son, birth ; that of the Spirit, procession (Greg. Naz. or. 25. 16 ; 29. 2 ; 31. 29.  Basil. ep. 38. 4-6 ; 105 ; 125. 3 ; 210. 4 ; hom. 15. 2.  Greg. Nyss. cat. mag. 3.  Apollin. l. c., pp. 255, 258, 269, 354).  This difference must be distinctly and clearly observed.  There are three individual persons, as were Paul, Peter, and Barnabas.  It is Marcellian or Sabellian to speak of one hypostasis or one prosopon, instead of one usia (Basil. ep. 125. 1 ; 69. 2).[2]  (c) But it is not by any means the purpose to subordinate one of these three persons to

---

[1] See the Philocalia and compare Basil's estimate of Origen, in Basil. de spirit. s. pp. 29, 73.

[2] In this criticism of Marcellus, all the points of difference with Athanasius (compare the latter's judgment in regard to Marcellus) are clearly seen.

the others in respect of divine nature or dignity. Divinity (θεότης) belongs to them all in the same way, for they possess the same energy (ἐνέργεια) and power (δύναμις) (Basil. ep. 189. 7, 8. Greg. Nyss. öhl. ii. 180, 196 f. 204 ff. 202 f. : "The Holy Trinity does not act apart according to the number of the hypostases, but every exercise of the good will is one, and an order is observed, from the Father through the Son to the Holy Ghost;" cf. Apollin. dialogi, pp. 272, 279, 277, 306, 313). But if there is an identical energy (ἐνεργείας ταυτότης) of the three hypostases, this implies their equality in dignity and nature (Greg. Nyss. ib. 182; Basil. ep. 189. 7). This is Origen's way of thinking upon the subject (supra, p. 149 f.). That which is common (the κοινόν) is brought into association with that which is peculiar (the ἰδιάζον, Bas. ep. 38. 5). Accordingly, we may speak of the divinity (θεότης) or nature (φύσις, οὐσία) common to the three hypostases. There is a sameness of nature (ταυτότης τῆς φύσεως, Bas. ep. 8. 3, 5). The hypostases are the same as to nature (ταὐτὸν κατ᾽ οὐσίαν, Greg. Naz. or. 30. 20). With the peculiarity (ἰδιάζον) of the hypostases stands contrasted the community (κοινόν) of the usia (Bas. ep. 210. 5. Greg. Naz. or. 29. 2). This relationship finds expression in the *homousios.* "Confessing the sameness of the nature, we accept also the *homousios.* . . For he who is by nature (κατ᾽ οὐσίαν) God is *homousios* to him who is by nature God" (Bas. ep. 8. 3; cf. Apollin. Dial. pp. 264, 267 ff.). This, he declares, asserts no more than that they are " by nature exactly alike " (ὅμοιον, Bas. ep. 9. 3).[1] Now that the idea of the separate hypostases stands in the foreground, the predicate in question receives a new shade of meaning : "They rightly say ὁμοούσιον, in order to set forth the equality of nature in honor (τὸ τῆς φύσεως ὁμότιμον, Bas. ep. 52. 2). It is the same nature (φύσις) and dignity of divinity (ἀξία τῆς θεότητος), an equality of nature in honor, which belongs to the three hypostases (Greg. Naz. or. 31. 9, 10, 28; 29. 2). The *homousia,* therefore, indicates the same divine substance or nature, but in consequence of this also the same dignity or glory, in the three hypostases.

(*d*) Thus arises the idea of the Triune God—three persons in

---

[1] The homousios originally sounded strangely to Basil, as is evident from a letter to Apollinaris (Draeseke, p. 102): "To such an idea, it seems to me that the meaning of the exactly equivalent *homoios* is even better fitted than that of the *homousios.* For light having no difference at all from light in being more or less, cannot, I think, be rightly said to be *the same,* because, in its own circuit of existence, it is different, but it may be accurately and exactly said to be *like in nature.*" Starting with this understanding, Basil interpreted the *homousios* in this sense, as appears above.

one Godhead. "The three one in divinity, and the one three in individualities" (ἰδιότησιν) (Greg. Naz. or. 31. 9; 28. 31; 39. 11, 12). The point of view which forms the basis of this conclusion is : " In order that the unmingledness (τὸ ἀσύνχυτον) of the three hypostases in the one nature and dignity of the God-head may be saved " (ib.), and "for God is not the more and the less, nor the former and the latter, nor severed in will nor divided in power . . . but undivided in the divided . . . the Godhead" (ib. 14). Thus the hypostatic distinction is pre-served, as well as the substantial unity : " But an indescribable and inconceivable (One) is discovered in these two things, the community and the distinction—neither the difference of the hypostases rending the continuity of the nature, nor the commu-nity as to substance dissipating the peculiarity of the marks of distinction" (Bas. ep. 38. 4). "The doctrine of piety knows how to behold a certain distinction of hypostases in the unity of nature " (Greg. Nyss. cat. m. 1). Hereby, it is claimed, is established the proper medium between Paganism and Arianism, as between Judaism and Sabellianism. Due recognition is given both to the unity and the multiplicity, to the nature (φύσις), and the persons (πρόσωπα): " Just as he who does not acknowledge the community of the essence falls into polytheism, so he who does not grant the peculiarity of hypostases is brought under Judaism " (Bas. ep. 210. 5 ; de spir. s. 30. 77. Greg. Nyss. cat. m. 1, 3 ; c. Eunom. iv.; Mig. 45. 644). But the formulas thus attained brought with them new problems. The Arians loudly proclaimed that this doctrine, and not theirs, was polytheism. If the three persons, Peter, James, and John, are three men, we must then speak here also of three gods (Greg. Nyss. öhl. ii. 188 ; Bas. ep. 189. 2 f. ; Apollin., κατὰ μερ, etc., p. 374 f.). But the increasing mystery was not regarded as a cause of offense (see above), and it was believed that the argument drawn from application of the number One to God was met by appeal to the quantitative nature of the conception of number (Bas. ep. 8. 2 ; de spir. s. 17, 18. Greg. Naz. or. 31. 18 f.). In reply to the objection made, appeal was taken to the authority of the Scrip-tures, which speak of one God (Greg. Nyss. ib. p. 192), but especially to the argument, that it is only by a misuse of terms that three persons are called three men. The word ἄνθρωπος designates the common element (τὸ κοινὸν) of the nature. Hence, in three persons there is one nature (φύσις), one essence (οὐσία); and hence it follows that, " in very accurate speech it would also properly be said, one man " (Greg. Nyss. l. c. pp. 192, 210, 222, 224, 226, 236). From this Platonic idea it was inferred concerning God: " We call the Creator of all things one God, although he is contemplated in three persons, or hypostases" (ib. p. 236). It is a relationship like that which existed between Adam and Eve and Seth : " Do not the clay (Adam) and that which is cut off from it (Eve) and the fruit from it (Seth) seem to you to be the same thing ? How can it be otherwise ? Are not things of the same nature (ὁμοούσια) the same ? But how can it be otherwise ? Let it then be confessed also that things subsisting differently are admitted to be of the same nature" (Greg. Naz. or. 31. 11, 14, 15, 32. Bas. ep. 210. 4). The three are one God, but : " It is plain that not the person (πρόσωπον) but the nature (οὐσία) is the God" (Greg. Nyss. l. c., p. 222; cf. Apollin. dial. de trin. p. 270 : " Is there therefore one hypostasis? No ") ; and : " The monarchy is not one which one person circumscribes . . . but one which equal dignity of nature determines and unity of purpose and sameness of action and agreement extending to the oneness of the things proceeding from it . . . so that although it differs in number it is not divided in essence" (Greg. Naz. or. 29. 2).[1]

(e) It is to be observed, finally, that the theologians here named zealously maintained the Homousia of the Holy Spirit, in this, too, following in the footsteps of Athanasius (supra, pp. 215, 227). Vid. especially Bas. de spir. s.; c. Eunom. iii. Greg. Naz. or. 31. Apollin. antirrh. p. 223 ff. 248 ff.; dial. de tr. p. 307 ff. They found in the prevalent usage the most various statements in regard to the Spirit. Some regarded him as an energy (ἐνέργεια); others as a creature (κτίσμα); others as God ; while still others thought it scriptural to refrain from any definite statement as to his nature (Greg. Naz. or. 31. 5. See also Cyril of Jer. cat. 16. 23, and compare the Macedonian in Apollin. with his oft-repeated question : " Where is it written, ' the Spirit is God ' ?" pp. 307, 324 f., 321, 323, 317, 328 f., 330). The earlier state of this doctrine (except in Irenæus—see p. 120 f.) is here but reflected. In opposition to this uncertainty it was not difficult—pressing forward upon the path once chosen—to prove that he is an hypostasis such as the Father and the Son, according to the Scriptures and the baptismal confession ; that he shares with them the same *energy;* and that to him belong accordingly the same divine nature (οὐσία) and dignity (ἀξία); that he is accordingly ὁμοούσιος, and is to be worshiped with the

---

[1] The Dialogi de trin. of Apollinaris are instructive in revealing this tendency to Tritheism. Here the deity is compared to the one humanity (ἀνθρωπότης) which belongs to the two hypostases, Peter and Paul (p. 272 ; cf. 254, 271 f.), or p. 281 : " Bishop, presbyter, and deacon are *homoousioi.* Hast thou not then confessed that Father, Son, and Holy Spirit are a *homoousion ?* "

Father and the Son (*e. g.*, Bas. hom. 15. 3; 125. 3; de sp. s.
1. 3; 10; 11; 16; 19. 49; 21; 25.  C. Eunom. iii. 1, 3.
Greg. Naz. or. 31. 4 f., 7. 9 f., 12.  Greg. Nyss. öhl. ii. 160,
170 ff. Apollin. pp. 327, 333, 334).[1]  The specific character of
his activity was seen in the completion and execution of the
work of redemption.  He unites the human race with the Logos,
and imparts to it the gifts of God (Basil de sp. s. 15. 36; 16.
38; hom. 15. 3.[2]  Greg. Naz. or. 34).  His relation to the
Father is described, in contradistinction from that of the Son
(otherwise there would be two Sons), not as a generation, but as a
sending forth (ἔκπεμψις) and a procession (ἐκπορεύεσθαι) (supra,
p. 228).  The formula, "from the Father through the Son," is
also found (Basil c. Eunom. iii. 6.  Greg. Naz. Apollin. dial. p.
213; cf. THOMASIUS D.G. i. ed. 2, p. 270 f.).

The modification which has here been made in the ancient
Nicene doctrine is very evident.  Athanasius (and Marcellus)
taught the one God, leading a three-fold personal life, who
reveals himself as such.  The Cappadocians think of three divine hypostases, which, as they manifest the same activity, are
recognized as possessing one nature and the same dignity.  The
mystery for the former lay in the trinity; for the latter, in the
unity.  It was with labor and difficulty that the latter guarded
themselves against polytheism.  But it was only in this way that
the Nicene doctrines were, for the Orientals, freed from the taint
of Sabellianism, and that the personality of the Logos appeared
to be sufficiently assured.  The Cappadocians interpreted the
doctrine of Athanusius in accordance with the conceptions and
underlying principles of the Logos-Christology of Origen.  They
paid, however, for their achievement a high price, the magnitude of which they did not realize—the idea of the personal God.
Three personalities and an abstract, impersonal essence are the
resultant.  In this form the οὐσία and φύσις are a heavy weight
upon the doctrine concerning God, for they are in conflict with
the personality of God.  It was a partial corrective of this that
they, after all—inconsistently—identified the Deity with the

---

[1] Appeal was made not only to the scriptural arguments, but to the Fathers,
Irenæus, Clement of Rome, Dionysius of Rome, Dionysius of Alexandria,
Origen, Gregory Thaum., Firmilian, Meletius (vid. Bas. de sp. s. 29, 72-74).

[2] He enlightens all for the knowing of God, inspires the prophets, makes
legislators wise, perfects priests, strengthens kings, restores the righteous,
exalts the prudent, exerts gifts of healing, revives the dead, sets free the
bound, makes children of the estranged.  Such things he does by virtue of his
birth from above. . . .  By him the weak are strong, the poor become rich,
the unpracticed in learning are wiser than the wise. . . .  He dwells entire
in everyone and he is entire with God.  He does not as a servant administer
gifts, but autocratically distributes benefits.

Father, which was again a relic of the earlier Subordinationism. The Father is the Deity as the Source whence the Son and the Spirit proceed : " The nature in the three is one : God ; but the union is the Father, from whom and to whom they are in their turn referred " (Greg. Naz. or. 42. 15 ; 20. 8. And especially : " For one and the same person of the Father, from whom the Son was born and the Holy Spirit proceeded. Wherefore also certainly the one who is the cause of the things caused by him you call One God, since he is also in them." Greg. Nyss. öhl. ii. 226 ;•Apollin. κατὰ μερ. etc., pp. 373, 273).¹ Thus, in place of the conception of the *one-natured, three-fold* God had come the doctrine of the *like-natured triune* God. That Athanasius was able to endure the latter, without ever zealously supporting it or condemning Marcellus, as he was urged to do (see Bas. ep. 125), may be understood from the foregoing.

Such was the teaching of the men who regarded themselves as the inheritors of the Nicene Creed (Bas. ep. 52. 1).² They believed that the God whom we worship as above the angels (Bas. hom. 15. 1) must be apprehended precisely in the terms of these formulas: " In regard to the doctrine of God, the different usage of terms is no longer so harmless, for what was a little thing then, is a little thing no longer " (Greg. Nyss. Öhl. ii. 192). The conflicts of the age and the toying with formulas produced an overstrained conception of orthodoxy. These Fathers—in league with the world—framed orthodoxy in the Grecian mould.

8. It was only through manifold reverses that the new orthodoxy pressed on to victory. Julian was really indifferent (persecuting Athanasius as " the enemy of the gods," Theod. h. e. iii. 5 ; Jul. ep. 6). Jovian reigned only ten months. Valens persecuted Homousians and Homoiusians alike (Theod. h. e. iv. 11 ff.; Socr. iv. 16). The East inclined more and more toward the orthodoxy of the West (embassy to Liberius of Rome ; council at Tyana, A. D. 367 ; see Socr. h. e. iv. 12 ; council at Antioch, A. D. 379 ; Mansi iii. 461 ff.). Basil the Great had now come to the front as leader. In the West, the Nicene orthodoxy had been able meanwhile to establish itself securely

---

¹ Apollinaris, indeed, also writes : " It is necessary not only that what the Father desires the Son shall also desire, but it is necessary that what the Son desires the Father shall also desire. Wherefore, the Son is placed after the Father in regard to those things which he desires and which are also enjoined, but which, if they are only enjoined, he even though not desiring, being under necessity, performs," Draeseke, p. 209 ; cf. Augustine.

² Cf. Apollin. dial. de trin. p. 264: " For when thou didst confess that the Son is *homousian* with the Father, then didst thou become a Christian ; " similarly, pp. 276, 280.

under VALENTINIAN and GRATIAN, and under the Roman bishop
DAMASUS (his first Roman council, A. D. 369 or 370, confesses
that " Father and Son are of one essence or substance, *essentiae
sive substantiae*, and also the Holy Spirit," Mansi iii. 444. The
Macedonians are also, upon the urgent desire of the Orientals,
condemned at Rome, A. D. 374 ; see Mansi iii. 488, and also
the Marcellians, A. D. 380 ; Theod. h. e. v. 11 ; cf. Hefele
CG. i., ed. 2, 739 ff. Rade, Damasus). THEODOSIUS THE
GREAT, in A. D. 381, established the Roman-Alexandrian orthodoxy in the East as the law of the empire (Cod. Theod. xvi.
1. 2 : " We believe in one deity of Father, Son, and Spirit,
under equal majesty and under a holy trinity. We command
that all who honor this law shall bear the name of Catholic Christians ; deciding that others, mad and insane, shall bear the in-
famy of heretical doctrine, to be punished, first, by divine vengeance, and afterward also by the avenging of our intention which
we have derived from the heavenly will ;" cf. 1. 6). The Apostles'
Creed and the Codex Theodosianus make the doctrine of the
Trinity the chief and fundamental dogma. But Theodosius, with
a prudent forbearance, recognized the new Oriental orthodoxy,
as is proved especially by the attitude which he assumed in favor
of MELETIUS of Antioch. Here had existed since A. D. 360
the much-talked-of schism between the homoiusian, neo-orthodox
Meletius and the old-orthodox Paulinus (s. Möller, PRE. ix.
530 ff.; cf. Harnack, DG. ii. 260, n.). The emperor summoned the former as the leader of the great final COUNCIL OF CON-
STANTINOPLE in A. D. 381. It was an assemblage of Oriental
bishops (Theod. h. e. v. 6 ; cf. Hefele CG. ii., ed. 2, 3). A hundred and fifty Orthodox and fifty-six Macedonian bishops (esp.
from the vicinity of the Hellespont) participated. The attempt
of the latter to win the day failed (Socr. h. e. v. 8). The council prepared an exhaustive treatise (τόμος) upon the orthodox
doctrine of the Trinity,[1] but framed no separate confession, being content to rest in the Nicene Creed, which had become the
shibboleth.[2]

---

[1] Perhaps the anathematizing paragraphs handed down as the first canon of
the council belong to this treatise (Tillemont, Mémoires, etc., ix. 221). They
profess allegiance to the Nicene Creed, and condemn the Eunomians or
Anomoeans, the Arians or Eudoxians, the Semi-Arians or Pneumatomachians,
as well as the Sabellians, Marcellians, Photinians, and Apollinarians. The
doctrine of Marcellus, which Rome had also in the meantime abandoned, is
here classed with Sabellianism.

[2] The so-called Niceno-Constantinopolitan (or simply Nicene) Creed is
*not* the confession of this council ; for (1) It is not mentioned as such before
the council of Chalcedon, A. D. 451 (see Greg. Naz. ep. 102 ; the council of
Constantinople, A. D. 382 ; the council at Ephesus). (2) The section upon

With this, the doctrine of Athanasius was acknowledged also in the East, though only in the interpretation above given.    The West was not entirely satisfied with the solution reached.    A desire was felt for a council, to be held, perhaps, at Alexandria or Rome (Mansi iii. 623, 630).    But Theodosius summoned a second council at Constantinople, A. D. 382.    At the same time a council assembled at Rome.    The former addressed a letter to the latter, professing adherence to the Nicene Creed, with reference also to the council at Antioch and the *Tomus* of the preceding year (Theod. h. e. v. 9).    The Nicene Creed had now gained the ascendency both in the West and in the East. The attempt of Theodosius, at Constantinople, A. D. 383, to win the Arians and Macedonians was a failure.    From this time forward, the State was upon the side of orthodoxy and opposed to the Arians (Socr. v. 10; Sozom. vii. 12).    Thus the civil argument prevails at the close, as at the opening, of the great controversy.    The church won its first dogma, in the stricter sense of the term, when the teaching-church became also a state-church, and ecclesiastical doctrine became a part of ecclesiastical law.    But this dogma was an outgrowth of the faith of the church at large.    Arianism continued for a little while, but its

---

the Holy Ghost does not suit the circumstances of that time.    (3) It is cited as early as A. D. 374 by Epiphanius (Ancorat. 119).    But this is really nothing else than the baptismal confession of the church at Jerusalem, prepared probably by Cyril of Jerusalem (Cyr. cat. 5. 12).    How it came to be attributed to the council of A. D. 381 cannot now be certainly known.    A. D. 500 it came into general use, displacing the Nicene Creed.    Cf. CASPARI in Ztschr. f. luth. Theol., 1857, p. 634; Sources, etc., i.    HORT, two dissertations, 1876, and esp. HARNACK PRE. viii., 212 ff.; KUNZE, Das nicänisch-constantinopolitan-ische Symbol (BONWETSCH-SEEBERG, Studien zur Gesch. der Theol. u. der Kirche, iii. 3), 1898.    It reads as follows : " We believe in one God, the Father Almighty, Maker of heaven and earth, and of all things visible and invisible. And in one Lord Jesus Christ, the only-begotten Son of God, begotten of the Father before all worlds, light of light, very God of very God, begotten not made, being of one substance with the Father, by whom all things were made ; who for us men and for our salvation came down from heaven and was incar-nate of the Holy Ghost and the Virgin Mary, and was made man ; and was crucified also for us under Pontius Pilate, and suffered, and was buried, and arose on the third day according to the Scriptures ; and ascended into heaven, and sitteth on the right hand of the Father, and cometh again with glory to judge the quick and the dead ; of whose kingdom there shall be no end.    And in the Holy Ghost the Lord, the Giver of life, who proceedeth from the Father, who with the Father and the Son is worshiped and glorified, who spake by the prophets ; in one holy catholic and apostolic church ; we acknowledge one baptism for the remission of sins ; we look for the resurrection of the dead and the life of the world to come."    Compared with the Nicene Creed, it lacks the "of the substance of the Father" and the anathemas ; compared with the more recent doctrinal development, it lacks the ascription of the ὁμοούσιος to the Holy Spirit.

day was past (Philostorg. h. e. xii. 11 ; Sozom. h. e. viii. 1).
It still made a passing demonstration among the German nations.

### § 22.  *The Completion of the Doctrine of the Trinity.*

1. Before entering upon the controversy concerning the two
natures in Christ, we must briefly note the final settlement of
the Trinitarian dogma. JOHN OF DAMASCUS († after A. D. 754)
marks the close of the controversy in the East, and AUGUSTINE
(† A. D. 430) in the West.

Later Monophysites, such as John ASCUSNAGES and John PHILO-
PONUS carried out the Cappadocian doctrine on the basis of the
Aristotelian philosophy (φύσις and ὑπόστασις=genus and individual) to the extreme of Tritheism (vid. Joh. Damasc. de haer. 83 ;
Leont. de sectis act. v. 6 ; Phot. Bibl. cod. 75 ; Joh. of Ephes. h. e.
v. 1-12, translated by SCHÖNFELDER, who discusses the doctrine
on page 275 ff.). To break the force of these deductions from
the system, JOHN OF DAMASCUS presented the orthodox doctrine
in his standard dogmatic work, *De fide orthodoxa*, following
especially the Cappadocians, but guarding the unity of God
more distinctly than they had done (opp. ed. Lequin, in Mign.
gr. 91 ff.; cf. LANGEN, Joh. of Dam., 1879).

2. The views of John of Damascus may be summarized as
follows : Father, Son, and Spirit are one God, or one substance
(οὐσία, fid. orth. i. 2), but not one person (ὑπόστασις or πρόσωπον):
" It is impossible to say that the three hypostases of the deity,
although they are united to one another, are one hypostasis "
(iii. 5 ; cf. iii. 15, p. 233). This one God is the Creator, Preserver, and Ruler of the world : " one substance, one deity, one
power, one will, one energy, one source, one authority, one dominion, one kingdom, in three complete hypostases, to be acknowledged and worshiped with one homage . . . united without mixture and continuously separated " (i. 8, pp. 132, 139,
140). Hence the Logos is the same in nature (αὐτὸς κατὰ τὴν
φύσιν) with the Father (1. 6). Accordingly, the three hypostases, although always to be thought of as realities, are yet not
related to one another as are three men (i. 8, p. 138). They
are one, but different in their mode of existence (τρόπος ὑπάρξεως):
" They are one in all respects . . . except those of non-genera-
tion, generation, and procession. The distinction is in thought ;
for we know one God, in the exclusive peculiarities of paternity
and sonship and procession " (i. 8, p. 139). This relationship
may be further defined as a mutual interpenetration of the three
hypostases without commingling (according to Jn. 14. 11):
" The hypostases are in one another. They are in . . . not so

as to be commingled with one another, but so as to be contained in one another ; and they move about within one another without any coalescing and without juncture " (i. 8, pp. 140, 138). " For the deity is, to speak concisely, undivided in the divided (ἀμέριστος ἐν μεμερισμένοις), just as also, in three suns contained in one another and unseparated, there is one blending and mutual connection of light " (ib.). Despite his radical rejection of Subordinationism, John of Damascus describes the Father as the Source of the Godhead (i. 7. 8), and accordingly represents the Spirit as proceeding from the Father, although, indeed, "through the Logos " (i. 12 ; per contra, vid. i. 8 fin.). This way of viewing the subject, which is simply a relic of the Greek Subordinationism, prepared the way for the controversy, long continued and never fully concluded,[1] between the Roman and the Greek churches, upon the procession of the Holy Spirit (*filioque*). See LANGEN, Die trin. Lehrdifferenz, 1876. GASS, Symbolik der griech. Kirche, p. 152 ff. KATTENBUSCH, Confessionskunde i., p. 323 ff.

3. The Western conception of the Trinity reached its final statement in the extensive and magnificent work of Augustine, *De trinitate*, which clearly re-states the Latin view of the Trinity—in its divergence from the Grecian, and which, by virtue of its method and the problems discussed, exerted a commanding influence upon the dogmatics of the Western church.[2] The Occident, as we have seen, stood unwaveringly upon the side of the Nicene theologians (Athanasius and Marcellus). The formulas of Tertullian were the means of preserving the recognition of the strict unity of God as not prejudicing in any degree the personal distinctions in his nature. The prevalent theory was not Sabellian, nor was there thought to be any reason for suspecting the Alexandrine theology of a Sabellianizing tendency. The Neo-Nicene orthodoxy was therefore, though tardily, acknowledged.

In this respect, Augustine is thoroughly Western in his point of view. It is not the Greek theology, nor even, in reality, the Council of Nice, which is decisive for him, but the " catholic faith," *e. g.*, ep. 120. 17 ; in Joh. tr. 74. 1 ; 98. 7 ; 18. 2 ; 37. 6 ; de doctr. chr. iii. 1 (cf. REUTER, Aug. Studien, p. 185 ff.).

As to Augustine's doctrine of the Trinity : BAUR, Lehre v. d. Dreieinigkeit, 1841, p. 828 ff. NITZSCH DG., i. 305 ff. THOMASIUS, DG. i., ed. 2, 281 ff. A. DORNER, Aug., 1873, p. 5 ff. BINDEMANN, Der heil. Aug. iii. 709 ff. GANGAUF, Aug. spekulat. Lehre von Gott, 1865.

[1] Cf. the Russian Catechism (Schaff, Creeds of Christendom, ii. 481 f., 461) and the negotiations between Old Catholics and Greeks at Bonn, A. D. 1874, reported in REUSCH, p. 26 ff.
[2] See the brief outline of the contents in Book xv. 3, § 5.

The basis of Augustine's theology is the unity of God. The
Trinity is the one and simple God, "not therefore not simple,
because a Trinity" (de civ. dei xi. 10; de trin. v. 7. 9; viii. 1;
de fid. et symb. 8. 20). "The Trinity itself is, indeed, the one
God, and one God in the same sense as one Creator" (c. serm.
Arian. 3). Accordingly, there belongs to the one triune God one
substance, one nature, one energy, and one will: "The works of
the Trinity are inseparable" (ib. 4; de trin. ii. 5. 9; Enchirid.
12. 38; de symb. 2; c. Maxim. ii. 10. 2; in Joh. tr. 18. 6; 20. 3,
7; 95. 1; 21. 11). These ideas are carried out to the fullest
extent. Even the theophanies of the Old Testament are not referred exclusively to the Son (trin. ii. 15 ff.). The Son (and
the Spirit) even takes an active part in his own *missio* into the
world, since this was not accomplished otherwise than through
"the Word of the Father:" "The incarnation . . . was
effected by one and the same operation of the Father and the
Son inseparably, the Spirit, indeed, not being separated from it;"
cf. Matt. 1. 18. "Since the Father sent him by his Word, it
was brought about by the Father and his Word that he was sent.
Therefore by the Father and the Son was sent the same Son,
because the Son himself is the Word of the Father" (trin. ii.
5. 9). But the fact that it is just the Son (and Spirit), and
not the Father, who is sent, is not because they are inferior to the
Father, but because they proceed from him (ib. iv. 20. 27; c.
serm. Ar. 4, cf. de symb. 9 and opp. viii. 1636). Father, Son,
and Spirit are, therefore, not three persons different from one
another in the sense in which three human persons differ although belonging to one genus (in Joh. tr. 39. 2 f.; 91. 4). On
the contrary, each divine person is, in respect to the substance,
identical with the others, or with the entire divine substance:
"For Father, and Son, and Holy Spirit together are not a greater
essence (*essentia*) than the Father alone or the Son alone, but
these three substances, or persons, if they be so called, are together equal to each one alone" (de trin. vii. 6. 11; viii. 1;
vi. 7. 9; 10. 12: "Neither are two something more than one."
In this sense, of the identity of substance, the term ὁμοούσιος is
used in Joh. tr. 97. 4). It is plain that Augustine's entire conception of the unity of God leads inevitably to the recognition
of his personal unity. Augustine felt this, but for him—and
long afterward—a distinct enunciation of this truth was prevented
by the triadic application of the term person (cf. de trin. vii.
4. 7; 6. 11).

The One (personal) God is thus for Augustine an established
fact. No less certain is it, however, that there are three persons
in the one God. Here lay for him, as for Athanasius, the

greatest difficulty—the real problem.    These are related to God, not as species to genus, nor as properties to a substance.    Every quantitative or qualitative distinction is excluded (*e. g.*, trin. v. 5-6 ; vii. 3-6 ; v. 11 ; viii. 1).    On the contrary, this terminology is designed to indicate the mutual inward relationship between the three : "They are so called, not with respect to substance, because they are thus called, not each one of them as related to himself, but as related mutually and the one to the other ; nor with respect to property, because what is called Father and what is called Son is eternal and immutable in them. Wherefore, although to be Father and to be Son are two different things, yet there is not a different substance ; for they are called thus, not with respect to substance, but with respect to that which is relative, which relativity is yet not a property, because it is not mutable" (trin. v. 5, 6 ; 8-9 ; viii. 1 init.; cf. "Another, not other (*alius non aliud*)," civ. dei. xi. 10. 1).    The one God is never either Father only nor Son only, but the three forms of existence of the one God, each requiring the others, are Father, Son, and Spirit.    They are hence substantially identical—the relation of dependence between them is a mutual one.    The Father, who commands the Son, is no less dependent upon him than is the latter upon the Father (c. serm. Ar. 3).    Father, Son, and Spirit behold in themselves the entire undivided Deity, only that it belongs to each of them under a different point of view, as generating, generated, or existing through spiration. "Father and Son, therefore, know one another mutually, but the one in begetting, the other in being begotten" (trin. xv. 14-23).    Between the three hypostases exists the relation of a mutual interpenetration and interdwelling (trin. vi. 7. 9).    For the designation of this relationship, the term *persona* (or *substantia*) does not altogether satisfy Augustine.    "Nevertheless, when it is asked, What are the three? human speech at once toils with great insufficiency.    Yet we say, three persons, not in order to express it, but in order not to be silent" (trin. v. 9, 10).[1]

That, with this conception of the Trinity, the Holy Ghost is regarded as proceeding not only from the Father "but from both at once," follows as a matter of course (xv. 17. 29 ; in Joh. tr. 99. 6).

According to Augustine, then, the one personal God, from an inward necessity, leads a three-fold, mutually-related personal

---

[1] The whole passage is important in elucidating the terminology of Augustine.    He translates μίαν οὐσίαν, τρεῖς ὑποστάσεις : *unam essentiam, tres substantias ;* but decides for the formula : *Unam essentiam vel substantiam, tres autem personas.*    Cf. vii. 5. 10, where, appealing to Ex. 3. 24, he prefers *essentia* to *substantia.*

life. The attempt is made to explain this view in a number of analogies, and thus prove the possibility of the three-fold life in the one God. These analogies are drawn from the human soul, because it was made in the image of God. Thus there is a trinity in sight ("thing seen, vision, intention of the will uniting the two" (trin. xi. 2. 2 ; cf. xv. 3. 5); in thought ("thus there is this trinity in memory, and inner vision, and the will which unites the two," ib. xi. 3. 6); in the human spirit (ix. and x.; xv. 3. 5: "mind, and knowledge by which it knows itself, and love by which it esteems itself and its knowledge—memory, intelligence, will"); in love (ix. 22 : "that which loves, that which is loved, and love itself"). These analogies not only give expression to the idea that three are equivalent to one, which the ancient teachers sought to illustrate from nature (cf. in Aug. de fid. et symb. 9. 17), but they present the idea of a harmonious spiritual entity, impelled and controlled from a three-fold centre. In this there was a distinct advance upon the representations of the older theologians, which constantly wavered between the unity and the trinity. Augustine made it impossible for later ages to overlook the fact, that there can be no Christian doctrine of the Trinity which is not at the same time an unequivocal confession of the one personal God. "Thrice have I said God, but I have not said three Gods ; for God thrice is greater than three Gods, because Father, Son, and Holy Spirit are one God " (in Joh. tr. 6. 2 ; cf. serm. 2. 15. 8 ; *trina unitas*). Augustine did not conceal his deep realization of the inadequacy of all these attempted explanations. He closes his work with the words : " Lord, our God, we believe in Thee, the Father and the Son and the Spirit. For Truth would not have said, Go, baptize, etc. (Matt. 28. 20), unless Thou wast a Trinity. . . . I would remember Thee ; I would know Thee ; I would love Thee . . . Lord, Thou one God, divine Trinity, whatsoever I have written in these books by suggestion of Thee, the One, mayest Thou the Three accept, if anything of myself, mayest both Thou the One and Thou the Three overlook it " (xv. 21. 51).[1]

Such is Augustine's doctrine of the Trinity. In it is collected a wealth of psychological observations and profound speculations. Theorists have hence always returned to it anew. It is but the more noticeable on this account that it really exerted but a slight influence upon practical piety. This is accounted for by the fact that the Augustinian theory was concerned only with the *imma-*

---

[1] Ambrose represented the Trinity in a way more in harmony with the Cappadocian ideas : three persons who are one by virtue of their "one substance, divinity, will, law." See de fide ad Grat. i. 2. 17-19; iii. c. 12, 26; ii. 8. 73 ; 10. 86 ; iii. 14. 108 ; iv. 6. 68 ; 8. 83, etc.

*nent* Trinity, without deducing this from the view-point of the *economic* Trinity ; whereas a practically religious conception of the Trinity can be secured only from a contemplation of the revealed Trinitarian activity of God.   It was because Augustine did not start at this point, that he was compelled to confess that men in theory acknowledged allegiance to the absolutely One, Triune God, whereas their practical ideas were always tinctured with Tritheism.   But, despite this, what a wealth of ideas and views has this doctrine of Augustine bequeathed to the church !

4.  This Augustinian conception of the Trinity was—in its fundamental features—embodied for the Western church in the so-called Athanasian Creed, or *Symbolum Quicunque* :[1]  " That we worship one God in Trinity and Trinity in Unity, neither confounding the persons nor dividing the substance.   For there

---

[1] The mention of this symbol, which was not produced until a later period, at this point is justified by the fact that it contains the theology of Augustine.

Of the recent literature we cite : KÖLLNER, Symbolik i., 1837. FFOULKES, The Athan. Creed, London, ed. 3. LUMBY, History of the Creeds, ed. 3, 1887. SWAINSON, The Nicene and Apostles' Creeds, etc., 1875, p. 195 ff. OMMANNEY, The Athan. Creed, 1875, and Early History of the Athan. Creed, 1880. G. MORIN in La science catholique, 1891, 673 ff., and in the Revue bénédictine xii., 1895, p. 385 ff. BURN, The Athan. Creed and Its Early Commentaries (Texts and Studies, ed. Robinson, iv. 1, 1896). HARNACK DG., ii. 298 ff. LOOFS PRE. ii. ed. 3, 178 ff.

The origin of the symbol, despite the most diligent efforts of scholars in recent years to discover it, is still unknown.   It is evident that it has no relation to Athanasius.   The following relatively certain data throw some light upon the question : (1) The manuscript copies of the text carry us to the eighth century.   (2) The ancient expositions would lead us still further back, if the *Expositio fidei Fortunati* (Burn, p. 28 ff.) can be attributed to Fortunatus († ca. A. D. 600), whom one manuscript represents as the author, while another manuscript names Euphronius the presbyter, who was bishop of Treves A. D. 555-572.   But the crediting of this Expositio, which would otherwise come to us anonymously, to two men who were personal acquaintances is very remarkable, and the apparently probable solution, that Euphronius as presbyter (hence about A. D. 550) composed it, must still remain uncertain.   (3) Parallels to the formula of the Creed appear in great numbers in Southern Gaul.   Especially important is the Pseudo-Augustinian *Sermo 244*, which has from ancient times been attributed to Cæsarius († A. D. 542).   But an *Expositio* discovered by Caspari in two Paris manuscripts (Anecdota i. 283 ff.) shows close relationship to *Sermo* 244, but does not contain the parallel to the Quicunque.   On this account the originality of *Sermo* 244 is assailed.   Caspari, Zahn, and Kattenbusch, however, zealously defend it. But if *Sermo* 244, in the form in which it appears in Pseudo-Augustine, was really composed by Caesarius, we then must here recognize, not only anticipations of the Quicunque, but an acquaintance at this early day with a completed formula.   Such a formula must then have existed as early as about A. D. 500. (4) Vincent of Lerins, when he wrote his *Commonitorium* in A. D. 434, had no knowledge of the Creed (Loofs).   (5) A council at Autun, at which Bishop Laodegar (A. D. 659 to ca. 683) presided, expressly mentions the " creed ( *fidem* ) of Saint Athanasius, the president."   Thus at this time

16

is one person of the Father, another of the Son, another of the Holy Spirit; but the Godhead of the Father and of the Son and of the Holy Spirit is one, the glory equal, the majesty coëternal. Such as is the Father, such is the Son, and such the Holy Spirit. . . . And yet there are not three eternals, but one eternal; just as there are not three uncreated nor three unbounded, but one uncreated and one unbounded . . . not three omnipotents, but

already the Creed bore at Autun the name of Athanasius. (6) The codex Paris, 3836, dating from the eighth century, cites among canonical material a Christological rule of faith which is intimately related to §§ 28-40 of the Quicunque, but which varies considerably in the wording. But the writer of the Paris codex had before him a Treves manuscript. From the fact that the Christological part of the symbol stands by itself in this document, it has been inferred that this second part was added later to the above-cited trinitarian portion (Swainson, Lumby, Harnack). But Loofs (p. 186) has correctly surmised that the part of the Treves manuscript cited by the writer beginning: "Domini nostri, Jesu Christi fideliter credat," is merely a fragment torn from § 27 of the Quicunque. From this he infers that there was a page wanting in the Treves manuscript in the hands of the Paris writer, and that he (about A. D. 750) had no knowledge of the Quicunque, or he would not have copied this. This is supposed to disprove the so-called two-source theory. Yet this entire argumentation does not appear to be at all decisive. The very circumstance that the creed designated as Athanasian at Autun about A. D. 670 should have been unknown to this writer of A. D. 750 is sufficient to shake our confidence in the conclusion. Nevertheless, the suggestion with which Loofs starts is correct beyond question; but the inference drawn by him is false. The proper inference can only be: Since a librarian living about the middle of the eighth century would be familiar with the Athanasian Creed, and it was such a man who transcribed the Christological part, he must have been yet in ignorance of this portion of the document. This might be said already of the writer of the Treves Codex. Thus the two-source theory concerning the codex of Paris, 3836, receives, in my opinion, an important support. It commends itself also from the fact that the transition from the first to the second part (§ 27) plainly betrays the attempt to artfully unite two documents in hand. Compare also § 40. It is evident, for example, that, according to the first part, the *fides catholica* embraces nothing more than faith in the Trinity (§§ 1-3). To this § 27 adds that it is necessary to eternal salvation that one believe *also* in the incarnation; while in § 28 the confession of the divinity and humanity of Christ is presented as the content of *fides recta*. This is evidently something new, which was not in view when § 3 was composed.

The history of the Quicunque must accordingly be somewhat as follows: The first part was composed from formulas of Augustinian theology for the elucidation of the Apostles' Creed. It may have attained a fixed form by about A. D. 500, and in South Gaul. But, in addition to this formula, there was also a second and Christological one, which was not much later in its appearance. It was probably bound up with the first named as early as the seventh century. Yet toward the middle of the eighth century there were scholarly people who knew nothing of the Christological formula. But, with this exception, the combination of the two formulas must be regarded as a fixed fact. Since the time of the Carlovingians, we find the Quicunque making its way into liturgies and then co-ordinated with the other two symbols as the Creed of Athanasius (Anselm, ep. ii. 41. Alex. of Hales, Summa iv. quest. 37, § 9, etc.). Thus the Reformers were also led to accept the symbol.

one omnipotent. . . . The Son is the only (son) of the Father ; not made, not created, but begotten. The Holy Spirit is of the Father and the Son, not made nor created nor begotten, but proceeding. . . . In this Trinity there is nothing before or after, nothing greater or less ; but the whole three persons are co-eternal together and coequal, so that in all things, as has been said above, both the unity in trinity and the trinity in unity is to be worshiped. Whoever, therefore, wishes to be saved, let him think thus concerning the Trinity " (§§ 3-26).

---

## CHAPTER II.

### THE DOCTRINE OF ONE PERSON AND TWO NATURES IN CHRIST.

§ 23. *Origin of the Controversies Upon the Two Natures of Christ.*

1. Two things had been transmitted by tradition as fixed : the reality of the humanity of Christ, with his human activity and sufferings (recognized in conflict with Docetism in the second century), and the reality and Homousia of his divinity. Divinity and humanity are now combined in one person ; there is a synthesis (σύνθετον, Origen), but as to the question how this union was conceivable, especially how two personal natures can constitute one person, there was no further investigation, despite the propositions put forth by the Dynamistic Monarchians. Only the West possessed, in Tertullian's view of one person in two substances, a formula which appeared to adequately meet the situation, and which had been confirmed by the fuller development of the doctrine of the Trinity. Western theologians, with this theory in hand, felt themselves relieved from the necessity of further investigation, and in the conflicts of the succeeding era they presented it as an adequate solution of all the questions raised in the Orient.

2. This was the situation when APOLLINARIS OF LAODICEA (born about A. D. 310) carefully stated the Christological problem and, at the same time, presented a clear and challenging attempt at its solution. The learned bishop was prominent as a humorist as well as noted for his acquaintance with the Scriptures and his intellectual acuteness.

Of his writings, the following are here of interest : The treatise attributed to Gregory Thaum., κατὰ μέρος πιστις; de divina incarnatione, frg.; die pseudo-Athanasian, περὶ τῆς σαρκώσεως τοῦ θεοῦ λόγου, and a number of fragments, vid. DRÄSEKE, in Texte u. Unters. vii. 34. CASPARI, Alte und Neue Quellen, etc., p. 65 ff. Further, in opposition : Athan. c. Apol. (genuineness questioned); cf. in Epiphan. h. 77 ; Greg. Naz. ep. ad Nectarium, epistolae ad Cledonium ; Greg. Nyss. Antirreheticus c. Apol.; Theodoret Eranistes dial. 5 ; haeret. fab. iv. 8. Theodore of Mopsuestia, frg. from his c. Apol. et de Apollinari. Compare DORNER, Entwicklungsgesch. d. Lehre v. d. Pers. Christi, i. pp. 975-1036. LOOFS PRE. ii. ed. 3, 177 ff. BURN, the Athan. Creed, Texts and Studies iv. 1. G. KRUEGER, PRE. i., ed. 3, 671 ff.

(a) The Christology of this enthusiastic champion of the ὁμοούσιος took its form in opposition, both to the Arian doctrine of the mutability of the Logos and that of the external juxtaposition of the two natures of Christ, as taught by the Antiochian "Paulinizing" (Paul of Samosata) theologians, who "say that the man that is from heaven is one, confessing him to be God, and the man from earth is another, saying that the one is uncreated, the other created" (ad Dionys. ep. p. 348 ; cf. ep. ad Jov. p. 342 ; cf. p. 381). The idea of the God, Christ, held his thought in positive thralldom. On the one hand, it was his aim to so construct Christology that no shadow of mutability might fall upon Christ. But this appeared to be possible only if this man was really God—if there was in him no free human will (de incarn. pp. 383, 387, 388). Otherwise, he would be subject to sin (fid. conf. p. 393 and Athan. c. Apol. i. 2 ; ii. 6, 8 ; Greg. Nyss. Antirrh. 40. 51 ; Greg. Naz. ad Cled. i. 10) and the redeeming death of Christ would be only the death of a man (de inc. p. 391 ; in inc. adversar. p. 395). On the other hand, the outward juxtaposition of the two natures does not help to overcome the difficulties. It is impossible to make the divinity and the humanity combine in their entirety into one person (de inc. pp. 384, 388, 389, 400). Two persons (πρόσωπα) would be the necessary result (ib. 387, 392). "That two complete things should become one is not possible" (Athan. c. Apol. i. 2). We would thus be led to a fabulous being like the Minotaurs or Tragelaphs, or we would be compelled to introduce a quaternity instead of the trinity (Greg. Nyss. antirrh. 42). Only because the flesh (σάρξ) of Christ is one person (πρόσωπον) with his divinity is it possible to worship Jesus without, at the same time, worshiping a man (pp. 389, 349, 350). Only thus is redemption a work of God. (b) From this it follows that the immutable divinity of Christ and the unity of the Redeemer's person can be preserved only by yielding the integrity of his human nature. Arius and his followers had, with a purpose diametrically opposite to that of Apollinaris, maintained the same position (in order to make all evidences of mutability or infirmity in Jesus applicable to the Logos), *i. e.*, that Christ was not made man, but only became incarnate, and therefore assumed only a human body and not also a human soul (see Confes. of Eudoxius in CASPARI, l. c. iv. p. 180 ; Athan. c. Apol. ii. 4 ; Greg. Naz. ad Cled. ep. ii. 7 ; Epiph. ancor. 33 ; cf. supra, p. 203). This same inference Apollinaris now drew with a different purpose and in a different sense. He regarded the trichotomy of man's nature as established by 1 Thes. 5. 23 (de inc. pp. 382, 388, 390). The Logos assumed the body and soul of a man, but the divine Logos itself took the place of the spirit (νοῦς) or intellectual soul (ψυχή νοερά). "Christ, having, besides soul and body, a divine spirit, *i. e.*, mind, is with reason called the man from heaven" (de inc. pp. 382, 401). Hence it may be said : "Thus the one living being consists of a moved and a mover, and is not two, nor composed of two, complete and self-moving beings" (de inc. p. 384); and thus Christ is one person with one personal life in mind and will and energy, *i. e.*, the purely divine (pp. 349, 399, 400, 401). "For, saying that 'the Logos became flesh,' he does not add, 'and soul ;' for it is impossible that two souls, a thinking and a willing, should dwell together in the same person, and the one not contend against the other by reason of its own will and energy. Therefore the Logos assumed not a human soul, but only the seed of Abraham" (de unione, frg. p. 401 ; cf. 396). The difficulties are thus overcome : "For God, having become incarnate, has in the human flesh simply his own energy, his mind being unsubject to sensual and carnal passions, and divinely and sinlessly guiding the flesh and controlling the fleshly emotions, and not alone unconquerable by death, but also destroying death. And he is true God, the unfleshly appearing in the flesh, the perfect one in genuine and divine perfection, *not two* persons (πρόσωπα), nor two natures (φύσεις). There is one Son ; both before the incarnation and after the incarnation the same, man and God, each as one. And the divine Logos is not one person and the man Jesus another" (κατὰ μερ. πιστ. pp. 377, 378). (*c*) But since Apollinaris in this way found in Christ one person, one harmonious being, he could also speak of his one nature (φύσις) and one substance (ὀυσία) (*e. g.*, 341, 348, 349, 352, 363), the Logos being unseparated and undivided (ἀχώριστος χαι ἀμέριστος) from his flesh (pp. 395, 396) and yet also distinguish two natures (de trin. pp. 358, 360): "For as man is one, but has in himself two different natures . . . so the Son, being one, has also two natures" (p. 358). Since this illustration from the nature of man is a proper one, it follows also that the relation of the two natures (συνάφεια, pp.

344, 346, 351, 367) is not to be conceived as a change (μεταβολή) nor as a mixing (σύγκρασις) and confounding (σύγχυσις) (c. Diodor. p. 366 sq.), for the Deity remains immutable (pp. 347, 393). (d) Apollinaris drew yet another notable inference from his premises, teaching, in a certain sense, a pre-existence of the σάρξ of Christ, appealing to Jn. 3. 13 and 1 Cor. 15. 47—not as though the Logos had the flesh already while in heaven and brought it with him to the earth (e. g., Ath. c. Ap. i. 7; ii. 10; Greg. Naz. ep. ad Nect. 3, ad Cled. i. 6; Greg. Nyss. antirrh. 13 f.), for this Apollinaris expressly denied (ep. ad Dionys. pp. 348, 349).[1] But he wrote: "The man Christ pre-exists, not as though the spirit, i. e., the divine Spirit, were that of another than himself, but in such a way that the divine Spirit in the nature of the divine man was the Lord" (de inc. p. 382 f.). Although this is obscure in some points, the meaning can scarcely be other than that the Logos was from all eternity predestined to become man, and was, in this sense, the pre-existent heavenly man.

Such was the teaching of this great bishop, which he, as an earnest exegete,[2] endeavored to establish upon biblical authority. "This man is certainly also God. If Christ had been only man, he could not have saved the world; and if only God, he could not have saved it through suffering. . . . If Christ had been only man, or if only God, he could not have been a middle one between men and God. The flesh is, therefore, an organ of life adapted to sufferings according to the divine counsels, and neither are the words of the flesh its own nor its deeds, and, having been made subject to sufferings as is suitable for flesh, it prevailed over the sufferings through its being the flesh of God." He believed that he was not in reality in conflict with the "dogmas" of the church in his day,[3] but in this he was self-deceived.[4]

[1] Epiphanius, indeed, heard this view expressed by pupils of Apollinaris (h. 77. 2, 14).

[2] This (cf. Hieron. vir. ill. 104) is shown, e. g., in the sensuous Chiliasm of Apollinaris (see Basil. ep. 263. 4; Greg. Naz. ad Cled. ii. 4).

[3] See ep. ad Dionys. p. 351: "We are not divided on account of these expressions. For to pretend that the things in the expressions which differ from the dogmas agree with them would be wicked; but to pretend that the things in the expressions which agree with the dogmas differ from them would be vain and foolish. But let those having this agreed upon, that Christ is God incarnate, and that he is from heaven and earth, in form a servant, and in power God, remain in unity, and neither be foolishly separated nor fall into the logomachy of the heretics, but rather esteem highly the simplicity of the church."

[4] Nor was Apollinaris able to free himself from the bonds of the Antiochian theology. Its statement of the problem remained regulative for him, and he could find no way to escape their solution of it except at the terrible price of the surrender of the human νοῦς of Christ. He substituted the human

From the decade A. D. 370-380, the Cappadocians assailed his views (see already Ath. c. Apol. and, perhaps, the Alexandrine Council of A. D. 362; tom. ad Antioch. 7). They were moved to opposition chiefly by their general sense of the integrity of the human nature of Jesus, as he is depicted in the Gospel narratives, and of its significance in the work of redemption. Only if Christ had a human mind ($\nu o \tilde{\upsilon} \varsigma$), could he redeem also the human mind—an idea which, from the standpoint of the deification theory of the Greek Soteriology, was not a mere phrase. On the contrary, the Athanasian Christology was against Apollinarianism: "If anyone imagines a man without a mind, such a one is really inconceivable and altogether not worthy to be saved. For that which cannot be added to cannot be cured; but that which is united to God is already saved. If the half of Adam fell, it was the half also which was added to and saved; but if the whole [Adam] fell, the addition was made to the whole that was born, and he was wholly saved" (Greg. Naz. ep. ad Cled. i. 7. Greg. Nyss. antirrh. 17). Apollinarianism was condemned at the councils of Rome, A. D. 374 and 376 ( "If therefore the whole man was lost, it was necessary that that which was lost should be saved" ), and also at Constantinople, A. D. 381.

3. But this did not answer the question raised by Apollinaris. It failed to explain how two personal natures could exist in one person. Apollinaris had stated the Christological problem for the ancient church. Its solution was attempted from two directions.

We must first note the view of the Antiochians, which had stirred Apollinaris to opposition. It was they who for some years manifested the deepest interest in the question (see Diodor. of Tarsus, † bef. 394, frg. in Marius Mercator in Gallandi Bibl. viii. 705. Theod. of Mopsuestia, † 428, dogmat. frgg. esp. from de incarn. and c. Apol. in Swete, Theod. comm. on ep. Pauli ii. 289-339; also Theodoret, see excerpts in Mar. Merc.). (*a*) A settled point is here the Homousia of the Logos. The Logos, by his birth from Mary, assumed a complete man as to nature, consisting of "soul and mind and flesh" ($\psi \upsilon \chi \acute{\eta}$. $\nu o \varepsilon \rho \acute{\alpha}$. $\sigma \acute{\alpha} \rho \xi$—Theod. expos. fid. p. 328). We are, therefore, to acknowledge in Christ two complete entities ($\tau \acute{\varepsilon} \lambda \varepsilon \iota \alpha$). This applies to the nature ($\varphi \acute{\upsilon} \sigma \iota \varsigma$) as well as to the person ($\pi \rho \acute{o} \sigma \omega \pi o \nu$): "When we attempt to distinguish the natures, we say that the person of the man is complete and also the person

"flesh" for the complete human being controlled by the Logos, because he was as little able as the Antiochian theologians to understand the divine-human nature and life of Christ (cf. also Cyril. ad reginas ii. 55).

of the deity " (Theod. de incarn. viii., p. 300). We can speak
of the deity as becoming man, only in appearance : " For when
he says ' he took ' (Phil. 2. 7) . . . he speaks according to the
reality ; but when he says ' he became ' (Jn. 1. 14), he speaks
according to appearance ; for he was not transformed into flesh "
(ib. ix., p. 300). (*b*) Since, therefore, the integrity of the
two natures, especially that of the actual and developing human
nature, must be preserved (Diod. p. 705), the conclusion was
reached that the Son of God dwelt within the son of David.
This was illustrated by examples. The Logos dwells in Jesus,
somewhat as God dwells in a temple, or as he dwelt within the
Old Testament prophets, or even, as in all Christian believers, but
it is emphasized that this occurs in another but a uniquely complete and permanent way in the case of Jesus (Diod. p. 705.
Theod. de inc. xii. c. Apol. iii., pp. 303, 313). The Logos
dwelt in the man Jesus "from his very first formation " on
throughout his whole life, "conducting him to perfection "
(Theod. c. Ap. iii. 2, p. 314). It is hence, not a natural, but
a moral union which exists between the two—not " according to
essence " (*οὐσία*), but "according to good pleasure " (*εὐδοκία*).
The man Jesus desires what God desires. Through him the Deity
becomes efficient. There is one willing (*θέλησις*) and one
energy (Theod. ep. ad Domn. p. 339). " But the unity of the
person is to be seen in this, that he does all things through himself, which unity has been effected by inhabitation, which is according to good pleasure " (Theod. de incarn. vii., p. 297). This
unity has become an indissoluble one, and has attained its completion through the ascension of Jesus ("making him immutable
in the thoughts of his mind, but also in the flesh incorruptible
and indissoluble," Theod. p. 326; de incarn. xiv., p. 308).
(*c*) In view of this connection (*συνάφεια*) of the two personal
natures through their unity of will,[1] we may speak of the one person : " For the natures are discriminated, but the person made
complete in the union is one " (Theod. de inc. viii., p. 300).
"The manner of this union, according to good pleasure, preserving the natures unmingled, shows also that the nature of the
two is inseparably one, and the will one, and the energy one, in
consequence of the abiding of one control and sway (*αὐθεντίας*

---

[1] The lineal relationship of Paul of Samosata, Lucian—Arius, Diodorus—
Theodorus—is here plainly traceable ; Christ, a man united with God through
*unity of will*—a demi-god thus joined with God—a man, thus one person
with the personal Logos. The theory became step by step more orthodox,
but the difficulties in its fundamental structure were not thereby solved.
Theodorus, indeed, declares Paul to have been an "angelus diaboli" (pp.
332, 318).

καὶ δεσποτείας) in them" (Theod. ad Domn., p. 339). Thus there are seen to be two different natures ("each of the natures remaining indissolubly by itself—the natures being discriminated"—de inc. viii., p. 299), but in their combination they are one person ("the natures combined into one person according to the completed union"—ib.; "difference of natures and unity of person," ib., p. 302 ; "the reason of the natures unconfused, the person undivided," ib. p. 292). But, in further explanation, the union of man and wife as "one flesh" is cited (ib. and p. 324); or, it is even said : "The one receives blessing, the other gives it!" (de inc. xi., p. 302).

(d) Upon this basis, the personal unity is little more than an assertion. According to it, in the sufferings of Christ "the deity was indeed separated from him who suffered (according to Hebr. 2. 9, citra deum=χωρὶς θεοῦ), . . . yet it was not absent according to love from him who suffered" (Theod. pp. 325, 310). The worship of Jesus is, therefore, possible only in so far as the worshiper combines in his thought his humanity and his divinity. "We adore the purple for the sake of him who wears it, and the temple for the sake of him who dwells within it—the form of a servant for the sake of the form of God" (Diodor. l. c.; Theod. pp. 308, 309, 316, 329). Thus also Mary, the mother of the man, can only in this metaphorical sense be called the mother of God (Diod. ib.; Theod. de inc. xv., p. 310 : "for she was mother of man by nature, since he who was in the womb of Mary was man, . . . but mother of God, since God was in the man who was being born ; not in him as circumscribed after the manner of nature, but in him after the manner of the understanding," κατὰ τὴν σχέσιν τῆς γνώμης). In view of these statements, we can understand the vigorous opposition of Apollinaris. The unity of the person is endangered. The divine cannot be said to have really become man, as there remains only the moral relative union (ἕνωσις σχετική) between two persons. The religious significance of this union is that Christ, in prototype and example, represented the union of man with God—in obedient will. As did the man Jesus, so may we also attain sonship to God "by grace, not naturally." His purpose was "to lead all to imitation of himself" (Theod. de inc. xii. 7, p. 306 ; xiv. 2, p. 308 ; cat. 8, p. 331).[1]

(e) The church is indebted to this school of theologians for the preservation of a precious treasure—the reality of the human and personal career of Jesus. To what extreme the ideas of

---

[1] Cf. the saying attributed to Ibas : "I do not envy Christ," he says, "that he was made God ; for what he has been made I have been made, because he is of my nature" (Gallandi viii. 705).

Apollinaris lead may be seen in the later Monophysites. But it cannot be maintained that the "historical Jesus" would ever have received justice at the hands of those who were content with this theory. The abstract conception of God which lay at its basis prevented any real and historical understanding of the nature of the God-man. Two difficulties were felt : (1) The unity of the personal life of Jesus remained problematical, although this problem was perhaps soluble. (2) The tendency of Greek Soteriology toward a mystical deification of the humanity through the medium of the God-man did not appear to harmonize with the theory as proposed by the Antiochians. The only significance remaining to the work of redemption appeared to be instruction and imitation. This explains the often unjustifiable opposition to this Christology. The theology of the Antiochians at least prevented the acceptance of Apollinarianism as a solution of the problem of Apollinaris.

4. The other Greek theologians attempted to solve the problem in a different way, following upon the track of Athanasius : the God-man is a concrete unit, in whom, however, we discriminate in the abstract two natures (supra, p. 211). The Cappadocians maintained essentially the same position. But, in facing the problem of Apollinaris, they, like the Antiochians, could not get beyond mere allegations. They spoke of two natures ($\varphi \acute{v} \sigma \epsilon \iota \varsigma$), but did not infer from this that there were "two Sons," although the two natures were to be conceived as each complete (Greg. Naz. ep. ad Cled. i. 7, 8). It was thought that the two natures coalesced in one. There is a miraculous commingling, the one deifying and the other being deified : "For both the taking and the taken are God, the two natures concurring in one ; not two Sons" (Greg. Naz. or. 37. 2); and "being that which deified and that which was deified. O, the new mixture ($\mu \acute{\iota} \xi \iota \varsigma$); O, the strange compound" ($\chi \rho \tilde{a} \sigma \iota \varsigma$)! (or. 38. 13). It is, says Gregory of Nyssa, a relation like that between a drop of vinegar mingled with the sea and the sea itself. This simile indicates how utterly unlimited was the range of thought which these men allowed themselves. Since the Logos becomes flesh, the human is transformed into the divine ("changed, a mixing up, $\grave{a} \nu \acute{a} \chi \rho a \sigma \iota \varsigma$, with the divine, a transformation, $\mu \epsilon \tau a \sigma \tau o \iota \chi \epsilon \acute{\iota} \omega \sigma \iota \varsigma$, of the man into the Christ "). Thus the infirmity, mutability, and mortality of the human nature are consumed by the deity : "He mixed his life-giving power with the mortal and perishable nature. . . . The Immutable appears in the mutable, in order that, having changed and transformed from the worse into the better the evil commingled with the mutable subject, he might, having expended the evil in himself, cause it to disappear from the nature. For our God is a

consuming fire, in which all wood of evil is thoroughly burnt up''
(Greg. Nyss. c. Eunom. v., Mi. 45, pp. 700, 693, 697, 705,
708, also Antirrh. 42). It is also held, indeed, that '' the beholding of the attributes of the flesh and of the deity remains
unconfused, so long as each of these is regarded by itself'' (ib.
p. 706). Thus the humanity weeps at the grave of Lazarus, but
the deity calls him to life. But viewed concretely, the deity, by
virtue of the union, affects the human just as well as the humanity
the divine : '' thus through the connection and union the (properties) of both become common to each, the Lord taking upon
himself the stripes of the servant, and the servant being glorified with the honor belonging to the Lord '' (ib. 705, 697).
The relation of the two natures is thus a different one from that
existing between the persons of the Trinity : '' God and man are,
it is true, two natures . . . but there are not two Sons nor two
Gods. . . . And if it is necessary to speak concisely : other
and other (ἄλλο καὶ ἄλλο) are the entities of which (τὰ ἐξ ὧν)
the Saviour . . . not another and another, ἄλλος καὶ ἄλλος. God
forbid. For both are one in the compound, God being human-
ized and man being deified . . . but I say 'other and other'
in a contrary sense from that in which it may be said of the
Trinity; for there it is 'another and another,' in order that
we may not commingle the hypostases, and not 'other and
other,' for the three are one and the same in their divinity ''
(Greg. Naz. ep. ad Cled. i. 4).

Unfinished as is all this, we may yet clearly see the aim of
these writers. The historical character of Christ compels them
to maintain the two complete natures as well as the intimate
union of these two natures. But their conception of redemption
leads them to think of this union as a commingling of the natures, as a transformation of the human into the divine. They
maintained in their relation to the Antiochians a religious position, and in opposition to Apollinaris a historical standpoint.
In view of this tendency—though by no means in the importance or clearness of their ideas—they are superior to both (cf.
p. 246, n. 4).

5. This view received its final formulation at the hands of CYRIL
OF ALEXANDRIA (bishop from A. D. 412, † A. D. 444).

Opp. ed. Aubert, 1638. Mi. gr. 68-77. Especially : Quod unus sit Christ.
Dial. de incarn. unigeniti. De incarn. verbi. De incarn. domini. Adv.
Nestorii blasphemias, ll. 5. Quod s. virgo deipara sit. L. adv. nolentes con-
fiteri s. virgo esse deiparam. Explicatio duodecim capitum. Apologetic.
pro duodecim capitibus. Apologet. c. Theodoret. De recta fide ad reginas,
ll. 2. Frgg. ex libris c. Theodor. et Diodor. Ep. 1 ff.; ep. 17 ad Nestor.;
epp. 45, 46; ad Succensum, in Mi. t. 75-77. Cf. LOOFS, Leontius v. Byz. in
Texte u. Untersuch. iii. 1, p. 40 ff.

(*a*) Cyril starts with the person of the Logos. This person
assumed complete human nature for our salvation. His formula
is : "one nature of the divine Logos, made flesh." He does
not speak of the one nature of the incarnated Logos, or Christ,
but habitually of the one incarnated nature of the Logos. The
Logos, as the subject contemplated, has thus the one incarnated
nature. It may, however, also be said of the Logos that he was
made man and incarnated (*e. g.*, c. Nest. v. 4, 7 ; ii. 10 ; ad
regin. ii. 4, 33). In detail, Cyril teaches : Two natures are to be
acknowledged, the divine and the human, both of them complete, so that the latter includes the reasoning soul (ψυχὴ λογικὴ)
(ad reg. i. 13, Mi. 76. 1221 ; ii. 55 ; inc. unig., Mi. 75. 1208 f.,
1220). Thus Christ is "of like nature (ὁμοούσιος) with his
mother as with his Father" (dial. c. Nest., Mi. 76. 252 ; ep.
40, Mi. 77. 192). In consequence of his becoming man, there
is a concurrence (συνδρομή) and union (ἔνωσις) of these two natures. How is this to be understood? Not as a conversion or
change, since "the nature of the Logos is immutable and absolutely unchangeable" (ad reg. ii. 2, 22 ; inc. unig., Mi. 75.
1192 ff., 1200, 1253). "Neither as a mixture nor compound"
(φυρμός, σύγκρασις, κρᾶσις); quod unus, Mi. 75. 1292 ; c. Nest.
ii. 11 ; ep. 4, Mi. 77. 45); yet not as a mere connection
(συνάφεια) or indwelling (ἐνοίκησις) (*e. g.*, c. Nest. ii. proem.
quod b. virgo 8). On the contrary, both natures retain their
own characteristics unmingled. The deity throughout all the
changes of its earthly lot remains in its full glory what it was before (c. Nest. ii. 1 ; ad reg. i. 4 ; ii. 9, 16, 27, 33, 37 ; inc.
unig., Mi. 75. 1216, 1220, 1221, 1229), and the humanity retains its complete Homousia with us (ep. 40, Mi. 77. 192 ; inc.
unig., Mi. 75. 1216 : Christ's body mortal). Cyril can, therefore, speak of two natures (vid. esp. quod unus, Mi. 75. 1292),
and he can compare the relation of the two to that between an
emperor in his proper character, and as appearing in the garb of
a consul (quod b. virg. 14); or to that of body and soul in man,
which yet together compose one man (c. Nest. ii. 12 ; inc. unig.,
Mi. 75. 1224 ; ep. 17, Mi. 77. 116 ; ep. 45, p. 233, quod unus,
Mi. 75. 1292). This illustration affords us a key to the interpretation of the above-cited formula of Cyril. The two natures
are, indeed, after their union the same as they were before, but
they are combined in indissoluble unity by means of the unity of
the person—the Logos, as also by means of the consequent mutual communication of their respective attributes. Thus the two
natures are kept distinct in abstract thought, although the concrete object of contemplation is the "one incarnate nature,"
which has the Logos as its controlling factor. The unity in this

sense is, therefore, one of hypostases (ἕνωσις καθ' ὑπόστασιν), as Cyril often describes it in his later writings, *i. e.*, it is the Logos-person which establishes the unity. Cyril, in opposing Theodoret, confesses the novelty of this formula, but maintains its import-ance in the combating of heresy. It asserts no more, in his view, than "simply that the nature (φύσις) or hypostasis of the Logos, *i. e.*, the Logos itself, is truly united (ἑνωθείς) with the human nature" (Apol. c. Theodoret, Mi. 76. 400). Inasmuch as the Logos-person of the God-man is for Cyril the self-evident postulate, he was not called upon to face the problem of Apolli-naris, and hence, of course, furnished no solution of it.

(*b*) But Cyril's ideas lead us also upon a different path. We are to acknowledge "one Son, one Lord, one Christ," and him as " of two perfects : " " the two natures proceed together in unbroken union, unconfusedly and unchangeably . . . we do not at all detract from the concurrent unity when we say that it is (derived) from two natures. From two and different natures is the one and only Christ" (ep. 45, p. 232 f.). For, just as the Logos was God before his sojourn on earth, so also, having be-come man . . . he is again one. Therefore he has called him-self a mediator between God and man (1 Tim. 2. 5), as being one from both natures" (quod b. virgo 12 ; cf. c. Nest. ii. 12 ; ep. 17, Mi. 77, 116 ; inc. unig., Mi. 75. 1220, 1221, 1233, 1253, 1208 : "We are accustomed to guard absolutely the un-broken unity, believing him to be the Only-begotten and the First-born ; the Only-begotten, as the Logos of God the Father . . . the First-born moreover in that he became man"). He is, therefore, one and the same before and after the incarnation : " for the Son according to nature from the Father, having taken to himself a physical and rational body, was carnally born . . . and, not turning into flesh, but rather taking it to himself, and ever mindful of his being God " (ad reg. ii. 2). " Being man, viewed outwardly ; but inwardly true God" (quod b. virgo 4). Cyril denies the charge that in his conception Christ is two-per-soned (διπρόσωπος) (inc. unig., Mi. 75. 1221 ; inc. dom. 31 ; ep. 46, Mi. 77. 241); but without fully recognizing its force. (*c*) But all these speculations assume a practical shape when Cyril comes to speak of the concrete form of the God-man. Here he be-comes really great. His conception of the historical Christ dom-inates his thought and lifts his ideas above their normal plane. " It is evident, therefore, that the mind beholds a certain dif-ference of the natures" (inc. unig., Mi. 75. 1221), but : " the fact is, that the Logos, not dividing but combining both into one, and, as it were, commingling with one another the attributes (ἰδιώματα) of the natures, escapes us through whatever the multitude of our words " (ib. 1244, 1249), *i. e.*, "bestowing upon the proper flesh the glory of the divine energy ; but, on the other hand, appropriating the things of the flesh and, as though in some way according to the economic union, also conferring these upon its own proper nature " (ib. 1241). Accordingly, the expressions of the Evangelists, applicable now to the divinity and again to the humanity, are not to be referred to two *hypostases* or *prosopa*: " for the one and only Christ is not double, as though he were to be regarded as derived from two and different things " (ep. 17, Mi. 77. 116). Since there is here but one person, all the attributes may be ascribed to the one Christ. The Logos is visible and tangible. His sufferings are the sufferings of God. Hunger and thirst, learning and praying, were parts of his experience ; while, on the other hand, the body of Christ was a " divine body," and the Son of man comes from heaven, returns to it, is worshiped, etc. (*e. g.*, inc. unig., Mi. 75. 1224, 1244, 1249, 1228, 1233 f.; ad regin. ii. 16, 36 f.; c. Nest. i. 6 ; ii. 3 ; iv. 6 ; quod unus 75. 1309; inc. dom. 75. 1469 ; ep. 45, Mi. 77. 234 ; 46, p. 245 ; cf. THOMASIUS DG. i., ed. 2, 348 f.). Hence, also, the designation of Mary as the "mother of God " is dogmatically correct. But this *communicatio idiomatum* at once finds its limitation in the inflexible immutability and impassibility of the Logos: "suffering excepted, in so far as he is thought of as divine " (quod unus, Mi. 75. 1337, 1357 ; c. Nestor. v. 4). Suffering could as little affect him as strokes falling upon a piece of glowing iron permeated by fire affect the fire (quod unus, Mi. 75. 1357). It was, therefore, an " impassive passion " (ἀπαθῶς ἔπαθεν).

(*d*) It is very difficult to give a correct summary of Cyril's view. If we begin with his fundamental formula, " one nature of the divine Logos, made flesh," and keep in mind his own explanations, we reach the result : The Logos-person assumed the (impersonal) human nature, uniting it with the divine nature. The Logos is now no longer fleshless (ἄσαρκος), but is not on that account a duplex personality, " but has remained one " (ep. 46, Mi. 77. 241). If, on the other hand, we start with the community of attributes, we come to the formula : " from two natures the one Christ," and to the conception of a divine-human Christ-person. Our faith in Christ reposes not upon the man, " but upon the God by nature and truly in the person (προσώπῳ) of Christ " (inc. unig., Mi. 75. 1233). In the first case, Cyril starts with the one Logos-person, who has a divine human nature ; in the second, we have the two natures, constituting one divine human person. Cyril did not realize the dissonance of these ideas, as his views were developed in contrast with those of Nestorius and not of Apollinaris. But a sound historic[1] and religious instinct led him to emphasize, as against the unhistoric tearing asunder of Christ, the unity of his person and of his manifestation. In this lies the significance of his teaching.

(*e*) Cyril's view, like that of Athanasius, grew upon religious soil. Since the Logos assumed the entire human nature, the latter becomes partaker of God and immortality : " For Christ the first man . . . the root, as it were, and the appointed first-fruit of those transformed by the Spirit into newness of life, was to effect the immortality of the body, and to make the human race already, both by grace and in its entirety, secure and safe, as in participation of the divine nature '' (inc. unig., Mi. 75. 1213, 1216 ; also 1241 f.; c. Nestor. iv. 6 ; ad reg. ii. 55). Other ideas connected with the Soteriology of Cyril demanded the same basis, *e. g.*, the conception of Christ as the mediator between God and man (c. Nest. v. 1 ; inc. unig., Mi. 75. 1245 ; quod b. virgo, 12), of redemption through his blood and the overcoming of the devil (ad reg. 7. 31, 36), of his life as an example (ib. ii. 41 f.).

6. We must notice, finally, the Christology of the contemporaneous Western theologians (cf. REUTER, Augustin. Studien, p. 194 ff.). It is to be said in general that the leaders in the Western church did not look upon the great question of the age as a '' problem.'' Since they firmly maintained the formulas of Tertullian, they no more questioned the unity of the person than the duplicity of the natures, only giving to the latter more prominence than did Cyril. As their formula gave some recognition to the ideas of both parties in the East, it was the formula of the future.

We can but glance briefly at the Christology of HILARY OF POITIERS.

† A. D. 366. His chief work was De trinitate. Works edited by Maffei, 1730, in Mi. lat. 9. 10 ; cf. DORNER, Lehre v. d. Person Christi, i. 1037 ff. LOOFS, PRE. viii., ed. 3, 57 ff. FÖRSTER, Zur Theol. d. Hilar. Stud. u. Krit., 1888, p. 655 ff.).

Christ is God and man (trin. ix. 19). As One, he is God just as he is man : " the whole in him is God the Word ; the whole in him is the man Christ—retaining this one thing in the

---

[1] The widely prevalent opinion, that the Antiochians were inspired by historical and Cyril by dogmatic or " speculative " interests, is incorrect. Cyril really came nearer than the Antiochians to the Christ of history, and he manifests an extraordinary zeal for a true understanding of the historical facts of the Saviour's life (*e. g.*, inc. unig., Mi. 75. 1196 f., 1215 ; ad reg. ii. 36, et pas).

sacrament of his confession, neither to believe that Christ is other than Jesus, nor to preach that Jesus is other than Christ" (x. 52-71). Compare : "in him is the nature of man, just as the nature of God" (in ps. 68. 25, or "person of both natures," trin. ix. 14). His strongly emphasized "evacuation" of the Son of God in the interest of the incarnation arrests our attention : "For, remaining in the form of God, he assumed the form of a servant, not being changed, but emptying (*exinaniens*) himself and hiding within himself, and he himself being emptied within his power, while he adapts himself even to the form of human condition" (xi. 48). But this asserts no more than that the Logos undertook a change of his condition. "The emptying (*evacuatio*) of form is not an abolition of nature" (ix. 14). The power of omnipotence remains to him (xi. 48 fin.; xii. 6 ; x. 15 ; ix. 51 f.). The divine nature did not and could not feel the sufferings (x. 23, 48, 24 : "that which is customary to a body was endured in order to prove the reality of the body''). Hence, the form of a servant implies a latency of the form of God.

AMBROSE († A. D. 397. See esp. de fide ad Gratianum, de incarnationis sacramento. Works edited by Ballerini, 1875 ff., Mi. lat. 14-17. Cf. FÖRSTER, Ambros., 1884) presented the genuine Western Christology of Tertullian : "the Son of God is said to be one in both natures, because both natures are in the same" (de fid. ii. 9. 77): "a two-fold substance (*substantia*) . . . both of divinity and of flesh" (ib. iii. 10. 65). The *distinctio* of the two natures or substances is to be sharply preserved (ib. ii. 9. 77 ; inc. 4. 23). The immutability and immunity from death of the divine nature (inc. 5. 37 ff.; 6. 55 ; fid. ii. 7. 57 ; 8. 60), as well as the completeness of the human nature, with the "rational soul" (inc. 7. 64 ff., 76), are guarded.[1]

Around the "immutable wisdom" has been thrown the "mantle of flesh" (ib. 5. 41). He, too, speaks of an emptying (*exinanire*) and a hiding (*celare*) of the divinity (inc. 5. 41, de spir, s. i. 9. 107), without thereby attaining any greater lucidity, inasmuch as the form of God and the form of a servant are, nevertheless, alike regarded as belonging to the incarnate Being (ep. 46. 6 ff.; cf. REUTER, p. 210 ff.). But the two natures are now combined in one person : "The One is of two-formed and two-fold (*biformis et geminaeque*) nature, partaking of divinity and of the body. . . . Not divided, but one ; because

---

[1] Ambrose says, de fide ii. 8. 61, indeed : "from the person of man he called the Father greater ;" but this must be interpreted in the light of the further remark, ib. 68 : "for it is not written from the person of the Jews . . . but the Evangelist speaks from his own person."

one and the other are both in each, *i. e.*, either in the divinity or in the body " (inc. 5. 35 ; fid. v. 8. 107 ; iii. 2. 8). " The Lord of majesty is said to have been crucified, because, partaking of both natures, *i. e.*, the human and the divine, he endured the sufferings in the nature of man " (fid. ii. 7. 58). This is the ancient theory of the Western church, which knew nothing of the problem of the age.

7. AUGUSTINE follows in the same path. It is not our task to present the Christology of Augustine in process of formation. Our interest lies in its final form. Yet a few remarks are necessary to a correct understanding of its appearance (cf. the thorough discussion of O. SCHEEL, Die Anschauung Augustins über Christi Person und Werk, 1901). Augustine had, as a Manichæan, denied the true humanity of Christ. When he found his way back to the church, the authority of the Scriptures led him first to recognize this (cf. Confessions, vii. 19. 25). The authority of the church's teaching then led him to accept also the divinity of Christ. But since his speculative spirit was controlled by Neo-platonic conceptions, and had from his early days been familiar with trinitarian ideas, his conception of the divinity of Christ was moulded by the Neo-platonic ideas of the divine νοῦς and the κοσμὸς νοητός. The eternal Word is conceived primarily in his relation to the world, and not in a purely religious way, in his relation to salvation and to human history. As, *e.g.*, all things are but copies of eternal ideas, and these ideas are in God (de oct. quaestionibus, q. 46. 2), so all things exist only in so far as God gives to them a " continuing and unchangeable form " (de lib. arb. ii. 17. 45). But the eternal ideas (*rationes*) of all temporal things are present in the Logos (de genes. ad litt. iv. 24. 41), and the Logos is the " form of all real things," " the unfashioned form " (*forma infabricata*), " without time . . . and without local dimensions." Of him it is said : " For he is a certain form, an unfashioned (*non formata*) form, but the form of all fashioned forms, an unchangeable (*incommutabilis*) form . . . controlling (*superans*) all things, existing in all things and a kind of foundation in which they exist, and a roof under which they exist. . . . Therefore all things are in him, and yet, because he is God, all things are under him " (serm. 117. 2, 3). These are clearly conceptions derived from Greek philosophy, regarding the Logos as the cosmic principle of idea and form. But, if we would rightly understand Augustine, we must also bear in mind that he always thinks of this Logos as the second person in the Trinity, as the Son of God immutably present with the Father, who in time became man. All ideas of Subordination-ism are utterly remote from his thought, however strongly the

17

Greek conception of the Logos might impel in that direction, as we have seen in the Apologists and in Origen. At this point, the church's doctrine of the divinity of the Son marked out for him an absolutely fixed path from which he never deviated. Nor did Augustine fail to draw from the divinity of Christ practical inferences in the sphere of Soteriology (vid. *sub*). But the starting-point of his doctrine, and hence its relation to other views, was always different from that of Athanasius.[1] Whilst the latter began really with the redeeming work of Christ, and upon this, as a basis, erected his homousian theory, Augustine started with an accepted ecclesiastical doctrine, which he interpreted for himself through speculative reflections, and from this drew his conclusions as to the redeeming work of Christ. Hence his Christology does not present the strikingly religious one-sidedness which marks the conception of Athanasius. Regarded as doctrine, its originality dare not at all events be too highly rated. Augustine maintained unconditionally the divinity of Christ, and he esteemed highly his humanity, as a fact of which he had gained knowledge in his personal experience. But in regard to the combination of the two natures, he did not advance beyond the views traditional in the West. The sources do not sustain the opinion of A. DORNER (Augustinus, p. 92) and HARNACK (DG. iii., ed. 3, 120), *i. e.*, that it was because of the susceptibility of the human soul of Jesus that the Logos appeared in it, nor justify the latter in declaring that "Augustine constructs the God-man from the standpoint of the human person (soul)," or that the chief interest of Augustine centres in the human soul of Jesus. We may, perhaps, characterize his fundamental tendency as in harmony with the positions taken in his *De civ. dei*, x. 23, 24. The oracular deliverance cited from Porphyry, "fountains can purify" (*principia posse purgare*), is correct, except that we can here speak of but One fountain. This fountain, the Logos, in entering humanity, purifies it : "Christ the Lord is the fountain, by whose incarnation we are purified. For neither the flesh nor the human soul (*i. e.*, of Christ) is the fountain, but the Word through which all things which were

---

[1] I mention here only the fact that this Christology, taking seriously as it does the idea of the divinity of Christ, cannot avoid questions concerning his activity before the incarnation. This is seen already in Paul and John. That is to say, since the work of Christ controls history to the attainment of the ends of the kingdom of God, and since there is a connection between the course of history before and after Christ, there must in some way be found a place for the direction of history by Christ also before the incarnation. We must, however, discriminate between such attempts and the purely cosmological discussions of the Greek philosophers, although the latter at a very early date influenced the structure of Christian thought.

made stand secure. Therefore the flesh does not cleanse of itself, but through the Word by which it has been assumed."

We now address ourselves to the examination of the DOCTRINE OF AUGUSTINE in detail. It is for him an absolutely fixed fact that in Christ two complete natures or substances (inclusive of the rational human soul; see in Joh. tr. 23. 6; 47. 9; conf. vii. 19; de agone christ. 19. 21) constitute one person : " Christ is one person of two-fold substance, because he is both God and man" (c. Maximin. Arian. ii. 10. 2). "Now truly has thus appeared the mediator between God and man, in order that, combining both natures in the unity of person, he might both exalt the ordinary by means of the extraordinary, and temper the extraordinary by means of the ordinary " (ep. 137. 3, 9, 12). " He assumed the man, and from himself and the latter made the one Jesus Christ, the mediator between God and men, equal to the Father according to his divinity, but less than the Father according to the flesh," i. e., according to the man. But this unification in the man-God (homo-deus, enchir. 25. 108) is different in kind from the indwelling of God in the saints, in whom the Word does not become flesh : " it is evident that, by a certain unique assumption, the person of this man has become one with the Word " (ep. 137. 12, 40; in Joh. tr. 72. 1; de agone chr. 20. 22). The idea is thus that the two natures are combined in the unity of one person (cf. enchir. 10. 35 ; 12. 40, 41 ; in Joh. tr. 27. 4). But this is evidently the person of the Logos. " The rational soul and the flesh entered into unity of person with the Word." " The Logos, who is the sole Son of God, and that not by grace but by nature, was made also Son of man, and this same, the One Christ, was both and from both." He remained that which he was. " He assumed the form of a servant, not abandoning nor diminishing the form of God " (enchir. 10. 35). There can here be no thought of any merit of the human nature of Christ as leading to the union. On the contrary, it is an exhibition of the same grace which justifies sinful men, that makes it impossible for the man Jesus to sin, viz., inasmuch as his nature was " taken up in a unique way into the unity of the person of the unique (unici) Son of God " (ib. ii. 36). " The only-begotten Son of God out of grace so united himself with his human nature, that he became man. The only-begotten Son of God, not by grace by nature, by nature uniting himself in such unity of person, that he, the same, was also man. This same " Jesus Christ, the only-begotten Son of God, i. e., the unique One, our Lord, was born of the Holy Spirit and the Virgin Mary " (ib. ii. 36, 37). But in all of this the Logos remains unchangeable (de agon. chr. i. 1 ; x. 11. 23, 25). But Augustine can also speak of the combination of the natures as a "mixture : " "the man is joined to, and in some way mingled (*commixtus*) with, the Word into a unity of person" (trin. iv. 20. 30). It is such a mixture as is found in every human person : " In that person there is a mixture of soul and body ; in this person is a mixture of God and man" (ep. 137. 3, 11 ; serm. 174. 2). But at the same time the immutability of the divine nature is still carefully guarded, and we accordingly read also : "the same who is man is God, and the same who is God is man, not in confusion of nature, but in unity of person" (sermo 186. 1). The idea of a change of the divine nature, or a denuding it of power in the interest of redemption, is entirely foreign to Augustine. The divine nature remains as it was, except that the flesh is added to it, and becomes with it the same person. "The Word does not come into the flesh in order to perish, but the flesh comes to the Word in order that it may not perish" (sermo 186. 1 ; 121. 5 ; 264. 4 ; ep. 137. 7, 10 ; trin. i. 8. 15).[1]

But the religious interest of Augustine does not centre entirely in the divinity of Christ, rather in this no less than in his humanity. In Christ the divine nature reveals itself. Its wisdom is thus offered to us as milk to babes (sermo 117. 10. 16 ; 126. 4. 5 ; conf. vii. 18). The love of God manifest in him awakens us to a responsive love. His humility overcomes our pride (de catechiz. rudibus 4. 7, 8 ; conf. vii. 18). His whole

---

[1] Augustine has also the following modification (afterward employed by Abelard): "the Word of God having the man" (*habens hominem*, in Joh. tr. 19. 15), but also : "he assumed the man" (de agon. chr. 11. 12 ; 18. 20 ; 19. 21 ; 20. 22 ; cf. Hilar. de trin. x. 22). He also teaches a predestination of the man Jesus (de praedest. 15. 30, 31 ; cf. SCHEEL, l. c., p. 215 f.). These terms of expression are, indeed, of value in aiding to a proper understanding of Augustine, since they show to what an extent he was able to grasp independently the idea of the humanity of Christ (cf. also such expressions as : "The Son of God assumed man, and in that man (*in illo homine*) suffered," de agon. chr. ii. 12 ; ib.: "in which [*i. e.*, that man] the Son of God offered himself to us as an example ;" ib. 23. 25 : " Thus we say that the Son of God suffered and died in the man whom he carried, without any change or destruction of his divinity"). But when SCHEEL (p. 216) infers from the predestination of Jesus a fundamental departure from the doctrine of the two natures, since only a person and not a substance can be predestinated (HARNACK similarly speaks of a " profound relationship with the Christology of Paul of Samosata, and Photinus," p. 121), he is in so far correct, that the ideas and formulas cited testify that Augustine could conceive of the human life of Jesus as relatively independent and like our own (vid. with reference to the childhood of Jesus, Scheel, p. 230). Yet in this Augustine by no means abandons his controlling scheme of thought, for the predestinating of the man Jesus means exactly that that the Logos should absorb him "in order through him as the mediator to bring grace to the predestinated." At all events, there are here points of view at variance with Greek conceptions, which became significant in the theology of the West.

life and conduct, in both its human and its divine aspects, serves as an example for believers (enchir. 14. 53; 25. 108). As man, he is the mediator between us and God (conf. x. 43 : " For in so far as he is man, in so far is he a mediator''); but only in so far as he is also God. As man he is the mediator (as Augustine always states with emphasis), for thereby he stands near to men ; but the nearness is the nearness of God. The man becomes the mediator, because he has God within him (enchir. 25. 108 ; conf. x. 42). Compare also in Joh. tr. 42. 8 : " His divinity whither we journey, his humanity where we journey," similarly tr. 13. 5 ; civ. dei xi. 2.

The West had, therefore—in independence of the East—its own Christological theory. It was more nearly in accord with the Christology of Alexandria than with that of Antioch, although not without points of agreement with the latter.

§ 24. *Nestorius and Cyril. The Third Ecumenical Council at Ephesus.*

Upon Nestorius, see Socr. h. e. vii. 29 ff., the letters of Coelestine ; his orations in Marius Mercator in Gallandi, bibl. viii. 629 ff., in Mi. lat. 48, cf. HEFELE CG. ii. 149 ff. LOOFS, PRE. xiii. ed. 3, 736 ff.

1. The great controversy arose from the discussion of a liturgical formula. Nestorius, who was called in A. D. 428 from Antioch to Constantinople, desired to controvert the heretics. He vigorously assailed the Arians, the Novatians, and the Macedonians, but joined hands with the western Pelagians. The designation of Mary as the mother of God, which was becoming current, aroused his polemics. He held the genuine Antiochian view : The Logos, being as divine absolutely immutable, was not born. This can be said only of his garment, or temple, *i. e.*, his human nature (or. 1. 2 ; 3. 2). Hence Mary was not to be called really the mother of God (θεοτόκος), God-bearing, but God-receiving (θεοδόχος), and man-bearing (ἀνθρωποτόκος), or Christ-bearing (χριστοτόκος) (or. 2. 8 ; 5. 2 ; ep. 1 ad Coelest. 3). It is only to the man Christ, therefore, that birth, suffering, and death can be ascribed (or. 2. 2 ; 3. 1). The man Jesus was the " organ of the divinity." Hence the Logos as God is strictly discriminated from the man, but without making two Sons or Christs : " We call our Lord Christ in view of his nature two-fold, in view of his sonship one (or. 3. 2); for to both natures belong, in consequence of their union, the same dignity and a common reverence : for there are two, if you regard the nature ; one, if you consider the dignity. I divide the natures,

but I combine the reverence " (or. 1. 2 ; 2. 6, 8). And, above
all, the Logos, after the incarnation, does not act except in union
with the man Jesus (Cyril c. Nest. ii. 7). Of the worship of the
human nature, he says : " I adore it as the animated mantle of
the King " (2. 6). When vigorous opposition was at once
manifested, Nestorius conceded the possibility of the θεοτόκος :
" the genetrix of God . . . on account of the Word united with
its temple," but he still thought that the term was calculated to
give aid to the Arians and Apollinarians (or. 4. 3 ; 5. 2, cf. ep.
1 ad Coelest. 3 ; ep. 2. 2). In his Christology there is evidently
nothing heterodox. It was only the usual doctrine of the Antioch school. Nothing was further from his thought than a
denial of the divinity of Christ, or of the doctrine of the two
natures.[1]

2. The controversy assumed larger proportions only when
CYRIL OF ALEXANDRIA (supra, p. 251) entered the lists. " Without Cyril there would have been no Nestorian controversy,"
Loofs. A passionate correspondence arose between the two
patriarchs. Cyril then thought it proper to inform Theodosius
himself, as well as his wife and sister, of the existing doctrinal
divergence. But the letters were very unfavorably received at the
court. He held firmly to the incarnated nature of the Logos, as
well as to the term θεοτόκος (supra, pp. 252, 254). He adduced an
exhaustive array of testimonies for his view from the Scriptures and
tradition. But he was, at this time and afterward, chiefly concerned
in pointing out the irreligious consequences to which the doctrine
of Nestorius would lead. According to Nestorius, we would be
redeemed by the sufferings of a mere man (c. Nestor. iii. 2 ; iv.
4 ; v. 1); a man would have become to us " the way, the truth,
and the life " (c. Nest. v. 1); we would worship a God-carrying
(θεοφόρος) man (ib. i. 2 ; ii. 10, cf. inc. unig., Mi. 75, 1232);
when we are baptized into Christ and by him, we would be baptized into a man (ad reg. ii. 52 ; c. Nestor. iii. 2 ; inc. unig.,
Mi. 75, 1240); we would in the Lord's Supper partake of the
flesh and blood of a man (c. Nestor. iv. 5 ; inc. unig., Mi. 75,
1241). Compare THOMASIUS, DG. 341 ff. Thus the Christian
world would be robbed by Nestorius of all the treasures which it
possesses in the historical Christ. All these things have now
only a human valuation ; and we no longer have in Christ God
himself. The whole religious energy of Cyril's views is here

---

[1] Lechler has prepared the way for a juster estimate of Nestorius, proving
that the latter taught the true divinity and humanity of Jesus, as well as the
union of the two in one person, but did not draw the inference of the *communicatio idiomatum*. Further, he maintains that it was chiefly love of conflict
and of debate which produced the controversy. Erl. Ed. 25, ed. 1, 304 ff.

revealed. The real point of controversy is, whether it was the man Jesus controlled by the Logos, or whether it was God himself, who was born, lived, taught, labored, and died among us. The positive teachings of Cyril have been already outlined. These writings of Cyril, viewed from the standpoint of church politics, are the works of a master hand. Theologically and morally, they make a different impression, giving evidence of a lack of capacity to understand and appreciate a theological opponent.

Rome was very soon drawn into the controversy. Nestorius wrote to Pope Coelestine as his colleague, and Cyril sought direction and instruction from the same source. Nestorius expressed his view in the charge which he brings against his opponents: "They confound, in the mutability of modification, both natures which, through the supreme and unconfused union, are adored in the one person of the only-begotten" (ep. 2 ad Coel. c. 2)— *i. e.*, he expressed himself—in word—in harmony with Western ideas.[1] Nevertheless Rome, after some delay, decided against him at a synod, according to her traditional policy making common cause with Alexandria (A. D. 430). Coelestine could find nothing to say to Nestorius except that he was a ravening wolf and a hireling, and that he must within ten days subscribe to the teaching of the Romish and Alexandrine church, or, failing to do so, be excluded from the church (see Coelestine, ep. 11-14).

3. Cyril now drew the lines of opposition most sharply at the Council of Alexandria, A. D. 430. He addressed a communication to Nestorius, containing an exposition of his teaching, and closing with twelve anathemas (ep. 17, in HAHN, Bibl. d. Symbole, ed. 3, p. 312 ff.): Mary is the mother of God (1). The one Christ dare not be divided in accordance with the *hypostases*, and the latter are not bound together only by their conjunction in accordance with their dignity, *i.e.*, their sphere of dominion or power, but through a physical union ($ἕνωσις φυσική$) (3). The expressions of the Scriptures are not to be divided between the two persons, *i. e.*, hypostases (4). Christ is not a God-carrying ($θεοφόρος$) man (5). The man assumed is not to be called God and, as such, to be worshiped as "one in another" (8). The flesh of the Lord is life-giving (11). The Logos of God suffered in the flesh, was crucified in the flesh, and tasted death in the flesh (12). Nestorius at once replied with twelve counter-anathemas (in Marius Merc., Mi. 48. 909): Christ is Emmanuel, God with

---

[1] It should be borne in mind that Coelestine had received an account of the teaching of Nestorius from Cyril (M. iv. 548 and Cyril's first letter to Coelestine). The sermons of Nestorius had also been sent to Rome.

us; Mary is the mother, not of the Word of God, but of Emmanuel (1). If anyone should say that flesh is capable of (containing) the divine nature . . . and call the very same nature God and man, let him be anathema (2). Christ is one according to union, not according to nature (3). The words of Scripture are not to be referred to one nature, nor are sufferings to be attributed to the Logos (4). If anyone dare to say that, after the assumption of man, the Son of God is one in nature, since he is Emmanuel, let him be anathema (5). He who was made of the Virgin is not the Only-begotten, but has only through his union with the Only-begotten received a share in his name (7). The form of a servant is not to be worshiped on account of this union (8). The flesh united with the Logos is not "through the possibility of the nature the giver of life" (11). The sufferings of Christ are not to be attributed to the Logos "without discrimination of the dignity of the natures" (12).

4. The Antiochians now declared themselves (see the letter of John of Antioch in M. v. 756) for Nestorius, charging Cyril with Apollinarianism. The emperor, in a very harsh letter, accused Cyril of pride, love of strife and intrigue (on account of his letter to the women of the imperial household) (M. iv. 1109). A general council was called at EPHESUS on Whitsunday, A. D. 431, in the interest of the salutary union between civil welfare and religious harmony (M. iv. 1111). The invitation found Augustine († Aug. 28, 430) no longer among the living. Nestorius and Cyril appeared before the appointed time. Coelestine was represented by three legates, who were instructed to act in all things with Cyril, and, beyond this, not to dispute but pass judgment (M. iv. 556). The arrival of John of Antioch was unduly delayed (M. iv. 1121, 1229, 1329 f.; cf. 1225). Despite the protests of Nestorius, 68 Asiatic bishops and the imperial commissary (M. iv. 1129 ff.; v. 765 f., 770 f.), Cyril and Memnon of Ephesus opened the council. 159 bishops (M. iv. 1123 ff., 1170 ff.) participated, sanctioned the teaching of Cyril as in accordance with Nicene doctrine, and condemned the "godless Nestorius." Many patristic citations were then read, and passages from Nestorius. "With many tears" he was then declared to be deprived of episcopal rank and of priestly fellowship (M. iv. 1212). The decision was reported to the "new Judas," the city illuminated, and the decision announced to the populace by posters upon the walls, and to the church at large by letters. Nestorius protested. John of Antioch arrived at this juncture. He at once, in the presence of the imperial commissioner, opened the properly authorized

council, which must be so called,[1] although it numbered but 43 members. Cyril and Memnon were deposed because they had illegally opened the council, and their followers excommunicated until they should be converted to the "Nicene faith." Nothing was said of Nestorius, nor of his doctrine (M. iv. 1260 ff.). The Romish legates now, for the first time, came to the front. Since Peter is "the head of the entire faith," they requested the decrees for "confirmation" (M. iv. 1289). John was three times summoned, but declared that he would have "no intercourse with deposed and excommunicated persons." The papal decision in regard to the Pelagians was approved (M. iv. 1337).[2] It was then resolved to report the action of the council to the emperor and the pope (M. iv. 1325, 1329 ff.). Such was the course of the third ecumenical council. One of the participants (Theodoret, opp. iv. 1335) declares: "No writer of comedies ever composed such a ridiculous farce, no tragic author such a mournful tragedy." The only positive result was that it was known that Cyril had been able to win the majority of those who participated in the proceedings.

Both parties now addressed themselves to the emperor. The followers of Cyril were able to cultivate a sentiment in their favor (Dalmatius). Opinion was divided in Constantinople. The emperor, weakling that he was, approved the action of both parties, and the depositions on both sides were confirmed (M. iv. 1396). Both parties now turned to him again. Nestorius voluntarily entered a cloister. The emperor received deputations from both sides. He inclined to the Alexandrines.[3] Cyril and Memnon received their bishoprics again, and the council was adjourned (M. iv. 1465).

5. But peace was not yet restored. Efforts were, therefore, made to effect a union. They proved successful, as the Antiochians surrendered Nestorius, who was now abused as a heretic, the assemblages of Cyril's followers being recognized as the legal council (see John of Antioch in M. v. 285, 289), and as Cyril was willing to subscribe to a union-symbol, prepared apparently by THEODORET OF CYROS (A. D. 433), without, indeed, retracting any of his former utterances (for further particulars, see

---

[1] The designation of the Cyrillian assemblage as "the Council of Ephesus" is justifiable only because it was afterward so recognized in the course of ecclesiastical politics, and John himself, the leader of the Antiochians, agreed to so regard it.

[2] As to the inner relationship of Pelagianism and Nestorianism, see Cassian. de incarn. i. 3; v. 1 ff.; vi. 14; cf. Faust. de grat. i. 1.

[3] It was said that Cyril, through his nephew, bribed influential persons (M. v. 819). For accounts of such "presents" of Cyril, vid. M. v. 987 ff.

HEFELE ii. 247-288).　The Creed of Antioch reads (HAHN, ed. 3, p. 215):

"We, therefore, acknowledge our Lord Jesus Christ, the Son of God, the Only-begotten, complete God and complete man, of a rational soul and a body; begotten of the Father before the ages according to (his) divinity, but in the last days . . . of Mary the Virgin according to (his) humanity; that he is of the same nature with the Father according to (his) divinity, and of the same nature with us according to (his) humanity. For a union of the two natures has taken place; wherefore, we confess one Christ, one Son, one Lord. In accordance with this conception of the unconfounded union, we acknowledge the holy Virgin to be the mother of God, because the divine Logos was made flesh and became man, and from her conception united with himself the temple received from her. We recognize the evangelical and apostolic utterances concerning the Lord, making the characters of the divine Logos and the man common as being in one person, but distinguishing them as in two natures, and teaching that the godlike traits are according to the divinity of Christ, and the humble traits according to his humanity."

The Antiochians had in this the rejection of Apollinarianism and the recognition of the two natures; Cyril, the one person,[1] the union of the two natures, and the θεοτόκος. Each party could read its own Christology into the symbol, and Cyril did this in a liberal way.[2] But inasmuch as the formula, which excluded both extremes, had been accepted, the submerging of the matter in the drawing of inferences was prevented. There was not lacking opposition upon both sides, but it was in part quelled by force. The Nestorians were persecuted, and were able to maintain themselves only in the Persian Empire (see HEFELE ii. 270 ff.).

---

[1] Whether the one person is that of the Logos or the divine-human person is not clear in the symbol.

[2] See the letters of Cyril in M. v., and, on the other hand, the attitude of Theodoret, who remained essentially in harmony with the Antiochian Christology. Yet he emphasized the unity of the person more strongly than his predecessors: see Eranistes u. haer. fab. v. Compare BERTRAM, Theodoreti doctrina christologica, 1883. His view is, in brief: "he showed in the one person the distinction of the two natures," i. e., Paul in Rom. 5. 9 (haer. fab. v. 14, opp. iv. 1. 433). Even after the incarnation there remain two natures: "that each nature remained also unmixed after the union" (Eranist. ii. opp. iv. 1, p. 101, also p. 99), and "we do not separate the flesh of the divine Logos, nor make the union a commingling" (ib. p. 102). The divine nature did not, indeed, depart from the human nature, either on the cross or at the grave, but "being immortal and immutable, it endured neither death nor suffering" (haer. fab. v. 15, p. 435; cf. ep. 113. 2).

§ 25.  *Eutychian Controversy and Councils of Ephesus and Chalcedon.*[1]

1.  Cyril may be designated either as a Dyophysite or as a Monophysite.  This explains his historical position.  The orthodox were trained under his influence, and he became the teacher of the Monophysites.  The Greek theory of redemption more and more repressed interest in the man Jesus.  Christ, in order to "deify" us, must be God, and practical Christianity constantly tended to find its entire expression in the doctrine and mysteries of the church.  That these really were divine and possessed the power of deifying man appeared to be certain only if the man Jesus was deified—if he was absolutely God.  The practical conception of Christ's personality demanded this view, and the administration of the mysteries in the ritual of the church gratified it.  The tendency to sensualize the spiritual, which marked the age, was here also manifest.  In this way arose a piety of Monophysite type.  But in theology there still survived a part of the Antiochian Christology.  We can understand it, therefore, that the energetic and shrewd successor of Cyril, Dioscurus (from A. D. 444 bishop of Alexandria), thought to best promote his own advancement by favoring the Monophysite conception.  In February, A. D. 448, the emperor had renewed the anti-Nestorian edicts.  The Alexandrine bishop zealously maintained intercourse with all Alexandrine territory, and thus, with a celebrated monk in Constantinople, Eutyches.

Opportunity for a decided stroke now appeared to be afforded him by the agitation aroused by this archimandrite.  The latter, after A. D. 433, was in the habit of accusing the Unionists of Nestorianism (see Leo ep. 20).  He was in consequence denounced by Eusebius of Dorylæum at a council at Constantinople, A. D. 448 (s. Hefele ii. 320 ff.).  After various refusals, he finally appeared before the council and declared : "I confess that our Lord was of two natures before the union, but after the union I confess one nature," and "until to-day I said that the body of our Lord and God was of the same nature with us" (M. vi. 744, 742).[2]  He opposed the union symbol of A. D. 433, but did not by any means accurately reproduce the doctrine of Cyril.  Eutyches can scarcely be said to have possessed a theory of his own upon the subject.  He was deposed and excommunicated as a reviler of Christ, with the proper accompaniment of tears (M. vi. 748).  But Eutyches did not rest quietly under condemna-

[1]  Loofs, PRE. v. ed. 3, 635 f.
[2]  Exceedingly characteristic is his earlier utterance : "Which Father has declared that the God Logos has two natures?" (M. vi. 725).

tion.  By the use of placards, he aroused the interest of the populace, and also of the emperor, in his cause and appealed to Pope
Leo of Rome (Leo ep. 21).  But bishop Flavian of Constantinople also laid his "burden of grief and multitude of tears" at
the feet of Leo (Leo ep. 22), declaring that Eutyches had
revived the teachings of Valentine and Apollinaris, and demanding that the pope inform his bishops of the heresies of Eutyches.
The pope had meanwhile, of his own accord, requested an accurate account of the affair, in order that he might pass judgment
upon it (ep. 23, 14).  Flavian complied with the request, and
implored the pope's approval of the "faith of the God-fearing
and Christ-loving emperor" (ep. 26).  The pope now sent to
Flavian his "doctrinal letter" (ep. 28).  He had thus definitely fixed the attitude of Rome, which is historically a fact of
the greatest importance, for it established a positive and powerful opposition to the Alexandrine doctrine.  But, meanwhile,
Dioscurus of Alexandria had entered the lists and secured the
summoning of a general council at Ephesus.  Theodoret was excluded from participation in the proceedings, and Dioscurus
presided.  Everything seemed to assure a Monophysite victory.

2. This resulted in the Robber Synod of Ephesus.  The
pope was here represented by three legates (ep. 31. 4), who
were informed that the Catholic doctrine was contained in the
"doctrinal letter" (ep. 29).[1]  But Dioscurus dominated the
council by brutal terrorism and nearly all yielded to intimida-
tion.  Discussion was not desired, but the faith of the Fathers
(*i. e.*, of the councils of Nice and Ephesus) was to be acknowledged (M. vi. 625).  Eutyches defended himself, and 114
of the 135 participants were of opinion that he was orthodox.
"Anathema to everyone who speaks of two natures still after the
incarnation" (M. vi. 737, 832 ff.).  Leo's letter was not even
read.  Eutyches was restored.  Flavian, Eusebius of Dorylæum,
together with Theodoret, Domnus of Antioch, and others, were
deposed (M. vi. 908 ff.  Theodoret ep. 113, 147).

3. The victory was thus with Dioscurus.  Measured by the
standard of his age, and compared with the people who followed
his leadership, we can scarcely pass a severe judgment upon him.
He had the courage to discard the traditional policy of the Alexandrine church in its compact with Rome.  He had vanquished
the New Rome without the aid of the Old Rome—had even
most seriously disabled the latter.  For one moment the Bishop
of Alexandria was lord of the church.  An Alexandrine priest

[1] As to the person of Eutyches, Leo expressed himself with remarkable forbearance.  ep. 29; 31. 4; 32; 33. 2; 38.

under his control became bishop of Rome (Leo ep. 53), and Leo was excommunicated by Dioscurus (M. vi. 1009). But Leo was shrewd enough to be true to Flavian, himself, and his "dogmatic epistle" (ep. 50, 51, 67, 68. 1, cf. 69. 1), since the latter was in harmony with Cyril and the first council of Ephesus. He became the refuge of the "humble and small," *i. e.*, the opposite party, who sought "help at the apostolic throne" (Theodoret ep. 113). His constant desire was to secure the annulling of the decrees of the Robber Synod and the summoning of a new council to be held in Italy under his leadership (ep. 44, 54. 70, cf. 55-58). Thus, and only thus, could he recover from the defeat experienced at the hands of the "Alexandrine bishop who usurps all things to himself" (ep. 45. 2). But Theodosius held fast to the confession of the second council of Ephesus as the "faith of the Fathers" (Leo ep. 62-64). Yet the pope's waiting was not in vain. Theodosius died (A. D. 450). He was succeeded by PULCHERIA, who was married to MARCIAN. It was decided that the desired council should be held—although in the Orient (ep. 73, 76, 77). It appeared to be a necessity, for it is scarcely correct to say "that the council of A. D. 449 had really pacified the church in the East" (Harnack ii. 365). If we consider the brevity of the period during which the second confession of Ephesus was in force, it will be evident that Harnack's conclusion is merely a dogmatic one. It follows from his assertion of the Monophysite-Apollinarian character of Greek Christianity. But there were other tendencies opposed to this! The Antiochian theology was not dead. The Union symbol had had many adherents. Individuals and whole groups of theologians in the Orient accepted the second confession of Ephesus. Neither the calling of the council of Chalcedon, nor its transactions, can be explained under Harnack's theory (vid. Liberatus Breviarium 12 b, Gallandi xii. 140. Theodoret ep. 113, cf. also the opinion of LOOFS, PRE. v. ed. 3, 647 f. ). Leo, indeed, no longer needed the council, and declared it now inopportune, especially as it was to be held, not in Rome, but at Nicæa. And, on the other hand, his *epistula dogmatica* was, without the aid of a council, finding ever wider acceptance in the East (ep. 82. 2 ; 83. 2 ; 89 ; 90 ; 94). But the emperor clung to his purpose, and the Council of Chalcedon (having been first summoned to meet in Nicæa), was accordingly held A. D. 451 (cf. M. vi. vii. HEFELE CG. ii. 410-544. Also, KRÜGER, Monophys. Streitigkeiten in Zusammenhang. m. d. Reichspolitik, Jena, 1884). The pope claimed the right to preside—in the person of legates —and considered his letter sufficient to decide the matters in controversy (ep. 93. 1. 2).

4. The contents of this letter (ep. 28) may be thus summarized : Christ is God and man, born of Mary, *her virginity being preserved* (c. 1, cf. c. 4). The two substances remain what they were, but combine in one person : "The peculiarity of each nature and substance being therefore preserved and entering into the one person, humility is received by majesty," etc. This is necessary in the interest of redemption : "One and the same mediator of God and men, the man Jesus Christ, should from the one be able to die, and from the other be unable to die." But, inasmuch as each nature retains its own peculiarity, the " emptying (*exinanitio*, cf. p. 256) by which the invisible makes itself visible . . . is not a loss of power " (3). There is, therefore, after the incarnation only one person, but the natures of this one person act in alternating fellowship : "For each form performs what is peculiar to it in fellowship with the other, *i. e.*, the Word doing that which is peculiar to the Word, and the flesh accomplishing that which is peculiar to the flesh. The one of these shines forth in miracles, the other succumbs to injuries." The one nature bewails the death of Lazarus ; the other wakes him from the dead (4). In consequence of the unity of person ("on account of this unity of person in each nature "), it may be said that the Son of man came down from heaven (Jn. 3. 13), and that the Son of God was crucified and buried (1 Cor. 2. 8), etc. (5). The confession of Eutyches, "before the incarnation two natures, after it one nature," is in both its parts equally profane. He who regards the death of Christ as a real death cannot deny "that the man whom he sees to have been passible was of our body " (6). This much-lauded document is nothing more than a reproduction of the Western Christology (Tertullian, Ambrose ; cf. Augustine). It does not enter at all upon the consideration of the problem which perplexed the Greeks, and the dogmatic simplicity of the pope is most strikingly revealed in his opinion, that the twelve propositions of the Apostles in the Creed sufficed for the refutation of this and other heresies (vid. ep. 31. 4 ; 45. 2 ; 28. 1). As to the Christology of Leo, see also ep. 35. 2 ; 59. 3-5 ; 88. 1 ; 114. 1 ; 119. 1.

5. The council itself (21 sessions in 14 days, HEFELE ii., 411 f.), attended by about 600 bishops—all Greeks—makes an exceedingly unfavorable impression. Not only was it as boisterous[1] as the Robber Synod ; but worse than this was the cowardly and senseless abandonment of Dioscurus and of the position taken two years before ("we have all been wrong ; we all beg for

---

[1] At the very first session, as Theodoret appeared : "Cast out the Jew, the adversary of God, and do not call him bishop ;" to which the opposing party responded : "Cast out the murderer Dioscurus. Who does not know the

pardon," vid. M. vi. 637 ff., 674 ff., 690, 827 ff., cf. 973 f., 1005). Dioscurus was self-consistent. With Athanasius, Gregory, and Cyril he professed to agree in the "one incarnated nature of the Logos." He did not question the "of two" (ἐκ δύο), but "the two (τὸ δύο), I do not receive" (M. vi. 684, 689). He was deserted by all, as his deposition had been a settled matter already at the first session. At the later sessions he did not appear—not even when summoned at the third session. A number of accusers of this "heretic and Origenist" now cried out that Dioscurus was a reviler of the Trinity, a desecrator of relics, a thief, an incendiary, a murderer, a licentious fellow, a traitor (M. vi. 1005 ff., 1012 ff., 1021 ff., 1029 ff.). But he was at length deposed for contempt of the "divine canons" and for "disobedience toward the council" (M. vi. 1093). As to the matters in dispute, the doctrine of the papal letter was approved : "This is the faith of the Fathers, this the faith of the Apostles. Thus we all believe. Anathema to him who does not so believe ! Through Leo, Peter has spoken . . . exactly thus taught Cyril ! Why was this not read at Ephesus ? Dioscurus kept it hidden" (M. vi. 971). It was thought that the harmony of Leo's teaching with the confessions of Nice, Constantinople (supra, p. 235, n.), and the First Council of Ephesus could be clearly established. Only the 13 Egyptian bishops refused to subscribe to it, and they were in earnest in their refusal : "We will be killed, we will be killed if we do it. We would rather be slain here by you than there (in Egypt). Have mercy on us ; we would rather die at your hands and the emperor's than at home " (M. vii. 53 ff., cf. the 30th canon of the council). Despite the opposition of the Roman legates, the letter of Leo was not given dogmatic authority, but the council at its fifth session adopted a new formula (M. vii. 112 ff.). The synodical letters of Cyril against Nestorius were adopted in refutation of Nestorianism, the letter of Leo to Flavian in refutation of Eutychianism. Those are condemned who teach a "dyad of sons," as well as those who dream of "two natures before the union, but one after the union." On the contrary : " We confess one and the same Son, our Lord Jesus Christ . . . the same perfect in divinity and the same perfect in humanity . . . of a rational soul and a body, of the same nature with the Father according to (his) divinity, and of the same nature with us according to (his) humanity, and we recognize the same one Christ, Son, Lord, and Only-begotten, in two natures (not, as the Greek text reads : of, ἐκ, two natures, cf.

crimes of Dioscurus?" M. vi. 589, cf. also the cry : "We shout for piety and orthodoxy."

HEFELE ii. 470 f.[1]), unmingled, immutable, indivisible, inseparable; the difference of the natures being by no means obliter-
ated by the union, but, on the contrary, the peculiarity of each
nature being preserved and entering into one person and one
hypostasis, not divided nor separated into two persons." It will be
observed that these definitions do not go beyond the statements
of Leo's letter. The Western Christology was forced upon the
Greeks, for the decree of the council marks a breach, not only
with Dioscurus and Eutyches, but also with the much-lauded
Cyril. The formula preserving the peculiarity (ἰδιότης) of the
two natures was contrary to Cyril's view, as also the terms, "unmingled, immutable." The Christological contradictions of the
Orient found no solution, to say nothing of a solution of the general Christological problem. But in the course of the development an element was fortunately—we cannot regard it otherwise
—introduced, which, in the form now assumed by the contest and
the terminology of the day, fixed a barrier against extreme views
in either direction. It must be remembered, too, that it is not
the office of symbols to establish dogmatic theories. They
merely give expression to the religious convictions of their age.
Such convictions found expression in the Chalcedon creed—
essentially, in consequence of the peculiar circumstances of the
period, in a negative form. As the formula of the one person
and the two natures was adopted as a fixed dogma, the historical
Christ was gained, although only in faintest outline, as the norm
and corrective for the ideas of the dogmaticians. This may be
seen most clearly in Luther.[2]

§ 26. *Movements Growing Out of the Christological Conflict
(Monophysite and Monothelete Controversies) and the Result
of the Agitation.*

1. The emperor condemned Eutyches and Dioscurus to exile.
Strict measures were employed against their followers and the
Apollinarians (M. vii. 476, 498 f., 502 f.).

[1] Originally the overwhelming majority, despite the letter of Leo, demanded
the formula: "ἐκ δύο φύσων." The reason for this is evident, as this formula
left open the possibility of speaking of *only one* nature even after the incarnation. Only after severe pressure had been brought to bear from above was the
victory gained for the ἐν δύο φύσεσι—thus saving the historic Christ.
[2] Leo endured the chagrin of having the council refuse to adopt his letter
as a dogma, increase the power of the bishop of Constantinople, and place
the bishop of New Rome, in view of the equal importance of the city as
an imperial city (nothing being said of Peter), by the side of the bishop of
Rome as second in dignity. Canon 28; cf. Leo ep. 104-107, 114, 119, 127,
135 f. At the opening of the council, the clerical delegates had requested

But peace was by no means restored.   On the contrary, the history of the ensuing years is marked through its whole course by the records of wild excitement and horrible deeds of religious fanaticism.   Within the limits of a general History of Doctrines the MONOPHYSITE CONTROVERSIES can be treated but briefly.

LITERATURE.   Vid. the KG. of Zacharias Rhetor, syr. in LAND, Anecdota syr. iii. (German by Ahrens and Krüger, Leipzig, 1899).   Evagrius h. e. l. ii.-v.   Johannes v. Ephesus h. e., translated from the Syrian by SCHÖNFELDER, 1862.   M. vii.-ix.   Cf. WALCH, hist. d. Ketzereien vi.-viii. SCHRÖCKH KG. xviii.   GIESELER, Comment. qua Monophysitarum opin. illustr. i.-ii., Gott. 1835, 1838.   HEFELE CG. ii. 564 ff.   KRÜGER, PRE. xiii., ed. 3, 372 ff.   KRÜGER, Monophys. Streitigkeiten, etc., p. 68 ff., Jena, 1884. LOOFS, Leontius oi Byzantium, 1888, p. 53 ff.

A strong party arose for the defense of Monophysitism, or the doctrine of Cyril—first in Palestine (Theodosius) and in Egypt (Timotheus Aelurus, Petrus Mongus), then in Antioch (Petrus Fullo), here in alliance with the Apollinarians.   All the efforts of the emperor could gain but superficial control of the movement and secure but temporary recognition for the confession of Chalcedon.   This was the situation under Leo I. (A. D. 457-474).   The usurper, BASILISCUS, by his *Encyclion* (A. D. 476) rejected the Chalcedon Creed, and about 500 bishops agreed with him (Evagr. h. e. iii. 4 ; Zachar. v. 2).   The emperor, ZENO, endeavored by his *Henoticon*, A. D. 482, to effect a union (Evagr. iii. 14 ; Zachar. v. 8).   The definitions of the councils of Nicaea, Constantinople, and Ephesus, as well as the twelve anathemas of Cyril, were here recognized, and Nestorius and Eutyches condemned.   Christ the true God and the true man is confessed to be of the same nature with the Father according to his divinity, and of the same nature with us according to his humanity, but " to be one and not two.   For we say that the miracles and whatever sufferings he endured in the flesh are (those) of one."   Whoever adopts another teaching ($\mu\dot{\alpha}\vartheta\eta\mu\alpha$) than this, whether taught now or heretofore, at Chalcedon or elsewhere, is anathematized.   Nothing is plain except the authority of Cyril and the rejection of Nestorianism and Eutychianism.   Beyond this, the disputed formulas are carefully avoided ; the rejection of the Chalcedon confession is implied but not distinctly expressed.   The agitation was not allayed by this formula.   Neither the strict Monophysites nor the orthodox were satisfied.   The former missed in the Henoticon the ex-

the exclusion of Dioscurus, because he had presumed to open an ecumenical council without the presence of Rome.   For the further history of the question, see HEFELE ii. 562 f., 568 f.   The foundation was thus laid for the schism between the East and the West.

press condemnation of the Chalcedon Creed and of the letter of
Pope Leo (Zachar. v. 7, 9 ; vi. 1). The latter, as in the days
of Chalcedon, took refuge in Rome. Pope FELIX III. turned to
the emperor in defense of the endangered Chalcedon creed and
excommunicated ACACIUS, the bishop of Constantinople, A. D.
484 (ep. 1-4, 6). The latter, in turn, struck the name of Felix
from the Diptychs. The breach with Rome had become complete. It was a necessity, as an agreement was not possible between the ancient Latin Christology and the Greek doctrine,
which inclined more and more toward Monophysitism. But
even in the East there were still elements which withstood the advance of the Monophysite views. The emperor, ANASTASIUS
(from A. D. 491), permitted the ''Henoticon'' to stand, but
favored the Monophysite interpretation of it. Nevertheless, there
were bitter controversies during the entire reign of Anastasius.
In Antioch, Severus, one of the Monophysite leaders, became
bishop, but the emperor yet labored to secure peace with the adherents of Chalcedon and the authorities of Rome. But it was
now evident that the situation had only become the more complicated, and that the Roman bishops were contending, not in the
interest of pure doctrine, but to secure the dominion of the entire church. Hence the transactions with Pope Hormisdas were
without result (cf. Krüger, PRE. xiii., 387 f.).

2. Anastasius was succeeded by JUSTIN I. (A. D. 518-527).
He was under the control of his nephew, JUSTINIAN, who succeeded him upon the imperial throne (A. D. 527-565). The
political plans of this great prince (cf. Krüger, PRE. ix., ed. 3,
650 ff.) required the pacification of the church. The ancient
universal empire was to be revived, and restraint put upon the
aggressions of the Germans. To this end there must be harmony in the government, the laws, and the church. He sought
for the formula of the universal empire and made everything
serviceable for his own purpose. ''He still lives in the *Codex*
and the *Hagia Sophia*'' (see delineation of his character in
RANKE, Weltgesch. iv. 2, p. 125 f.). No one before him had
attempted to carry out in so comprehensive and reckless a way
the idea of the state church. The ecclesiastical doctrines and
ordinances became state laws, and heresy and heathenism were
forbidden by the civil government. The power of the church
was thus vastly increased, but it at the same time lost every ves-
tige of independence and distinct character as contrasted with
the state. The emperor was unwearied in his efforts to
strengthen the power of the clergy, but he at the same time
ruled in the church with despotic power. Great as was his
power, however, he was confronted by immense difficulties in

the prosecution of his final plans.   The old unity of the Greek
and Roman churches had been dissolved.   Rome and Constantinople were now independent centres, and it was sought to
combine them in one.   The church of the East was to be harmonized and again united with the church of the West.   The
restoration of the orthodoxy of Chalcedon was hence, from
the start, the watchword.   It was a difficult undertaking, as the
power of the Monophysites was yet unbroken in the East, and
they enjoyed the sympathies of the empress, Theodora, not to
mention the favor of hosts of pious believers.   The creed of
Chalcedon must remain in force—that was now clearly seen—
and an interpretation of it found which would be tolerable for
the Monophysites.   The ecclesiastical primacy of Rome must be
recognized in principle (vid. Novella 131. 2 : " that the pope of
Old Rome is the first of all priests, but that the most blessed
archbishop of Constantinople, the New Rome, has the second
seat after the holy apostolic seat of Old Rome "), but the
power of the popes practically overcome.   Such was the task,
as complicated as the circumstances and the purpose which
gave it birth.   The first attempted policy, that of the forcible
suppression the Monophysites (Zachar. h. e. viii. 5 f.), was soon
abandoned by Justinian as fruitless.

3. The theology of Justinian's age accommodated itself to the
tendencies of the emperor.   This was particularly true in the case
of the "Scythian" monk, a relative of Vitalian, LEONTIUS OF
BYZANTIUM (about A. D. 485-543.   See especially his publication in three "books" against the Nestorians and Eutychians in
Mi. gr. 86. 1267 ff.; cf. LOOFS, L. v. B., 1888.   RÜGAMER, L. v.
B., 1894).   The formulas of Chalcedon are here recast in accordance with Aristotelian categories (οὐσία, γένος, εἶδος, represented by the εἰδοποιοὶ διαφοραί, or ποιότητες οὐσιώδεισ, ἄτομον,
see LOOFS, p. 60 ff.): φύσις and ὑπόστασις are related to one another as εἶδος to ἄτομον.   But now a nature (φύσις) exists only
as a substance (ὑπόστασις), just as an image exists only as a body
(Mi. 86. 1278, 1280).   Therefore the acknowledgment of two
natures would lead to two hypostases, or to Nestorianism (ib.
1276 f.).   Leontius escapes this consequence by introducing the
idea of a nature as being intrahypostatic (ἐνυπόστατος).   That is,
one nature may combine with another to form a unity in such a way
that, although it retains the peculiar characteristic of its own existence, yet it has its substance (ὑπόστασις) in the second nature.
It is then not without hypostases (ἀνυπόστατος), but (ἐνυπόστατος),
e. g., a man composed of body and soul, or a burning torch ; indeed, "it has given of its attributes interchangeably, which continue in the abiding and uncommingled peculiarity of their own

natures " (ib. 1304, 1278 ff.). Thus the problem of the time appears to be solved—two independent natures, and yet only one hypostasis. The Chalcedon creed is justified, and Cyril is justified, for the hypostasis of Christ is thus the hypostasis of the Logos. "Our author stands for an orthodoxy leading back as far as possible to the Alexandrine theology. This is the permanent impression left by all his discussions" (LOOFS, p. 71).

This theology made it less difficult to approach the Monophysites, which was done by the recognition of the enlarged Trisagion first introduced in Antioch by Peter the Fuller : "Holy God, holy Mighty, holy Immortal, crucified for us, have mercy upon us." It was thus acknowledged that one person of the Trinity had suffered, and the Scythian monks gave their approval. The same end was served by a religious conference held with the Severians at Constantinople (A. D. 533 or 531, vid. Loofs, p. 283), as also by the condemnation of the former leaders of the Antiochian theology, Theodore of Mopsuestia, Ibas. Theodoret (vid. decrees in M. ix.),[1] which occurred in the course of the Three-Chapter controversy (A. D. 544). The East soon acquiesced, but the West resented this condemnation of its honored teachers, who had died at peace with the Church (s. esp. Facundus Hermian, pro defensione trium capitum, in Mi. lat. 67). The part taken in all these controversies by the Roman bishops was, on the other hand, but a pitiable exhibition of their weakness—a wavering between the spirit of the West and fear of the emperor, a kicking against the pricks and a half or entire surrender (Hormisdas and the Trisagion, Johann II., Agapetus I., and the Theopaschite supplement, Vigilius and the Three-Chapter controversy, the fifth ecumenical council).

4. The FIFTH ECUMENICAL COUNCIL, A. D. 553 (M. ix. HEFELE CG. ii. 854 ff.) was called primarily to sanction the condemnation of the Three Chapters. The bishop of Constantinople presided. About 150 bishops participated. Pope Vigilius, who was present, protested against the condemnation. He was in consequence denounced as a liar in view of some of his earlier utterances, and the council resolved to strike his name from the Dyptichs. The Three Chapters were condemned : "A Theodore, a Judas." "His defenders are Jews ; his adherents heathen. Many years to the Emperor !" (cf. can. 12-14). The council of Chalcedon was recognized, Origen condemned (can. 11), the

---

[1] The church politics of Justinian and the world-embracing church mark a visible decadence of intellectual and spiritual energy. Heathenism was forbidden, Judaism repressed, the Manichæans destroyed. The ancient school of Athens was closed A. D. 528, Origen condemned A. D. 544, and, finally, the Antiochians surrendered.

doctrine of the Theopaschite supplement adopted (can. 10). Pope
Vigilius subsequently acquiesced in the decisions of the council
(HEFELE ii. 905 ff.), as also the African bishops (ib. 913).[1] The
ecclesiastical politics of the emperor had proved successful.

5. But the emperor had not yet accomplished what he desired.
The situation was made more hopeless by the dissensions which
arose among the Monophysites themselves.   Monophysitism was
primarily but an opposition to the Chalcedonian and Cyrillian
theology.   Its adherents spoke of the "heresy of the Dyophy-
sites" in opposition to the doctrine of "believers," who hold to
the one nature ($\mu i \alpha \ \varphi \acute{\nu}\sigma\iota\varsigma$).   It was acknowledged in theory that
Christ is $\acute{o}\mu oo\acute{\nu}\sigma\iota o\varsigma$ with the Father as well as with man.   Apollinaris and Eutyches were rejected (Timoth. Ael. in Zachar. h. e. iv.
12 ; v. 7).   Dioscurus was the "apostolic man" who would not
worship the "idol image with two faces that was set up by Leo
and the assembly at Chalcedon" (ib. iii. 1).   But their temper
became more pronounced, and the views of the Monophysites
themselves became more and more divergent.   There was also,
from the beginning, a group of more strict partisans, who held
about the position of Eutyches (vid. e. g., Zachar. h. e. iii. 9. 10).
The two chief parties were known as SEVERIANS and JULIANISTS,
so named from their later leaders, Severus and Julian of Halicar-
nassus.   Severus taught essentially the Christology of Cyril :
"Of two natures one Christ."   He expressly recognizes the
reality of the two natures after the union, in which he accords
with Nestorius.   But there is an "unmixed union," in which,
as Cyril says, the distinction can be noted "at a single glance."
He appropriates the Areopagite formula of a "new theandric
energy ($\dot{\epsilon}\nu\acute{\epsilon}\rho\gamma\epsilon\iota\alpha$) of Christ."   He is unable to accept the Chalcedon creed, because it leads to two persons, and even to a
"duad of wills."   This is all in the spirit of Cyril.   It makes no
real difference, that Cyril starts with the Logos without flesh
($\check{\alpha}\sigma\alpha\rho\kappa o\varsigma$) and Severus with the Logos in the flesh ($\check{\epsilon}\nu\sigma\alpha\rho\kappa o\varsigma$),
as the latter conception occurs also frequently in Cyril (despite
Loofs, p. 206 f., frg. of Severus in antiquorum patr. doctr. de verbi
inc., in Leont. Hierosolym. c. Monophysit., Eustathius. ad
Timoth. de duab. nat., in Mai Scriptur. vet. nov. coll. vii.; vid.
also Mi. gr. 86 and several letters in Zachar. h. e. ix. 11, 13,
16, 20, 22, 23.   Cf. DORNER ii. 1. 166 ff., LOOFS, l. c. p. 54
ff.).   The inference from this view is that the body of Christ

---

[1] A number of bishops of Upper Italy, indeed, renounced church fellowship
with Pope Pelagius I. in consequence of the Three Chapter agitation (HEFELE
ii. 914 f.).   The downfall of the Lombards (A. D. 568) released the Roman
pontiff from the critical situation.   Subsequent bishops of Rome were compelled to exert themselves with energy for the healing of the Italian schism.

was, according to its nature, capable of suffering and corruptible.
Hence its opponents spoke of it as *Phthartolatry*. Its advocates
did not even shrink from the inference that the human soul of
Christ was not omriscient (AGNOETAE). The JULIANISTS, on the
contrary, taught that Christ assumed our flesh "in order that he
might deliver it at once from corruption and from sin." His
human nature, being sinless, is therefore not corruptible
(Julian Anath. 6, 7, in GIESELER, comment. de Monoph., etc.,
ii. 6). On the contrary, the body of Christ is, from the moment
of the union, glorified, incorruptible, and of the same character
as after the resurrection (Gieseler ib. 11. 7). Hence, Christ's
capability of suffering is not natural to him, but rests upon his
free-will (octo quaesit. 4, in Gieseler ii. 7). Julian did not in
this way by any means wish to deny the Homousia of Christ's
human nature with our humanity. By the "incorruptibility"
he understood, not a Docetic character, but the freedom of
Christ's nature from all the human infirmities which have resulted from the entrance of sin. Christ assumed such a body
and soul as Adam possessed before the fall (cf. KRÜGER, PRE.
ix. ed. 3, 608). In the face of this position, the task of the
Severians was a difficult one ; for, in the denial of the *Aphthar-
sia* of the human nature of Christ, his divine unity, which they
asserted, appeared to be lost. Hence the Julianists accused
them of Aphthartolatry. Yet the Severians maintained that
there was a Docetic element in the theory of Julian, charged
him with holding the doctrine of Eutyches, and reviled his followers as *Aphthartodocetes* or *Phantasiasts*.

(Upon Julian, vid. ZACHAR. h. e. ix. 9 ff. Leontius, de sectis, 10, Mi. gr.
86. 1. 1260 ff. Joh. Damasc. haer. 84. ASSEMANI, Bibl. oriental. ii. 168.
WERNER, in Vien. Mus. lv. 321 ff. GIESELER, l. c. Krüger, PRE. ix. ed.
3, 606 ff.)

Other Monophysites (the GAIANITES) carried out their ideas
to the absurdity, that the body of Christ, from the time of the
union, was uncreated. They were called ACTISTETES. Stephen
Niobes held that all distinction of the divine and human in
Christ must be totally denied (ADIAPHORITES).[1]

6. Justinian tolerated the Monophysites (Joh. v. Eph. h. e.
i. 4 f.). Even in the capital they had honored representatives
(Theodosius, John of Ephesus); and the restlessly wandering

[1] We have here the germ of the later Syrian Monophysite pantheism, vid.
FROTHINGHAM, Stephen ben Sudaili, 1886 ; his teachings, p. 28 ff. If the unity
of the divine and human in Christ was granted as a natural characteristic, the
inference might easily be drawn that the two natures are essentially one. Thus
this form of Greek Christian philosophy reverts to the pantheism of Greek
philosophy.

Jacob el Baradai was able to accomplish much for the unification and strengthening of the party. The emperor has held the church under his control, but he has not achieved his purpose. We can easily understand from this situation how he, at the close of his career, should conceive the idea of unifying at least the church of the Orient by the adoption of Aphthartodocetism. Death prevented the execution of the edict, which he fully purposed to enforce (Evagr. h. e. iv. 39). That which he failed to accomplish, his successors (Justin II., Tiberius, Mauricius) were equally unable to attain, although they spared neither the arts of persuasion nor force. Monophysitism steadily advanced to a permanent position in church life among the Syrian Jacobites and in the Coptic, Abyssinian, and Armenian churches.

7. The efforts to win the Monophysites gave occasion, further, to the MONOTHELETE CONTROVERSIES. Here, too, political aims furnished the controlling motive.

(Vid. Acta, in M. x., xi., cf. G. KRÜGER, PRE. xiii., ed. 3, 401 ff. WALCH, Hist. d. Ketzereien ix. SCHRÖCKH, KG. xx. 386 ff. HEFELE, CG. iii. 121 ff.; OWSEPIAN, Die Entstehungsgesch. des Monotheletismus, Leipz., 1897.)

The policy was to gain support for the empire, which was hardly pressed by the Persians and Saracens, by gaining over the numerous Monophysite elements in the Eastern church—preserving, of course, at the same time the Chalcedon creed. The patriarch SERGIUS of Constantinople advised HERACLIUS (A. D. 610-641) to employ for this purpose the formula, that the one Christ performs divine and human acts "by one theandric energy" (thus already Dionys. Areop. ep. 4 and Severus supra, p. 277). Although this formula served its purpose in Egypt and elsewhere, it was necessary to abandon it because of the opposition of SOPHRONIUS of Jerusalem. Whether there is one energy or two, is not a proper matter for investigation, thought Sergius. One will (ἓν θέλημα) was, however, postulated of Christ as self-evident. In this spirit Sergius wrote to HONORIUS OF ROME (M. xi. 529 ff.), and the latter responded approvingly, "that the question, whether there be one energy or two, is not biblical, and belongs only to the sphere of the grammarians. Among the uninstructed populace, one energy might be interpreted as having a Eutychian sound and two as savoring of Nestorianism." It follows, on the contrary, from the fact of the incarnation : "Wherefore also we confess one will of the Lord Jesus Christ" (M. xi. 537 ff.). In a second letter, the pope again rejected the question concerning the energies, and employed Leo's formula, that each of the two natures "works in fellowship with the other" (M. xi. 580). Sergius, therefore,

secured the publication of his Ἔκθεσις πίστεως, A. D. 638):
Two natures with their peculiarities, "but one hypostasis and one
person of the divine Logos, together with rationally-animated
flesh;" "we ascribe all divine and human energy to one and
the same incarnated Logos . . . and do not by any means permit anyone to maintain or teach either one or two energies of the
incarnate Lord." The two energies would work confusion, as
they would give occasion for the inference : "And there preside
two wills of those who are in opposition to one another," which
even the impious Nestorius would not have dared to assert. It
is thus impossible to accept "two, and these opposing, wills in
the same (person)." Following the Fathers in all things, it is
to be said: "We confess . . . one will of our Lord Jesus
Christ" (M. x. 992 ff.). The Roman legates of Severinus,
the successor of Honorius, declared themselves ready to adopt
the Ecthesis; but as early as A. D. 641, JOHN IV. of Rome
condemned Monotheletism (M. x. 607), while, at the same
time, he endeavored to defend Pope Honorius from the suspicion of a Monothelete type of doctrine, maintaining that
the latter had in mind only the human will of Christ, and
denied that there were two contrary wills in Christ (vid. his
Apol. pro papa Honor., M. x. 682 ff.). His successor, Theodore I., desired the rejection of the Ecthesis (M. x. 702,
705 f.). The Africans assumed the same attitude (Hefele iii.
205 ff.). The emperor, CONSTANS II., yielded in the τύπος of
A. D. 648. The problem is to be banished from the world forever, as had been attempted in the Ecthesis. The latter is surrendered, and questions are to be decided in accordance with
the five ecumenical councils, the utterances of the Fathers, and
the doctrinal positions held before the controversy, just "as it
would have been if no such controversy had ever arisen." "We
decree that our subjects abiding in orthodoxy . . . shall, from
the present time, not have permission to carry on any controversy whatsoever among themselves concerning one will or energy,
or two energies and two wills," etc. Any who may disregard this
decree are threatened with severe punishments (M. x. 1029 f.).
It may be seen from this brutal composition to what tyranny the
secularized church was compelled to submit.

8. But at Rome there were hopes of accomplishing something
more. The monk, MAXIMUS, proved in writings and disputa-
tions that Dyotheletism is a necessary inference from the two
natures of the Chalcedon creed (his writings were edited by
Combesis, 2 vols., Paris, 1675; see esp. the interesting dispu-
tation with Pyrrhus in Combes. ii. 159-195; M. x. 709 ff.;
cf. upon Maximus, Wagermann-Seeberg, PRE. xii., ed. 3,

457 ff.).[1] We must devote some attention to the Christology of Maximus. He was inspired by a keen interest in the reality of the humanity of Christ. Without a human will, he maintained, Christ would not have been a man (opp. ii. 105-108). On the other hand, the doctrine of the Trinity demands Dyotheletism; for since, according to the Fathers, the Trinity has a will, the theandric will of Christ must also be the will of the Trinity (ii. 163). This is impossible. The real human nature of Christ requires a human will, and with this the divine will united itself. The unity of the two is effected through the one hypostasis which is common to both (ii. 164). Christ lived as God and man (ii. 165). Since the Logos assumed human nature, he received also a human will, which acts in a way corresponding with its natural psychological character. But this will was not compelled, as is ours, to decide between opposites, but, by virtue of its union with the Logos, it received a permanent, fixed moral inclination. In this way the true doctrine is distinguished from that of Nestorius (ii. 13, 14). The celebrated formula of the Areopagite ($\vartheta\varepsilon\alpha\nu\delta\rho\iota\varkappa\dot{\eta}$ $\dot{\varepsilon}\nu\dot{\varepsilon}\rho\gamma\varepsilon\iota\alpha$) itself proves the presence of two energies, but is merely the expression of the empirical relationship (ii. 51). The opinion of Maximus is therefore: that the Logos appropriates to himself the human will of Christ, since he by this union with it gives to it a fixed inclination, which, however, exerts itself in many separate free human choices. The theology of Maximus rightly defined the nature of the man Jesus, positing it in the spiritual will, and it exerted itself with energy to maintain this nature intact within the lines of the two-nature theory. This gives to it its historical significance. It is remarkable to observe how, toward the end of the great controversies, ideas again came to the front which had at the beginning been advanced by the Antiochians.

We return to the contemplation of the course of external events. Pope MARTIN I., without waiting for the imperial approval, conducted a large synod (105 bishops) at Rome, A. D. 649. He here declared himself opposed to the Ecthesis, as contradicting the two natures, and also opposed to the Typos, which he dismissed with the perfidious charge, that it denies to Christ will and energy, and thus every kind of nature. The synod decided in accordance with his wishes, adding to the Chalcedon creed: "two natural wills, divine and human, and two natural operations" (M. x. 1150). With great energy the pope now sought to interest the Frankish church and the two kings in his cause,

---

[1] Reversing the process, the Monotheletes from the one person inferred one will, e. g., M. x. 709.

and endeavored to gain influence in the Oriental churches among
the Saracens.    It was even charged that he gave money to the
Saracens in Sicily.    The emperor treated both the pope and
Maximus as traitors.    They died in exile, A. D. 655 and 662.
EUGENE I. and VITALIAN of Rome adapted themselves to the situation, their scruples apparently met by the reflection that the
two natural wills unite in one hypostatic will.    We may, therefore, speak of one will as well as of two, accordingly as we use
the term.    Rome, on the other hand, would know nothing of
this, as the doctrine of Maximus had there full sway.

9. Constans was murdered A. D. 668 and succeeded by CON-
STANTINE POGONATUS (A. D. 668-685).    The constantly obtrud-
ing antagonism between Rome and Constantinople induced the
emperor to call a council and to yield, as far as possible, to the
demands of Rome—the greater part of the Monophysites being
in any event lost to the Byzantine empire.    This resulted in the
Sixth Ecumenical[1] Council, held at Constantinople, A. D. 680.
There were about 170 participants (proceedings in M. xi.; cf.
HEFELE iii. 249 ff.).    The letter of Pope AGATHO here played an
important part.    It is presented as the doctrine of the Romish
church, which has never departed from the way of truth, or the
apostolic tradition, that—as an inference from the doctrine of
two natures—the will of Christ is two-fold, having in it "two
natural wills and energies just as two natures" (M. xi. 239).
Accordingly, the council decided, after the reading of volumes
of patristic excerpts—not, indeed, without opposition (Poly-
chronius, a Monophysite, seeking by his formula to call a dead
issue to life)—in accordance with the wishes of the emperor
("Thou hast established the completeness of the two natures of
our God," M. xi. 656) and the pope ; but Honorius of Rome
was anathematized as well as the Monothelete patriarch of Constantinople.    The doctrinal decree recognizes the letter of
Agatho and the five ecumenical councils.    After citing the
formulas of Chalcedon, it proceeds : "Two natural willings
($\vartheta\epsilon\lambda\acute{\eta}\sigma\epsilon\iota\varsigma$) or wills ($\vartheta\epsilon\lambda\acute{\eta}\mu\alpha\tau\alpha$) in Christ and two natural energies,
inseparably, immutably, indivisibly, without mixture, according
to the teaching of the holy Fathers. . . .    It follows that his
human will is not in opposition or conflict with, but, on the contrary, is subject to his divine and almighty will. . . .    For just
as his flesh is called and is the flesh of the divine Logos, so also his
proper human will is called and is the will of the divine Logos.
. . .    His flesh deified is not divided . . . so also his human

----

[1] It was not the original purpose to summon an "ecumenical" council, s.
HEFELE iii. 260.

will deified is not divided . . . for each form performs what
is peculiar to it with the fellowship of the other form '' (M. xi.
637).

The revival of Monotheletism at a later date (A. D. 711-713)
by the emperor, Philippicus Bardanes, and the Monotheletic
church of the MARONITES, which persisted in Lebanon until the
Crusades, are of no dogmatic significance.

The Council of Constantinople marks the termination of the
great intellectual movements which had agitated the church from
the days of Apollinaris, and of Nestorius and Cyril.   It did not
originate any new ideas nor intellectual tendencies, as the age did
not furnish the necessary inner religious force.   This was evident
from the fact that, as in all ages of deterioration, there was lacking the courage to undertake anything new.   Passages of the
'' Fathers '' were anxiously sought after.   Citations were gathered by the volume, and it was not ventured to maintain any
position until some word of one of the great Fathers of the
earlier age could be found for support and protection.   Thus the
council did nothing more than  draw an inference from the Chalcedon creed, and this was attached to  the latter in a quite external way.   It was, however, a just inference.   It thus, in its
own way, gives evidence that the Chalcedon creed was not a
Trojan horse for the church of the Orient.   On the contrary, it
made it necessary for her theologians to pursue the doctrine of
the two natures to its profound depths.   The two natures must
be apprehended in their full significance, as extending not only
to the external φύσις, but also to the internal spiritual life with
its centre, the will.   In this way the problem became more and
more difficult : Two inner wills and yet only one inner person.
The council presented, not a solution, but an assertion.   Yet it
stated distinctly a fact, and one which summoned Christian
thought to a serious task.   There was, however, lacking in the
Greek Christianity of the age the energy necessary to a proper
discharge of this obligation, and the church of the West felt no
interest in the problem as such.

10. The historical development which we have reviewed in
the above paragraphs was a most remarkable one.   Forces which
appear to have everything in their favor succeed in making
their way but feebly, and their power is broken by cold formulas.
Intellectual forces which appear to have been entirely overcome
continue to exert a silent influence.   The formalism of Greek
philosophy comes to the assistance of the church's dogma.   External considerations of church policy become the decisive factors in the discussions of doctrine.   A reckless abandonment of
old and a compulsory adoption of new formulas alternate with

one another, and, as the result of it all, the recognition of a certain *inner* necessity !

We must note a few details of the process. The great Athanasius had, in the interest of practical religion, established the
Homousia of the Son. The man Jesus served the divine Logos
as the organ through which he acted. But this idea was capable
of many interpretations, although the Homousia was the fixed
premise for them all. One might adopt the bold course of
Apollinaris, who treated the human nature of Christ as did Arius
his divinity, *i. e.*, mutilated it. Or, one might conceive the
problem in the sense of the first view of the Antiochians, and
lay all stress upon the inner personal unity of the Logos with the
man Jesus—a view which, as an intellectual formula, if not as an
actual theory, continued to be influential even after it had been
condemned in the person of Nestorius. Or, again, one might,
with Cyril, centre his theory in the divine-human unity of
Christ, his deified nature, and thus be led—under the increasing
pressure of the mystical materialism of the age—to the Monophysite position. It is evident that the broad current of Greek
piety flowed within this channel. Finally, one might face the
problem with the formulas of Tertullian in hand, and constantly oppose these formulas, as a canon, to all assaults of the times. Rome
possessed these formulas. But Rome was a political power. The
desire to preserve intact the unity of the East and the West made
the Greek emperors dependent upon the dogmatic teachings of
Rome. They were compelled to give due recognition to the
Roman formulas ; and this became but the more necessary, as
there were never lacking among Greek theologians and believers
earnest opponents of Monophysitism. All who had any realization of the problem as stated by the Antiochians could adopt the
Western formulas, but not the views of the Monophysites. It
was political considerations, indeed, but not these alone, which
compelled the emperors to join in league with the dogmatics of
Rome. Thus was brought about the second decisive event in the
history of Christology, ranking in importance with the adoption
of the Nicene creed, *i. e.*, the construction and adoption of the
creed of Chalcedon, marking the triumph of Western Christology in the East. That this was possible, and that the Chalcedon creed, despite the most bitter opposition, was not only
able to maintain itself, but controlled the entire development of
the future, proves very clearly that it is a great mistake to place
the oriental Christology simply upon the plane of Monophysitism.
But if the Chalcedon creed had really won a secure footing in
the East, then the entire course of subsequent events is intelligible. Such theologians as Leontius and Maximus must labor to

interpret the now accepted creed as far as possible in harmony with the teachings of Cyril.   Monophysitism and Monotheletism must be driven from the church.   The sixth ecumenical council was compelled to decide as it did, and John of Damascus could not tolerate any other doctrine.   All this followed by necessity upon the adoption of the creed of Chalcedon.

It may be said, in view of the above : Thus it was the political scheming of the calculating demagogues at Rome and of the imperial advisers at Constantinople that framed the faith of the church !   This is not untrue, and yet it is not correct.   It is not untrue, for without the political ambitions of the age, the creed of Chalcedon would not have been constructed, nor could it have secured the approval of Justinian, and the sixth ecumenical council would never have been held.   On the other hand, the statement is not correct, for without the faith of the Greek church, Monophysitism and Monotheletism could never have been permanently banished.   In order to realize this, it is only necessary to consider the Christology of Maximus, who was a thorough-going Greek and a fanatical Areopagite.   Thus was formed the Christology of the Greek church.   It is Chalcedonian, but limits the humanity as far as possible.   It is Cyrillian, but also anti-Monophysite.   Cyril and the Chalcedon Creed are the authorities by which it is determined.   The two tendencies which, at the beginning of the controversy, struggled for the mastery—the Antiochian and the Alexandrine—were, as a result of the controversy, in a measure, united, having both found their secure unity in the Christological scheme of the West. Politics led to this result, but politics could never have chosen this way if the course of inward development in the church had not required it.   The Western Christology was taken into account, not only in order to satisfy Rome, but also in order to gratify those in the East who were not in accord with the Monophysite doctrine.

The position recently taken, especially by Ritschl and Harnack, that Greek piety was Monophysite in type, and that, in consequence, the conception of Soteriology here dominant, can have represented only the Christology of Dioscurus or Julian, cannot be sustained in view of the actual facts.   It generalizes upon an observation which is, in itself, correct.   Generalizations of this character may be an effectual aid in the establishment of particular theories, but they cannot be permanently maintained.   This is manifest from the account above given, but others also, as, *e. g.*, Loofs and Krüger, have begun to call attention to the one-sided nature of this modern interpretation of history.

11. John of Damascus gave the final form to Christology

also upon Grecian territory (see his Ἔκθεσις πίστεως, cf. supra, p. 236). The dogmatics of this leader again mirror the character of the preceding centuries. Faith is the "not over-curious assent" to the incomprehensible doctrine of the triune God, the dogmas of the church, and the utterances of the Fathers (iv. 9, 10, 11; i. 1), along with which many strange things are advocated (adoration of the cross, the manger, the socket of the cross, saints, relics, images, celibacy, iv. 11 f., 15 f., 24).[1] (a) John is a thorough Chalcedonian and Dyothe-lete in his Christology (vid. book iii. of De fide orthodoxa: "One hypostasis in two natures"). From the latter it necessarily follows that Christ also possessed two natural wills and energies (iii. 13-15). We can no more accept the idea of one will (iii. 14) than we can speak of one composite nature (iii. 2). In the Cyrillian formula: "One nature of the divine Logos, made flesh" (μία φύσις τοῦ θεοῦ λόγου σεσαρχωμένη), the term "made flesh" indicates "the essence (οὐσία) of the flesh" (iii. 7, p. 215, c. 11, p. 221). (b) The union of the two natures is im-plied in the acknowledgment of one hypostasis. Here John follows Leontius.[2] It is, indeed, true that no nature (φύσις) is without hypostasis (ἀνυπόστατος), and no essence; (οὐσία) is with-out person (ἀπρόσωπος); but it is possible for two natures to have a common hypostasis. The flesh of Christ has no other hypostasis than that which the Logos also has; "but is, on the contrary, en-hypostatic in the same hypostasis" (iii. 9). The Logos-hyposta-sis, therefore, became the hypostasis of the formerly impersonal flesh: "For he assumed a germ of our clay, not used before as an actual hypostasis and atom and thus taken to himself, but having its existence in the same hypostasis. For the hypostasis of the divine Logos became an hypostasis in the flesh, and in this

---

[1] The divisions of this work are as follows (cf. Origen, Theognostos, supra, p. 147, n. 2, 186, n. 1, and Gregory of Nyssa, Augustine, Peter Lom-bard, Melanchthon): Book I. treats of God, his incomprehensibility, revelation, the Trinity, divine attributes, etc. Book II. discusses the world, the devil, heaven, the air, winds, paradise, man—including under the last-named head-ing the whole range of psychology, free-will, etc. Book III. treats of Christ, the two natures, the one hypostasis, the trisagion, the mother of God, the life, energies, and will of Christ, his unblamable emotions, his fear, his prayers, his sufferings, the descent to hell, etc. Book IV. deals with the state of the risen Saviour, redemption, baptism, faith, the cross, the mysteries, worship of saints, images, the Scriptures, the Jews, celibacy, circumcision, Antichrist, the resurrection, etc. That this outline became—not to the advantage of dog-matic theology—a model for later discussions, cannot be denied. We look in it in vain for an answer to the question, What is Christianity? or, What is the Gospel?

[2] Whom he often uses and in iii. 11 expressly names (although Harnack, DG. ii., ed. 3, 410, n., declares that Leontius is "never mentioned").

way ' the Logos became flesh ' " (iii. 11. pp. 220, 221 ; c. 2 :
"The Logos himself became an hypostasis in the flesh "). This
is the conception of Cyril and Leontius, and also of Apollinaris.
But, since the term "hypostasis" does not exactly correspond
with our term "personality," but indicates as well simply individual existence (iii. 7), the Damascene speaks of a "composite hypostasis" of Christ. As Christ is God and man, there
belongs to him the separate divine-human existence, or hypostasis.
Hence John can say : " The hypostasis of the divine Logos before the incarnation was single and incomposite and non-corporate
and uncreate ; but it became incarnate and a hypostasis in the
flesh, and became compounded of divinity, of which it always
partook, and of flesh which it assumed, and it bears the properties
of the two natures, being seen in two natures, so that this one
hypostasis is uncreate in its divinity and create in its humanity,
visible and invisible" (iv. 5 ; similarly iii. 3, 4, 5, 7, 14).
(c) With this unity of the hypostasis is involved the mutual participation and interpenetration of the two natures : "The Logos
participates in the human (attributes) . . . and imparts of its
own to the flesh in the way of exchange through the mutual
revolution of parts and the hypostatic union, and because it was
one and the same performing both the divine and the human acts
in either form with the participation of the other " (iii. 3, the
closing part cited from Leo ; see also iv. 18). But this interpenetration proceeds only from the side of the divine nature (iii.
7 fin.). The human will of Christ is deified, so that he voluntarily wills what the divine will of Christ wills (iii. 17, 18). His
humanity is also omniscient (iii. 21). Christ does not know any
choice (προαίρεσις, iii. 14). The declaration of Lk. 2. 52
is to be understood as a revelation of the wisdom which dwells in
him, or as indicating that he assumes as his own the progress
made by the human nature (iii. 22). The prayers referred to
in Matt. 26. 39 and 27. 46 are simply for our instruction, or de-
signedly vicarious (iii. 24). The divine nature has no direct
relation to the sufferings of Christ (iii. 15). This is illustrated
by various similes. If we strike a tree upon which the sunlight
is falling, the sun is not struck, but remains without suffering ;
and if we pour water upon glowing iron, the fire is extinguished,
but the iron remains, according to its nature, unconsumed (iii.
26). From the hypostatic union is inferred, indeed, the propriety
of worshiping the flesh of Christ (iii. 8 ; iv. 2) and of employing
the term "mother of God" (iii. 12 : "For this name involves
the whole mystery of the economy "), and it is taught that Christ
effects our salvation according to his two natures (iii. 14); but this
does not overbalance the one-sided intoning of the divine nature

in the Christology of John.  He is the diligent recorder of the doctrinal development up to his own day, but there is no ground for the extolling of the truthfulness and profundity of his view (as is done by THOMASIUS DG. i. 391).  His ideas followed the lines of the Chalcedon creed and his spirit was Cyrillian ; but he did not succeed in giving effectual prominence to the valuable features of Cyril.  He presents the result of Greek Christology— *i. e.*, the Chalcedon creed triumphed, but it triumphed in alliance with Cyril.

<hr />

## CHAPTER III.

GENERAL CONCEPTION OF CHRISTIANITY.  COMPLETION OF DOC-
TRINAL CONSTRUCTION IN THE EAST (NICAEA, A. D. 787).

### § 27.  *Greek Christianity.*

We can here make but a few general comments upon this theme.  The material is inexhaustible.

We shall depend chiefly—after the writings of ATHANASIUS ; those of the three CAPPADOCIANS ; the homilies of CHRYSOSTOM († A. D. 407 ; opp. ed. Montfaucon, 1718 ff.  Mi. gr. t. 47-64); the 50 homilies of MACARIUS THE GREAT († about A. D. 390, ed. Floss, 1850. Mi. gr. 34)—upon the comprehensive presentations of the subject by CYRIL OF JERUSALEM in his catechisms († after A. D. 381, ed. Touttée, 1720.  Mi. gr. t. 33); the large catechism of GREGORY OF NYSSA ; the De fide orthodoxa of JOHN OF DAMASCUS ; the works of MAXIMUS THE CONFESSOR (ed. by Combesis, 1675), and of ANASTASIUS SINAITA (Mi. gr. 89), etc.; and finally the writings of PSEUDODIONYSIUS AREO-PAGITA (de coelesti hierarchia, de ecclesiastica hierarch., de divinis nominibus, de mystica theologica, epistulae 10, ed. Corderius, 1634, also 1644 and 1755 in Mi. gr. 4, translated and scrutinized by ENGELHARDT, 1823 ; cf. HIPLER, Dionys. der Ar., 1861 ; STIGLMAYR, Das Aufkommen der ps.-Dionys. Schriften, etc., 1895 ; H. KOCH, Das Aufkommen der pseudodionysian. Schriften, in Theol. Quartelschr., 1895, 353 ff.; BONWETSCH, PRE. iv., ed 3, 687 ff.  BARDENHEWER, Patrologie, 1894, p. 284 ff.[1]  Cf. further KUNZE, Marcus Eremita, 1895 : HOLL, Enthusiasmus u. Bussgewalt beim griech. Mönchtum, 1898.  HARNACK DG. ii., ed. 3, 441 ff.).

[1] There is yet no general agreement as to the time when these writings appeared.  They are first mentioned at a synod at Tyre, which was held not later than A. D. 513 (Zachar. rhet. h. e. vii.; 12 in Land, Anecdota Syr. iii. 228), and by Severus (bishop of Antioch, A. D. 512-518, vid. Mai, Vet scriptor. nov coll. vi. 1, p. 71); then at the religious colloquy at Constantinople, A. D. 533 (M. viii. 817 ff.; vid. also Liberat. breviar. 10 ; and BONWETSCH, l. c. 689).  It appears safe to place its appearance at the close of Cent. v. in Syria.  As the writings now stand (have they been revised ?) they appear (despite the arguments of Hipler to the contrary) to be a designed forgery (cf. STIGL-MAYR and KOCH).  Suspicion is aroused by the relationship of the eighth letter

1. " Orthodoxy " and "good works," according to Methodius, constitute Christianity (supra, p. 190, and Clem. Al., p. 146). Cyril of Jerusalem names " the teaching, μάθευμα, of the dogmas " and "good works " (cat. 4. 2 ; cf. Const. ap. iii. 12). But among the Greeks the emphasis was laid more and more upon the " orthodox " doctrine. The doctrine of the church as such, in its technical and detailed form, was regarded as an object of faith. This explains the acrimony in the conduct of controversies, and the bad habit of denying life and salvation to the adherents of another doctrinal formula. The " tradition of the Catholic church," *i.e.*, the dogmas of the Trinity and the two natures in Christ, is to be accepted and believed to be true (*e. g.*, Cyril. cat. 16. 24 fin.; 5. 12 ; 11. 20 init. Greg. Nyss. cat. m. 1-3 ; 39. Joh. Dam. iv. 10). It is only necessary to observe the style employed in the documents named in order to realize that the bread is here already beginning to turn into stone. The dogmas are state laws whose acknowledgment the state requires of its citizens. It therefore persecutes with its own weapons opposition to the doctrines of the church. But these same doctrines are also an expression of the most ancient convictions of Christian truth. It is only by their acceptance that a saving view of the truth can be obtained. But such a view is made dependent upon a merely intellectual apprehension of the truth. Here, then, appears the office of the mysteries. He who participates in these is lifted above the world in the experience of salvation. Here becomes manifest the life-giving fountain of religion. The doctrines are the theory of life : the mysteries bestow this life. But only he who accepts the theory can experience that which it contains. It is easy to understand that the conception of the inward nature of Christianity should thus be gradually lost. The Pauline doctrine of justification was never comprehended by the Greek church. The internal element which it contains did not become a motive for the regulation of piety. To believe means " simply to obey," *i. e.*, the traditional doctrine, and how this can bring salvation to a man, cannot be made plain to the inner consciousness (see, *e. g.*, Cyril. cat. 5. 5 ; the homilies of Chrys. upon Romans 1. 17 ; 4. 7 ; 3. 21 ; Gal. 2. 8, 16 f.; Heb. 11). Faith is nothing more than the acceptance of a doctrine, with its mysteries and with the injunctions to the performance of pious works. But when faith has been robbed of its true character, the church must find for herself a substitute. The church

(cf. eccl. hier. iii. 3. 7) to that which Dionysius of Alexandria wrote against Novatian (Eus. h. e. vii. 8 f.); and also by the relation of a passage of the letter (§ 5) to the *ep. ad Cononem* of Dionys. Al., § 3 (in Pitra, jur. eccl. Graecorum hist. et Monum. i. 547 ; cf. 549 f.).

19

of the West chose "good works;" that of the East, worship
and its mysteries, mystic consecrations, relics and saints, amulets
and images.   Thus there is poured into the church the whole
current of religious materialism, which seeks to realize the
spiritual and eternal in sensuous, tangible and audible forms.
Christianity *is* participating in worship, subjection to ecclesiastical ordinances.   The sacred symbols are commended to the multitude, and the spirit of reverence for them cultivated—as in the
" dreadful hour " when the "terrible mystery " of the eucharist is presented (cf. Chrysost. de sacerdot. iii. 4 ; ep. ad Olym-
piad. 2. 2 init.; the 9th homily upon repentance).   This is represented as Christian piety.   The same may be said of all parts
of the " second order of Christianity," and even of the mystery of the dogmatic formulary itself.   The interest of the populace in the dogmatic controversies was, after all, only that of
veneration for a formula.   There is nothing left to awaken de-
vout longings and hold  reverence in the " beholder " (Dionys.
Ar.) but the venerated symbol.   Thus visible sacred symbols
were relied upon to lead the soul to the  vision of the spiritual :
" Since it is not possible for the spirit in our state to pass through
to that immaterial imitation and contemplation of the heavenly
hierarchies unless it makes use of the material guidance to it, we
regard the visible beautiful things as reflections of the invisible
loveliness, and the sensible odors as typifications of the spiritual
largess, and the material lights as images of the immaterial
glory, and the *sacred doctrines* as channels for the satisfying of
the mind contemplatively. . . .   In which way he would lead
us through things sensible to things spiritual " (Dionys. coel.
hier. 1. 3 ; eccl. hier. 1. 2, 4, 5 ; 3. 2 : "the multitude catching
a glimpse only of the divine symbols;" 3. 3. 12 ; 4. 3. 1).
It is the flourishing period of the *arcana disciplina*.

2. This reveals the fundamental thought of the work of
DIONYSIUS AREOPAGITA, which became so influential in the East.
(*a*) Christianity is the representation of the ladder of sacred
symbols, mysteries, consecrations, which come down from God
to men through the medium of divinely-enlightened hierarchs—
and the persuading of men to climb upward upon the ladder of
these mysteries to God.   Grace reveals itself in a complex of
purifying and consecrating mysteries.   In this connection, the
" hierarchy "—in a way peculiar to the Orient—finds its place.
(*b*) God is the unpredicated, supersubstantial Existence.   This
"primeval source " (div. nom. 1. 3, 5), this "darkness above
light " (theol. myst. 1. 1), this "unapproachable Light," and
this " divine darkness " (ep. 5) is not approachable to man.
But God allows himself to be known by man by means of the

hierarchical ladder. (c) The hierarchy is hence a sacred order and agency through which God, extending his energies from person to person, *purifies*, *illuminates*, and *perfects*—or actually *deifies*—those whom these energies reach (coel. hier. 3. 1, 2 ; 7. 2, 3 ; 9. 2 ; 10. 2 ; 12. 2 ; eccl. hier. 1. 1, 3 ; 5. 1. 4, 7 ; 6. 3. 6, 1, 3 : " For as one, in speaking of all taken together, calls the order of the priests a hierarchy, so evidently, when speaking of the chief priest (hierarch), he means the inspired and divine man who presides over all sacred knowledge. . . . The source of this hierarchy is the fountain of life . . . the one cause of existing things, the Triad, from whom come both existence and prosperity to existing things through his goodness. . . . And this is the common aim of the entire hierarchy, an intimate affection for God and divine things . . . the gnosis of existing things, in which all things exist . . . the vision and understanding of sacred truth, the inspired impartation of the unique perfection of this One as far as possible, the feast of contemplation spiritually nourishing and deifying him who attains to it "). (d) This hierarchy is primarily the heavenly hierarchy of angels, which in its three orders bears a graduated relation to the Deity (coel. hier. 4-9). Through it God revealed himself under the old covenant (ib. 4. 3). Then follows the earthly hierarchy, whose source, essence, and power is Jesus, the supremely-deified and supersubstantial mind (ὁ θεαρχικώτατος νοῦς καὶ ὑπερούσιος). Through him, or the Holy Trinity, according to the declarations of the sacred Scriptures, the hierarch is filled with divine knowledge and inducted into the "sacred and spiritual vision" (ib. 1. 2, 3 ; 3. 2. 1 fin.; 3. 3. 14). But there is here also a three-fold gradation (hierarch, priest, deacon), which is regarded as absorbing God, not in a local way, but according to capacity (ep. 8. 2), in which process purity becomes the portion of the deacons, illumination that of the priests, and perfection that of the hierarchs (cf. ib. 5. 1. 5, 6 ; 6. 3. 5). Furthermore, the incumbents of the higher orders possess also the endowments of the lower (ib. 5. 3. 7). (e) By means of the sacred mysteries, the hierarchs perform their official duties toward the people, purifying, enlightening, and perfecting them. These symbols are baptism (ib. 2), the eucharist (ib. 3), the holy oil (ib. 4), the consecration of the priesthood (ib. 5), monastic consecration (ib. 6 : "possessors of the most perfect philosophy"), consecrations and prayers for the dead (ib. 7). The aim of all these symbolical acts is union with God through the luxurious contemplation of his Being (coel. hier. 3. 2 ; eccl. hier. 1. 3): "Trinity more than nature, more than God, and more than good ! Thou guardian of the wisdom of Christians, lead us to the more than unknown and more than lofty and unapplauded summit of the mystic doctrines, where the simple and absolute and unchangeable mysteries of theology are veiled in the more-than-light darkness of the crypto-mystic science, shining with superlative brilliancy in the superlatively dark, and more than filling unfettered souls in the absolutely intangible and invisible (realm) of super-lovely glories" (theol. myst. 1 init.).[1] Rightly did a philosopher term our author a "patricide" (ep. 7. 2). The Neo-Platonic premises of this opponent of heathenism are everywhere very apparent. "All transitory things are but a parable—the insufficient here is that which occurs." Such is the Neo-Platonism of the Areopagite. It is a distinct expression of the Greek Christianity of a later period. The Christianity of dogmatic formulas has been paralyzed by the devotional symbols, although the veneration of formulas finds in this very devotional tendency its strongest support. The great majority were satisfied with the formula, and the latter might easily become a mere formula of enchantment.

3. Recognizing this fact, we feel that less importance attaches to the separate doctrines presented by the Areopagite. We must constantly keep in mind his fundamental principle. Greek Christianity evolved no "dogmas," in the strict sense of the term, except those above discussed. We note particularly the lack of interest in matters pertaining to personal religious life. Men spoke of sin and grace with the same unsophisticated piety, or unsophisticated rationalism, in the centuries following as in those preceding the Nicene period. The problems which held the interest of Augustine leave no trace in the East. Yet it would be incorrect to regard the Oriental church as Pelagian, as the problem upon which Pelagius and Augustine joined issue does not even occur to their minds.

The state of man fallen into sin is, after as before the Nicene age, painted in the darkest colors. The devil has gained possession of the soul ; the serpent dwells as a second soul within our own (Macar. hom. 15. 35, 49): "Thus the evil prince clothed the soul and its whole substance with sin, and polluted it entire, and made it entire a prisoner to his kingdom, and did not release nor set free from him a single part, not the reasoning powers, nor the spirit, nor the body, but he clothed the soul in a garment of darkness. . . . The evil one put upon the whole soul, i. e.,

---

[1] Observe the transcendental character of the Neo-Platonic conception of God. Of God, as the Absolute Existence, everything existent must be affirmed and again denied (div. nom. i. 5-7 ; 7. 3 ; theol. myst. 3-5, cataphatic and apophatic theology). This accounts for the many combinations with ὑπέρ and α privitive in the Areopagite.

the essential member and part of man, its malady, *i. e.*, sin, and thus the body became passible and mortal" (Macar. h. 2. 1; Marcus Erem. c. Nestor. 18). Thus the whole man, with all his powers, is imbued with sin. He is separated from God. The devil holds sway over his soul. Sensuality overpowers the reason. Man, originally destined for immortality, becomes transitory and subject to death—in all things the very opposite of his original character and condition (Greg. Nyss. cat. 5. Athanas. c. gent. 3 f. Dionys. eccl. hier. 3. 3. 11). He has forfeited grace and boldness toward God, and has won for himself "mortality and the dullness of the flesh." He is "sentenced to death" and "subject to perdition" (Joh. Dam. iii. 1), the emphasis being laid finally upon the latter. Sin is at the same time regarded not so much in the aspect of guilt as in that of infirmity or weakness—of mortality and death. This is a different attitude from that of the West. It directs the thoughts not only upon the forgiveness of sins, but upon the contemplation of the state of sin and its conquest by means of a new inner life.

That the entire human race fell into this condition through the fall of Adam is acknowledged. But, although the idea of the inheritance of sin may at times appear to be advanced (Greg. Nyss. cat. 16 : "The pleasurable pain of human birth teaches   .   .   . the beginning of death, having been made in one, has passed through upon the whole human nature" (de orat. 5): "to speak again of the common debts of human nature, in which each and everyone who shares the lot of nature bears a part" (Oehler iii. 300. Dionys. Ar. eccl. hier. 3. 3. 11 : "Having had its origin in corrupt births, it naturally pursues its course in a way conformable to its beginning"), yet it is only meant, after all, that since Adam the human race has been subject to corruption. In view of the conflict between the spiritual and the sensuous inclinations of man, it is difficult, or altogether impossible, to abstain entirely from sin (Greg. Nyss. l. c., p. 302). Hence we occasionally find new-born children referred to as "sinless" (Cyril. cat. 4. 19 init.); or we read of "many" who have kept themselves "free from sin" (as Jeremiah and John); or the opinion is expressed that this would have been possible if obedience had been rendered to the law (Athanas. c. Arianos serm. iii. 33 ; de incarn. 12). Commenting upon Rom. 5. 19, Chrysostom remarks that it is inconceivable that we should have become sinners through Adam's sin, but that we through Adam's sinning and becoming mortal have also become mortal. It is not meant that all are in Adam sinners, but that we have through him become mortal and thereby lost the power to give to the spirit dominion over sensuality.  The terrible thing is not guilt, but subjection to death.  " But whence did the evil spirit come and take up its abode with him?  It first assailed him from without through the nearing, then proceeded through his heart, and took possession of his whole being, and thus, he being subjugated, the whole creation beneath and above him was carried along with him " (the illustration of a chained nobleman with his vassals led after him has been used in the context).  " For through him death gained dominion over every living soul and darkened the whole likeness of Adam on account of his sin, so that men were transformed and came to the worship of demons " (Macar. hom. 11. 5; cf. 12. 1).  Marcus Eremita says likewise, that, since Adam had been given over to death on account of his sin, "we have all, whether sinners or righteous, fallen from eternal life " (adv. Nestor. 18).  Only death and not sin, properly speaking, is inherited.  The latter is expressly denied by Marcus (de baptism. Gallandi viii. 50 D; 54 B).  Thus Adam is to blame for the wretchedness which has resulted, since it was through him that death gained the mastery and ruined the original image of Adam in us.  There has, however, remained to man the *liberty* of deciding for God when grace is offered to him. This is the conclusion to which the view in question leads.  The soul is free and lord of itself; the devil cannot drive it to do anything against its will, and God will not do so, since righteousness would otherwise not receive its merited crown (Cyril. cat. 4. 21. Macar. h. 15. 40; 27. 9, 11. Joh. Dam. ii. 25 ff.). There still remains something good, therefore, in every man. It is his inner nature, his reason, or free will.  Only a stimulus is needed, and man can then decide in favor of the good.  But the free will is always in such connections innocently embraced in the thought, as a " good co-operation ($\sigma \upsilon \nu \acute{\epsilon} \rho \gamma \epsilon \iota \alpha \; \alpha \gamma \alpha \vartheta \acute{\eta}$) for the attainment of salvation " (Maxim. i. 414).  But it is also often strongly insisted that no one can by his own strength overcome or drive out sin, and that to accomplish this divine help is always necessary (Macar. h. 2. 4; 3. 4. Greg. Naz. or. 37. 13). "And it is not the case, as some, misled by false doctrines, say, that man is totally dead and utterly unable to do anything good.  For even a child, although it is not able to accomplish anything, nor to walk upon its feet to its mother, yet rolls upon the ground and calls and cries because it yearns for its mother.  And this moves the mother's heart to pity, and she is pleased that her child, with struggle and outcry, seeks to come to her.  And although the child cannot come to her, yet the mother, in view of this great yearning of the child, goes to it, constrained by love for the child, takes it up and cherishes and feeds it, with great love:

this does also the man-loving God for the soul that approaches
and yearns for him '' (Macar. h. 46. 3). It may be said, in
brief, that the Fathers of this period remained throughout the
entire range of their teaching upon the basis of the second and
third centuries (vid. supra, p. 115 f., 139, 157). The fall of
Adam made us mortal, giving free reign to sensuality. Since
Adam, we are all sinners. Without his help there is no salvation.
But we, by virtue of our liberty, may secure and accept his
assistance.

4. The redemption achieved by Christ brings salvation. Here,
too, the ideas of the past are adopted, without reduction or revision. In accordance with the conception of the primitive
church, salvation is, first of all, dependent upon the death of
Christ. The Damascene summarizes as follows : '' For the whole
activity and wonder-working of Christ is most great and divine
and wonderful ; but his precious cross is the most wonderful of
all. For by nothing else was death destroyed, the sin of our
first parent atoned for, hell despoiled, resurrection bestowed,
power given to us to disdain things present and death itself, the
restoration to original blessedness accomplished, the gates of paradise opened, our nature seated at the right hand of God, we
made children of God and heirs of heaven—but through the
cross of our Lord Jesus Christ. For through the cross have
all things been set right '' (fid. orth. iv. 11 ; cf. iii. 20). This,
of course, does not set forth all the ideas accepted in the period,
as such summaries never do (Eusebius demonstr. ev. iv. 12 and
esp. Epiphan. ancor. 65). The ancient ideas are developed
more at length : the innocent Christ became a sacrifice, a ransom, which was brought to the Father that we might be made
free from condemnation (Joh. Dam. iii. 27). It is also asserted
that he intercedes with the Father for us (Greg. Naz. or. 30.
14). On the other hand, he has by his death freed us from the
dominion of the devil (ib. iv. 4. Dionys. eccl. hier. 3. 3. 11).
At the same time we find in its crassest form the idea, that he ransomed us from the devil by making satisfaction for Adam's guilt
(Macar. h. 11. 10). The devil had a certain right to man,
whom he had made his slave through lust. The justice of God
prevented him from snatching us from the devil by force. Therefore Christ was offered to him as an object of exchange and ransom. In this is displayed the kindness of God toward us, and
his justice toward the devil. But his wisdom also appears in the
transaction. In order not to alarm the devil at the outset, the
divinity of Christ is concealed in the flesh. With the bait of
the flesh the devil swallows also the fishhook of the divinity.
Since life now appears in death, death is brought to nought.

The devil is outwitted (thus Greg. Nyss. cat. 22-24 ; cf. Cyril.
cat. 12. 15). Gregory of Nazianzum, indeed, rejected this
offering of a ransom to the devil as outrageous (ὕβρις), as did
also the Damascene (Greg. or. 45. 22 ; Joh. fid. orth. iii. 27):
but they did not altogether break away from the idea (vid. Greg.
or. 39. 13. Joh. fid. orth. iii. 1). In this, as in the sacrifice
brought to God, is manifested the goodness, justice, and wisdom of God (Cyril. cat. 13. 33. Greg. cat. 23. Joh. Dam.
iii. 1).[1]

But the real central thought of the Greeks in connection with
the doctrine of redemption was, after all, a different one. The
conceptions of sin which we have traced are based not so
much upon the idea of deliverance from the torment of the devil
and from the wrath of God, as upon the thought that we are to
receive life and be freed from the power of the devil. The controlling conception here was that, since God himself entered the
human race in Christ, humanity has been deified and made immortal—a conception which may be traced back through Athanasius, Methodius, Irenæus, and Ignatius to John. We have
cited passages of this character from Athanasius, the Cappadocians, and Cyril of Alexandria (supra, pp. 212 ff., 251, 255).
" For, since he has made us partakers of his own image and his
own spirit, and we have not guarded it, he in exchange became
partaker of our dull and weak nature, in order that he might
purify and immortalize us, and make us again partakers of his
divinity" (Joh. Dam. iv. 13). Since one member of the body
of humanity (Christ's body) becomes immortal, the whole body
of humanity becomes so : "just as when anyone of all the race is
alive, the resurrection of the part, being communicated from the
part to the whole, penetrates the whole in consequence of the
continuity and unity of the nature " (Greg. Nyss. cat. 32).
The Logos assumed a " man, who became a divine man
(κυριακὸς ἄνθρωπος) in order that we might thereby become
what he is. The Logos became flesh in order that the flesh
might become Logos" (Marc. Er. ad Nicol. 9). The object of the creation, and likewise of the incarnation, is that we
may secure a part in the divine nature and in eternity (Maxim.

[1] Also the power of God : That the almighty nature is even able to conde-
scend to the humble things of humanity is a greater display of power than the
great and supernatural features of the miracles. . . . What an overflow of
the power that knows no restraint in things beyond nature is the condescension
to humble things (Greg. Nyss. cat. 24 init.). Gregory denies the charge that
his theory of the outwitting of the devil introduces a fraud, maintaining that
justice demands that the deceiver be deceived, and, moreover, the latter will
by this means be himself restored in the end (ib. 26 ; as to the restoration, see
also 35 fin.).

i. 519, 525). God's will in regard to man is the deification (ϑέωσις) of the latter (ib. i. 345). The religious application of these ideas may be studied in Athanasius (vid. supra, p. 212 ff.). The deification of man is, on the one hand, a mystical conception. Man is drawn up into the Eternal Existence. In the symbols of worship the Eternal Existence comes near to him. He through them feels himself one with God, and has become a partaker of the divine nature, or of immortality. But these ideas are always capable of a spiritual interpretation. With them is intimately connected the thought, that Christ is the lawgiver, pattern, and example. Christ restores again in and through himself the original nobility of human nature together with immortality, but he imparts this to us by teaching us the knowledge of God and virtue. This idea is very distinctly expressed by John Damascenus (iv. 4): "In order that through and in himself he might restore that which was according to (his) image and likeness, and might teach us the excellent way, having through himself made it easy of ascent for us, and in order that, having become the first fruits of our resurrection, he might in the fellowship of life free us from corruption and restore the antiquated and shattered tabernacle, having called us to the knowledge of God in order that we might be ransomed from the tyranny of the devil . . . and that he might teach us to overthrow the tyrant by patience and humility." Good works are, therefore, by no means excluded by the deification of the believer. On the contrary, the path of deification is the path of virtue. Man attains the divine life of Christ by striving for the holy innocence preserved by him (Dionys. eccl. hier. 3. 3. 12. Joh. Dam. iv. 13; iii. 1. Greg. cat. 35).

It remains only to observe how this conception of Soteriology fits into the general view of Christianity presented by the Areopagite. The consciousness of being deified and immortal was to be awakened by the mystical worship in its intimate association with the imagination and the senses, and the demand for instruction and ethical inspiration was met by the symbolical acts. "How otherwise could the imitation of God be engendered in us than by our having the recollection of the most holy works of God constantly refreshed in the sacred benedictions and services?" (Dionys. eccl. hier. 3. 3. 12 init.; cf. 11). The symbol is the actual presence of that which is symbolized: "The sign of Christ (the cross) is, therefore, to be worshiped; for wherever the sign is, there will he also be" (Joh. Dam. iv. 11, p. 265). We must, therefore, be careful not to understand the term, deification, which has a strange sound to our ears, in a one-sided, physical way, as do Ritschl and Harnack. There is not lacking in it, indeed, the hyperphysical hypnosis of natural mysticism, wrought by means of the holy symbols. But this does not exhaust its content. It always embraces also the inward, gracious, moralistically conceived influence of Christ. The worshiper becomes one with the immortal Christ, but this embraces as a means the keeping of his commandments and the imitation of his divine life.

5. This bring us to the means by which salvation is to be appropriated. With the increased importance attached to the forms of worship is intimately associated a comparative neglect of indoctrination looking to the moving of the will. Of course, there is still some effort to arouse the will by instruction and the Scriptures.[1] But the chief means relied upon were the formula and form of worship. Worship naturally centred about the ancient ecclesiastical sacraments (especially the eucharist). To these were added further mysteries (chrism, priestly and monastic consecration, prayers for the dead ; see the Areopagite, p. 291). Then followed a whole array of mystic signs and consecrations. Thus there was a veneration of the cross, the nails, the lance, the clothes of Christ, the manger, the socket of the cross, etc. (Joh. Dam. iv. ii. Cyril. cat. 4. 10 ; 13. 6). The saints who intercede for us in heaven are to be adored (e. g., Greg. Naz. or. 43. 80), as also the "mother of God" (e. g., Greg. Naz. or. 24. 11. Joh. Dam. iv. 16) and the relics of the saints : "Christ the Lord gives us as fountains of salvation the relics of the saints, pouring forth blessings in many ways, distilling the oil of a sweet odor. Let no one neglect them" (Joh. Dam. iv. 15, p. 278). Amulets and images must be added to the list (e. g., Chrysost. ad cat. 2. 5. Joh. Dam. iv. 16). These were all means of salvation, "for where the sign is, there will he himself also be" (p. 297). But to what an extent this paganized Christianity, with its demoralizing faith in miracles and demons, had forced its way into the church, may be seen most strikingly in the biographies of the holy ascetics.[2]

---

[1] See e. g. Macar. hom. 39 : The Holy Scriptures are letters of the King to us. Similarly Chrysost. in 2 Thes. hom. 3. 4. We meet very frequently in the homilies of Chrysostom discussions of the practical significance of the reading of the Scriptures and urgent exhortations to the practice of it ; e. g., in Col. hom. 9. 1 ; in 1 Thes. hom. 7. 3 ; in 1 Tim. hom. 13. 1 ; in 2 Tim. hom. 8. 3. 4 ; 9. 1 ; de poenit. hom. 4. 1. Vid. also Cyril. catech. 4. 35 ; 9. 13 ; 16. 2 ; 17. 34. Athanasius, Festal Letter 39, in ZAHN, Gesch. d. Kanons ii. 212. Marc. Er. de leg. spirit. 4 ff., 24. 87. Upon the pedagogical significance of the Bible, see in Eph. hom. 21. 1 ff. ; cf. Basil. serm. 22. 2 (de legendis libr. gentilium, ep. 2. 3). Also, Joh. Dam. iv. 17. In addition to this is the reading of the Scripture in religious services, see Dionys. eccl. hier. 3. 2 ; 3. 3. 4. and the liturgies.

[2] Harnack DG., ii. 442, n.: "It fell to the lot of monasticism, especially in

These life-portraits make a wonderful impression. Here the miracle still survives. Here visions and revelations are yet the order of the day. The old Grecianism appears to be unconquered ; only all has become more crude and coarse. The entire range of Hellenic superstition finds covert in the manifestations of the Spirit. Yet, in the midst of all these strange phenomena, it must not be forgotten that there still remained, in the consciousness of the presence of God, an element of true religion ; but it is, it must be confessed, a sensualized and externalized religion. In close relationship to these things stood also the sacraments. Under the circumstances, even the relatively small interest attaching to each of these must follow the lines of the general theory of the sacraments. Distinction is made between the metabolic and the symbolic view ; but there is no good reason for ascribing credit to the advocates of the former, for it is commonly among them that the spiritual and religious character of Christianity is most seriously misunderstood. In addition to this, the distinction above noted is a modern one, and cannot be detected in the period under review. The symbol—as was in a Neo-Platonic way conceived—is the reality. In the symbolic act, the reality itself is received. " The things sensibly sacred are images of the things perceived in thought and a guide and way to them " (Dionys. hier. eccl. 2. 3. 2). In picture or cross, in water or in bread and wine, Christ himself is present and is imparted (cf. also HARNACK DG. ii. 429).

6. Of the separate sacraments, BAPTISM is effectual in laying the foundation of the Christian life. It brings to the individual regeneration and renewal, and makes him a member of the church (Basil. serm. 13. 4, 7). Hence, in contrast with the misguided custom of the fourth century, it was urged that its administration be not postponed (Basil. serm. 13. Greg. Naz. or. 40. Chrys. ad catechum. i. 1, cf. Joh. Dam. iv. 9 fin.). The requirements for its reception were faith, as a recognition of the doctrine of the Trinity (Basil. de spir. s. 12. 28. Greg. Nyss. cat. 39. Joh. Dam. iv. 9), and a penitent frame of mind (Cyril cat. 3. 15). It effects the blotting out of sins, which are " washed away as with a flood " (Chrys. in Rom. hom. 2. 6), and the new life in Christ ; and it bestows immortality. " Baptism, release to the imprisoned, the pardon of debts, the death of sin, the new birth of the soul, a garment of light, an inviolable seal, a chariot to heaven, an ambassador of the kingdom, the chrism of sonship "

the East, to play the role of mediary between the Christianity of the first and that of the second type. It contributed, perhaps, more than any other influence, to introduce the watchwords of the former into the latter and the spirit of the latter into the former."

(Basil. ep. 189. 5. sermo 13. 5 closely following Cyril. procat.
16 init. Greg. Nyss. cat. 33, 35). There are references also to
the dying of the old and the arising of the new man, as set forth
in Rom. 6. If we meet the term "forgiveness of sins" frequently, the idea conveyed by it is that of a κάθαρσις or καθάρσιον,
*i. e.*, the cleansing, or blotting out, of sin in the individual (Chrys.
ad catechum. 1. 3. Greg. Naz. or. 39. 1, 14. Cyril cat. 3.
4): although "not indeed completely banishing" (Greg. Nyss.
cat. 35). But baptism imparts to the individual the obligation
and impulse to "follow Christ by imitation." It is now his
duty, striving to walk in the footsteps of Christ, to contend
against sin, and thus, since God has healed the wounds of the
past, to guard against new offenses in the future, or to heal them
by repentance (Cyril. cat. 18. 20; cat. myst. 2. 5, 6. Basil. de
sp. s. 15. 35; sermo 13. 1 fin. Greg. Nyss. cat. 35, 40. Const.
ap. ii. 7. Chrys. ad catechum. 1. 4. Dionys. eccl. hier. 2.
3. 7. Joh. Dam. iv. 9, 13). With this, the sacrament assumes
a tangible and practical character. The mystery in some way
blots out sin, but its chief significance lies in its symbolic stimulus to the recipient himself to strive against sin and overcome it.
The question as to the relation between the visible symbol and
the divine agency is answered by "the divine being present with
the occurrences," or "by the ceremony being performed in accordance with divine directions" (Greg. Nyss. cat. 34). The
important point was, that the presence of God is not lacking in
the observance of the outward symbol : "for the things seen are
symbols of the things spiritually discerned" (Joh. Dam. iv. 9).
Essentially, it made but little difference whether it was said : "if
there is any grace in the water, it is not from the nature of the
water, but from the presence of the Spirit" (Basil. sp. s. 15.
35), or whether the "sanctifying power dwelling in the water"
(Cyril. cat. 3. 3 ; but see also cat. myst. 2. 5) was spoken of, or
it was said : "By the energy of the Spirit the visible water is
transmuted (ἀναστοιχειοῦται) into a certain divine and indescribable power, and it furthermore sanctifies those among whom
it may be found" (Cyril. Al. in Joh. under 3. 5, Mi. 73. 245).
Under all forms of expression, there is the conception of the
mystery which has been above outlined. But he who has now
become pure in baptism must contend against sin, and, if he is
overcome, repent, since repentance (μετάνοια) is the fulfillment
of the commands of Christ. In accordance with the Greek
conception of sin, the idea in repentance was not only the satisfaction rendered to God in order to secure forgiveness, as in the
West, but rather a discipline for amendment, an inward purification and sanctification. Thus Clement and Origen had regarded

the matter (vid. supra). Something of this idea long lingered, even in the presence of the ecclesiastical ordinance of penitential discipline. The duty of confessing all their sins—even their secret thoughts—which was imposed by Basil upon the monks, was not, indeed, extended to the laity (vid., *e. g.*, Chrysost. hom. 4; in Laz. 4); but the injunction to confess sin to God, in order thereby to deepen one's own conviction of sin, was often repeated in homiletic exhortations (ib.). Upon the history of the ordinance of public repentance in the Greek church the History of Doctrines has no occasion to enter (cf. HOLL, l. c., p. 240 ff.).

The EUCHARIST is, above all, enwrapped in the awe of mystery, as the chief symbol (ἀρχισύμβολον, Dionys. hier. eccl. iii. 1; 2. 1, cf. supra, p. 290), since all the angels hover around the priest as he offers the "awful sacrifice" (Chrys. de sacerd. vi. 4, and accounts by him of actual appearances of angels). Regarded from a dogmatic point of view (cf. STEITZ's discussions of the doctrine of the Greek church concerning the Lord's Supper, in Jarbb. f. d. Theol., vols. ix.-xiii.), we may distinguish a more scientific symbolic tendency from the practical metabolic view, a difference which did not, however, produce any actual conflict (cf. p. 299). Basil says, for example: "He called his whole mystic life (ἐπιδημία) flesh and blood, and taught a doctrine composed of practical and natural and theological elements, by which the soul is nourished and meanwhile prepared for the contemplation of things existing" (ep. 8. 4 fin.). Other teachers speak in a similar way of spiritual food, or spiritual reception of the flesh of Christ (Athan. ad Serap. iv. 19; in ps. 80. 17. Macar. hom. 27. 17). But it is not hereby intended to question a real presence of Christ. The difference between this and the metabolic view is, therefore, not so great. The latter regards Christ as himself miraculously dwelling in the elements. This is very plainly taught by Cyril of Jerusalem in his "mystagogical catechisms." By means of the invocation, the miracle of Cana is repeated; the bread becomes body, and the wine blood (i. 7; iii. 3; iv. 1, 2). We are not to allow ourselves to be deceived by the sense of taste (iv. 6, 9). On the contrary, we call upon God "to send forth the Holy Spirit upon that which lies before us, in order that he may make the bread the body of Christ and the wine the blood of Christ. For, if the Holy Spirit should touch this at all, it would be sanctified and changed (μεταβέβληται)." But with this we must also keep in mind the declaration: "For in the type of bread is given to thee the body, and in the type of wine is given to thee the blood, in order that, partaking of the body and blood of Christ, thou mayest become of the same body and blood (*σύσσωμος* and *σύναιμος*) with him '' (iv. 3). Now this body of Christ imparts itself to our body and makes it a partaker of the divine nature (iv. 3 ; v. 15), and thus the eucharist works for us immortality. The Origenist, Gregory of Nyssa, expresses himself in essentially the same way in his ''large catechism '' (c. 37). As the soul is purified in baptism through faith, so the eucharist bestows an antidote for the poison which has penetrated the body : '' The body (of Christ) immortalized by God, being in ours, tranforms and changes the whole into that body itself.'' Bread and wine, as the natural means of nourishment, are the potency of every body, including that of Christ. Hence, it is said : '' Well do we, therefore, now believe that the bread consecrated by the word of God is transformed into the body of the divine Logos.'' But the design of this is ''in order that, by this union with the immortal, man might also become a partaker of incorruptibility.'' During the Christological controversies it became customary to regard the body of Christ, spoken of in connection with the Lord's Supper, as identical with the body which the Lord bore when on earth (thus Cyril. Al., supra, p. 262, cf. Chrys. in Tit. hom. 2. 4 ; in Eph. hom. 3. 3). Here again the Damascene summarizes the thought for us (orth. fid. iv. 13): He who framed for us a body from the blood of the Virgin, by the power of the Spirit also changes bread and wine into body and blood. The elements are now not ''a type of the body and blood '' (pp. 271, 273), nor are they the body come down from heaven ; but they are transformed : '' The body is truly the body from the Holy Virgin united with divinity, not that the ascended body comes down from heaven, but that the bread and wine are transformed into the body and blood of God '' (p. 269). A remarkable conclusion, which reveals how little of a religious character attaches to this system ! The purpose of the bestowal of the body and blood is the forgiveness of sins—but, above all, unification with Christ ; and this means deification, or the bestowal of immortality (pp. 271, 272). To this is added ''communing, and being through this united with one another '' (p. 273).

Side by side with this line of interpretation runs the other, which regards the eucharist in the light of the '' unbloody, mystic, God-appeasing sacrifice,'' as a repetition of the sacrifice of Christ (Euseb. vit. Const. iv. 45. Joh. Dam. de imag. or. 2. 17. Chrysost. de poenit. hom. 9), which only a priest can administer (Chrysost. de sacerd. iii. 4, 5 ; vi. 4), and which is efficacious for the living and the dead (Eus. l. c. iv. 71. Chrysost. in 1 Cor. hom. 41. 5 init. Greg. Naz. ep. 240).

§ 28. *Iconoclastic Controversies. Final Dogma of the Greek Church.*

LITERATURE. Vid. the Byzantine chronographies in Corp. sacr. hist. Byz., esp. Theophanes Chronographia, edited by DE BOOR, 1883. For details of the proceedings, vid. M. Act. conc. xii., xiii. JOH. DAMASC. de imaginibus orat. tres. THEODOR. STUDITA, opp., in Mi. 99. Also the modern delineations of WALCH, Ketzerhist. vol. x. HEFELE CG. iii., ed. 2, 366 ff. HERGENRÖTHER, Kirchengesch. I. 528 ff. HARNACK DG. ii. 450 ff. SCHWARZLOSE, Der Bilderstreit ein Kampf der griech. Kirche um ihre Eigenart u. um ihre Freiheit, 1890. THOMAS, Theod. von Studion u. seine Zeitalter, Leipz., 1892. BONWETSCH, PRE. iii., ed. 3, 222 ff.

The 36th canon of the synod of Elvira (A. D. 306, or, perhaps, as early as A. D. 300) reads: "It seems good to us that there ought not to be pictures in the church, nor should that which is worshiped and adored be painted upon the walls." This principle was carried out also in decisions and in action (Eus. ep. ad Constantiam, Mi. 20. 1545, cf. h. e. vii. 18. Epiph. opp. ed. Dindorf iv. 2, p. 85). But it was not the view of the theologians which influenced public conviction in the matter, but the latter compelled the acquiescence of the teachers (*e. g.*, in Joh. Dam. or. i. 27; 2. 23; 3. 42). It was an outgrowth of the exaggerated culture of mysteries (p. 290).[1]

That an assault upon images should cause a profound excitement, may be readily understood. It is not so easy to discern the motive which prompted it. Neither respect for the Jews nor regard for the Saracens can have been the stimulating force. The Emperor LEO THE ISAURIAN appears to have received the suggestion from Phrygia (Bishop Constantine of Nicolaea). To a man holding a legalistic conception of the Old Testament, the idea seemed self-evident (the imperial edict based its argument upon the Old Testament prohibition of images, Ex. 20. 4; 2 Ki. 18 4; cf. Joh. Dam. or. i. 4 ff., and the first letter of Pope Gregory to the emperor); and it was as natural for the emperor to command the church in the matter as the limitation of the latter's power was desirable.[2] In A. D. 726 the emperor forbade the worship of images (HEFELE iii. 378 ff.), on the ground that they take the place of the idols of the heathen, and that the worship of them is forbidden in the Scriptures. We dare not worship "stones, walls, and boards." With the approval of the patriarch Anastasius, the agitation was renewed in A. D. 730.

Energetic opposition was at once aroused upon the part of the

---

[1] The controlling idea, that God is present in pictures of the Deity, is antique (see the Apologetes) and Neo-Platonic (see Zeller, Philos. der Griechen iii. 2, ed. 3, pp. 626, 697).

[2] The discussion by SCHWARZLOSE (p. 45 ff.) of the imperial "politics" is not satisfactory.

people as well as among the theologians, *e. g.*, GERMANUS of
Constantinople (in M. xiii. 100 ff.), GREGORY II. of Rome
(M. xii. 959 ff.), JOHN OF DAMASCUS (Mi. 94. 1227 ff.).
Appeal was made to tradition and custom, to the miracles
wrought through the images, to which at any rate only veneration (*προσκύνησις*) and not worship (*λατρεία*) was rendered, to
the cherubim, etc.    The Roman bishop also reflected that " the
dogmas of the church are not an affair of the emperor, but of
the bishops," and pointed to the position of Peter "whom the
kingdoms of the West regard as the earthly God," at the same
time, in the most offensive manner, charging the emperor with
outrageous folly.[1]

John of Damascus published a comprehensive defense of the
images.    The images of Christ and the saints may and must be
honored, not, indeed, by divine worship (or. 3. 29 ff.), but by
veneration.    God himself is the originator of the use of images,
having sanctioned it by the method of Old Testament revelation,
the forms of Old Testament worship, and his own visible appearance in Christ (or. 3. 12, 18, 21 ff., 26 ; 1. 14, 20 ff.).
Everything on earth is a picture of God (1. 11).    The spiritual,
and, therefore, the revelation of God, can be revealed to us only
through matter (*ὕλη*).    We honor the images just as we honor
the gospels, the eucharist, the cross, the spear and sponge, or
Golgotha (1. 16 ; 2. 14, 19)—not the materials composing
them as such (2. 19), but as being bearers of the divine.
The controlling idea of the age here finds expression : " Things
made by our hands are holy, leading us through matter
to the immaterial God (2. 23), through bodily vision to
spiritual vision" (3. 12, 25).    We must either surrender
our veneration for the "parchments of the gospels" written with ink, and for the elements of the eucharist, or acknowledge " the veneration of images of God and of the precious things consecrated to the name of God, and thus overshadowed by the grace of the divine Spirit " (2. 14).    Images
are, therefore, means of grace, since the material copy brings to
us God himself ("therefore I revere, *σέβω*, and through the
unseen draw near and venerate, the material object through which
salvation comes to me.    But I revere it not as divine, but as
filled with divine energy and grace," 2. 14).    Such character is
possessed by them not only as the " books of the unlearned "
(3. 9).    Hence, to deny them veneration is Manichæism (1. 16 ;

---

[1] SCHWARZLOSE'S attack upon the genuineness of the two letters of Gregory
has not convinced me.    We may, at the most, acknowledge some alterations,
which may perhaps be charged to the account of a contemporary Byzantine
translator, who was familiar with the writings of the Damascene upon images.

2. 13). Not only does God himself, with his whole revelation to man, thus defend the veneration of images, but it is just as fully supported by the tradition of the church (1. 27, 23; 2. 23; 3. 42). To abandon the veneration of images is a worse offense than fornication (3. 13). At any rate, the emperor has nothing to do with the inner life of the church : "The emperor's sphere is the right conduct of political affairs; the management of ecclesiastical affairs is the province of pastors and teachers" (2. 12).

To the punctilious legality and Cæsaropapy of the emperor is here opposed the historically well-defined Greek Christianity, not without suggesting the idea—in spite of recent events—of the independence of the church. In so far the worshipers of images were right. But it is Christianity as represented in the lower form which magically sinks the spiritual in the material (*e. g.*, power of images against demons, 1. 27, p. 231; miracles performed by them, 1. 22; 3. 41—hence religious veneration). In this—impartially considered—lies the error of the image worshipers, and of the piety of the church which they represented.

It must be left to Church History to trace the outward course of the resulting controversies. CONSTANTINE V. (Copronymus, A. D. 741-775) proceeded against the images with the greatest energy, particularly after an insurrection of their defenders under his brother-in-law, Artabasdus, had most seriously endangered his throne. A general council was now planned to set the stamp of ecclesiastical authority upon the emperor's view. It met at Constantinople, A. D. 754 (see the *horos* of the council in M. xiii. 205 ff.). Since the devil could not tolerate the adornment of "glorious doctrines" in the church, he was constantly re-introducing idolatry. As God in ancient times equipped the apostles to contend against ancient idolatry, so now has he endowed the apostolic emperors with the spirit of wisdom for the conflict against images. The council realizes that the "iniquitous art of painting" reviles the incarnation of Christ, since Christ can be painted only by a Nestorian separation, or by a Eutychian confusion, of the divine and the human. Bread and wine in the Lord's Supper are the only authorized pictures of Christ. The Scriptures forbid images (Jn. 4. 24 ; Deut. 5. 8 ; Rom. 1. 23, 25, etc.). Accordingly, images dare neither be made, nor placed in churches or private houses, nor kept in secret. Any cleric who violates the prohibition shall be removed from office ; any layman or monk so transgressing anathematized, in which case he is amenable to the civil law as "an opponent of the commandments of God, and an enemy of the dogmas of

20

the Fathers.'' These decrees were executed with great energy. The clergy yielded, but the monks resisted. Pictures were destroyed, plastered over, or replaced with landscape and hunting views. The emperor pursued all who resisted with terrible cruelty. The monks were treated with special severity. The emperor went so far as to forbid the veneration of relics and prayers to the Virgin Mary and the saints (Theophan., p. 439 ; cf. Cedrenus, hist. compend. ed. Bekker ii., p. 3).

Leo IV. (Chazarus, A. D. 775-780) espoused the principles of his father, but his cunning and ambitious wife, Irene, was friendly to the images. After the death of her consort, she felt herself constrained, in order to retain her position as guardian of her son, to depend upon the support of the image-venerating party (cf. Ranke, Weltgesch. v. 89, 91 f.). Advancing by slow stages, she crowned her efforts by securing the assembly of the Seventh Ecumenical Council at Nicaea, A. D. 787. The members of this council approved the veneration of images, supporting it by the Scriptures (ark of the covenant and cherubim, Gen. 32. 24), and a great number of patristic citations, and refuting at length the *horos* of A. D. 754. The council's own *horos* laid stress upon the assertion, that it held to the doctrines of the first six ecumenical councils. With respect to images, it was maintained, with appeal to tradition, that veneration is to be shown, as to the cross, so also to images of Christ, of the stainless lady, the angels and saints, whether depicted in colors or on stone, upon vessels, clothing, walls, or on the streets : '' for, as often as they are seen from time to time in pictorial representation, so often are those who behold them incited to the recollection of and desire for the prototypes, and to render to them affection and deep veneration ; not, indeed, true worship according to our faith, which is properly rendered only to the divine nature, but in such a way as to the symbol of the precious and life-giving cross and to the holy gospels, and to the other sacred objects, and to make a presentation of incense and lights for the honor of such, as it was customary among the ancients piously to do. For the honor rendered to the image passes over to the prototype.'' Clerics refusing to conform to these requirements are to be deposed, laymen excommunicated. The decree was subscribed by those present. With loud salutations of the new Helena and the new Constantine, and with abundant anathemas against all heretics, especially such as refuse to venerate the images and reject tradition, the seventh and chief session closed. A feature of Greek Christianity was saved, but it is a peculiar illustration of the irony of history, that the same city, Nicaea, in which the first dogma was framed, was also the birthplace of this last Greek dogma. The two councils of Nicaea mark the course of Greek Christianity—from dogma to images.

The further history of the iconoclastic controversies does not belong to the sphere of the History of Doctrines. The restitution of the images naturally followed, and was accomplished without bloodshed. The superstitious practices in connection with images passed all bounds (see passages in THOMAS, Theod. v. Studion, p. 101). The Armenian, LEO V., renewed the warfare against them. MICHAEL II. (Balbus), and THEOPHILUS followed in his steps. But the populace and the monks, led by the powerful abbot of Studion, THEODORE, resisted, despite all oppressive measures (THOMAS, p. 98 ff.). THEODORA, the wife of Theophilus, restored the images, A. D. 842, and in celebration of this act it was appointed that the "festival of orthodoxy" should be annually celebrated.

With this, the dogma of the Greek church reaches its consummation; for neither the separation between the Greek and Roman churches (Photius, Michael Cerularius, A. D. 1054) nor the later attempts to unite them (A. D. 1274, 1439) fall within the domain of the general History of Doctrines. The same is to be said of the heretics in the Russian church and the great schism dating from the age of Nicon, A. D. 1654. The study of these agitations furnishes nothing beyond what has been presented in the two preceding paragraphs. As to the conditions of the present, see especially LE ROY BEAULIEU, das Reich der Zaren, vol. iii.

---

## CHAPTER IV.

FOUNDATION OF ANTHROPOLOGICAL DOGMA (SIN AND GRACE). DEVELOPMENT OF THE CHURCH IN THE WEST. DOCTRINE OF AUGUSTINE.

### § 29. *The Fundamental Religious Ideas of Augustine and His Place in the History of Doctrines.*

LITERATURE. The WORKS OF AUGUSTINE, Maurine ed., 11 vols., Paris, 1679 ff. Reprint edit. tertia Veneta (from which we quote), Migne Lat. 32-46. Cf. BINDEMANN, Der h. Aug., 3 vols., 1844 ff. BÖHRINGER, Aurel. Aug., ed. 2, 1877 f. DORNER, Aug., sein theol. System u. sein rel. phil. Anschauung, 1873. REUTER, Augustin. Studien, 1887. HARNACK DG. iii. 54 ff. FEUERLEIN, Aug. Stellung in der Kirchen. u. Kulturgesch., Hist. Ztschr. xxii. 270 ff. DILTHEY, Einleitung in die Geisteswissenschaft, 1. 335 ff. EUCKEN, Die Lebensanschauungen d. grossen Denker, 1890, p. 258 ff.

CUNNINGHAM, Saint Aug. and his Place in the History of Christian Thought, 1881. BESTMANN, Qua rat. Aug. notiones phil. graec. adhib., 1877. LÖSCHE, De Aug. plotinizante, 1880. STORZ, Die Philos. d. h. Aug., 1882. SCIPIO, Des Aur. Aug. Metaphysik im Ramen s. Lehre v. Uebel, 1886. SIE-BECK, Geschichte der Psychologie, i. 2, p. 381 ff.

The general conception of Christianity which prevailed in the Western church in the third century has been seen (p. 198) to have been that of a legal relationship between God and man, whose result is the salvation of souls (*salus animarum*). " The whole foundation of religion and faith proceeds from obedience and the fear of God" (*observatione ac timore*, Cyprian, de hab. virg. ii.; cf. supra, p. 194 f.). We have seen, further, that in the Trinitarian and Christological controversies the West maintained its characteristic position (illustrated in Tertullian, p. 125 f.; also pp. 237, 255). Nevertheless, the Renaissance movement in the Eastern church made itself felt even here, as is manifest in the views of HILARY, and no less in the writings of AMBROSE, who was largely dependent upon the Cappadocians (especially Basil), and in the prevalence of the allegorical method of exegesis (cf. also Jerome). Such a man as the orator Victorinus, in a way which reminds us of Augustine, applied the Neo-Platonic theory of ideas in the interest of Trinitarianism and— which is of special interest to us—was able to reproduce Paul's doctrine of justification, although not, indeed, without exhibiting a naive Pelagianism (vid. Mi. viii., also Dict. of Christ. Biograph. iv. 1129 ff. R. SCHMIDT, M. Victorinus Rhetor, KIEL, 1895). At the same time, the chacteristic ideas of the West were not lost sight of, but even more fully developed. In the doctrines of original sin and grace (where Tertullian is still the controlling influence, vid. p. 122; cf. also Cyprian and Commodian, p. 192), Ambrose largely anticipated Augustine (vid. supra). The agitation which prevailed throughout the Western church from the days of Augustine was not without its forerunners. AMBROSE was an Augustine before Augustine, and remained for the latter the controlling authority. But such a man as the Docetic TYCONIUS likewise prepared the way for Augustine, not only in his views concerning the church, but also by his emphasizing of grace. At this point begin the labors of Augustine, who combined in himself all the elements of the culture and religion of his age, and yet produced something quite new. He is the dominating force for the History of Doctrines in the West during the following periods. The ideas which he expressed gave birth to the dogmatic history of the West; the form of piety which he represented remained as a model, and became one of the most powerful co-efficients in the intellectual and spiritual life of the race. The labors of scholasticism no less than the emotions of the mystics, Roman hierarchy as well as the antihierarchical parties of the Middl Ages, Rome and Wittenberg, alike leaned upon him and found support (cf. Reu-TER, p. 479 ff.). His formulas, his statement of the perplexing problems of theology, and his religious temper, are constantly reappearing as we pursue the subsequent History of Doctrines. Even where an entirely different spirit is manifest, there is no escape from the masterful influence of his thoughts and terminology.

The history of his conversion is well known. AURELIUS AUGUSTINE (A. D. 354-430) was, despite his fervid sensuous temperament and the errors into which it led him, a noble soul, free from everything sordid. He was inspired with an intense yearning after truth and life. A disciple of the Manichæans, he was won by the glory of the Catholic church (conf. v. 14; vi. 1. 5, 11; vii. 19), the examples of her confessors (ib. viii. 2, 5, 6 f.), and the power of the grace of Christ (ib. vii. 5. 18 f.; viii. 8 ff.). The allegorical interpretations of Scripture in the preaching of the day (ib. vi. 5. 11; cf. vii. 1), the teaching of Paul (ib. vii. 21 init.; viii. 6), and the spirit of the Neo-platonic philosophy prepared the way for him into the communion of the church. The universal significance of Augustine results from his return to the original Christian temper of soul. He was from his youth distinguished by an insatiable longing for happiness, life, and wealth. Not quiet contemplation, but the utmost exertion of every power, was from the very beginning of his career the ideal of this daring genius. The will is the essential part of man. It turns away from God and toward nothingness. It is, accordingly, the cause of all misery. On the other hand, the new will, inspired by God, i. e., love, is the real blessing bestowed by divine grace. Only when God's will controls the will of man is man free (vid. conf. vii. 16. 22; viii. 5. 10; xiii. 10. 19; de civ. dei xxii. 22. 1; de sp. et lit. 30. 52). But God is the almighty Will, which controls and ordains all things. Over against and beneath the divine Will, stands the will of man. To be controlled and permeated by the will of God constitutes salvation and blessedness. Regarded from this point of view, religion is subjection to God in love. But from this same point all the positive and empirical ordinances of the church could appear to Augustine to exist rightfully, because designed and appointed by God. But to this principle of Augustine, which, in the last analysis, rested upon the primitive Christian recognition of the sovereignty of God and the subjection of the human will, was added the Neo-Platonic element in Augustine's sphere

of thought.  Fundamentally considered, it is the will which leads
man to knowledge.  That which is willed becomes a constituent
part of the soul, since the latter knows it.  " For certainly a
thing cannot be loved unless it is known" (de trin. x. 1. 2).  But
knowledge arises not only from the perception of these heavenly
truths.  There is innate in the soul an " interior sense," which
apprehends the nature of things through their intelligible forms
(per intelligibilem speciem, de civ. dei, xi. 27. 2).  This species
intelligibilis is not attained, but innate.  But here Augustine
launches out into the "intelligible world" of the Platonic system—into the contemplation of the ancient fantasies of the original forms of all existing things.  The contemplation of the eternal becomes for him—in genuinely Greek spirit—salvation (cf.
de quaest. oct. l. 46. 2).

These are the fundamental intellectual lines within which the
thought of Augustine moved.  First, voluntarism (God is Will
and man is will; love is blessedness).  Then, the Neo-Platonic
intellectualism (the contemplation of the intelligible world is
blessedness).  Both are, in a marvelous way, interwoven,
and over all lies the enchantment of inner and personal experience.

It was in the midst of earnest struggle that Augustine found
salvation in the fellowship of the living God, of whom he could
so impressively speak.  All that he has written bears the marks
of its origin in the depths of his personal life and earnest striving.  There exist for him but two great realities: God and the
Soul.  God is light, truth, life; in the soul dwell darkness,
misery, death.  But where the soul lays hold upon God and God
lays hold upon the soul, there is clearness of vision and the power
to do good—there is blessedness.  A few citations will best reveal this fundamental religious temper of the man : "What,
therefore, dost thou desire to know? . . .  State briefly.  God
and the soul I desire to know.  And nothing more?  Nothing at all."  But this limitation of interest is a consequent upon
the declaration : "I love nothing else but God and the soul"
(soliloq. i. 2, 7 ; viii. 15 ; xv. 27).  "Thou dost stir us up
to find delight in praising Thee, because Thou hast made us
for Thyself, and our heart is restless until it rests in Thee"
(conf. i. 1).  "For in this I sinned, that I sought pleasures,
sublimities, truths, not in Himself but in his creatures, myself
and others.  And thus I rushed into griefs, confusions, errors"
(ib. i. 20).  "Who will give to me that I may find rest in Thee?
Who will give to me that Thou mayest come into my heart and
intoxicate it, so that I may forget my evil ways and embrace Thee
as my only good?  Say to my soul : I am thy salvation" (ib.

i. 5). "Too late I have learned to love Thee, Loveliness so ancient and so new—too late I have learned to love Thee. And behold, Thou wast within and I without, and there I sought Thee; and I, unshapely, rushed upon the shapely things which Thou hast made. <u>Thou wast with me and I was not with Thee.</u> Those things held me far from Thee, which would not be if they were not in Thee. Thou hast called and cried aloud, and broken through my deafness. Thou hast sparkled and shone and driven away my blindness. Thou hast broken and allured my spirit, and I pant for Thee. I have tasted, and I hunger and thirst. Thou hast touched me, and I have been consumed with Thy peace" (ib. x. 27). "And I sought a way of gaining the strength that would be capable of enjoying Thee, and I found it not until I embraced the Mediator between God and men, the man Christ Jesus" (ib. vii. 18). "His coming is his humanity; his remaining is his divinity. His divinity is the whither we are journeying; his humanity is the where we are journeying. Unless he had become for us the where we are journeying, we could never have come to him where he dwells (in Joh. tr. 42. 8). I have entered the depths under Thy guidance, and I have been able, since Thou hast become my helper. I have entered and have seen, as with a certain eye of my soul, above this same eye of my soul, above my mind, the unchangeable Light. . . . O eternal Truth and true Love, and lovable Eternity, Thou art my God. . . . And since I first have known Thee, Thou hast taken me to Thyself, that I might see that that exists which I should see, and which I who see am not yet . . . and I have trembled with love and terror" (conf. vii. 10). "For when I seek Thee, my God, I seek blessed life. I will seek Thee, that my soul may live. For my body lives from my soul, and my soul lives from Thee" (ib. x. 20). "For me, to cling to God is good; this is the whole good. Do you wish anything more? I grieve that you so wish. Brothers, for what more do you wish? There is nothing better than to cling to God" (in ps. 72. 34). "God is to be worshiped by faith, hope, love" (enchirid. iii.; cf. soliloq. i. 7. 14). "Give what Thou appointest, and appoint what Thou wilt" (conf. x. 37; cf. solil. i. 1. 5). "Do Thou suggest to me, do Thou show me, do Thou grant me help by the way . . . increase in me faith, increase hope, increase love" (solil. i. 1. 5). "But there is a delight which is not given to the wicked, but to those who willingly worship Thee, whose joy Thou Thyself art. And this is blessed life itself, to delight one's self toward Thee and on account of Thee; this it is, and there is no other" (conf. x. 22).

A new spirit breathes through these utterances, and they illus-

trate at the same time the enrapturing diction of Augustine.
The very existence of man is sin and misery ; but God is his
salvation—not by virtue of fixed laws, not by way of reward
or punishment, but in the direct personal fellowship of life and
love.  These are the ideas upon which rests Paul's view of sin
and grace.  But Augustine now proceeded, while maintaining
as his central position that above indicated, to unfold his religious
ideas within the lines of the traditional formulas and ideals of the
church.  He "deepened" and transformed the latter.  But he
had also from the start demanded submission to the authority
of the church (vid. de utilitate credendi ix. ff.; c. ep. Mani-
chaei 5. 6 : " But I would not believe the gospel, unless the
authority of the Catholic church impelled me ").  This has been
manifest in our study of his Trinitarian and Christological utterances (p. 238).  It comes to view again in his doctrine of sin
and grace, as developed in the conflict with Pelagianism, although
here the characteristic religious elements of his theology assert
themselves with peculiar force.  In the same light are to be
viewed his utterances touching the church and the sacraments
during the anti-Donatistic controversy, as well as his acceptance
and ennobling of nearly all the teachings of the popular Catholicism.  He remains himself almost everywhere, but he is yet, at
the same time, an orthodox Catholic teacher in the church of his
age.  He did not, like Origen, develop a theological system,
but he furnished to his age a wealth of fruitful religious and
speculative ideas, giving back to it in a purified and profounder
form what he received from it.  His " doctrine " is deficient in
unity, combining the most violent contradictions (gospel and
philosophy, Catholic tradition and religion, voluntarism and intellectualism, etc.); but his writings proved stimulating in an
unparalleled degree.  He was a theologian and a philosopher ;
but he was also more, a religious genius and a great man.

It will be necessary for us to examine : (1) His doctrine of
the church and the sacraments, in opposition to Donatism.  (2)
His doctrine of sin and grace, in opposition to Pelagianism.  (3)
His general view of theology and the church, in tracing which we
must follow the lines of his only comprehensive dogmatic work,
the *Enchiridion ad Laurentium.*

§ 30.  *Donatistic Controversy and Further Development of the
Doctrines of the Church and the Sacraments by Augustine.*

LITERATURE.  OPTATUS of Mileve, de schismate Donatistarum ll. 7 ed.
Ziswa in Corp. scr. eccl. Lat. 26 (written perhaps A. D. 368, but see ii. 3).
Synodal Acts and fragments of the same in M. iv.  Original sources in Opp.
Aug. xvii. 2446 ff.  Also DEUTSCH, Drei Aktenstücke z. Gesch. d. Donat.

1875. VÖLTER, Der Ursprung d. Donat, 1883. SEECK, Quellen u. Urkunden über die Anfänge des. Donat., Ztschr. f. KG. x. 505 ff. RIBBECK, Donatus u. Aug., 1858. HEFELE, in Wetzer u. Welte's Kirchenlex. iii. ed. 2, 1969 ff. THÜMMEL, Zur Beurteilung des Donatism, 1893. F. HAHN, Tyconius-Studien (Bonwetsch-Seeberg, Studien zur Gesch. der Theol. u. der Kirche, vi. 2), 1900. BONWETSCH, PRE. iv., ed. 3, 788 ff. Of the works of Augustine: c. epistulam Parmeniani, ll. 3 (ca. A. D. 400); de baptismo c. Donatistas, ll. 7; c. litteras Petiliani, ll. 3; de unitate eccl. (after A. D. 400); c. Cresconium, ll. 4 (ca. A. D. 406); de unico baptismo c. Petilianum (ca. A. D. 410); breviculus collationes cum Donatistis (A. D. 411); ad Donatistas post collationem (A. D. 412); de gestis cum Emerito (A. D. 418); c. Gaudentium ll. 2 (ca. A. D. 420). Upon Aug's conception of the church, vid. KÖSTLIN, Die Cath. Auffassung v. d. Kirche in ihrer ersten Ausbildung, in Deutsche Ztschr. f. chr. Wiss. u. chr. Leben, 1856, p. 101 ff., 113 ff. H. SCHMIDT, Des Aug. Lehre v. d. Kirche, in Jarbb. f. deutsche Theol., 1861, p. 197 ff. REUTER, Aug. Studien, pp. 231 ff., 47 ff. SEEBERG, Begriff d. Kirche, i. p. 38 ff. SPECHT, Die Lehre v. d. Kirche nach dem. h. Aug., 1892. Upon his doctrine of the Sacraments, vid. HAHN, Die Lehre v. d. Sakr., 1864. DIECKHOFF, Theol. Ztschr., 1860, p. 524 ff.

## 1. THE DONATISTIC CONTROVERSY.

(*a*) The greatest schism in the ancient church arose from personal and local conditions in the congregation at Carthage. As in the case of the Novatian schism, a persecution furnished the occasion. Various courses of action were advocated in North Africa in response to the demand for the surrender of the Scriptures during the Diocletian persecution. Bishop MENSURIUS OF CARTHAGE represented the milder view (surrender of other writings of indifferent character permitted). He and his archdeacon CAECILIAN also opposed the exaggerated veneration of confessors and martyrs. SECUNDUS OF TIGISIS advocated a rigoristic view. After the death of Mensurius, Caecilian, who was hated by the strict party in Carthage, was chosen bishop and consecrated to the office by FELIX OF APTUNGA, whom the strict party regarded as a "traditor." This election awakened great indignation among the "pious" (Lucilla), which was encouraged by the foreign rigorists. The Numidian bishops had sent Docetus from Casae Nigrae to Carthage as vicar of the bishopric. An assemblage of 70 bishops in Carthage (A. D. 312) declared the ordination invalid. MAJORINUS was then elected Bishop of Carthage. His successor was DONATUS THE GREAT. Through a combination of many influences, this conflict led to the formation of two warring churches sharply opposing one another, the Catholic and the Donatistic. The pride of the martyrs, the spirit of piety quickened anew under the stress of persecution, the idea of the holiness of the church, archaistic religious reminiscences, the pressure soon brought to bear by the civil authorities, the league of the Catholic church with the state, social distress, perhaps also national motives, all

united to expand the personal dispute into the great schism
which distracted the church of Africa for a century.   The African church was really split in two (in A. D. 330 there were 270
Donatistic bishops at a council, and in A. D. 311, at Carthage,
266).   Outside of Africa, Donatism secured no following
worthy of mention (a bishop in Spain and another in Rome are
spoken of, gesta collationis i. 157), only Caecilian and his followers being recognized.   The emperor, Constantine, after being
drawn into the matter by the Donatists, assumed a similar attitude.   He ordered an investigation of the subject; then examined it himself, deciding that Caecilian and Felix were innocent, but that their assailants were contemptible slanderers.
Stringent laws were enacted against the latter, but, proving in-
effectual, they were soon revoked.   But the most important
measure was that adopted, under the influence of Constantine,
at the council of Arles (A. D. 316, according to Seeck, l. c., p.
508 f.; cf. Eus. v. C. 44, 45), *i. e.*, the establishment of the
milder view on the ground of principle.   It was here decreed
that even the ordination administered by a " traditor " is valid,
provided only that the persons so ordained " remain reasonable "
(can. 13); also, that persons who had been baptized by heretics
should be questioned only upon the Creed, and that, if it be found
that they have been baptized in the name of the Triune God,
only the laying on of hands shall be further administered to
them (can. 8).   According to this, ordination and baptism are
not dependent upon the worthiness of the administrant.   Thus
a doctrinal difference runs parallel with the personal and historical conflict.   The agitation spread with great rapidity, especially
among the lower ranks of society.   Socialistic ideas as to property
and a reckless fanaticism, leading to a complete outward separation, to frightful deeds of violence, and to wanton and con-
temptuous surrender of life, became distinguishing marks of the
church of the saints (Circumcelliones, Agonistici, vid. Opt. ii.
18 f. 21 ; vi. 1 f.; iii. 4.   Aug. unit. eccl. 19. 50 ; c. ep. Parm.
ii. 3. 6 ; c. Crescon. iii. 42. 46 ; brev. iii. 11).   Against this,
church and state were alike powerless.   Restrictive measures
under CONSTANS and CONSTANTIUS, as under JOVIAN, VALEN-
TINIAN, GRATIAN, and HONORIUS, were unable to suppress the
movement.   The most serious obstacle encountered by the party
was its division into mutually antagonistic groups (Rogatus,
Tyconius, Maximian, and Primian)—the fate of all separatists.
Augustine, soon after entering upon the episcopacy, addressed
all his energy to the work of reconciling the opposing factions.
This resulted in the three-day conference at Carthage in June,
411 (vid. gesta collationis in M. iv. and Aug. brevic. coll.).

Both the historical and the doctrinal questions were here discussed. No reader of the proceedings of this assembly can escape the impression that the Donatists here appear in the light of embittered fanatics, incompetent but vain, adepts in the most trifling legal quibbles, in questions of formality and in intrigue, always seeking to impede the progress of the proceedings. The imperial presiding officer (Marcellin) accorded the victory to the Catholics upon both points of dispute. His decision was a just one. Augustine continued to labor in the same spirit. Strict imperial edicts forbade the assemblage of the Donatists upon penalty of death, and their churches and church property were given over to the Catholics. The power of Donatism was broken, and it soon after disappears from church history.

(b) The doctrinal difference between Donatists and Catholics may be briefly expressed. Donatism does not question the episcopal foundation of the church. It demands only that the bishops be holy men, and maintains that only when they are such are the sacraments administered by them effectual. In this, as at other points, it could appeal to Cyprian. It was well known that Cyprian denied the validity of heretic baptism (p. 184). He taught that there was no virtue in the sacrifices or prayers of fallen priests (referring to Jn. 9. 31), and warned against the contamination of their touch (p. 181, n. 1). When the Donatists appealed to the miracles performed by their bishops, to visions and dreams (Aug. unit. eccl. 19. 49), they had in this also a precedent in Cyprian (p. 181, n. 3). They maintained, further, that they were the only true and real Catholic church (gesta coll. i. 148, 202; iii. 22, 91, 165), the holy, persecuted church of the martyrs (ib. i. 45; iii. 116). The Catholics are not a church, but adherents of Caecilian, traditors, and blood-thirsty oppressors (Optat. ii. 14, 18; gest. i. 148; iii. 14, 29, 258). The Donatist church is in reality the holy bride of Christ, without spot or wrinkle, because it requires holiness of its bishops and its members (ib. iii. 75, 249, 258. Optat. ii. 20; vii. 2). They apply the term, Catholic, "not to provinces or races," but : "the name Catholic is that which is filled with the sacraments" (*sacramentis plenum*, gest. iii. 102, cf. Aug. brev. iii. 3), or, "thou shouldst interpret the name Catholic, not from the fellowship of the whole world, but from the observance of all the divine commandments and of all the sacraments" (Aug. ep. 93. 7. 23). In accordance with the holiness of this church, its members are to carefully avoid association with all who are not in its fellowship,[1] all such being re-

---

[1] Vid. Optat. i. 4; iv. 5; vi. 3. Aug. c. litt. Petil. ii. 83. 184. At the

garded as no better than heathen.[1] Any connection whatever
of the church with the civil government is regarded with abhor-
rence : " What have Christians to do with kings, bishops with
the palace?" (Opt. i. 22 ; Aug. c. litt. Petil. 92. 202).[2] The
dogmatic reason for this separateness lies in the invalidity of the
Catholic sacraments. The moral unworthiness of the bishops of
the traditor-church robs their sacraments of value : " How can
he give who has nothing to give?" (Opt. v. 6 ; cf. gest. iii.
258). Hence the repetition of the sacraments, the second baptism, and the repetition of extreme unction are necessary (Opt.
i. 5 ; iii. 2 ; iv. 4 ; v. 1. 3 f.; vii. 4). Yet it is going too far
to regard re-baptism as, without any modification, a characteristic mark of Donatism. The Donatist Tyconius advocated the
validity of the Catholic sacraments, and maintained that this was
the genuine Donatist view—a position that is supported by historical evidences from other sources (Aug. ep. 93. 43 ; cf.
HAHN, Tyconius-Studien, p. 102 ff.). But, since the Donatists
have the full observance of the sacraments, they are the Catholic
church. Hence, Christ and true baptism are to be found only
among them : " For how can it be, if the church is one and
Christ undivided, that anyone located without may obtain baptism (gest. iii. 258)?"

The Catholic position, on the contrary, is as follows :[3] The
orthodoxy of the Donatists is acknowledged, as well as the
validity of their sacraments, and they are regarded as Christian
brethren (gest. i. 16, 55, 62 ; ii. 50. Opt. i. 4 f.; iv. 2):
" Both among you and among us there is one ecclesiastical life
(conversatio), common texts, the same faith, the same sacraments
of the faith, the same mysteries" (Opt. v. 1). Even their baptism
is unassailable, for baptism is baptism, even though administered
by thieves and robbers (gest. i. 62); for it is not a man, but the
holy Trinity, which here bestows a gift (Opt. v. 7). The Trinity
is necessary in baptism, and also the faith of the recipient.
These elements are unchangeable ; but the administrant is a
variable element. "Administrants may be changed, but the
sacraments cannot be changed. If, therefore, you consider all

religious colloquy at Carthage, the Donatists could not be induced to sit with
the Catholics (gest. i. 45 ; ii. 3).

[1] Optat. iii. 11 (cf. vi. 8): You say even to the clergy, " Be Christians,"
and you dare to say to everyone : " Gai sei Gaia seia : adhuc paganus es aut
pagana" (translating the Punic words, vid. remarks in Ziswa's edition, p.
277).

[2] Yet the Donatists themselves called upon Constantine to act as umpire,
and, as it appears, did not at a later day disdain the assistance of the secular
arm (gest. iii. 194. Aug. brev. iii. 11).

[3] We take no account for the present of ideas specifically Augustinian.

who baptize, they are administrants, not lords ; and the sacraments are holy in themselves and not through men '' (Opt. iv. 4, 1). Thus regarded, the Donatists are also a part of the church. But they are not so in the full sense of the word, since they lack catholicity and are only *quasi ecclesia.* They build a ''ruinous wall'' (Ez. 13. 10). There is no other house beside the house of God. What they build is only a wall, and that not even resting upon the corner-stone : '' your part is a quasi-church, but is not Catholic'' (Opt. iii. 10). They array '' novelty against antiquity '' (ib. iii. 2), and cut themselves off from the root (iii. 7). Among the Catholics, on the contrary, is found the house of God and the one Catholic church. It is the latter, because, according to the promise of Christ, it spreads abroad over all nations and is not confined '' to a small part of Africa, to the corner of a little region '' (Opt. ii. 1, 5 ; iii. 2, 3). But it is also the *holy* church, and this not because of the character of the men belonging to it, but because it has the ''symbol of the Trinity, the chair of Peter, the faith of believers, the salutary precepts of Christ '' (ib. ii. 9, 10 ; vii. 2), and, above all, the sacraments : '' whose holiness is derived from the sacraments, not measured by the loftiness of persons '' (ib. ii. 1). When the Donatists refuse to accord holiness to the church because some bishops at the time of the Diocletian persecution became traditors, they magnify what is irrelevant, if true, and what is, moreover, historically incorrect (gest. i. 16, 55. Aug. brev. iii. 19 ff.). There are, indeed, unholy persons in the church, but we are forbidden to cast these out before the time by the parables of the tares and of the net in which are gathered good and worthless fishes (gest. i. 18, 55. Opt. vii. 2). Those passages of Scripture which speak of a state of unmixed holiness in the church are to be understood as referring to her condition of final blessedness (Aug. brev. iii. 9. Opt. ii. 20). The church, therefore, as a whole, is holy in the present day by virtue of the divine agency exerted within its bounds in the sacraments, and it will one day be holy in all its members. The error of the Donatists consists in seeking to realize this final state before the time. It is certain that, viewed dogmatically, the Catholic position was the more correct, yet its victory was not a clear step in advance. The ancient idea, that the people of God should consist of holy children of God, was forced another step backward.

2. AUGUSTINE'S DOCTRINE OF THE CHURCH, THE SACRAMENTS, AND THE RELATION OF CHURCH AND STATE.

(*a*) Augustine's doctrine of the church is a complicated structure. Ideas evolved in the conflict with the Donatists, the popular conception of the church, his own doctrine of grace, and certain Donatistic tendencies are here brought into combination. Augustine was influenced especially by Tyconius' conception of the church. This Donatist maintained, indeed, that the church is composed of saints only, but he also taught that empirically the church for the present embraces evil as well as good persons, and that this is so by divine ordering. True, this mixed condition of the church is, according to his view, soon to be terminated, and to this end Donatism is a beginning (vid. HAHN, Tyconius-Studien, p. 80 ff.). As opposed to Donatism, Augustine thus formulates the point at issue : " The question is, indeed, discussed between us, Where is the church, whether among us or among them?" (de unit. eccl. 2. 2). With Optatus, Augustine holds that the great church is the *one Catholic* church by virtue of the distribution of the latter throughout the whole world (c. litt. Petil. ii. 38. 91 ; iii. 2. 3 ; de unit. eccl. 6. 11 ff.) and by virtue of its connection with the church of the apostles, whose successors the bishops are (c. Cresc. iii. 18. 21 ; de unit. eccl. 11. 30, cf. in Joh. tr. 37. 6). Outside of this one Catholic church, the body of Christ, there is no truth,[1] no salvation (ep. 141. 5 ; de unit. 2. 2). Separation from it is a *sacrilegium* (c. ep. Parm. i. 8. 14; 10. 16). Only chaff is blown off by the fan (bapt. v. 21. 29); only pride and lack of love can impel a Christian to split the unity of the church (c. Cresc. iv. 59. 71 ; c. litt. Petil. ii. 77. 172). The declaration of Augustine is not, however, inspired by hierarchial motive, but rests ultimately upon the thought that it is only in the Catholic church that the Spirit and love are bestowed upon man. But the saints are to be found only in the Catholic church. In this connection, Augustine championed the motto, *Extra ecclesiam nulla salus*, no less positively than Cyprian ; but, at the same time—as a result of the different character of the opposition—displayed less of hierarchical interest than the latter (cf. REUTER, l. c., p. 253 ff.).

(*b*) The idea of the ROMAN PRIMACY likewise receives no special elucidation at the hands of Augustine. We find a general acknowledgment of the " primacy of the apostolic chair " (*e. g,*, ep. 43. 7), but Augustine knows nothing of any special authority vested in Peter or his successors. Peter is a " figure of the church " or of the " good pastors," and represents the unity of the church (serm. 295. 2 ; 147. 2). In this consists the significance of his position and that of his successors (thus also Cyprian, p. 183). As all bishops (in contradistinction from the

---

[1] *E. g.*, it is manifest, faith admits it, the Catholic church approves it, it is true (serm. 117. 4. 6).

Scriptures) may err (unit. eccl. 11. 28), so also the Roman
bishop. This view is plainly manifest from the bearing of
Augustine and his colleagues in the Pelagian controversy (vid.
p. 355 f., cf. ep. 177, 191 ; pecc. orig. 21. 24, cf. 8. 9). The
infallible authority of the pope in the church at large was a
dogma in which only the popes believed (vid. the letters of
Innocent, p. 355 ; cf. as to Leo, p. 268, and Callistus, p. 177).
Dogmatically, there had been no advance from the position of
Cyprian. The Africans, in their relations with Rome, played
somewhat the role of the Gallicanism of a later period (cf.
REUTER, p. 291 ff.).

(*c*) The opposition between the Donatistic and Catholic
churches was based upon their different conceptions of the sacraments. From the time of the Council of Arles (p. 314), the
great point of discussion was whether baptism and ordination
administered by an unworthy person retained their validity.
Augustine's views concerning the sacraments, by an inner necessity, determined his attitude upon this question (cf. REUTER, p.
278). The sacraments are gifts of God, and the moral condition of the administrator cannot detract from the value of the
gift conveyed : "What he gives is, nevertheless, real (*verum*),
if he gives not what is his own, but God's" (c. litt. Pet. ii. 30.
69 ; unit. eccl. 21. 58). Only thus is the result certain, and salvation dependent upon God, not upon men. It is not the
intercession of men, but that of Christ, which helps us (c. litt.
Pet. i. 3. 4 ; c. ep. Parm. ii. 8. 16). "No reason is shown
why he who cannot lose baptism itself can forfeit the right of
administering it. For each is a sacrament, and each is given to
man by the same consecration—the one when he is baptized, and
the other when he is ordained : therefore, in the Catholic church
neither dare be repeated" (c. ep. Parm. ii. 12. 28). This is explained by the fact that these sacraments impart to the recipient
a permanent character : "just as baptism, so ordination *remains
whole* in them" (ib.). Baptism and ordination impress upon
man a fixed "*dominical character.*"[1] This military form of expression implies that, as there is a military brand (*nota militaris*)
whose significance continues through the whole life, so also
baptism and ordination have a perpetual and indelible (the term
employed in the Middle Ages) force for the recipient (c. ep. Parm.
ii. 13. 29). There remains in him something sacred, a *sanctum*.
The spirit is preserved to him, not in a moral sense, but in the
sense of an official equipment. He may have committed heinous

---

[1] Augustine introduced this term into theology. He was also the first to
use the expression *obicem opponere* (ep. 98. 9).

crimes—may have severed himself from the church, yet this *character* once impressed upon him remains, and the sacraments administered by him retain their force.  If he be converted, there
is no need for a repetition of the sacrament (c. ep. Parm. ii. 11.
24; 13. 28 f.; bapt. iv. 12. 18; vi. 1. 1; de symbol. 8. 15;
de bon. conjug. 24. 32: "in those ordained, the sacrament
of ordination remains;" bapt. vi. 5. 7; in 1 Joh. tract. 5. 7).  It
is evident that this *character indelebilis* may be employed as
the most telling argument against Donatism ; but it also brought
Augustine into new difficulties.  If the sacraments have bestowed such a character, how can objection be brought against
the Donatistic church ?  It was necessary, therefore, to maintain
the validity of the Donatist sacraments, and yet to condemn
them as seriously defective.  This was accomplished by discriminating between the sacrament itself and the *effectus* or *usus
sacramenti*.  By failing to observe this distinction, Cyprian and
others were led to the view " that the baptism of Christ cannot
exist among heretics or schismatics."  By observing it, we may
say : " its effect or use, in liberation from sin and in rectitude of
heart, could not be found among heretics " (bapt. vi. 1. 1).
Baptism imparts to the recipient an abiding character, but if he
do not live in the church, the " effect " in the forgiveness of sin
does not follow.  The baptism cannot, indeed, be repeated ; but
only when the individual is converted to the *unity* of the true
church does it become effectual : " He who has received the
baptism of Christ, which they have not lost who have separated
themselves . . . in any heresy or schism, in which sacrilegious
crime his sins were not remitted, when he shall have reformed
and come to the fellowship and unity of the church, is not to be
again baptized, because in this very reconciliation and peace it is
offered to him, that the sacrament which, when received in
schism, could not benefit, shall now in the unity (of the church)
begin to benefit him for the remission of his sins " (bapt. i. 12.
18; v. 8. 9; vi. 5. 7).  In the case of ordination, it was held
that the *character* remains, bringing, however, to the individual
himself not blessing, but the contrary : "the Holy Spirit . . .
fails, indeed, to effect his salvation . . . yet does not desert his
ministry, by which he works through him the salvation of
others " (c. Parm. ii. 11. 24 ; de bon. conjug. 24. 32).  By
this means the Donatist theory is discountenanced and, at the
same time, the necessity of the return of its adherents to the
Catholic church is made evident.

(*d*) The means by which the church is built up are the sacraments, especially baptism and the Lord's Supper, and also the
Word.  "Blood and water flowed (Jn. 19. 34), which we know

to be the sacraments by which the church is built up " (civ. dei,
xxii. 17). "God begets sons from the church . . . we are,
therefore, spiritually born, and we are born in the Spirit by word
and sacrament. The Spirit is present, that we may be born "
(in Joh. tract. 12. 5; serm. 88. 5; ep. 21. 3). The term,
*sacramentum*—corresponding exactly to μυστήριον—is applied
also to other ecclesiastical acts, such as confirmation (bapt. v. 20.
28; c. Faustum xix. 14), the presentation of the consecrated
salt to catechumens (de catechizandis rudibus, 26. 50), ordination (bon. conjug. 24. 32; c. ep. Parm. ii. 13. 28; cf. supra),
exorcism (serm. 27). But the proper sacraments are the two
which proceeded from the side of Christ (civ. dei, xv. 26. 1; in
Joh. tract. 15. 8; 120. 2; 50. 12; doctr. christ. iii. 9. 13), to
which is to be added ordination. The representation of the
divine agency exerted is essentially the same in the word and in
the sacraments.[1] The human transaction is accompanied by a
divine, inwardly effectual act. The word is read in the hearing
of others, preached, sung, and chanted by men : " we enjoy
the hearing of it, the truth speaking to us without sound inwardly " (in Joh. tr. 57. 3; 40. 5; 71. 1; 77. 2; bapt. v. 11.
24). Augustine is thus the first to formulate a doctrine of
the word as a means of grace. The problem is here presented,
how the spoken human word can be the medium through
which the divine Spirit operates. In the same way in the sacraments as in the word, men work outwardly, God inwardly (c.
ep. Parm. ii. 11; bapt. v. 21. 29; ep. 98. 2 : "the water,
therefore, presenting the sacrament of grace outwardly, and the
Spirit inwardly effecting the benefit of grace "). It is to be,
however, here noted that the outward observance of the sacrament
and the inner work of grace do not always correspond (bapt. iv.
25. 32; in Lev. iii., quaest. 84; enarr. in. ps. 77. 2).

We are now in position to define Augustine's conception of a sacrament. We must, first of all, discriminate carefully between the
outward sign and the inward power and efficacy : "the sacrament is one thing, the virtue of the sacrament another " (in Joh.
tr. 26. 11). Viewed in the first aspect, the sacrament is purely
symbolical. There are needed, says Augustine, in genuine Neo-
Platonic spirit, in religious associations "signs (*signacula*) or visible sacraments " (c. Faust. xix. 11). The visible signs are
symbols of an invisible content : "they are, indeed, visible
signs of divine things, but in them are to be honored the invisible things themselves " (de cat. rud. 26. 50). "They are
called sacraments, because in them one thing is seen, another thing

---

[1] Even the word is included among the signs (*signa*), doctr. christ. ii. 3.

understood'' (serm. 272). The symbol has at the same time a
certain resemblance to that which it represents (ep. 98. 9). Accordingly, the visible symbols become what they are through the
interpreting word : ''the word comes to (*accedit*) the element and
it becomes (*fit*) a sacrament—itself also, as it were, a visible
word.'' The ''*fit*'' is used here not in the objective, but purely
in the subjective sense : '' Whence is there in the water such
virtue that it can touch the body and purify the heart, unless the
word effects this ?—*not because it is spoken, but because it is believed*'' (in Joh. tr. 80. 3). In the light of this explanation,
Augustine would seem to have a purely symbolical view of the
sacrament ; and it is beyond doubt that the Neo-Platonic caste
of his thought at least inclined him in this direction. But we must
not overlook the fact, that an actual exertion of divine energy, as a
rule, accompanies the sacrament. God really forgives sins in baptism, in it, as in ordination, imprinting a character upon the recipient. In the Lord's Supper there is really an effectual refreshment
(*salubris refectio*) in the Lord's flesh and blood. Thus to drink is
to live ; a spiritual eating and drinking accompanies the visible
reception (serm. 131. 1). The two-fold aspect of the sacramental theory of the ancient church here comes into distinct prominence : The sacraments are purely symbols, but the reception of
the sacraments brings real, objective exertions of divine energy.
In Augustine, indeed, the whole conception is wavering, since
there is no fixed connection between the sacrament and the gracious divine energy. Here, too, is felt the influence of his
theory of predestination. As to the sacramental *character*, see p.
319.

(*e*) The peculiarities of the separate sacraments may be briefly
stated. (*a*) Baptism, as the *sacramentum remissionis peccatorum*,
(bapt. v. 21. 29) works the forgiveness of sins, primarily the
forgiveness of the guilt of original concupiscence ; in this consists its chief efficacy (cf. p. 314). Augustine frequently speaks of
a blotting out of sins (*e. g.*, by baptism . . . sins are destroyed,
*delentur*, in ps. 106. 3). Discrimination is to be made between
this forgiveness once granted and the recurring forgiveness of
daily sins in response to the fifth petition of the Lord's Prayer
(*e. g.*, serm. 58. 5. 6). Augustine, however, made the latter
dependent upon the former : '' by that which is given once it
comes to pass that pardon of any sins whatsoever, not only before but also afterward, is granted to believers.'' Prayer, alms,
and good works would bring no forgiveness to the Christian if he
were not baptized (nupt. et conc. i. 33. 38). But this idea was
obscured by the penitential discipline (vid. sub) and by the
relatively unimportant place of the forgiveness of sins in the

consciousness of Augustine (p. 346 f.). Compare Dieckhoff, l. c., p. 536 ff.). (β) In contradistinction from Ambrose (e. g., de fide iv. 10. 124 : "through the mystery of the sacred prayer they are transfigured into flesh and blood "), the symbolical character of the sacraments comes in Augustine into distinct prominence : "The Lord did not hesitate to say, 'This is my body,' when he gave the sign of his body" (c. Adimantum Manich. 12. 3 ; in ps. 3. 1). The blessing, or gift, of the sacrament is conceived in harmony with this. The body of the Lord is the mystic body, or the church : "hence he wishes the food and drink to be understood as the fellowship (societas) of his body and of his members, which is the holy church " (in Joh. tr. 26. 15, 14 ; serm. 272 ; civ. dei, xxi. 25. 2); or, "this is, therefore, to eat that food and to drink that drink—to remain in Christ and to have him remaining in us " (in Joh. tr. 26. 18 ; civ. dei, xxi. 25. 4). Augustine can even say that the eating of the body of the Lord is "delightfully and profitably to store away in memory that his flesh was wounded and crucified for us " (doctr. christ. iii. 16. 24).[1] It is true, there are not wanting passages in which Augustine expresses himself differently and more fully, speaking of the reception of the body of Christ, etc. (e. g., serm. 131. 1 ; bapt. v. 8. 9); but his real thought is even here not that which the words seem to convey, although he still has in mind the bestowal and reception of a real gift. Thus Augustine's theory of the Lord's Supper has more of a really religious character than his doctrines of baptism and grace, since the personal nature of fellowship with God here finds due recognition. It is to be observed, further, that in the view of Augustine, Christ is, indeed, omnipresent according to his divine nature, but according to his human nature he is in one place in heaven (ubique totum praesentem esse non dubites tanquam deum . . . et in loco aliquo caeli propter veri corporis modum, ep. 187. 12. 41). In this again we see the model after which the medieval theories were patterned. The genius of Augustine is manifest in his interpretation of the sacrifice of the mass : the congregatio sanctorum presents itself to God in good works under its head, Christ. "This is the sacrifice of Christians : Many one body in Christ"

---

[1] I purposely omit the famous passage which is usually cited in this connection (by Löscher already, in the Weimar edition, ii. 742): "Why preparest thou the teeth and the stomach ? Believe, and thou hast eaten " (in Joh. tr. 25. 12), for, in the context in which this occurs, the author has not the Lord's Supper in mind. The food to which he refers is the God-given commandment, to believe on Christ ; and in order to receive (eat) this, the teeth are not needed, but faith. Compare the similar statements (ib. 26. 1): " for to believe in him, this is to eat living bread ; " " he who believes eats ; " and 35. 3 : " with the mind, not with the stomach."

(civ. dei, x. 6). Of which thing [the sacrifice of Christ] he wished the sacrifice of the church (which, since it is the body of him, the Head, teaches that it offers itself through him) to be a daily sacrament [symbolical imitation] (ib. x. 20). (γ) As to the sacrament of ordination, see p. 319 f., and cf. REUTER l.c., 253, 264 ff.

(ƒ) But we have thus far seen but one side of Augustine's conception of the church. When we remember that the infusion of the Spirit and of love makes the Christian (p. 347 f.), we realize that we are brought to face another line of thought. (α) The good, who have the Spirit and love, constitute among themselves a communion (*congregatio*, *compages*). These saints are the unspotted bride of Christ, his dove, and the house of God, the rock upon which the Lord builds his church, the church which possesses the power to loose and bind (unit. eccl. 21. 60 ; c. litt. Pet. ii. 58. 246 ; bapt. vii. 51. 99). It is not being outwardly in the church, nor partaking of the sacraments, that decides, but belonging to the church in this sense : "Nor are they to be thought to be in the body of Christ, which is the church, because they become corporeally participants in its sacraments . . . they are not in the union (*compages*) of the church, which, in the members of Christ, grows through connection and contact to the increase of God" (c. litt. Pet. l. c.). It is this communion of the saints,[1] united by the Spirit and love, through whose intercession sins are forgiven, and through whose mediation the gifts of grace are bestowed. To it, and not to the officials of the church, are given these great promises. "God gives the sacrament of grace, indeed, through evil men, but not grace itself except through himself or through his saints. And, therefore, he effects remission of sins either through himself or through the members of that dove, to whom he says : If to anyone ye remit, they are remitted" (bapt. v. 21. 29). "Or does the sacrament and a secret dispensation of the mercy of God, perhaps, through the prayers of the spiritual saints who are in the church, as through the continuous cooing of the dove, accomplish the great thing, that even the sins of those who have been baptized, not by the

---

[1] The term, *communio sanctorum*, is found in the first canon of the Council at Nimes (A. D. 394. HEFELE, CG. ii., ed. 2, 62) and among the Donatists (Aug. in ps. 36 ; serm. 2. 20 and opp. xvii. 2532). In Augustine's own writings, serm. 52. 3. 6 ; cf. *congregatio sanctorum* (civ. dei, x. 6 ; bapt. i. 17. 26); *communis unitatis corporis Christi* (bapt. i. 4. 5); *societas credentium* (bapt. vii. 53. 102); *christiana societas* (*c. litt. Petil.* ii. 39. 94); *bonorum societas* (ib. ii. 77. 174); also *communio malorum* (bapt. vii. 25. 49). At a later date, as is well known, it appears in the Creed (Nicetas v. Romatiana in Caspari, Anecdota, 355. Faust. v. Riez, ib. 338. Ps. Aug. serm. 240, 241, 242 ; cf. vol. xvii. 1960).

dove but by the hawk, are remitted?" (ib. iii. 17. 22 ; 18. 23).
This is the essence of the communion of the good and pious:
They love God and one another, and they pray for the church.
This is the "invisible union (*compages*) of love" (bapt. iii. 19.
26 ; de unit. eccl. 21. 60) with the invisible anointing of love
(*unctio caritatis*, c. litt. Petil. ii. 104. 239). But this exists, and
is conceivable, only within the Catholic church, separation from
which is at once a renunciation of the Spirit and of love (ep.
141. 5, and citations on p. 318). Only in the Catholic church
is the spirit of love thus present. But Augustine here thinks not
only of the efficacious working of the sacrament, but also, and
particularly, of the working of the Spirit upon the spiritual life
through the personal fellowship of the believing and holy with
one another. He has not, therefore, yet reached the position of
medieval Catholicism.

(β) But is not the church then split into two churches,
the mixed church of the present and the pure church of the
future (Donatist criticism, brev. iii. 10. 19)? Augustine meets
this objection with a variety of illustrations. The question is
one solely of a present relationship. Good and evil are commingled in the church. According to the instructions of Christ,
the latter cannot be outwardly excluded, although they are inwardly entirely separated from the pious (c. ep. Parm. iii. 2. 12 ;
c. Cresc. iii. 65. 73 ; bapt. vi. 3. 5 ; vii. 51. 99), just as are
heretics : " Whether they seem to live within or are openly without, that which is flesh is flesh. . . . And even he who in carnal obduracy is mingled with the congregation of the saints is
always separated from the unity of that church which is without
spot or wrinkle " (bapt. i. 17. 26 ; also vii. 51. 99 extr.). But :
" he tolerates the wicked *in communione sanctorum*" (serm. 214.
11). It is a relationship like that between the wheat and the
tares upon the same threshing-floor (bapt. v. 21. 29); between
belonging to a house and being in the house (ib. vii. 51. 99);
between the outer and the inner man (brev. iii. 10. 20); or even :
"thus there are in the body of Christ in some way evil humors"
(in 1 Joh. tr. 3. 4). We may, therefore, speak of " the true and
the commingled, or counterfeited, body of the Lord," or of a
" commingled church." Hence, in the proper sense, the church
consists of only the good and holy : the wicked and heretics only
apparently belong to it by virtue of the temporal commingling
and the communion of the sacraments " (doctr. christ. iii. 32.
45). We can see that Augustine takes some account of the demand of the Donatists ; but he effects only in thought the separation which they sought to realize in fact. "We understand
the departure (*recessio*) spiritually, they corporeally " (serm. 88.

20. 23). From a critical point of view, the Donatistic objection is not without justification, for the church of the sacraments and the church of grace can only with the greatest difficulty be intellectually harmonized.

(γ) This difficulty is intimately connected with Augustine's definition of grace, and it becomes still more serious when the doctrine of predestination is taken into account. "The invisible union of love" is not identical with the "number of the predestinated." As the latter may extend beyond the bounds of the church (p. 351), so, on the contrary, some may belong to the church who are not in the number of the predestinated, and, therefore, do not have the "gift of perseverance" (corr. et grat. 9. 22; don. pers. 2. 2). Practically, indeed, Augustine did not realize this discrepancy any more than that between the inward and the outward church. That it nevertheless exists, cannot be denied, although Augustine only occasionally combines the conceptions, church and predestination.[1] We may, accordingly, speak of a two-fold, or even a three-fold, definition of the church in Augustine. Cf. REUTER, l. c., p. 47 ff. SEEBERG, l. c., 49 ff.

(g) It must be mentioned, finally, that Augustine applied the term, KINGDOM OF GOD, also to the church of the present, whereas the ancient church, as represented in other teachers, regarded the kingdom as the result and goal of the church's development,[2] looking to the future for the highest good. But Augustine says : "The church is even now the kingdom of Christ and the kingdom of heaven" (civ. dei, xx. 9. 1 ; cf. de fid. et op. 7. 10 ; serm. 213. 7 ; 214. 11). This utterance means primarily only that the saints are the kingdom of Christ and reign with him. But this dominion is at once attributed to the leaders (praepositi) "through whom the church is now governed" (ib. § 2). The kingdom of God is thus for Augustine essentially identical with the pious and holy ; but it is also the episcopally organized church. The contrast between the city of God (civitas dei) and the city[3] of

[1] We read, de bapt. v. 27. 28 : The church as an enclosed garden, paradise, etc., consists of the sancti and justi. Then appears as equivalent : "the certain predestinated number of saints," and from this again : "the number of the just." Yet many of the predestinati are now living carnally and unworthily—are heathen and heretics. And yet these are all to be considered as included in the enclosed garden, the church, which originally consisted of the holy and righteous. Cf. SEEBERG, p. 53.

[2] Vid., e. g., Did. 10. 5. Cypr. de op. et eleem. 9; de unit. eccl. 14. Hieron. adv. Iovin. ii. 19. Also Augustine himself, serm. 131. 6. 6 ; esp. brev. collat. iii. 10. 20 ; 9. 16.

[3] Civitas is here used as meaning "city" (civ. dei, xv. 1. 25), a signification which in general historical connections passes over into that of "state." Vid. REUTER, p. 131 f.

the world (*civitas mundi*), or of the devil, is for him that between Christanity and heathenism (in the first 10 books): between the good and the bad, including the devil and angels (civ. dei, xii. 1 ; 27. 2), or between the saints and the wicked even within the church; between the spiritual and the carnal, the love of God and self-love, grace and nature, those foreordained to glory or to torment (*e. g.*, xx. 9. 3 ; xiv. 1 ; 4. 2 ; 28 ; xv. 1. 2 ; 16. 3). The evil world is never represented, indeed, as itself equivalent to the state. But since the *civitas dei* may be and is conceived as the empirical church, the reader very naturally thinks of the *civitas mundi* concretely as equivalent to the state (*e. g.*, xiv. 28 ; xv. 4 ; i. 35). This is encouraged by the fact that, although Augustine recognizes the necessity of the (Christian) state and the civil law (xv. 4 in Joh. tr. 6. 25 f.), yet everything really and permanently good is found upon the side of the church. From this it follows, that it is the duty of the state to execute the commandments of Christ, or of the church (xv. 2, ep. 138. 2. 14 ; 105. 3. 11). From this point of view, Augustine—in conflict with his earlier convictions (ep. 93. 5. 17)—desired the state to employ force against Donatists and heretics : "Compel them to come in" (Lk. 14. 23 ; vid. ep. 93 and 185 in Joh. tr. 11. 14). Here, as so frequently, he falls into the current of the popular Christianity of the day. The great work upon the "City of God"— capable of many interpretations (a double line of aims and means running through the work, just as through Plato's "State") —became the criterion for the development of the church polity of the Middle Ages. Cf. REUTER, p. 111 f.

Such, in outline, was Augustine's conception of the church. The power of the historic Catholic tradition, the opposition of the Donatists, the fundamental tendency of his doctrine of grace, the predestination theory, and a grandly broad view of the course of history—were the threads woven into the texture. In it the best and the worst elements appear side by side. It is Evangelical and Catholic ; superior to the world and compromising with the world ; at once, true and untrue. Theoretically contemplated, it is a malformation without parallel : practically considered, a redundancy of large conceptions and impulses--not an organism, but a vessel full of fermenting elements.

Augustine prepared the way for the medieval ecclesiasticism ; but he also revived and gave practical efficacy to a central idea of primitive Christianity—the present kingdom of God. He embraced the many treasures of Christianity in the one treasure— the kingdom of God, and thus made them concrete and historically visible. He also, in his conception of the church, saved from the confusion of Donatistic ideas the primitive truth of the church as the communion of saints. In connection with this, he definitely asserted the natural character of the *charismata*. The Spirit, who creates new life, is the great gift of divine grace to the church. It may be said that Augustine was the first since Paul to renounce the grace of visions, dreams, and inner suggestions (cf. Cyprian and the Donatists), since he understood grace as consisting in the spirit of love animating the church. Not only could Rome appeal to Augustine, but the Evangelical theory of the church finds in him as well a champion.

§ 31. *Establishment of the Doctrine of Sin and Grace in the Conflict with Pelagianism.*

LITERATURE. WALCH, Ketzerhistorie iv. v. WIGGERS, Pragmat. Darstellung d. Augustinismus u. Pelagianismus, 2 vols., 1821, 1833. JACOBI, Die Lehre des Pelag., 1842. WÖRTER, Der Pelagianismus, 1866. KLASEN, Die innere Entwicklung d. Pelagianismus, 1882. DIECKHOFF, Aug. Lehre v. d. Gnade, in Theol. Ztschr. von Dieckhoff u. Kliefoth, 1860, p. 11 ff. LANDERER, Das Verhältniss v. Gnade u. Freiheit, Jarbb. f. deutsche Theol., 1857, p. 500 ff. LUTHARDT, Die Lehre vom fr. Willen u. sein Verh. zur Gnade, 1863. ROTTMANNER, Augustinismus, 1892. DORNER, Augustin, p. 113 ff. HEFELE, CG. ii., ed. 2, 104 ff. REUTER, Augustin. Studien, p. 4 ff.; THOMASIUS, DG. i., ed. 2, 456 ff. HARNACK, DG. iii. 151 ff. WÖRTER, Beiträge zur DG. des Pelagianismus, 1898.

1. DIVERGENCES OF THE EASTERN AND WESTERN CHURCHES. We have had occasion to observe (§ 27) that the Eastern church laid great emphasis upon the freedom of the natural man. This is done especially in moral exhortations, while, at the same time, when treating of the work of redemption, the state of the natural man was often depicted in the darkest colors (*e. g.*, by Athanasius). We must bear in mind that the attitude of the Greeks toward the problem of free-will was fundamentally different from that of the Latins. They began with the intellect, to which the will was simply subordinate, as an organ through which it operates. Whatever a man thinks, that he is also able to will. The Romans, on the contrary, assign an independent position to the will. In the utterances of such a practical Greek teacher as Chrysostom, we find indeed both conceptions embodied, but that of human freedom holds the place of prominence: "For God created our nature self-controlling" (αὐτεξούσιος, in Genes. hom. 19). Accordingly, it is only the separate acts of man that are regarded as evil. There is no sinful *habitus:* "Thou shouldst not acknowledge any substantial (ἐνυπόστατος) power, but the evil deed, always coming into being and vanishing, not existing before it has occurred, and disappearing again after it has occurred" (in Rom. hom. 12). The

result of the fall for us is that, as Adam thereby became mortal, so his descendants are also mortal (hom. in ps. 51). The conception of grace is in harmony with this view. Man makes the beginning in that which is good, and grace comes to his aid : " For it is necessary that we first choose the good, and when we have chosen it, then he also brings his part. He does not anticipate our wishes, in order that our freedom may not be destroyed. But when we have chosen, then he brings great help to us . . . it is ours to choose beforehand and to will, but it is God's to accomplish and lead to the result" (in Heb. h. 12 ; in Rom. h. 16 ; in Joh. h. 17). This expresses very fairly the position of the Eastern church, in which, moreover, the conception of grace itself becomes confused by its connection with the worship of the mysteries. Cf. Förster, Chrysostomus, 1869, pp. 63 ff., 139 ff. August. c. Jul. i. 6. 21 ff.

In contrast with the above, we may place the teaching of a Western theologian, AMBROSE († A. D. 397), the forerunner of Augustine upon the subject of sin and grace. In his conception of sin we can still trace the beginnings of a doctrine of original sin which we discovered in Tertullian, Cyprian, and Commodian (pp. 122 f., 193).[1] (a) In his practical addresses, Ambrose also occasionally used strong language in placing the responsibility for evil deeds upon the free will of man (e. g., enarr. in ps. 1, § 30 ; de Jac. et vit. beata i. 10). But his thought is dominated by the view, that through the fall of Adam we come into the world as sinners, that sin is an attribute which belongs to us from our conception, and that we, therefore, being from the outstart sinful, must sin even when for the time being we do not desire to sin : "Adam was, and in him we all were. Adam perished, and in him we all perished " (in Luc. vii. 234, 164). " I fell in Adam, I was in Adam ejected from paradise, I died in Adam " (de excessu fratr. sui Satyri ii. 6).[2] " No one at all who has been born under sin can be saved, whom that very inheritance of

---

[1] Hilary at this point betrays the influence of the Greeks, e. g., in ps. 118 lit. N. 20 : "There is, indeed, in faith a gift of continuance from God ; but the source of the beginning is from us, and our will ought to have this of itself as its own, that it wills. God will give an increase of the beginning, because our infirmity does not through itself attain the consummation ; nevertheless, the merit of reaching the consummation is, from the beginning, of the will." Yet he uses also the term, *vitium originis*, and says : " In the error of the one Adam, the whole race of men went astray" (in ps. 119 lit. N. 20; P. 6; in Matt. 18. 6). Cf. LANDERER, l. c., p. 591 f.

[2] Cf. also the so-called Ambrosiaster upon Rom. v. 12 : "It is manifest that in Adam all sinned, as it were, in the mass; for all whom he who was himself corrupted through sin begat were born under sin ; from him, therefore all are sinners, because from him we all are." Vid. also the (apparently not Ambrosian) Apol. ii., David, § 71.

guilty condition has constrained to sin '' (in ps. 38, § 29). '' Before we are born we are defiled by contagion, and before we enjoy
the light we receive the injury of our very origin ; we are conceived in iniquity.'' In response to the question, whether this
last assertion relates to the mother or to the child, it is said :
'' But see whether it may not be known which. The one conceived is not without sin, since the parents are not without fault.
And, if the infant of one day is not without sin, much more are
all the days of maternal conception not without sin. We are
conceived, therefore, in the sin (*peccato*) of our parents and in
their faults (*delictis*) we are born '' (apol. David, 11. 56). Hence
also : '' We are led unwilling and reluctant into guilt '' (*culpam*),
and : '' For our heart and our meditations are not in our power ''
(de fuga seculi i. 1 ; ii. 9). According to these citations, Ambrose really taught the propagation of Adam's sin ; but we do
not find in his writings the idea of the imputation of Adam's
guilt to the race sprung from him. He recognizes a physical, but not a moral, original sin (cf. FÖRSTER, Ambr., p.
154 f.).

(*b*) As to his doctrine of grace, we note that Ambrose very
strongly emphasized the activity of grace, but yet knows nothing
of its alone-activity. '' He who follows Christ, when asked why
he resolved to be a Christian, can respond : ' It seemed good to
me ' '' (Lk. i. 3). '' When he says this, he does not deny that it
seemed good to God, for *the will of men* is *prepared by God*.
For that God may be worshiped by a saint is from the grace of
God '' (in Luc. i. 10). But also : '' By free will we are either
disposed toward virtue or inclined toward vice. And, therefore,
either free affection draws us toward error, or the will, following
reason, recalls us '' (Jac. et vit. beat. i. 1 ; de poenit. ii. 9. 80). It
is Christ, coming to us and into us, who effects this '' (in Luc.
x. 7). But this occurs chiefly through baptism. The efficacy
of the latter is seen in the blotting out of iniquity (*iniquitas*, the
sinful *habitus*), the forgiveness of sins, and the bringing of the
gift of spiritual grace (*spiritualis gratiae munus*) (apol. Dav. 13.
62): '' Thus perfect virtue destroys iniquity, and the remission
of sins every sin '' (de myst. 4. 20; ep. 7. 20 ; 41. 7 ; in Luc.
ii. 79). If, indeed, after the manner of the ancient church,
room is here found for the blotting out of sins by the endowment with new spiritual power, yet Ambrose could, nevertheless,
write : '' I will not glory because I am righteous, but I will
glory because I have been redeemed. I will glory, not because
I am empty of sins, but because my sins have been forgiven me ''
(Jac. et vit.; b. i. 6. 21 ; cf. in ps. 44. 1 ; ep. 73. 10). It
is easily seen that this forerunner of Augustine was not unac-

quainted with Paul.[1] We find in him, it is true, a certain synergism. But while the Eastern theologians represent man as making the beginning for the attainment of salvation, and then ascribe a *synergia* to God, here it is God who begins the work, and the *synergia* is upon the part of man. The Eastern teachers think of a divine, the Western of a human synergy.

Cf. FÖRSTER, Ambrosius, 1884, p. 139 ff. DEUTSCH, Des Ambros. Lehre von der Sünde u. Sündentilgung, 1867 (Program of the Joachimsthal Gymn. in Berlin). EWALD, Der Einfluss der stoisch-ciceron. Moral auf die Darstellung der Ethik bei Ambr., 1881.

## 2. PELAGIUS AND PELAGIANISM.

SOURCES. PELAGIUS, epistula ad Demetriadem in the Works of Jerome, ed. Vallarsi, xi. 2. 1 ff. Ep. ad Livaniam, in fragments only in Augustine and Jerome. Marius Mercator, in his Commonitorium super nomine Caelestii, and in the Liber subnotationum in verba Juliani. Eulogiarum liber, fragments

[1] We must not fail to note also the remarkable teaching of the monk, JOVINIAN (in Rome and Milan, about A. D. 390), although the sources do not enable us to form a perfectly reliable opinion in regard to him. Jovinian made a vigorous assault upon the low estimation of marriage, in which the influence of Manichæism and heathenism was so plainly seen ; maintained the moral equality of marriage and celibacy, as also of fasting and the receiving of food with thankfulness ; and asserted an equality of reward for all believers (Jerome adv. Jovin. l. ii. 5 ff.). A difficulty meets us in his assertion (ib. i. 3): "That those who have been with full faith regenerated in baptism cannot be subverted by the devil" (in ii. 1, "cannot be tempted," or, according to Julian of Eclanum, who had read the work of Jovinian, "cannot sin ;" vid. Aug. op. imperf. i. 98). It is beyond question that Jovinian expresses this view, but it is also to be observed that he does so with appeal to Jn. iii. 9 ; v. 18 (ii. 1), and that he did not deny to the baptized the possibility of repentance : "Although ye have fallen, repentance will restore you" (ii. 37). His real opinion can scarcely be other than that expressed in ii. 27 : "But if the Father and the Son make their abode with believers, where Christ is guest, *there* can be nothing lacking." Hence, they in whom Christ dwells, who are baptized and believe, are good, and fundamentally free from sin. They constitute the one true church (ii. 18, 20, 27 ; i. 2). So far as their salvation is concerned, it matters not whether they are married or unmarried, whether they fast or not; and every sin is of equal guilt (11. 30 f.). They shall receive at last the same reward. It must be noted, however, that he taught that "before baptism it is possible to sin or *not to sin*" (Julian, l. c.), and : "But whoever shall yield to temptation (*tentati fuerint*) are proved to have been baptized by water only and not by the Spirit, as we read of Simon Magus" (ii. 1). That the former of these citations represents his view cannot well be doubted, and it proves that his theory of sin was not as yet of the Ambrose-Augustinian type. It is surprising that Jerome does not take more advantage from the second. Jovtinian probably means that baptism is of immediate (vid. ii. 37) benefit only when received in faith (i. 3). The student of the History of Doctrines will note in Jovtinian premonitions of the interest soon to be awakened in the great problems discussed by Augustine. Upon Jovinian, vid. NEANDER, KG. ii. 2, p. 574 ff. GRÜTZMACHER, PRE. ix., ed. 3, 398 ff. HARNACK, Die Lehre v. d. Seligk. allein durch den Gl. in d. alt. K., in Ztschr. f. Theol. u. K., 1891, p. 138 ff. W. HALLER, Jovinianus, 1897.

in Augustine, de gestis Pelagii, and in Jerome in his Dial. c. Pelag.  Fragments of the work of Pelagius, De natura, in Augustine's De nat. et grat.  Of Pelagius, De libero arbitrio, ll. 4, also only fragments in Augustine.  Commentary upon the Pauline epistles in the works of Jerome (Migne, 30. 645-902).  Libellus fidei ad Innocentium in Hahn, Bibl. der Symbole, ed. 3, p. 288 ff.

Of the many writings of CAELESTIUS only fragments remain, especially from the Definitiones in Augustine's de perfectione justit.  His confession of faith is found in the Appendix to the works of Augustine, xvii. 2728 ff.  Vid. also citations in Marius Mercator (Migne, 48. 65 ff.).

Of JULIAN OF ECLANUM, who wrote Libri 4 and Libri 8 adversus Augustinum, we have very many fragments in August. c. Julianum, ll. 6, and especially the Opus imperfectum.  Vid. further the Confession, Hahn, ed. 3, p. 293 f., and Aug. opp. xvii. 272 ; also Marius Mercator (Migne, 48. 109 ff.).

Further, the Pseudo-Augustinian work, De vita christiana (opp. Aug. xvii. 1941), ascribed to Bishop FASTIDIUS, and other writings (letters and tractates) perhaps belonging to a Briton, AGRICOLA, in Caspari, Briefe, Abhandlungen u. Predigten, etc., 1890, pp. 1-167.  Vid. especially Opp. August. and Opp. Hieron.  The Liber apologeticus of OROSIUS, ed. Zangemeister, p. 601 ff.  Collections may be seen in M., Acta conciliorum iv., and in the appendix to the works of Augustine, xvii. 2649 ff.

PELAGIUS, a British monk of austere morality, began before the close of the fourth century to preach repentance with great earnestness.  He seems to have been under Greek influence (Marius Liber. subnot. praef. i. 2).[1]  The starting-point of his exhortations was the natural moral ability of man.  When confronted, as he speedily was, with the Augustinian : "Grant what Thou commandest, and command what Thou wilt" (Aug. don. pers. 20), it but confirmed him in his theory and led him to express himself the more positively.  Two fundamentally different conceptions of Christianity were here brought into contact.  The hitherto unharmonized doctrines of man's free will and the influence of divine grace presented a serious problem.  Pelagius soon won, in the eloquent CAELESTIUS, a disciple who stated the problems with keen discrimination and formulated them in a most aggressive way.  Contemporaries spoke not without reason of the "Pelagian, or Caelestian, heresy."  Their adherents were not few nor insignificant.  After A. D. 418, the diplomatic and prudent Pelagius and the radical Caelestius were reinforced by the young bishop of. Eclanum, JULIAN, a keen-witted but fundamentally rationalistic disputant, as champion of the new views.  That these three men present a progressive development cannot be denied.  The practical ideas of Pelagius are followed by the doctrinal formulation of Caelestius, and the con-

---

[1] In the theory of sin, following Theodore of Mopsuestia, through the medium of a Syrian, Rufinus, who, according to Jerome (in Hierem., lib. i. 1 praef.), appears to be identical with Aquileia.  Vid. also Aug., De pecc. orig. iii. 3.

ceptions of Julian, wrought out as component elements in his cosmogony, go beyond them both.

As we are in other connections to follow the course of the controversy, we shall here attempt merely to set forth clearly the Pelagian view of Sin, Liberty, and Grace. "Whenever I am called upon to speak upon moral training and the course of holy living, I am accustomed first to display the power and quality of human nature and show what it is able to accomplish, and then from this to incite the mind of the hearer to (some) forms of virtues, lest it profit nothing to summon to those things which it would have thought to be impossible for it." In these words of Pelagius (ad Demetr. 2 init.) we recognize distinctly his moral temperament. (*a*) God has commanded man to do that which is good ; he must, therefore, have the ability to do it. That is to say, man is free, *i. e.*, it is possible for him to decide for or against that which is good : "But we say that man is (always) able both to sin and not to sin, so that we confess ourselves to have always a free will" (Pel. in his confession). "Freedom of the will . . . consists in the possibility of committing sin or of abstaining from sin" (Jul. in Aug. op. imp. i. 78). This "possibility" has distinguished man ever since the creation : "For God, wishing to endow (his) rational creature with the gift of voluntary good and with the power of free will, by implanting in man the possibility of either part, made that to be his own which he may choose, in order that, being by nature capable of good and evil, he might choose either and bend his will to either the one or the other" (Pel. ad Dem. 3, cf. de lib. arb. i., ii., in Aug. de gr. Chr. 18. 19 ; 4. 5).[1] It, therefore, constitutes his essential nature, and is accordingly inamissible. Whether I will do good or do evil is a matter of my free will, but the freedom, "the possibility of this free will and of works," is from God : "By no means can I be without the possibility of good" (Pel. lib. arb. iii. in Aug. de gr. Chr. 4. 5). The ideas of Pelagius move within the limits of this scheme of freedom of the will, a scheme alike insufficient as seen from the religious or the moral point of view. It follows from it, that there is no such thing as a moral development of the individual. Good and evil are located in the separate acts of men. The separate works finally decide whether a man is good or evil. But it is possible for one, by a free use of the "possibility" of well-doing, to lead a holy life. This natural goodness (*bonum naturae*), historically regarded, made very many heathen philosophers capable of the most lofty

[1] In this and the following citations from Augustine, the first figure refers to the chapter and the second to the numbered paragraph in the parallel notation.

virtues; how much more, then, may Christians expect from it?
(Pel. ad Dem. 3. 7). There is no shrinking back from the inference, that an entirely sinless life is possible : "I say that
man is able to be without sin, . . . but I do not say that man is
without sin" (Pel. in Aug. nat. et grat. 7-8 ; de gr. Chr. 4. 5).
Despite the cautious statement of the passage cited, this declaration was very sincerely interpreted by the Pelagians ; see Aug.
de gest. Pel. 6. 16 ; ep. 156 (letter of Hilary from Syracuse to
Augustine). Caelest. definitiones in Aug. de perfect. justit.,
and the Pelagian in Caspari, pp. 5. 114 ff. (ep. de possibilitate
non peccandi).

(*b*) From this position we can understand the doctrinal
teaching concerning sin. This consists, as a matter of course,
only in the separate acts of the will. There is no such thing as
a sinful character or a sinful nature. Otherwise, sin would not
be sin—not something which can be avoided ; and God could
not charge sin to our account as guilt and punish it (Caelest. in
Aug. perf. grat. 2. 1; 6. 15). Since sin cannot have been
created by God, it is not a thing (*res*), but an act (*actus*) (ib.
2. 4). It is a fault, not of nature, but of the will (in Aug. de
pecc. orig. 6. 6 ; op. imp. i. 48). Man's peculiar nature, the
justice of God, and the reality of sin, alike forbid us to speak of
an "original sin." If such were the nature of sin, a deliverance from it would be impossible : "Even if we should wish not
to be able not to sin, we are not able not to be able not to sin,
because no will is able to free itself from that which is proved to
be inseparably implanted in (its) nature" (Pel. in Aug. nat. et
grat. 49, 50, 57, 58). "If original sin be contracted by the
generation of original nativity . . . it cannot be taken away
from infants, since that which is innate continues to the very end
of him to whom it has adhered from the occasion of his ances-
tors" (Jul. op. imp. i. 61). Inasmuch as sin consists only in
separate acts of the will, the idea of its propagation by the act
of generation is absurd. Adam was certainly the first sinner,
but such a connection between his sin and ours cannot be established. The sins and guilt of parents no more pass over to their
children than do those of children to their parents (op. imp. iii.
14, 19 f.). "If their own sins do not harm parents after
their conversion, much more can they not through the parents
injure their children" (Pel. in Marius Com. 2. 10). The view
of Augustine is habitually referred to by Julian as Manichæism
(*e. g.*, op. imp. vi. 10 : "Your doctrine differs in nothing
from the Manichæans"). In contravention of God's Word, it
pronounces marriage and the desire for carnal intercourse sinful
(de nupt. et concup. i. 1, 2 ; ii. 1. 2). Julian refuses to recog-

nize Augustine's distinction between marriage (*nuptiae*) and
concupiscence : "Natural sin within cannot be asserted without
defamation of sexual intercourse" (op. imp. v. 5). Adam's little,
childish sin (op. imp. vi. 21) is an act of disobedience which
has only a temporary significance for him, *i. e.*, until his conversion (op. imp. vi. 11 f.), and none at all for us. Adam's death
was not a punishment for sin, but only conformity to a law of
nature (Aug. de gestis Pel. 11. 23 f.; op. imp. ii. 64, 93 f., but
also vi. 30). Accordingly, new-born children are sinless, and
baptism cannot in their case have any sin-remitting effect (vid.
Caelest. in Aug. pecc. orig. 6. 6 ; Marius Lib. subnot. praef. v.;
also Jul. op. imp. i. 53 : "He bestows his gifts according to the
capacity of the recipients").[1] The passage, Rom. 5. 12, merely
asserts "that sin has passed from the first man upon other men,
not by propagation, but by imitation" (Aug. de peccator.
meritis et remiss. i. 9. 9); or the term πάντες does not mean
absolutely all (Aug. de nat. et grat. 41. 48).

   (*c*) This brings us to the Pelagian explanation of the universality of sin, which all experience testifies. It is attributed to
imitation, the "long practice (*longus usus*) of sinning and the
long habit (*longa consuetudo*) of vices" (Pelag. ad Demetr. 8).
"For no other cause occasions for us the difficulty of doing good
than the long custom of vices, which has infected us from childhood, and gradually, through many years, corrupted us, and thus
holds us afterward bound and addicted to itself, so that it seems
in some way to have the force of nature" (ib. cf. 17 fin.). To
this must be added the natural sensuous and worldly character of
man (Pel. in Aug. de gr. Chr. 10. 11). This line of thought
reveals the final conclusion reached by the naive Pelagianism of
the Greeks: There are really no sinners, but only separate
wicked acts. A religious conception of sin is hereby excluded, and nothing more is needed than the effort to perform
separate good deeds. But just as truly is a religious conception
of the history of the race impossible, since there are no sinful
men, but only wicked acts of individual men.

   (*d*) The religious and moral superficiality of this way of re-

---

[1] It is of dogmatico-historical interest to observe that the Pelagians were,
on the one hand, charged with undermining infant baptism (Council of Carthage, vid. Aug. ep. 157. 3. 22. Innocent in Aug. c. duas epp. Pel. ii. 4. 7 :
"They seem to me to wish to annihilate baptism itself"); and that they were,
on the other hand, very anxious to free themselves from the charge (Aug. pecc.
orig. 19. 21 ; c. duas epp. Pel. iv. 2. 2); the confession of faith of Pelagius and
Julian, Caelestus, op. imp. iii. 146 ; i. 53 ; HAHN, Bibl. ed 3, 294, in reference to which Augustine indeed says : "You fear to say, Let them not be
baptized, lest not only your faces be defiled by the spittle of men, but your
heads softened by the sandals of women" (c. Jul. iii. 5. 11).

garding the subject is very plainly manifest in the doctrine of grace. The necessity of grace for the attainment of salvation is not denied. On the contrary, Pelagius has declared that grace is needed "not only for every hour or for every moment, but even for every separate act of ours" (Aug. de gr. Chr. 2. 2 ; 7. 8 ; 32. 36 ; de gest. Pel. 14. 31 ; Pel. ep. ad Dem. 3 fin.; Jul. in op. imp. iii. 106 ; i. 52).

Over against this affirmation of the "help of grace," or "divine assistance," Caelestius, indeed, declares in his fashion, "that the will is not free if it needs the aid of God," and that "our victory is not from the assistance of God, but from (our) free will" (Aug. de gest. Pel. 18. 42). This is but a blunt statement of the logical inference from the position of Pelagius. The latter wrote : "grace is given in order that what is commanded by God may be *more easily* fulfilled " (Aug. de gr. Chr. 26. 27), from which Augustine rightly infers : "that even without this, that which is divinely commanded can be done, although less easily." What do the Pelagians then understand by grace? Really nothing more than the "good of nature," or the endowment with free will, *i. e.*, the possibility of doing good or evil. So Pelagius distinctly expressed himself at the council at Diospolis : "this he calls the grace of God, that our nature, when it was created, received the possibility of not sinning, since it was created with a free will" (in Aug. de gest. Pel. 10. 22). The endowment with reason (Pel. ad Dem. 2) and free will is primarily grace. This was sufficient in the primitive age of the race (ib. 4 ff. 8). But when ignorance and the habit of sinning gained the upper hand among men, God gave the law (Pel. ad Dem. 8), and again, when the law proved too weak to break the power of evil habit, he gave the teachings and example of Christ (Aug. pecc. orig. 26. 30). Pelagius, indeed, writes : "We, who have been instructed through the grace of Christ and born again to better manhood, who have been expiated and purified by his blood,[1] and incited by his example to perfect righteousness, ought to be better than those who were before the law, and better also than those who were under the law" (ad Dem. 8); but the whole argument of this letter, where the topic is simply the knowledge of the law as a means for the promotion of virtue (9, 10, 13, 16, 20, 23), as well as the declaration, that God opens our eyes and reveals the future "when he illuminates us with the multiform and ineffable gift of celestial grace " (Aug. de gr. Chr. 7. 8), proves that for him that the "assistance of God" consists, after all, only in instruction. Augustine is correct

---

[1] The same idea occurs in Julian, op. imp. i. 171.

in maintaining that, in addition to nature and the law, it is only the teaching and example[1] of Christ which are thought of by Pelagius as embraced in the term, grace (de gr. Chr. 41. 45 ; c. duas epp. Pel. iv. 5. 11). "Briefly and summarily I reply to thee : ' He is a Christian in whom are to be found those three things which ought to be in all Christians : knowledge, faith, and obedience—knowledge, by which God is known ; faith, by which (our) acceptance is believed ; obedience, by which the compliance of servitude is rendered to the one believed ' " (ep. de possibil. non peccandi, 5. 1. Casp., p. 119). Christianity is law, and, as compared with the Old Testament, an enlarged law (ib. p. 71). It is, therefore, good works which decide whether anyone is good : " For the wicked are so called from their wicked works ; thus, on the contrary, the good are so named from their good works " (de vit. chr. 10). The Christian reads the "word of God" as a *law*, which requires to be not only known, but also fulfilled (Pel. ad Dem. 23). He acts, therefore, in accordance with it, and seeks to " extinguish habit by habit," since " it is habit which nourishes either vices or virtues " (ib. 17. 13). He abandons the " imitation of Adam," and lays hold upon the " imitation of the holiness of Christ " (op. imp. ii. 146). This doctrine of grace is in entire harmony with the theory of sin. Sin is overcome through free will enlightened by the reason, or by the giving of the law. This, properly speaking, is grace. That which is occasionally said of atonement through the blood of Christ, of the forgiveness of sins, and renewal through baptism, is inconsistent, and beyond the range of Pelagian ideas.

Instead of attempting a summary, I cite in conclusion the six propositions into which the first antagonist of Pelagianism, Paulinus of Milan, compressed the Pelagian doctrine : " Adam was born mortal, and would have died, whether he had sinned or not sinned. The sin of Adam injured only himself, and not

---

[1] For the Pelagian idea of following Christ (also de vita christ. 6, 14 ; Jul. in op. imp. ii. 146 ; ii. 223 ; Aug. de gr. Chr. 2. 2), vid. Caspari, pp. 5, 20, 40, 121. Julian emphasized the truth that we are by Christ incited to a responsive love toward God : " God, as is well known, did whatever he did toward us with inestimable love, in order that we might, though late, love him in return " (op. imp. i. 94). Pelagius could not clearly explain wherein consisted the unutterable impartation of grace which he maintained. He mentions, indeed, in reference to Rom. 4. 7, the forgiveness of sins (" in addition, faith is first imputed for righteousness in order that he may be absolved from the past and justified in the present, and prepared for future works of faith," Mi. 30. 688). But, under the Pelagian theory of sin, the significance of forgiveness is very slight, the more so since such forgiveness applies only to the sins committed before the renewal wrought in baptism (Aug. c. duas ep. Pel. iii. 8. 24 ; iv. 7. 17 ; de gr. Chr. 34. 39).

22

the human race.   Children who are now born are in the state in
which Adam was before the fall.   Neither does the whole human
race die through the death or fall of Adam, nor does the whole
human race arise from the dead through the resurrection of
Christ.   The law sends into the kingdom of heaven in the same
way as does the gospel.   Men were impeccable, *i. e.*, without
sin, even before the coming of the Lord '' (in Marius Common.
1. 1 ; cf. 1 subnot. praef. 5).

### 3.  AUGUSTINE'S DOCTRINE OF SIN AND GRACE.

Of the works of Augustine, the following are of chief importance for us :
Liber de 83 quaestionibus (about A. D. 388 to about A. D. 396), De libero
arbitrio (A. D. 388-395).  Quaestiones ad Simplicianum (397).  Confes-
siones, ll. 13 (400).  In connection with the Pelagian controversy : De peccatorum meritis et remissione, ll. 3 (412).  De spiritu et littera (412).  De
natura et gratia (415).  De perfectione justitiae hominis (415).  De gestis
Pelagii (417).  De gratia Christi et de peccato originali, ll. 2 (418).  De
nuptiis et concupiscentia, ll. 2 (419).  Contra duas epistulas Pelagianorum,
ll. 4 (420).  Contra Julianum, ll. 6 (421).  De gratia et libero arbitrio (427).
De correptione et gratia (427).  De praedestinatione sanctorum (428).  De
dono perseverantiae (429).  Opus imperfectum contra Julianum, ll. 6 (until
his death).  Also a number of letters, vid. Opp. xiv. 1705 ff.  Compare the
literature referred to at the beginning of the section.

A.  The controlling factor in giving to Augustine's doctrine of
grace its peculiar form was not primarily the nature of his conversion, although this helped to mould his theory ; nor the Pelagian doctrine which he was compelled to face, although this gave
form to many details in the statement of the doctrine ; least of
all, the Augustinian conception of the church.   Historically
considered, Augustine, following Ambrose, gave recognition to
the religious common sense of the West, and was moulded by
the ideas of the Epistle to the Romans.   His doctrine was complete in its essential features before the beginning of the great
controversy (cf. the remarks, don. persev. 20. 52).

The first utterances of Augustine upon this subject remind us
of the view of Ambrose.   Indeed, they are even more moderate
than the latter.   The human race is a "mass of sin" (l. de 83
quaest. 68. 3, 4).   No one, not even new-born children, is free
from original sin (*peccatum originale*, conf. i. 7 ; v. 9 ; ix. 6).
Concupiscence or lust, ignorance, and death, reign in the human
race (qu. 66. 1; lib. arb. i. 4. 9 ff.; iii. 20. 55 : "lust comes from
a perverse will ; '' conf. viii. 5. 10), "because it was just, that
after our nature had sinned  .  .  .  we should be born animal and
carnal " (qu. 66. 3).   But our nature sinned in Adam (66. 3-5 ;
lib. arb. iii. 20. 56).   Yet Adam sinned as a free man.   Evil
in the world is a result of freedom, as Augustine very frequently
reminds the Manichæans (vid. esp. de. lib. arb.).   The law

can accomplish nothing toward releasing from the state of sin, since it can only convince of sin (66. 1, 3). There is need of grace. "And since no one is able to will unless admonished and called, either internally where no man may see, or externally through the spoken sermon or some other visible signs, it comes to pass that God works in us even to will itself" (68. 5). But, although grace here produces the will (to do good), yet Augustine thinks : "But God would not have mercy . . . unless the will had preceded," and says the reason why God has mercy upon some and rejects others lies " in the most hidden merits " of the former, since God is not unrighteous (ib. 68. 5, 4). Of fallen man, it is said : " It was fitting that God should not only not hinder, but should even assist him in willing" (lib. arb. iii. 20. 55). The capacity for striving after salvation remained to his will (ib. iii. 22. 65). He is able of himself to believe and to will, but God must give him the power to do good (exposit. quarundam proposit. ex ep. ad Rom. 61 ; cf. retract. i. 23. 3 ; de praedest. 3. 7). The form of doctrinal conception may here be summarized as follows : Man has, through the fall of Adam, become subject to ignorance, lust, and death. In response to the call (*vocatio*) of God, he is indeed able to believe and to will that which is good, but it is only grace that works in him the power to perform it.

But, under renewed study of the Epistle to the Romans (vid. quaest. ad Simplician. i. quaest 2), Augustine revised this theory (vid. remarks, praed. sanct. 3. 8). The subject there under discussion is the election of Jacob, according to Rom. 9. Works can in this instance not be the ground of the election, nor can the divine prescience of the " merits of the faith " of Jacob (l. c. qu. 2. 2. ff.). According to Rom. 9. 16 and Phil. 2. 13, the resolution to save lies solely in the mercy and good pleasure of God. Hence salvation must be attributed solely to grace. It has its beginning in man in faith. Even this faith is a work wrought by grace—namely, through the divine call (10). But to this it might be objected, that grace of itself is not sufficient, but that the human will must be combined with it. To this Augustine replies : " But this is manifest, that we will in vain, unless God have mercy ; but I do not know how it can be said, that God has mercy in vain unless we will. *For if God has mercy*, we also will ; our willing belongs to the same mercy " (12). Therefore, it depends solely upon the omnipotent will of God, whether anyone shall will or not will. When this idea is combined with that of the divine call, it results in the discrimination of two classes : the elect (*electi*) who are suitably (*congruenter*) called, whom God calls " in whatever way was suitable for them;' and the called (*vocati*), to whom the call indeed came, but "because it was of such a character that they could not be moved by it and were not suitable (*apti!*) to accept it, they could be said to be called indeed, but not chosen" (*electi*) (13). That Esau was not chosen is, therefore, because God did not have mercy upon him, and did not effectually call him (14). There can be no thought here of any unrighteousness in God, since no one has a right to be delivered from the "mass of sin." But the judgments and ways of God are inscrutable (Rom. 11. 23). God "therefore laments with justice and mercy" (16). It is, hence, not the willing and the conduct of man which lead to salvation, but solely the grace of God, which has mercy upon some and effectually calls them, but leaves others to their merited fate. It is interesting to observe here that the peculiar effect of grace is held to be, not the awakening of faith, but an upright life : "But grace justifies, in order that the justified man may be able to live justly (righteously): the first thing, therefore, is grace ; the second, good works" (3, cf. 12 : "the will of man alone does not suffice, that we may live righteously and rightly"). This may be understood in the light of Augustine's personal Christian experience. He learned to lay hold upon the grace of God, not because it awakened in him, as in Luther, the assurance of faith, but because it overcame his unwillingness to lead a Christian life. He apprehended it as he read the exhortation to moral conduct in Rom. 13. 13 f.: "Neither did I wish to read any further, nor was there any need; for immediately with the end of this sentence, the light of assurance being, as it were, poured into my heart, all the shades of doubt were dissipated" (conf. viii. 12. 29, cf. 30 : "Thou didst convert me to Thyself, that I might desire neither wife nor any other hope of this world ; " also the prayer x. 1).

But we notice also in this connection the influence of the conception of God entertained by Augustine. Profoundly and fully as he recognizes the personal God holding intercourse with man, yet there is also a foreign element in his conception of the Deity. He thinks of God as pure Being, absolutely simple, immutable, and indestructible (*e. g.*, soliloq. i. 1. 4 init.; de trin. vi. 6. 8 ; in Joh. tr. 13. 5 ; 1. 8).[1] This absolute Subsistence (*substantia*) is the Good. All that exists either is this Subsistence or is derived from it. Hence it follows, that everything that exists is good. "Therefore every subsistence is either God or from God, be-

---

[1] The last passage reads : "What is formed in my heart when I say God ? A certain great and supreme Subsistence is thought of, which transcends every mutable carnal and animal creature."

cause all good is either God or from God" (lib. arb. iii. 13. 36). Hence, the base and the evil are not subsistences. "And that evil of which I inquired whence it was, is not a subsistence, because if it were a subsistence it would be good" (conf. vii. 12. 18).[1] Evil bears a privitive character as a *privatio boni* (civ. dei, xi. 22). It has no "efficient cause," but only a "deficient cause" (civ. dei, xii. 7). It is a lack of existence, not a subsistence. Evil has its basis, not in God, but in free will: "And I inquired what iniquity was, and I found not a subsistence, but the perversity of a will turned away from God, the supreme Subsistence, to the depths (conf. vii. 16. 22). The evil will is the source of all evil (enchirid. 4. 15 ; civ. dei, xii. 7 ; op. imp. vi. 5).

But if evil be thought of in this (Neo-Platonic) scheme as a nonentity in man, then grace can be regarded only as a creative act of God, making of the nonentity an entity, by transforming the basis of the former, the *evil will*, through the *inbreathing of a good will*. It is only from this point of view that we can entirely understand Augustine's doctrine of grace. He has in view primarily, not the establishment of a personal communion, but a creative act. Grace is effectual as the almighty, creative Will, which infuses into man a new subsistence, the moral will.

B. These principles remained as normative for the exhaustive treatment given to the subject by Augustine in opposition to Pelagianism.

(a) God created man good and upright. He knew nothing of concupiscence. His will was positively good. Being thus good, he was in consequence truly free. "God made (man) therefore, as it is written, upright, and hence of a good will. . . . Therefore the decision of the will is truly free whenever it does not serve vices and sins" (civ. dei, xiv. 11. 1 ; 10 ; op. imp. v. 61). In this condition man served God, and found supreme satisfaction in doing so. The body meanwhile, with all its impulses, served the soul, and reason reigned in man (civ. dei, xiv. 24. 1 ; 26 init.; nupt. et conc. ii. 15. 30 ; pecc. merit. ii. 22. 36). But this condition was one of freedom : "It should be within his choice, either that he should always wish to be in this (good will) or that he should not always thus wish, but should change from it to an evil will without compulsion from any source" (op. imp. v. 61). The divine assistance (*adjutorium*) was within his reach, by means of which he was *able*, but *not compelled*, to persevere in the good. This was the "first grace" (corrept. et grat. 11. 31). There was a *posse non peccare*, but not a *non*

---

[1] Ib.: "Therefore whatever things exist are good."

*posse peccare*, and, in connection with this, a *posse non mori*, but
not a *non posse mori* (ib. 12. 33 ; op. imp. vi. 16), and hence :
" He had a possibility, but not a necessity, of sinning " (op.
imp. vi. 5). Man was, therefore, created with an inclination
of the will toward the good and was by God preserved in it, but
in such a way that, through his freedom, it was possible for his
inclination to be turned in another direction.

(*b*) All of this Adam lost in the fall. Since he transgressed
the commandment of God, which he might so easily have fulfilled, his will became evil. Pride was the cause of it. Man
was not willing to obey God, but wished to be his own master.
But, since man refuses obedience to God, God assigns it as his
punishment, that his flesh shall cease to serve the spirit, that
ignorance shall take possession of his soul, and the potential mortality of body and soul shall become a reality. " An evil will
preceded, by which credence was given to the wile of the serpent, and evil concupiscence followed, by which he stood gaping
before the forbidden food " (op. imp. i. 71 ; vid. also civ. dei,
xiv. 11 ff.; xiii. 3. 13 ; nat. et grat. 25. 28). Adam has not
merely done a single act, but has become a sinner.

(*c*) This character of Adam has now passed over to his posterity. Through the punitive decree of God, Adam has become
a different man, and human nature has thereby been changed :
" Nature (was) vitiated by sin : our nature, there transformed
for the worse, not only became a sinner, but also begets sinners ;
and yet that languor in which the power of living aright has
been lost is certainly not nature, but defect " (nupt. et conc. ii.
34. 57 ; 8. 20; c. Jul. iii. 24. 53 ; op. imp. iii. 11 ; ii. 163 ;
civ. dei, xiii. 3 ; cf. in Joh. tr. 44. 1 : "defect grew, *inolevit*, instead of nature "). But now all men were in Adam : " All men
were that one man " (pecc. mer. et rem. i. 10. 11); hence, according to Rom. 5. 12 (ἐφ' ᾧ = in quo): "in Adam all then
sinned " (ib. iii. 17. 4 ; nupt. et conc. ii. 5. 15 ; op. imp. ii.
176). They were all, indeed, contained in him. From this it
follows : (1) That his moral character becomes theirs. (2)
That the penalty pronounced upon him (of being subject to concupiscence and death) passes over also upon them. We have his
sin, and are burdened with his guilt. " Wherefore condemnation in view of the magnitude of that sin has changed nature for
the worse, so that what preceded penally in the first sinning men,
follows naturally in other men in birth. . . . But what the
parent man is, that is also the offspring man. . . . To such an
extent was human nature vitiated and changed in him that it
should have to endure the disobedience of concupiscence warring
in its members, and be subject to the necessity of death, and

thus that which sprung from fault became penalty, *i. e.*, he should generate those subject to sin and death " (civ. dei, xiii. 3, 13, 14; op. imp. iv. 104; vi. 22; i. 47). Thus, in Adam the whole human race has become a "mass of perdition" and is condemned in him. "For all men were thus seminally in the loins of Adam when he was condemned, and, therefore, he was not condemned without them" (op. imp. v. 12). From this no one is exempt, not even new-born children (c. Jul. i. 6. 22; op. imp. i. 56; iii. 154; cf. the scriptural proof in pecc. mer. et rem. i. 27. 40 ff.). This is attested by the sufferings which the righteous God appoints for men, and especially by the sufferings of children (pecc. mer. et rem. iii. 10. 18) and by exorcism at baptism (c. Jul. vi. 5. 11). As original sin simply as such brings condemnation, it must have this effect even in the case of children, although there is meted out to them "the lightest condemnation of all" (pecc. mer. et rem. i. 12. 15; 16. 21). From all the above it follows, that there is in us a "necessity of sinning" (op. imp. i. 106; v. 61; perf. just. 4. 9). Of this life, it is said : "whether mortal life or vital death, I know not" (conf. i. 67; cf. civ. dei, xiii. 10 init.). But, above all else, the absolute unfitness of man for salvation must be emphasized. It is the energy with which Augustine maintains this idea, embracing all human activity under sin and guilt (the virtues of the heathen being but "splendid vices ;" cf. civ. dei, v. 12 ff.; xix. 25),[1] which marks his advance beyond Ambrose, and constitutes the religious significance of his theory. That nothing good and no salvation can be found except in Christ was the thought impressed upon the church by these discussions.

Original sin is regarded in the light of real sin, as well as of guilt. It is sin, and is a divine penalty. It is propagated among men, not in the way of imitation (c. Jul. vi. 24. 75), but by generation. "Through one man it entered the world, and it passes through all men" (pecc. mer. et rem. i. 12. 33). Although marriage is a moral good (pecc. orig. 37. 42; 33. 38; though celibacy is to be preferred, vid. op. imp. v. 17), yet generation never occurs without sinful concupiscence, as is proved clearly enough by the sense of shame associated with the act (nupt. et conc. ii. 5. 14), and the concupiscence passes over upon the children. This is the case even when the parents are regenerate, " as from the seed of an olive springs nothing but a wild olive " (ib. ii. 34. 58). " Yet, when it shall come to the act of generation, it is not possible that allowable and honorable inter-

---

[1] This term does not itself occur in Augustine, but it admirably summarizes his view ; somewhat as the *credo quia absurdum* attributed to Tertullian ; cf. supra, p. 127.

course should occur without the burning of lust, so that what springs from reason might be transmitted, and not what springs from lust. . . . Of this concupiscence of the flesh, which I grant is in the regenerate not imputed as sin (previously described as 'venial sins'), but which is not found in nature except from sin—of this concupiscence of the flesh, I say . . . whatever offspring is born is by virtue of its origin (*originaliter*) bound to sin " (nupt. et conc. i. 24. 27). There is "a defect (*vitium*) of the seed " (ib. ii. 8. 20). In the question of Traducianism or Creationism, Augustine could reach no conclusion (de anima et ejus origine, ii. 14. 20 ; 15. 21 ; retract. i. 1. 3). There is, consequently, at this point a lack of clearness in his theory of sin. He certainly represents sin as propagated by lust in copulation, but this is not to be understood as though he regarded the intercourse of the sexes as in itself sinful or unworthy of man. His idea is only, that man, being a sinner, can generate offspring only in a sinful way. The sinful state, to his mind, logically precedes the sinful act. It is, therefore, not correct to trace this idea to unvanquished Manichæan dualism (HARNACK, DG. iii. 191, note 3), as was done already by Julian of Eclanum. It may be said that the "monastic temper of Augustine favored " it (LOOFS, DG., ed. 3, p. 215), but beyond this we cannot go. In evidence against the suggestion, we may recall that even yet there lies in the background in Augustine's mind the conviction that sin has no subsistence, but is only a *privatio boni*, a μὴ ὄν (nat. et grat. 20. 22 ; c. Jul. 1. 8. 37 ; enchir. 11 ; cf. p. 341). From original sin, which is thus a " necessity," proceed the individual sins of man, which he adds to the former " of his own free will, not through Adam " (pecc. mer. et rem. i. 15. 20 ; conf. v. 9 init.). Yet, despite all this, we may speak of a free will (*liberum arbitrium*) even in the case of the sinner, though not in the sense of the Pelagian *possibilitas utriusque partis*, for a man cannot be at the same time both a good and an evil tree (grat. Chr. c. 18, 19, § 19 ff.). The *libertas* of paradise has been lost, *i. e.*, "to have with righteousness full immortality ; " for this freedom ("free to live well and uprightly ") now exists only by virtue of the influence of "grace," which is precisely what is lacking in the sinner's case. But the freedom to sin of his own will has, however, remained to him. " We do not say that by the sin of Adam free will perished from the nature of men, but that it is capable of sinning . . . but it is not capable of living well and piously, unless the will of man has itself been liberated by the grace of God " (c. duas ep. Pel. ii. 5. 9 ; op. imp. i. 94). Hence, " we are not such against our will."

(*d*) In harmony with what we have before observed, the

words of Augustine just cited indicate clearly that, in his view, righteousness is a "living well and rightly." This gives us a clue to his conception of the nature of original sin. It cannot be, as in Luther, unbelief. According to Augustine, it is above all, *evil* or *carnal concupiscence*, which finds its subject, indeed, in the soul : "for the flesh does not lust (*concupiscit*) without the soul, although the flesh is said to lust, because the soul lusts carnally" (perf. just. 8. 19). In this dominion of sensuality over the spirit we are to recognize the penal consequence of the first sin, but not its cause. "The corruption of the body which oppresses the soul is not the cause, but the penalty, of the first sin ; neither does the corruptible flesh make the soul a sinner, but the sinful soul makes the flesh corrupt" (civ. dei, xiv. 3 ; cf., as to the term, flesh, ib. c. 2). With this degradation of the spirit i. intimately connected the "horrifying depth of ignorance." This enables us to understand why man surrenders himself to his passions and to vain things. "But these are all characteristics of wicked men, yet they come from that root of error and perverted affection with which every son of Adam is born" (civ. dei, xxii. 22. 1). Lust finds its explanation in ignorance. And both have their foundation in the perverted inclination of man. He turned away from God and toward himself, and in this fell a prey to the world. He wanted to love himself, and abandoned his love to God ; he is, in consequence, given over to the lust which loves and pursues the husks of the world. This "love of self" is the real essence of sin. That such is Augustine's conception is manifest from his magnificent presentation of the subject in *Sermo 96. 2. 2 :* "The first ruin of man was the *love of himself.* . . . That is, his making it his will that he should will to love himself. . . . For, having forsaken God, he begins to love himself and is driven away from himself to the loving of the things which are without. . . . Thou hast begun to love thyself : remain in thyself, if thou canst. What is without ? . . . Thou hast begun to love what is without thee ; thou hast destroyed thyself. Therefore, when a man's love passes from himself to the things which are without, he begins to lose himself (*evanescere*) in vain things and to squander his strength like the prodigal. He is emptied, poured out, rendered destitute, and feeds swine." Such is the nature of sin : love of self, ignorance, concupiscence. Man falls away from God, wishing to serve himself, and he is drawn into the whirlpool of worldliness. Henceforth his existence is but death. Of our first parents, it is said : "Therefore, although they lived many years afterward, yet they began to die in that day in which they received the law by which they should grow into the decay of old age" (pecc. mer. et rem. i. 16. 21). The whole host of evils now overwhelms man.

Thus life in the world was by sin transformed into a hell, from which only Christ was able to deliver (civ. dei, xxii. 22. 4). But, in discussing original evil, Augustine does not forget the *original good*. Men generate men,[1] and God permits the latter through his "efficacious power" to become men, with intellectual likeness to God. "In original evil there are two things, sin and penalty; in original good, two other things, propagation and conformation. Yet there is not entirely extinct within man a certain spark of the character (*scintilla rationis*) in which he was created after the image of God" (civ. dei, xxii. 24. 1, 2, 3).

Such is Augustine's doctrine of sin. Here at length sin is treated from a purely religious point of view, as the absolute opposite of the good, and as the condition of the race, which can be changed only through Christ. But here, too, sin is regarded as the sin of *man* himself and of the *race*. The way is thus opened for the recognition of the spiritual character of man as in itself consistent, and for a proper conception of the historical development of the race. Augustine's doctrine of original sin is not only a matter of religious interest, but it is also a scientific advance in the realms of psychology and ethics, as well as a massive conception in the sphere of history.[2]

(*e*) In harmony with his doctrine of sin, Augustine attributes the salvation of men to grace alone. Grace begins the good in man, and it remains actively influential in him after it has liberated his will. "It goes before him when unwilling, that he may will; it follows him when willing, that he may not will in vain" (enchir. 9. 32). God "prepares the will, and by co-operating completes what he begins by operating. Since he, in beginning, operates that we may will, who, in perfecting, co-operates with us when we will" (grat. et lib. arb. 17. 33). It is thus only under the gracious influence of God that man comes to the good and remains in it. We have already observed (p. 341) that Augustine conceives of grace as divine creative power in action. We understand, therefore, how it can be described as a "wonderful and ineffable power" which effects in man "not alone true revelations, but also good wills" (grat. Chr. 24. 25), and how its influence can be pronounced necessary even in the state of integrity in paradise (ep. 186. 11. 37; enchir. 25. 106). Grace is simply the resistless creative power of God, which ex-

---

[1] Observe the point of view under which Augustine could here regard the act of generation.

[2] I fail to find a proper recognition of this and other aspects in SEYREICH'S dissertation, Die Geschichtsphilosophie Augustins, Chemnitz, 1891.

erts its influence in the hearts of men as the power of the good. This must be kept in view when we follow Augustine's delineation of the work of grace. Not man himself, not doctrine, not example, not the law, can help. The bare commandment is powerless against concupiscence. Only through grace and faith can salvation be attained: "what the law of works demands with threatening, that the law of faith secures by believing." Here the motto is: "Grant what Thou commandest;" there, "Do what I command" (sp. et lit. 13. 22). The first blessing is the *forgiveness of sins*, which man receives through baptism. With it begins *renewal* (*renovatio*), which finds here its basis (pecc. mer. et rem. ii. 7. 9 ; 27. 43 ; conf. i. 11). Sin is, therefore, forgiven through baptism. Concupiscence, however, yet remains even in the baptized ; but it is no longer sin, because God no longer so accounts it (nupt. et conc. i. 25. 28 ; 31. 36 ; pecc. mer. et rem. i. 37. 70). It is to be noted, however, that the forgiveness of sins is not brought into such unvarying connection with faith as in Paul. The Christian life begins with faith, which is wrought by God (supra, p. 339) as the "beginning of our religion and life." Faith is described as " to agree that what is said is true " (sp. et lit. 31. 54) or " to meditate upon with assent " (praedest. sanct. 2. 5). Faith is, therefore, the *assensio* to the preached truth (cf. enchir. 7. 20 ; conf. vi. 5 ; in Joh. tr. 40. 9 ; 79. 1). This explains why a higher stage is supposed to be reached in knowledge (*cognitio*), according to Isa. 7. 9 : "unless you had believed, you would not know " (*e. g.*, sermo 43 ; in Joh. tr. 27. 7 ; 22. 5 ; 29. 6 ; 48. 1 ; 112. 1 : "he can believe before he can know ;" ep. 114. 7 ; 120. 3). We meet, indeed, statements which appear to lead us beyond this definition, as, for example, when the idea of "justification through faith " is occasionally reproduced (vid. sub), or when it is said that men would not be free from sin, "unless united and joined by faith to his body " (*i. e.*, Christ's, sermo 143. 1), or when a distinction is drawn between " believing Christ " and " believing in Christ," and the latter is described as constituting Christian faith (sermo 144. 2). But just here the thought becomes clear, as Augustine explains : " For he believes in Christ who both hopes in Christ and loves Christ . . . to him Christ comes, and in some way is united to him and is made a member in his body ; which cannot occur unless both hope and love are added " (cf. in Joh. tr. 29. 6). Here, again, faith points beyond itself to a higher stage. Instead of knowledge, this is now love.[1] The

---

[1] Through love there is effected also an advance in knowledge, in Joh. tr. 96. 4.

nature of faith is not that trustful attitude of heart which apprehends present grace, but it is the preparatory step toward a righteousness not yet attained.  It is, therefore, also the ability to
pray for this righteousness : "the spirit of grace brings it to
pass that we have faith, so that through faith we may by praying
secure the ability to do what we are commanded" (grat. et lib.
arb. 14. 28 ; sermo 168. 5 ; enchir. 28. 117).  Faith in itself
is thus the belief of the truth of revelation.  But it becomes
Christian faith only when it is a "faith which works by love"
(fid. et op. 16. 27 ; serm. 168. 2 ; cf. in Joh. tr. 6. 21).

( f ) The chief work of grace is really the *infusion of love*,[1]
or of a *new and good will*, by the Holy Spirit.  "They who
have love are born of God ; they who have not, are not born
of God" (in Joh. tr. 5. 7).  This is not effected by external
commandments, nor by the example of Christ ; but "he gives an
increase internally by shedding abroad love in our hearts by the
Holy Spirit" (sp. et lit. 25. 42 ; pecc. mer. et rem. i. 9, 10),
or there is even said to be an "*inspiratio* of good will and work"
(corr. et grat. 2. 3).  Thus evil desire is crowded out by desire
for God and his will : "the Spirit inspiring good *concupiscentia*
instead of evil—that is, shedding abroad love in our hearts"
(sp. et lit. 4. 6 ; enchir. 32. 121).  The endowing with new
moral power, and thus the transforming of the man ("nature repaired by grace," sp. et lit. 27. 47), is for Augustine the proper
meaning of the term, justification.  Its essential nature consists
in this, that man becomes actually righteous, and is, hence, able
to perform righteous works.  "For what else is it to be justified,
than to be made righteous (just), *i. e.*, by him who justifies the
ungodly man, that from being ungodly he may be made righteous" (ib. 26. 45 ; grat. et lib. arb. 6. 13).  "Through the
gift of the Spirit we work righteousness" (sp. et lit. 18. 31).
Thus the individual becomes a new man—from being an ungodly, he becomes a righteous man ; from being a dead, becomes a living man.  "He heals the sick in spirit and revives
the dead, *i. e.*, he justifies the ungodly" (nat. et grat. 26. 29).
"When the soul lives in sin, it is its death ; but when it becomes righteous, it becomes a participant in another life, which is
not the same as before, for, by lifting itself to God and inbreathing God, it is justified by him" (in Joh. tr. 19. 11).  This
instilling of the good, justifying will by the Spirit is progressive
and marks the entire Christian life, since concupiscence remains
even in the regenerate (nupt. et conc. i. 25. 28): "We are
justified (have been made righteous), but righteousness itself

---

[1] The expression is derived from Rom. 5. 5.

grows as we go forward " (serm. 158. 5). Although the essential nature of justification lies in the " inspiring of a good will,"
yet, in a wider sense, the forgiveness of sins may also be ascribed
to it ; in such a way, however, that the emphasis still rests upon
the inspiration.    " Nor is this grace only the remission of sins
. . . but it effects that the law is fulfilled and nature set free "
(grat. et lib. arb. 14. 27 ; cf. op. imp. ii. 165 ; civ. dei, xii.
22).    " For grace assists in both ways—by remitting the evil
things that we have done, and by aiding us to depart from the
evil and do the good " (op. imp. ii. 227 ; vi. 15).

We have thus secured a clear conception of Augustine's doctrine
of grace.    Grace is the action of divine omnipotence which makes
man's will good, or capable of doing good.    The view corresponds exactly with his doctrine of sin.    Ignorance is overcome
by the bestowal of faith ; the love of self, together with lust by
the imparting of the good will and of love to God and his law ; the
sinner's state of death, by the process of grace through which he
is made righteous and alive.[1]

Notable above all else in this doctrinal structure is the energy
with which everything is referred to the grace of God, to the exclusion of all human work.    But whoever scrutinizes carefully
the real character of the operation of grace as thus depicted will
observe how imperfectly this theory meets the requirements of
the fundamental religious impulse of Augustine.    The Pauline
character, which so largely distinguishes the latter, fails, after all,
to rise to the height of Paul's conception of the righteousness of faith.    Augustine cites the formula of Paul times
without number ; but he interprets it as meaning, that we
reach the conviction that righteousness is granted to us by
God without antecedent works upon our part, or that faith justifies because it works by love.    " This is the righteousness
of (ex) faith, by which we believe that we are justified ; that is,
made righteous by the grace of God through Jesus Christ our
Lord, so that we may be found in him, not having our own righteousness, which is of the law, but that which is through the faith
of Christ.    Which righteousness of (ex) God in faith, is in faith
in this way, that we by faith believe that righteousness is divinely
granted to us, not achieved by us by our own strength " (ep.

---

[1] Augustine's order of salvation (following Rom. 8. 29 f. ) includes the following heads : " (Praescience) predestination, vocation, justification, glorification " (in Joh. tr. 26. 15 ; corr. et grat. 9. 23).    Or : " Remission of sins,
thine infirmities are healed, redemption from corruption, the crown of righteousness" (serm. 131. 6. 8).    Or : " Before the law, under the law, under
grace, in peace " (enchir. 31. 118).    " By the grace of God we are regenerated, purified, justified " (c. litt. Petil. iii. 50. 62).

186. 3. 8). " For we read that they are justified in Christ who believe in him, on account of a mysterious secret communication and inspiration of grace, by which whoever clings to the Lord is one spirit" (pecc. mer. et rem. i. 10. 11). Accordingly, it. may be said that even this great disciple of Paul, powerfully as he was influenced by the apostle, yet misunderstood him at the crucial point.[1]

(g) Grace, as being irresistible, is characterized by Augustine as *predestinating* grace. Many lines of thought are concentrated in this term : the Platonic tincture of Augustine's doctrine of God, his personal religious experience, his recognition of the sole agency of grace, and exegetical considerations (p. 340). If grace lays hold of man, there can be no resistance, for God carries out his will in the human heart no less than in nature. " It cannot, therefore, be doubted that human wills are not able to resist the will of God, so that he may not do what he will, who has done all things which he has willed in heaven and in earth, and has done even those things which shall be, since, even with respect to the wills of men themselves, he does what he will when he will . . . who nevertheless does not do so except through the wills of men themselves ; having beyond doubt omnipotent power of inclining hearts whithersoever it may please him" (corr. et grat. 14. 45, 43 ; enchir. 21. 95). The difference between grace and the " primary grace," or " assistance," granted to Adam lies in the fact that the latter could be voluntarily relinquished, whereas the former produces the will (corr. et grat. 11. 31, 38). To the question, whether the freedom of man's will is hereby destroyed, Augustine replies in the negative. On the contrary, grace heals and restores the free will, so that it is able to freely choose the good (sp. et lit. 30. 52 ; enchir. 25. 105). Man does not, as the Pelagians would have us believe, attain grace by freedom, but freedom by grace (corr. et grat. 8. 17). But when we remember that a new will is in an irresistible way implanted in man, and this will then " indeclinably and insuperably" controlled by the divine power (*virtus*, corr. et grat. 12. 38), it cannot be open to question that the claim of freedom is here meant to be taken in a very peculiar sense. It can be understood only in the sense that God

---

[1] Yet Augustine—as many of the pious in the Middle Ages—was able to find his chief consolation in the forgiveness of sins, *e.g.*: " And this our righteousness, although it is a true righteousness on account of the end of real goodness at which it aims, yet is in this life of such a nature that it consists rather in the remission of sins than in the perfection of virtues. A witness to this is the prayer of the whole kingdom of God, ' Forgive us our debts'" (civ. dei, xix. 27).

deals with man in a way consonant with his endowment with a will, so that man survives the transformation of his will as a creature still (formally) possessing the power of willing (see above citation). In this way man becomes free, *i. e.*, from the power of concupiscence. The state of spiritual subjection to God divinely wrought in him, by virtue of which he withdraws himself from the control of sensuous motives, is his freedom. The same result is reached if we consider the doctrine of perseverance in grace. This is a work of grace, the *donum perseverantiae* (don. pers. 1. 1). Here also applies the rule : " God effects that they may will " (corr. et grat. l. c.). A real freedom, in the metaphysical sense of the term, is thus excluded. This, again, is a consequence of Augustine's conception of grace as a creative energy (*virtus*) and not as a personal, spiritual relation.

But it is necessary to face the fact, that not all who are called (*vocati*) are subdued by grace. Augustine explains this on the ground of *predestination*. Before the creation of the world, God formed the resolution to redeem certain men in Christ and to apply to them his grace. "The predestination of God, which is in the good man, is a preparation . . . for grace, but grace is the effect of this predestination (praedest. 10. 19 ; don. persev. 9. 21). There is a "good-pleasure of his (God's) will," which has nothing to do with human merits, not even with such as were foreseen by God. On the contrary, the determination (*propositum*) of God is the ground upon which the good will is imparted to this or that one (praed. 18. 37). There is a strictly definite number (as maintained already in de bapt. v. 27. 38) whom God has thus foreordained to grace : "There is a number so fixed, that neither can anyone be added to them nor taken from them " (corr. et grat. 13. 39).[1] Predestination is the cause of salvation. All saving ordinances are means for realizing it, and therefore really serve and benefit only the predestinated. Only to the *elect* comes the effectual "peculiar calling of the elect" (praed. 18. 37), so that he may follow him who calls : others are not so (*non ita*) called (don. pers. 9. 21). The elect alone has the "gift of perseverance," whereas the foreknown (*praesciti*) may still fall away even in the last hour (corr. et grat. 9. 22 ; don. pers. 8. 19). All, therefore, rests in the hands of God, depends upon his choice : "Therefore whoever have in the most provident ordering of God been foreknown, predestinated, called, justified, and glorified, although yet, I will not say unregenerated but even yet unborn, are now the sons of God

---

[1] The fixity of the number is evident from Augustine's view that the elect are to form a substitution for the number of the fallen angels (enchir. 9. 29 ; 15. 62 ; civ. dei, xxii. 1).

and can by no means perish" (corr. et grat. 9. 23). The predestinated is saved, commonly becoming a *called* and *justified*
member of the church.   But it must be held as possible that
such an one may not come into contact in any way with historical Christianity, and yet be saved—because he is predestinated
(ep. 102 quaest. 2, §§ 12, 14, 15; cf. with praedest. 9, §§ 17-
19 ; also REUTER, Aug. Stud., p. 90 ff.).  The unpredestinated,
or *foreknown*, on the other hand, under all circumstances, fall
into ruin, as parts of the *massa perditionis*.  Even if they appear
to be true Christians, called, justified, regenerated through baptism, renewed—they will not be saved, because they have not
been elected (don. pers. 9. 21).   No blame attaches to God ;
they are alone to blame, as they simply remain given over to
their just fate :  " He who falls, falls by his own will ; and he who
stands, stands by the will of God" (don. pers. 8. 19).[1]  In
such God reveals his justice, as in the elect his mercy (ib. 8.
16).   To the question, Why he chooses some and leaves others to
their fate, the only answer is :  "I so will," at which the creature
must humbly bow before his Creator (ib. 17).[2]

In these conceptions, Augustine's doctrine of grace culminates.   Grace and nature, mercy and justice, are seen in direct
opposition to one another, as formerly in Marcion, and a solution is offered as paradoxical as was his, and as unsatisfactory to
the religious sense.   The profoundly religious spirit of Augustine
is as manifest as is the fact that certain foreign and unevangelical
threads have found their way into the texture of his thought.
He had learned to present faithfully the *sola gratia*, but his doctrine suffered detriment from the fact that he did not understand
the *sola fide*—that the God whose fellowship his heart could so
wonderfully portray was yet for his intellect not the God of the
gospel.   Assurance of salvation cannot—according to this theory
—be attained (corr. et grat. 13. 40 ; 9. 22 ; civ. dei, xi. 12).
" Nevertheless, this is good : not to be too wise, but to fear"
(don. pers. 8. 19), says the man who yet so well knew that religion is something more than the fear of breaking off a covenant
relationship.   But however deeply this mighty intellectual structure may be enshrouded beneath the shadows of the age, yet it
stated the problem for the doctrinal history of the future.   In

---

[1] Augustine commonly expresses himself in this way, but he also speaks of
those "predestinated to eternal death" (in Joh. tr. 43. 13, cf. 110. 2 ; civ.
dei, xv. 1. 1 ; enchir. 26. 100).
[2] Augustine escapes the force of opposing passages of Scripture, especially
Tim. 2. 4, by peculiar interpretations, as that no one is saved unless God wills
it (enchir. 24. 103), or that "all" means the predestinated, "because the
whole race of men is in them" (corr. et grat. 14. 44).

tones that can never be forgotten, it taught the church : There is only one thing to be feared—rebellion against God, or evil in the heart ; and there is only one thing good and great—the effectual grace of the living God.

4. HISTORICAL COURSE OF THE CONTROVERSY.

The direct opposition between the positions of Pelagius and Augustine is manifest. It was natural that a violent controversy should ensue, in which the leadership should fall to the lot of Augustine. The ideas with which he confronts his opponents may be readily inferred, *i. e.*, that Pelagianism knows nothing of grace, and that it is not freedom of the will, but the grace of God, which saves man. If man were free in the Pelagian sense, then would Christ have come into the world in vain (nat. et grat. c. 19 ff., § 21 ff.). If it was only a question of teaching and example, then why did not the pious Abel long since become the chief of the righteous ? (ib. 9. 10). Christian experience, no less than the prayer of the whole church for the forgiveness of sins, testifies that man cannot by his own power avoid sin (serm. 181). Further, the universality of the penalties imposed by a righteous God, from which even children are not exempt, makes against the Pelagian view (op. imp. iii. 154). In this connection, Augustine strongly emphasizes infant baptism. Either new-born children are sinful, or they are not. In the latter case, they need no baptism (pecc. mer. et rem. i. 23. 33 ; 18. 23 ; op. imp. ii. 222)—an inference, indeed, against which the Pelagians protested (p. 335, note). Finally, Augustine appeals to a number of passages of Scripture (Rom. 5. 12 ; 7. 14-26 ; 8. 26. Gen. 2. 7. Ps. 51 ; 143. 2. Eph. 2. 3. Joh. 8. 36). He even endeavored to produce a proof from the history of the church's doctrinal development (c. Jul. i. ii.). THOMASIUS (i. ed. 2, 543 ff.) has treated exhaustively this critique of Pelagianism.

The controversy was started when CAELESTIUS was endeavoring to secure an appointment as presbyter in Carthage. The first offense appears to have been taken at the claim of the followers of Caelestius, that infant baptism does not aim at the forgiveness of sins (Aug. pecc. mer. et rem. iii. 6. 12).[1] Paulinus, a deacon of Milan, brought charges against him ( vid. the charges in Marius Commonit. 1. 1, supra, p. 337 f. ) at a council in Car-

---

[1] In the discussion, Caelestius laid emphasis upon the necessity of baptism for infants. In the Relatio of the theses in Lib. subnot. praef. 5, Marius has the declaration : " Since infants, although they are not baptized, have eternal life." This is therefore, perhaps, original. All these instances give evidence that the assertion of Caelestius in regard to baptism referred to in the text fixed attention upon the subject.

23

thage (A. D. 411 or 412). Caelestius was excommunicated and went to Ephesus, where he secured—on Greek territory—appointment as a presbyter. Pelagius, who had also been in Carthage, had gone to Palestine. He, too, secured a following But Jerome wrote against him (ad Ctesiphontem [ep. 133] and dialogus c. Pelagianos ll. 3).[1] Reports from the West impelled John of Jerusalem to summon a council (Jerusalem A. D. 415, vid. account of Orosius in Liber apologeticus 3-6) to consider the case of Pelagius. But John unequivocally defended the thesis of Pelagius, that man may easily keep the commandments of God, i. e., by divine help. Orosius, therefore, requested that, as Pelagius was a Latin, the matter be referred to Rome. Under the urgency of two exiled Gallic bishops, Heros and Lazarus, another council was called, A. D. 415, at Diospolis, or Lydda (cf. Aug. de gestis Pel.; also Mansi iv. 311 ff.). Pelagius adroitly satisfied the minds of the bishops, affirming that man can indeed do everything good, but only with the divine assistance (adjutorium). Assertions ascribed to him he pronounced apocryphal. He disclaimed responsibility for the positions of Caelestius, but with the remark : "But the things which I have declared to be not mine, I, in accordance with the opinion of the holy church, reprobate, pronouncing an anathema against everyone who opposes." This was a cowardly untruth. The council pronounced him orthodox.[2] But the Africans did not rest. A council at Carthage and another in Mileve (both A. D. 416) sent letters to his "Holiness," Pope Innocent I., at Rome. Then came an exhaustive and instructive private communication by five bishops (including Augustine—among his letters ep. 175-177), cautiously urging to energetic action. The situation is depicted, the doctrine of Pelagius described and confuted, the unique authority of the Roman bishop extolled (ep. 175. 2 f.; 176. 1; 177. 19), and the latter urged to take the matter in hand. Pelagius, who gloried in the decision of the Eastern

---

[1] This work, bitter and passionate in style (Jerome heaps upon the head of Pelagius the names of nearly all the heretics), proved that Jerome wished to please Augustine, but in the question itself stood not very far from Pelagius (e. g., ep. ad Ct. 6. 10, dial. ii. 5 ff.; iii. 5. 6, cf. ZÖCKLER, Hieronymus, pp. 420 ff., 311 ff.).

[2] Pelagius shrewdly emphasized his orthodoxy upon the Trinity (Aug. gest. Pel. 19. 43), and also the fact that the question in dispute did not affect any "dogma." "I anathematize them as fools, not as heretics, if there is no dogma" (ib. 6. 16). This is to be explained not by a disinclination to enlarge "the sphere of the dogmatic" (HARNACK iii. 162, n. 1), but it is simply a means of defense, just as Caelestius declared at Carthage : "This is a matter of inquiry, not of heresy" (Aug. pecc. or. 3. 3, cf. the Roman confession of Caelestius in Aug. pecc. orig. c. 23. Julian's term, quaestiones indiscipli-natae, in Marius l. subnot. 6. 12).

theologians (ep. 177. 2), was required to recall his statements or
to acknowledge the saving nature of infant baptism and the insufficiency of nature for the attainment of salvation (ep. 175. 6).[1]
The pope lost no time in answering the letters (vid. in the letters of Aug., ep. 181-183). In the labored style of the Curia,
there is, first of all, an acknowledgment of the praiseworthy and
proper observance of the discipline—now observed by the whole
world—in appealing, as all churches do, to the decision of
Rome (ep. 181. 1; 182. 2). But in the discussion of the doctrinal question, this pope, as some of his predecessors, showed
himself a poor theologian. The Africans have, indeed, spoken
rightly and said all. It is superfluous for any person of orthodox
views to dispute concerning grace and freedom (ep. 181. 7, 9;
183. 5), for it is clear that man needs the divine assistance for
his salvation (ep. 181. 4-6, 8; 182. 3 f.). In other words—
the Africans are of course in the right, because the doctrine of
their opponents is correct! The dogmatic helplessness of the
pope in this instance, having no finished scheme at his command, is comical. As to other phases of the difficulty, speedy
help must be given against the pestilent poison (181. 2 f., 8).
The pope does not believe that Pelagius and Caelestius can be
converted (181. 8)—he doubts also if decision was really given
in favor of Pelagius at Diospolis—they are both to be excluded
from the church (ep. 181. 8; 182. 6).[2]
A strictly orthodox confession of Pelagius now found its way
to Rome. The questions at issue were but briefly touched upon,
infant baptism and the freedom of the will acknowledged (but
with the limitation "we are always in need of the help of
God"), and emphasis laid upon complete subjection to the
pope[3] (HAHN, ed. 3, p. 288 f.). Innocent had died (March,
417), and the confession fell into the hands of his successor,
ZOSIMUS. Caelestius, having in the meanwhile gone to Constantinople and been driven thence, had also appeared in Rome.
He acknowledged baptism for the remission of sins and the infallibility of the papal decision, but denied that "sin is born
with man" (HAHN, ed. 3, p. 292 f.). Zosimus was entirely satisfied, and in this he did not come into collision with the dogmatics of his predecessor. A council at Rome (A. D. 417)

---

[1] This practical inference in the letter from Carthage is interesting, as it
falls back upon the starting-point of the controversy.

[2] I do not interpret these letters in the customary way, nor as does HAR-
NACK (iii. 165). The pope did not leave "back-doors" open behind him—
but he simply did not understand anything about the matter.

[3] The words: "We execrate those who, with Manichæus, condemn first
marriage," are evidently a stab at Augustine.

certified to the orthodoxy of Caelestius. The confession of
Pelagius, which appeared soon afterward, to the support of
which the bishop of Jerusalem cast his influence, caused jubila-
tion. The pope was imprudent or honest enough to send a
report of this in two letters to the African bishops, and to re-
prove them sharply from the lofty station of the apostolic chair
for their lack of due consideration in the matter (vid. Zos. ep.
3, 4).[1] But a council at Carthage (A. D. 417, or early in 418)
explained to the pope that good reason had not yet been
shown for the various transactions, and that they would still
recognize as valid the condemnation pronounced by Innocent
(Mansi iv. 376, 378). The pope, alarmed, replied that Peter
received the authority to loose and bind, and that no one
dare oppose the pope, but that he would take counsel with
the Carthaginians in the matter, in which meanwhile no positive steps had been taken (ep. 15). At this point the great
African GENERAL COUNCIL, A. D. 418, was assembled at CAR-
THAGE, with 200 participants (Mansi iii. 810 ff.; iv. 377 ff.).
Condemnation was here pronounced against the doctrines: That
Adam was created mortal without respect to sin; that children
are not subject to original sin inherited from Adam; that grace
does not help with reference to future sins; that grace consists
only in doctrines and commandments; that grace only makes it
easier to do good; that saints utter the fifth petition of the
Lord's Prayer not for themselves, or only from humility. But,
at the same time, the practice of appealing to Rome, "beyond
the sea," was placed under the ban. This interdict was repeated
A. D. 419 at Carthage (occasioned by the meddling of Zosimus
in African affairs). The emperor had (A. D. 418) issued an
edict against Pelagius, Caelestius, and their followers, which expelled them from Rome and threatened more serious measures
(Aug. opp. xvii. 2720 ff.). Zosimus now yielded and published
the *epistola tractoria* (frg. vid. Coustant-Schoenemann, pontiff.
Rom. epp. i. 709), which he requested all bishops to subscribe.
Eighteen bishops refused to accede to this request (Aug. c. duas
ep. Pel. i. 1. 3). The leader of the latter was JULIAN OF
ECLANUM, who in two letters to the pope (in Mar. l. subnot. 6.
10-13. Aug. opp. xvii. 2728 ff.) defended their course, upon
the ground that it was not right to condemn the absent without a
hearing, and announced the adherence of these men to a rather
mildly-expressed statement of Pelagianism (the paradoxes of
Caelestius being rejected). From this time, Julian (having lost

---

[1] The pope learned also from Caelestius that the quarrel was about en-
tangling questions and useless dissensions (s. ep. 3. 7).

his bishopric) assumed the offensive, and proved the most energetic, combative, and voluminous opponent of Augustine, charging Augustine and his adherents, for whom, as heretics, he invented the title· *Traduciani*, with Manichæism, contempt of
marriage,[1] unscientific spirit, and unreasonableness (vid. frgg. in
Aug. nupt. et conc. ii.; c. Jul.; op. imp.). He became more
and more extreme, reaching at length the boldest rationalism :
" What reason disputes authority cannot prove " (op. imp. ii. 16,
137, 144). Questions are to be decided, not by assemblies of
clerics who have scarcely mastered the categories of Aristotle,
nor by the uncouth populace, but by the small number of the cultured (c. Jul. ii. 10. 35-37, cf. KLASEN, Entwicklung des Pel.,
p. 98 ff.). He appealed to the testimony of reason and the
Scriptures, neither of which recognizes original sin. Sin resides
in the will. Infants have no will, and hence no sin (ii. 28). Imitation leads to sin (ii. 48. 209). The generating act is pure
(iv. 6). Augustine's view leads to Manichæism. Christ re-
deems us, in that he brought to us our nature and his will, and
thereby gave to us a mirror and a rule, namely, that our sin, as
also our righteousness, consists in the will (iv. 84). Under his
hands the teachings of Pelagianism became more and more
secular and self-sufficient. But all of this exerted no influence
upon doctrinal history. Pelagianism extended over considerable
territory. We meet its adherents not only in Rome, Southern
Italy, and Sicily, but also the district of Aquileia (Dalmatia),
Brittany, and in the district of Arles. The council of Ephesus
(A. D. 431), to the great gratification of the pope, confirmed the
rejection of Pelagianism (vid. p. 264 f.).

§ 32. *Summary of Augustine's Theological and Ecclesiastical
Views in the Enchiridion ad Laurentium.*

We are reminded of Origen (*de principiis*) and his school,
Gregory of Nyssa (*catech. magna*), John of Damascus (*de fide
orth.*), Lactantius (*Institut.*), as we undertake to review Augustine's brief general survey of Christianity, written about A. D. 421.

" God to be worshiped in faith, hope, and love," is the theme of
the book. The question is : " What ought to be believed, what
to be hoped, what to be loved?" Truths which may be learned
by our natural intelligence are to be defended by reason. Those
which lie beyond this province "are to be believed without any hesi-
tation upon the testimony of the witnesses by whom was composed

---

[1] In connection with this point, Augustine was denounced by Pelagius before Comes Valerius (vid. nupt. et conc. i. 1, 2).

that Scripture which has hitherto been justly called divine, who,
divinely assisted, were enabled, whether through the body or
through the spirit, to see, or even to foresee, these things'' (4).
This is the '' beginning of the faith which works by love,'' whose
higher stage is attained in vision (5).    This is the Catholic conception of faith (cf. *assensio*, 7. 20, and supra, p. 347) and the
scholastic division of Christian doctrine into natural and revealed
truths.[1]  Succinctly stated, faith has its object in the Creed ; hope
and love find exercise in prayer (the Lord's Prayer, 2. 7).
In discussing the question, ''What is to be believed pertaining
to religion ? '' we are not to think of insight into the physical
laws of the universe :    '' It is enough for the Christian to believe that the first cause of created things, whether celestial or
terrestrial, . . . is nothing other than the goodness of the Creator . . . and that there is no nature which is not either the
Creator himself, or from him '' (3. 9).    This God is the God of
the Trinity.    The world was made good, and even evil fits into
its harmony (10).    Evil is the lack of good (*privatio boni*, 11).
That which is, is good, since it comes from God.    Even evil, so
far as it really is, is good : '' corruption cannot consume the
good except by consuming nature '' (4. 12).    Evil, as a lack of
existence, presupposes an existing good :  '' evil cannot be unless
there be something good '' (13 ff.).    The Christian must be ac-
quainted, not with the general order of the universe, but with
the causes of good and evil things, that he may be able to avoid
error and misery (5. 16).    To err is to accept the false as true
(17).    The worst error is for a man not to believe that which
leads to eternal life, but to believe that which leads to eternal
death (6. 18).    Not every error is sin, and the opinion of the
Academy, that all assent must be held in suspense, is false.    There
would then be no faith :  '' if assent be taken away, faith is taken
away ;  because without assent nothing is believed '' (7. 21).    In
matters not connected with the way which leads us to God, nor
with the faith in Christ which works by love, error (faith being
preserved) is no sin, or at all events only ''the least and
lightest sin ; '' but even then it is to be counted among
the '' evils (*mala*) of this life '' (21).    But every lie is a sin,

---

[1] It is to be noted that Augustine excluded from the objects of faith a series
of physical and metaphysical speculations (3. 9 ; 5. 16 ; 7. 21 ; 15. 58 f.,
66 ; 29. 86, 92).    Catholic truth is summarized in the Creed (in Joh. tr. 98.
7).    The content of '' believing well '' is the trinitarian God and the incarnation of the Word (ib. 18. 2 ; 74. 1 ; ep. 120. 2) ; but the true Catholic faith
excludes also the teachings of Pelagianism (in Joh. tr. 67. 3).    The highest
normative and only infallible authority is, for Augustine, the Holy Scriptures,
*e. g.*, doctr. christ. ii. 8 ; ep. 82. 1. 3, unit.; eccl. 3. 5 ; 13. 33 ; 11. 28 ;
bapt. ii. 3. 4 ; civ. dei, xi. 3 ; enchirid. 1. 4.

since "words were instituted, not that men might through them deceive one another, but that each might through them bring his thoughts to the knowledge of the other" (22). What we need to know, therefore, in order that we may not fall into sin, is the causes of good and evil, namely : "that the cause of good . . . things is nothing else than the goodness of God, but that of evil things is the will of a mutably good being—first of an angel, afterward of a man—forsaking the immutably good" (8. 23). The first evil (*primum malum*) of man is his unwillingness to do (*nolle*) that which God wishes. From this results the "ignorance of things to be done, and the lust of things injurious ;" hence "error, distress, fear, *i. e.*, the whole misery of men, as well as the death of the body" (24 f.). Adam by his sin "vitiated his posterity . . . at the root, made them subject to the penalty of death and damnation." All who are begotten "through carnal concupiscence" have original sin (26). The entire race is thus living in wickedness and subject to the "most just wrath of God." This is evident both from the fact that the wicked willingly indulge their concupiscence, and the further fact that they are, against their will, visited with punishment. God is, however, not only just, but also merciful,[1] and he, therefore, does not abandon men to their merited fate (27). Inasmuch as the angels are not bound together by natural descent, the fall of the evil angels had no effect upon the good (9. 28). It is designed that men shall (in, perhaps, larger numbers) take the place of the fallen angels (29). But that portion of the human race to whom God has promised deliverance attains that end not through the exercise of free will, for this has been lost, but only through grace. As servants of God, they become truly free (30). Faith itself is a gift of God (31). God alone works in us to will and to do (Phil. 2. 13. Rom. 9. 16). "He precedes him who is unwilling, that he may will ; he follows him who is willing, that he may not will in vain." It is false to say : "the will of man alone is not sufficient, if there be not also the mercy of God," for God works all things (32). "When men were, through original sin, under this wrath, the more seriously and ruinously they had added to this more and greater (offenses), the more necessary was a mediator, that is, a reconciler, who *should placate this wrath by the offering of one sacrifice.*" The wrath of God is not a "disturbance, such as that in the heart of an angry man," but it is "his vengeance, which is nothing but just" (10. 33). The mediator became man (his divinity not being changed

[1] This contrast, which we have met before (pp. 120, 295, 340, and already in Marcion, p. 102 f.), has been normative in dogmatics since the time of Augustine.

into flesh), sinless, "not such as is born from the two sexes through the concupiscence of the flesh with inevitable tendency to wrong-doing," but of the Virgin, whose "integrity" was not impaired at his birth (34). Christ was God and man (35). It was no merit of the man Jesus which secured this combination, but only the grace of God (11. 36). His human birth itself was a work of the Holy Spirit (37). But Christ is not, therefore, according to his human nature a Son of the Spirit, as he is according to his divine nature a Son of the Father (12. 38 f.). But the grace of God is manifested in the incarnation " by which man, no merits preceding . . . was joined with the Word of God in such unity of person, that the very same who was the son of man was the Son of God, and the very same who was the Son of God was the son of man " (40). The absolutely sinless Christ has now been pronounced "sin" (2 Cor. v.), since in the Old Testament the sin-offering was thus designated. Christ is, therefore : " a sacrifice for sins, through which we might be able to be reconciled." He became sin " in the likeness of the sin of the flesh, in order that . . . he might thus, in a manner, die to sin, when he dies to the flesh in which was the likeness of sin . . . and might by his resurrection seal our new reviving life from the old death in which we would have died in sin " (13. 41). Hence, Christ died as a sacrifice for sin, as our representative, and he arose as an evidence of the new life brought to us by him. We have a reflection of this in baptism, as we die to sin and live through the washing of regeneration (42). All, therefore, have need of baptism. Children thereby die to original sin, and adults also to the further sins actually committed (43). The aim of baptism is the "remission of sins" (44 and 51 ; cf. supra, pp. 322, 349). It is asserted, not without probability, that children are bound also by the sins of their parents—not alone of the first human beings, but also their own parents of whom they were born " (cf. Ezek. 18. 2). But baptism has essentially to do with deliverance from original sin, as individual sins may also be atoned for through repentance (46). Original sin, as the root of all sins, is removed and destroyed only through the one mediator, the man Jesus (14. 48). The baptism of Christ was significant, not for him, but for us : " in order that his great humility might be commended." The same is to be said of his death : " in order that the devil, overcome and vanquished by the truth of justice, not by the violence of power, since he had most unjustly slain him who was without any desert of sin, might most justly lose those whom he for desert of sin held in his power " (49). It is only as new-born in Christ that we can become free from the condemnation which rests upon all through Adam (51). As to the way in which this is accomplished : "just as true death has occurred in him, so true remission of sins in us ; and just as true resurrection in him, so true justification in us." The former takes place in baptism, which, however, has the latter as its goal (52, cf. supra, p. 322). As Christ is in this our pattern, so also in his whole history " in order that to these things, not only mystically spoken, but also done, the Christian life which is lived here might be conformed " (53). The coming of Christ to judgment is here excepted (54). That which we designate the doctrine of the Work of Christ is treated by Augustine under three aspects : as the sacrifice for sin, by virtue of which we receive the forgiveness of sins in baptism; as deliverance from the devil ; and as a pattern and example for believers.[1]

---

[1] Sections 41, 42, 48, 51, 52, 53 reveal quite fully the aspects under which Augustine regards the work of Christ. We add a few remarks. The dominating thought is : Christ is the Head ; the church (the predestinated, in Joh. tr. iii. 1) is his body. All who are his and whom he has won belong to the church (pecc. mer. et rem. i. 26. 39 : civ. dei, xvii. 15 ; in Joh. tr. 21. 8 ; 108. 5 ; serm. 117. 10. 16). He who became man and yet remained God is, as man, the mediator or the way to God (often, following 1 Tim. 2-5, *e. g.*, civ. dei, xi. 2 ; xxi. 16 ; ix. 15. 2 ; in Joh. tr. 82. 4 ; 105. 7). Hence, the rule is : From the man Jesus to God : " If thou wishest to live piously and christianly, cling to Christ according to that which he has done for us, in order that thou mayest come to him according to that which he is and according to that which he was " (in Joh. tr. 2. 3 ; 13. 14 ; cf. the passages cited on p. 261). The Head now reveals and secures salvation as a whole for his members (civ. dei, x. 32. 3). Regarded more closely, Christ (1) has by his blood brought us the forgiveness of sins; by his sacrifice cleansed us from our sins, paid a ransom for us, taken away the wrath of God, bestowed upon us righteousness, reconciled us with God, and has become our advocate (*e. g.*, in Joh. tr. 92. 1 ; 98. 2 ; 119. 4 ; 3. 13 ; 41. 6 ; 4. 2 ; 123. 4 ; 14. 13 ; civ. dei, vii. 31 ; x. 24 ; doctr. chr. i. 15, 17 ; serm. 134. 4, 5 ; 155. 8 ; 19. 3 ; conf. ix. 13 ; x. 43). (2) He has freed men from the power of the devil, who without any right seized upon the flesh of the righteous Christ, and to whom that flesh proved a *bait* (serm. 134. 3. 4 ; 5. 6 ; in Joh. 52. 6). (3) He has, as Mediator, in his person and work revealed to us God, his wisdom and love in : " That we have, therefore, been reconciled to God by the death of his Son, is not to be understood as though the Son had reconciled us to him, so that he should now begin to love what he had hated, as when an enemy is reconciled to an enemy, so that they are thereafter friends, and they who have mutually hated now mutually love ; but we are now reconciled to him who loves us, with whom we have been at enmity on account of sin " (in Joh. tr. 110. 6 ; cf. 2. 16 ; serm. 174 ; 126. 4. 6); by this love we are moved to love him in return (de cat. rud. 4. 7, 8). (4) He has given us an example and pattern of humility, patience, and trust in God (*e. g.*, civ. dei, xviii. 49 ; in Joh. tr. 4. 13 ; 25. 16, 18 ; 51. 11 ; 58. 4 ff.; 113. 4 ; 116. 1 ; 119. 2); but " the animal man . . . does not perceive what the cross of Christ confers upon those who believe, and thinks that by this cross was accomplished *only* that an example for imitation should be given to us as we contend even to death for the truth " (in Joh. tr. 98. 3). (5) He has through his incarnation, and especially through his death and resurrection, brought to us immortality,

After thus treating of God, creation, sin, grace, and of Christ, Augustine, following the order of the Creed, comes to speak of the Holy Spirit. The church depends upon the Trinity : " The proper order of confession requires that the church be subordinated to the Trinity, just as to the tenant his house, to God his temple, and to the founder his city." In this we are to have in view, not only the Christians yet sojourning on earth, but also glorified saints and angels (15. 56). There is then a discussion of angels, in which the author confesses his ignorance as to the orders of celestial beings, and the propriety of numbering among them the sun and the moon (Orig., supra, p. 151), or the kind of corporeality involved in the appearances of angels on earth (58 f.). It is more important to discriminate when Satan transforms himself into an angel of light, in order that we may not follow him upon his paths of error[1] (60). The church is thus to be divided into the earthly and the heavenly. The redemption wrought by Christ extends also, in a certain measure, to the angels, inasmuch as by it the enmity between them and sinful men is removed, and the places vacated by the fallen angels are filled. Hence, as affirmed in Eph. 1. 10, the heavenly is by Christ united in peace with the earthly, and the earthly with the heavenly (61, 62). This peace shall be complete for us only in the full vision of the future world, but it exists here already through the forgiveness of sins. Hence, the next item in the Creed is the forgiveness of sins. Renewal begins (*incipit renovatio*) with the blotting out of original sin in baptism, yet everyone needs beyond this the forgiveness of sins, since he is, though perhaps without crime (*crimen*), not without sin (64). But even in regard to crimes, we dare not despair of the mercy of God. The church excommunicates the criminal ; but let him repent. In this, not the extent of time, but that of the sorrow, is important. Since now it is only in the church that sins are forgiven, there are fixed "times of repentance, in order that it may be exercised to the satisfaction of the church as well" (65). The regenerate are also subjected to temporal penalties, in order that their guilt may

---

in order thus to make us gods : "to make us gods who were men, he who was God was made man " (serm. 192. 1 ; 166. 4); but also : "by loving God we are made gods" (serm. 121. 1). Augustine presents not a consistent theory, but elements of religious truth which are genuinely Christian. In this he has again furnished dogmatic material to the church of the West. Cf. KÜHNER, Aug. Anschauung von der Erlösungsbedeutung Christi, 1890. SCHEEL, Aug. Anschauung über Christi Person und Werk, 1901.

[1] This is, indeed, difficult, but the very difficulty of this thing is beneficial in that no one may be hope for himself, nor one man for another, but God for all his own.

not be charged against them for eternity (66). But there are Catholic Christians[1] who hold that, if they have been baptized and believe, *i. e.*, do not renounce the name of Christ, they will be saved despite the most grievous sins, "which they neither wash away by repenting nor atone for by alms," that "they will be saved by fire—punished, doubtless, in proportion to the magnitude of their offenses and the duration of their shameful deeds, yet not with eternal fire" (cf. 1 Cor. 3. 11 ff.). Only faith manifesting itself in works saves : faith without works does not save (67). The fire in the scriptural passages under discussion refers to the pain endured in the giving up of that which is fervently desired (68). Augustine leaves it an open[2] question whether a purifying fire does not exist also after this life for such as through repentance, and especially through almsgiving, have secured for themselves forgiveness— whether "some believers are not saved more tardily or more speedily, through a certain purgatorial fire, in proportion as they have more or less loved the things that perish" (69). He adds, in explanation, that one cannot indeed daily atone by alms for sins which exclude from the kingdom of God, nor, forsooth, by them purchase for himself the right to sin in the future (16. 70).

Turning now to the practice of repentance, Augustine declares: "But for brief and light daily sins . . . the daily prayer of believers makes satisfaction" (*satisfacit*), *i. e.*, the fifth petition of the Lord's Prayer. But this prayer also blots out grave offenses, when the believer forsakes them—and when he also forgives those who trespass against him. For forgiveness is also an *alms*, just as are all good works done for those in need. "There are thus many kinds of alms, when we perform which we help to secure the remission of our own sins" (71, 72). Forgiveness of others and the love of enemies are the best alms (73). Only he who is ready to forgive receives forgiveness (74). Only he who also reforms his life becomes pure through alms (17. 75). Indeed, in a certain sense, everything is included in alms, if we give to ourselves the alms of charging guilt upon ourselves, *i. e.*, if we by the mercy of God seek

---

[1] As to the view of these "lay brethren," see retract. ii. 38 ; de fide et operibus ; civ. dei, xxi. 19 ff. These people are in no kind of harmony with the evangelical view of justification by faith (despite HARNACK, Ztschr. f. Theol. u. K., 1891, p. 165 ff.). On the contrary, they anticipate the most extreme Catholicism : He who has accepted the teachings of the church, been baptized, received the Lord's Supper, and remains in the church, will be saved, without any regard to his moral character, the deficiencies of which will be re paired in purgatorial fire.

[2] Thus also civ. dei, xxi. 26. 4.

out ourselves in our misery (76; also serm. 87. 9. 10). The division of sins into *peccata levia* and *gravia* cannot be carried out fully by any means in our power; but it is established by such passages as 1 Cor. 7. 5 ff.; 6. 1 ff. (78). Some which seem light to us ("thou fool") are grievous according to the Scriptures (79), while many which are really grievous are from force of habit regarded by us as light (80). We cannot resist sins, whether arising from ignorance or from infirmity, "unless we are divinely assisted" (19. 81). The mercy of God also impels us to repentance (82). He who does not believe, or despises, the forgiveness of sins in the church is guilty of the unpardonable sin against the Holy Ghost (83).[1]

---

[1] Augustine's view of repentance is, in its essential features, fully presented in his *Enchiridion*. It is merely a continuation of the Ancient Catholic teaching upon the subjects (supra, p. 195). Although the East also possessed a penitential ordinance (vid. Greg. Thaum. ep. canon. and Basil. ep. 199, 217), yet the penitential discipline of the church never there attained so rigid a development as in the West (cf. the homilies of Chrysostom upon repentance, and *supra*). The antecedent of the Western view is the distinction drawn between venial, daily, petty sins, and damnable or great (*grandia*) sins, such as idolatry, the *constellations of the mathematicians*, heresy, schism, murder, adultery, fornication, robbery, theft, false witness (perf. just. 9. 20; in Joh. tr. 12. 14; op. imp. ii. 97; serm. 56. 8. 12). If we include repentance before baptism, there are three kinds of repentance : (1) Repentance for sins committed before baptism; in the case of children, "the faith of those by whom they are presented prevails" (serm. 351. 2. 2). (2) Repentance for the lighter daily sins, "whose committal runs through the whole of this life," the daily repentance, which brings to man a daily medicine of forgiveness (Augustine is fond of describing grace as *medicina*). This occurs through the daily use of the Lord's Prayer (fifth petition), as well as through alms and fasting (serm. 351. 3. 3 ff.; 352. 2. 7; 18. 5; 58. 5. 6; de symbolo ad cat. 7. 14; civ. dei, xxi. 27. 4; cf. Ambrose, de poenit. ii. 5. 35 : "He who exercises repentance, *agit poenitentiam*, ought not only to wash away his sin with tears, but also to hide and cover his greater offenses by better works, so that sin may not be imputed to him"). (3) Repentance in the proper sense of the term ("the more serious and painful repentance, in which they are properly called penitents, *poenitentes*, in the church") has to do with those who, on account of grave sins (forbidden by the Decalogue), have been excluded from the holy communion (*communio sacra*, Ambros. ib. i. 15. 78), or the Lord's Supper (Aug. serm. 355. 4. 7). Such must make confession to the bishop, who assigns to them an appropriate "satisfaction," and, if the matter has been publicly known, directs them to repeat the confession before the church (vid. 351. 4. 7-10; 352. 3. 8; ep. 265. 7. Also can. 30 of the council of Hippo, A. D. 393, HEFELE CG. ii., ed. 2, 58). This repentance is, like baptism, to be granted but once (ep. 152. 2; 153. 3. 7; cf. Ambrose, l. c. ii. 10. 95; the decretal letter of Pope Siricius to Himerius, A. D. 385, c. 5). Thus repentance becomes a continuation of baptism (ep. 56. 8. 12 init. Ambrose, l. c. ii. 11. 98: "Repentance is therefore a good thing; for, if it did not exist, all would have to defer until old age the grace of cleansing"). But in this way repentance is externalized and set in opposition to grace, and thus was a new stone fitted into the hierarchical structure: "Let him come to the overseers (*antistites*), through whom the keys are administered for him in the church . . . let him receive from those placed over

Augustine treats, finally, of the Resurrection. After some remarks in regard to the resurrection body of the abortive fœtus
(20. 85 f.) and of monstrosities (87), he declares that the material of the human body is for God not lost (88); that in the resurrection God will restore the entire body, it being not implied,
however, that every particle of the matter shall become a portion
of that member to which it once belonged (89). The bodies
will not be all alike (*e. g.*, the notes of an anthem), nor will they
be repulsive (wan or corpulent). They will be spiritual bodies,
but in substance still flesh (*caro*), although serving the spirit in
all things (90, 91; cf. civ. dei, xxii. 12 ff., 19 ff.). The lost
have also a body; a continual dying and decaying is their fate
(92). This is the second death. Condemnation (*damnatio*) is
graded according to the measure of guilt, being lightest for children. "Certainly the lightest punishment of all will be that of
those, who, beyond the sin which they have inherited from their
ancestry, have superadded none" (93). It is only in the two-
fold outcome of human life that we shall learn why one was saved
and another left to condemnation. It will become clear how
certain, immutable, and most efficacious is the will of God (21.
94, 95). Since God permits evil, its existence must be good; otherwise the almighty Will would not allow it (96). What God wills,
that he does. But he wills that all men be saved (1 Tim. 2. 4;
cf. 23. 27), and yet by far the greater number are not saved (97).
God in mercy turns the evil will of some into a good will, without any regard to future works. To others he is simply just (22.
98 f.). The will of God rules in all, even in the wicked: "so
that . . . even that which is contrary to his will does not occur
without his will" (23. 100 f.). Therefore: "he does not do
anything wicked, nor does he do anything unless he wills to do
it, and he does all things whatsoever which he wills to do" (102).
At this point Augustine takes up 1 Tim. 2. 4 (103) and endeavors by a forced interpretation to bring it into harmony with the
above (supra, p. 352). The will of man is always free, even
and particularly when it can no longer will to do evil (25, 105).
But free will would not have sufficed even in paradise to merit immortality: even there the divine assistance (*adjutorium*) was
needed—how much more since the fall! (106). Hence, strictly
speaking, eternal life is a matter, not of reward, but of grace. "It
is to be understood, therefore, that even the good merits of man
themselves are gifts of God, to which when eternal life is given,

the sacraments (*praepositi sacramentorum*), the mode of his satisfaction"
(sermo. 351. 4. 10). "Where, if ministers are wanting, how great ruin follows those who depart from this world either not regenerated or bound" (ep.
228. 8).

how is grace given except (in exchange) for grace?''[1]  God's mercy is the ground of salvation; therefore let no one boast (107). Even the Mediator through whom salvation is secured is not only man but God.  In description of his work, it is declared: "it was necessary for us to be reconciled to God in order to the resurrection of the flesh unto eternal life."  Through him the resurrection is set forth, the devil conquered.  Further, "an example of obedience is by the divine man set before contumacious man."  He showed to men also in his person how far they had departed from God (108).

After death and before the resurrection, the souls of men are in a secret retreat (*abdita receptacula*), where it goes well or ill with them according to their deserts.  For the alleviation of their condition, their friends may avail themselves of the sacrifice of the mass and of alms.  But the latter avail as "*propitiationes*" only for those who on earth have deserved that the benefits of these things should now be enjoyed (those who were "not very wicked," 20. 110; vid. also serm. 172. 2; civ. dei, xxi. 27. 6). The *civitas dei* and the *civitas diaboli*, both of which include men and angels, will continue to exist in eternity (111).  There can be no doubt of the eternal duration of the punishments of hell.  The most that could be deduced from Ps. 76. 10 would be a temporary alleviation or interruption.  That condition itself is one of dreadful torment: "to depart from the kingdom of God, to be an exile from the city of God, to be alienated from the life of God, to be deprived, with so great a multitude, of the delightful fellowship of God" (112 f.).

These are the doctrines "which are to be faithfully believed." Out of faith spring hope and love.  What we hope is shown by the Lord's Prayer.  We hope only in God, not in men nor in ourselves.  "Therefore only from the Lord God ought we to seek whatever we hope either to do well or to receive (in exchange for good works)" (27. 114).  Then follows a short exposition of the Lord's Prayer, as given in Matthew and Luke (115 f.).

Then comes Love.  "When it is asked whether anyone is a good man, it is not asked what he believes or hopes, but what he loves . . . he who does not love, believes in vain, even though the things which he believes are true."  True faith is that which works in love.  Love is shed abroad in us by the Holy Spirit; it annihilates concupiscence and fulfills the law" (28. 117; cf. supra, p. 348).  The course of moral development is then sketched:

---

[1] For this strained interpretation of the term "merit," see further in Joh. tr. 3. 10: "he crowns his gifts, not thy merits;" grat. et lib. arb. 7. 16. Augustine, of course, uses the term also in the ordinary sense, *e. g.*, ep. 214. 4; grat. et lib. arb. 1 init.

(1) "Living according to the flesh, reason making no resistance —this is the first state (*haec sunt prima*) of man." (2) "Recognition of sin through the law," but "sinning knowingly . . . this is the second state of man." (3) Faith in the help of God : "and that the man has begun to be moved by the Spirit of God, he lusts against the flesh by the stronger power of love . . . his whole infirmity not yet being healed, pious perseverance—this is the third state of the man of good hope." (4) "Final peace remains—after this life. Of these four different stages, the first is before the law, the second under the law, the third under grace, the fourth in full and perfect peace." The history of salvation has followed the same course (118). But grace brings the forgiveness of sins and removal of guilt (*reatus*, 119). Every commandment of God has love as its aim. "Therefore, that which is done either from fear of punishment or with any carnal aim, so that it cannot be traced to that love which the Holy Spirit sheds abroad in our hearts, is not yet, although it may seem to be, done as it ought to be done" (121).

The treatise does not furnish the outlines of a doctrinal "system," but a connected presentation of that which Augustine regarded as essential in Christian teaching. The great underlying current of his thought runs through the composition. Into it he has interwoven his profoundest ideas upon sin, grace, and predestination. The metaphysical background is clearly traceable in his doctrine concerning God ; and the distinctively hierarchical elements are to a remarkable degree overshadowed. He skillfully arranged his ideas in harmony with the orderly statements of the Creed ; but, as in all his teaching, so even in this brief epitome, he has introduced nearly all the elements of the popular Catholicism of the day (ideas of merit, fastings, alms, together with hierarchism, sacramental magic, saint worship, veneration of relics, and the ascetic ideal of life). Wherever he stepped, the scene became one of verdure and flowers. He could attach the profoundest ideas to the most external things (*e. g.*, his exposition of merit and alms). Stones under his hand became bread. His influence upon the church is explained—in part, at least— by this wonderful power of assimilating and glorifying. But it may also be readily understood, in view of this same trait, that the loosely-connected elements of his general view, harmonized in him only by the power of his religious genius, were unable to exert a thoroughgoing reformatory influence upon the entire scope of ecclesiastical doctrine. He possessed the creative power of the reformer, but he lacked the talent required for tearing down. From this characteristic we may explain also the multitude of inconsistencies and self-contradictory tendencies in his teachings (*e. g.*, predestination and church, church and church, Christ and grace, grace and sacraments, the knowledge of God and the definition of God, faith and love, etc.). And yet the ideas of this man furnished the themes for the piety and theology of more than a thousand years. No one possessed the "whole" Augustine, but all lived upon the fragments of his spirit, from which each appropriated and understood what was "adapted" to his own wants.

---

## CHAPTER V.

### AUGUSTINIANISM AS THE DOCTRINE OF THE CHURCH. COMPLETION OF DOCTRINAL DEVELOPMENT IN THE ANCIENT CHURCH OF THE WEST.

### § 33.   *The Semi-Pelagian Controversies.*

1. Augustine won the day in the conflict with Pelagianism, but his views were not by any means generally accepted in all their details (vid. p. 357). Offense was taken, especially at his doctrines of man's absolute inability to do good and of predestination, however for the time being his illustrious name and the charm of his writings may have smothered opposition. But, even before his death, doubts were openly expressed upon these points. In the cloister at Hadrumetum there were some, he reports, who "preached grace in such a way that they deny that the will of man is free," and all discipline and works were thus abolished (Aug. ep. 214. 1 ; cf. corr. et gr. 5. 8); while others held that "the free will is assisted by the grace of God, in order that we may know and do what is right" (ib.). Augustine agrees with the latter, for he was concerned above all else to counteract the ethically perilous consequences to which the view of the former group would lead. He thus formulates his position : " Both the will of man and the grace of God, without whose assistance it cannot be converted to God nor advance in God, are free " (ib. 7). This he sought to establish in his publications, *De gratia et libero arbitrio* and *De correptione et gratia* (cf. p. 350 f.). On the other hand, violent opposition arose in South Gaul, especially in Massilia. PROSPER of Aquitania and a layman named HILARY reported (Aug. ep. 225, 226) to Augustine that men in high positions and of lofty character, who were in other

points great admirers of Augustine (ep. 226. 9) were most strenuously opposing his doctrine of predestination, and, in doing so,
were citing the latter against himself (ib. 3). That doctrine—it was
claimed in the land of Irenæus—is new and of no value ; it col-
lides with the intuitions of the church (*ecclesiasticus sensus*),
with antiquity, and the opinion of the Fathers (226. 2 ; 225.
2, 3); it is dangerous, because it cripples the force of preaching,
reproof, and moral energy (226. 2, 5 ; 225. 3), and plunges
men into despair (226. 6); finally, "under this name, predestination, there is introduced a certain fatal necessity, or the Lord
the Creator is said to be of diverse natures" (225. 3). Pelagius
may be refuted without resort to this theory (226. 8). All have
sinned in Adam (225. 3), and no one can free himself by his
own wilı (226. 2); but "everyone who is sick desires to be made
well." Hence man wishes to have the Physician, *i. e.*, he believes on him (226. 2. 4). This believing (*credulitas*) is a deed
of man, his merit (225. 6, 4). Grace now interests itself in
behalf of the man through the "sacrament of regeneration"
(225. 4). God assists the human will to do that which is good ;
but man, and not God, makes the beginning. "In order that
he who has begun to will may be assisted, not that the power to
will be also given (226. 2), they wish grace to be regarded as
concomitant, and not prevenient to human merits" (225. 5).
God wishes to save all (*indifferenter universos*) and the *propitiatio* of the blood of Christ avails for all (225. 4, 3). Predestination is therefore based upon fore-knowledge. The latter
extends to the case of children dying in infancy, and to the historical diffusion of the gospel (226. 4 ;[1] 225. 5). Accordingly,
there is not "a definite number of persons to be elected or rejected," "since he wishes all men to be saved, and yet not all
men are saved" (226. 7). Hence, only the will of man is to
blame. The motives, as well as the tendencies, of these Semiaugustinians are here plainly revealed. Augustine replied in the
publications, *De praedestinatione sanctorum* and *De dono perseverantiae*, in which he maintained his position without modification.

2. But the struggles between the doctrine of Augustine and
that of the Semipelagians were yet long continued. The name
Semipelagians is not very appropriate ; for the majority of that
party might be more accurately described as Semiaugustinians,
inasmuch as the influence of Augustine upon them was very
marked, and they really found their starting-point in his teach-

---

[1] The appeal to Sap. 4. 11 is here rejected " as not canonical ;" but see,
on the contrary, the 36th canon of the council at Hippo (HEFELE CG. ii., ed.
2, 59) and also Aug. doctr. Christ. ii. 8 ; retract. ii. 4. 2.

24

ings. The scene of these conflicts was the Gallic church. For
almost two and a half centuries the African church held in its
hand the leadership of Western theology. It was now, under the
pressure of political conditions, compelled to surrender this
leadership to the Gallic church. The views of this Semiaugus-
tinian circle are clearly seen in the writings of JOHANNES CASSI-
ANUS (de coenobiorum institutis ll. 12. Collationum ll., 24 ed.
Petschenig in Corp. scr. eccl. lat. 13, 17, and in Migne lat.
49; cf. HOCH, Die Lehre des Joh. Cassianus von Natur u.
Gnade, 1894). In the background is the monastic temper. The
ideal of "evangelical perfection," as the fulfilling of the evangelical commandments and counsels, is to be attained by the
most severe ascetic discipline (coll. iii. 7; xi. 8, 10; xvi.
22; xix. 9; xxi. 5, 7 ff.). The most painstaking carefulness is
made a duty. But with the contemplations (*contemplationes*,
coll. 1. 15; xiv. 8), flights (*excessus*, iii. 7), and profoundest
emotions (*secretissimi sensus*, iv. 2), alternate anxiety and
sadness (iv. 2; vi. 10). Accordingly, human sinfulness, and
that in its sensuous aspects, is strongly emphasized,[1] and, on the
other hand, man's moral activity is made equally prominent.
The sin of Adam is a hereditary disease (inst. xii. 5);[2] since
the fall, there has been an *infirmitas liberi arbitrii* (coll.
iii. 12 fin.). The Pelagian theory is very positively rejected
(coll. xiii. 16; cf. de incarn. 1. 3; v. 1). Two principles concerning divine grace are firmly held by Cassian : that we are unable to do anything good without the help of God (coll. xiii. 6),
and that the freedom of the will must be preserved : "For
through these things which we have presented we have not
wished to remove the free will of man, but to prove that the
assistance and grace of God are necessary for it every day and
moment " (coll. iii. 22). From this it follows that grace and
free will *co-operate :* "And thus the grace of God always co-
operates for that which is good with our will and in all things
assists, protects, and defends it " (coll. xiii. 13; iii. 12, cf. inst.
xii. 14). By grace, Cassian understands illumination and instruction through the law, as well as the *illuminatio* of the spirit
for the spiritual understanding of the law, and *divina inspiratio :*
"To breathe into anyone the principles of salvation and to im-
plant the fervor of a good will" (vid. inst. xii. 18; coll. iii. 10, 14,

---

[1] The eight *principalia vitia* are : Gluttony, fornication, covetousness, anger,
melancholy, taedium, vainglory, and pride, coll. v. 2, also inst. v.-xii. Upon
this list, which is found also in Evagrius and Nilus, vid. ZÖCKLER, Das Lehr-
stück von den 7 Hauptsünden, 1893, p. 16 ff. Upon the list of the seven chief
crimes, which may be traced to Gregory the Great, see ib., p. 40 ff.

[2] Original and actual sin, coll. xiii. 7.

15 ; xiii. 6, 18). Together with the imparting of the law, there
is hence also an infusion (*infundere*) of grace (inst. xii. 16 fin.;
cf. coll. vii. 1 : "The gift of chastity infused by a peculiar
blessing "). Cassian occasionally attributes the willing, as well
as the doing, of good to the working of grace ("the beginning
of our conversion and faith," coll. iii. 15): Man cannot even
preserve his own faith intact by the power of his will (ib. 16). Yet
it is meant by this only that " he is not able to perform anything
without the assistance of God, which produces industry," and
that no one "may think that his work is the cause of the divine
bounty " (coll. xiii. 3). Conversion is effected in this wise :
" Who, when he has observed in us a certain beginning of a good
will, immediately illuminates this and comforts and incites it
toward salvation, bestowing an increase upon that which either
he himself has implanted or which he has seen to arise from our
own effort " (coll. xiii. 8, 7), and "the beginnings of good
wills sometimes precede, which, nevertheless, unless they are
directed by the Lord, cannot proceed to the attainment of virtues " (ib. 9, cf. inst. xii. 14). Man may, like Zacchæus,
make the beginning ; or God, as in the cases of Paul and
Matthew (coll. xiii. 11, 12, 17, 18). The chief thing is the co-
operation (ib. 13), and that "the consummation of our salvation be attributed, not to the merit of our works, but to celestial
grace " (ib. 18); but, at the same time, the freedom of man
must be preserved both at the beginning and through the various
stages of the process (ib.). At this point, as in its assertion
that God really desires to save all (ib. 7), this theory opposes
Augustine. The idea of Cassian is, that the human will has indeed been crippled by sin, but that a certain freedom has yet
remained to it. By virtue of this, it is able to turn to God, and, just
as though God had first turned to it, it is able, with the assistance
of divine grace, setting before it the law and infusing the needed
power, to will and to do that which is good. Hence the sinner is not dead, but wounded. Grace comes to view, not as
*operans*, but as *cooperans;* to it is to be attributed not alone
activity, but synergy. This doctrine is theoretically as well as
practically[1] untenable, but its appearance is a very severe arraign-

---

[1] The opinion has, indeed, been expressed that this doctrine of grace is "as
a theory *entirely correct*, but as an expression of self-condemnation before
God, *entirely* false " (HARNACK, iii. 223, n.); but, aside from the discrepancy
between theory and praxis, which to my mind is not clear in this proposition,
every doctrine of grace is " entirely false " which is not deduced from the idea
of a personal intercourse of God with man or directly from "grace alone."
That this is not the case in Cassian is evinced by the inconsistent double
origin of conversion in his theory. This leads not to a life with God, but only
to the idea of a parallel working of God and man.

ment of Augustinianism, as it proves that the doctrine of "in-fused grace," which Cassian had adopted from Augustine, was tolerable to the Christian consciousness only in combination with the conception of God as the Lawgiver and with man's relative freedom to obey the divine commandments. It was an instruc-tive attempt to preserve the personal and spiritual relationship of man to God. But the attempt of necessity surrendered that which was the best in Augustine—the *sola gratia*.[1] "For this it is to be under grace—to perform the things which grace com-mands" (coll. xxi. 34). The effort thus led back again to about the ancient Latin position.

3. The controversy upon grace and freedom was protracted through the following decennia in the Gallic church. The oppo-nents of strict Augustinianism did not hesitate to draw the most appalling inferences. They feared the annihilation of man's freedom, the introduction of fatalism and Manichæism. Baptism and the divine call are robbed of their force and value. God does not wish all men to be saved. Christ did not die for all. Sin and the fall are to be attributed to God's planning. God creates man and directly compels him to sin and crime. This, they contended, is contrary to the teachings of the Scriptures (esp. 1 Tim. 2. 4), as well as to the intuitions of the church, and makes predestination coëxtensive with foreknowledge, etc. (vid. the separate propositions in Prosper's writings : *Pro Aug. responsiones ad capitula calumniantium Gallorum* and *Resp. ad objectiones Vincentianas*, Migne 51. 155 ff.; also, Aug. opp. xvii. 2887 ff.). On the other hand, Prosper, in the writings named and in his *Liber contra collatorem* (Cassian, cf. his poem, *De in-gratis*) defended the Augustinian position and made fierce assaults upon his opponents. But he not infrequently ascribed to them Pelagian conclusions which they themselves did not draw, and in his positive statements he did not advance beyond a repetition of the ideas of Augustine (cf. WIGGERS, Augustinianism and Pela-gianism, ii. 136 ff., 183 ff.). His intemperate zeal can only have drawn the lines more sharply between the opposing parties. And the attempt to bring the Augustinian doctrine into closer accord with the religious intuitions, made in the anonymous book, *De vocatione gentium* (Migne 51. 647 ff.), can hardly have produced any large results. The ideas of Augustine are here reproduced, though in a diluted form. By the fall of Adam, it is said,

---

[1] This is confirmed by the further soteriological views of Cassian. Vid., upon the definition of *merit*, WIGGERS, Augustinianism and Pelagianism ii., p. 81 f.; upon his theory of *repentance* as a satisfaction rendered by good works to an offended God, coll. xx. 3-8.

human nature has been depraved (*vitiata*, i. 6 f.): "the choice
(*judicium*)) of the will has been depraved (*depravatum*), not
abrograted.  Therefore, what has not been slain by the wounder
is not annihilated by the healer.  He who is endowed with
the power of willing is cured ; his nature is not removed.  But
that in the nature which has perished is not restored except by the author of the nature " (i. 8).  Accordingly,
it is not the human will by its merits that makes the beginning toward salvation (ii. 7), but the elective will of God
(i. 18), who works everything good in us and upholds us in it
(i. 23).  "There is given to everyone without merit that by
virtue of which he tends toward merit " (ii. 8).  Christ died
for all (ii. 16).  Yet it is a fact, that not all are saved, as
especially children dying unbaptized (1. 16, 22 ; ii. 20, 22) and
the heathen world.  This leads to the insoluble problem, "Why
he who wishes all men to be saved does not save all men?"
(ii. 1).  Though utterly unable to solve this fundamental question, the author labors earnestly to make the course of God comprehensible.   In the first place, he emphasizes the fact that the
gracious working of God does not exclude the free exercise of
the human will :  "but the will of man is also subjoined to and
conjoined with (*subjungitur et conjungitur*) it . . . so that it co-
operates with the divine work within itself and begins to exercise
for merit what it received for the awakening of energy (ii. 26)
from the seed implanted from above," and also, "it does not
take away from those who will persevere the mutability which can
refuse to will " (ii. 28).  He then presents the thought peculiar
to himself, that God proclaims his desire that all men be saved,
not in the first instance through grace, or a special call (*vocatio
specialis*), but from the very beginning through general grace
(*generalis gratia*) as a revelation made in nature (ii. 25. 4).
The latter has always existed ; the former is now announced to
the whole world ("no part of the world is now excluded from
the gospel of Christ," ii. 33).  But since this general assistance
(*auxilium generale*) does not suffice for salvation, and since, on
the other hand, from ancient times some, although indeed very
few, from the heathen world, " have been separated by the Spirit
to the grace of God " (ii. 5, 15 fin.), it is evident that this whole
scheme does not solve the problem, but only complicates it.
The author finds only the precarious ground of consolation, "the
more difficult this is to understand, the more laudable is the faith
that believes it.  For he has great fortitude of faith (*consensionis*)
for whom authority suffices to lead to acceptance of the truth,
although reason remains dormant " (ii. 2).  Augustine's conception of religious truth is thus supported by the medieval idea of

faith : the more unintelligible the matter in hand, the greater the merit of the faith which accepts it !

4. Semipelagianism, or the old Western view, continued its assaults upon the advocates of Augustinianism, and the latter' may here and there have been betrayed into the extreme conclusions attributed to them. The anonymous book, *Praedestinatus* (Migne 53), written about A. D. 450, professes in its second part to be the literary production of a Semipelagian, who, by presenting the horrible doctrines said to be taught by a predestinarian sect, seeks to awaken in the pious a sense of alarm in order that he may more effectually administer consolation.[1] But there were also doubtless Ultra-Augustinians, who allowed themselves to be led from grace to libertinism. In consequence, Augustinianism itself was charged with leading to immoral conclusions. VINCENT of Lerinum, on the other hand, called attention to its novelty and its lack of support from the tradition of the ancient church (*novitatis adinventores*, vid. Commonit. 32).[2]

But the Semipelagian view of grace found an especially zealous champion in the highly-esteemed Bishop FAUSTUS of Riji († ab. A. D. 495, vid. his writings in the corp. scr. eccl. lat. xxi. ed. Engelbrecht, also Mi. 58 ; cf. WIGGERS, l. c. ii. 224 ff. KOCH, der h. Faust. 1895. R. SEEBERG, PRE. v. ed. 3, 782 ff.). Faustus contended (vid. esp. *De gratia*) sharply against Pelagius and his denial of original sin, and of the necessity of grace (i. 1). He himself represented the Semipelagian view. All men have original sin, and that "from the carnal delight of their progenitor" (i. 2, p. 12[3]), and are, in consequence, sub-

---

[1] Yet it is to be remarked that objections of no inconsiderable force may be urged against this now prevalent solution of the historico-literary problem presented by this publication. It is not impossible that there were libertines of grace, and that the terrifying portraiture of predestinarian consequences, which was continually drawn by their opponents, was utilized by them as a pillow for their consciences (did not heretical tendencies influence these Augustinians?). We cannot here go into details. But let the polemical and not "symbolical" character of the book (the publisher says it was used as a symbol, Mi. 53. 628) be observed, and also the statements of Lucidus (FAUST. ep. 1, p. 162, ed. Engelbrecht). But see recently VON SCHUBERT, Der so-genannte Praedestinatus, 1903.

[2] At this point should be considered the remarks of GENNADIUS upon Augustine and Prosper, vid. De scriptoribus ecclesiast. 38, 84, as also Gennadius' own doctrine of grace, vid. De ecclesiastic. dogmatibus, c. 21, 56. This chapter may not be free from interpolation. Chapters 22-51, which develop the Augustinian doctrine of grace in exact harmony with the Council of Orange, are also, upon the testimony of preserved manuscript, an interpolation (vid. ELMENHORST in Mi. 58. 1023).

[3] Ib. p. 13 : "But whence comes that connection which produces posterity? . . . Through the impulsive ardor of accursed generation and through the seductive embrace of both parents. For since thou seest that he alone is

ject to death (i. 1, p. 11). But man has not lost his freedom through sin. There is no "necessity of an ordained and imposed perdition," but a "power of choosing." The free will has, indeed, been weakened, and freedom has lost the "bloom and vigor of its grace" (i. 8, p. 24 f.). "The power of choice of the human will has been attenuated . . . not abrogated" (i. 16, p. 50; ii. 10, p. 88). We are to speak, not of impossibility, but of infirmity and difficulty (ii. 8, p. 76). "We see, therefore, that the consent of the human mind may pass over to the good or to the contrary side" (i. 12, p. 41; i. 10, p. 32). Hence, even fallen man possesses "the possibility of striving for salvation" (ep. 1, p. 163). The appropriation of salvation by man is effected in such a way that grace and the human will co-operate: "we always associate grace with work" (i. 16, p. 51; cf. i. 6, p. 21 f.; ep. 1, p. 163). "And thus these two are combined, the power to draw near, and the impulse to obey, just as if a sick man should attempt to rise and his faculty should not obey the mandate of his spirit, and he should, therefore, beg that a right hand be extended to him" (i. 16, p. 52). From this it follows, that man makes the beginning. He believes in God, and God increases in him this faith and helps him to good works (i. 6, p. 22). The word "assistance" implies equally two (persons), one working and the other co-working, one seeking and the other promising, one knocking and the other opening, one asking and the other rewarding" (ii. 12, p. 91). Thus also in baptism, the "desire of the will" comes first: "The will of the applicant is first required in order that the grace of the regenerator may follow" (ii. 10, p. 84). It appears sometimes as though faith itself were regarded by Faustus as a gift of grace (ii. 5, p. 67 f.), but in such cases the meaning is only that the author regards the will itself as a gift of creative grace ("that I am indebted to God for the will itself," ii. 10, p. 84; also ii. 12, p. 90; cf. KOCH, l. c., p. 92 ff.). The matter can also be conceived in this way: That God, as in the case of the prodigal son, by his providential guidance gives to man the stimulus to serious reflection (i. 11, p. 38). But to comprehend fully the variance from the Augustinian position, it is necessary to consider, further, that Faustus understands by grace, not an inwardly illuminating and renewing power, but, after the manner of Pelagius (p. 336), the preaching, the comfort, the threatenings, and the promises of the

---

exempt from original contagion who was conceived not by flesh but by spirit, and not with the passion that makes ashamed . . . behold the cause of original sin, that one is born from the delight of conception and from the vice of carnal pleasure." This is the monastic idea of original sin. Consider also the reference to the origin of Jesus.

Scriptures. Thus is the "drawing" of the Father (Jn. 6. 44)
explained (i. 16, p. 52), and the "divine assistance" is more
closely defined as the law and the prophets, the evangelical
oracles and divine laws (i. 10, p. 33[1]). If this representation
of the view of Faustus be correct, he is yet further removed
from Augustine than Cassian (p. 371 f.) and nearer to Pelagius
(cf. WIGGERS, ii. 264 ff.). In harmony with the general character of this theory, predestination and foreknowledge merge
into one. "Foreknowledge foresees the things that will come
to pass; predestination afterward defines the retributions to be
meted out. The former foresees merits; the latter foreordains
rewards. And thus, until foreknowledge shall have explored,
predestination decrees nothing" (ii. 3, p. 63). From this view-
point, the problem, why not all men are saved, may, so far as
human freedom is concerned, be easily solved (i. 16, p. 50 f.).
The question as to children dying unbaptized, man is not able
to answer (i. 13, p. 45 f.). Thus, the Semipelagian doctrine,
as related to Cassian, had been further developed, i. e., had
approached nearer to Pelagianism. Two councils were held, at
Arles about A. D. 473 (cf. Engelbrecht's prolog. to his edition,
p. 15), and soon after, at Lyons, in the spirit of Faustus, and against
the "error of predestination" (de grat. prolog., pp. 3, 4). It
was under the instructions of these councils that Faustus wrote the
work above analyzed (vid. the prolog.). The document, as
well as the letters exchanged by Faustus and the predestinarian
presbyter, LUCIDUS, give us some knowledge of the spirit of
these assemblages (ep. 1. 2, pp. 161-168). Lucidus had championed certain ultra-predestinarian propositions (that the foreknowledge of God appoints men to death; that a "vessel of
wrath" cannot become a vessel of glory; that Christ did not die
for all, vid. ep. 1, p. 162). He, under moral pressure, anathematized these propositions and, going still further, of his free
will acquiesced in the *praedicandi statuta* of the council (vid.
ep. 2, p. 165 f.).[2]

[1] In this very passage, indeed, side by side with the law, is mentioned a
working of grace: (he gave) "divine precepts; to those observing them
through the duties of laborious servitude, grace co-operating, he has promised a
celestial kingdom."

[2] In his letter, addressed probably to the second council (at Lyons), Lucidus announces his agreement with the "council's recent statutes for preaching" (Fausti ep., p. 165 f.), and then cites a series of theses which do not
entirely correspond with those presented to him for his recantation. We may
probably see in them the decrees of the council at Arles. He condemns: (1)
Those who say that, after the fall of the first man, the choice of the will is
totally extinct. (2) That Christ . . . did not undergo death for the salvation of all men. (3) That the foreknowledge of God violently compels men

5. Various causes combined to check Semipelagianism. In the first place, its approach to Pelagianism, which was especially perilous while the latter was still in existence. Secondly, the literary assault upon the Traducianism of Faustus by the philosopher, Mamertus Claudianus (vid. Faust. ep. 3 and 5, also Mam. Cl. de statu animae), and the condemnation of Traducianism as heresy by Pope Anastasius II. (ep. 6, v. 23 ; Aug. 498).[1] But it must be emphasized, in the third place, that Rome clung to the Augustinian doctrine, though, indeed, only in the sense of Innocent I., *i. e.*, with an ignoring of predestination. The popes, maintaining this position, always pronounced Pelagianism heretical, and also expressed themselves against Semipelagianism. Vid. COELESTINE I., ep. 21. 2, where the Semipelagians are charged with "preaching things contrary to the truth." Hilary and Prosper are lauded, and the rule laid down : "let novelty cease to assault antiquity."[2] LEO opposes Pelagianism, appealing to the doctrinal instructions of Rome (vid. ep. 1, 2 of A. D. 442 ; so also GELASIUS I.; vid. ep. 4. 2, 3 ; 6. 1, 4, 5 f., 7, 8 f.). This pope from Africa expressed himself with exceptional thoroughness upon the subjects of original sin and grace (vid. also his Tractatus adv. Pelagian. haeresim, Thiel, epp. pontif., p. 571 ff.). The Romish position appears most fully in a dissertation upon grace preserved as a supplement to the 21st letter of Coelestine: In Adam all lost their natural power and innocence (5). Hence, no one, without the help of God, can, of himself

to death. (4) That whoever sins after baptism legitimately received dies in Adam. (5) That some are destined to death, others predestined to life. (6) That from Adam to Christ none of the Gentiles were saved through the primary grace of God, *i. e.*, through the law of nature, until the coming of Christ, because they had lost their free will entirely in our first parent. (7) That the patriarchs and prophets, or some most lofty saints, were living in the dwelling place of paradise even before the times of redemption. (8) That there are no fires nor infernal regions. Under the last thesis, vid. p. 167: "I confess, indeed, that eternal fires and infernal flames have been prepared for capital offenses, because divine judgment justly follows human faults persisting to the end." To this is added the positive assertion of the mere weakening of the will by the fall, and the proof from Scripture and tradition that Christ died for all.

[1] The pope was able to answer very easily, to his own satisfaction, the dogmatic question of whose solution Augustine despaired : According to Jn. 5. 17, the Father worketh always. He, therefore, gives souls also (c. 1. 4). It has been established that the child receives its spirit four weeks after conception (2. 5). Hence, Traducianism is heresy (3. 6). Nevertheless the sin of parents reproduces itself in the children (4. 7). The whole Scriptures teach Creationism, and, in view of Psalm 99. 3, it is said : "in this clearest trumpet tone all iniquity is silenced."

[2] That the force of these deliverances was felt in Gaul is evident from the perversion of the words by Vincent, comm. 32.

be good (6); even those who have been renewed through baptism attain steadfastness in the good only by the daily help of God (7). All merits are gifts received from God (9). God works the free will in man by giving him holy thoughts and the good will (10). This is also the end had in view in sacerdotal prayers (12). Hence: " By these ecclesiastical rules [utterances of Innocent, and Zosimus, and the African decrees], and by the documents received by divine authority . . . we are assured that we should acknowledge God as the author of all good emotions and works, and of all efforts and all virtues . . . and that we should not doubt that all the merits of man are preceded by the grace of him through whom it comes to pass that we begin to will and to do anything good—by which assistance and gift of God free will is not abolished, but liberated, so that instead of darkened it becomes light; instead of evil, right; instead of sick, well; instead of imprudent, provident. For such is the goodness of God toward all men that he wishes those things which are his gifts to be our merits. . . . Wherefore he effects in us that we will and do what he wills . . . so that we are also co-operators with the grace of God " (14). Finally, it is said: " We hold that as we dare not despise, so it is not necessary for us to affirm, the more profound and difficult parts of the questions before us, which those who opposed the heretics have fully treated, because we believe that, for confessing the grace of God, whatever, according to the proclaimed canons of the apostolic chair, the Scriptures have taught us, is sufficient, so that we simply do not regard as Catholic that which has appeared to be contrary to the universally accepted opinions " (15). Thus the non-Augustinian doctrine of grace is rejected as uncatholic, while predestination is, not indeed discountenanced, but yet not designated as an absolutely necessary element in the church's doctrine of grace. This important document plainly indicates the attitude of the Roman chair toward the doctrine of grace during the fifth and the early part of the sixth century.[1] It is Augustinian, but avoids committing itself to the extreme positions of Augustinianism. Pope HORMISDAS also, in his decision

---

[1] From the last section it is evident that Prosper cannot have been the author of the document. That it is not a part of the 21st letter of Coelestine is plain. The date of composition cannot be placed later than A. D. 431, since only utterances of Innocent I. and Zosimus are made use of (vid., however, expressions like those of Gelasius, ep. 4. 3), and no mention is made of the condemnation of Pelagianism at Ephesus (p. 264). On the other hand, Dionysius Exiguus found it so early as the days of Symmachus (A. D. 498-514) bound together with the letter of Coelestine (Mi. 67. 270). It may be included under the *capitula* of Hormisdas (ep. 124. 5); but it is, perhaps, already presupposed by Leo (ep. 1. 2) and Gelasius (ep. 4. 3; cf. 5. 2).

called forth by the assaults of the Scythian monks upon the orthodoxy of Faustus, pursues the same line. He goes even further, as
he describes the Catholic doctrine as being simply the Augustinian
(''it may be seen in the various books of the blessed Augustine,
and chiefly in those addressed to Hilary and Prosper,''[1] ep. 124.
5). The same controversy called forth the (now lost) publication
of the Augustinian FULGENTIUS OF RUSPE, *Contra Faustum*, ll.
7 (vita Fulg. 28. 54). He, in a number of other writings,
championed the strict Augustinian doctrine of grace, including
the '' double predestination, the one of the good to glory, the
other of the wicked to punishment '' (vid. ad Monimum, ll. 3,
and especially vol. i. de veritate praedestinationis ; also ep. 15
in Mi. 65 ; cf. WIGGERS, ii. 370 ff., 419 ff.).

6. Thus Semipelagianism, as a theory, failed to secure acceptance in the most influential quarters.   Then appeared a man in the
church of South Gaul, who was by personal religious conviction an
Augustinian, but who, nevertheless—or perhaps also therefore—
was able to look beyond the sacred paradoxes of predestination,
CAESARIUS OF ARLES († A. D. 542. Morin is preparing an
edition of his widely-distributed homilies.   Portions in Mi. 67 ;
cf. ARNOLD, Caes. von Arel., 1894.   As bearing upon our
question, see esp. 312 ff. and 533 ff.).   But opposition arose
against the view of grace advocated by Caesarius,[2] which may
have been increased by political and practical considerations
(vid. ARNOLD, p. 344 ff.).   His teaching, however, really con-
flicted with the legally binding decrees of Arles (p. 376).
The council at VALENTIA (A. D. 529) was accordingly summoned to oppose him.   Caesarius was prevented from attendance, but sent representatives to conduct his cause, who argued
that no one can of himself make spiritual progress, unless
previously called by ''prevenient grace,'' and that the will
of man becomes free only through Christ's redeeming work
(vita Caesar. i. 5. 46).[3]   The decrees of this council have been

---

[1] *I. e.*, the strict predestinarian books, De predest. and De don. persev.,
vid. p. 368.

[2] Caesarius did *not* write the work attributed to him, *De gratia et libero
arbitrio*.   The statement to that effect in Gennad. de scr. eccl. 86 is a rather
late interpolation (cf. ARNOLD, p. 498 f.).

[3] That the council of Valence was held before that of Orange is to-day
almost universally admitted (vid. HEFELE CG., ii. 739 f.).   The passage cited
from the Vita Caes. permits no other conclusion.   The council of Orange does
not, indeed, directly mention it, but indirectly in the statement that Caesarius
(after the council of Val.) presented the proof from apostolic tradition for the
view of his delegates (not of the council of Valence, as Hefele states, p.
738), and that Boniface II. confirmed this.   Of course, Caesarius was not
''flatly accused of Semipelagianism '' (KOCH, Faust. p. 53) at Valence.   On
the contrary, his accusers were Semipelagians.

lost,[1] but that they bore a Semipelagian character does not admit of doubt.[2] Before the summoning of this council, Caesarius had appealed to Pope Felix IV., who sent to him "a few chapters." These, which have been preserved substantially in Can. 9-25 of the decrees of Orange, were taken from the Sentences of Prosper. When Caesarius, while in attendance at the dedication of a church at ARAUSIACUM (Orange, A. D. 529), learned of the Semipelagian decrees of Valence, he took advantage of the assemblage to reaffirm his views upon the doctrine of grace. He added to the Sentences sent by the pope, the introduction, the final confession, and decrees 1-8.[3] Thus originated the decrees

---

[1] But see further remarks below upon the decrees of Orange.

[2] Vid. ARNOLD, p. 349 f., especially, as otherwise the biographer of Caesarius would not have failed to mention the acceptance of the arguments of the latter's delegates at Valence.

[3] As to the origin of the Canons of Orange, ARNOLD is substantially correct (p. 534 ff.). We remark briefly: (1) N. 9-15 a, except n. 10, is derived from Prosper's Sentences (22-372, vid. the Maurine ed. of the works of Augustine, xvii. 2818 ff. HEFELE, ii. 730 ff.). These are the *capitula* sent by the pope. Caesarius inserted n. 10 and made some modifications (esp. n. 13, but not n. 18, where Arnold labored with a false LA. (2) The preface and the final confession, n. 25 b, are from Caesarius. (3) N. 1-8, in form and content different from the other sentences, are also the work of Caesarius, *i. e.*, of the synod. This is confirmed particularly by the fact that Caesarius has presented to the pope for his approval the proposition "that even faith is a gift of grace," and that the papal letter accordingly enlarges upon this proposition. But this is the leading thought in n. 3-6. (4) Caesarius framed the canon with a wise moderation and consideration for the opponents (avoidance of the double predestination, 25 b; insertion of baptism, 13, 25 b; the relation of grace to perseverance in good works, 10). (5) The question as to the motive for the construction of n. 1-8 is thus answered by Arnold : N. 1 and 2 are directed against Pelagianism ; 3-6, against Faustus ; 7, against the earlier Augustine ; 8, against Cassian (p. 557). But this does not harmonize with the concrete situation in which Caesarius was placed. It would be an astonishing thing if he had framed these sentences with a view to considerations of doctrinal history. Caesarius, as we know, sent with his own document to the pope the letter of a certain priest, Mansi viii. 737. This letter must have some reference to the Sentences of his opponent, the condemnation of which he was endeavoring to secure. It contained, in other words, the Sentences of the assembly at Valence. If Caesarius regarded the sending of these as necessary for the understanding of his canon, it then follows that n. 1-8 (but also the other comments and modifications of the documents received from Rome) were constructed in the light of the canons of Valence. And this is, in fact, in view of the entire situation, the only probable conclusion. This opens to us the possibility of reconstructing—in their fundamental features—the decrees of Valence. These began with a condemnation of strict Pelagianism. Not only death, but also sin, has come upon the race through Adam (according to n. 1, 2). Grace delivers man, if the latter calls upon God, desires to be pure, believes in God and the gospel message, and manifests an earnest longing and striving after grace and baptism (3 7). At the same time (according to Caesarius), there was left open the possibility that in some cases grace should make the beginning (8); while, on the other hand, as testified

of Orange, designed to put an end to the Semipelagian controversy. Pope Boniface II. (in Mansi viii. 735 ff.) confirmed
them, A. D. 530 or 531 (Hefele ii. 737 f.).

The leading ideas of this doctrinal decision[1] are as follows :
Both Pelagianism and Semipelagianism are in conflict with
the "rule of Catholic faith." By the sin of Adam, he himself and all his posterity were ruined in body and soul. Not
only death, but sin also, has through Adam come upon the whole
human race (1, 2, 8). " No one has of himself anything except
falsehood and sin " (22[2]). The free will has been inclined and
weakened in such a way that man of himself can neither believe
in God nor love him (25 b). If man even before the fall was
unable without the help of his Creator to maintain his original
integrity, "how shall he be able without the grace of God to recover what he has lost?" (19). The grace of God works in us
the impulse to call upon God and to strive after purification, as
also faith. Grace is an "*infusio et operatio*" of the Spirit (4).
That we believe, and that we will or are able to do these things as
we ought, is wrought in us through the infusion and inspiration of
the Holy Spirit (6. 5). Faith is " to consent to the preaching of the
gospel" (7, cf. ib.: " in consenting to and believing the truth").
The faith thus inspired by God impels us to baptism (25 H., p.
152). It is baptism which renews our will : " the choice of
the will, weakened in the first man, cannot be repaired *except*

by examples in the Old Testament, the natural goodness (the *bonum naturae*)
of man might stand at the beginning of the process (25 b). Finally, assault
is made upon the double predestination, and the evisceration of baptism and of
morality which it involves (cf. n. 10, 13, 25 b). This was the ancient Semipelagian position, which has close affinity with n. 3-7 of the Sentences of
Arles (supra, p. 376, n.). It was maintained with a certain moderation (the
preface of the Canons of Orange attributes the doctrine to the "simplicity " of
its adherents) and an energetic rejection of Pelagianism.

The origin of the Canons of Orange may accordingly be thus explained. But
if Caesarius was able to inform himself as to the canons of Orange only by
means of a letter, then it follows that the council of Orange was held immediately after that of Valence. This conclusion is demanded also by the
preface. It was only after assembling at Orange that information was secured
concerning the departure from the rule of faith (*esse aliquos*, etc.). But then
Caesarius had already, before the council of Arles, requested the papal advice,
and probably received it immediately before the council of Orange. Caesarius
did not summon the council for the purpose of conferring with them upon this
point, but merely embraced the opportunity afforded. The pope calls the
Canons a *collatio* (M. viii. 736). We may thus understand also the silence of
the *Vita* in regard to them.

[1] Vid. the decrees in HAHN, Bibl. d. Symb. 143 ff., and a revised text of
MAASSEN in Mon. Germ. Leg. sect. 3 ; concil. t. i. (1893), p. 44 ff.

[2] As to the solution of the problem bequeathed in this thesis to modern
Catholic theologians, vid. ERNST, Die Werke und Tugenden der Ungläubigen
n. Aug., 1871, p. 228 ff. (appendix).

*through the grace of baptism*" (13). God, therefore, works in us to every good work. "The assistance of God must always be implored even by the regenerated and restored (var. reading = saints) in order that they may be able to attain to a good end, or to persevere in the good" (10). Thus every good deed is to be traced back to God (20, 23 f.). Accordingly, our worthiness before God depends not upon our merit, but upon the gift of God. "God loves us for what we are to be by his gift, not for what we are by our merit" (12, cf. 18). The double predestination is expressly anathematized (25 b). We present as a summary the leading sentences of the concluding confession : " We ought to preach and believe, that the free will has been so inclined and weakened by the sin of the first man, that no one since would be able either to love God as he ought, or to believe on God, or to work what is good before God, unless the grace of the divine mercy had preceded him. We believe that, grace having been received through baptism, all the baptized are able and under obligation to perform by the assistance and co-operation of Christ the things which pertain to the salvation of the soul, if they have resolved to labor faithfully. But that some have by the divine power been predestinated to evil, we not only do not believe, but even if there are any who are willing to believe such an evil thing, we with all detestation pronounce an anathema upon them. He, no good merits preceding, inspires in us faith and love of himself, so that we may both seek in faith the sacraments of baptism, and may be able after baptism, by his assistance, to perform those things which are pleasing to him." Thus the doctrine of "grace alone" came off victorious ; but the Augustinian doctrine of predestination was abandoned. The irresistible grace of predestination was driven from the field by the sacramental grace of baptism. The doctrine of grace was hereby brought into a closer relationship with the popular Catholicism, as also by the exaltation of good works as the aim of the divine impartation of grace.[1]

## § 34. *Tradition and the Papacy.*

1. We have now traced the genesis of dogma in the ancient church of the West. The doctrines of Anthropology and So-

[1] HARNACK says : "It is a fact which has not hitherto been duly considered, that the Catholic doctrine did not continue Semipelagian simply because it declared the sexual passion sinful " (iii. 233). This is false, since it was just Pelagianism (vid. Faust., supra, p. 374) which presented the strongest statements upon this point, and because the controversy between the Semipelagians and the Augustinians really culminated elsewhere.

teriology were the most distinctly original products of Occidental Christianity.   But even in the development of the doctrines of the Trinity and of Christology, the influence of the Western church was, as we have seen (supra, pp. 217, 272), of very great significance.   Thus the Western theologians made themselves felt in the formation of both the Nicene and the Chalcedon creeds, and retained their peculiar conception of God and Christ in the forms of the Augustinian theology.   The Trinitarian and Christological dogmas are hence common to the Eastern and Western churches, while the Greeks have given expression to their peculiar religious tendency in the doctrine of images, and the Occidentals in the doctrine of sin and grace.   In the West, there was also a close and scrupulous adherence to the orthodox definitions and the heaping of condemnations upon heretics.   This is clearly proved alike by the anti-heretical writings of the period (Augustine, Philaster) and by the efforts made to present a summary statement of Catholic truth (Vincent of Lerinum, Gennadius, Fulgentius of Ruspe[1]).   But in close association with this regard for dogma stand the views and ideals, the superstition and cus-

---

[1] Vid. the writings of Faustus and Gennadius, cited by the latter, de vir. ill. 85, 100 ; the works attributed to Vigilius of Tapsus (in Mi. lat. 62); also the writings of Fulgentius (Mi. 65).   As summaries, GENNADIUS, de ecclesiastic. dogmatibus (Mi. 58. 979 ff.), and FULGENTIUS, de fide (Mi. 65. 671 ff.) are of special interest.   Gennadius treats of the Trinity and Christology, the resurrection, the creation, man and his soul, freedom (c. 21 ; as to c. 22-52, vid. supra, p. 374, n., and ARNOLD, Caesar., p. 535), then of baptism, the eucharist, repentance (54, 80), in condemnation of sensuous Chiliasm, upon angels, marriage, temperance, the Virgin Mary, relics, the necessity of baptism to salvation, the eucharist (c. 75 : "pure water ought not to be offered in the sacrament in order to deceive some by the symbol of sobriety"), the resurrection, the influence of the death of Christ upon the dead, etc. Fulgentius, under the heading of Redemption (22 f.), gives a more exhaustive treatment of the Trinity and Christology in the spirit of Augustine.   This constitutes the first part of the work, entitled by the author, *De trinitate*.   The second part teaches : "What thou shouldst believe without doubt concerning created things" (24), viz.: creation from nothing (25, 29), the omnipresence of God, angels, freedom, and the possibility of falling, predestination and the leaving of some, especially of children dying unbaptized, to perdition (31); that original sin expresses itself primarily in unbelief (*infidelitas*) (34); eternal death and eternal life, wherein no "indulgence" follows repentance (36), whereas in repentance on earth : "if thou shalt have with the whole heart renounced past sins, and shalt have shed tears of the heart . . . for them, and shalt have been careful to wash away the stains of evil works by good works, thou shalt have at once indulgence for all thy sins" (37 ; cf. 82 : "to wash away . . . thy sins by alms, fastings, prayer, or tears"); that baptism is not to be repeated ; that "without association with the Catholic church neither can baptism profit anyone, nor works of mercy (42); that perpetual continence is better than a good marriage" (43); then follow forty rules which, for the most, are a repetition of what has preceded ; § 84 : "that the wicked are mingled with the good in the communion of the sacraments," *i. e.*, in the church.

toms, of the popular Catholicism. In this also Augustine prepared the way for the later development (p. 367). We may, accordingly, refrain at this point from a portrayal of the Christianity of the period, as this will form a fitting introduction to Book II. (cf. p. 24).

At the beginning of the course of development, whose conclusion, relatively speaking, we have now reached, we met the ideas of Irenæus and Tertullian upon Tradition (p. 136 f.). In the present period VINCENT OF LERINUM, in his *Commonitorium* (A. D. 434, in Mi. 50. 637 ff.), gave to this always influential consideration a form in harmony with the views of his age, at the same time recording some interesting remarks upon the development of doctrine. The Catholic faith is fundamentally distinct from heresy in the fact that it is based " primarily, of course, upon the authority of the divine law ; then, likewise, upon the tradition of the Catholic church." Although the canon of Scripture is complete, " and of itself is sufficient and more than sufficient for all things," yet tradition is needed for a proper understanding of the Scriptures : " in the Catholic church itself the greatest care must be exercised to hold that which has been believed everywhere and always and by all."

Genuine tradition is, hence, that which has in its favor *universitas, antiquitas* and *consensio* (c. 2). Heresy is innovation : " when well-established antiquity is subverted by wicked novelty " (14). This is confirmed by the study of the historical heresies (*e. g.*, Apollinaris, Nestorius, Origen, Tertullian). Let us, therefore, be on our guard against the darkness of heretical illumination. " If novelty is to be avoided, antiquity is to be cherished ; and if novelty is profane, age is hallowed " (21). There is, indeed, progress in history, " but yet in such a way that it advances truly in the faith, not a transformation." The knowledge of the church grows, but " in its own kind (*genere*), in the same doctrine, in the same sense (*sensu*), in the same opinion " (*sententia*). There is a growth, just as the child becomes a man—a development, as the plant comes from the seed. " Whatever, therefore, has in the agriculture of God been planted in this church in the faith of the Fathers, this same flourishes and matures, this same advances and is completed. For it is right that these primal doctrines of celestial philosophy should, in process of time, be carefully studied, refined, and polished ; but it is nefarious that they should be changed, abbreviated, mutilated " (23). Accordingly, the councils have only furnished more precise definitions of the ancient doctrine. " What else has ever been produced by the decrees of councils, except that what had before been believed in simplicity (*simpliciter*), this same was afterward believed more heartily ; what had before been preached more moderately, this same was afterward preached more vigorously ; what had before been cherished in greater security, this same was afterward cultivated with greater solicitude ? " (ib.). That which was "not a new doctrine (*sensum*) of the faith " was now designated by the " peculiarity of a new appelation." The heretics, on the contrary (*e. g.*, Pelagius, Sabellius, Novatian, Priscillian[1]), produce one innovation after another, and do not fail to adduce abundant proofs for their views from the Scriptures (Paul of Samosata, Priscillian, Eunomius, Jovinian), in this following Satan's example (24 ff.). The church must oppose to all heresies either the decisions of the councils or—if there be none applicable to the case in hand— the concensus of the ancient Fathers, *i. e.*, of those who remained until their death in the *communio catholica*, and, even in their case, not their obscure and private opinions upon minor points, but the fundamental views common to them all. Whatever has been plainly, frequently, and persistently accepted and handed down, either by all or by the majority, in one and the same sense, is to be regarded as true (28). Finally, as the letter of Pope Coelestine (p. 377) is quite evidently used as fully as possible *against* the Augustinians, this Semipelagian betrays his determination to apply his canon against the doctrine of Augustine. The doctrine of the ancient Fathers is, therefore, the truth, in comparison with which the authority of the Scriptures retreats into the background. Tradition was for Irenæus a tributary line of evidence for the establishment of the identity of the religious views of the church with the truth revealed in the Scriptures. Here tradition has become an independent entity, and really the chief consideration. From this time forward, side by side with the Scriptures—and in fact above them, runs the Catholic tradition. With this is combined the idea that the development of doctrine should and dare be nothing more than the formal restatement of the teachings of the Catholic Fathers —an idea which must stanu or fall with the false presumption, that those Fathers had exhausted the contents of the gospel. The decreasing prominence of the episcopacy in this connection is worthy of note, but we dare not fail to observe also that the

---

[1] Upon Priscillian († A. D. 385) vid. Prisc. quae supersunt, ed. SCHEPSS, 1889 ; also PARET, Prisc. ein Reformator des 4. Jarh. 1891. HILGENFELD, in Ztschr. f. wiss. Theol., 1892, p. 1 ff. The solution of the historical problem presented by the theology of Priscillian (in which Gnosticizing, popular- Catholic, and archaistic elements are combined) does not lie within the province of the History of Doctrines. I regard PARET'S attempt as unsuccessful. Cf. also the instructive study of F. LEZIUS, Die Libra des Dictinnius (in Abhandlungen für Alex. von Oettingen, 1898).

25

episcopate is regarded as self-evidently the means for the preservation of the tradition.

3. When considering the evidence for the truth of the church's dogmas, mention must be made of the Papacy. It is the province of Church History to trace the extension of the temporal power of the popes; we can deal only with the dogmatic authority of the papal deliverances. The popes themselves with ever-increasing boldness referred to their doctrinal utterances as simply the truth (Callistus, p. 176; Stephan, p. 184; Leo, p. 271; Innocent I., p. 356); but they did so at first in the ancient sense (vid. Iren., p. 137, and also Tertul. praescr. 36, 20), that they were the representatives of the ancient doctrine—that, as the successors of Peter, they have the doctrine of Peter in their keeping (Stephan, p. 184; cf. Coelestine, p. 321). However lofty their utterances may sound, they are yet very far from asserting the " I am tradition " of a later age. The first traces of this theory may, indeed, be already noted, as at the council of Ephesus, A. D. 431, where the papal legates declare: "who (Peter) until the present and forever both lives and decides in his successors " (Mansi, iv. 1296). So also the ep. decret..Gelasii de recip. et non recip., libr. i. (Thiel, p. 455): "The Roman church has been exalted above other churches by no synodical decrees, but has obtained the primacy by the evangelical voice of the Lord and Saviour, Matt. 16. 18." But the councils by no means blindly acknowledge the papal claims, but subject them to scrutiny (e. g., at Chalcedon, p. 272, at the sixth ecumenical council, p. 282; cf. Mansi, xi. 331 ff.). This explains how a pope could be expressly condemned for error by a council and by another pope (Honorius, p. 282; also Jaffé Reg. pontif. Rom. i., ed. 2, n. 2118). The bishops always ascribed the highest value to the authority of the pope when that authority was enlisted, or thought to be enlisted, in favor of their own opinions (e. g., Aug., supra, pp. 354, 318; Caesar., vid. passages in ARNOLD, p. 298, n.). Where this was not the case, they were ready enough to set over against Matt. 16 the course of Paul, described in Gal. c. 2 (Cyprian, p. 183, Aug. and the Council of Carthage, p. 356 f.). Highly esteemed as was the papal authority—dogmatically, the views entertained scarcely went beyond the deliverance of Jerome: " But thou sayest that the church is founded upon Peter. Granted, that this same thing is in another place said with relation to all the apostles, and that they all received the keys of the kingdom of heaven . . . yet one was selected among the twelve in order that by the appointment of a head the liability to schism might be removed " (adv. Jovin. i. 26; cf. Cypr., p. 183; Aug., p. 318). Very similar

was the attitude of the emperors toward the popes. The actual power wielded by the latter forced from them expressions of the highest esteem, but they were never inclined to treat the papal teachings as infallible (cf. pp. 222, 235, 268 f., 272, n., 276 f., 281, 303, 356). In fact, the first decided interest was awakened by the edict of Valentinian III. (A. D. 445), which aimed to bring the Western church into complete subjection to Rome : "For then at length will the peace of the churches be everywhere preserved if the whole world (*universitas*) acknowledges its ruler ; " and " let this be law for them all, whatever the authority of the apostolic chair has sanctioned or shall have sanctioned " (Leon. ep. 11). The Justinian laws had only added emphasis to this. But that the papal utterances were even yet in the last analysis controlled by the traditional conception of the matter is best attested by the *Exemplum libelli* of Hormisdas : "Our chief safety is to guard the rule of the true faith, and by no means to deviate from the ordinances of the Fathers. And since the opinion of our Lord Jesus Christ when he said, ' Thou art Peter,' cannot be disregarded . . . these things which have been said are to be attested by the actual results, because in the apostolic chair the Catholic religion has always been preserved immaculate. Whence . . . following in all things the apostolic chair and preaching all its ordinances, I hope that I may merit to be with you in the one communion which the apostolic chair preaches, in which is the whole and true solidity of the Christian religion " (A. D. 515, ep. 7. 9 ; Thiel, ep. rom. pont., p. 754 f.). Cf. LANGEN, Das vatikan. Dogma vom Universalepiskopat u. der Unfehlbarkeit des Papstes, 4 parts, 1871-6. DÖLLINGER, Das Papsttum, 1892. Vid. Sources in MIRBT, Quellen zu Gesch. des Papsttums., ed. 2, 1901.

4. In the doctrine upon the subject of tradition there is again brought to view the harmony between the theological ideas of the later period of ancient dogmatic history and those of the second century, but none the less distinctly the departure of the former from the latter. The doctrines of the ancient church were constructed upon the basis of the primitive Catholic Christianity. In this process we may again remark (vid. p. 383) that the Trinitarian and Christological dogmas were a common product of the Orient and Occident, whereas the Soteriological dogma was an entirely Western construction.[1] This dogma, or these dogmas, became the basis of the entire doctrinal structure of the church and of the religious conceptions of the Chris-

[1] The condemnation of Pelagianism at Ephesus (p. 264) was merely an accident.

tian world. This explains the inestimable importance of a famil-
iarity with the course of doctrinal development in the ancient
church in order to a correct understanding of the doctrines now
held in the church. But we are led, on the other hand, to the
conviction, that the established dogma of the ancient church does
not present the final truth, but is capable of and requires development, expansion, and continual recasting and progressive revision. For the evangelical believer, the Gospel of the Lord
and of the apostles is the norm for the criticism and revision of
the dogma of the ancient church. Inasmuch as the latter excludes certain conceptions, and, in their stead, formulates an
actual statement of religious principles in the philosophical forms
of antiquity, it has been a leaven modifying the course of further
development. It transmitted a gift to posterity which, like
every spiritual legacy, became of necessity for the recipient[1] a chal-
lenge to labor. The further course of dogmatic history must reveal
to what an extent the church of later times understood the
problem, and what progress was made toward its solution.

[1] Cf. FRANK, Syst. d. chr. Warh. i., ed. 3, 161 f.: " It is no less unjustifiable
to regard the fixed formulas of the church as of such a character that in them
is established a complete dogmatic conception of the topic under consideration,
whereas, in fact, they furnish, or attempt to furnish, nothing more than
the most suitable terms in which it is possible to define the realities of
faith as such ; " and further, " that this is not to be so understood as though
the formula once established in consequence of the Arian controversy, and
since then handed down in the church, were in itself, and in this external form,
the basis for our dogmatic investigations. It is this only because, and in so far
as, in it finds expression a treasure of faith which . . . as an inherited legacy,
but one which, requiring, in order to its actual possession, to be appropriated
anew from generation to generation, leads us constantly forward." Vid. also
RITSCHL, Rechtfertigung u. Versöhnung, ii., ed. 2, 18 f.: ' Even Philippi
( Kirchl. Dogm. ii. 150) attributes but a *negative* value for theology to the doctrinal formulas of the church. Yet this value is to be understood as *positive*
in character, in so far as these formulas keep within the range of view problems
whose solution has been attempted in the articles of faith, even though a more
careful scrutiny may have convinced us that the solution sought has not been
attained in them. Viewed in this light, both aspects of the doctrinal statements of the Lutheran church endure the test as a direct contribution toward
the derivation from the New Testament of the authentic content of the Christian religion."

# INDEX.

## A.

Ability, Human. In Judaism, 31; Hermas, 61; Barnabas, 71, 73; Apostolic fathers, 80; Ebionites, 91; Apologists, 115; Antignostic fathers, 122, 139; Tertullian, 123; Clement of Alexandria, 144; Origen, 147, 151, 157; Methodius, 187; John of Damascus, 286; Dionysius, 294; Eastern Church, 328; Western Church, 318; Chrysostom, 328; Ambrose, 329; Pelagius, 332 f., 337, 355; Cælestius, 332, 336; Augustine, 339, 341, 344, 350, 353, 359, 365; Pelagianism, 353; Cassian, 370 ff.; Faustus, 375; Lucidus, 376 n.; Council of Orange, 380, 381; Council of Valence, 379, 381 n.

Acacius of Caesarea, 225, 225 n.

Acacius of Constantinople, 274.

Actistites, 278.

Adam, sin of, 335, 337; original state of, 341.

Adiaphorites, 278.

Aelurus, 273.

Aeon, Christ as, 96.

Aëtius, 223, 225.

Agapetus I., 276.

Agatho, Pope, 282.

Agency, Divine. In Paul, 38; Apostolic age, 52; Apostolic fathers, 79; Augustine, 309 (see Will of God, Grace).

Agnoetae, 278.

Agonisti, 314.

Alcibiades, 90.

Alexander of Alexandria, 205, 216.

Alexandria, Council at (A. D. 362), 226; (A. D. 363), 227; A. D. 430), 263.

Alexandrine Fathers, works of, 140; aim of, 140; moralism of, 161; *vs.* Gnosticism, 161; estimate of, 160; on confession, 158; on divinity of Christ, 161; on rule of faith, 160, 161.

Almsgiving. In Clement, 76; Cyprian, 195; Augustine, 363, 367.

Alogi, 163.

Apollinarianism, condemned, 234; repressed, 272; and Antiochians, 246; and Cappadocians, 247; and Monophysites, 277; on Logos, 245.

Apollinaris, works of, 227, 244; problem of, 247, 250, 253, 255; and Cappadocians, 247, 250 ff.; on person of Christ, 233 n., 240, 284; on incarnation, 245; on Chiliasm, 246 n.

Apologists, The, 109-118; aim of, 110; *vs.* Judaism and heathenism, 111; estimate of, 110, 118; legalism of, 118; on God, 112; person of Christ, 113 f.; Trinity, 114; work of Christ, 115; human ability, 115; sufferings of Christ, 116; the church, 116; worship, baptism, eucharist, 117; resurrection, immortality, 117.

(389)